The Big Book of HOME MAINTENANCE

Roy Day

The Big Book of
HOME
MAINTENANCE
Roy Day

This edition produced exclusively for

WHSMITH

THE BIG BOOK OF HOME MAINTENANCE

Acknowledgements

The publishers would like to thank the following for their helpful advice and use of photographs: Blue Hawk Limited, Burtt and Parker of Lightwater, FIDOR Fibre Building Board, ICI Limited (Paints Division), Kwikform Limited, Maclamp Company Limited, MEM Company Limited, MK Electric Limited and The Rawlplug Company Limited.

Line drawings by Gay John Galsworthy/Tony Truscott, Stuart Perry, Bob Mathias, Raymond Turvey

**This edition published exclusively for
W H Smith**

Published by
The Hamlyn Publishing Group Limited
London · New York · Sydney · Toronto
Astronaut House, Feltham, Middlesex, England

Copyright © The Hamlyn Publishing Group Limited 1981
ISBN 0 600 37459 9

The material in this book has been published previously by The Hamlyn Publishing Group Limited under the titles *Decorating Your Home, House Repair and Home Maintenance, Plumbing and Central Heating, Home Electrics, Brickwork, Stonework and Concrete.*

Printed in Czechoslovakia
52051

Contents

Introduction

The days of having the decoration and maintenance of your house done for you are rapidly becoming a thing of the past. Even assuming that you have sufficient funds available to pay for certain jobs to be carried out by the professional, it can often be a frustrating business finding a reliable tradesman who will attend to your requirements without a long delay.

This book has been written with the wide cross section of the public in mind, who are either limited in their means, or would desperately like to carry out work for themselves in their own homes if only they had sufficient knowledge of what to do. This applies to so many sections of the community, both young and old, male and female, and particularly to the ever growing number who live alone through choice or circumstance.

Confidence in undertaking many of the jobs which occur about the house and garden grows from doing those first simple jobs well. It is for this reason that much of the book is concerned with relating how basic services such as plumbing and electricity work, and explaining the basic techniques of getting to grips with the everyday problems which are likely to arise when decorating and maintaining your home.

A wide range of tools, equipment and materials are now readily available to meet all of your needs, but advice is still sadly lacking at the point of sale on how to use successfully the items which you buy.

To get the very best value out of the money that you spend and to obtain satisfaction from the work that you do, plan a maintenance programme which is long-term and on-going. Tackle the urgent jobs first, and to avoid frustration have an indoors/outdoors schedule of jobs which you can pick up to suit the day-to-day variations in the weather. Your home is the one big investment in your life, so never put off until tomorrow what you can do today. If you do, the result could prove more costly than you bargained for.

Decorating Your Home

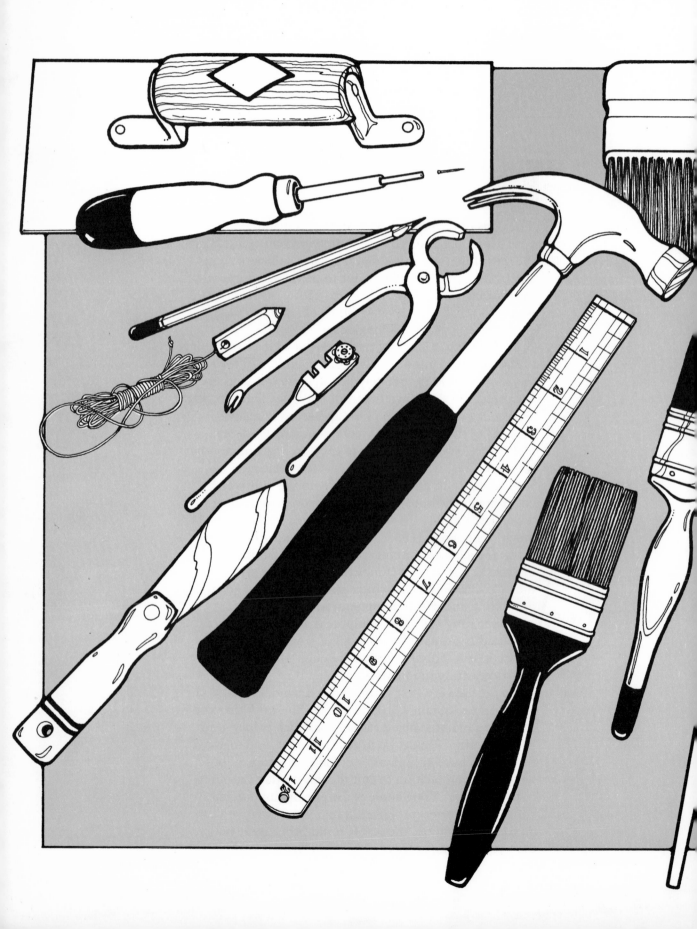

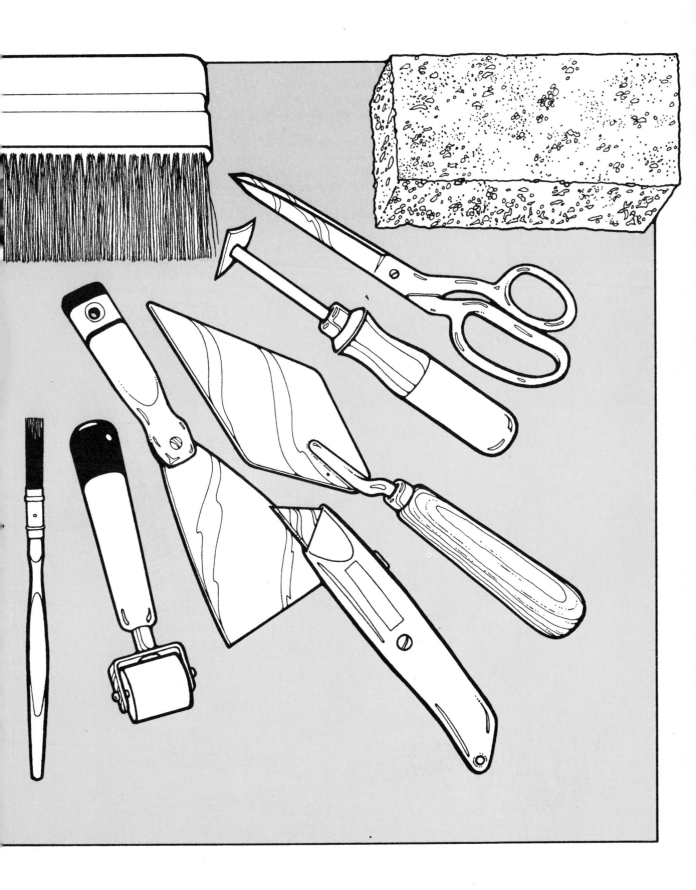

Decorating can be a real headache sometimes. What you thought was going to be a simple exercise, completed in a few days with the minimum of fuss and upheaval, can suddenly become a monster.

Problems crop up unexpectedly, you find you have not got the right sort of equipment, materials or know-how with which to tackle them, and all the time your carefully worked out budget keeps rising.

In the end the job takes weeks. The final effect is nothing like you anticipated and, what is worse, a few short months later the room looks shabby again.

If you are one of the thousands who can identify with this situation, or if you are a complete beginner, then you will find this book invaluable.

Some people, usually those who are good at it, enjoy decorating as a hobby. The vast majority, like you, only put on their working clothes when a room needs a facelift, a floorcovering has to be laid, or any general decorating job has to be done.

What you want is the basic knowledge which will enable you to do a first class job quickly. You do not want to know about expensive tools and equipment, just the economical necessities.

There is a widespread belief that to produce excellent decorating results, the very best tools and the most expensive paints and wallcoverings are essential.

This is not so. Expensive tools are of value only if you know how to use them and will be making enough use of them in future jobs to justify their expense.

The best materials only look effective when they have been applied correctly. If you put the most costly wallcovering material on to a poorly prepared surface it will still look unsightly – assuming that is that it does not peel off before you have had time to notice how bad it looks.

It is worth remembering that doing it yourself saves money only if you do it properly yourself.

Knowing which wallcoverings suit particular situations, how to benefit from the vast selection of modern paints, how to lay floorcoverings successfully, how colours and patterns can be used to the best effect, what other forms of decorating materials are available for you to stamp a mark of individuality on your own home; these are the things the beginner needs to know about.

Planning the Work

Despite the introduction of new materials that are supposed to take the sting out of decorating, most people still look forward to the job even less favourably than to a visit to the dentist. It is hardly surprising, though, if the approach and techniques to be used are still the traditional ones.

To start with, summer holidays are earmarked up to a year in advance for a confrontation with stepladders and paint. So, at a time when you should be lying on the beach, enjoying a well-earned rest from the rigours of work, you are going to be shut away in the house for two weeks as an emulsion-spattered recluse.

When you have given yourself most of the year to chew over that daunting prospect, you can not really be expected to relish the thought of finally getting to grips with the job.

However, there really is no sense in committing yourself to a solid slog for a whole fortnight.

A room, any room, can be decorated from top to bottom over a period of a couple of months simply by doing things in well-planned stages.

Work periods must be restricted to reasonable amounts of time.

Remember, that working for too long a stretch breeds carelessness. At the beginning of the day, you are prepared to do things properly; the rate of progress takes second place. But towards the end of the evening, after more than a full day's work, when the room seems to have quadrupled its size, the paint is splashed on and wallpaper is cut roughly to shape – anything goes in order to get as much finished as possible.

Allowing yourself to get into this state is totally amateurish and its reward is inevitably an amateurish finished effect.

If you have ever employed a professional decorator and have been pleased with his results, then try to remember how he worked. It is most unlikely that he took ten minutes for

A room can be decorated while it remains in normal, everyday use.

lunch, skipped tea and kept at it until the dead of night.

His working day will have been as well organised and run as any insurance office. Probably there was a ten-minute mid-morning break, a full lunch hour (with a proper sit down meal) and another ten minute break for a cup of tea in the afternoon. And all these probably spent outside the house in the fresh air or at least in another room.

The secret of successful decorating is to work only when you are enthusiastic and fresh. Whenever a finished effect fails to live up to the original concept, then you can bet your bottom dollar that tiredness and bad planning were among the main causes.

You should decorate only when you are really in the mood. If you feel like doing eight hours with suitable breaks, then that is fine, but if you only fancy working for ten minutes or a quarter of an hour in an evening, well that is fine too.

Organising the work to cause as little inconvenience and upheaval to the rest

of the family as possible, is the next thing to think about.

But what usually happens? Furniture cleared out of one room blocks hallways, landings, stairs and living rooms; wallpaper peelings are trodden into every carpet in the house; a congealed bucket of paste lies in the bath; brushes, bottles of white spirit and cans of paint on the sideboard, in the kitchen and under the television. All this, when the art of successful decorating is to restrict domestic upheaval to a minimum.

Yet with a little careful thought and effort, it is quite simple to decorate a complete room by carefully re-arranging the furniture to suit work areas. In some circumstances, it is possible to give a new look to a room, even a complete floor to ceiling revamp, while the room remains in normal, everyday use.

Let us assume that you intend to paint the ceiling and the woodwork,

11

and also paper the walls. A real face-lift, in fact. Remember, the room is completely furnished so the only way to work is in gradual stages. The furniture can be constantly repositioned to suit.

You will need a dust sheet to protect the floorcovering of course. Any old bed sheet or disused piece of curtain will do, since the work will be confined to small areas.

Incidentally, although polythene dust sheets are excellent for covering groups of furniture, or for covering floors when working in dry conditions, they are not to be recommended as a floor protection where water is likely to be splashing about, as the water will remain on them in pools.

A stout step stool or a small table step ladder which enables you to reach the ceiling comfortably is ideal.

The height of the stool or ladder is important for two reasons. If you have to stand on the top step and really strain to touch the ceiling, you could

quite easily topple over, no matter how young and agile you are. And falls from small heights are responsible for an enormous number of domestic injuries.

The second reason, and this applies to all work, is that having to strain and stretch the whole time will quickly make your arms feel like lead weights. So always arrange to work within comfortable reach of the ceiling. The time spent rearranging your steps or stool will be repaid in terms of less physical wear and tear.

A gleaming coat of paint on the ceiling, by itself, works wonders for a room. So if this is as much as you have time to do this month, or indeed can afford financially to do, then it is still a job well done. You will see how much brighter and fresher the whole rooms seems to be.

Now, what sort of paint should you use? Quite probably you will be totally confused by the number of paint types that adorn the shelves of your decorating shop. On page 53 you can

find out all about the modern paint ranges.

With the ceiling completed, the time is right to sit back and, at your leisure, really consider the rest of the room. Decide what you want on each wall – paper, paint, cladding, panelling – the choice is wide.

Really thinking about a room is the first stage of good interior design. A successful room has continuity about it but each wall should be complete in its design concept; this is the basic rule.

You may be in the habit of choosing a conventional wallpaper pattern for an all-over look. But why not try something different for a change? Modern materials are made in so many attractive designs and colours that the introduction of these, even in one feature area, will give the room more character.

When work is confined to small areas, protect the floorcovering with a piece of old bedspread or disused curtain.

Table step ladder.

Make sure you can reach the ceiling comfortably. Never stand on the top step of a stool.

Not everyone likes their feet to leave the ground. Here, a long handled, squeegee-type mop is invaluable for washing down.

The ideal feature areas are often part of the room's structure; alcoves, chimney breasts, a staircase in an open plan room. These can be given another dimension by covering with a contrasting paper or paint. You can use colour and pattern to highlight or detract from certain areas.

If you are a little more adventurous, you can really give a room a character of its own.

To make the fireplace recede use darker colours in the recesses.

A strong colour on the chimney breast with a lighter colour on adjacent recesses will make the chimney breast dominate the room and take away that 'square' appearance.

Lose recesses and fireplace projection by using a colourful pattern throughout.

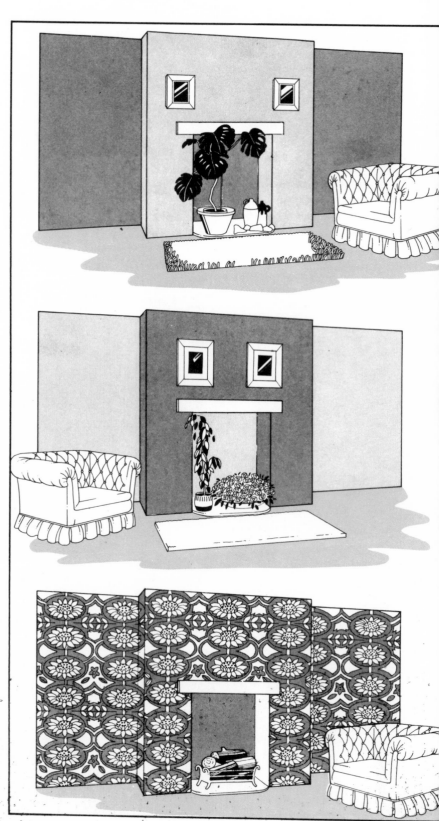

Use two buckets or bowls for washing down. Use plenty of clean water when rinsing off.

You can create all sorts of effects
with mirrors or mirror tiles. Use
them in alcoves, recesses or small,
normally unused areas. Couple with
concealed lighting to create an eye-
catching corner. The light can
highlight ornaments, flowers, a
painting, or simply cast shadows to
throw light on to wall decorations.
On a complete wall, mirrors can give
a double-length appearance to a small
room.

Of course feature areas need not be confined to single elevations.
Colour can be used to split a room in two. Create a double L shape by painting adjacent walls in contrasting colours.
Alternatively, especially in a long room, you can separate areas by using a contrasting colour or texture on one end wall.

If you can't be persuaded away from using a traditional effect such as an all-over white for the walls, why not use the door to bring some colour to the room? Add a splash of yellow, blue, red, orange or whatever you like. Perhaps use a colour to match the carpet. You can paint the panels in a contrasting shade, or give a more subtle effect by highlighting the mouldings to match the overall scheme. In a room with a vinyl wall covering, continue the pattern on to the door by using the same vinyl to cover the panels.

Using two colours on a panelled door can make the panels appear deeper or more shallow. For the deeper effect, choose a light colour for the surround to match the general scheme, and cover the panels in a darker contrasting paint. Reverse the procedure, dark surround and light panels, to give a shallow effect.

A simple pattern or motif is an easy way to bring a door to life. You can use a stencil to produce designs.

Some of the Tools You Will Need

BRUSHES

Do not buy cheap brushes; they will prove more expensive in the long run. Avoid those with a 'mouth' running through thin bristles as they will hold very little paint. Choose one in the medium price range which has plenty of bristles. The ideal brush size for a ceiling is 3in. to 4in. wide.

The best quality brushes have first grade pure hog's bristle. This will wear well and have a 'springy' feel.

Work out your new brush on brickwork after dipping it in water. This will remove any loose hairs. Then wash it thoroughly and allow to dry before using.

Before immersing it in the paint for the first time, twirl the brush in your palms a few times to remove final loose hairs.

PAINT PADS

I would recommend a paint pad every time for a beginner to use on a ceiling, especially when decorating in a room which is still at least partly furnished and there is only a single small sheet to protect the floor covering. If used correctly, a paint pad is less likely to throw paint splashes around.

A paint pad is simply a foam square base with a top covering of short bristles. The whole thing is mounted on a plastic handle.

A pad will apply the same amount of paint as a well brushed-out coat and yet it is less tiring to use than a brush or roller.

ROLLERS

Rollers are especially useful for applying paint to large areas. Roller applications are probably quicker than a brush or pad. They give a thicker coat but great care must be taken when using them or you can flick paint everywhere. Properly applied, a roller coat of paint can look just as good as a brush or pad coat.

There are several types of roller

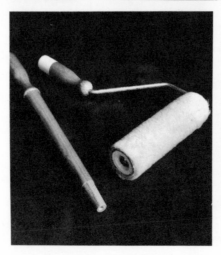

Opposite page
A 6in. × 4in. pad is the best for ceilings, walls and flush doors. The smallest is for painting around window frames and other more delicate work.

With experience you will soon develop the correct technique for loading a pad. Only immerse the bristles in the paint. Any excess paint can be wiped away on the side of the container.

Work in random strokes and don't brush out the paint too far. As you move the pad forward, tilt it slightly on to one edge; on the completion of the forward stroke, tilt it on to the opposite edge and draw the pad backwards.

Use a lambswool or mohair pile roller for ceilings.

To load a roller, immerse about half the pile into the paint in the roller tray. Roll out the roller on the 'dry' end of the tray to ensure an even covering of paint and to remove any excess. Do not allow the roller to spin as it is taken towards the ceiling or paint will splash off it.

Left
Use the roller in random directions and join up paint edges before they dry.

A roller will not reach into corners so finish off with a 1in. brush.

Keep the roller tray clean by lining it with a sheet of cooking foil. Throw the foil away afterwards.

available. Lambswool and mohair rollers are best for ceilings. A short pile lambswool type is probably the best buy for all-round use. Use a mohair type for gloss.

For textured ceilings use a long-pile lambswool roller. Cheaper all purpose foam types are also available. They are quite good, but not as good as those already described.

GLASSPAPER

There are various grades of glasspaper and waterproof abrasive paper from coarse to fine. The coarser grades are for heavier duty, the finer grades are for lighter work.

Since these papers are bought in sheets, it is inconvenient – and wasteful – to use them as they are. So cut each piece into three or four smaller pieces.

To use the paper efficiently, wrap a piece around a small, flat-sided block of wood or cork so that the face of the wood or cork is exactly covered. The remainder of the paper should be folded to the back of the block and retained in position with the hand.

Use the block with the paper held flat against the surface.

Types to have in your kit: Waterproof abrasive paper: 220 grade: covers most jobs.

Use 280 and 320 grade: for fine rubbing down.

Use F2 grade glasspaper for rubbing down oil-based, eggshell paint or emulsion.

Use M2 grade for coarser work on all rough surfaces.

For Woodwork: Before painting, rub down bare woodwork with F2 glasspaper. (If the surface is coarse, use M2 initially, finishing off with F2). Work in the direction of the grain only. Rubbing across the grain will cause scratches.

After the priming coat has been applied, the fibres in the wood may rise. Allow the primer to dry thoroughly and then rub down with F2 as above.

For Plaster: There is no need to rub down new plaster before painting.

This will only tend to scratch the surface and the indentations will show through the new paint. After stripping old wallcoverings, use M2 and/or F2, dependent on the state of the surface.

For Oil-base or eggshell surfaces: These surfaces are best rubbed down after they have been washed. Use waterproof abrasive paper. Normally, 220 grade can be used throughout, though a real craftsman would probably finish off with 320 grade.

The technique for using this paper differs slightly. Here, work in a circular motion using firm pressure.

To prevent paint clogging the face of the paper, dip it in clean water occasionally and rub it against a clean piece of paper. A small amount

of soap rubbed on the face of the paper keeps it lubricated while working, making the paper slide over the surface.

Waterproof abrasive paper lasts longer than ordinary glasspaper (since it can be cleaned) but it is more expensive. It does not create dust either.

M2 or F2 glasspaper can be used for oil-base or eggshell paint – dependent on the roughness of the surface.

For Emulsion: Never wet an emulsion before rubbing down. The surface could soften and scratches result under the rubbing action. F2 glasspaper treatment is adequate here before new emulsion is applied. Use the paper lightly though.

Preparation of the Work

SOME GENERAL POINTS

Where there are door architraves,
skirtings, picture rails and window
frames to be painted, these should be
done before a new wall covering is
used. Assuming that the paintwork
is in pretty good condition and you
want to repaint in a gloss finish then
first of all rub it down with wet-or-dry
glasspaper. Then wash down well to
make sure that all grease and polish
is removed. Use sugar soap or liquid
detergent and rinse thoroughly with
plenty of clean water. Then allow to
dry before painting.

Most people choose gloss paints for
woodwork. They are the most durable,
an important factor where the surface
is likely to be subjected to a fair
amount of knocks; on skirtings, for
example.

There is an important technique
associated with washing down walls
prior to painting. Start washing down
at the skirting level and finish at the
top of the wall or the ceiling rail. The
logic behind this might seem a little
obscure, and you might think that it is
pointless to allow dirty water to stream
down over a previously washed and
presumably clean surface. In fact,
though, the dirty water streaming
down the wall will flow freely over the
lower, wet area, thus avoiding dirty
streaks of water adhering to the surface
and drying out in lines.

Allow the wall to dry out before
painting.

Where possible, repaint a previously
glossed surface with a gloss or eggshell

**Wash walls down starting at the
bottom. Use the same washing down
technique and materials as for
ceilings. Take in three or so inches of
adjacent walls, when painting one wall
at a time.**

**If walls are clean just brush them down
to remove dust before repainting.**

finish. Emulsion paint used on a gloss surface is liable to flake, especially where steam and moisture are likely as in a kitchen or bathroom. It is therefore important to give a good key to the gloss surface.

Emulsion or other paints can be used on an existing paper but remember the pattern will show through as relief or texture and the paper will be more difficult to remove at a later date.

If you are using emulsion, but changing the colour, use a thinned down coat of the new emulsion colour as a primer.

The success of any covering material whether wallpaper, paint, floor tiles or whatever it is, depends to a large extent on the preparatory work. If you have ever been disappointed with a finish either immediately or a few months after the work has been completed, then you will realise the importance of correct groundwork. Peeling wallpaper, flaking or blistered paintwork or bumps and ridges under a brand new floorcovering are typical tell-tale signs.

Apart from the visual effect, skimped groundwork can be costly and, in the long run time-consuming. Covering materials will have to be removed and new ones bought. So it makes sense to do the job properly in the first place.

There is a wide variety of decorative coverings available today and each group demands a specific treatment. Sometimes you can get away with a minimum amount of materials and a few simple tools, but elsewhere major surgery involving a good deal of time and expense will be involved. Never deliberately fool yourself that a simple repair will suffice; look at the surface objectively and err on the side of pessimism if you are at all uncertain.

If putting emulsion on a gloss surface, rub down first to give a good key for the new paint. A piece of wet-or-dry glasspaper, used with clean water, will prevent dust when rubbing down. Alternatively use a pumice block and water.

A plank resting on stepladders provides a continuous working platform.

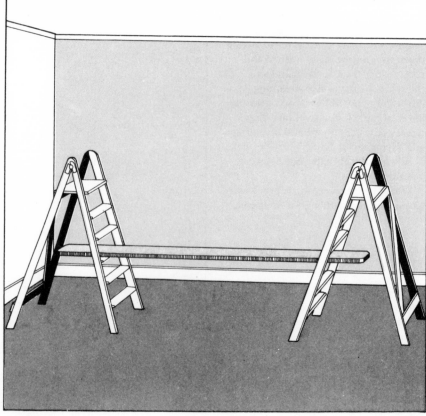

WOODWORK

Never remove old paintwork which is in a sound condition. Very often, the old layers may have been built up on an uneven surface to form a smooth covering. If you remove the paint, you have to start this build-up again and any minor bad areas can be dealt with by filling in without removing the lot.

There are four ways to remove paint. By burning it off; by using a chemical stripper; or by dry scraping and sanding, or by sanding alone.

METHOD 1 : Paraffin blowlamps are difficult for the amateur to use, so a blowtorch is preferable. These are used with bottled gas cartridges and you just fit a cartridge and light up.

The basic technique involves adjusting the flame to suit your working speed and keeping the blowtorch on the move, using a scraper to lift the softened paint away. If you stop, you may scorch the wood and cause a lot more preparatory work to be done, as the scorched surface must be removed.

Strip flat surfaces from the bottom upwards.

After stripping, rub down the woodwork with M2 glasspaper to remove final nibs of paint.

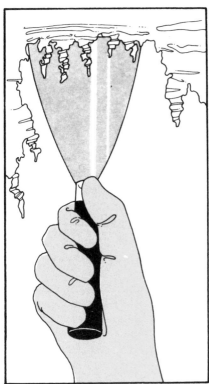

One method of removing paint is using chemical stripper applied with a brush.

With a blowtorch or chemical stripper, when the paint wrinkles, it can be stripped off. It is wise to wear a pair of old leather gloves, to protect the skin from being burnt by hot, melted paint peelings.

Blowtorches and chemical strippers are used in conjunction with a stripping knife (for large, flat areas), a chisel knife (for narrower, flat areas), and shavehooks (for mouldings and other awkward corners and crevices). Two types of shavehooks are used: one is triangular, the other has a multi-edged blade.

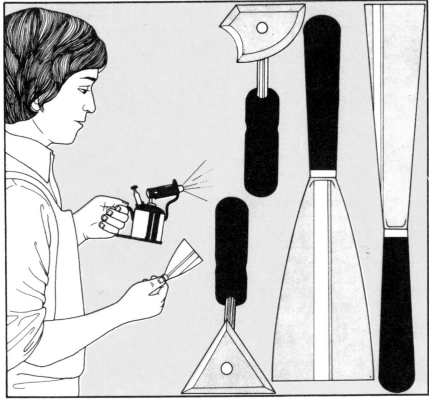

METHOD 2 : Proprietary chemical paint strippers are preferable for anyone who feels unsafe about using heat.

Use of chemicals is not confined to removing paint from woodwork as they can also be employed to strip paint from metal and plaster.

Some types dissolve the paint, others shrivel it, causing it to bubble and wrinkle, similar to the effect that heat has on paint.

Avoid the cheaper types of stripper which have caustic soda as a base. No matter how thoroughly the surface is cleaned afterwards, these often leave small residues behind which might bleed through the new paintwork and ruin it.

The best types have paint solvents as their base. These are very efficient when dealing with oil-based paints, which is the most likely type you will have to deal with. Some types remove emulsion.

Follow manufacturer's instructions closely when using chemical strippers.

Two safety points to note are: First, no form of heating must be nearby while you are working. Second, the chemicals emit noxious fumes so keep windows open to give plenty of ventilation.

The big disadvantage with chemicals

It is a good idea, when stripping with either heat or chemicals, to keep a tin container below to catch paint peelings.

Wear old gloves to protect the skin. Use an old, worn out paintbrush to apply a liberal coat of stripper. Transfer a small amount of stripper into a suitable container for use.

After a few seconds the paint will shrivel and can be removed.

Be especially careful where working overhead is unavoidable. The only safe way to prevent splashes falling into your eyes is to wear protective goggles.

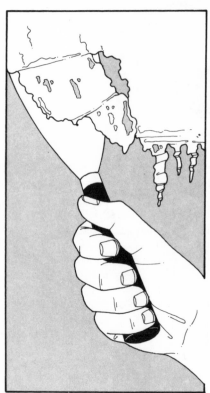

Take care when using a Skarsten scraper not to damage the surface by 'digging out' stubborn paint.

To remove wallpaper you need a bucket of water, a sponge, and a 3in. wide scraper. A small amount of domestic detergent or proprietary wallpaper stripper added to the water sometimes help to remove stubborn areas.

Lay newspapers on top of the dust sheet. When they are soaked and covered with peelings, gather them up into a bundle and transfer them to a polythene bag.

Use the scraper square to the wall to avoid digging it into the plaster. Take off all the small bits as you proceed.

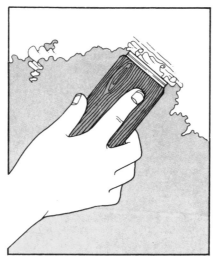

is their cost, especially noticeable when dealing with large areas. Also thick or stubborn paint might need two or three applications before it is removed. For small areas, however, chemical strippers are very useful.

An especially useful aspect of chemicals comes to the fore on such things as panelled doors where there are lots of mouldings and crevices which can be difficult to reach.

Here, the stripper can be applied and, when the paint wrinkles, wire wool, used lightly, and a pointed stick (for reaching right into corners) can remove the paint.

Use an old, worn brush to apply the stripper; leave it for a few seconds, until the paintwork starts to wrinkle and shrivel and then it can be removed with a shavehook or scraper.

When all the paint is off, use white spirit or water – according to the maker's instructions – to wipe down all surfaces thoroughly. Usually 24 hours must be allowed to elapse before any paint is applied.

It cannot be over emphasised, that chemicals can burn the skin. Therefore always wear gloves when using them.

METHOD 3: The cheapest, but also the hardest, stripping method is to use a scraper and glasspaper. These are generally useful for odd, small areas.

A Skarsten scraper is very good as it has a serrated blade for initial scoring and a plain blade for final stripping. After scraping, use the glasspaper wrapped around a cork block for final smoothing.

METHOD 4: Power tools fitted with a sander are useful for stripping paintwork. These save a lot of elbow work. However, they really cause the dust to fly so, where possible, with removable doors for example, take the work outside.

A drum sander, which can probably be obtained from a local hire shop is ideal for large areas. The abrasive paper is fitted to a foam rubber wheel.

Use it lightly, starting with a coarse abrasive and, for the final finish, switch to a fine grade. Do not use disc sanders unless you are experienced with them. Used incorrectly, they will leave scratch marks or circular marks through the grain of wood, giving you another repair job to do.

Finish off by hand with a fine abrasive wrapped around a cork block.

Filling for Woodwork: Hollows, cracks and other surface indentations will ruin the finished paintwork so they must be filled. It would take many coats if you used paint alone to bring the surface level even with minor defects.

New or stripped paintwork should first be rubbed down with F2 glasspaper working in the direction of the grain. Rubbing across the grain will cause scratches. Use a coarser glasspaper, M2 grade, if you are dealing with rough timber.

Fill cracks with a proprietary wood filler which should be pressed into the cavity with a filling knife, left to harden, and rubbed flat with F2 glasspaper. Gaps around electrical socket outlets fitted to skirtings *must* be lined with a dry timber backing for the filler.

Removing old wallpaper: Stripping off old wallpaper can almost be a pleasant job when the old, tired wallcovering peels off the wall in long lengths. A task that you had reservations about suddenly looks as though it might be completed in an hour.

However, those long lengths of paper indicate something about wallpapering and decorating, that is worth remembering.

Although the paper may have appeared to have been well stuck to the walls, the effect that water had in loosening its grip so easily is an indication of what would have happened had you attempted to decorate over it.

Had fresh paper been applied, the new paste would have soaked through the old paper and loosened the grip of the old adhesive. Thus the original paper would have come away bringing with it the new covering.

The same would have happened with new paint. The paint would have soaked through and loosened the adhesive, so you have an answer to those people who scoff at the idea of removing the existing paper before redecorating.

Of course some people do decorate successfully without removing the old paper. If the paper is thick and the paste is of the correct strength then it often works. The trouble is that the only way to find out is to try it.

Testing a small area – or even a whole wall is no guide to the way the other walls were decorated. If a weaker paste was used in some areas or the surface was not properly prepared then you will suddenly encounter trouble.

Incidentally, when paper can be pulled off without wetting, then this can be attributed to papering over old distemper or papering over a damp wall. So this time, make sure the surface is prepared correctly. The cause of any damp must be traced and attended to before proceeding.

The other argument against painting over paper is that any pattern or texture will probably show through the paint.

A couple of coats may obliterate a pattern but heavy textures may need further coats to hide them. However, a pattern or texture can sometimes be attractive under fresh paint.

Floor protection: Laying newspapers along the skirtings is a good way to catch any water and paper peelings dropping down on to the floor. However it is only a good idea if you conscientously pick up the newspapers when they are soaking – and before they start to stick to the floor.

If you are a self-confessed 'messy worker' then forget the newspapers and use pieces of cardboard torn from grocery packing cartons.

Use Sellotape to stick the pieces of cardboard together until they stretch continuously around the perimeter of the room.

Proprietary wallpaper strippers: There are proprietary wallpaper strippers on the market which are added to the bucket of water used to soak the paper. However, there is no point in buying one of these until you are certain that it is needed. They become a worthwhile investment when a good soaking has insufficient effect on the paper, but even then, a few drops of a household detergent often achieves the same effect of helping to loosen the old paste.

METHOD OF WORKING: So, first of all, soak all the walls with warm water applied with an old, large distemper brush, or a sponge.

Punch the water well into the surface but do not cause a mini-Niagara Falls situation where water just pours down the walls.

When you return to the starting point, test with a scraper to see if the water has had any effect in the ten minutes that has probably elapsed.

If the scraper will not lift the paper easily, go right around again. You might have to do this two or three times.

When the water seems to be having the desired effect, concentrate on removing about 2 or 3 square yards at a time. A final light sponging with water may be necessary before you can scrape off the paper easily.

Use a 3-inch scraper and use it carefully. Avoid digging into the plaster. The temptation will be there with stubborn pieces of paper but resist it. Otherwise you will have a lot of extra hole filling work to do later on.

When all the paper is off the walls, wash them thoroughly to remove all traces of hard paste, before filling any cracks with filler.

If you encounter walls with two or three layers of paper, each layer will have to be removed individually, since the water will not soak through several layers.

Dealing with washable papers: Washable papers can cause headaches.

Soaking alone will not break down the surface of the paper and allow the water to soak through and the old adhesive to become soft. There are a few alternatives to try but it is really hard going whichever method you opt for. The surface must be broken up first by 'scrubbing' with a wire brush, or using coarse glasspaper or even an old hacksaw blade.

You can hire a steam stripper to do the softening up work, and they certainly save time and effort. But unless you have had previous experience in using one, it would probably be better to employ a professional to do the work, since misuse can cause a lot of plaster to come away.

Heavy-relief papers can be extremely tricky to strip: sometimes a steam stripper is the only answer. Even so, the paper was probably stuck down originally with special adhesive and a lot of plaster could come away with it.

It might not be a bad idea to consider panelling with tongued and grooved cladding or ordinary wood panels instead of repapering.

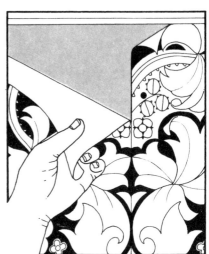

Steam strippers should be filled with water, the burner ignited and, when steam emerges, held close to the wall. After a while the steam will penetrate through and soften the old adhesive.

Strippable papers can be removed simply by peeling away from the wall. This will leave a backing paper which is ideal for painting over or as a backing for a new wallcovering, provided it is well stuck down.

Hang lining paper horizontally, taking ½in. on to each return wall.

Use the seam roller to smooth down all edges.

The use of lining paper: If walls are sound but crazed, or there is a fair amount of unevenness due to bad plastering, hang lining paper first. Lining paper will improve the finish of any decorative wallcovering. Paste as for normal wallpaper (see page 37).

The lengths on the wall you start on should turn on to the side walls for about ½in. Always start at the top of the wall and hang each length horizontally. Allow for the turn when cutting the lengths.

Carefully, butt the edges of successive lengths. Remember, any overlaps will show through the covering material whether using paper or paint over it.

Continue to hang horizontally around the room, cutting the lengths carefully into the completed corner and turning ½in. on to the unfinished wall. On the last wall, cut neatly into both corners.

Walls with only limited defective areas can be feather edged lined to add strength to a repair. Tear off a piece of lining paper, about 1ft. wide. Paste the central 6in. with cellulose paste and brush it over the repair leaving the 'dry' border hanging down. Allow to dry thoroughly.

Tear off the border to leave an edge which feathers out into nothing. Prime the area with emulsion and allow to dry.

Finally, to complete the invisible repair, apply a thin coat of filler over the feathered edge to completely disguise it and prime with emulsion.

Whether or not you use lining paper beneath a wallcovering, it is worthwhile applying glue size first. Mix the powder with water according to the instructions and brush it on to the walls with an old distemper brush. If you use cellulose paste to hang the paper, this can also be used to a size. Sizing seals porous walls. If it is not used, the paper might not stick properly.

Expanded polystyrene covering:
(See illustrations on next page)
If walls are subject to condensation

(kitchens and bathrooms especially) line them with expanded polystyrene. This is bought in rolls and can be papered over or painted with emulsion.

Prepare the wall by washing and removing all loose material.

If there is mould, fungus or mildew on it wash it down with a fungicide.

Special adhesive is used to hang the polystyrene and so, to provide a key for it if the surface has been previously painted, score with a wire brush. The adhesive is brushed on to the wall immediately prior to hanging a length.

Washing and repairing vinyls: If the covering on your wall is vinyl, you may find that you do not need to replace it. The big advantage of vinyl wallcoverings is that if they get stained – a strong possibility with children about – they can be cleaned. By cleaning, I mean scrubbing, not just a light sponging.

It is all very well when you have to deal with a wallcovering that you put up yourself but, when the covering is one that you inherited from a previous occupant, you can not always tell whether you are faced with a washable type or not. If you wash ordinary paper, most likely it will come away from the wall, tear, or the colours will start to run.

There is only one sure way of finding out and that is to make a test on a small, inconspicuous area. For example, behind a bookcase or other bulky piece of furniture in the room which is likely to remain in one position until the room is completely redecorated.

Apply a little clean water with a sponge. Should any of the things listed above be the result then it is ordinary paper and there is no point in continuing.

Should the water remain on the surface, try sponging it a little more heavily. If nothing happens, use a nail brush to scrub it lightly. At the end of this test, if the covering remains sound, you should be able to wash the paper without causing any damage.

A word of warning if a stain you are

trying to remove covers a join between two lengths of wallcovering.

Whether the stain needs a simple sponging or more vigorous nail brush treatment, work in an up and down vertical movement. If you work horizontally, you could lift the vinyl away from its paper backing.

Patching an 'impossible' stain can be done with matching material, but if the covering has been on the wall for a long time, the patched area will be obvious as the original colour may have faded a little.

However if a patch were to be as obvious as that then the room probably needs redecorating anyway, so most people would prefer to live with the damage for a while. You never know, it might even provide the incentive for you to get started and redecorate.

If you keep all the old bits and pieces of paper remaining after covering a wall with vinyl then you will have a ready supply of 'patches' at your disposal.

To repair a vinyl, cut out a piece which corresponds in pattern to the damaged area. It needs to be about ½in. larger all round than the damage.

Stick it in place with a little wallpaper paste. Place a straight-edge about ½in. inside the edge of the patch and, using a sharp knife, cut through the patch and wallcovering. Repeat round the patch. Remove the patch and the old vinyl to leave the backing paper only on the wall. Remove the paper from the back of the patch and stick it in place using latex adhesive.

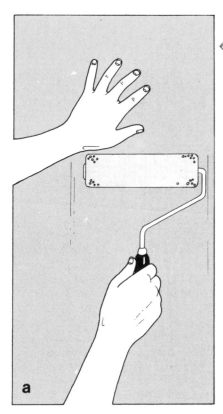

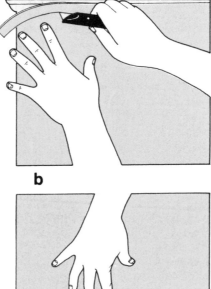

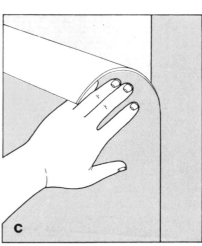

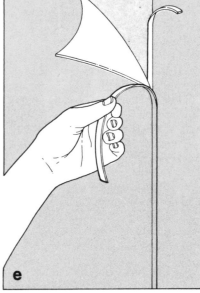

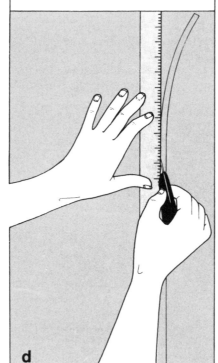

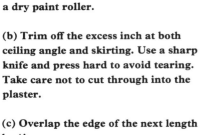

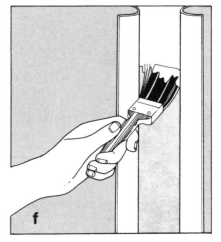

Expanded Polystyrene (see text on previous page).

(a) Hold the roll of polystyrene in position and press it into place with a dry paint roller.

(b) Trim off the excess inch at both ceiling angle and skirting. Use a sharp knife and press hard to avoid tearing. Take care not to cut through into the plaster.

(c) Overlap the edge of the next length by ½in.

(d) To get a neat butt join at edges, use a straight-edge as a guide for the knife and cut through both thicknesses.

(e) and (f) Gently peel off the top strip and then the bottom, working carefully. It may be necessary to apply more adhesive to restick the edges.

Condensation

The signs to look for: Pools of water on window sills and steamed up windows are the traditional signs of condensation in a house.

Many people recognise this for what it is but assume that only the window areas can be affected. When damp patches appear on walls, ceilings and floors, they are thought to be caused by damp from outside or a leak in the plumbing system.

This need not be so. It could equally well be condensation.

The trouble is that when damp patches disappear, as they often do for a time, they are forgotten until the next time they reappear.

Eventually, however, the constant effect of wetness will cause the condition of decorations to deteriorate, possibly ruining them all together.

So two things must be done. First, the problem has to be analysed to establish whether or not condensation is the enemy. Remedial treatment for damp is different.

Second, an attempt has to be made to cure or even lessen the effects.

It is pointless to continue shrugging your shoulders and wiping down windows and mopping up the water that collects on sills. Strategically placed towels or strips of sponge fixed to the window afford some protection but this should only be a last resort when some effort has been made to remedy the situation in other ways.

So how can you differentiate between damp and condensation if their appearance is the same?

An accurate evaluation can usually be made by noting the weather conditions.

On a cold, dry day condensation is more likely. Streaming windows and damp patches on outer walls are the obvious signs. On the other hand, damp patches forming on walls and floors on a wet and muggy day are more likely to indicate damp from outside.

If damp patches appear on floors, there is a simple test that can be made to find out which the cause is.

Fix a small piece of glass to a ring of putty or plasticine arranged on the floor so that the air space inside the putty and below the glass is completely sealed off.

After a few days, moisture will form either on top or below the surface of the glass.

If it forms on top, the problem is condensation. If it forms below, the problem is damp.

The causes of condensation: In order to effect treatment, the causes of condensation must be understood.

Condensation is formed when warm, moist air contacts a cool surface. In rooms where the air is often filled with water vapour – bathrooms and kitchens especially – beads of moisture will form on wall tiles. In living rooms, irregularly spaced and shaped damp patches will occur on walls and ceilings.

The air in a room is moistened through steam given off by normal household activities – washing and cooking; the burning of gas, solid fuel or paraffin.

These activities make rooms warmer but, at the same time, they increase the amount of water vapour carried in the air, so warm, moist air is created. When this contacts a cooler surface, the water vapour condenses.

At a given temperature, air will hold a certain amount of water vapour. When the temperature is lowered, the amount of water in the air drops proportionately. That is when the vapour condenses.

A small piece of glass, pressed down onto a ring of putty on the floor is a good way to test for damp or condensation.

How to prevent it: The complete prevention of condensation is not always possible but it is usually possible to reduce it.

This can be done by taking certain measures – keeping rooms warm, disposing of steam and water vapour, avoiding cold surfaces and making sure that there is adequate ventilation in the room.

It might sound paradoxical to say 'keep rooms warm and provide adequate ventilation' but a happy balance can be struck between warmth and fresh air.

The main rooms to concentrate on are the kitchen and the bathroom. If you get rid of the steam at its source, then there will be little left to spread into other rooms in the house. So ventilation is the first thing.

An air brick bought from a builders' merchant can be fitted in the wall. Louvres in windows and doors are useful, since they can be opened to allow fresh air in without causing uncomfortable draughts.

Steam created during cooking can be removed by a cooker hood which takes it out through an external wall. Another good idea is an extractor fan. There are many types available which come with full fitting instructions.

The problem is which to buy. The fan must not be too small for the size of the room, since it will not extract the steam efficiently. For an average-sized kitchen a fan of at least 6in. diameter is needed, but discuss this aspect fully with your supplier.

In the bathroom, $\frac{3}{8}$in. or $\frac{1}{2}$in. thick expanded polystyrene tiles will prevent condensation forming on the ceiling.

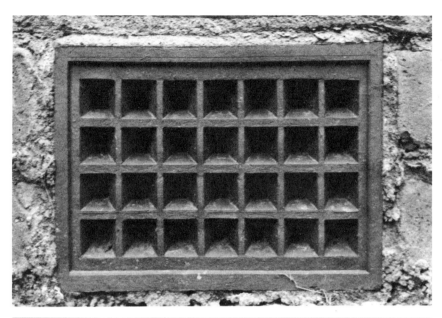

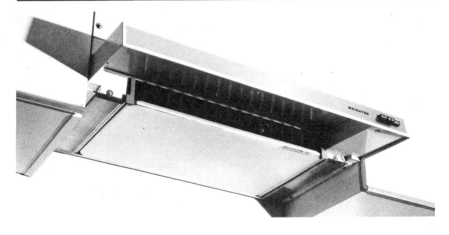

An air brick can be fitted in the wall.

Louvres on inside walls, doors and windows are useful.

A cooker hood will take steam out through an external wall.

More about these on page 70.

Flame retardant polystyrene tiles should be used where there is a fire risk. If you want to paint the tiles, use a fire retardent paint such as Timonox.

If you take out a fireplace and build a new surround, or simply cover the chimney breast with wallpaper (after bricking up the hole in the wall), then you have blocked off the ventilation point of the flue. Make sure you leave an air brick when you block off a chimney or damp patches will soon appear on the chimney breast.

The ideal heat for the prevention of condensation is dry heat – radiators, electric convectors, radiant fires, and so on.

Paraffin heaters cause condensation. For every gallon of paraffin they burn, a gallon of water vapour is released into the air.

Other remedies: If the problem persists try lining the walls with sheet expanded polystyrene.

If this does not work, the last resort is cavity wall insulation, an expensive step but it does make a house warmer and reduce fuel bills. This is a specialist job involving filling the cavity between the walls of a house with foam or mineral wool fibres. Firms which carry it out can be found in the Yellow Pages directory.

Solid floors: On solid floors, a cork underlay or a reflective-faced building paper under the floorcovering will cure condensation. Both materials are available from builders' merchants. However, good carpet and underlay will prevent condensation in normal circumstances.

Sheet expanded polystyrene and adhesive.

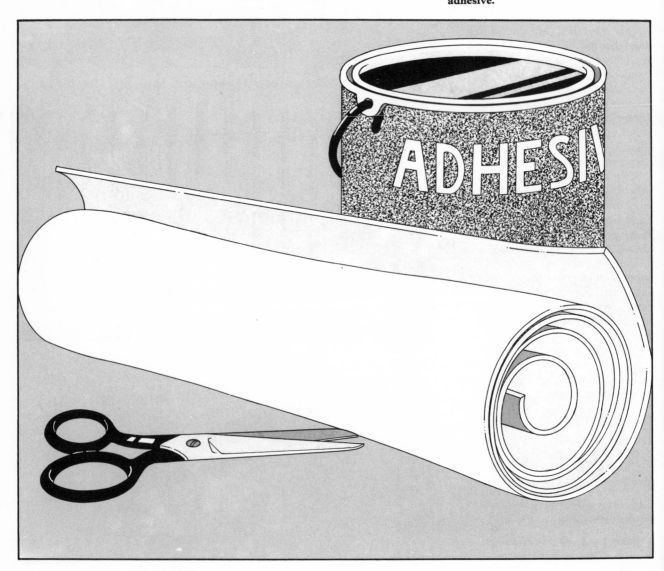

Hanging Wallpaper

Tools and equipment: A fold-away pasting table is a good buy if you have a lot of papering to do. This is where all cutting and pasting is done. An old 5in.-wide distemper brush makes an ideal pasting brush.

YOU WILL NEED: a bucket for the paste, and a pair of shears about 8in. long are right for the beginner. These enable you to get a good straight cut when finishing off at picture rails or ceilings.

For intricate cutting around fireplaces, socket outlets, etc., use an ordinary pair of scissors.

A wallpaper brush is needed to smooth the paper into position.

For smoothing down the edges of each length, you use a wooden seam roller. This should not be used on textured papers.

Use a sharp knife with vinyl wallcoverings for trimming around fireplaces etc. Do not cut into the plaster as the plaster could lift away later.

A folding boxwood rule is used to measure lengths and narrow widths at corners.

It is important to hang the first length of paper vertically, so you will need a plumb bob.

Keep a pencil handy for marking cut lines on the paper and vertical lines on the wall.

To indicate starting lines for ceiling paper you use a piece of chalked string. Transfer the chalk line to the ceiling by pulling the supported string gently away at the ceiling and releasing.

Keep a sponge handy for wiping away paste. A clean bucket of water should also be on hand to wash the sponge out occasionally.

Buy the correct type of paste for your wallcovering. Your supplier will advise you on this.

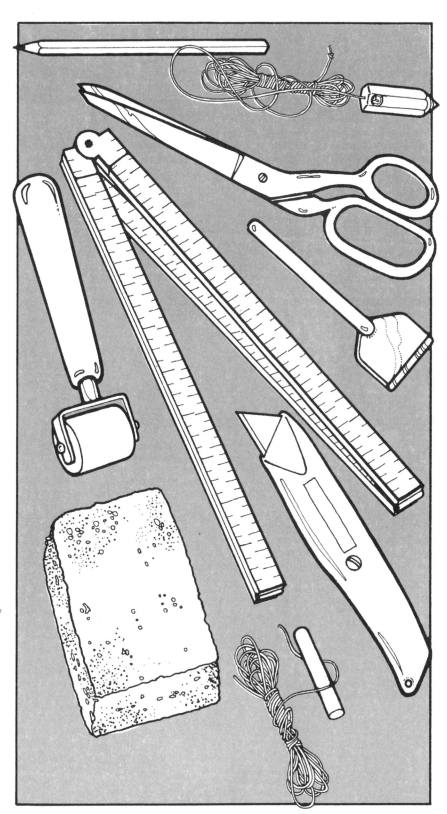

Using a plumb line: As, apart from lining paper, wallpaper is hung vertically, before the first length is hung, a plumb line must be suspended from a drawing pin pushed into the wall as high up as possible to find a true vertical. Do this irrespective of whether you start by a window frame, door or centrally over a fireplace. It is equally important to use a plumb line when cutting a length into a corner if this is your starting point, to make sure that the corner is vertical.

Window frames, doors, plastered edges or corners must never be taken as being vertical without checking.

If you intend to use a wall covering on the walls, then the old paper should be stripped off. See section on preparation (page 26). It is at this stage of decorating that the results of your work can often spread into every room in the house. Strips of paper are picked up on shoes and trodden everywhere. So work in gradual stages, cleaning up as you proceed.

Ready pasted papers: The ideal wall coverings to use when decorating a partly furnished room, are ready-pasted papers or vinyls. They avoid all

This could happen if you do not hang the first length vertically.

If starting at a corner, hang the plumb line 20in. from the corner, (assuming the roll is 21in. wide).

When the line stops swinging, mark its position on the wall in three or four places. Using a straight-edge and pencil, join up the marks and you have a vertical start line to work to. A plumb line must be used on each wall in turn to test for a true vertical.

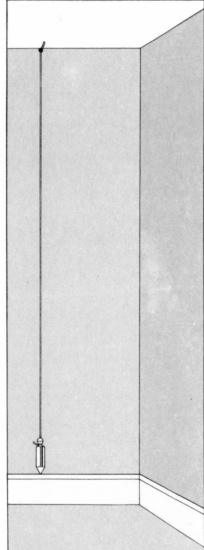

the usual trappings and mess associated with conventional wallpapers, pasting table, bucket of paste, brush and so on. The paste is already on the back of the paper in a dry state, ready to be activated by pulling the paper through a water trough. The trough is usually supplied with the paper.

The only preparation needed, apart from covering the floor, is to cut a couple of strips of paper and to fill the trough with water.

Take hold of the top corners and withdraw the roll slowly from the trough. Leave the tail of the paper immersed to ensure that all the water runs back into the trough. Hang the length in the usual way (see section on hanging wallcoverings, page 37) leaving the tail of the paper in the trough until the last moment.

Do not panic if a lot of adhesive squelches out from beneath the paper; this is quite usual. The porosity of wall surfaces is so varied that, to allow for every situation, manufacturers apply

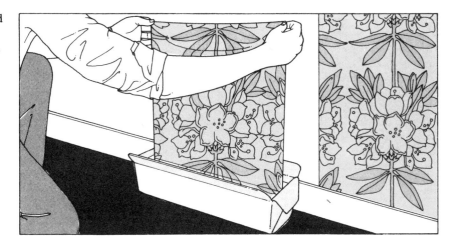

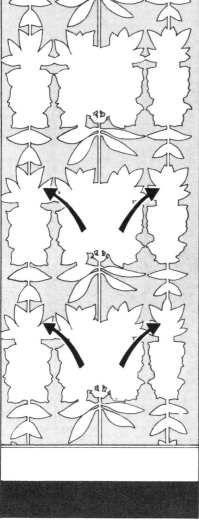

Cut ready pasted paper to length, then roll it up and immerse it in the water trough (pattern facing outwards) and leave it there for the recommended time, usually about a minute. Pull it out slowly or the paste on the back won't become activated.

Withdraw the paper by holding the corners. Leave the tail immersed to ensure that the water runs back into the trough.

Some manufacturers recommend using a sponge rather than the conventional brush for smoothing out the paper. A clean paint roller can also be used. Work in the direction of the arrows.

much more adhesive to the back than is normally necessary. This caters for highly porous surfaces which soak up a lot of paste.

The big advantage of ready-pasted wallcoverings is that you can hang as few or as many lengths of paper as you want to in any one work session. You will not keep wasting a lot of mixed-up paste.

Other papers: Papers come in a wide variety of textures, weights and patterns. Avoid thin, cheap papers if you are a beginner as they tear easily; unless you get the positioning right first time you will be in trouble. Go for medium or heavyweights. You can distinguish light papers from heavier weights by the feel. The price is also a guide.

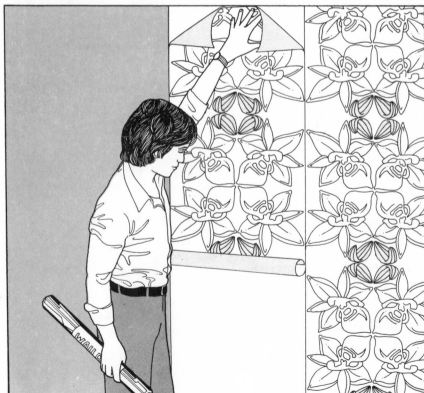

Random patterns avoid the wastage associated with pattern matching, especially in a room with lots of corners.

Large prominent patterns create a lot of wastage and could mean breaking into part of a spare roll.

36

Estimating wallpaper needed: To find out how many rolls of paper to buy, use the chart (right).

The important measurements are the height of the wall from the skirting board and the distance around the walls. Include doors and windows in this.

Remember, it is always worth buying an extra roll at the outset. Wallpaper is manufactured in batches and sometimes the colours of one batch differ very slightly from the next – even though the pattern is identical and the colours are supposed to be an exact match. If you need an extra roll through underestimating or ruining a couple of lengths when hanging, then it might not be possible to get a spare roll from the same batch.

Arrange with your supplier a sale-or-return transaction. If the spare roll is not needed and the wrapper remains intact you will get your money refunded. It is better to be sure than sorry.

Measuring and pasting: Make up sufficient paste for the amount of paper to be hung in one session.

Measure the first length by holding a prominent part of the pattern (which makes for easier pattern matching) to the starting point, probably the picture rail or ceiling. Allow 3in. for trimming at the bottom and top. Hold the paper in position on the wall and cut off the length. If you find this awkward to manage, then simply mark the paper to indicate the cut line and transfer the work to your working table.

Lay the paper face down on the table for pasting. Leave each length for the amount of time needed for the paste to soak in. Anaglyptas and heavy papers need up to five minutes. Thin papers and vinyls can be hung almost immediately.

Uniform soaking time is needed to prevent the paper from stretching unevenly, making pattern matching impossible.

Hanging: Carry the folded, pasted paper over your arm to the wall.

You must be able to reach the ceiling comfortably when hanging the top of the length, so arrange your step ladder to suit the most convenient working position.

A good wallpaper brush is expensive so as an alternative, (if you only have one room to paper in the forseeable future) you can use a clean, dry paint roller to smooth out the paper.

Wipe any paste from the face of vinyls and washable papers before it dries. Take good care to avoid any paste getting on to the face of non-washable papers. Remove any paste from skirtings, picture rails or ceilings before it dries.

Neighbouring lengths must meet with a neat butt join; the edges must not overlap.

If you use a paint roller for the main brushing out, use a small wood seam roller for smoothing back the

Distance round the room in feet	Height in feet from skirting						
	7 to 7½	7½ to 8	8 to 8½	8½ to 9	9 to 9½	9½ to 10	10 to 10½
	Number of rolls required						
30	4	5	5	5	6	6	6
34	5	5	5	5	6	6	7
38	5	6	6	6	7	7	8
42	6	6	7	7	7	8	8
46	6	7	7	7	8	8	9
50	7	7	8	8	9	9	10
54	7	8	9	9	9	10	10
58	8	8	9	9	10	10	11
62	8	9	10	10	10	11	12
66	9	9	10	10	11	12	13
70	9	10	11	11	12	12	13
74	10	10	12	12	12	13	14
75	10	11	12	12	13	14	15
82	11	11	13	13	14	14	16
86	12	12	14	14	14	15	16
90	12	13	14	14	15	16	17
94	13	13	15	15	15	16	18
98	13	14	15	15	16	17	19

top and bottom edges at ceiling and skirting. Do not use rollers on textured papers.

After hanging a length, examine it for air bubbles. Bubbles indicate either trapped air (peel back enough of the paper to smooth out the bubble), dry spots on the back of the paper or insufficient soaking time (you may have to remove the paper and re-paste).

High spots indicate excessive paste, which can generally be smoothed out. Sponge away any paste from the table before pasting the next length.

Corners: Corners are the only points where paper edges should overlap, as here small overlaps will not be noticed. You must always cut the paper to the width required when turning corners. Never try to take more than 1in. of paper around a corner. 1in. is the maximum on external corners; on internal corners only $\frac{1}{4}$in. must be taken on to the return wall.

Always ensure that the length is cut correctly so that the pattern will still match when it is hung.

If the corners are badly out of square, avoid vertical patterns which will highlight the fault.

Never stand the rolls of paper upright; the edges will be damaged. Most papers are packed ready to hang. Check this when purchasing. If necessary, get the shop to trim off the selvedge.

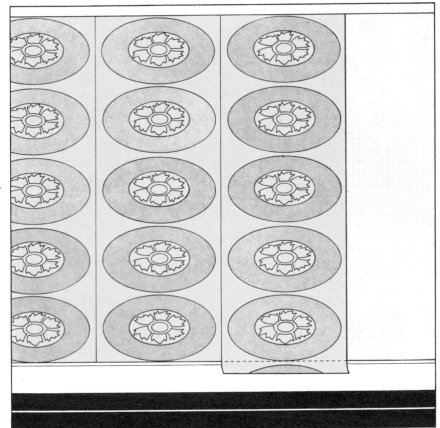

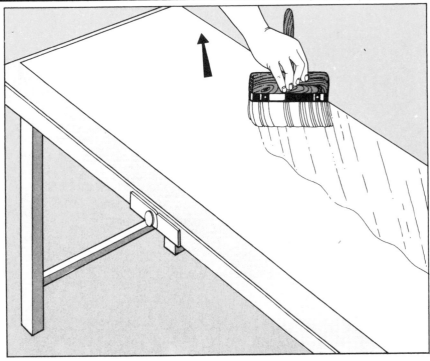

Make sure a prominent part of the pattern appears at the top. Allow 3in. excess at the skirting for trimming.

Tie a piece of string across the paste bucket and use this to wipe the brush on to remove excess paste. This will avoid any paste running down the outside of the bucket.

Line the paste bucket with a polythene pedal bin liner. When the paste is used up, remove it and throw it away. This saves a cleaning job.

Lay the paper face down on the table and brush on the paste smoothly in herringbone fashion. Slide each edge of the paper to the corresponding edge of the table. Always brush from the centre outwards. This will prevent the paste from getting on the table.

(a) Fold over the pasted half to the centre of the length.

(b) Paste the other half then fold it over to meet the first length in the centre.

(c) Carry the folded paper to the wall over your arm.

(d) Soaking time must be uniform for all lengths. Otherwise the paper will stretch irregularly and the pattern will be impossible to match.

(e) Unfold the top half of the paper and position the edge against the vertical pencil line already marked on the wall. Position the top to allow for the 3in. overlap for final trimming.

(f) When the positioning is correct, brush out the top half of the length. Brush down the centre first; then work in herringbone fashion out to the edges. Do this carefully to avoid any air remaining trapped under the paper. This would cause bubbles on the surface.

(g) Unfold the bottom half of the paper and brush out in the same way. Do not let the lower half drop down and swing. This will cause stretching and make pattern matching impossible.

(h) When the paper is firmly fixed, trim it to fit the ceiling (or picture rail). Press the back of the shears into the paper, following the line of the under side of the picture rail. This will leave a crease on the paper.

(i) Pull the paper away from the wall and cut along the crease line with the shears. A knife must not be used on standard papers as they will ruck up and tear.

(j) Brush the paper back into position. Repeat at skirting.

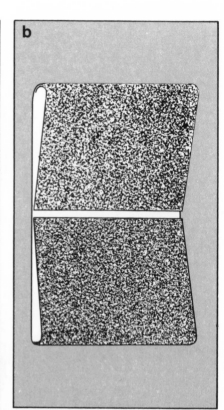
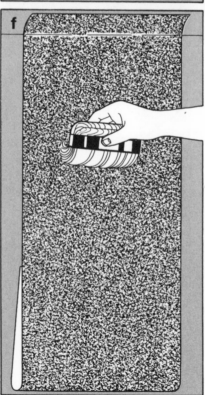
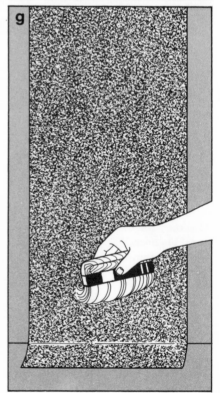

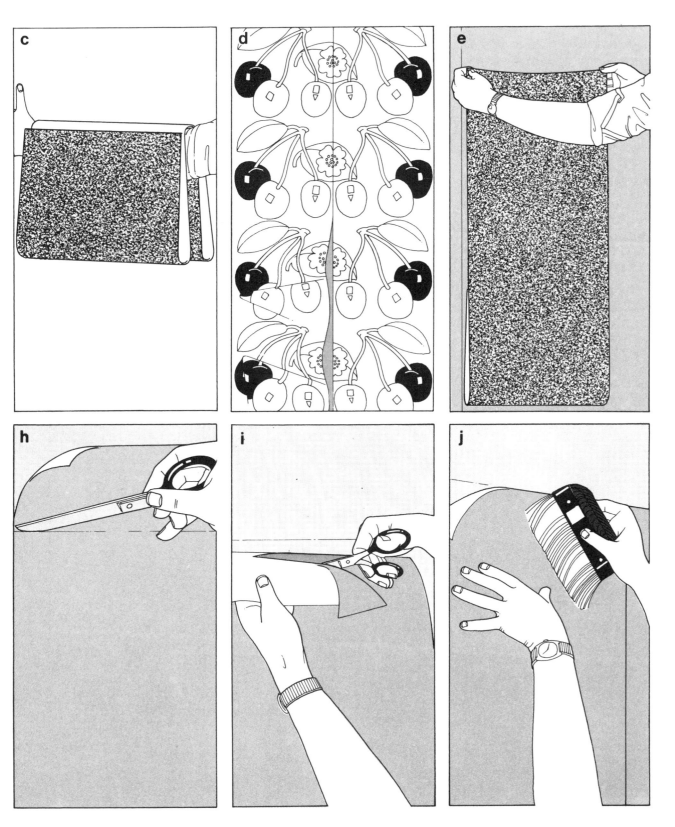

A sharp Stanley knife is ideal for trimming vinyls. Cut at an angle to the wall. If you use the knife square to the wall, you may cut into the plaster; the vinyl could pull it away on drying.

Unfold the top half of the next length and line up the pattern. Slide the edges together to form a neat butt joint. Brush out as before.

Release the bottom half of the length; this is where the vertical plumb line begins to pay off. The edge of the length will automatically form a neat butt joint with the first length.

Use a small wood seam roller to smooth out all edges.

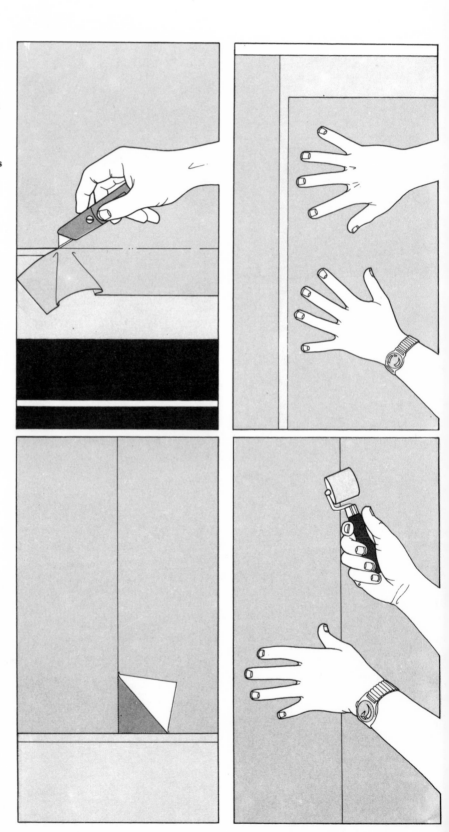

As soon as a length is in place, examine it for bubbles. A switched-on electric bulb held close to the wall will indicate these. Brush out bubbles immediately, working towards the edges; or preferably pull the paper back beyond the bubble and brush out as before. If the bubble is caused by a dry spot, pull the paper away from the surface, brush paste on to the paper and smooth the paper back, working in both directions from the centre to the edges.

For corners, measure the distance from the edge of the last length to the corner. Take 4 measurements at different points. These may vary. Add ¼in. to the greatest distance (in the drawing 10in.) and cut this amount from the length on the table. Hang the first portion as usual turning ¼in. on to the return wall. Press the paper well into the corner.

Use the plumb line on the return wall to mark a true vertical for the edge of the next length. The line will be about 10¼in. from the corner (assuming you are using the other half of the paper you have already cut).

On the adjoining wall, hang the matching portion of the length with the edge following the vertical plumb line. Try to match the pattern in the corner as well as possible but do not worry if it will not line up completely. The difference will be slight and unnoticeable.

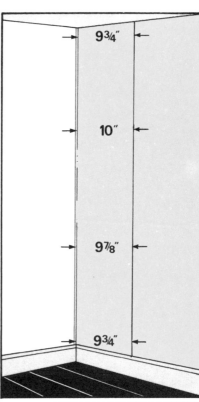

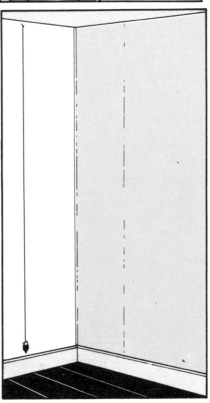

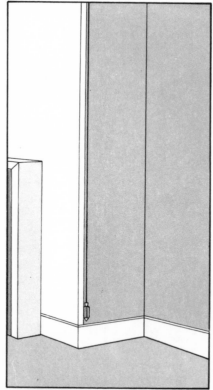

Light switches and socket outlets:
Two methods can be used for dealing with light switches and socket outlets depending on whether or not they can be unscrewed from the wall. If you have the screw-on type then turn off the electricity at the mains before releasing the screws. If you have the fixed type they will have to be dealt with in situ.

Halls and landings: Before decorating a stairwell, make sure the dust sheets on the stairs are well fixed down. A loose dust sheet can cause an accident.

Arrange a safe working platform which will enable you to reach the top of the wall comfortably. Re-arrange the platform as you proceed, to suit the work area. Do not assume that long spans of boards will support your weight. Provide intermediate support.

Opposite page

When the top half of the paper is in position, press the paper gently against the switch to ascertain its position. Cut a square from the paper about ¼in. smaller all round than the size of the switch plate.

Tuck the edges behind the switch plate and hang the rest of the length.

Tighten up the screws to conceal the cut edges.

Cut the paper star-shaped around a fixed switch.

Cut off the star shape and brush the paper back in place. Always undercut initially when trimming. You can always take a little extra off later. Over-cutting will leave an ugly gap.

Never attempt to turn uncut widths into a window recess. You must cut out separate pieces, working first in the recess itself.

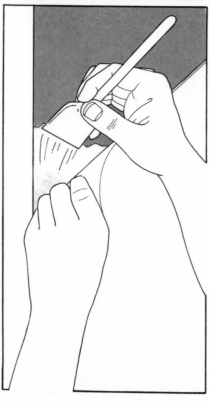

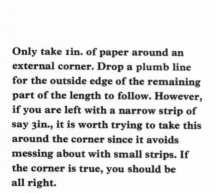

Only take 1in. of paper around an external corner. Drop a plumb line for the outside edge of the remaining part of the length to follow. However, if you are left with a narrow strip of say 3in., it is worth trying to take this around the corner since it avoids messing about with small strips. If the corner is true, you should be all right.

When overlapping vinyls in corners, it will be necessary to use latex adhesive to stick down the overlapping edge. Use the wood seam roller to smooth down the overlapping edges.

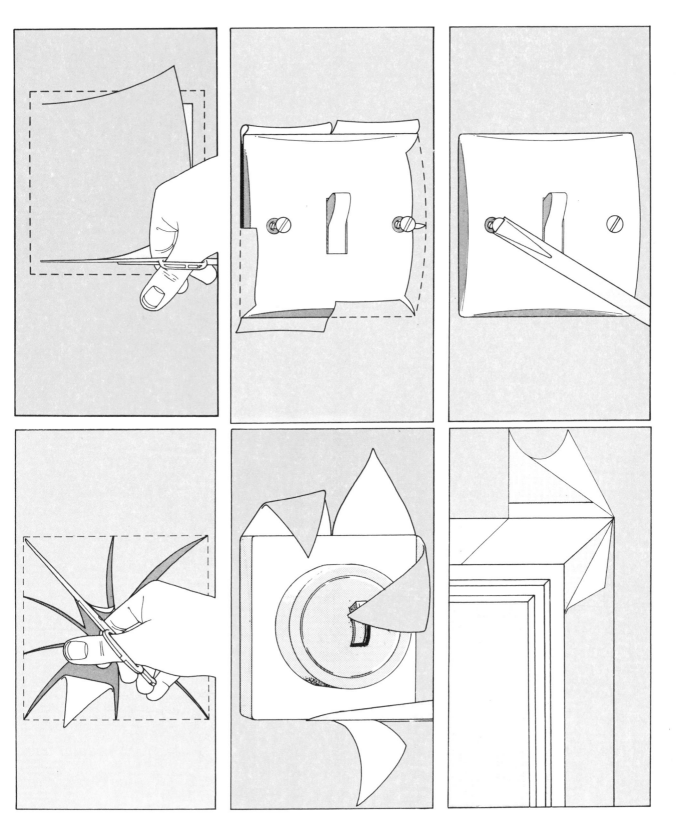

The overlapping paper on the outside wall must be cut exactly to the shape of the corner. When pasted down it conceals the $\frac{1}{2}$in. margin of paper turned on to the outside wall from the recess.

To tailor paper to a fireplace surround, first hang the paper down to mantel level. Then cut off most of the surplus from the area below.

Make a series of angled cuts to suit the fireplace projections, crease the paper to fit and then snip off, using small scissors.

At door frames, crease the length to fit the frame with the back of the shears and make an angled cut towards the corner of the frame. Trim off surplus and fit length.

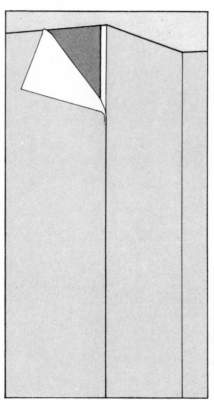

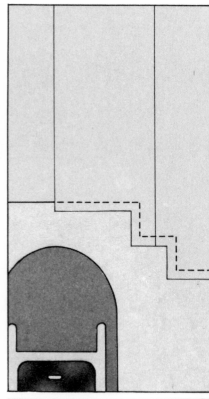

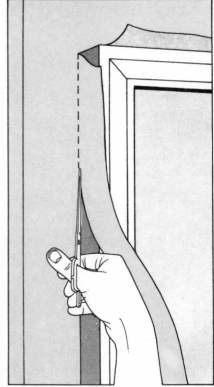

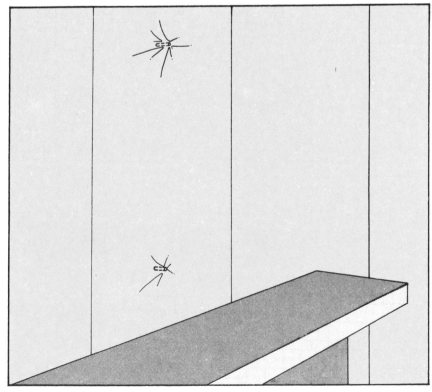

An 'all-over' look can be given by
smoothing the edges of surrounding
lengths behind a radiator. Here a
'wood-grain' paper has been used.

Stick matchsticks in screw holes to
identify their position.
Paper over the matchsticks and push
through.

OTHER DECORATIVE WALL COVERINGS

There is a wide selection of decorative
wall coverings on the market which
many people are reluctant to try
because they have no knowledge of
hanging techniques.

This is a pity because by bringing
them into consideration, a whole host
of alternative decorative effects are
possible.

There is also sometimes a feeling
that these wall coverings are suitable
only for a professional to hang because
some special knowledge is needed.

In truth, nothing of the kind applies.

No specialist knowledge is needed
but, as with all other wall covering
materials, the key to success lies in
thorough preparation of the surfaces
and care and attention to detail when
hanging the materials.

Old wallpaper must be removed, or
paint rubbed down to provide a key
for the new material.

Cracks must be filled and smoothed.
From there, hanging flocks,
hessians, Japanese silks, grasscloths
and so on is a straightforward job.

Although some of these materials
are costly, they will give longer wear
than ordinary decorative papers. If
used in feature areas – alcoves, single
walls, recesses and so on, they provide
an eye-catching contrast to other
decorations.

All these materials have unique
qualities and different hanging
techniques must be employed if they
are to be used successfully.

The following points should be
watched carefully when hanging them.

A typical flock wallpaper design.

Flocks: These tend to move about on the pasting table when under pressure from the pasting brush. This can cause damage to the delicate, decorative surface.

A way to avoid this is to put a sheet of lining paper underneath when pasting.

If any paste gets on to the patterned surface, it may cause a stain, so be very careful.

Flocks present no particular problems when hanging, but do not press the face of the material with your fingers when positioning a length on the wall. Use the flat of the hand.

To smooth out, use a felt roller, gently.

The introduction of vinyl flock wall coverings has made this type of decorating material far easier to hang. Like ordinary vinyls, flock vinyl can be roughly handled, allowing paste and other deposits to be vigorously washed from the surface.

Grasscloths: These are traditional Japanese wallcoverings and usually have simple yet beautiful designs.

Special care is needed when preparing the surface of the walls.

Walls, especially where painted, should be rubbed down with coarse glasspaper to provide a good key and then be lined with white lining paper.

Cut the grasscloths into lengths with about ⅝in. trimmed from each edge, using a sharp knife and a metal straight-edge.

Never cut narrow widths when the material is wet.

Use paste to a creamy consistency. The material should be left to soak until it becomes supple, but it must not be allowed to oversoak. Follow manufacturer's instructions very closely for the soaking time.

Do not stretch grasscloths when hanging. Always use a felt roller in order to smooth them down.

Use a seam roller to smooth down butted edges between lengths.

Do not turn the material into an internal angle. Butt it tightly into the corner.

At external angles, grasscloths can be turned round about 2in.

Anaglypta: This is an embossed paper that gives a low-relief texture. It is particularly suitable for disguising cracked surfaces on ceilings and walls.

Fill the cracks first with cellulose filler and then follow the techniques used to hang ordinary wallpaper.

If the walls were previously gloss painted, manufacturers recommend hanging lining paper or applying a primer to walls or ceilings before hanging Anaglypta paper or relief panels (see below).

A good quality starch paste or heavy duty cellulose adhesive is essential.

The main thing about the paste is that it must not be too thin, so add water sparingly.

Use a wallpaper brush to smooth out each length on the wall. A felt roller can also be used for smoothing.

Avoid stretching the material. When a length is in position, firm the edges by tapping down with a brush. Never use a seam roller as this will flatten the texture.

When dry, anaglypta can be decorated with any colour emulsion paint. Two coats produce the best effect.

Anaglypta high relief panels: When used on ceilings and walls, these panels provide distinctive architectural effects.

They may seem a bit stiff, which makes them more awkward to handle, but they can be made pliable by sponging their reverse sides with warm water.

It is important to use Dextrine adhesive for fixing. Decorating shops stock this.

Panels must not be turned into an internal angle; place them so that they butt up in the angle. They can be turned round external angles.

You must remember that the adhesive takes time to work. Fine panel pins can be tapped into the panels to hold them temporarily in place until the adhesive takes effect.

Avoid touching the face of the panels as much as possible; slide them into position with a sponge.

Where cut pieces are needed, lay the panel on a clean, firm surface and use a sharp Stanley-type knife held against a straight-edge to cut it.

Again these panels can be decorated with emulsion when dry.

Cork: Cork wall coverings are made by applying cork panels of irregular shape and size to a coloured background paper to create a textured effect.

The random design is intended to be retained, so horizontal lines should not be matched up when hanging.

All walls must be lined before hanging cork.

The cork must be trimmed first with a sharp knife against a 4ft. long metal straight-edge.

From then on normal wallpaper techniques are used.

A thick mixture of decorator's prepared paste must be used. Ask for this at the decorators' shop.

When the material has become supple on the pasting table it can be hung.

A length must not be repasted so, in case edges have started to dry, rub the wet paste brush along the edges only.

Sponge off any paste that gets on the face of the cork. If it is allowed to dry it will cause a stain.

Hand-printed wallpapers: These provide a luxury-look wall covering but are expensive.

Large-drop patterns are a feature of these papers so work from alternative rolls and match the pattern at eye level.

They may need to be trimmed after purchase, but leave this job to an expert. Your supplier should be able to arrange for this to be done for a small charge.

Avoid overpasting and hang each length within five minutes of pasting.

Hessian: These are fabric-type wall coverings, some of which are paper-backed to facilitate hanging.

The different types involve different pasting techniques.

Those with a paper backing are pasted and hung as with normal wallpaper. With unbacked hessians the wall, not the material, must be pasted before hanging.

Both types can be wider than ordinary wall coverings, a point to consider if you have a normal size pasting board.

The walls should be lined before hanging.

Since there are different types produced, individual manufacturers instructions should be checked before hanging.

Avoid getting paste on the face of the material as it may stain.

Smooth out each length with a felt roller or a brush; butt up all joints.

Use a sharp knife and metal straight-edge for cutting.

Lincrusta: This wall covering is embossed to simulate natural effects such as wood grains.

Though it is quite thick, lincrusta has a smooth back so any nibs of paint or uneven plaster will show through when it is in position.

So pay great attention to getting the walls completely smooth, clean and firm.

Use lincrusta glue or Dextrine adhesive for the paste.

Before applying it, sponge the surface of the material to remove any French chalk and trim the edges with a sharp knife and a straight-edge.

Get a helper to feed the lincrusta across the pasting table. If the dry end hangs down over the edge of the table it might crack.

The thinner types of lincrusta can be turned into an internal angle but when hanging the thicker types, trim with a knife.

Do this also at external corners, and meeting edges can be covered with angle beading or any small gaps can be filled with cellulose filler.

A lustre or satin finish emulsion can be used over the material when it is dry.

Supaglypta: This has an embossed decoration with a deep relief texture.

Apply the paste liberally and allow plenty of soaking time so that each length becomes pliable. Hang as for wallpaper.

It can be decorated with emulsion when dry.

Vynaglypta: This heavyweight moulded, white vinyl relief wall covering can be painted with emulsion. Vinyl adhesive is used to hang it.

Bubbles can form if the material is hung too soon after pasting, so make sure it is allowed to soak for the full time recommended by the manufacturer's directions.

After pasting a section, roll it up loosely; do not fold it over. From then on follow normal wallpaper hanging techniques.

Murals: Printed paper panels which take the place of murals painted onto the actual wall.

Thinned-down prepared paste is used to fix them. It is most important to hang these murals really vertically.

After pasting a section, fold it back so as not to crease the paper. Use a seam roller to roll out any bubbles which tend to form near the edges. If bubbles remain after rolling edges, nick the paper with a sharp knife to release the air.

Papering Ceilings: Start papering a ceiling by the window wall and hang the lengths parallel to the window, working away from the light.

Size the ceiling first to facilitate sliding the paper around a little.

The paper must be folded, concertina-fashion, after pasting. Be sure that adjoining edges of successive lengths are butted up and do not overlap.

Arrange a working platform to span the width of the room. Your head should be only two or three inches from the ceiling.

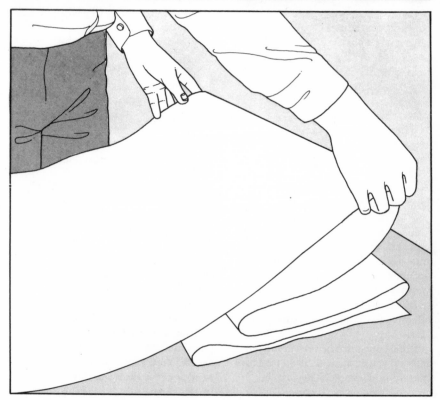

Snap a chalk line on the ceiling, ½in. less than the width of the paper away from the window wall. Tie the string to a small nail at one side of the room, pull it taut than pluck it to leave a chalk line on the ceiling. On a white ceiling use a coloured chalk.

Fold the pasted paper concertina fashion.

Support the paper with a spare roll. Face the window and line up the edge of the paper with the chalk line. Unfold and smooth out each section as you work. If you find this operation tiring, get a helper to support the paper from the ground with a soft broom.

Alternatively, get a helper to support the lower half of the length while you hang the top half. If it is allowed to drop down unsupported, it will certainly stretch, making pattern matching impossible. Irregular soaking time will also make pattern matching impossible.

Once on the ceiling, the suction will hold it and will enable you to brush out the paper smoothly. If you spot bubbles, do not be afraid to pull away the paper from one edge, in towards the centre to release the air before smoothing out again.

Use the back of the shears to crease the paper into the ceiling angle before removing the 2in. surplus at the end.

Fit the paper around a ceiling rose by piercing the paper in the required position and pulling the rose through. Continue hanging the length before returning to the rose for finishing off. Use ordinary scissors to trim off the surplus paper before smoothing it into place.

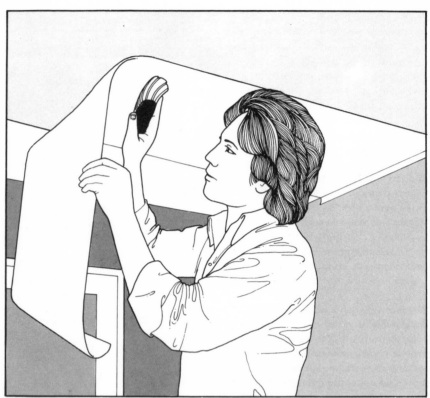

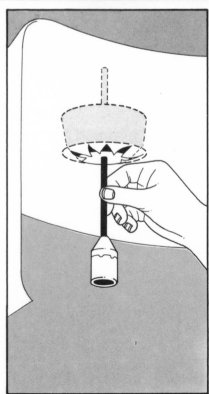

Painting Indoors

PAINT TYPES

The variety of strange-sounding names on the myriad paint cans adorning the shelves of any large decorating shop can cause the layman's mind to go into a whirl.

Satin, eggshell, polyurethane, latex, vinyl emulsion – these are just a few of the names you have to conjure with.

A few years ago, it was a much more simple task to select the right paint for the job. The choice was basic and traditional – emulsion for the walls and ceilings, gloss for the woodwork. Your only concern was picking an attractive colour from the shade card.

All the new names may sound confusing but they are there for the express purpose of enabling you to do a better, more satisfying job.

The increase in paint types means that you can now find a paint which will not only give you the colour you want, but provide a specific texture or effect, so enhancing the finished appearance of the room. So a background knowledge of paint types is important if you are going to make full use of the modern range of paints.

All paint is comprised of three main ingredients – pigment, binder and thinner.

Pigments provide the paint with its colour and covering power.

Open tins of paint with a broad lever. A narrow screwdriver could damage the lid.

If using old paint, carefully cut around the edge of skin with a sharp knife. Try to lift it from the can in one piece.

Stir the paint with a broad stick.

To remove particles, strain the paint through fine muslin or a nylon stocking.

The binders bind the pigments together to form a hard-wearing, continuous film, enabling the paint to adhere to the surface being painted.

The thinners enable the paint to flow over the surface. They evaporate as the paint dries.

Gloss paint is for interior and exterior woodwork and metalwork – and other areas demanding a tough finish.

Though many modern emulsion paints are suitable for exterior use and woodwork, they are still thought of, and used mainly for interior decoration on walls and ceilings.

In the past linseed oil was used as the binder in gloss paint, which is why all gloss paints are put under the heading of oil-based paints. Nowadays though, synthetic resins are used – alkyd and polyurethane are the most common.

Emulsion paints do not contain any oil. In manufacture, the binder (synthetic resin particles) is suspended in the thinner (water) to form an emulsion. When the emulsion is brushed on, the water evaporates, allowing the resins to join together to form the film on the surface. Those strange-sounding names on the tins are merely references to the synthetic resin that has been used in the binder.

When shaking paint, wrap rag over the lid tightly to prevent it flying off.

When closing the lid, clean all paint from the rim and then use a wood block and a hammer to tap it on securely. This ensures the lid remains tight-fitting and reduces the chances of skin forming.

Work out a new brush on brickwork with water to remove any loose hairs. Then wash and dry thoroughly before use.

Transfer the paint in small quantities to a paint kettle. When used up, add more paint. This avoids having to carry around a full can while working.

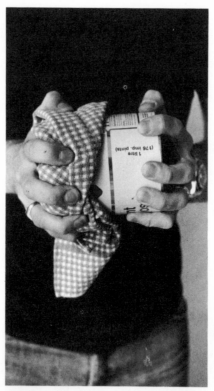

Acrylics and vinyls – two of the most widely-used resins – apart from providing a hardwearing surface, also ensure that the paint will retain its colour better.

However, just because resins such as these have been added to an emulsion, there is no guarantee that it will produce good results. The whole production technique of the manufacturer is important. This is one reason why you should always buy one of the reputable brand names such as Dulux or Crown.

It is worth making brief mention here of the recently developed paint which is a cross between gloss and emulsion, making it a very useful paint for the handyman.

Let us compare the different qualities of gloss and emulsion paints.

The smell of gloss paint will remain for some time after it has been applied, while emulsion hardly smells at all, either during or after application.

Gloss paints take a lot longer to dry – overnight drying must be allowed usually before a second coat is applied. Emulsions are quick drying and another coat can usually be applied in a couple of hours.

Gloss paints are normally thinned with white spirit or turpentine. Emulsions are thinned with water.

Though a primer is required on previously unpainted surfaces before applying gloss, emulsions only require a primer when the wall or ceiling is very porous or absorbent.

Selecting the right paint – gloss or emulsion – is not the end of the story – another decision has to be made – the degree of gloss required. Traditionally, emulsion dried to a matt finish and gloss to a shiny finish.

Now the degree of gloss you can have is varied. In between the two extremes is a wide choice – silk, satin, eggshell, semi-gloss, lustre – each having their own sheen.

The 'glossier' finishes provide a surface that is much more hardwearing and easier to clean.

The level of durability is proportionate always to the level of the gloss – the higher the gloss, the more durable is the finish.

An oil-based, silk finish is tougher than an emulsion silk finish, for example. So, if you want a steam resistant finish for the kitchen, you would be better off opting for the oil-based variety.

The condition of the surface to be painted is important also when selecting the degree of sheen.

Remember that the higher the paint sheen, the more it will emphasise any cracks, bumps, ridges or other faults in the surface.

Another decision you will have to make when choosing paints is that between liquid or non-drip paints. With nearly all oil-based types you have the choice; with emulsions, the choice is not always there to be made.

As many amateurs have found to their cost, if you overload a brush or 'slap' it about when using liquid paint, there will inevitably be a shower of drips all over the floor, and runs of paint down the surface being covered.

For those who just cannot get the hang of loading and using a brush correctly, the non-drip paints are a boon.

Non-drip paints were known, formerly, as thixotropics. Since this tended to add even more confusion to modern paint names, the term non-drip is now accepted.

The difference between non-drip and liquid paints becomes obvious when you first take the lid off a can of paint. Whereas the liquid will move easily if you tilt the can (do not, of course make this test with a full can of paint) the non-drip will stay put.

To load a brush, dip the bristles about halfway into the paint and wipe away excess on the side of the can or paint kettle if you are using one.

The liquid paint can be stirred easily. On the other hand the non-drip, being in a jelly-like state, will actually hold a light 'stirring' stick upright in the can. If you stir the non-drip it will become liquid quite quickly. Leave it alone for a while and it will return to its jelly-like state.

This is an excellent indication of what happens when it is transferred from the can to the wall. As it is lifted on to the brush, it will cling to the bristles in a lump. Then, as it is brushed out on to the wall, it breaks up and becomes almost liquid. You will notice, however, that it does not start to trickle down the wall, causing runs which have to be brushed out. This is because it is immediately returning to its jelly-like state.

Obviously, for the beginner, the non-drip paints offer more likelihood that the finished job will have a professional finish.

Earlier, mention was made of thinners.

There is a great deal of confusion about which paints should be thinned and which should not be thinned.

New oil-based finishing paints and undercoats do not usually require thinning. They are intended to be used straight from the can after stirring. Non-drip paints are, not, of course, stirred.

Oil-based non-drip paints must not on any account be thinned or they will not remain non-drip for very long.

The normal thinner for ordinary oil-based paints is white spirit used in accordance with the directions on the tin.

(a) Use a 3in. wide brush to paint a wide, flush surface. First, apply the paint with the grain in vertical strokes.
(b) Wipe off the surplus paint on the side of the can.
(c) Without reloading the brush, brush out across the grain.
(d) Again wipe the brush on the can.
(e) Without reloading, brush with the grain in light strokes.

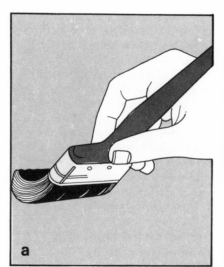

a

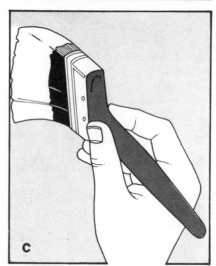

c

d

b

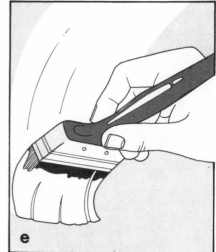

e

Always stir the paint thoroughly after thinning. An occasional stir is always a good idea whether you are adding thinner or not.

Emulsion paints, are sometimes used as primer on porous surfaces. Here, usually, they have to be thinned with water. The instructions on the can will advise on the correct amount of water to add.

Normally, emulsions can be used straight from the can for ceilings or walls.

Estimating paint needed: No one wants to be left with a half-full can of paint when the job in hand is completed, especially if it is an unusual colour which cannot be used elsewhere in the house. Though there are places such as the insides of house gutters, where colours will not be seen from the ground and that provide an outlet for left-overs, a half-full can can hardly be described as left-overs.

Average spreading figures issued by Dulux for their range of primers, sealers, emulsion and gloss are given in the chart and are reasonably representative of all manufacturers.

Being average figures, they take into account the nature of the surface, the method of application (roller, brush or pad), and even the technique of the painter.

Textured surfaces such as pebble-dash will take more paint than a flat area of the same dimensions. If the texture is rough, it might require twice as much paint.

Porous surfaces found on plaster walls absorb much paint, especially the priming or sealing coats.

Thinning emulsion to use it as a primer makes it go further but it might still be necessary to allow up to 50% more paint than the table shows.

The number of coats required is the other influencing factor.

Where the existing paint is in a good condition, one coat may be sufficient – provided that no significant colour change is being made. If a much darker colour is used, two coats will usually be sufficient. If a lighter colour is used, three coats may be necessary.

Extra coats of finishing paint can apply to emulsion, eggshell and matt and gloss finishes.

Liquid gloss paints are used (in colour change situations) with an undercoat recommended by the makers.

Non-drip gloss paints are usually applied without an undercoat.

Paint is now sold in metric quantities: $\frac{1}{2}$ litre and 1, $2\frac{1}{2}$ and 5 litres. These replace the imperial sizes of 1 pint, quart, $\frac{1}{2}$ gallon, and gallon.

Average spreading rate of 1 litre

	sq. metre	sq. yd.
Wood primer	8	10
Aluminium sealer	17	20
Primer sealer	9	11
Masonry sealer	12	14
Metal primer chromate	11	13
Undercoat	11	13
Gloss finish	17	20
Non-drip gloss	12	14
Eggshell	16	19
Vinyl matt emulsion	15	17
Vinyl silk emulsion	15	17
Vinyl gloss	15	17

PAINT SYSTEMS

Under that gleaming top coat of paint which goes on and on in tip-top condition is a complete paint system, not just a couple of coats of gloss.

The so-called finishing coat is only as good as the undercoats, sealers and primers used under it.

Irrespective of the material you are painting – wood, metal, plaster or whatever it is, each stage in the build-up of the paint system must be attended to carefully.

There are various types of primers and sealers and the right one to choose depends on the surface being treated.

Primers and sealers are not used together with every material. Sometimes one can be omitted, sometimes the other.

Let us look at each type in the order that they are used – sealers, primers and undercoats.

Sealers: Sealers prevent the following paint coats from soaking into an absorbent surface. They also prevent wood resins, chemicals in plaster and preservatives, from rising to the surface and attacking the top coat of paint.

Another use for them is in binding powdery surfaces such as cement paint, old distemper and limewash.

Primers: Primers help to fill in any irregularities in the surface, thus leaving a perfectly flat surface for the undercoat and top coat.

They do two other jobs, too. They waterproof the surface and they provide a key for the following paint coat.

On metal surfaces sealers are essential to prevent moisture from reaching the metal and setting up corrosion.

Primers are often used in place of a sealer.

Undercoats: Undercoats are becoming less used nowadays because finishing paints can now be applied in much thicker coats, which have more covering power. Thus they do much of the work of an undercoat which is largely that of obliterating the old colour underneath.

So why use an undercoat at all?

The most obvious place to use one is where the existing paintwork is in good condition but a drastic change of colour is being made – say from dark red to a pale green. Here the undercoat will be beneficial.

However, if you want a really top-quality finish then the undercoat is a stage that cannot be omitted.

It produces a coat of uniform colour and obliterates any textures in the surface which would show up under the top coat of gloss.

Having defined the basic qualities of each type, we can see how they are used on different surfaces.

Preparing Woodwork: The first stage is to seal any knots in the wood with a substance called knotting. This prevents any resin bleeding through the paint coats.

Use shellac knotting. This is a quick-drying varnish. Apply a thin coat to knots and other resinous areas. It dries in a couple of minutes.

Aluminium wood primers are an alternative. These both seal knots and prime the surface. Brush out well to avoid runs; work well into the grain.

When priming dense hardwoods such as oak, it is usually necessary to thin ordinary wood primer. Check instructions on the tin first. Normally a 10 parts primer; 1 part white spirit ratio is about right. Aluminium primers are not usually thinned.

Plaster, cement, brick: Priming with an oil-based primer is not usually necessary when using emulsion. If a surface is particularly porous or absorbent, a sealing coat of diluted emulsion can be used. Check Instructions on the tin. Normally 4 parts of emulsion to 1 part water is about right.

If an oil-based paint is to be used on these surfaces then emulsion can be used as a primer – but only on interior surfaces. The alternative for indoor or outdoor use is an oil-based primer of the alkali resistant type.

On powdery surfaces, remove all loose flaking material by scraping, brushing and washing. Allow to dry, then apply the sealer, or a stabilising primer. Omit this and the new paint will flake off in time.

Primers for metal surfaces: Use calcium plumbate primer on galvanised iron; zinc chromate primer for aluminium after suitable pre-treatment.

BRUSH TECHNIQUES

Different brush techniques are needed when applying free-flowing gloss paints and non drip thixotropic paints.

With non drip, you must get a thick, even spread of paint and do the minimum of brushing out or it will run.

An immediate, even spread is not so important with free flowing paints as these have to be well brushed out to avoid drips or runs.

Beginners are never certain why it is so important to make the final

stroke of the brush following the grain of the timber. The final stroke is called 'laying-off'.

Any hard parts of the grain that have not been glasspapered smooth, leave ridges on the surface.

If you lay-off the paint across the grain, the brush will drag paint off the ridges thus leaving an uneven spread of paint.

When one part of, say, a door has been completed, apply paint to an adjoining part and lay-off, brushing towards the wet edge of the first part. To hide the join line between sections, the tips of the bristles should leave the surface obliquely when the wet edge of the first section is reached.

Painting faults: When the finished paint effect is faulty, there is no use blaming the paint. It is extremely unlikely that anything will have been wrong with that.

Nowadays, quality control in paint manufacture is of an extremely high standard. The fault will be due to something omitted in the paint system you have used or the way the paint was applied. There is more about paint 'systems. on page 59.

Always choose a reputable brand of paint. Below are described typical painting faults together with likely causes and remedies.

Bittiness: This is most noticeable on glossy surfaces. There will be a covering of specks of dust or grit under the dry paint film.

Cleanliness is an important part of the painting technique. The lack of it causes bittiness.

Before painting a surface, it is important to get it really clean. Even those cracks and crevices which are difficult to clean out must be attended to. Any dirt trapped in them can be drawn out by the bristles on the brush and rubbed over the surface.

When the paint is drying, do not start sweeping up anywhere in the room. Small dust particles will fly through the air and land on the sticky paint. Keep all brushes and other equipment clean at all times.

Always clean the can of paint before taking the lid off, otherwise dust on the lid might drift into the paint, contaminating it.

Always keep the lid on the paint can when it is not in use. Transferring small quantities of paint to a paint kettle is a good idea as it means that if any of the paint in the kettle gets dust in it, this will not affect the whole can. Should this happen, clean out the kettle before pouring in more paint.

If you have got bittiness on the surface, when the paint has hardened – allow a week for this as it may seem hard before then but probably will not be underneath – rub it down lightly with fine waterproof abrasive paper. Then rinse with water, allow to dry thoroughly and apply a second top coat.

Blisters: These are usually caused by painting on a damp surface. This is why it is essential to allow woodwork to dry off after washing, or after a fall of rain.

Not using a sealer over resinous areas or knots is another possible cause. Painting in hot sunlight is also a risk.

If paint is applied over an old, thick soft coat of paint, the new paint film will swell up, and, dependent on the extent of the damage, you may have to scrape off the whole paint system and start again. An isolated blister or two, however, can be scraped off and the bare area primed and undercoated before finishing with top coat.

Brushmarks: These are obvious on a dry surface. The most likely cause is the brushwork technique. Spreading an even coat of paint and finishing with light strokes is essential if this is to be avoided. If this has been done, then look to poor rubbing down at the beginning or bad-quality brushes. Too thick paint can also cause the same problem. So, if the brush seems to be dragging when applying the paint, the latter must be thinned. Rub down lightly and repaint.

Slow drying: When the paint is still tacky the day after application – and the day after that – then you could be heading for a lot of work. If it dries after a couple of days, it may be dull (if gloss) or it could be bitty – since dust will stick to a tacky surface.

Here, simple rubbing down and a new coat of paint is the answer.

If it has not dried at the end of three or four days, then there is no solution but to clean off the whole lot with paint thinner and start again.

What causes it? The main things are painting over a damp surface (or a greasy one), not stirring the paint properly or using the wrong type of thinner.

Flaking and peeling: A bad case necessitates stripping off the whole lot and starting again from scratch.

Odd areas can be dealt with by stripping, filling up to surface level with fine surface filler (Polyfilla fine surface filler, for example) and recoating.

Poor preparation is the root cause – painting over damp, dirt or grease; not rubbing down hard gloss paint; not using a primer; painting over generally poor old paintwork.

Loss of Gloss: The reasons listed for flaking also apply here. Also, it can be due to painting over a still-wet undercoat or brushing out too much when finishing off the top coat.

For the last cause the remedy is simple. Apply another top coat after the existing one is completely dry.

Runs and sags: Too heavy or too thick paint applied unevenly is the prime cause. More often than not this happens towards the end of the day's work when through tiredness the paint tends to be slapped on.

If runs or sags are caught early enough they can be brushed out. If the paint is tacky when you notice a run or sag, leave it for a few days. Then rub down with waterproof abrasive paper and repaint.

Care of brushes: After use with oil paint, wipe out the excess paint by drawing the bristles across the edge of a knife and then rub out the brush on an old rag or newspapers.

Immerse the bristles in white spirit.

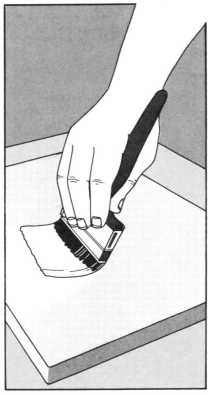

After using a brush, press down on the bristles to work out all paint. Paraffin can be used here and it is cheaper.

After rinsing, shake out the water by spinning the brush. Leave to dry. If traces of paint are found in the stock of the brush after cleaning, repeat the whole cleaning procedure.

Wrap the clean, dry brush in newspaper secured with an elastic band and store it in a dry place.

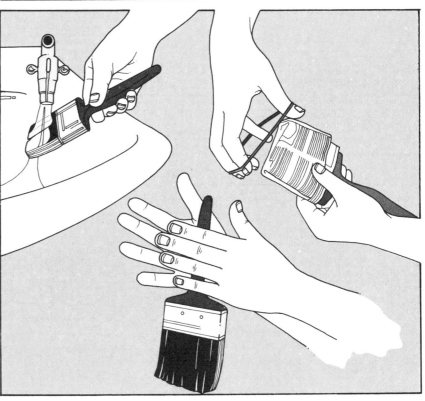

Wipe the spirit out on a clean rag. Work a small amount of brush cleaner into the bristles before rinsing off in soap and water.

Simply rinse brushes used for emulsion paints in clean water immediately after use until they are clean.

Some oil-based paints can be washed off brushes with ordinary household detergent mixed with water. Check the instructions on the can.

Follow the procedures described above for individual paints when cleaning pads or rollers.

Preparing the paint: Skinning on paint in the can occurs mainly with gloss and can be a problem. It is unlikely that this will happen with a new can. If it has happened, return it to the supplier.

Never stir paint with a screwdriver or a narrow stick; the settled pigment will not be lifted from the bottom of the can. If any small particles of skin remain after stirring, then the paint must be strained into a fresh container. This is always a wise precaution before using old paint.

A partly full tin of thixotropic paint can have minute particles of skin which are hard to detect. If in doubt, brush some of the paint out on a clean board when the particles will be clearly seen. If necessary, stir the paint throughly and then strain it into a fresh container. After straining, the paint will return to its jelly-like consistency.

Always shake gloss paint thoroughly before use if you are certain that skin is not present. Do not shake thixotropic.

PAINTING DOORS

Before painting, remove all door furniture – handles, keyhole plates, finger plates, hooks and so on. Clean out the keyholes to remove all dirt and grease.

Plan to complete the painting in one continuous session. If paint edges are allowed to dry, they will show through the finished work.

On panelled doors, use a 1in. and

2in. brush. Although you can get by with only the 2in. brush, the smaller one will make it easier to cut into mouldings.

Complete the panels and mouldings and then brush away any paint from the corners of the mouldings. This will prevent tears building up and causing runs.

On flush doors, you will have to work faster to avoid leaving 'dry' edges. Use a 2½in. or 3in. brush, a pad brush or nylon short-pile roller.

Beginners will find it easier to use a roller.

If using a non drip paint, this

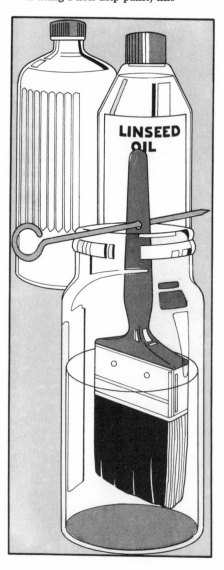

should be stirred by pouring it into a tray to make it slightly thinner.

If you are using a brush for oil paint over a long, continuous period, drill a hole in the handle and suspend it from a skewer or length of thick wire in a solution of linseed oil and white spirit. The pigment will fall from the stock.

When ready to resume painting, wipe out the solution on the edge of a knife. Then rub the brush out well on a clean piece of wood before re-use.

Paint a panelled door in this order. Finishing on the handle side means the door can be moved easily if necessary. To prevent it moving when actually painting, tap a wedge under the bottom.

A ıin. brush makes it easier to cut into mouldings.

It is worth while painting the top edge for easier cleaning later. Paint this first.

While the paint is still wet, clean out screw slots to leave them free from paint. Next time you have to remove screws, you will not have to scrape away dried paint to get the screwdriver in.

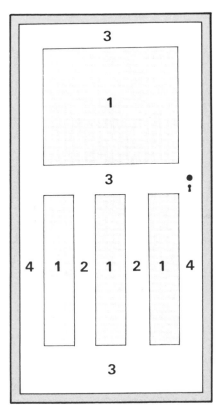

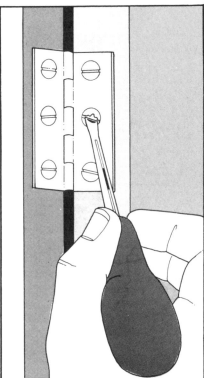

Make a particular point of clearing away any dirt or flaking paint from the bottom of the frame. This excessive breakdown of the surface is caused by moisture from condensation running down the glass on to dust. Double glazing cures this problem by preventing dust getting through and reducing condensation.

To prevent too much paint getting on the glass, use a cutting-in brush. You can buy these or make one yourself by cutting the bristles of an old ½in. brush at an angle.

If you prefer you can use a paint shield for this job.

Or you can use masking tape. Pull this away when the paint is touch dry. If the paint dries hard, the paint film on the frame may also be pulled away.

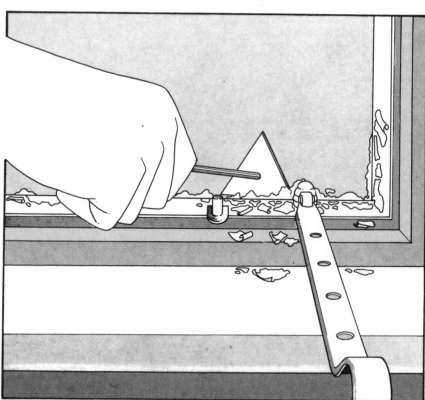

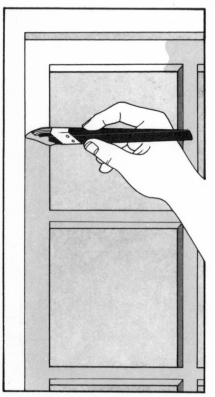

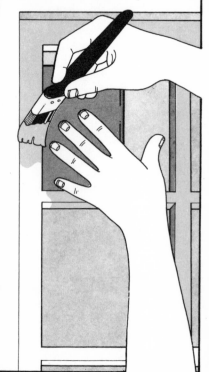

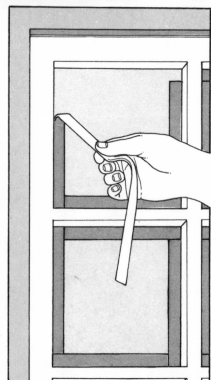

INTERNAL WINDOW FRAMES

The general rule for painting window frames is to paint any surface which shows inside the room when the window is open, in the interior colour. To paint a sash window, first raise the top sash and lower the bottom sash to allow the meeting rail to be painted.

The main problem is to prevent too much paint getting on to the glass. It is advisable, though, to take an ⅛in. paint margin on to the glass to prevent moisture infiltrating between glass and frame.

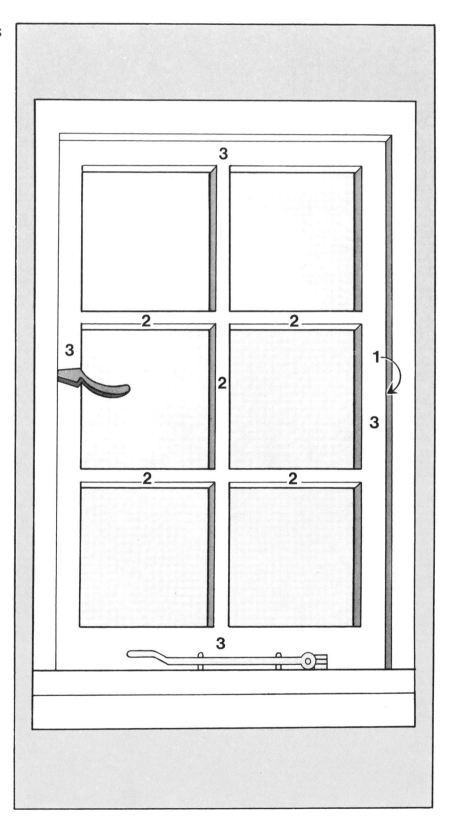

Paint a casement window in this order.

Paint this edge in the interior colour.

Paint a sash window in this order.
Paint the meeting rail first by raising
the top sash and lowering the bottom
sash.

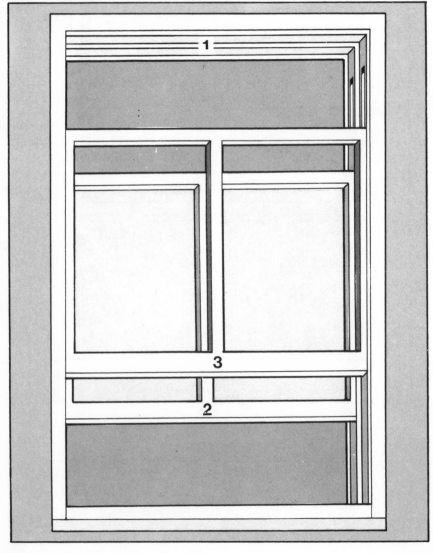

PAINTING WALLS AND CEILINGS

Always paint a complete wall without
a break. Once an edge has dried it
will show through after the job is
finished.

A paint pad will form a clean line
between adjoining walls and wall and
ceiling, which is important where
different colours are to be used in the
same room.

Remember, a 1in. brush should be
used along edges when using a roller.
The latter will not get into corners.
A roller will give an even spread of
colour which is important where
darker colours are used.

PAINTING CEILINGS SAFELY

The most important consideration
when painting a ceiling is comfort
and safety.

This is probably the most tiring
painting job of the lot and even a
small ceiling can seem to take on the
proportions of a football pitch after a
short while.

With this in mind it is important
that you are as organised as possible.

The essential thing is that your
head should be only a few inches from
the ceiling so that you will not have to
stretch.

Earlier on this aspect was discussed
when we were dealing with decorating
without removing the furniture.

If the room is not being lived in
and the furniture has been grouped in
the centre, then a working platform can
be organised spanning the length or
width of the room. This means that
continual climbing up and down is
minimised.

The platform must be sound. Two
stepladders with a scaffold board
stretched between them, or a board
between two trestles is ideal. With
the latter, two boards side-by-side
across the trestles will make the
platform a little wider.

If you have neither of these things
on hand, but you do have an old
kitchen table, then this is a possible
alternative.

Anyone who feels unsafe at heights can hire the necessary frames, boards and castors to make up an enclosed mobile platform. Local tool-hire shops will help there.

Before painting the ceiling, close the windows to keep the speed of drying of the paint down. This gives more time to join up wet sections.

Start painting at the window end of the room and then work away from the window. This makes it easier to see which areas have been painted, especially when painting with the same colour as before. Paint in sections about 2ft. wide and join up wet edges quickly. When the ceiling is completed, open the windows to speed drying.

When painting walls, work in 1ft. vertical bands across the room, starting at the top when using emulsion paints. If an oil based paint, gloss, eggshell etc. is used, paint in 2ft. squares following this sequence.

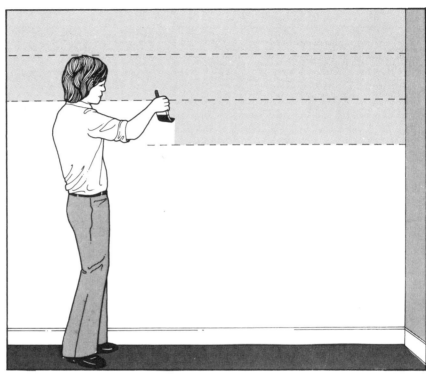

Ceiling Cove and Tiles

Cracks at the wall to ceiling angle are a common problem. They are caused by normal house movement. There is no point in filling them with plaster or cellulose filler since they will soon reappear.

Ceiling cove, nowadays usually made of expanded polystyrene, can be used to hide the cracks for good and, at the same time, give the ceiling angle an attractive curved appearance.

Cove can be used also to cover pipes or wiring.

After fixing, any suitable form of decoration, preferably emulsion paint can be applied over the cove surface.

Standard cove lengths are 6ft. 6¾in. For fixing mix up the special adhesive bought with the cove, following manufacturers' instructions. Do not mix up more adhesive than you can use in thirty minutes, otherwise it will start setting before you can use it. Use a spatula to butter it on to the back of the cove.

Pencil guide lines on the ceiling and wall, 2⅜in. from the angle for 4in. cove.

Scrape away any paper or flaking paint within the guide lines and scratch the area to make a key for the adhesive. Brush away any remaining dust.

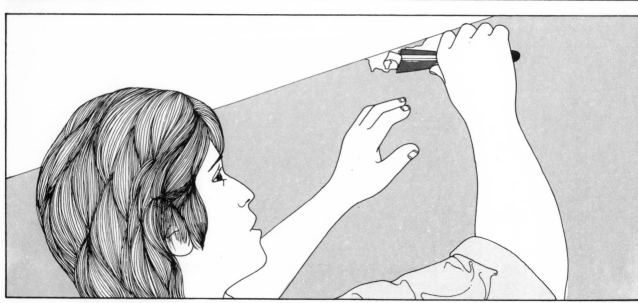

Dampen the fixing area before pushing the cove firmly into position. On long lengths, get someone to support the other end.

If the adhesive does not hold the cove after a few seconds, drive a nail into the wall to act as a temporary support.

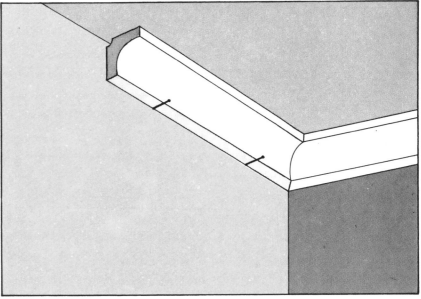

At corners, the meeting ends of lengths have to be mitred. A cardboard template should be supplied with the cove. Use this to mark out the appropriate mitre for an external or internal corner.

Use a fine tooth saw to cut the cove. Saw from the front face.
Use glasspaper to smooth any ragged sawn edges.

Leave an ⅛in. gap between the edges of lengths. Use adhesive which squelches to the surface to make good any gaps between edges of lengths. Remove excess adhesive from the edges with a scraper. Use a damp brush to clean any traces of adhesive from the face of the cove.
If lengths will not stick, knock nails below surface. Fix a nail every 24 inches. Fill all nail holes with cellulose filler.

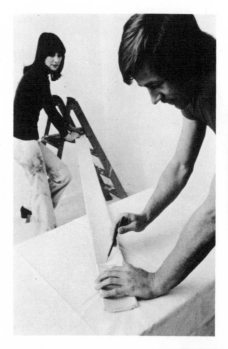
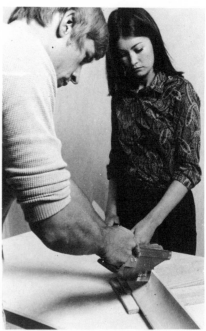

OTHER CEILING COVERINGS
Ceiling cladding: Tongued and grooved boards can be used to cover a poor but structurally sound ceiling. The same fixing methods are used as for walls (page 80) except that here the joists are used as fixing points instead of wall battens.

To indicate the position of joists on the ceiling, use a pointed implement to punch a series of holes through the ceiling on either side of the joists.

As for ceiling paper, use a line to ascertain the correct position of the first length. Plane the inside edge so that the outer edge is level with the line.

Use a nail punch to sink pin heads below the surface and into the joists above.

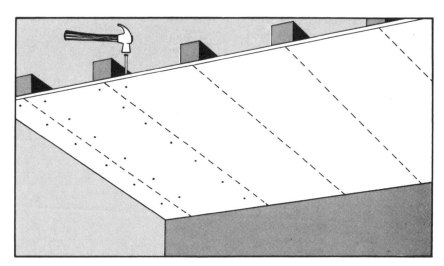

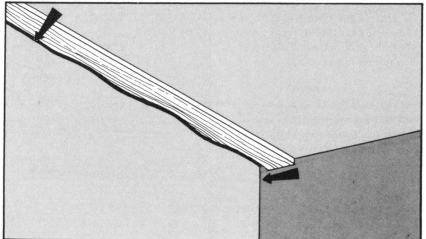

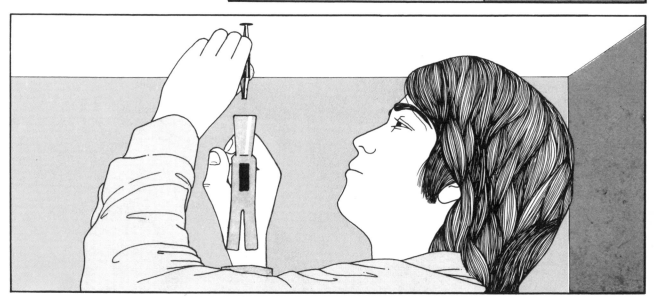

Polystyrene ceiling tiles: Polystyrene ceiling tiles have excellent insulation qualities and are an ideal way of creating an entirely new ceiling surface.

The tiles are feather light and are available in plain or patterned varieties. Plain tiles or those with a random pattern are easiest to apply since there are no problems with pattern matching.

White is the standard colour but the tiles can be painted. Where they are to be used in kitchens, especially, it is advisable to use a fire resistant paint. It is far easier to paint the tiles before fixing them on the ceiling.

Standard sizes are 1ft. and 2ft. square.

Use an old paint brush to apply the adhesive all over the back of the tile. Follow the manufacturer's directions when mixing the adhesive.

Find the middle point of opposite walls and stretch string lines across. The starting point is where the strings cross. Check with a try square that the lines cross at right angles. If necessary, adjust them.

Aim to leave an equally wide row of cut tiles along each border. If a narrow strip of, say, 1in. will be left on either side of the room, then move the first tile across half a tile's width to provide a wider border along both walls.

Use a sheet of plywood or hardboard to press the tile on to the ceiling. Do not press the tile with your fingers otherwise you will leave indentations in the surface.

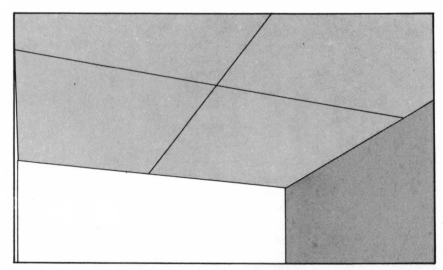

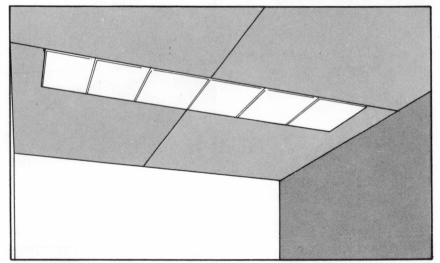

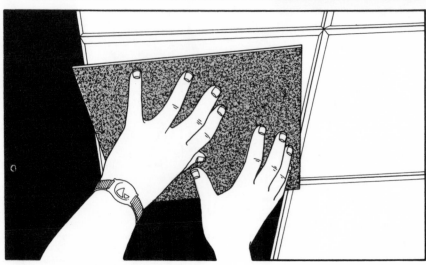

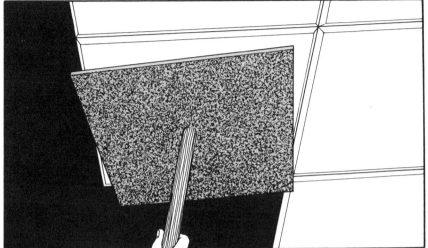

A broom handle can be used to press the plywood. Butt all the bevelled edges of the tiles closely together. The adhesive will support the tile after a few seconds.

Work off-cut tiles as for ceramic wall tiles. Lay the tile on a level surface, decorative face uppermost. Using a straight edge as a guide, cut firmly into the surface with a sharp knife.

Polystyrene cove can be used to hide a ragged border. Butt cove edges tightly.

To cut round a ceiling rose, make a cardboard pattern of the shape first and transfer this to the tile. Make sure that when the cut tile is in position, its edge lines up with neighbouring tiles.

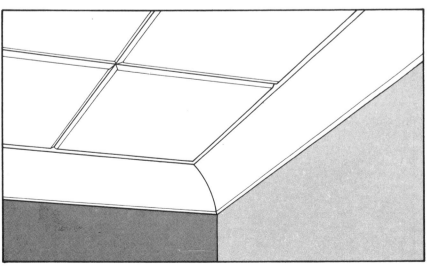

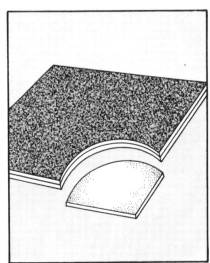

Ceramic Tiles

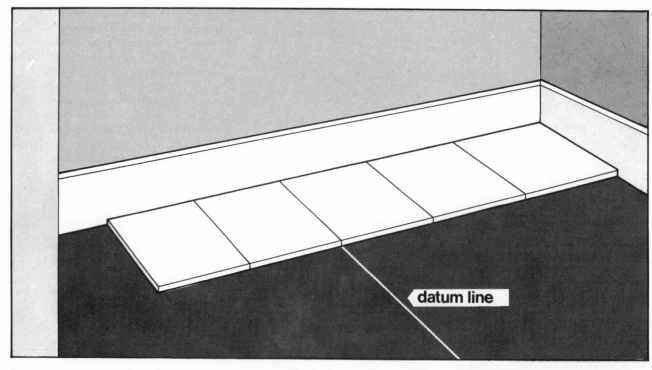

datum line

Spacer or Field tiles have lugs along each side to ensure correct spacing. These tiles are usually about 108mm. square and 4mm. thick and can be applied to most wall surfaces, as well as over existing tiled areas.

The RE tile has one rounded edge and is used for external corners and along the top row of half tiled walls. The REX tile has two rounded edges and is used at the top external corner of a half tiled wall. RE and REX tiles do not usually have spacer lugs along the remaining edges.

Border tiles have glazed edges and are without spacer lugs. These will require the use of spacers when fixing and can be used effectively for external corners.

Planning is the major consideration. Although the tiles are easy enough to cut, this is the most time consuming part of the job. So work out the best possible starting point to leave the minimum amount of cutting at edges and obstacles.

Avoid being left with thin strips of less than ½in. wide. These *are* difficult to cut. However, somewhere

Pieces of tile of less than ½in. are difficult to cut. Laying a row of tiles on the floor along the skirting is the best way to ascertain the starting point so that the gaps to be filled at each end are equal in width.

Spacer tiles have lugs along all four edges. RE tiles have one rounded edge; the three remaining edges are usually without lugs.

or other you will have to cut a tile to fit round an obstacle such as a sink or bath side. You will be lucky indeed if this situation does not arise.

72

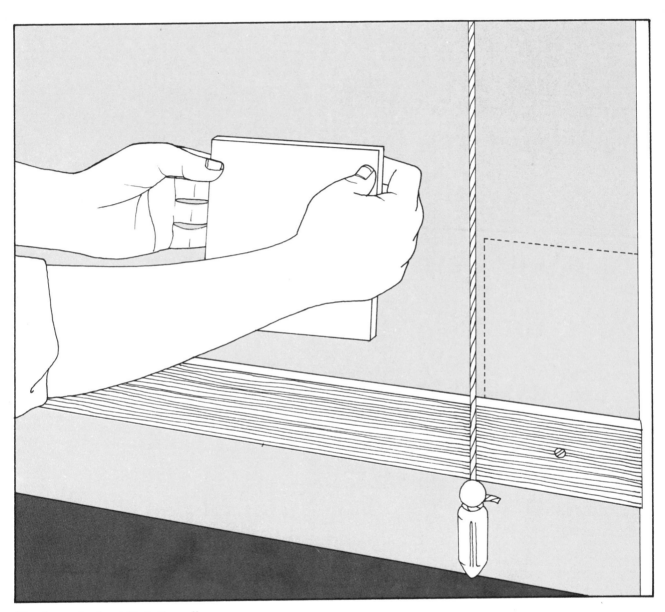

Fix a batten horizontally to the wall
with its top edge a tile width from
the floor. Check it with a spirit level.
This batten forms a support for the
bottom row of tiles, which in turn,
supports the next row and so on, until
the tile adhesive has set and each tile is
secure. The batten is then removed
and tiling completed down to the floor.
Drop a plumb line to find a true
vertical for the edges of the first
vertical row. Adjust it as necessary to
limit the amount of cut tiles at edges.
The first tile is positioned as shown.

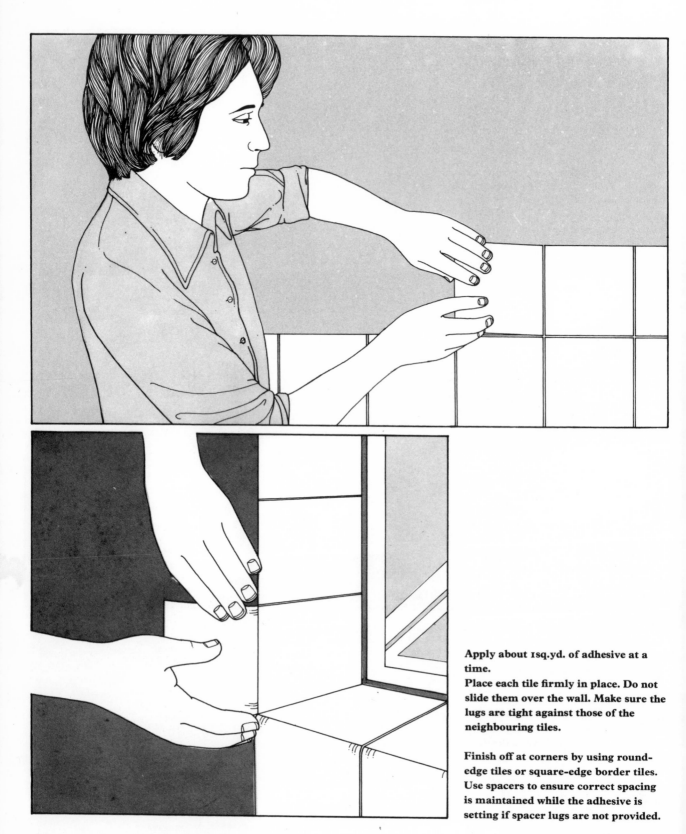

Apply about 1sq.yd. of adhesive at a time.
Place each tile firmly in place. Do not slide them over the wall. Make sure the lugs are tight against those of the neighbouring tiles.

Finish off at corners by using round-edge tiles or square-edge border tiles. Use spacers to ensure correct spacing is maintained while the adhesive is setting if spacer lugs are not provided.

There is only one way to cut a tile to shape successfully and it demands a great deal of patience.

First, make a cardboard template of the required shape. Position this on the tile and pencil on to it the outline of the cardboard.

Now, using a straight-edge as a guide, score along the pencil line with a tile cutter until the glaze of the tile is cut through right along the marked line.

Now comes the bit where patience is needed. The waste part of the tile must be gradually nibbled away with pincers. Do not attempt to take off a chunk all in one go or the tile will probably crack right across. With care, you will be able to nibble away all the waste to leave a smooth edge. If not, secure the tile in a vice and file along the cut edges until they are square.

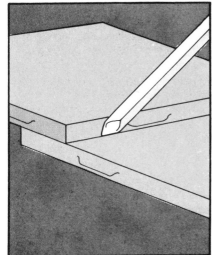

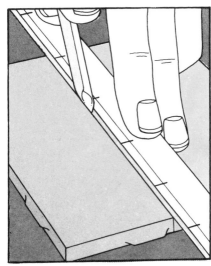

There are two ways of cutting tiles. For a straight cut, mask off the portion of tile needed, using the last full tile as a guide. Alternatively, make a cardboard pattern of the space and use this to cut out the tile.

Lay the tile on a smooth surface. Score a line with a tile cutter.

Place a matchstick under the score line at one end and apply downward pressure with the thumbs on each side of it to break the tile cleanly.

The only way to cut out a shaped tile is to gradually nibble bits away using pincers or tile side nipper, working towards a really deeply scored cut line.

Smooth the ragged edges up to the scored line, with a file.

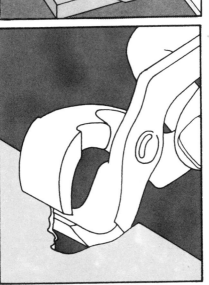

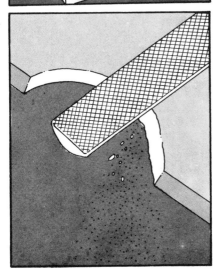

When the tiles have been in position
for at least 12 hours, the joint
lines between them have to be filled
with white grouting cement. This is
bought in powder form – your tile
supplier will stock it – and mixed
with water to a smooth paste.

Use a damp sponge to rub the grout
into the joints, and sponge excess
from the surface of the tiles.

**The joint lines betweeen the tiles are
filled with grouting cement. This is
sold in powder form where you buy
your tiles. Mix it with water to a
creamy consistency. Use a damp
sponge or a square of card to work it
well into the joints.**

**Wipe away excess grout from the face
of the tiles.**

**For a neat finish at bath edges, use
bath trim. This is sold in kits.**

**If the tiles have been laid over old tiles
in a half tiled room, the top of the tiles
can be finished off neatly with a strip
of beading. This can be varnished or
painted.**

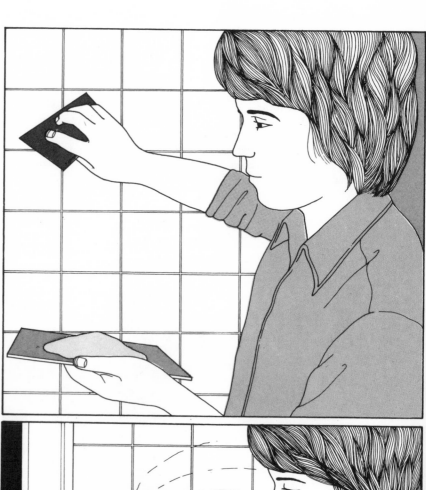

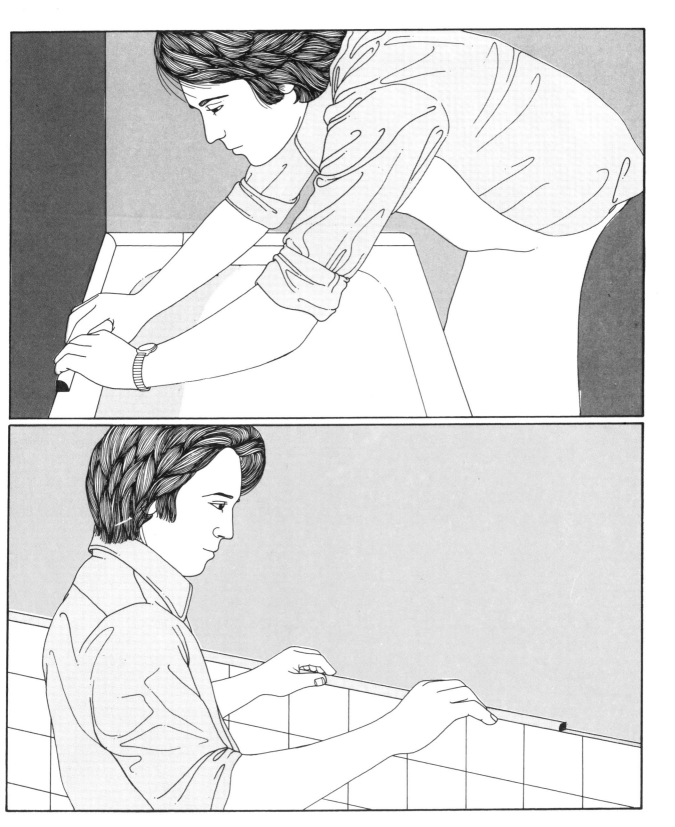

Mosaics: Ceramic mosaics can be bought in panels containing small mosaics held together by a net backing. Each panel has bands of adhesive on the back, covered by protective paper.

Original patterns can be created by cutting individual ceramics from a panel and substituting some of different colours, cut from other panels.

As for tiling, use a plumb line and horizontal spirit level to ascertain starting points.

Strip off the protective backing to activate the adhesive backing.

Press the panel firmly into place.

Work grouting cement into the joint lines as for tiles.

Remove individual pieces to fit a panel around light switches and other obstacles.

Cut through the net backing to remove individual pieces and substitute other colours when creating a patterned effect.

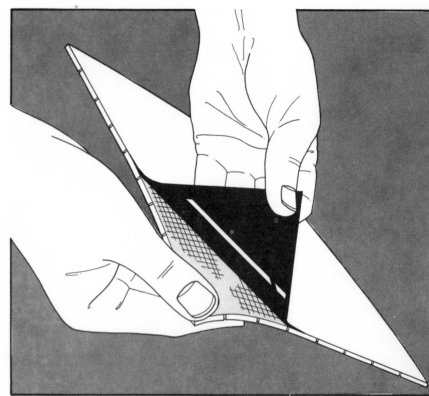

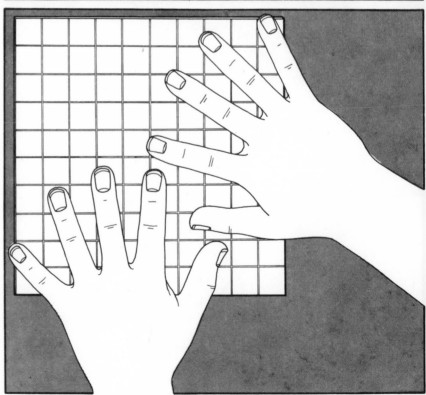

Tongued and Grooved Cladding

Tongued and grooved boards fixed to a framework of battens provide an entirely new and attractive wall surface. This is the ideal method of covering up really poor walls where extensive plastering would be needed to make them presentable.

The boards are maintenance-free and will last a lifetime. Although expensive, the fact that you need never decorate again gives them a built-in advantage over other decorative materials.

Even a single boarded wall, used as a feature area, will give a room a new appeal.

Although the boards can be fixed horizontally or vertically, the latter is more popular in the average room since it makes a ceiling seem higher.

A board is 4in. wide, including the tongue. Remember however, when planning quantities required, that when the tongue of one board slides into the groove of its neighbour, the two only span 7 inches, *not* including the tongue still exposed on one side.

Eight to ten feet-long boards are available. Buy the correct length for your walls.

Carefully prise away door architraves, and picture rails. Take care if you intend to refix the architraves.

Screw battens firmly to the wall using 2½in. gauge 8 screws with suitable plugs to get a really good fixing. Countersink all screwheads below surface.
Use a steel straight edge to ensure that all battens are plumb.
Where necessary, use packing pieces to level battens.
Fix a complete framework of battens at 16in. spacing.

Use a plumb line to find a true vertical for the outside edge of first board.

Use a nail punch and hammer to sink pin heads below the surface. Fix them diagonally through the tongue. This allows the groove of the next board to slide into position over the tongue.

Use a wood block to protect edges when tapping boards into position. A uniform gap of $\frac{1}{16}$in. should be left down the length of all boards where the tongue has engaged a groove. If the boards were locking tightly, and expansion took place, there would be no way for the boards to move easily and they would bulge.

If you were not too successful in cutting the boards square at the ends, use quadrant moulding to give a good finish.

It will be necessary to fit a new metal wall mounting box to the wall surface. A new cover plate can then be used to finish off.

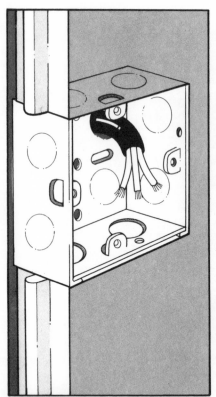

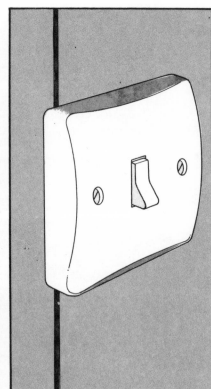

There are one or two points to bear in mind. Ideally all the tongued and grooved boards and the battens should be stored in the room where they are to be used for a couple of weeks before work begins.

This ensures that the moisture content of the wood will become the same as that of the room and the wood will not warp later on.

It may not, of course, be convenient to stack them in the room. In this case use a different room in the house.

The second point is that damp may arise in the walls (outside walls especially) and attack the timber from the back.

To prevent the effects of this, prime the timber battens with primer paint before fixing. Do not worry about getting a perfectly even coat or avoiding runs, since the battens will not be seen. A good, over-all coverage is important though.

Expanded polystyrene can be fixed between the walls and the cladding to insulate the room against moisture, cold or damp.

WOOD PANELLING

Wood panelling is available in an assortment of finishes and textures. Many types can be fixed direct to walls using adhesive recommended by the makers or Bostik stikpads, but since perfectly smooth walls are essential, a framework of battens will usually have to be fixed as one does for tongued and grooved cladding.

Remove all architraves, picture rails and mouldings.

Always cut the boards to the required size and shape before applying the adhesive to the battens.

Fix battens at centres shown or in accordance with manufacturers instructions. Follow the same fixing procedure for tongued and grooved cladding, starting in a corner.

For recessed skirting, use a foot wedge to raise each board whilst knocking home support pins into the top of each panel. Pins can be used throughout instead of adhesive. Pin panels are needed every 4in. along all edges and at every 8in. into intermediate battens.

A Shelving system for walls:
Children love to pin pictures of
footballers or pop stars on their
bedroom walls. The trouble is that,
when removed, the pins leave a
network of holes all over the wall
surface.

An excellent way to overcome the
problem is to create a special wall
surface on one or all walls, using
either Sundeala board or a cork
wallboard.

The boards can, if you like, be
secured to wall battens using a
proprietary adjustable shelving system.
A number of these systems comprise
vertical support rails containing a series
of holes into which the shelf brackets
are fitted at convenient heights.

To ring the changes, a top fascia
of chipboard, faced with laminate, can
be used.

With careful planning, wires to
electrical fittings can be hidden behind
the board. Since the board is just
screwed in position, access to the wires
is easy.

**A fabric covering of hessian or vinyl
can be applied to the Sundeala board.
The screws of the rails secure the
Sundeala board to the vertical wall
battens.**

Mirror Tiles

Need a mirror? the most economical method is to use mirror tiles. These are available in a whole range of sizes from 3in. × 2in. to 4ft. 6in. × 1ft. 4in.

There are two weights, 24oz. and 32oz. The heavier weight though slightly more expensive is a better proposition as, in my experience, the thinner types tend to splinter.

One essential is a flat backing. Fix ¾in. chipboard or plywood direct to the wall using 3in. long by gauge 8 screws to get a secure fixing.

If you are lucky enough to have really smooth walls and do not need chipboard backing, rub a little contact adhesive on to the wall in the position each pad will occupy before fixing. This will overcome the problem of a porous wall surface to which the pads may not, by themselves, adhere. Use this practice on a porous chipboard or plywood. Once in position the tiles are very difficult to dislodge so you must get each one correctly positioned first time.

Apart from their basic use as a mirror, mirror tiles can be used to make a small room appear larger if used to cover a whole wall, to increase the light in a room, or simply to reflect flowers, ornaments on shelves or other decorative features in a room.

On the back of each tile there are four adhesive pads. Just strip off the protective covering and press the tile in place on the wall. The pads will take up any *slight* unevenness in the surface.

The tiles are not precision made so there may be slight differences in sizes. Edges may not, therefore, align. Over a wide area errors will be accumulative and the final effect will look unsightly and distort reflected images. To avoid this, lay out the tiles on the chipboard backing before it is screwed to the wall to find the best sequence. Number each tile and write its number on the board in its fixing position.

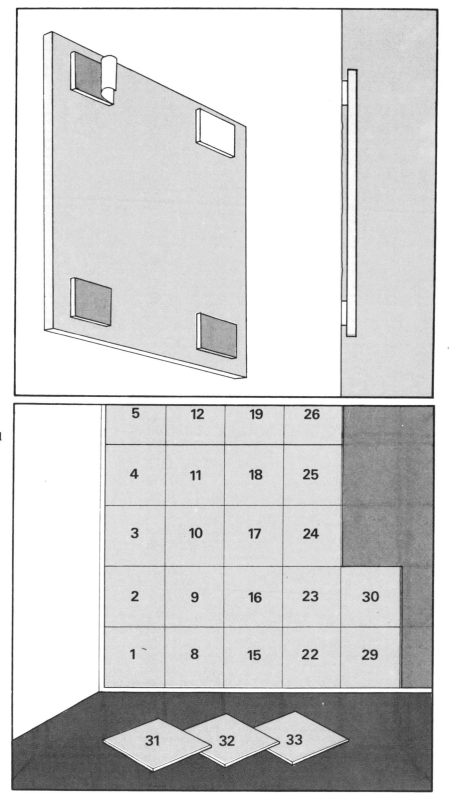

To avoid having to cut any tiles, work
out from the range of sizes a
convenient plan. If necessary use a
narrow row of tiles on one side.
However, you can tailor the framework
to suit the area covered by same-size
tiles.

To leave a flush join between the
framework and the tiles, use a strip
of plywood screwed to the chipboard
and faced with laminate.

Wall Mirrors

Mirrors can be bought in a standard range of popular sizes from manufacturers – 2ft. 6in. × 1ft. 6in., 4ft. × 2ft., 5ft. × 1ft. 6in. and 4ft. × 1ft. 3in. – these are just a selection.

Of course, if you need a size outside the standard range, it can be supplied, though it might work out to be a little more expensive per square foot.

Another possible source of mirrors is old furniture bought from second-hand shops or at jumble sales. Very often a token price is placed on a unit which contains a perfectly good mirror and in this way you would be paying a cheap price for an expensive item. If you are a keen woodworker, there is the bonus of obtaining a supply of possibly excellent timber from the piece of furniture.

It is not difficult to fix a mirror to a wall, but the fixing method must be selected in relation to the overall size of the mirror.

You should not, for example, attempt to support a 6ft.-long mirror set in a wood frame by fixing a chain to it and hanging it from a picture hanger on the wall.
This method is suitable only for a smaller, face mirror.

Hang small mirrors from a picture hook or a No. 8 gauge chromium plated screw, 1½in. long. The screw must be well secured in the wall.

Larger mirrors can be fixed in a variety of ways using screws, plugs, washers or clips.

Usually when you buy a mirror, the correct fixing aids will be included. If they are not, then discuss this aspect with your supplier.

If inadequate fixings are used and the mirror falls from the wall the result can be disastrous.

In a solid wall of brick or concrete, either screws or corner clips can be used for fixing. Where screws are used, the mirror will have to be drilled through to form holes for the screws.

If you have never drilled holes

in a mirror, then get your supplier to do this for you. It is not worth risking cracking an expensive item.

Make the screw holes in the wall after the mirror is drilled, so that the centres will be identical.

To make sure of this, get someone to hold the drilled mirror in place while you mark off the positions of the holes by feeding a pencil or sharp implement through the holes to the wall behind.

The screws will be supplied with a plastic sleeve which prevents the head of the screw coming into contact with the surface of the mirror.

Get someone to support the mirror until all the holding screws have been inserted and tightened.

As a guide, a 6mm. plate glass mirror needs 2 fixing points up to 3sq.ft. of area. Four fixing points are essential up to 15sq.ft. Above this size, the mirror also needs to be supported on a firm ledge if it is to be safe.

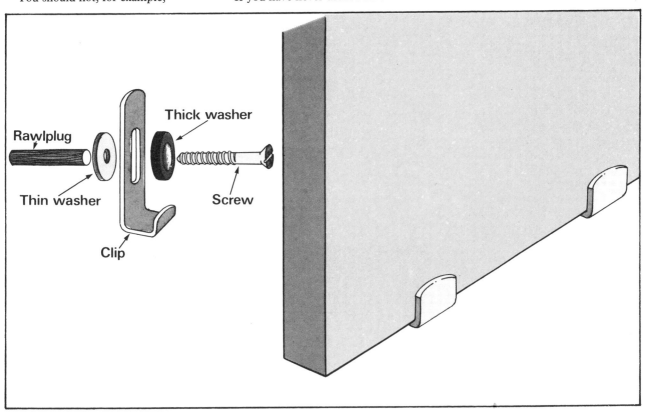

Rawlplug
Thin washer
Clip
Thick washer
Screw

Floor Coverings

CERAMIC FLOOR TILES

The most annoying aspect of laying any floor covering material is that the room is put out of action or, at the very best, is made very inconvenient to use while the work is in progress.

Where kitchens are concerned, this can be really upsetting. However, by dividing the room up into convenient sections and confining all tools and materials to one area until it is complete, the aggravation will be removed and the room can remain in constant use. This is especially useful if fitting ceramic floor tiles, which cannot be walked on for 24 hours after fixing.

Ceramics have all the hardwearing qualities of wall tiles and, as they absorb heat, they are warm underfoot in a heated bathroom.

The tiles have a special rough-glazed surface which makes them slip resistant.

Round edge tiles are used to finish off step edges, at skirtings and at external corners. Fixing methods are the same as for wall tiles.

A plywood base (about 9mm. thick) should be screwed to timber floors, using countersunk screws at 1ft. centres.

Stretch string lines from middle points of opposite walls. Where the lines cross at right angles, this is the starting point. Adjust as necessary to avoid leaving too narrow a strip at edges. (See section on ceiling tiles). Aim to complete one section of the room per day – more if the layout of the room makes this possible.

There must be no hollow spots under the tiles, otherwise they will be cracked by heels or furniture legs. A solid bed of ¼in. thick adhesive should be spread on to an area of about ½sq.yd. As a safety precaution against hollow spots, spread a thin coat of adhesive on the back of each tile as well. It is better to be safe than sorry. Complete each section, including any cut edge tiles.

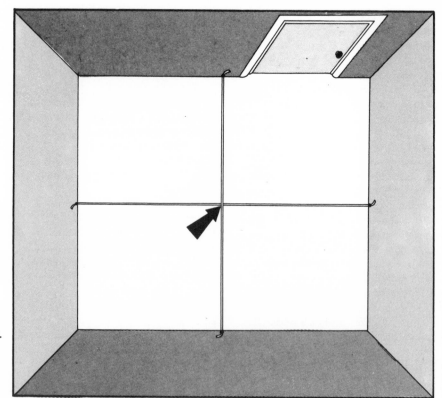

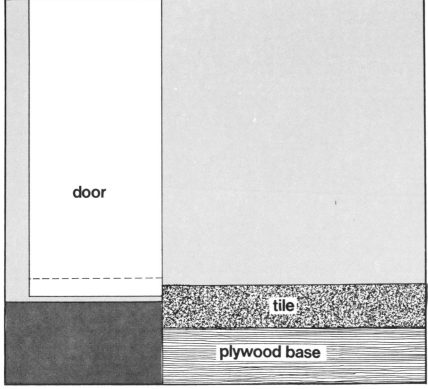

Remember, the plywood base and the tiles build up the height of the floor so it may be necessary to remove the door and plane a little off the bottom edge if it will not clear the tiles.

At skirtings, there are two finishing-off methods. You can use round-edge tiles in place of the skirting or remove the skirtings, lay the edge tiles and then replace the skirting to leave a flush finish.

Finish off by grouting the joints. Use a proprietary grout cement or mix your own, using one part of cement to three parts of sand. The mix, in both cases, should be easily workable.

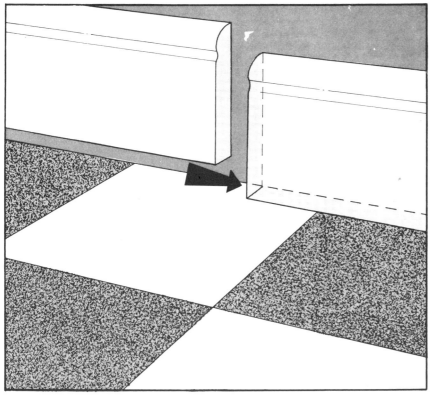

VINYL TILES

Vinyl is an ever-popular material for kitchen or bathroom floors. Tiles are generally preferred to sheets of vinyl by the amateur since they are easier to lay. In rooms where obstacles such as sink pedestals and pipes are many, a good deal of accurate cutting is needed. If a mistake is made in cutting one tile, it can be discarded and a new one cut quickly.

Do not throw away a spoiled tile since it could well be used in another place.

Tiles which have an adhesive backing are easiest to lay. The protective paper backing is peeled off before fixing the tile in position.

Vinyl can become brittle in cold conditions, so lay the tiles out in a warm room before work. This will make them more supple and easier to handle.

Use the same basic planning and starting point methods as for ceramics.
Sheet vinyl: The main advantage of sheet vinyl is that it provides a

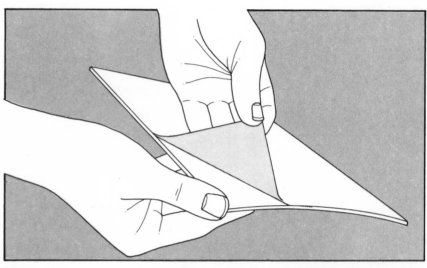

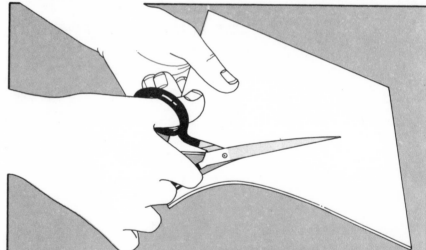

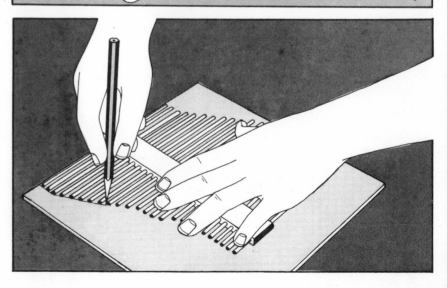

Do not peel off the paper backing until you are ready to fix the tile in place. If you make a mistake in laying, then pull the tile up and reposition it immediately. Do not do this more than three times to each tile as the adhesive will lose its holding power.

Cut vinyl with sharp scissors or a knife.

A proprietary shape tracer can be used to transfer awkward shapes to the tile to be cut. However, where only a few shaped tiles are required, it is more economical to use cardboard patterns.

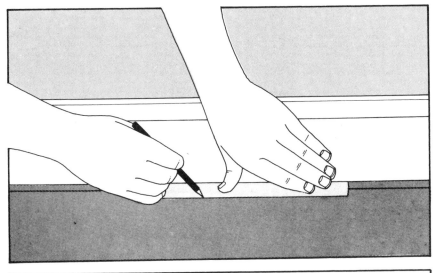

continuous floor surface and affords
a vast range of patterns and colours
from which to choose.

However, cutting is critical. If a
mistake is made it could leave an ugly
gap somewhere in the room.

When you get the rolls of vinyl
home after buying them, leave them to
stand in a warm room for 24 hours
before laying, so that they will
become flexible.

**For sheet vinyl, overcome irregular
skirtings by pulling the edge of the first
length slightly away from the skirting.
Hold a rule against the skirting and run
it along the complete length, tracing
its line with a pencil.**

**Overlap adjoining seams by about ½in.
and leave for 24 hours before
trimming to fit. Use a rule and knife
to cut through the two layers. Allow
1in. for trimming at edges. Check
carefully to allow for pattern match
between butting edges.**

**Fix to one half of the floor by
spreading the adhesive in position. Roll
back the loose half to apply the
adhesive.**

**If you make a mistake in edge cutting,
use quadrant moulding to leave a
flush finish.**

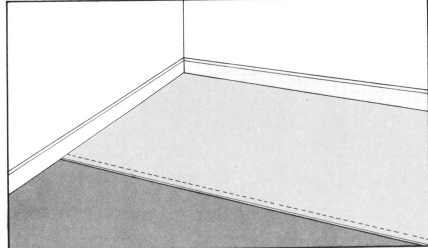

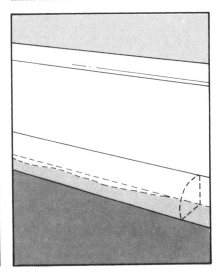

PARQUET PANELS

Thanks to the introduction of cheaper parquet tiles, this kind of floor is within the reach of everyone. Laying a wood floor costs no more than fitting a medium-priced carpet.

Several types of floor systems are available including tongued and grooved 'Lynx' panels which are removable should you decide to move house or want to take them up and re-lay them elsewhere.

The panels, about 18in. square, have a plywood backing with an oak veneer surface. There are tongues on two opposite edges and grooves on the other two opposite edges. When slotted together, a basket weave pattern is formed automatically.

The panels are laid over a cork and bitumen underlay which is supplied in rolls. Leave a gap of ½in. at the skirtings and between each strip.

Knock up a square of nine panels using the wood strip provided by the makers to protect each tile edge from damage from the hammer.

Saw off the tongues that will touch the skirting.

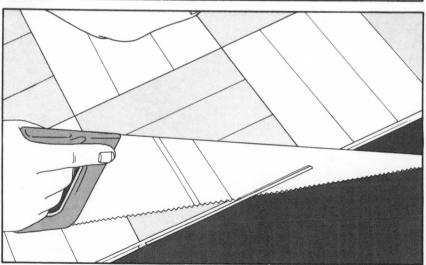

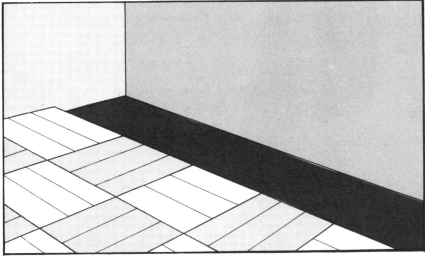

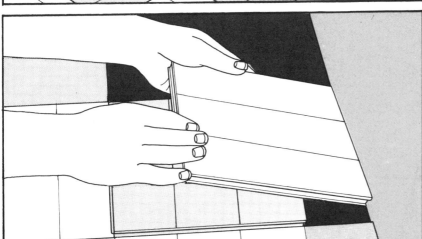

If the walls are square, you can push the first panel into the corner and proceed to add more panels. However, if the walls are not square, lay the tongue edge (sawn off) against the skirting leaving a gap of just under one panel's width between the grooved edge and the adjacent skirting. Cut panels to fill the gaps.

To mark off a cut panel, place a complete panel over the last one in the row, with the grain running at right angles. Place another panel on top with its edge butted against the skirting.

The middle panel is the one to be fitted. Mark a cut line in pencil as shown. Saw along marked line.

Use the wood strip and hammer to knock the cut panel into position.

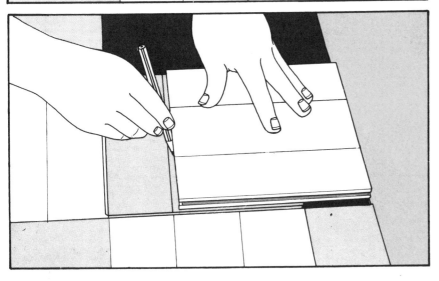

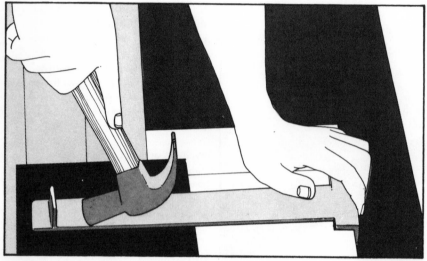

A special tool supplied by the makers
enables you to knock edge panels into
position along other skirtings.

When completing the last corner, it
will not be possible to fit a part panel
using the previous marking method. A
simple way of overcoming the problem
is to saw off the lower edge of the
groove and slide the panel into place.
Apply some adhesive to the groove for
added strength.

Reducing strip is used to finish off at
doorways.

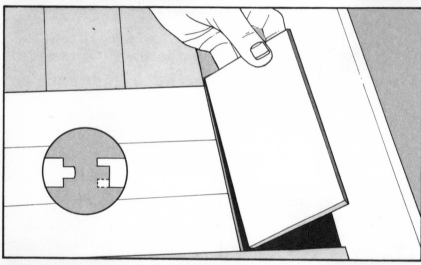

LAYING A CARPET

Fitting a good quality Axminster or
Wilton carpet is a job for a
professional. The carpet has to be
stretched correctly before it is secured.
However, a foam backed carpet should
present few difficulties.

Unroll and loosely position the carpet,
remembering to allow a tuck of 2in.
at each edge.

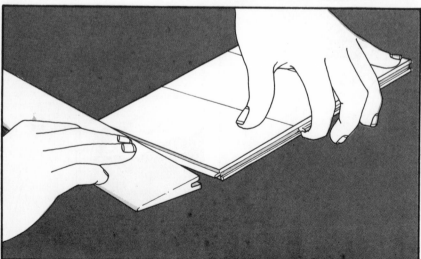

Start at the doorway. Use a sharp
knife to trim the carpet to the shape
of the frame. Tack this area in position
using carpet tacks. Hammer these
well down into the pile.

Start fitting the carpet along the
longest wall. Turn under 2in. and
knock in tacks at 9in. intervals. Use
1½in. tacks.

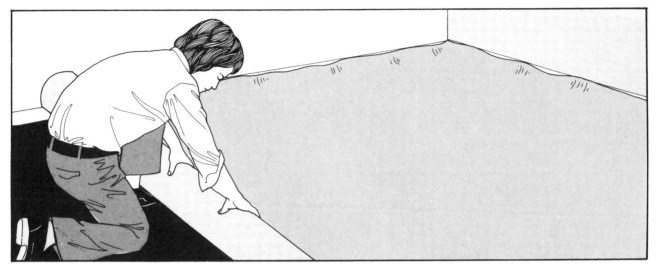

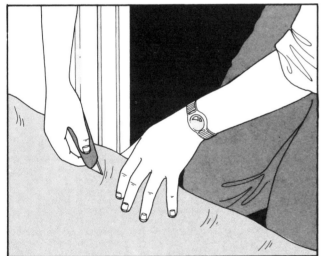

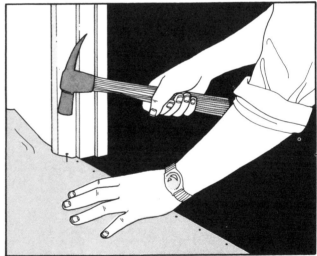

When the first side is tacked in place, pull the carpet to the opposite wall and repeat the tacking procedure.

If necessary, shuffle across the carpet to remove any wrinkles. This is a simple form of stretching.

To prevent the carpet springing back into wrinkles, knock in temporary tacks about 2ft. from the skirting to hold it in place. These can be removed when the carpet edge is secure.

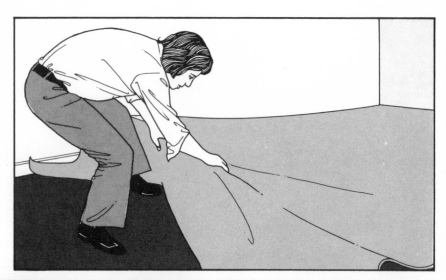

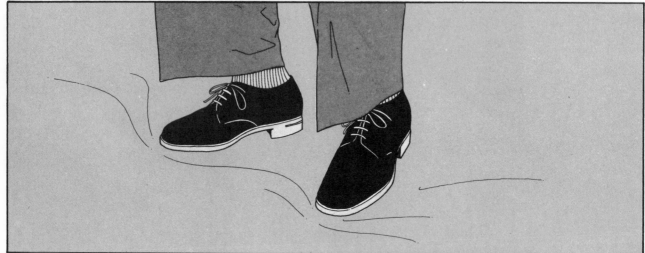

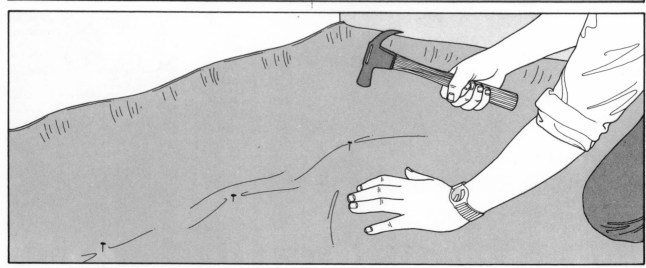

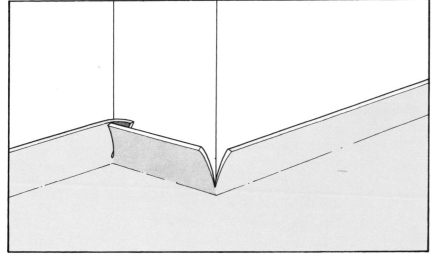

To fit the carpet at external corners, cut down to just above the floor level.

If laying a carpet with a separate underlay, cut off any surplus carpet to leave a 2in. tuck under to butt up to the underlay when tacked in place.

If fitting new skirtings, fix these after laying the carpet. This avoids the necessity of accurate edge trimming to leave a flush finish.

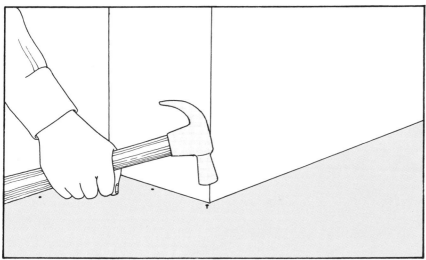

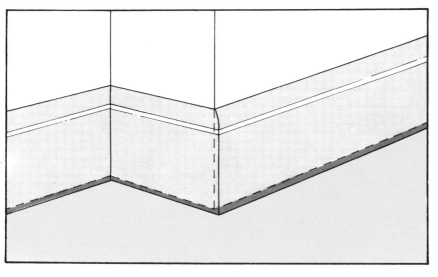

FITTING STAIR PADS

Open-tread stairs are now popular, especially in modern houses. These can only be fitted with stair pads, rather than stair carpet.

A simple, yet secure method of fastening the pads is to use Velcro tape. This comes in two parts. One part has a complete covering of tiny hooks; the other part has a backing of corresponding loops. When pushed together the hooks grip the loops firmly.

Any of the three methods shown can be used. Use whichever you prefer, dependent on the type of finish you want.

Use nails, staples or adhesive to secure the hook strip to the stair.

Use adhesive to secure the loop strip to the back of the carpet. Use 40mm. wide strip in all cases.

The pad can be wrapped around both edges of the tread; around just one edge; or simply fitted to the top of the tread.

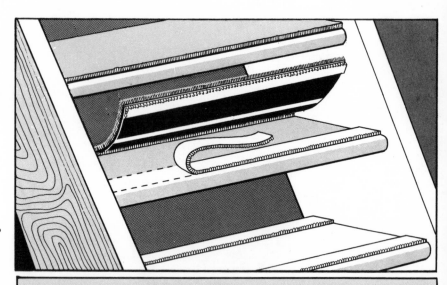

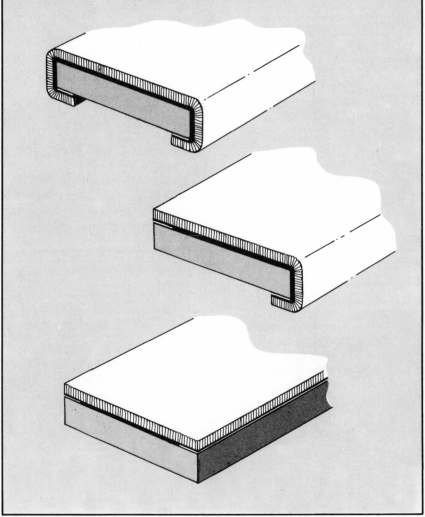

Paints for Outside

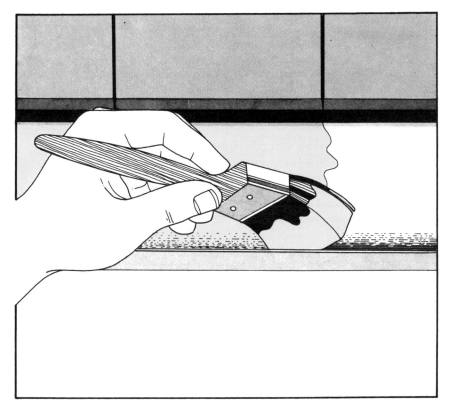

Use up old gloss paint on the inside of gutters. This gives added protection and the colour will not be seen from below.

Specialised paints are made for outside walls. None of these paints should be applied to dusty or powdery surfaces. Remove as much of the loose material as possible by scrubbing and brushing. Rinse off, using plenty of clean water. Allow to dry, then apply a coat of stabilising primer which will bind all the remaining material together to make a stable base for the finishing coats.

Cement paint provides a flat finish. It can be applied to brickwork, cement rendering, roughcast or pebbledash. It must be thinned with water following instructions on the tin. It must not be applied over gloss or emulsion surfaces.

Masonry paint: This is thicker than ordinary gloss paint. It must be thinned with white spirit, and dries more quickly than normal gloss. It is durable and long lasting, and provides a smoother finish than stone paint.

Stone paint: This is exterior grade emulsion and provides a flat or semi-gloss finish. It is ideal for filling up hairline cracks in wall surface due to the addition of crushed rock particles, mica and nylon fibres in the paint.

Soffits comprising asbestos cement panels should be painted with bituminous paint.

Interior Design

A great deal has been written in the past about the technique of interior design. For the homeowner who needs only a basic brief, outlining the simple principles involved, much of the information one reads is unnecessary.

So, in this final chapter, I am going to concentrate on a few basic ideas and principles which anyone can translate into their own living room, hall or other rooms.

At the outset, two things should be made clear. First, these basic rules are not mandatory – you do not have to follow them for fear that you will not otherwise produce a room scheme that would grace the pages of a Sunday colour supplement.

Certain colours and patterns should really not be used in certain sized rooms or in the wrong combinations, but if it pleases you to disobey these rules, then that is entirely your concern. After all, you have to live with the decorations.

So if you follow the design laws to the letter and end up feeling uncomfortable or unhappy in your own living room then the room scheme has failed your particular needs.

Generally, though, most people will prefer to use colours and patterns in a certain way because they will make the best possible use of a room's dimensions.

The second point is that, no matter how closely the rules are followed, there is no guarantee of success if the practical work is carried out sloppily and carelessly.

Many a room, which has all the right colours or patterns in an ideal blend of position and proportion, fails because the paintwork smudges on to an adjacent wall or the wallpaper pattern is lopsided.

But I am concentrating on design in this last chapter, as you should by now be able to do the actual decorating without too many mistakes.

Successful interior design is the result of several 'elements' coming together in the right blend and balance. These elements are form, colour,

pattern and texture – all combined with a furnishing layout that fulfils the functional purposes of the room.

It would be nice to assume that everyone has lots of money to spend on new furnishings so that they can carry on merrily and produce any effect that they choose. But money is the first stumbling block.

The existing furniture and furnishings usually have to stay, so these must be taken into consideration. Perhaps your three-piece suite is a vivacious colour or has a patterned cover; or perhaps the carpet is a neutral colour.

True, the first could possibly be covered or the second dyed but, assuming that you like them just as they are, they will have to blend in with any new decorating scheme. So the existing furnishings could limit design possibilities straight away.

There are many other things to consider before you reach for a paint colour chart or borrow a wallpaper pattern book from the local decorating shop.

It is worthwhile sitting down and really looking at a room; the role it plays in the house, and how it might be used in the future.

Room size: The room's dimensions and position are important.

Is it of rabbit-hutch proportions or really spacious? Colour and pattern can be used to make it seem bigger or smaller.

Light: Or again, many people have decorated their new house quickly without having any regard as to whether the room is a sunny one or inclined to be dark. This can be frustrating afterwards if you have chosen the wrong scheme for the wrong room.

Many houses are positioned so that, for example, the front rooms are bathed in sunlight from dawn to late afternoon, the back rooms only get the benefit of the sun for the last hour or so before it sets.

If you have chosen a bright scheme for the sunny room, that is not so bad.

Bright, sunny rooms put people in a more enjoyable frame of mind.

However, a subdued scheme in a dark room will make it very depressing – especially in the winter.

If you have been in residence for a reasonable time, this point will not have eluded you. If, on the other hand, you had intended to start decorating your new home before the furniture van has reached the bottom of the road, then curb your impetuosity or discuss the amount of light in the rooms with the previous occupant.

Basically, though, it is never a good idea to get straight on with the decorating before you have lived in a house for a few weeks. After a while you get a 'feel' for the rooms and the part that they play in your house.

This brings me to the next point. What is the function of the room?

Bathrooms and toilets are the only single-purpose rooms in the house. The kitchen may have to double as a dining room/workroom/sewing room, so this should be borne in mind when planning the layout of furnishings and lighting.

Bedrooms: Bedrooms may also be dual-purpose, especially where there are children.

In smaller houses bedrooms are often the only escape for essential privacy. So they must take on a sitting room atmosphere as well.

Utilising the bedroom in this way is a commonsense attitude to modern living. Space is always at a premium, so it is pointless to use the bedrooms only for sleeping. The rooms are out of action most of the time, while the family congregate en masse in the lounge.

Children invariably need space to play games or pursue their hobbies or do their homework. Adults with a penchant for listening to music or reading need a 'den' where they can escape for an hour. So it is important to create a 'living room' atmosphere in the bedroom.

The furnishings should include an armchair or desk, or be arranged to leave the maximum amount of space on the floor for train sets, dolls houses or whatever else it may be.

Clutter does not create an agreeable atmosphere in which to relax and pursue a pastime. Built-in furnishings which incorporate sufficient space for storage are essential.

If storage is ample there is no danger of clothes, make-up containers, shoes and so on making an unsightly display.

The colour scheme to match the mood of a place to relax should be warm and tranquil.

Children's rooms: In a nursery or children's room, decoration should be selected with an eye to the future. Adults may be content to live with exactly the same decor for four or five years, but children's tastes and interests can alter dramatically in two or three years. A ten-year-old girl's tastes can have altered out of all recognition by the time she is thirteen or fourteen. Or a boy could be replacing his international footballer posters on the wall with pin-ups of a very different kind.

So in the early stages of a child's life the decor must be easily adaptable. Pictures alone can alter the whole appearance of the room.

In an earlier chapter, I described how a pin-up board could be fixed to the wall, if necessary covering the whole of one elevation. This can be used for the child's pictures. The rest of the decor could be ordinary wallpaper provided that one does not select a paper which quickly becomes outdated.

Toddlers generally manage to create havoc in their nursery bedroom. Greasy little fingers leave their tell-tale signs all over the place and inevitably, crayons or spillages can ruin walls and carpets. So use washable papers or vinyl emulsion paint which can be sponged down easily when damage is done.

The floor is more of a problem. A carpet is important for a toddler to crawl – and fall – upon. But, as every parent knows, at the end of the day, biscuit crumbs, orange juice and so on remain as a testimony to the day's activities.

Cleaning a carpet is impossible in the evening when the toddler is asleep in the same room. In any case time has to be allowed for it to dry out after cleaning, which may not happen before the following morning.

A solution is to lay carpet tiles in the nursery. If any do get stained they can be picked up, cleaned, dried and replaced.

With carpet tiles irreparable damage is less of a problem too. An 'impossible' stain does not have to mean the introduction of a discreetly placed rug. The affected tiles can be replaced with spares bought at the outset.

Incidentally, rugs are not a good idea anyway, where there are toddlers, They just create another hazard in the room.

The living room: The living room gets the most wear and tear of all. It is here that the family gather to watch television, play games, talk, have snacks and hot drinks, entertain guests and do many of the other things that form the overall pattern of family life.

This room, therefore, must be the most carefully planned of all since the family will, collectively, spend more hours here than anywhere else in the house. The layout must cater for all the conflicting and unified activities.

The furnishings play a critical part in the design. These must be kept to a minimum yet be adequate to cover all regular needs. And they must be sited discreetly to make the best possible use of the central floor area.

Probably the television is the most important single item in many rooms, so the position of this and adequate seating for the 'viewers' must be planned so that the family can settle down for the evening without having to drag chairs into position to see the screen.

Ideally, chairs should be arranged so that they are not blocking traffic 'lanes'. Anyone should be able to move anywhere in the room without stumbling over feet or climbing over furniture.

Storage space is required for those items needed for individual hobbies or for general family interests.

Books, model boats, drinks – the possibilities are endless. The exact size and type of storage space can be decided only by the nature of the family's needs.

In many living rooms the problem of knowing where to site cupboards and other storage is readily answered by the presence of alcoves on either side of the chimney breast.

The floor space in recesses is very often not used at all, which is quite a number of square feet going to waste.

Built-in storage units make the best possible use of a recess, since they use up every square inch of space, if necessary going right up to the ceiling.

The one disadvantage they have is that the room can no longer be easily changed or adapted. However, since only that part containing the recesses is not going to be flexible, this is not likely to worry too many people.

The dining room: The dining room is probably the easiest room in the house to design.

It is usually a single-purpose room and thus needs only a centrally placed table with chairs, plus a sideboard or other storage unit.

Nowadays, if there are recesses, it is fashionable to install fitted units as for the living room. This, though, is largely a matter of personal preference.

Since the function of a dining room is purely and simply a place for the family to assemble at mealtimes, it is closely linked to the kitchen where the meals are cooked.

Ideally the room nearest the kitchen should be made into the dining room. This means that the shortest possible route is taken when ferrying food from the cooking area to the dining table.

Also, of course, it is the shortest route for transporting the 'empties' back to the kitchen for washing-up.

Using the shortest route means that

there is less risk of spillages, and it is often said that it also ensures that the meals are served hot. However, I never think that this can be used as a reason in the average modern house, where an extra few feet is not going to make all that much difference. In a mansion, it may well be true.

The ideal arrangement, of course, is to build a serving hatch in the partition wall between dining room and kitchen so that crockery can be passed through directly on to a serving table positioned below.

Dining room and living room combined: Where there is only one room in a house which has to perform the dual function of a living room and dining room, greater care has to be taken to segregate the two areas.

Clearly the area allocated for the dining room section will need far less space than the main living zone, so dining table and chairs can be put in the least used part of the room.

A serving hatch would overcome the problem of having to carry trays across the room to the dining table. In many houses nowadays the dining area is the one adjoining the kitchen wall.

The decor in the room can be used to segregate the dining and living areas visually. The area of the walls encompassing the dining area could be covered in a colour contrasting with the rest of the room. This change in decor will form a demarcation line, which could be accentuated further by a change in the floor covering materials.

For example, carpet could give way to an area of parquet or vinyl tiles.

A decorative screen partition could be another dividing feature.

Colours, textures and patterns: Now let us look at colours, textures and patterns and how they can be used to alter the visual effect of a room.

If these three things are totally lacking in a room, there will be no contrast and the room will be dull and lifeless. If on the other hand they are over-done the decor will become confusing and irritating to the eye.

Patterns are used to give interest and variety to a room scheme. Ostentatious designs are best used to bring interest only where it is needed. They should not be used excessively, since they become over-bearing and their impact is lost completely.

In a small room, beware of using a large pattern; it will swamp the room and not allow the eyes to rest. The same effect will be produced if a large pattern is chosen for a feature area – an alcove, for example.

And even if the pattern motif is small, a zig-zag or similar type of jazzy pattern used on every wall will become irritating.

Patterned wallcoverings must be selected bearing in mind the wall surface.

If the wall is uneven, avoid any design incorporating long unbroken lines. These merely emphasise the faults. Go instead for an irregular broken effect with plenty of colour change and this will disguise the defects.

Large patterns are acceptable in big rooms which need to be scaled down visually. A small pattern in this situation will produce the opposite effect.

Vertical stripes will give a room more height while horizontal stripes create the illusion of extra length.

A room with more than its fair share of corners, angles and recesses can seem fussy. These can be 'lost' if a smallish, busy-patterned wall covering is used throughout the room in conjunction with matching curtains. Matching wallcovering and curtain sets are readily available nowadays.

It is sometimes inevitable that pipes, a meter box, or other eyesores are situated in a room. Obviously, most people want to disguise their presence as much as possible.

Boxing them in is the first thing to consider. This is not a difficult task since the only requirements are a couple of softwood battens covered with plywood or hardboard and fixed

to the wall over the offending item.

But remember, in the case of a meter, that access will be needed from time to time, so the box construction should be designed with accessibility in mind.

A 'box' fixed to the wall can be covered with the same decorative paper used in the rest of the room, so making it merge with the background.

Whatever you do, unless you have a liking for pipes, meters and so on, never paint them in a contrasting colour – this will make them a focal point.

Be cautious about using two wall covering patterns in the same room. It rarely works.

If you want two types of paper, you should follow the principle of having a patterned area enclosed by a plain colour and a plain area enclosed by a pattern.

Furniture in the scheme of things: The carpet or a three piece suite is often the cornerstone of a whole room scheme.

It is all too easy to forget about these when the room has been cleared for decorating. Then, when the work is finished, the new decorations might well appear to be quite unsuitable as soon as the old furniture is moved back in.

Bear in mind that a busy-patterned carpet will never blend with a busy wall covering. It is far better to go for plain colour walls.

So base the colours and patterns of the walls on one of the items of furniture that is likely to be a dominant feature of the room. Select a main colour from the feature and use this as the basis for the scheme.

When we think of patterns we tend to associate them only with the designs on wall coverings, curtains, cushions and so on. Yet furniture itself in a room creates patterns, and textures as well.

If all the walls and the ceiling in a room were painted white, when empty it would look bare, clinical, cold and uninteresting, even though, in a smallish room, the plainness would make the room seem bigger. Yet, when the furnishings are moved back, the outline of the table, chairs, television, bookshelves, and so on will create patterns against the plain backcloth.

Furthermore, the textures of the wood, picture frames, carpets and everything else will add the essential interest that the eye automatically searches for.

Many designers, in fact, believe this to be a foolproof method of creating a good visual effect.

The use of colours: Colours fall into two categories – called the definite and the indefinite.

These names are an exact indication in one word as to the effect the use of colour will produce.

Definite colours are those like yellow, orange and red.

Set against a pale background, an object painted in one of the definite colours will stand out vividly.

The indefinite colours are hues such as those with a blue base; blue-violet or blue-green. If these are used on an object or a wall, they will detract from its importance.

The colours chosen depend on the effect they are intended to have on the overall dimensions of a room, whether an ugly feature is going to be disguised or a nice feature emphasised, and whether the room needs to have a cool or a warm appearance.

Taking the size factor of a room first, colours can be used in much the same way as patterns.

Using pale colours or white walls in a room will make it appear bigger. The opposite effect is achieved with dark colours.

A high ceiling in a room can be 'lowered' by using a strong, dark colour, or even a patterned paper, in conjunction with plain walls.

Low ceilings are oppressive – especially in small rooms. In this situation, dark walls and a dark ceiling – even in a contrasting colour will produce a claustrophobic effect.

Ideally, in a small room, you should think only of pale colours.

If you must go for dark walls, then you will be well advised to paint the ceiling white. This will make a low ceiling look a couple of feet higher.

A long, narrow room can well take on the appearance of a hallway or an upstairs landing. To create a more 'square' appearance, use dark colours or a heavy pattern on the end walls with a pale shade on the long walls.

When choosing colours, do not be hindered by any of the conventionally accepted combinations. 'Reds and greens should never be seen' is a basic design rule. But, if you happen to like reds and greens together, then by all means use them.

Most colours will combine with each other provided that not too many are used in one room.

The important point to watch is the way you combine the different shades of the colours. Closely related colours are always the best though.

The following six colours are those seen in a rainbow: yellow, orange, red, violet, blue and green. They are not clearly defined in the rainbow, since they merge into each other.

If you want to make a colour chart of your own to get a clearer picture of the related colours that will merge with each other easily, it can be done simply with paper and pencil.

Draw a circle and mark around the perimeter twelve equidistant points, like the numbers on the clock.

On the 12 o'clock mark write red and then continue in the following sequence right around the 'dial': red-purple, purple, blue-purple, blue, blue-green, green, yellow-green, yellow, yellow-orange, orange, orange-red.

The colours nearest to each other will merge successfully and you can see why red (in the 12 o'clock position) and green (in the 6 o'clock position) are never supposed to be seen together.

The definite colours are described as the warm colours and the indefinite colours as the cool.

As I said before there are definite rules to follow for dark or sunny rooms, but it is entirely up to you whether or not you follow them. However, the rooms on the North side of the house which get little or no sun would feel warmer if the colours used were selected from the definite shades in the top half of the colour chart.

The rooms which are bathed in sunlight for the most part of the day can be decorated in the cool, indefinite colours.

You may think that some of the rules on using colours are contradictory or do not fit into the layout of your home.

For example, the smallest room (which needs light colours to give an illusion of space) may face North (therefore needing the definite colours to make it feel warmer).

In this example, though, you could get the best of both worlds by choosing pale oranges, reds or yellows.

If there is not an obvious compromise, something will have to suffer and you must make your own choice. By and large, though a happy mixture usually can be found.

House Repair and Maintenance

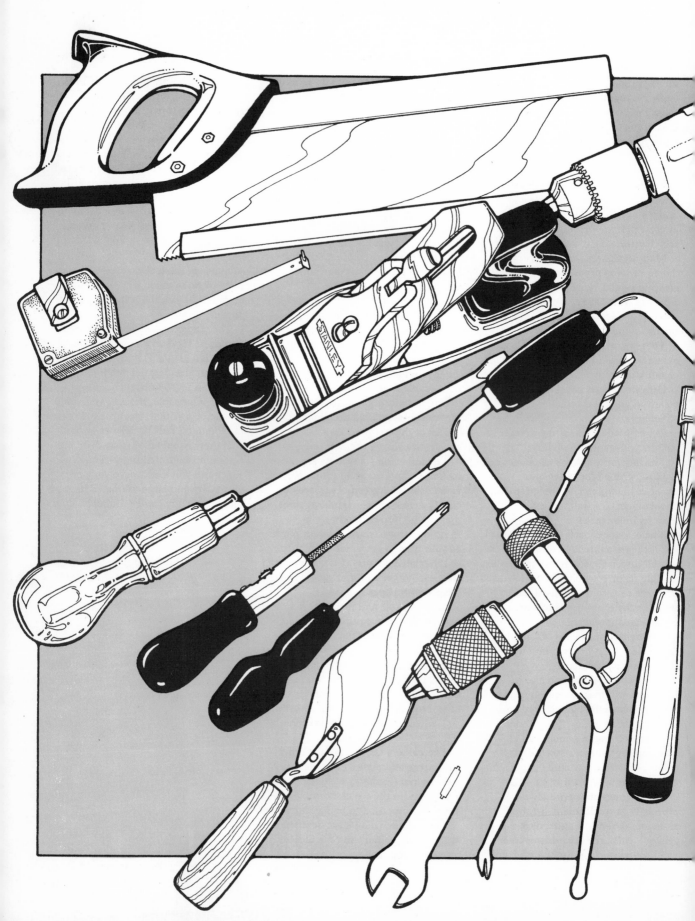

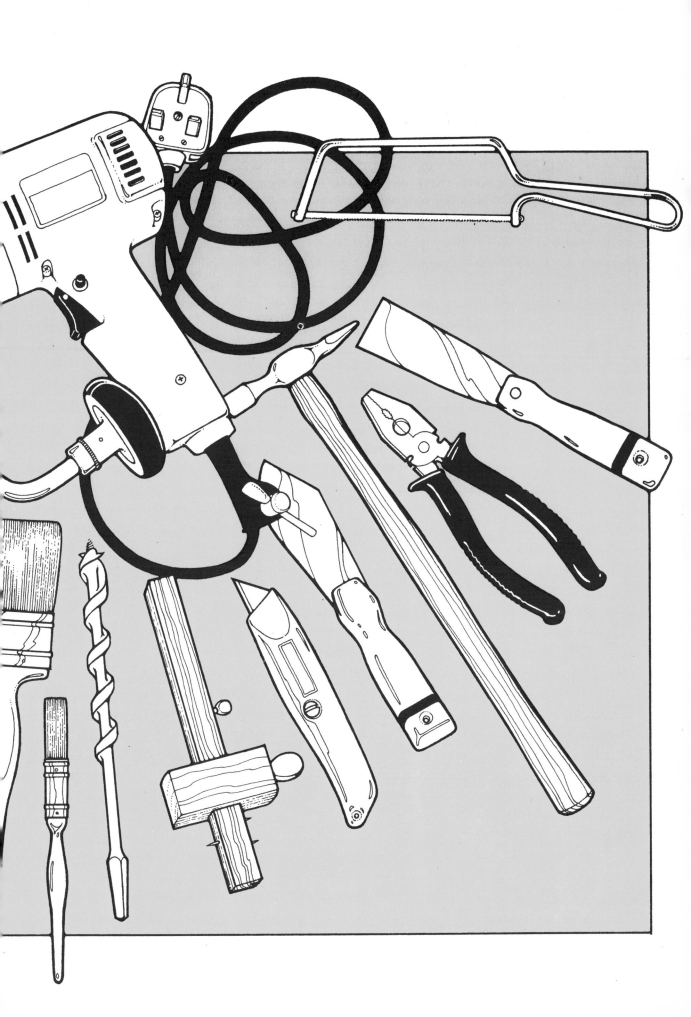

Looking After Walls

BRICKWORK

Efflorescence – a white powdery substance that forms on brickwork – is caused by water drawing the soluble salts in the bricks to the surface.

Since water causes the trouble, do not attempt to wash away the substance; this will add to the problem.

Damp walls may give rise to vegetation or fungus growth. Here, use a stiff broom (not a wire brush) to clean down the wall before brushing on a coat of fungicide. The cause of the damp (see page 120) must be cured or the trouble will reoccur.

Efflorescence and fungus growth can appear on interior walls and spoil wallpaper. In this case, there is no alternative but to strip off the paper, complete the remedial work and then redecorate. As an added precaution use a wallpaper paste containing a fungicide.

Often solid brick walls which face the prevailing winds can be saturated by driving rain, which can cause efflorescence. A liberal application of silicone solution to the brickwork in dry summer conditions will prevent rain soaking into the bricks.

Rust can occur in the mortar joints between the bricks. One of the ingredients used to make mortar is sand. The rust is caused by ironstone present in the sand. Chip out the old mortar and fill the joints with freshly mixed mortar.

Repointing If the mortar joints have started to crumble or crack, the whole wall will soon look shabby. Even sound, discoloured joints can ruin the appearance of attractive brickwork. In both cases it is worthwhile raking out the old mortar and filling the joints with new.

If any mortar drops on to the face of the bricks, do not try to clean it off immediately; you will only succeed in spreading it further over the surface. Allow it to dry and then scrape it off with a trowel. Then lightly brush the

There are three types of joint. Make sure you repoint (make good) defective joints to match those used previously. Flush joints are the most common. These leave a flat surface. They should be used where a wall is to be painted.

Weathered joints are slanted to make sure rainwater slides off, thus preventing it settling and sinking into the mortar. Rubbed joints are formed with a half round length of metal or timber.

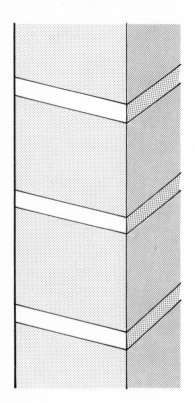
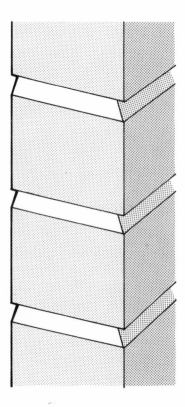
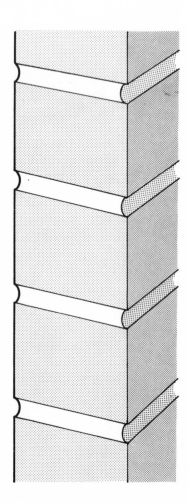

surface of the brick with a stiff brush.

The correct mortar mix should be used when re-pointing and as a small amount will go a long way it is adviseable to purchase a proprietary ready-mixed bag such as Marley Mix. Water is then added as required.

Match up to the existing mortar joint which will usually be a rubbed, flush or weathered joint.

If a large amount of mortar is needed, make it by mixing Portland cement, fine sand and some pva adhesive (plasticiser) – and water. The mix must be neither too stiff nor too runny. A 'buttery' consistency is best. Follow manufacturer's instructions when using pva adhesive.

Use a small sharp cold chisel or plugging chisel and club hammer to chip out the old mortar to a depth of ¾in. Brush out all dust and soak the cavity with water. Wetting first prevents the bricks from absorbing too much moisture from the mortar.

Use a trowel to press the mortar into the cavities. Leave the mortar slightly proud of the surface.

When the mortar is partially dry, rub off the excess. Use a half round length of timber or a short length of pipe.

Use the edge of the trowel to shape the horizontal joints. The mortar must slope outwards to the bottom edge.

Weathered pointing is more difficult to master. Complete the vertical joints by drawing the trowel back towards the right-hand bricks while pressing inwards with the left side of the trowel. Use the edge of the trowel to slice surplus mortar off the face of the bricks.

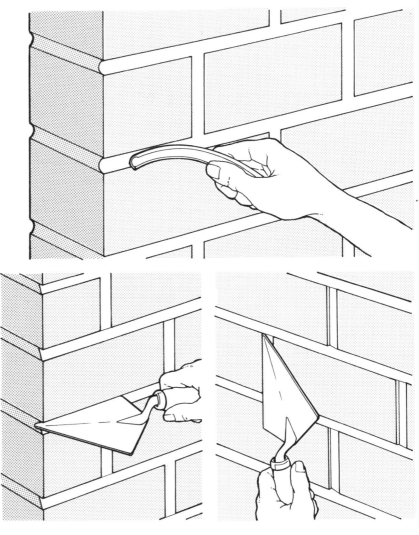

Damaged bricks A single damaged brick can be removed and replaced quite easily. If the wall is to be painted it is not important to buy a matching brick. If it is not being painted, then see if a builders' merchant can supply a used brick of the same type.

The space (usually 2in.) between the outer and inner leaf of a cavity wall prevents rainwater reaching the inside wall of the house and causing damp problems. If any of the pieces of brick being removed drop into and become lodged in the cavity they will form a bridge for rainwater to cross to the inside wall. So be careful when chipping out a brick. Make sure that the line of mortar around the four sides of the hole are also chipped clean, so that fresh mortar can be pressed around the replacement brick.

When chipping out a brick from a solid wall, use a small, sharp cold chisel to clean out the brick and surrounding mortar. If a club hammer and larger brick bolster are used, it is all too easy to damage the internal brick and for the plaster to be cracked and dislodged from the inner wall.

Use a cold chisel and club hammer to chip away the damaged brick. Work from the centre outwards. It is very important to use a small sharp cold chisel and take out only small pieces of the brick at a time to avoid internal damage in a solid brick wall.

'Butter' mortar around the new brick and slide it into the cavity. Tap the brick into its final position by using the handle of the trowel. Wedge small pieces of slate at top and bottom of brick to hold it in the correct position before completing the pointing. Take care not to push the brick too far into a cavity wall as it will be difficult to extract. Complete the pointing as before.

A continuous crack down a wall can indicate a major fault in the foundations. Get qualified help as repairs will certainly have to be carried out by a professional builder.

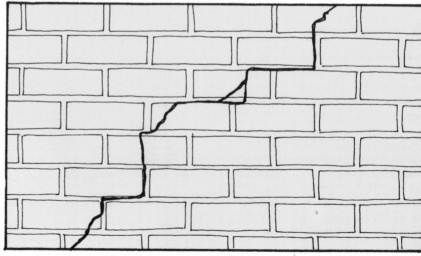

Replacing an airbrick The grid formation of an airbrick allows fresh air to pass through the walls but prevents birds or vermin getting inside. If it is damaged it must be replaced immediately.

There are two types of airbrick. The type for a solid wall comprises a brick and louvre which are fixed to the outside and inside of the wall respectively. A cavity wall airbrick extends right through the wall.

Knock out the damaged airbrick using a cold chisel and club hammer. Work from the centre outwards. Remember to see that all airbricks around the house are above path level and not blocked up by soil or any other obstruction piled against them. Blocked vents will prevent the air circulating and can cause wet rot in the ground floor joists and floorboards.

Spread a ½in. layer of mortar on the base of the hole and a similar thickness around the new airbrick.

Push the brick into the hole and wedge with slate before matching up the pointing.

RENDERING REPAIRS

The rendering over the brickwork of a house wall (on solid walls) prevents rainwater reaching the bricks of the outer face of the wall and thereafter crossing to the inner walls to cause damp patches which ruin decorations.

Should a damp patch appear, check the outside wall to see if the rendering is cracked or damaged. Sometimes defects are not immediately apparent; gentle tapping along a suspect area with a hammer will find defective patches – they will sound hollow and could fall out even under a light tap. For repairs, use a mortar mix of 1 part Portland cement to 6 parts sand. The sand should be a mixture of soft and sharp sand.

For smaller cracks use a proprietary mix, available from d-i-y shops in small bags.

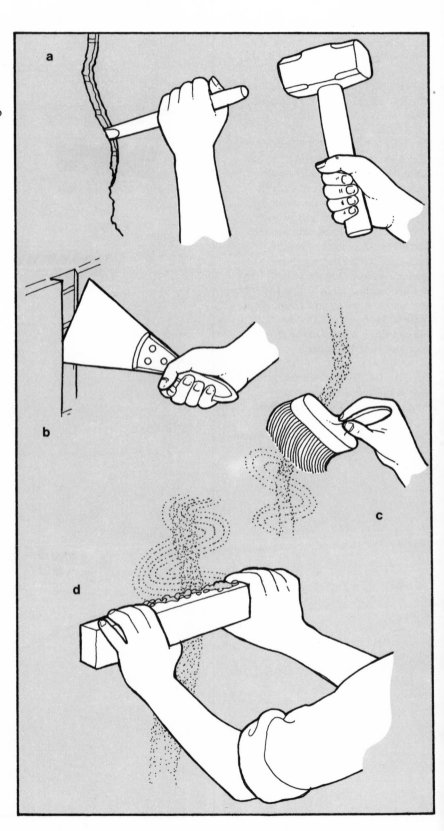

Use a sharp cold chisel and club hammer to widen the crack. (a)

Undercut the edges with a scraper so that the new mortar can be pressed behind the crack. Remove all loose material using a wire brush. Brush a pva bonding agent, proprietary type, into the crack. (b)

Press the mortar well into the crack using a trowel. Remove excess mortar immediately, using an old damp brush. (c)

Allow the mortar to dry partially before damping down and smoothing off with a trowel or a block of wood. (d)

PEBBLEDASH

An 'invisible' repair can be made to an area of damaged pebbledash by adding some pebbles to mortar spread over the damaged area before painting.

Use a mortar mix of 1 part Portland cement and 6 parts sand. Try to buy pebbles from a builder's merchant as near as possible in size to the existing pebbles.

Cut back all damaged pebbles and mortar to leave sound edges around the damage. If necessary, chip back to brickwork using a broad cold chisel. (a)

Trowel mortar into the cavity, level off and, while it is still wet, throw on the pebbles. (b)

Press the pebbles well into the mortar using a wood float. (c)

When the mortar is dry, use a large worn brush to punch paint well into the wall surface. Gloss paint provides an easy-to-clean finish and helps to make the repair invisible. (d)

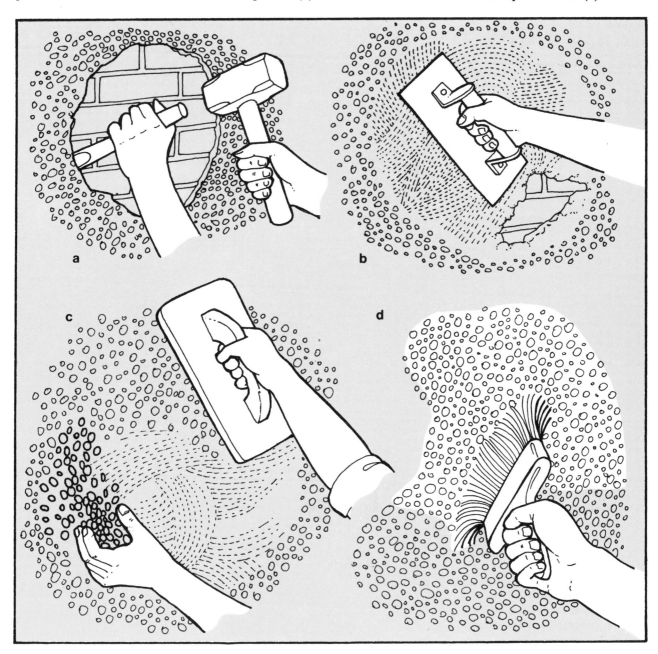

CRACKS IN CEILINGS AND WALLS

The method of repairing holes and cracks in ceilings and interior walls depends on the extent of the damage and the situation.

Smaller cracks can usually be repaired with a cellulose filler whereas large cracks in ceilings will need different treatment.

Wide cracks Wide ceiling cracks or those which re-open after filling indicate excessive ceiling movement. This is a common problem. If you fill these cracks with a cellulose filler you will probably be back to square one in no time.

However, it may be possible to achieve a permanent, invisible repair by using a scrim mesh and, if necessary, lining paper.

Whether in ceilings or walls, fill all nail holes and smaller cracks with cellulose filler such as Polyfilla. Before filling a crack you must first undercut it with a filling knife. Undercutting means deepening the cavity behind the crack to form a V-shape. The V should be widest at its deepest part.

Dust all loose material from the crack and fill the cavity with the filler. Allow to set before rubbing flush with the surface using glasspaper wrapped around a wood block. A flush finish can also be achieved by drawing the filling knife at right angles across the surface. A 3in. filling knife with a flexible blade is ideal.

For large areas it is more economical to use a plaster such as Sirapite. Dampen the crack beforehand and apply the plaster with a trowel. Sirapite sets quickly so work in a continuous session.

To get a flush finish, draw a timber straight-edge across the wet plaster to level it off. Rub a steel float across the area when the plaster is touch dry. This will leave a smooth surface.

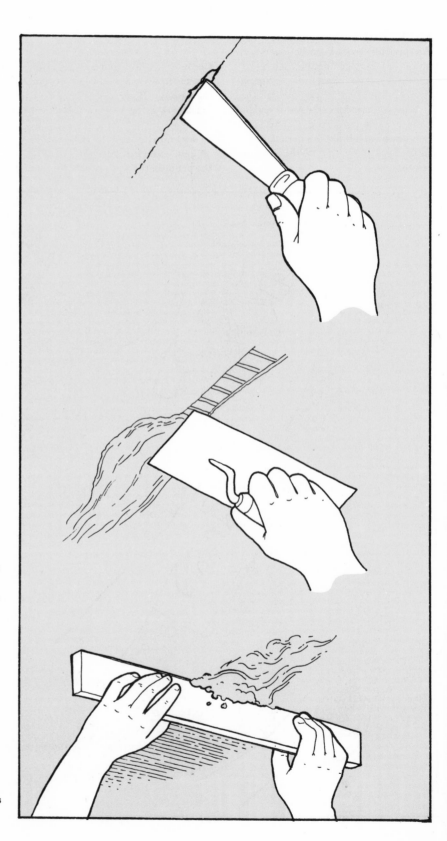

If you prefer, fill the bulk of the cavity with plaster. Allow to dry and then 'top up' with cellulose filler, as before, using a filling knife.

Alternatively fill the crack with cellulose filler. Cut out some scrim mesh (available from decorating shops; it is sold in rolls) and stick it over the crack with cellulose paste. The scrim should be slightly longer than the crack. (a)

When dry, cover the mesh with filler, using a filling knife. When dry, rub down the surface if necessary with fine glass paper over a sanding block. (b)

To add more strength to the repair, tear off a piece of lining paper about 1ft wide. Paste the central 6in. with cellulose paste and brush it over the repaired area leaving its 'dry' border hanging down. (c)

When dry, tear off the border to leave a feathered edge on the ceiling. To completely disguise the feathered edge, apply a thin coat of cellulose filler, having first primed the surface with emulsion paint. (d)

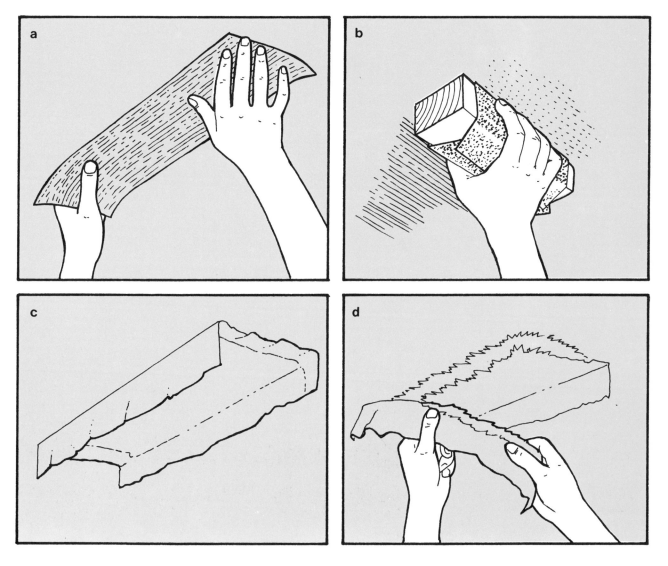

Fix a timber straight-edge to an external corner as a guide when repairing with plaster.

Loose plaster Chimney breasts and other areas near fireplaces are likely points at which to find whole chunks of loose plaster. These should be lifted out with a broad knife, if necessary going right back to the brickwork. Repairs can then be made with Sirapite.

When repairing an external corner of a window or doorway, use a hard-setting plaster. This dries rock hard and will stand knocks.

Any plaster of this type which is left too long before use will start to harden in the container. Do not add fresh water to the mix to activate it or it will set hard immediately. So always use fresh material.

Plastering electric cable channels Before working in the vicinity of electrical wires, always turn off the current at the mains.

Where possible, run cables through conduit to wall switches, or alternatively fix cover plates before plastering.

It will be necessary to unscrew the switch cover in order to plaster around the switch box sunk in the wall.

FIXING DECORATIVE COVERINGS

Laminate This is bought in large sheets, about $\frac{1}{16}$in. thick, and cut down to the required size. A variety of colours is available. The surface of

Run cables throughout conduit and brush out all dust from the cavity before plastering.

Dampen the cavity with fresh water before plastering. Make sure that the plaster is well packed around the switch box and the plastic conduit. Allow the plaster to dry before refixing the switch cover. All power should be switched off when undertaking this type of repair.

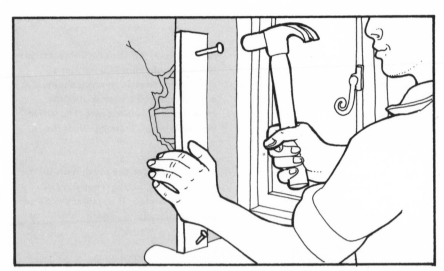

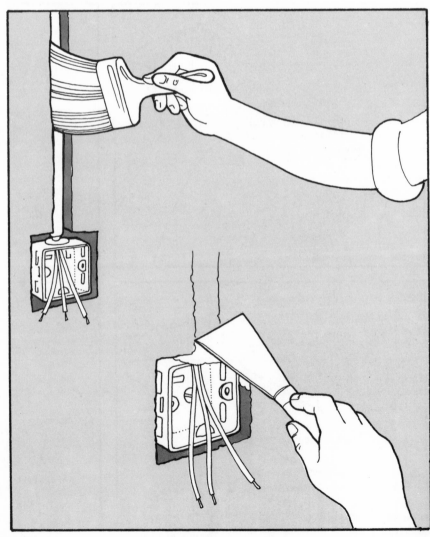

laminate will resist all normal domestic stains.

It is simple to cut, using a Stanley knife fitted with a special laminate blade. Alternatively, a fine-tooth handsaw can be used. Cut the laminate about ⅛in. oversize. Trim off this surplus edge when the piece is glued firmly in place.

Adhesive is used to fix the laminate. Contact adhesive can be used though here you must get the positioning absolutely right first time since the laminate will stick firmly immediately it touches the surface. A water-based resin adhesive such as Cascamite does allow time for the laminate to be repositioned, but it must be clamped while drying.

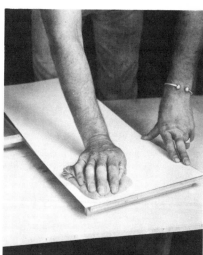

To cut laminate, lay it on a flat surface. Score along the decorative face with a laminate blade held against a straight-edge. Continue scoring until the sheet is cut at least halfway through.
Holding the straight-edge firmly down, fold the waste side upwards, to break the laminate cleanly. If preferred, the sheet can be cut right through without the need to snap along the line.

If using contact adhesive, place battens on the surface and position the laminate over them. Gradually remove battens, working from one end, and press the sheet into place. This is a useful method of getting the positioning right first time. Finish off by sliding a smooth block of wood over the surface and tapping firmly with a hammer to form a firm bond between laminate and the core board.

If pva or a resin-based adhesive is used, the sheet will have to be clamped in position until the glue has set.

Trim off the surplus ⅛in. with a sharp block plane. Alternatively, use a fine file.

Edges can be lipped with hardwood, laminate or a special edging strip obtainable at d-i-y shops. It is advisable, wherever possible, to fix the edging strip first.

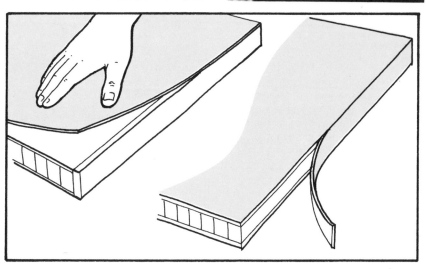

Mirror tiles Mirror tiles are sold in a whole range of sizes so you can plan each area so as to avoid having to cut any tiles.

These tiles are not precision made so widths and lengths of 'same-size' tiles can vary slightly. It is best to lay out the tiles 'dry' to ascertain the best arrangement. Number each tile on the surface and indicate its position, using a grease pencil or lipstick.

Other coverings Self-adhesive flexible coverings such as Fablon are simple to cut and fit. A wide choice of patterns and designs is available. These coverings must be fixed to a dry, clean, smooth surface.

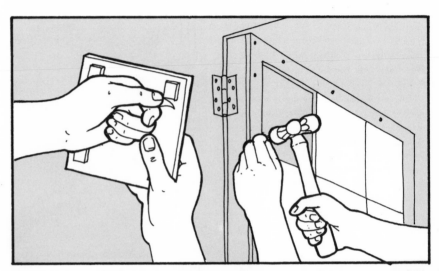

Each tile has four adhesive pads on the back covered by a protective paper. This is stripped off and the tile pressed firmly into place. The positioning must be right first time since, once they touch the surface, they are well stuck down.

If covering a door, to avoid cutting any tiles the door can be framed with plywood, covered with laminate. Build the frame up to leave a flush surface with the tiles.

Cut Fablon to size with scissors.

Smooth it in place on the surface, avoiding wrinkles.

For dry lining, screw a framework of battens to the wall. The battens will have to coincide with the edges of the wallboard when it is fixed. Check for horizontal and vertical alignment with a straight-edge. Where necessary, use packing pieces to bring the battens true.

Around windows, fireplaces and recesses arrange a framework of battens. In these areas smaller pieces of cut board will be used.

DRY LINING

In older houses, especially, it is not
unusual for the plaster to be in such a
poor state, that the whole lot has to be
scraped off back to bare bricks.

Here a new plaster surface can be
created using Gyproc wallboard fixed
to battens. This is called dry lining,
i.e. little or no water is used. Wallboard
can be cut with an ordinary handsaw.

The boards have a paper surface, so
be careful not to tear this when nailing
the boards to the battens. Your
supplier will advise on the correct
nails to use.

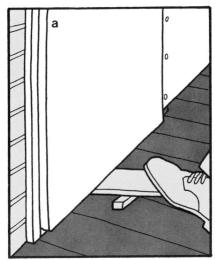
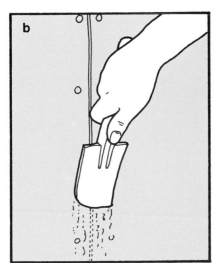

**Cut each board about 1½in. less than
room height. Lift them into position
with a simple foot-lifter made from
softwood. Nail each board onto the
backing battens at 6in. intervals. (a)**

**A special applicator is needed to fill the
joints between the boards. Joint filler is
used here – mixed according to the
instructions on the packet. (b)**

**Press a complete length of joint tape
down the joint, using a taping knife. (c)**

**Apply another band of filler over the
tape immediately. Wipe off the surplus
filler from the joint edges before it
starts to set. (d)**

**Two bands of joint finish (mixed
according to instructions supplied)
should be applied with the applicator.
The first layer should be about 8in.
wide. Feather out the edges with a
sponge, working in light, circular
strokes. When this band is partially
dry, apply a second band about 1in.
wide all down. Repeat the above
process. (e)**

**A final, thin coat of finish applied over
the complete surface of the wallboards
will even up the texture between the
main surface and the joints. (f)**

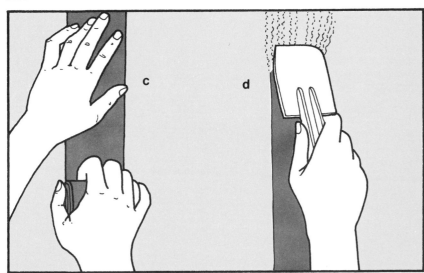
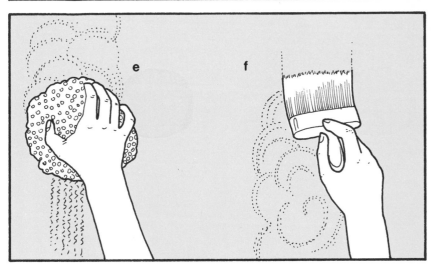

Dealing With Condensation

Damp and condensation are two of the greatest nuisances of winter. Wet patches appear on ceilings and walls, ruining decorations, while moisture runs down windows to form puddles on sills, eventually breaking up the paintwork and causing the wood to rot.

Damp and condensation are entirely different things though their effect is basically the same. Before remedial action can be taken, you have to establish which of the two is causing the trouble.

Condensation is caused by warm, moist air contacting a cool surface. Moisture on kitchen and bathroom windows or beads of water on ceramic wall tiles are the more obvious signs. Damp patches on living room walls is another tell-tale sign.

The air is moistened by such things as steam from cooking, washing, burning paraffin heaters – even breathing.

These combine to raise the room temperature and load the air with water vapour. When this moist air contacts a cool surface, the water vapour condenses on it.

So on a cold day, streaming windows and damp patches on walls indicate condensation.

To combat condensation, four things can be done. Keep rooms warm, dispose of steam and water vapour, provide ventilation, and avoid cold surfaces.

The kitchen and bathroom should be the main places to watch as most of the troubles spring from there. An extractor fan fitted in a window will help to remove water-laden air.

The manufacturers of the fan will tell you the recommended thickness of glass needed to support a fan.

Cutting a circle in an existing window can be a difficult task. It is

easier to remove the glass and take it to your glass supplier for cutting, or get a replacement piece from him. Alternatively, look at the possibility of setting an extractor fan in an external wall. A wall cupboard could be placed over it with a vent in the base of the cupboard.

Most fans are easily fitted in two or three stages. Follow individual makers' instructions closely.

Very cold bathroom walls can be kept warm by fitting a black tubular heater that operates at 60 watts per foot.

CEILINGS
Line the ceilings with expanded polystyrene tiles. These give good insulation value and resist condensation forming. Use flame-retardant types in kitchens or in any room where fire is a risk.

Fix flame retardant polystyrene ceiling tiles to bathroom and kitchen ceilings to reduce condensation forming.

Cut the tiles with a Stanley-type knife, held against a straight-edge. Press down firmly on the knife to make a clean cut. Spread the special adhesive all over the back of each tile before fixing in place.

FIREPLACES

Fireplaces used to provide ventilation; by blocking them in, ventilation is reduced or cut-off completely. Always allow for an air-brick when bricking up a fireplace. No flow of air in the chimney can cause damp patches on living room walls, especially on chimney breasts.

Paraffin or oil heaters contribute towards condensation problems. Radiators, electric convectors or radiant fires – any dry-heat types in fact – should be used. Even with these, however, correct ventilation is needed. An open window or a ventilator that can be controlled will enable you to allow the correct amount of air into the room according to the seriousness of the condensation problem.

WALLS

The simplest way to insulate walls against condensation is to line them with sheet expanded polystyrene which is sold in rolls at decorating shops. Wallpaper can be applied over the polystyrene in the normal way.

Cavity wall insulation is another method of wall insulation. This is discussed on page 126.

FLOORS

Less of a problem, usually, is condensation on solid floors. Many people imagine that damp patches are a sign of rising damp. There is a simple way to find out if they are.

Fix a small piece of glass to the floor with putty all round its edges so that air is trapped in the space between the glass and the floor.

If moisture forms on the bottom of the glass (after a short while) the problem is rising damp. If the moisture appears on the top of the glass, then you are up against condensation.

A good underlay beneath a carpet will help, as will any type of warm flooring material such as cork or cushioned vinyl.

WINDOWS

Double glazing will help against,

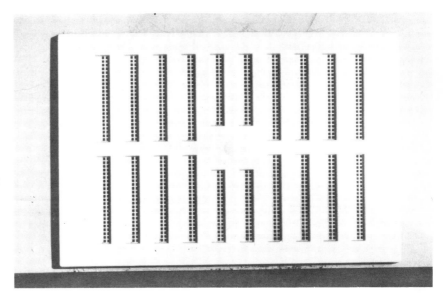

A blocked off chimney means it is no longer ventilated. Eventually damp patches will appear on the breast. An air brick or grill must be fitted in every room.

Mould, mildew or fungus on walls means having to strip off the wallpaper. Wash the wall with a fungicide before repapering, and use a paste containing a fungicide.

Walls affected by condensation should be lined with sheet expanded polystyrene. This is bought in rolls and can be papered over in the normal way.

Strip off the old wallcovering and hang the first length of polystyrene. Your supplier will advise you on the special adhesive needed to stick it to the wall. Use a roller to smooth out the length.

Trim with a sharp Stanley-type knife at the skirting and ceiling line. Press down hard with the knife to cut the material cleanly. Carefully butt the edges of successive lengths.

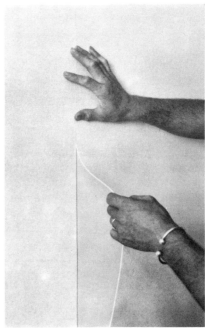

though may not always cure, condensation. The various systems are discussed more fully on page 126. Anyone with double glazing already installed who still gets condensation will find that some silica gel crystals (available from chemists) placed between the panes of glass will help. These absorb all the moisture, but they eventually become saturated and have to be dried out in an oven before re-use.

Dealing With Damp

If the weather is wet and muggy and damp patches appear on walls and floors then the problem is damp.

Damp is caused by such things as broken tiles (see page 148), defective flashings (see page 150), cracked down-pipes and gutters (see page 152). All these must be fixed immediately or the trouble will spread – it is no use redecorating hoping all will be well – it won't.

Usually the rain which is absorbed by the house walls dries out when the weather is dry. Sometimes, however, the water reaches the interior house walls. This can happen for a number of reasons.

Most modern houses are built with cavity walls, that is an inner and outer wall separated by an air cavity. The two walls are held together with steel ties. Normally there is no way that rainwater can cross the cavity and reach the inside wall (the steel ties are constructed to prevent them forming a 'bridge'). However, if, during wall construction, mortar is allowed to drop on to the ties a 'bridge' will be formed and the rainwater will cross.

Painting the outside wall with a silicone water repellent is the answer here. This seals the brickwork against rain but still allows the bricks to breathe so that trapped moisture vapour can escape.

Not all solid walls give rise to damp problems but many do. The more exposed walls facing the prevailing winds from the south-west are most likely to be affected. Damp patches in severe cases could extend over an entire internal wall.

Here again, a coat of silicone water repellent will help.

Other safeguards against water penetration are to make sure the pointing between the bricks is in good condition (see page 106), and any exterior grade decorative paint will also help.

Gaps around windows must be sealed. These gaps round a wooden window frame will widen and narrow as the frame expands and contracts

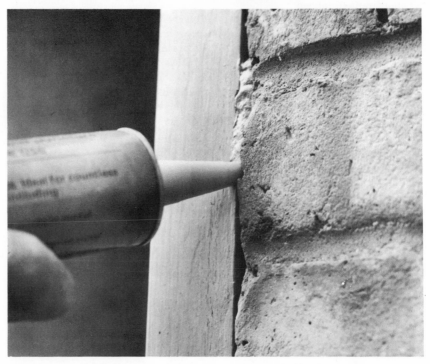

If the brickwork of the house walls is porous and the wall ties in the cavity between the inner and outer walls were covered with mortar droppings when the walls were built, then the ties form 'bridges' for rainwater to cross to the inside wall. Brush a proprietary damp-resisting liquid, usually silicone solution, on to the outside wall.

Seal any gaps between door and window frames and brickwork with a proprietary flexible mastic sealer. Do not use cellulose filler as this will crack and eventually fall out due to normal movement of the timber frame.

in its normal seasonal movement. It is no use filling them with Polyfilla or other cellulose filler; this will crack up and fall out after a short while. Use a mastic compound. This material is flexible and will expand and contract along with the frame, thus keeping the gaps permanently sealed.

DAMP-PROOF COURSES

The damp-proof course in the house wall prevents damp rising above the first few brick courses. Take a look at the lower part of the wall; you should see a horizontal layer of material set into the pointing.

This material spans both walls of the cavity and is usually slate or bitumen felt. It continues, unbroken, around all the walls. Normally damp will be stopped when it reaches the damp-proof course. However, should earth be piled up against the wall or a path raised too near the damp-proof course level there could be problems. The damp-proof course will be bridged and moisture from the earth will soak into the bricks. In heavy rain, water could splash up above it from the raised path.

So keep earth piles away from the house wall and make sure that the damp-proof course is at least 6in. above the level of paths. If you have to, then lower the level of a path by break-it up and re-laying it. Or else apply cement to the house wall to form a skirting. The cement must contain a waterproof agent, but whatever you do, it is worth while applying a water repellent liquid to the wall as well.

If the existing damp-proof course is faulty there are several firms who will carry out one of a number of methods of curing the trouble. Their addresses are in the yellow pages directory.

You can do the job yourself, though, using a damp repelling liquid – Stroma is one make. There are two grades – one for the inside walls and one for the outside walls. This liquid forms a barrier by penetrating right through the brickwork.

In older properties there may not be a damp-proof course at all. In days

Rising damp can be caused by earth piled against the house wall over the level of the damp proof course or by a blocked airbrick. If these are not the causes get specialist advice.

past, builders often relied on the thickness of materials to prevent rising damp – and often it did not work. The firms referred to above will help here, but they use systems which have to be carried out by specialists.

121

Insulation

The heat generated in a house is lost through several places – roofs, walls, windows, floors, chimneys, doors and odd gaps around door and window frames. Since fuel bills are forever rising it makes sense to consider insulating the house properly. Most insulation methods must be regarded as a long-term investment. If the work is done properly, then fuel bills will be reduced.

The length of time it takes to recoup the initial outlay will depend on various factors – the size of the house and its position, whether all the 'escape routes' have been sealed effectively, and so on.

Double glazing, one aspect of insulation, is discussed on page 126. Here we are looking at the cheapest and simplest methods of insulation for roofs and ceilings, and around windows and doors.

Because warm air rises, a good deal of the heat in a house is lost through the roof. Without insulated ceilings, the heat will rise into the loft and, if the roof is not lined, it will go out through the tiles.

INSULATING A LOFT

Whether or not you insulate ceilings to keep the warm air in bedrooms depends on whether the loft is being used as a living space. If it remains empty, except for storage, you should insulate and there are three good alternative types of insulation which can be used for the job, one is vermiculite, a loose-fill material made from mica, the others are blanket materials supplied in rolls of varying widths. Laying loose-fill materials like vermiculite between the joists in the loft is an easy job. Or a blanket insulation material of glass fibre or mineral wool can be used to give the necessary amount of insulation. If there are lots of nooks and crannies, the pellets or granules will probably be easier to pour into place. These are also best used when the spacings between the joists are not standard.

However in a windy loft space they can get blown about whereas a

Use foam plastic lagging to cover all pipework. Ask your builder's merchant for the right diameter to suit the size of your pipes. The foam has a split along its length so that it can be fitted quickly on to the pipe, and be taped in position.

All joins between pieces of lagging can be sealed with a waterproof plastic adhesive tape. Use the tape to seal any gaps in the foam which open at bends in the pipework.
Cut a T-shape plywood spreader to even out pellets or granules. These should be laid between the joists to an even depth of at least 4in.
Use a broom or the back of a rake to get into awkward corners.

blanket will stay put.

A 4in. layer of vermiculite is preferable. The material, supplied in bags, is poured between the joists and levelled out to the required thickness.

The alternatives are glass fibre and mineral wood in blanket form, which are laid between the joists.

The fibre blanket is sold in rolls about 45in. long and 16 to 18in. wide. Being comprised of glass or other mineral fibres, it can be irritating to the skin so gloves should be worn if you are so affected.

If the situation demands it, there is nothing to prevent using the blanket in one area and the pellets in another more inaccessible spot.

There is another form of blanket – quilt material which is draped over the joists. Here though, since the joists will be obscured, boards will have to be nailed over some of them to walk on when using the loft.

Whichever method you use, do not insulate the area immediately under the cold water tank. The warm air current must be allowed through from below to prevent this freezing. Finally, fix some insulation on the loft side of the trap door. These trap doors are of considerable area and account for much heat loss.

In addition to insulating the loft, you can stick expanded foam polystyrene tiles on the ceilings of rooms immediately below. However, while these are quite acceptable in kitchens and bathrooms, not everyone likes to see them in bedrooms. An alternative is to use more expensive tiles such as cork or fibre.

When heat is prevented from getting into the loft, it is important to insulate all the loft plumbing with lagging material. The loft will be much colder than before and, in winter, frozen pipework becomes more of a possibility.

If the loft space is to be used for living purposes, it will need to receive heat from the rooms below. So there is no point in insulating the ceiling or loft floor. So, the main concern is the roof itself. Modern roofs are usually underfelted. In older houses an alternative is to pin building paper to the rafters.

Where the loft is to be decorated,

Starting at the eaves, tuck the blanket well down so that wind cannot blow underneath.
Unroll the length, tucking the edges up against the sides of the joists.
When the end of the loft is reached, tear off the blanket and again tuck the end down into the eaves.

Cover the ceiling hatch with a square of blanket. Glue it in place with pva adhesive. Do not cover the floor under the cold water tank – the heat that comes up from the room below will help prevent it freezing in cold weather. The tank itself can be lagged with strips of blanket.

plasterboard or insulating board should be fixed to the rafters over the building paper.

Remember, though, there must

always be sufficient space between the insulation material and the roof to ensure that rot does not form on the rafters.

PLUMBING – FROST PROTECTION

All pipework and the cold water tank should be insulated to prevent freeze-ups in cold spells. A hot water cylinder must also be insulated to prevent heat escaping and thereby increasing fuel bills.

Wrap a blanket of glass fibre around the cold water tank and a specially made insulating jacket around the hot water cylinder. These jackets are available from most plumbers' merchants and are simply tied in place.

DRAUGHTS

Gaps around window and door frames can cause considerable discomfort from draughts apart from allowing valuable heat to escape, and it is amazing how much cold air can come through letterboxes and even keyholes. The solution here is to fix special flaps (available from d-i-y shops) to both the insides of letterboxes and keyholes.

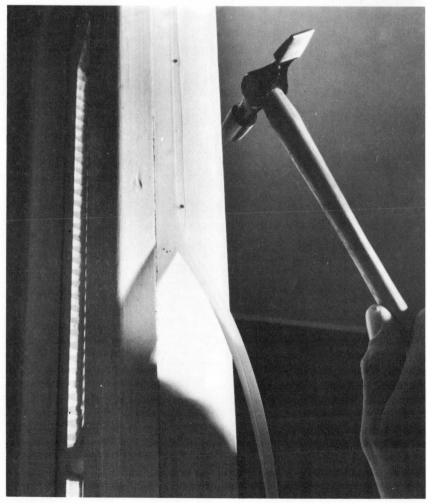

Plastic strips are the cheapest. They usually have to be replaced each year though. Just peel off the backing paper, cut to length with scissors, and stick them to the frame. This type will only effectively block normal gaps. Wide gaps can be blocked off using two plastic strips which come together when the door or window is closed.

Plastic strips with a layer of felt at the bottom are stuck in place after removing the protective paper backing. Cut to length with scissors.
Spring metal strip or a different kind of plastic strip can be tacked around the door or window rebate. It is not seen when the door is closed. Cut to length with scissors or wire cutters.

There are several draughtproofing systems available for sealing gaps around door and window frames.

The cheapest system (and the simplest to fix) is self-adhesive rubber or foam strips. When bought, these have a protective covering on the back which is peeled off and the strip is then stuck to the frame after making sure it is clean and dry. These strips are not suitable for sash windows.

Aluminium or phosphor bronze strips are also effective. These are fixed to the frames and then bent outwards. The door or window closes against the strip thus forming a tight seal.

They are slightly more difficult to fit since accuracy of positioning is essential and care must be taken to ensure that no kinks are formed in the metal.

Special draught excluders are made for metal windows though foam plastic strips will be adequate provided the metal is clean before sticking them on. Gaps under doors are notorious for letting through draughts. Though a $\frac{1}{4}$in. thick batten nailed across the threshold often forms an efficient seal (provided that carpets of the same thickness are used on both sides of the door to prevent people tripping over the batten), it can look unsightly and will only be partly effective if the gap is more than $\frac{1}{4}$in. Commercial draught excluders are made from rubber mouldings, aluminium section or a combination of metal and plastic. Other types come in halves – one being fixed to the door, and other to the threshold – which lock together when the door is closed.

Seal metal windows with a proprietary aluminium strip system available at d-i-y shops. The strip clips to the outside of the frame and is secured with corner pieces.

A threshold strip can be fixed to the floor.

Rise and fall draught excluders are available where the door has to clear a door mat. These are very effective though they can be tricky to position correctly.

UNDERFLOOR DRAUGHTS

Although a flow of air under timber floors is essential to prevent rot, the draughts that can come up through the floorboards can cause a lot of discomfort.

Filling gaps in floorboards is discussed on page 140. Here, it is worth saying that mastic can be used to plug any minor gaps.

WALL INSULATION

The walls of a house are the biggest cause of heat loss. All building materials have a U value. This, in essence, represents the measure of heat loss – the higher the U value, the lower the insulation value of a material.

For example, a sealed-cavity 11in. external wall, plastered on one side, has a U value of ·30. If ½in. insulating fibreboard fixed to battens replaces the plaster, the U value would be ·18. However, if the cavity were filled with insulating material such as mineral wool or foam, the U value would be ·09 and ·07 respectively.

So you can see from this how beneficial the cavity wall insulation materials are. Assuming that all other insulating work is carried out as well, the claim that cavity wall insulation could reduce fuel bills substantially does not seem unreasonable.

There are two systems of cavity wall insulation which will reduce heat losses through walls by about 70%.

Rentokil Limited uses dry mineral rock wool blown into the cavity and packed to a uniform density. The other system, used by many manufacturers, involves urea formaldehyde foam, which is pumped into the cavity where it sets in the form of an insulating layer.

Side benefits of this type of insulation are that the house walls will be free from damp and condensation. Damp will not rise through capillary action since both materials are water repellent.

Cavity wall insulation is not a d-i-y job, however. It should be carried out by professionals, using an approved material. The actual work usually takes a day to complete in an average size house. Holes are drilled in the mortar joints between the bricks to allow the material to be injected. At the end of the day, the contractors will fill in the holes leaving the walls looking as they did before.

Solid walls Of course cavity infill can only be used if there is a cavity between the house walls. External 9in.-thick solid brick walls need to be lined for proper insulation.

One method is to fix ½in.-thick insulation boards to the plaster, and then plaster over the boards. Alternatively, the insulation boards can be hidden behind plasterboard, hardboard or plywood. The boards can be of non-combustible fibre or polystyrene. Decorative insulating boards are available which would not need to be covered with anything else. Plain boards, though, have the advantage that they can be painted or papered and your choice of colour or design is not limited.

A second method of dealing with solid walls is to nail insulating quilt material to battens fixed to the walls. Fix more battens over the quilt and fix insulating fibre board to the battens.

DOUBLE GLAZING

Because of rising fuel bills, more and more people are installing double glazing to reduce heat losses and increase comfort in the home.

It should be said that double glazing alone will not reduce fuel bills dramatically. It has to be used in conjunction with other insulating methods discussed on page 118.

Assuming you attend to the other forms of insulation, which are comparatively cheap, the types of double glazing available and their benefits can be considered.

The heat generated in a house escapes through various channels. In an average size semi, insulated to current minimum standards of Building Regulations, with a window area of about 20% of the total area of the external walls, the windows account for 22% of heat losses.

Double glazing cuts the heat loss through the windows by 50%, that is, the heat loss from the house through the windows is cut to 11%. Thus 11% of the cost of the heat generated in the house can be saved, meaning a minimum saving of £11 per £100 heating costs. Of course, this is not a hard and fast rule since so many variations in house design are to be found.

Actual fuel cost savings, therefore, depend on several factors. For example, if a house has more than 20% area of outside glazing, then proportionately more heat escapes through the windows.

Therefore by halving these larger heat losses, double glazing will be reducing the fuel bill proportionately more. Similarly, if the house is surrounded by open spaces, or is in an enclosed urban area, this can affect heat losses and therefore, in turn, affect the heat cost reductions which can be achieved.

The human element must also be considered. Control of a central heating system does affect the amount of heat that needs to be generated to maintain an even, warm temperature.

Cold windows Double glazing can also provide other benefits to make a house more comfortable. It reduces cold down draughts from the window; eliminates the cold window area of a room thus enlarging living space; reduces noise irritation and controls condensation.

So there should be no more huddling around the fire, or radiators, and using only a small part of the room that is not cold.

Noise The reduction of noise level entering the room from outside is a really valuable asset of double glazing. Excessive noise can cause stress, in extreme cases mental disorder and temporary loss of vision, and lack of proper sleep.

For sound-insulation the main factors to be considered are:
(a) the elimination of gaps and cracks both in the complete window assembly and in the fixing into the main structure;
(b) the space between the two panes of glass;
(c) the weight of the glass – in general, the thicker the better.

When secondary sash (double window) systems are installed to achieve sound insulation, the efficiency of the system is increased if the sides of the air space are lined with sound absorbent materials.

The minimum air space between the two panes in double glazing should be 4in., although an air space of 8in. is generally the optimum for sound insulation.

Now let us look at the types of double glazing that are available. Double glazing can be either a complete, hermetically sealed replacement unit or an additional secondary window. The main systems are:

Insulating glass: A factory-made, hermetically sealed double glazing unit which requires cleaning on two sides only (as with ordinary glazed windows). There are two kinds:

The standard type looks like a single sheet of glass but in fact consists of two pieces of glass joined together with a sealed metal, alloy or plastic edge, and is usually purpose-made. The air between the two panes is dried to prevent misting. In existing houses, it may be necessary to alter the rebates of the window frames for a neat appearance. Installing this type is not really a job for an amateur.

The second type (a stepped-unit) is a modified version of the previous unit, with one glass bigger all round than the other. It is ideal for converting single glazed frames to double glazing without altering the frame. Good draught-proofing of opening window frames adds to the effectiveness of both types of insulating glass.

Secondary sashes This is a simple system whereby a second pane of glass is added within the existing window openings and is tailor-made. It can be fixed, sliding or hinged. A glazed secondary sash is usually removable and can be lifted out of the surrounding framework for cleaning. This type can usually be installed without disturbing the original window.

A third system is called *coupled windows*: Here a single glazed window has another window coupled to it so that both move together. Fitted with hinges and fasteners, the frames can be separated for cleaning. A coupled window is more often specified for new buildings although they can be used to improve existing homes provided modifications are made to the original surrounds. Secondary sashes and coupled windows are generally more suitable for sound-insulation.

Last of all is a simple and cheap *do-it-yourself* system which uses flexible channels to hold the second pane of glass, the glass itself being obtained separately from glass merchants.

The makers supply various types of channels which can easily be cut to the required size. Special clips and screws are provided and, after the glass has been fixed inside the channel, it is a simple matter to fix the secondary sash to the original frame or surround.

Manufacturers of double glazing systems like this will provide assembly and fixing instructions.

When deciding on the type to use, consider the window's location in relation to prevailing winds, safety and the design and strength of the primary window.

For up-to-date costs of double glazing get estimates from individual manufacturers. The Insulation Glazing Association will advise you further if you need help in choosing the correct system. They will also provide a list of member firms whom you can contact for estimates.

The secondary sash is easily fixed with special clips.

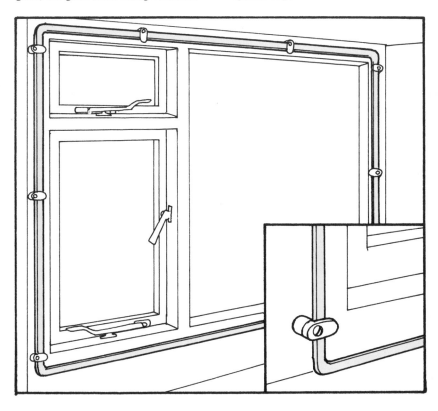

Taps and Stop-cocks

Taps An annoying trickle of water from the cold tap over the kitchen sink when it is turned tightly off indicates that a new washer is needed.

Re-washering a tap is avoided by many people because they envisage a sudden uncontrollable flood of water pouring from the dismantled tap. Yet it is an easy enough operation.

The first thing you must do – to prevent that 'uncontrollable flood' – is to turn off the main stop-cock which usually is found under the sink, though it could be in a purpose-made pit outside the house. No doubt, though, you will know where your stop-cock is situated. Turn it off completely. Now turn the kitchen sink tap on fully and wait until no more water gushes out.

Your kitchen tap may have an easy clean cover and usually this will unscrew by hand after unscrewing the top.

Next, use a padded wrench to grip the lower part of the tap's body; use another wrench to grip the nut securing the headgear and remove it.

Inside will be the jumper. The washer will be attached to it. Grip the stem of the jumper with a wrench and remove the nut that holds the washer in place.

Position the new washer and replace the nut to secure it. You can then re-assemble the tap and turn on the water again.

Sometimes the nut cannot be removed easily. The best solution here is to fit a new jumper and washer.

If a tap over the sink has a shrouded head, simply remove this and proceed as before. It will probably be necessary to use a screwdriver to prise off the plastic tab on the head of the tap (which has a small C, for cold on it) in order to reach the screw holding the shrouded head in place.

Bathroom taps usually have a slightly different arrangement. The jumper and washer is pegged into the headgear. This is necessary since the low pressure of water under which they operate may not be enough to raise the jumper when the tap is turned on.

Unscrew the nut holding the jumper and washer together. Remove them both and replace with a new jumper and washer.

Since the new jumper will not be pegged into the headgear, it might be necessary to taper the stem of the jumper so that it will fit tightly in the headgear.

Before re-washering bathroom taps (whether hot or cold the method is the same) there is no need to turn off the main stop valve. If there is a stop valve on either the cold supply pipe to the hot water cylinder or on the cold supply pipes to the bathroom taps, turn off which ever is appropriate depending on which tap you are re-washering.

If there are no stop valves, then tie up the ball valve to the main cold storage tank and then drain the tank.

There is no need to switch off the immersion heater or turn out the boiler provided, that is, that the hot water system has been properly designed.

A final word on bathroom taps, in fact on all mixer taps. For re-washering purposes these can be thought of as two independent taps to be re-washered as before. Just ascertain from the spout which tap is dripping after it has been turned off. This is simple to do since the spout is partitioned down its middle.

STOP-COCKS

If the stop-cock starts to leak it can be repaired easily. The leaking water is by-passing the gland packing. By turning the first nut through which the spindle of the tap passes (called the gland adjusting nut) the drip will be stopped. Half a turn or perhaps one full turn is usually enough.

After the gland nut has been adjusted over a period of time, the packing inside will have to be renewed. Screw down the stop-cock to prevent the water from flowing past and release the screw holding the handle in place.

Completely unscrew the gland nut and remove it. Rake out all the old packing and replace with knitting wool coated with Vaseline. Pack it down tightly before replacing the gland nut and handle.

The workings of a tap.

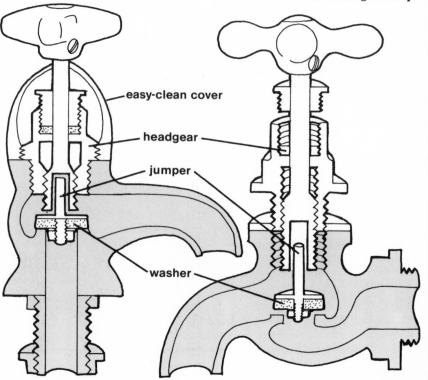

easy-clean cover

headgear

jumper

washer

Keeping Drains in Order

The underground drains in a house drainage system are laid in straight lines at a slight gradient. Since they can become blocked from time to time, every part of the underground system must be accessible to drain rods so that they can be cleared.

Near the house there will be an inspection chamber (or manhole) to take the branch drains from the yard gulley and the house soil pipe. The branch drains connect to a 4in. diameter drain which runs to another chamber probably situated just inside the garden boundary.

If the house is an older one, the inspection chamber nearest the house could have an intercepting trap fitted, which is intended to prevent rats and sewer gases entering the house. It impedes drainage, however and is the likely cause of blockages.

If the water in the w.c., sinks or basins drain away slowly, or if a water gulley overflows, check this first chamber initially. It is the most likely trouble spot.

Normally a blockage here can be cleared easily, using drain rods which can usually be hired locally. A plunger (a 4in. diameter rubber disc) is screwed to the end of the rods to do the work.

Above the entrance to the trap there will be a stopper fitted into the end of a rodding arm. This arm enables blockages between the intercepting trap and the sewer to be cleared.

Sometimes, the stopper can fall out of the arm into the trap causing a blockage. A simple way to avoid this re-occurring is to cement a small glass disc in place of the stopper. If ever access to the rodding arm is needed the disc can be broken and replaced with another.

Screw two drain rods together. Fit a corkscrew head and push the rods down the manhole. Never turn the rods anti-clockwise or they will become unscrewed in the drain. If more than one drainpipe enters the manhole, push the rods down each one until the blockage is clear.

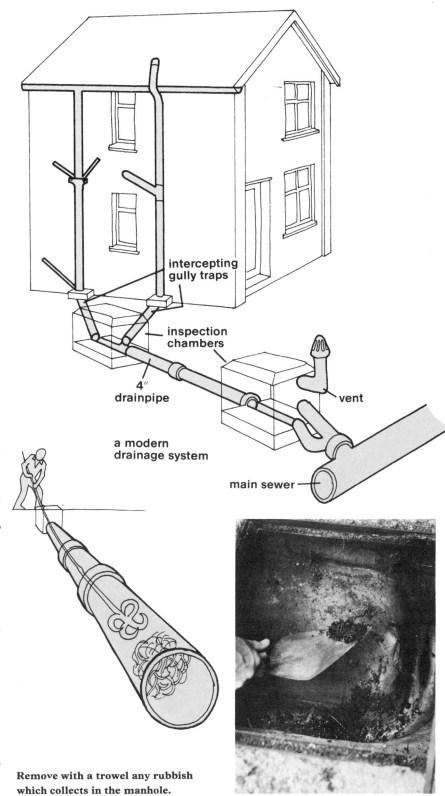

intercepting gully traps

inspection chambers

4″ drainpipe

a modern drainage system

vent

main sewer

Remove with a trowel any rubbish which collects in the manhole.

Most blockages in the sink waste pipes are easily cleared with a plunger. It is worth while buying one of these and they are often inexpensive. Stuff the overflow outlet in the sink with a wet rag. Position the plunger over the drain hole and let about 1in. of water into the sink; then pump vigorously. The water will usually drain away quickly.

More stubborn blockages occur when the U bend of the waste pipe below the sink gets filled with matchsticks, hair, or other rubbish. Modern plastic pipe fittings are easy to deal with and normally only a U bend section or a bottle trap has to be unscrewed and cleaned out.

Old metal pipework can be more of a problem. In the bottom of the U bend is a drain plug which can be difficult to budge. An old chisel will often give sufficient leverage to move it.

A plunger will clear most blockages. When removing a bottle trap, U bend or drain plug, keep a bucket underneath to catch the sink water as it gushes out.

A really stubborn plug in old pipework may need a wrench to budge it.

If, after removing the bottle trap, U bend or drain plug, the blockage still does not clear, feed a flexible curtain wire fitted with an eye down into the waste outlet of the sink and prod away the obstruction.

If a blockage is in the waste pipe on the other side of the U bend, feed the curtain wire into the waste pipe from outside the house.

The grid over the outside drain can become blocked by leaves and other debris. This can cause drains to smell. Lift out the grid and burn off all the debris by holding it over a fire made in the garden. Flush out the drain with hot water and soda before replacing the grid.

Doors New and Old

A door which jams in winter yet opens in summer is usually the result of humidity changes swelling and shrinking the timber. Minor problems could be caused by excessive coats of paint. In both cases the paint on the edge of the door will have to be stripped back to bare wood. With a plane, shave off a little more of this than necessary to ease the door to allow for the thickness of new paint.

Only paint when the timber is thoroughly dry. Remove the door from its hinges and apply two liberal coats of primer to both the top and bottom edges if it is these that are sticking. Allow to dry thoroughly and rehang.

High spots on the closing edge can always be located by closing the door over carbon paper. The areas showing marks along the edge can then be planed back after opening the door and holding it firm with wedges.

Loose hinges can cause a door to sag and not close properly. Try retightening the screws. If they remain loose, remove them, fill the holes with wood plugs and reinsert the screws. Check also that the hinges are set deep enough into the door and frame so that the gap is equal along

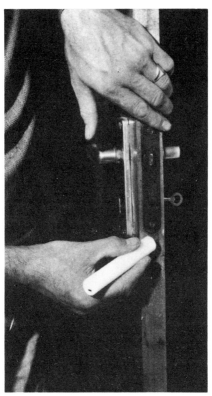

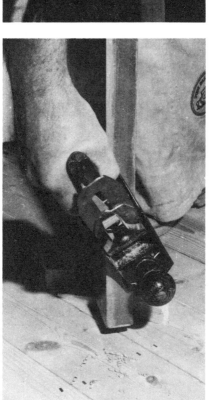

Minor sticking problems can often be cured by rubbing the closing edge with a candle.

Ascertain sticking points by closing the door on a sheet of carbon paper. The carbon will leave tell-tale marks.

Secure the door with wedges before planing back to bare wood.

Altering the position of hinges by cutting the hinge rebates deeper will cure too wide a gap on the hinged side of a close door. If the door is binding on the hinge side insert thin wood packing pieces into the hinge slots.

both vertical edges of the door when it is in the closed position. A wider gap down the hinge side may indicate that the hinge rebates require to be slightly deepened with a sharp chisel. If, however, the hinges have been set too deeply into both door and frame, they can be raised by removing the hinges and fitting one or more thicknesses of card under the hinge before screwing back into position.

Remember that large gaps can also be dealt with by fixing draught excluders to the frame surround.

RATTLING DOORS

Usually caused by the door catch not resting firmly against its stop. The latch keep (or strike plate) has to be repositioned nearer to the stop.

Carefully check the distance between door face and the door jamb on the lock side. Then remove the plate and extend the recess and mortice correspondingly with a sharp chisel, carefully keeping all edges of the cut timber square. Before screwing the plate back into position plug the original screw holes with timber.

Wide gaps can be overcome by fitting a weatherstrip or draught excluder (see page 124).

Measure the distance from the jamb to the face of the door. The keep plate must be moved back by this amount Remove the keep – it is screwed in place – and use a chisel to extend the existing recess to the required position. Extend the mortises as required. Refit the keep plate after first plugging the old screw holes with timber plugs.

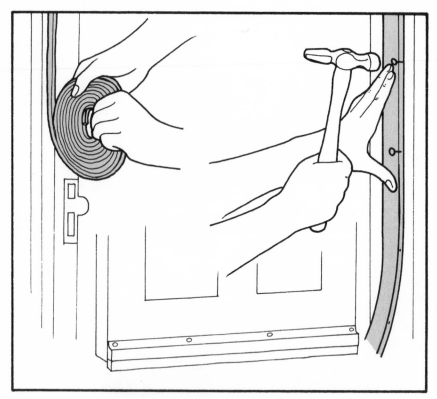

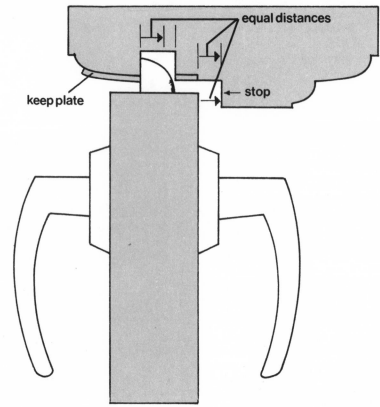

equal distances

keep plate

stop

PANELLING A DOOR

The simplest way to flush panel a door is to face it with hardboard or plywood, leaving a border around the perimeter. This obviates the need to cut new holes for the keyhole and handle in the facing material.

If hardboard or thin plywood is used to flush panel a door completely, the two long edges must be lipped with solid timber in order that the facing material does not rub or fray at the edges.

Completely flush panelling a door is made rather more complicated by having to reposition the door catch to allow for the extra thickness of the door and to accommodate the handle and lock. The door will have to be removed for this operation.

If you are using hardboard for the flush panel, this must be conditioned first to the room's atmosphere to prevent it buckling later on. This is done by damping the rough side of each sheet with water. Two pints to an 8ft. × 4ft. sheet is about right. Lay the sheets flat (wet side to wet side) for 24 hours in the room in which they are to be used.

Any loose or flaking paint must be removed from the face of the door and the surface rubbed down with fine glasspaper as a key for the adhesive.

As the door has already been removed fixing the panel will be easier if you lay it flat on the ground.

Apply a coat of primer to the facing material before painting.

Pack out all the panels with plywood to bring them level with the stiles and rails. Use pins and adhesive to fix the plywood and the facing panel to the door. Punch all pin heads below the surface. Fill all the pin holes with filler (such as Polyfilla). The door is now ready for priming and painting.

Flush panelling a door with hardboard or thin plywood will require lipping down both long edges. This will mean cutting new mortices and recesses for hinges and lock.

FITTING A NEW DOOR

If you have to fit a new door it must be exactly the same height, width and thickness as the old one. They are readily available from timber merchants and will be delivered with protective pieces (called horns) projecting from the top and bottom. Saw off these flush with the edges.

First remove the horns and then hold the door in the frame and mark off the outline of the frame on to the door, using a pencil. There should be an ½in. gap between both sides of the door and the frame so remember to trim down slightly past the pencil lines. The top edge must also be trimmed to allow an ½in. gap at the top and a sufficient gap at the bottom to clear the floorcovering by ¼in. (a)

Rest the door on battens to protect its edge and then plane down to just beyond the pencil lines. (b)

Hold the trimmed door in the frame and mark off the positions of the hinge slots.
When fitting a new door, use the old hinge recesses cut in the frame. Hold the new door in position in the frame and mark off the hinge positions on the door. Get help to keep the door raised while marking, or support it with wedges. (c)

Hold each hinge in position on the door and mark off its width and length. Scribe the lines about ⅛in. deep, using a mortice gauge, or mark off accurately with a pencil. (d)

Use a chisel and hammer to chop out the hinge recesses. The hinge must lie flush with the surface. Use the chisel squarely against the timber when cutting – keeping the flat back of the chisel fractionally inside the line. A hammer can be used on the chisel if it has a plastic handle – otherwise use a mallet on a wooden handle chisel. (e)

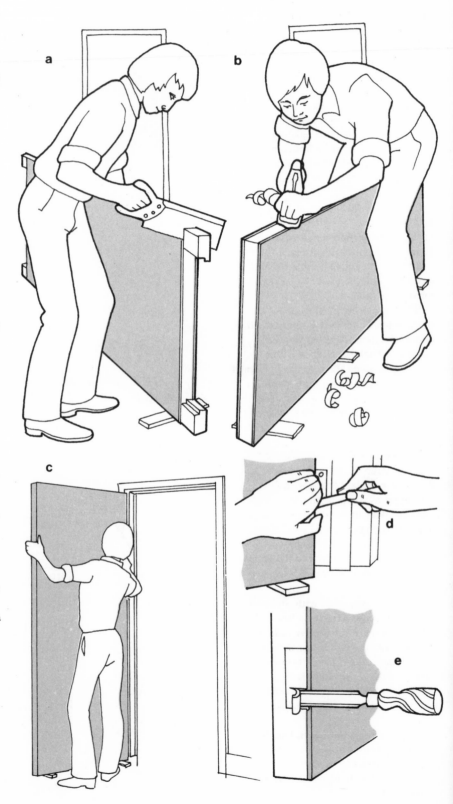

It is usually easier to fix the door furniture – lock, letterplate, etc., before hanging it. If it is to have glass panels, any glazing must be done after the door is in place.

You will probably have to trim a little off the door for it to fit the frame, as the frame may not be quite true.

Get a helper to hold the door in place while you mark off any trimming lines and the hinge positions. If help is not available to hold the door, a couple of wedges will provide support.

Remember to prime thoroughly and paint the bottom edge before hanging the door as, once in position, there will not be another opportunity to paint this edge again.

Drill starter holes for the screws to prevent them splitting the wood as they go in. (f)

Secure the hinges with 1½in. countersunk woodscrews. Countersunk screws are needed so that their heads do not protrude above the hinge surface to prevent it closing tightly. (g)

When fitting rising butts (see next page), mark off the top of the door where it meets the door stop. Mark off the centre of the door at the top; draw a diagonal line between this point and the door stop line on the hinge side. Plane off the waste material to leave a bevel to give the door clearance. (a)

Mark off the outline of the socket plate on the door. Scribe the lines with a cutting gauge, and chisel out the recess. (b)

Lift the door and lower the socket plate on to the spindle plate. (c)

Use only one screw initially in the frame side of each hinge in case adjustment of their positions is needed. Test that the door opens and closes freely before fixing remaining screws. (d)

HINGE MAINTENANCE

Since the hinges are the only things supporting a door, they must be of a sufficient size and be the correct type to take the weight of the door.

For exterior doors always use non-ferrous metal hinges to prevent rusting.

Hinges should be oiled regularly with only a little oil used on each occasion. Have a rag handy to wipe away any surplus oil that runs down the door. On outside hinges use grease rather than oil which will evaporate quickly.

LOCK MAINTENANCE

An easy way to lubricate cylinder locks (such as the Yale type) normally found on the front door is to drop a little oil on to the key before inserting it into the lock.

The spring of a conventional back-door lock needs greasing occasionally. You can get at the spring by taking the lock off the door and unscrewing the back plate. If it is a mortice lock, first remove the door handles and then withdraw the lock from the door. Then you can separate the lock casing.

RISING BUTTS

These are popular hinges because they automatically raise the door over a floorcovering as it opens.

They come in two parts; a spindle plate that fits to the door frame and a socket plate that fits on the door.

It will probably be necessary to fill the existing screw holes in both the frame and the door with small wood plugs as the positions of the new holes may not correspond.

FITTING A LETTER PLATE

A new letter plate is usually fixed to the middle rail or the stile of a new door.

The easiest way to cut an apperture in solid timber is to drill a hole in each corner of the proposed opening and then saw along each line in turn by inserting a padsaw into each of the holes.

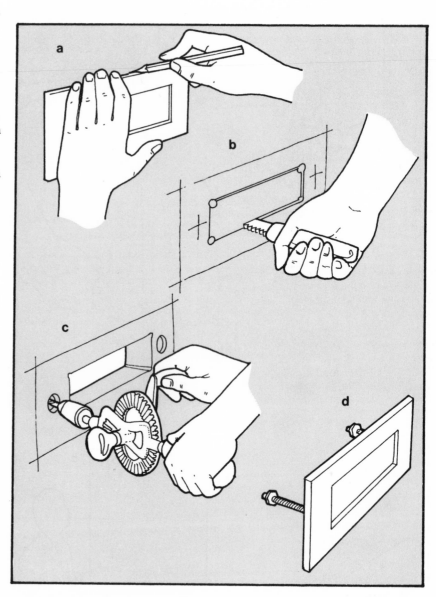

Pencil the outline of the letter plate on to the door (a). Drill holes through each corner of the slot through which the letters go. Cut along the pencil lines using a pad saw (b). Remember to position a block of wood on the reverse side of the door to prevent the drill bursting through and splitting the grain. It is easier to do this if the door is first removed and laid flat.

Hold the letter plate in position and mark off the positions of the sockets. Drill ½in. diameter holes, ½in. deep. In the centre of these, drill smaller holes right through the door the size of the letter plate bolts. (c)

Fit the letter plate and tighten the fixing nuts of the bolts. (d)

Ceiling Repairs and Ceiling Coving

MENDING A PLASTERBOARD CEILING

Mending a large hole in a plasterboard ceiling is not as difficult as it may sound.

Plasterboard is obtainable at builders' merchants. A new piece can be nailed to a softwood framework fixed to the joists above the ceiling.

Cut out the damaged area of plasterboard with a saw to form a square recess. The opposite sides of the opening should be cut flush with the internal face of the joists. (a)

A new softwood framework should be fixed to the joists. Nail the new plasterboard to the four sides of the framework, leaving a small gap at the edges. (b)

Spread a band of joint filler around the edges of the new plasterboard. (c) Then spread scrim tape along the edges. Proceed as for wall lining, page 117.

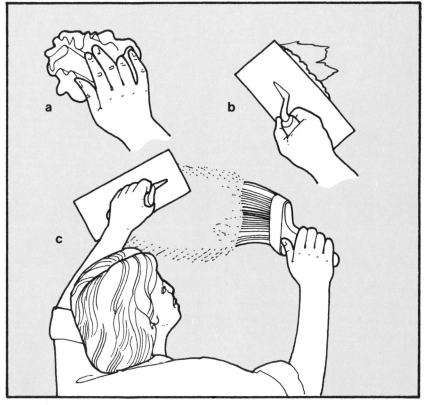

For damaged areas in lath and plaster ceilings (see next page), brush away all dust and push in paper backing, if it is needed, leaving a space of ½in. for the plaster. (a)

Use a trowel to apply the plaster. Leave the first coat slightly below surface level. (b)

Dampen the surface with fresh water before applying the final coat of plaster – or cellulose filler if you prefer. Brush lightly over the repaired area with water to feather out the edges. (c)

LATH AND PLASTER CEILINGS

Small holes in a lath and plaster ceiling can be repaired with cellulose filler or plaster applied directly to the laths.

A large hole, say 3in. wide, should be plugged with stiff, dampened paper or expanded metal nailed to the laths. This will provide a backing for the new plaster.

Expanded metal is a fine metal mesh in sheet form which can easily be cut to size with snips.

FIXING A CEILING COVE

Cracks which appear along the ceiling-to-wall angle are caused by normal house movement. No matter how often these are filled they are almost bound to re-open again.

The permanent answer is to hide them behind ceiling cove.

Blue Hawk cove is 4in. wide and 6ft. long and is fixed with special adhesive.

Corners have to be mitred. These are easy to cut with a fine tooth saw, using a template supplied by the makers.

The special adhesive is mixed to a creamy consistency according to instructions supplied. Only mix the amount you can use in 30 minutes or it will dry out.

After fixing, the cove can be painted.

Draw pencil guide lines along the wall and ceiling 2⅝in. away from the angle. Remove any wallpaper, flaking paint or dust from within the lines. Scratch the area to provide a key for the adhesive. (a)

Butter the adhesive on to the back of the cover. (b)

Push the cove into position. If the adhesive does not take immediately, knock a couple of nails to act as a temporary support. (c)

Make good the joints between lengths with adhesive. Use enough so that it squelches to the surface. (d)

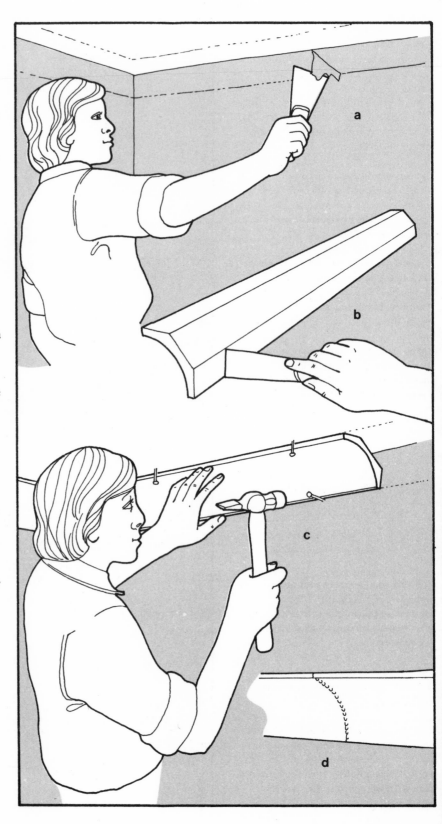

Floors

Dependent on the type of house you have, and its age, you will encounter either wood or solid floors. Pre-war houses will probably have wooden floors; those built after 1945 could have solid floors, though there is no hard and fast rule.

Normally repairs are essential to prevent undue wear to floorcovering material.

Wood floors are comprised of floorboards, either those which simply butt up to each other, or the more modern types called tongued and grooved. The latter interlock by means of thin strips of timber on one edge which slot into matching gaps in the edges of neighbouring boards.

The boards are supported on joists which run at right angles to them and are, in the ground floor of a house, supported on low walls called sleepers. The sleepers have gaps in them to allow air to circulate freely beneath the timber, thereby preventing damp. This system is called a hollow timber floor.

Tongued and grooved boards are far the best, since even if movement has caused the boards to come apart a little, the projecting tongues will still be partly in the grooves, preventing dust from rising up to the surface.

If you want to find out which type of boards you have and they are still fairly tight together, then force a thin knife blade down into the gap at several points along the length of two adjoining boards. If the blade meets an obstacle, they are tongued and grooved. If it pushes down a way or all the way, they are the butt edge type. You need to know this should you have to remove a board. There is a different technique for removing each type.

When confronted with bare boards, perhaps before laying a carpet, you can make a detailed examination to find spots that may need attention.

The first thing to do is to look for any nails protruding from the floor. Nail heads can snare the backing of a covering material so they must either be knocked below the surface or extracted and replaced by countersunk screws.

To sink the heads you need a hammer and a nail punch. A nail punch is a steel pencil-like tool. Place the tip on the nail head and tap the other end with the hammer.

If a nail is in crooked or it won't sink down for any reason, then remove it with a claw hammer or pincers and

A squeak can be caused by two boards rubbing together. A simple, cheap remedy which often works is to puff some talcum powder down between the edges.

A loose screw can cause a squeak. Find the squeaking area, knock in some floor brads and then drive a couple of woodscrews through the board and into the joist below. The positions of nail heads indicate where the joists are located beneath the boards.

Remove crooked nails with pincers or a claw hammer. In upstairs rooms it is preferable to use screws to re-secure the boards. Hammering can damage the ceiling plaster below.

Protruding nail heads can tear into the back of the floorcovering, so they must either be removed and replaced by countersunk screws or else be punched below the surface, using a nail punch and hammer.

replace it with a fresh nail. In upstairs rooms where hammering may damage the ceiling below, it is better to use screws.

Drill a starter hole for the screw to avoid splitting the wood as the screw goes in.

The next most obvious fault is boards which have shrunk apart leaving gaps between them. Even if the gap is still actually sealed by the subsurface tongue, it may be quite wide on the surface and could cause wear of floor coverings. So it is important to remedy the situation and in any case the boards could move again in the future and the gap could widen.

Small gaps need cost practically nothing to repair if papier mâché is used as a filler.

To make papier mâché get plenty of newspapers and soak them in water until they are soggy.

Tear them into small pieces and then squeeze them until all the moisture is drained out. To this raw material, add some glue size. Mix up a stronger solution than directed on the packet for its normal use in preparing walls for wall papering. Dip the newspaper pulp into the mixture and mould the lot together keeping it on the dry side.

Using an old knife, press the papier mâché into the gaps between the floor boards, forcing it well down until the gaps are filled. Leave it to dry out for a while and then sand it flush with the adjacent boards, working in the direction of the grain. This is a quick and cheap remedy for an all-too-familiar floorboard fault.

Wider gaps between boards need different treatment since the papier mâché would just fall through the gap between butted boards. Provided there are not too many gaps, the answer is to fill them with wood battens, slightly thicker than the boards. For easy working the maximum length for any batten must not exceed about 3ft. If, therefore, a gap exists along an entire floorboard length, several will be needed.

Cut the batten to length and form it into a wedge shape with a plane. Cover the lower part of the batten with glue and tap it down into the gap until it is a tight fit. Allow plenty of time for it to set before planing down the protruding edge to floor level.

Creaks and squeaks can be very

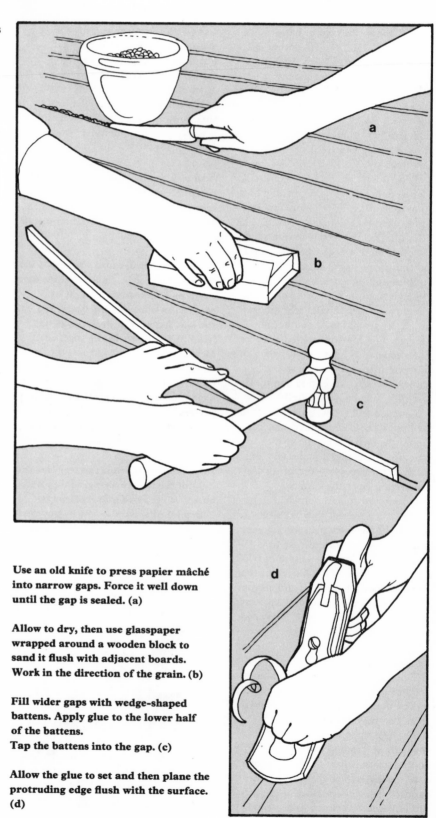

Use an old knife to press papier mâché into narrow gaps. Force it well down until the gap is sealed. (a)

Allow to dry, then use glasspaper wrapped around a wooden block to sand it flush with adjacent boards. Work in the direction of the grain. (b)

Fill wider gaps with wedge-shaped battens. Apply glue to the lower half of the battens.
Tap the battens into the gap. (c)

Allow the glue to set and then plane the protruding edge flush with the surface. (d)

irritating, but they can simply be a pointer to two boards rubbing together. To find out, walk across the room in all directions, making sure that a good deal of pressure is exerted on all areas until you hear a tell-tale squeak.

If it is boards rubbing together, a simple remedy which can be effective is to puff talcum powder well down between the edges of the boards. This will act as a lubricant and cure the squeak. Failing this, you might have to buy an aerosol of timber lubricant to squirt between the rubbing edges.

Creaks can sometimes be attributed to a loose board. Refixing loose nails or screws might be the answer, so try this first. If it fails, buy some floor brads, about 1½in. longer than the thickness of the boards and hammer them into the loose area, using a nail punch to sink them below surface. Follow up by inserting a couple of woodscrews through the board end into the joist below. Locating the joists is easy. Just find the existing nail heads.

SMOOTHING A LARGE AREA
When floor boards have warped they create an undulating surface that must be levelled off before laying a floorcovering.

A lot of hard work is involved in sanding boards smooth if hand tools are used. Most people would prefer to simplify the job by using an electric floor sanding machine. These can be obtained from hire shops.

Before using a sander, or even a plane, to smooth floorboards make sure that all nail heads are knocked below the surface, using a hammer and nail punch. If you possess a sharp plane this can be used to smooth small areas of floorboards but is very laborious work over a whole floor.

A floor sander works like a vacuum cleaner. An abrasive belt does the work and the dust created is automatically collected in a bag. Even so, this can still be a fairly dirty operation so keep the door of the room shut and open windows for ventilation.

Ask for a selection of abrasive sheets

at the hire shop. These are fitted in sequence. A coarse grade is used for the initial work, the medium grade is needed to give a smooth finish and the final 'sweep' is made with a fine grade abrasive.

With a coarse grade abrasive belt fitted to a floor sander, work diagonally across the room.
When using a medium or fine grade abrasive, work in the direction of the boards.
The sander will not reach into corners, so use a sanding disc fitted to an electric drill.

REPLACING FLOORBOARDS

When a floorboard is in such a poor state that replacement is the only sensible solution, think carefully and shop around before buying new timber. Floorboards are an expensive item – timber prices being what they are today – and since you might not be able to buy timber to match the thickness of the existing boards, go for something a fraction thicker and trim back with a plane when the board is in position with the nails driven well below the surface. The older type of boards can be removed with a bolster chisel and a club hammer. Remember, however, to turn off the electricity at the mains before you start work. Electric cables and water pipes run under floorboards so work with great care until you can see what may be there. Since economy is important when using timber, it may be possible only to replace part of a board.

Here, locate the joist nearest to where the board is to be cut and mark a cut line in pencil just in front of the nails.

Sawing through floorboards in situ is impossible with an ordinary hand saw. The ideal tool to use is a pad saw which has a very thin blade and can be operated in restricted areas. But even for the pad saw, you have to make a starter hole into which the blade can be inserted. Do this by drilling two or three holes closely together to form one big one.

When you have sawn across the width of the board, insert a bolster chisel into the cut and prise up the end. Push a batten under the raised end to keep it up before sawing through the board immediately on top of the joist at the other end. It can then be lifted clear.

Support the new piece of board with a small batten screwed firmly to the joist. Use screws to fasten down the new piece of board.

Tongued and grooved boards are more of a problem to remove since you have to saw through the tongues first before prising up the board.

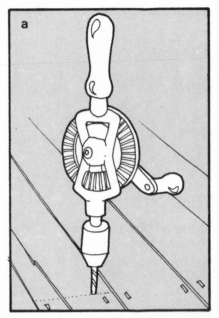

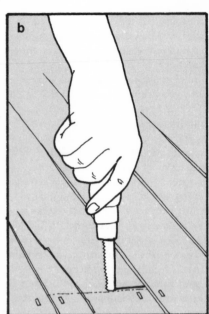

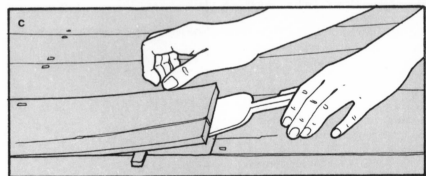

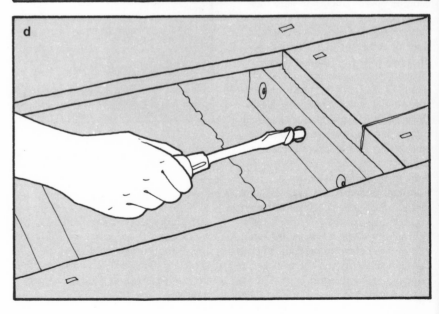

It is very much a professional's job to lay a complete tongued and grooved floor and there are, anyway, some ideal and much simpler alternatives.

When faults in boards extend over a wide area, it really is not worth your while to attempt repair. The same thing applies where you encounter other faults such as extensive woodworm or rot bad enough to mean extensive replacement.

Where damage is confined to wear and tear, you can lay a new surface of hardboard sheets. Hardboard is bought in 8ft. × 4ft. sheets and, for this purpose, should be sawn into 4ft. × 2ft. panels.

The sheets have to be conditioned to the room's atmosphere before laying. This involves damping the sheets with water – two pints to an 8ft. × 4ft. sheet is the usual amount.

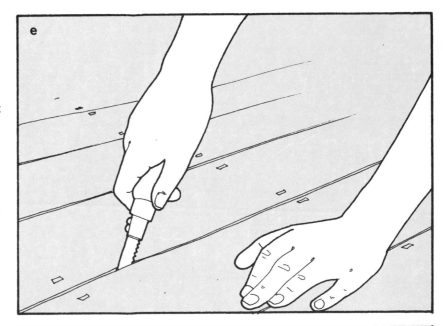

To replace part of a board, draw a line across the board in front of the nails securing it to the joist.
Make a starter hole for a pad saw by drilling three holes closely together to form a gap big enough for the saw to operate. (a)
The thin blade of the pad saw is essential for working in restricted areas such as this. (b)

Keep the cut end raised with a batten. It may be necessary to prise up the cut end with a bolster chisel to tap in the batten. Saw through the other end of the board immediately on top of the joist. Then lift the board clear. (c)

Screw a batten to the joist to support the new piece of timber. Fix the new board with screws. (d)

For tongue and grooved boards, drill starter holes for the saw and cut along the tongue before prising it up with a bolster chisel. (e)

As if dealing with a butt-edged board, lever it out in the same way, after removing the nails or screws holding it to the joists. (f)

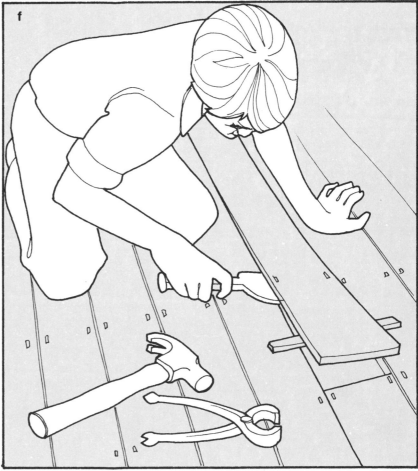

Lay the hardboard in the room where it is to be used for 48 hours before fixing. Use hardboard nails to secure the sheets and stagger all joining edges. And, as always, punch the nail heads below surface.

LAYING A NEW SURFACE

Where complete removal of the boards is necessary, a new surface can still be formed quite easily by laying chipboard sheets over the joists. The chipboard must be 18mm. flooring grade. It is simply a matter of cutting out the sheets to coincide with the formation of the joists and ensuring that all edges are well supported.

Fix the chipboard to the joists with 2in. screws inserted no more than 1ft. apart. Where necessary, perhaps in an awkward corner, fix battens to the joists as supports for the edges of the chipboard. And remember, that access to underfloor wiring or pipes will still be needed, so cut inspection panels in appropriate places that can be removed quickly when necessary.

SOLID FLOORS

And now for solid floors. Problems here are likely only to be slight. Cracks, possibly undulations, will be the only faults.

The simple solution is to cover the whole floor with a screeding compound. Special self levelling types are available from d-i-y shops. You simply mix the powder with water according to the manufacturers instructions and spread it over the affected area with a stiff broom, and smooth it roughly with a trowel, leave it to dry and it will set perfectly level.

STAIRS

Stairs are notorious for squeaks. The problem here is usually found in loose wooden wedges which hold the risers and treads in place. They can shrink, crack or work loose.

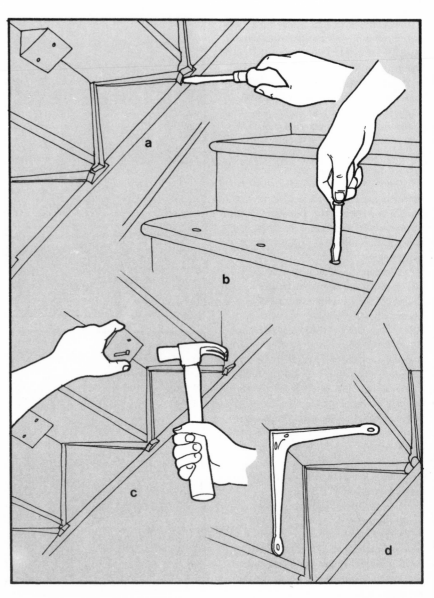

For creaking stairs, remove any defective wedges, apply adhesive and tap them firmly back into place. If a wedge has shrunk too much, make a new one. (a)

It is not always possible to get under the stairs, of course. Here, a couple of screws driven through the squeaky treads into the risers will usually cure the problem. (b)

If a carriage block works loose, refit it with pins and glue. If the block remains a loose fit, cut a new one from softwood. (c)

Alternatively, screw angle brackets in position. The arm must be a little shorter than the steps. (d)

SKIRTINGS

Skirting boards take a constant
pounding from vacuum cleaners, toys,
furniture and anything else likely to
come into contact with them. As a
result they quickly become chipped,
cracked and generally an eyesore.

If you have to replace a skirting and
you prefer conventional ones made of
timber, you can get replacement
lengths from builders' merchants or
timber yards. Where these skirtings
meet at corners, the ends have to be
mitred to give a neat join. Skirtings
with ready mitred ends can be bought
and it is advisable to get this type since
cutting neat mitres is not an easy job.

You might, however, decide to opt
for making your own maintenance-free
skirtings from chipboard or plywood
faced with laminate.

Skirtings are fixed by nailing them
to wood battens or plugs set in the
walls.

**Use a claw hammer or a crowbar to
prise the skirting away from the wall.
To prevent damage to the plaster
above, interpose a timber batten
between the hammer and the wall.**

**To help locate the positions of fixing
plugs after the new skirtings are
positioned over them, mark their
positions on the floor.**

**Fit new timber skirtings by driving
nails into the existing plugs. Sink the
nail heads below the surface and fill
the holes with wood filler before
painting.**

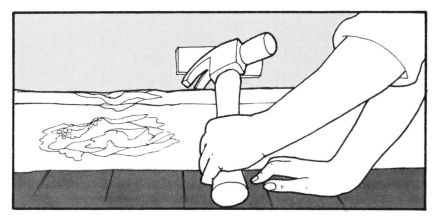

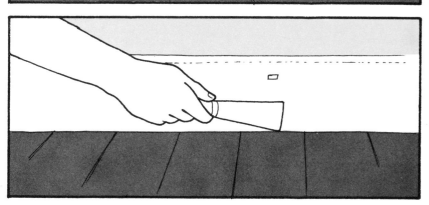

To cut mitres, use a mitre block.

Butt the mitred corners closely together before nailing.

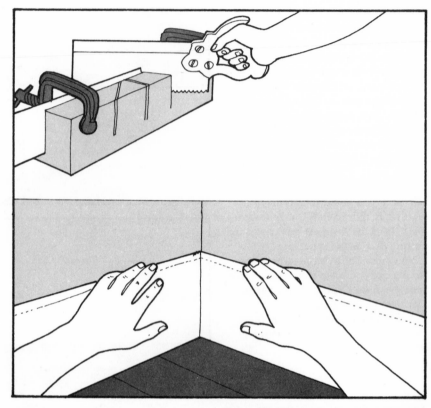

For blockboard or plywood skirtings use nails or screws to fix lengths of blockboard or plywood to the existing wood plugs. Sink all screw or nail heads below the surface. When possible, the top edge or lipping should be applied and trimmed before fixing the lengths to the wall.

Fix the laminate facings in position (see page 115). Then trim back with a file when the lengths are on the wall. This provides a concealed fixing.

Being thin, quadrant moulding is flexible enough to be able to follow any slight unevenness in the boards and hide it.

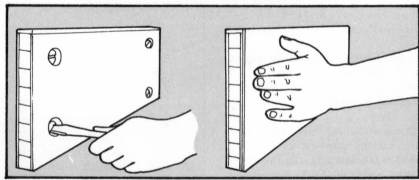

Uneven floors Where a floor is uneven, an ugly gap will be left at intervals between the bottom of the skirting and the floorboards.

Two choices are open to you here. The simplest solution is to fit the skirting board and then conceal the gap by nailing quadrant moulding to the skirting.

The alternative is to cut the skirting to match the shape of the floor.

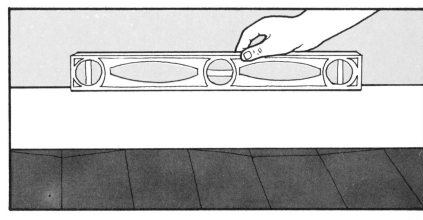

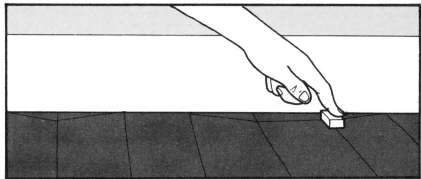

The alternative is to pin the skirting in position; checking with a spirit level that it is horizontal.

Cut a block of wood that is a little thicker than the widest gap between the skirting and the floor.

Run the block along the skirting, following its path with a pencil.

Cut along the pencil line with a saw and the skirting should fit perfectly. Remember that if the skirting is fixed ¼in. clear from the floor, a fitted carpet can be tucked under it. If the carpet is butted to the skirting, any gaps will be hidden.

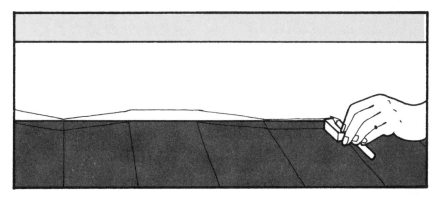

Roof Repairs

The most important aspect of working at a height is safety. The essential thing before attempting any roof repairs is to get the proper equipment and secure it correctly before using it.

A ladder must extend at least three rungs above the level of the eaves. From there, you will need a roof ladder or a duckboard which spans the distance between the eaves and the ridge of the roof. This equipment can usually be hired locally. Ask your supplier for specific instructions on fixing the duckboard or roof ladder securely to both the ridge and to the main ladder. If you feel unsafe at height then get professional help. The use of ladders and scaffolding is covered in detail in a later chapter.

Many people wait until the roof gives trouble before attempting a repair. This is a bad policy.

It is essential to make a regular inspection of the roof since a lot of damage can be caused before the tell-tale signs of leaks start to appear on ceilings and walls.

A reasonable overall inspection of the roof can be made from the ground using binoculars, though a close-up examination of suspect areas will then be needed.

Go up into the loft when it is raining heavily and look and listen for any drips or splashes which will indicate cracked or displaced tiles or slates.

Very often the defect will be some distance from where the water is actually dripping. Use a torch to trace the water back to the trouble spot.

Pre-war houses generally have roofs of slates or plain clay tiles. Thereafter roofs were covered with single-lap concrete tiles or plain, triple-lapped concrete tiles. The single-lap tiles interlock with adjacent tiles through tongues and grooves in their sides. There are various types and patterns available.

In plain tiling the roof battens are about 4in. apart. The tiles should overlap by not less than 2½in. They are secured to the battens by two projecting nibs. The tiles in some courses may be nailed, depending on the design of the roof and the tiles used.

TILE ROOF REPAIRS

Old tiles must be replaced if they are crumbling or cracked. To remove a defective tile, lift the edges of adjoining tiles and insert wedges to hold them up while the defective tile is removed.

Where a tile is nailed, a trowel can often be used to lever out the nail holding the tile. If not, you will need a ripper. This tool has a hooked blade. They can usually be hired locally.

Hook the blade around the nail and pull sharply to cut through the nail.

To fit the new tile, push it back until the nibs hook over the battens. It cannot be nailed if the overlapping tiles are not removed.

Some old roofs are covered with nibless tiles nailed to the battens. If a tile slips down, the only remedy is to lift and renail all the tiles in position.

Finding matching replacement single-lap tiles is often difficult. Many of the older patterns are no longer made. Very likely, though, the particular type you want will have been used in a lot of other houses in the area. So hunt around nearby builders' merchants or demolition firms as one may stock some of the type you need. But be careful. Before buying old tiles make sure they are not crumbled or cracked.

If you do locate a source of matching tiles, it would be worth while taking a few extra ones home and storing them in case they are needed in future.

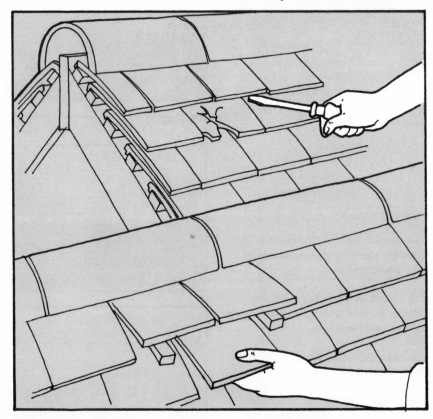

Lift the tiles in the course above the damaged tile. Raise the damaged tile upwards to release the holding nibs from the battens. Slide out the damaged tile.

Wedge up the tiles above and slip the fixing nibs of the new tile over the roof batten to lock it in place. Remove the wedges and lower the tiles above back into place.

SLATE ROOFS

A single slate or two can be replaced quite easily, but a bigger job involving cutting or drilling is best left to a professional.

Slates are brittle and difficult for the amateur to cut to shape or drill through.

Cracks and breaks are the usual problem with slates though the fixing nails can corrode leaving a slate loose.

Slate tiles can be bought with predrilled holes either at one end of the slate (mainly for fixing at the ridge of the roof or the eaves) or in the centre (for slates fixed elsewhere). Always replace a slate in the same way as it was fixed before.

They are nailed to battens in the roof in such a way that a single slate overlaps two in the row below.

Various slate sizes are in common use and some types are thicker than others.

A special tool called a ripper will be needed to remove damaged slates.

If a slate slips because the fixing nails have corroded, it can be re-fixed with a strip of lead, zinc or aluminium, 1in. wide or, alternatively, heavy gauge copper wire nailed to the batten through the slight gap between the pair of slates below.

The new slate is pushed into position and the projecting end of the clip is turned up and over to grip the tail of the slate.

If they are sound, there is no reason why old slates should not be used again,

Slide the ripper under the broken slate so that its end locks on to the slate's fixing nails.

Pull or tap the ripper backwards to break the nails. Slide the broken slate gently out.

Nail a strip of lead, about 1 ft. long, to the batten through the remaining slates.

Slide the new slate into place and curl the lead strip around it to hold it in place.

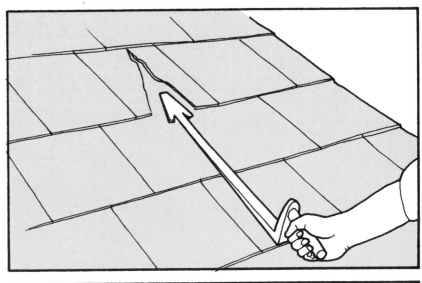

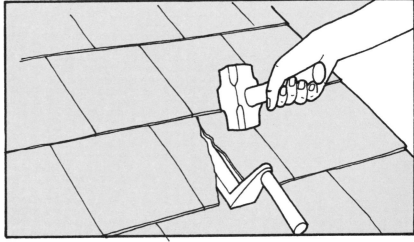

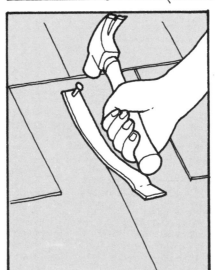

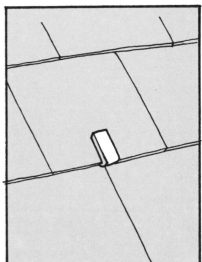

and stocks of slates recovered from demolished houses are often kept by builders' merchants in the locality. These second-hand slates, because they have been weathered, often make a better colour match than new ones, but examine them for defects before buying. To be sure of getting a good colour match, take the defective one with you to your supplier.

REMOVING MOSS FROM ROOFS

Moss forms easily on many roofs. If simply scraped off it will almost certainly reform. The best way to treat the problem is to scrape the area clean, scrub it thoroughly, and then brush on a good coat of suitable fungicide bought from a hardware shop.

RENEWING FLASHING

The point at which the roof of an extension meets the house wall is usually sealed with mortar, or a strip of zinc or lead which is called the flashing.

Mortar is a poor sealer since it inevitably cracks under normal house movement. You can anticipate and avoid trouble by fixing zinc flashing over the mortar.

Old damaged flashing can be levered out with a cold chisel and hammer and replaced with zinc.

When renewing flashing rake out the mortar from the joint in the brickwork above the roof. Clean it out to leave a 1in. deep cavity.

Use the dresser to form a ¾in. wide edge at right angles on the strip of zinc.

Hammer down the other side to suit the angle between the roof and the wall.

Wet the cleaned-out mortar cavity with clean water before slotting the flashing into place. Wedge it in place and fill the joint with a mix of 4 parts sand to one part cement.

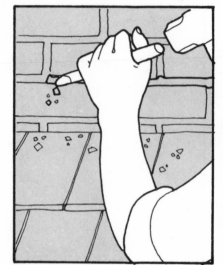
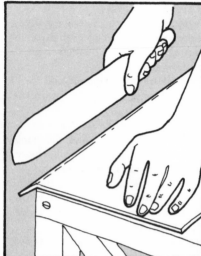
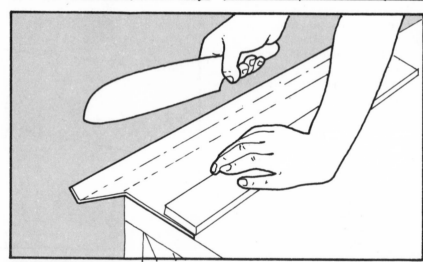

A builders' merchant will supply a flat piece of zinc for you to shape to the contours of the roof and wall. They might, however, be prepared to shape the zinc as required if you give them detailed instructions.

If not, you will need to hire a special wooden tool called a dresser. This will enable you to beat the zinc into shape. Ask for the zinc to be supplied in 1ft. wide strips cut to the required lengths. Normally each strip will be 8ft. long.

CORRUGATED ROOFS

Older corrugated garage roofs are often made of iron which is a difficult material to cut to size. But a sound repair can be made quite easily with Novolux plastic sheet.

If necessary, raise the flashing between the roof (of an attached garage) and the wall by bending it upwards temporarily to free the existing corrugated material.

If you use Novolux plastic sheet, buy the special fixing screws and washers at the same time.

Drill all holes through the raised corrugation of the sheet before inserting the screws.

Cut through the raised corrugations, and then reverse the sheet and complete cutting from the other side. A wood batten can be used to guide the saw cut. Saw through the raised corrugations when cutting lengthwise.

Overlap sections by at least two corrugations.

Insert fixing screws through the raised corrugations into the roof battens.

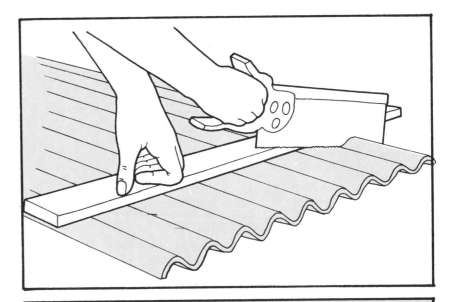

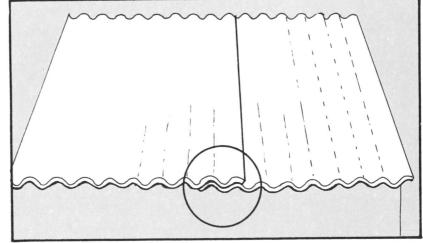

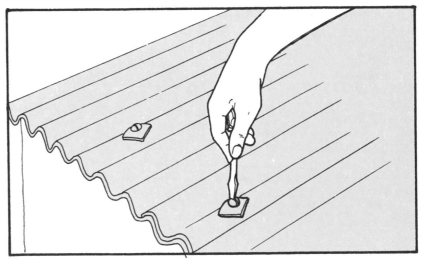

Gutters and Downpipes

The house gutters are fixed to the fascias and connected to the downpipes. Since the gutters are supposed to carry rainwater to the downpipes (from where it goes to the house drainage system) they must be kept in good condition – free of blockages and leaks. A once-a-year check is well worthwhile.

Older gutters were made of metal which can rust away and if you ever have to replace a complete guttering it is worth while changing to the modern plastic types. These will not rust and never need to be painted, though they can leak if a poor joint is made between sections. However, their lightness will make it easier to repair the joint.

Although minor repairs to gutters, or replacing a small length, are within the scope of the average handyman, replacing a whole system is a tricky operation best left to a professional.

Metal gutters are heavy and replacing even a section of these is very much a two-handed job, so get help or once again leave it to a professional.

PREVENTING BLOCKAGES
Trees close to the house will cause leaves to blow into the gutter, so it is a good idea to fit plastic mesh over it to keep out leaves and other debris.

LEAKS
After cleaning a metal gutter, examine the inside for rust spots. Any corroded areas should be cleaned, using a wire hand brush or a wire cup brush fitted to an electric drill.

Coat the cleaned area with a rust inhibiting liquid or with good metal primer.

Repaint with gloss or bituminous paint. If bituminous paint was used before, you cannot use gloss paint over it, because the bitumen will bleed through. A simple test for finding out if it has been used is to apply some white gloss over a small, hidden area. If the existing paint is bituminous, the white gloss will quickly turn brown.

If using gloss paint over old gloss

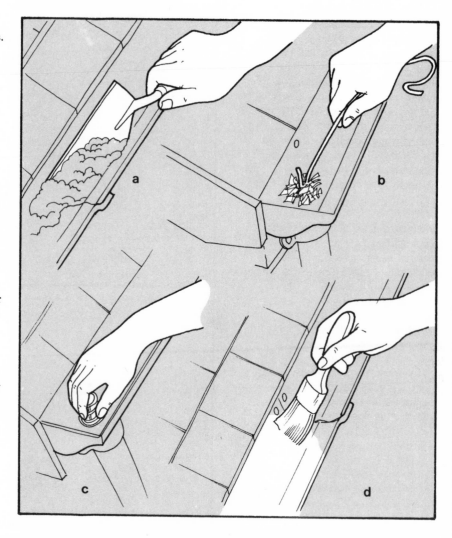

Use a trowel to scrape all leaves and other rubbish from the gutter. Wash out the entire length of the gutter before treating rust spots and priming with metal primer. (a)

Use a piece of stiff wire to lift rubbish from the mouth of downpipes. Birds often nest in the top of a downpipe and sometimes the nest gets washed by rainwater into the pipe. Be careful when hooking a nest out; if it is accidentally pushed further into the pipe it will cause a serious blockage. (b)

Prevent birds building nests on the downpipe by fitting a wire cage to the top. These are simply pressed into position. Get one that is the same diameter as the downpipe. (c)

Minor leaks can sometimes be cured by applying a couple of coats of bitumastic paint after cleaning the affected area. (d) you can use up old cans of any colour. The colour will not show from the ground since it will be on the inside only.

Cracks and holes must be repaired carefully after cleaning away rust. If holes are large, a new length of gutter will be needed.

Cast iron gutter joints Leaks from the joints of a cast iron gutter means uncoupling the overlapping sections and applying a sealing compound or putty before rejoining the lengths.

DISMANTLING A METAL DRAINPIPE

If a downpipe gets blocked and the obstruction cannot be removed from the top, the downpipe will have to be dismantled and cleaned with a long cane with a cloth pad tied to the end.

Each length of metal downpipe just slots into the section below. Overflowing water at a joint will indicate the position of the blockage. Downpipes retaining brackets are nailed to wooden plugs inserted in the house walls. If a plug has worked loose, it has to be replaced with a larger one.

Fill cracks or holes with bituminous mastic compound or plastic padding. Follow maker's instructions. (a)

The overlapping sections of the gutter are joined by a nut and bolt. Unscrew the bolt and prise the sections apart. (b)

Use an old chisel to scrape away the existing sealing material. Spread a new layer of sealing compound or putty. (c)

Press the two sections together again; tighten the fixing bolt. Trim away the surplus mastic and apply a coat of bituminous paint or a mixture of old left-overs from your gloss paint. (d)

Use a claw hammer to lever out nails from the wood plugs in the walls. (e)

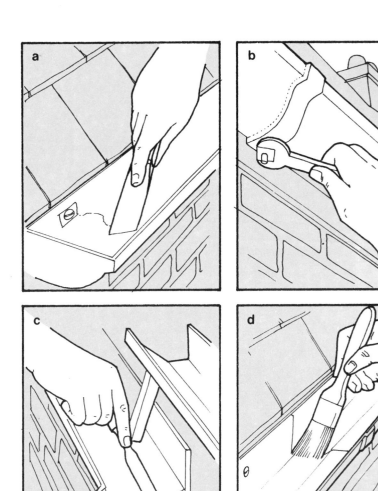

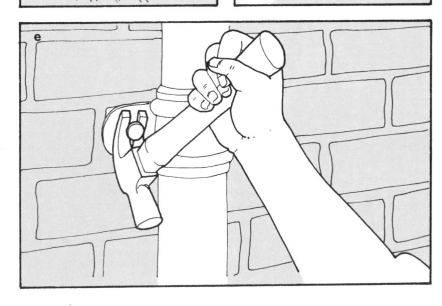

Pull apart the interlocking sections of downpipe and clean them out. (a)

When refitting the downpipe, it may be necessary to cut longer and thicker conical-shape wood plugs to fit tightly into the holes in the wall. (b)

Knock back the securing nails that hold the brackets to the plugs. (c)

If leaves collect around joints, water may settle and turn to ice, eventually splitting the pipe. Seal off any joints between sections with proprietary mastic and apply a coat of bitumen paint. (d)

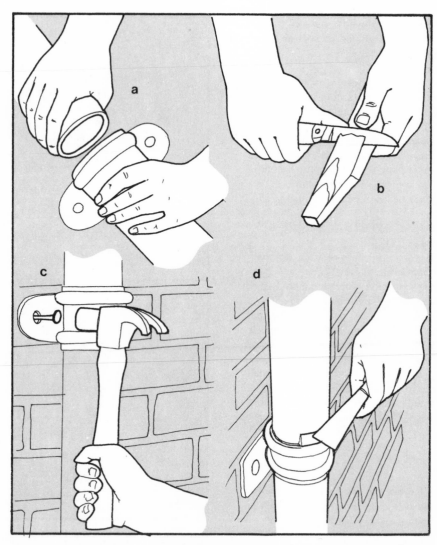

PLASTIC GUTTER LEAKS

If a joint in a plastic gutter leaks soon after fixing it is most often the result of a poor joint having been made and it must be re-done.

If the leak occurs after the guttering has been in place for a considerable period, then the foam plastic seals on the joining pieces that hold the sections together will have to be replaced. There are several makes of plastic gutters and therefore several types of seal. Make sure you get the right type for your particular gutter system.

Free the joining piece between sections by squeezing its front edge inwards. Remove all traces of the old seal.

Fit the new seal, making sure that the edges of the joining piece are covering its edges.

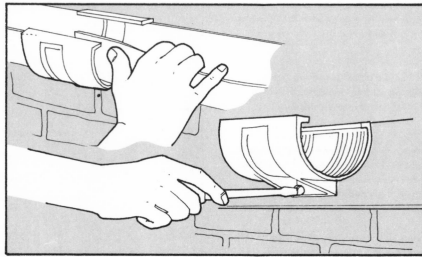

ALIGNING A GUTTER

In order that rainwater can flow into the downpipes, gutters have to be set at a slight slope. This can vary according to individual systems so check first with the manufacturers of the system you have before attempting installation or repair work. The minimum fall is usually 1in. in 10ft.

If water overflows at the centre of a gutter which is already installed, check that the fall is correct. If the trouble is due to a broken or loose bracket causing the gutter to sag in the middle, this can easily be refixed.

If the fault extends along the complete length the whole system will have to be taken down and re-positioned. This is really a job for an expert.

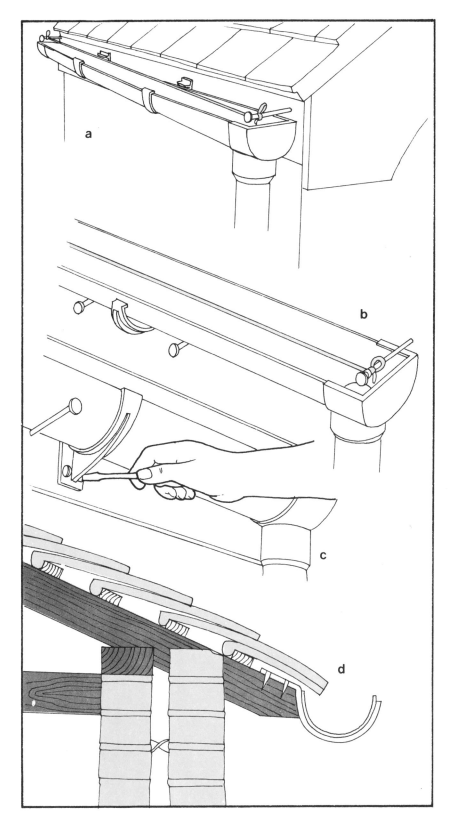

To correct a slightly sagging gutter, first stretch a taut string line along the top of the gutter. Check with a spirit level that the gutter falls evenly to the downpipe. (a)

Before removing bracket screws, knock a couple of nails into the fascia to support the gutter temporarily in its new position. (b)

Insert the screws through the brackets in their new positions. The temporary nails and the string line can now be removed. (c)

If the bracket is fixed to the rafters, a tile has to be removed to reach the old bracket and to refix the new one (see page 148). (d)

Rust

Rust can have a devastating effect on metalwork. Removing it is a really painstaking and time consuming job. The best approach to the rust problem is to put all your efforts into preventing it. The time and money needed is negligible compared to that required for its removal.

Iron and steel are the metals prone to rust attack. These are the ferrous metals which, in their original state, are iron oxide. Rust is the outward sign of them trying to return to their natural state.

Water, oxygen and carbon dioxide, combining to attack the metal, causes the corrosion. The electric potentials of varying parts of the metal differ during the attack and when moisture (rainwater, for example) bridges the parts, currents flow between the negative and positive areas. A chemical change takes place in parts of the metal which is seen as rust.

Assuming then, that prevention is the best cure, what can be done?

Paint is often assumed to be a complete protection against rust; this is not so. Extra paint coats will simply make it more difficult for moisture vapour to penetrate through to the metal surface. They do not keep it out all together.

Even tiny cracks in the paint surface are an open invitation to rust so regular checks are essential on exterior metalwork to make sure that the paint film is unbroken on all surfaces.

If any cracks in the paint are spotted, deal with them immediately.

Not all exterior metal surfaces are painted however. Where this is so, and where damp is likely to be encountered, apply a liberal coat of grease or oil. Hard-to-reach areas can be treated with a film of water-displacing fluid available from builders' merchants.

Garden tools At the end of the summer, it is traditional to put all the tools and gardening equipment into storage – often in the shed at the bottom of the garden. In an uninsulated shed without any form of continuous, even heat, rust attack is likely.

If possible, bring all metal equipment into the house during the winter. If tools have to be stored in a shed, put them in drawers or boxes allowing just a little air to infiltrate. A thorough coating of grease on all the metal parts is essential. Check the equipment during the winter and repeat the greasing treatment. Specially impregnated rust inhibiting paper for wrapping them in is available that will keep the corrosion at bay for a good while.

Cars The family car is one of the most likely targets for attacks from corrosion. The chassis and underside are most prone to attack and even if the car is garaged, it is no protection.

Ideally when the car is new, the underside should be protected with underseal and this is a wise investment, provided it is done immediately.

If this was not done – or the car was bought second-hand – then check the undersides for rust. Never be deceived by shiny bodywork – this is no indication as to what is going on underneath.

Hose down the underside of the car to remove all caked mud and grime. Then spray the whole area with moisture displacing oils. A hosing down is important too after a snowy spell.

When the authorities spread salt on the roads, this is inevitably thrown up on to the underside of the car and will cause corrosion if it is not washed off.

WATER TANKS
Because the domestic water tank is tucked away out of sight in the loft it is often ignored – until it is too late and corrosion has started. Certainly, if it is an older type it will be galvanized and will corrode in time.

A simple protection is to suspend a sacrificial anode into the water. The anode wastes away instead of the galvanizing on the tank. It is also worth while draining the tank and applying a couple of coats of bitumen paint. This colourless, taintless paint will provide excellent protection over a number of years.

But what if, after draining the tank of water, it is found to be hopelessly corroded? Well, in one way, you have been lucky in finding this out in time. Had the tank finally burst, an awful lot of water would have found its way down into the rooms below.

If the tank is beyond repair – that is, the corrosion is severe – there is no alternative but to replace it, but get a plumber to do this.

As a replacement it is best nowadays to buy a polythene type; at least one rust problem will be solved for good.

On the other hand, if the corrosion has only reached the loose, flaking rust stage, this can be dealt with.

Use a wire brush to remove all the

flaking rust. Even better, and less hard work, is to use a wire cup brush fitted to an electric drill. Any minor spots of rust left can be cleaned up with emery paper.

Only attempt to remove the loose rust. The remainder can be painted with a rust inhibiting liquid which will neutralise it to form a hard, inert layer. When dry, this can be painted over.

The alternative is to paint the tank with zinc-base cold galvanizing paint. This kills the rust action and puts an extra layer of zinc on the tank.

RUST REMEDIES
When prevention was overlooked, there is no alternative but to remove the rust as quickly as possible. First of all clean away all signs of rust with one of the methods mentioned earlier.

The metal does not have to gleam but it should be as bright as possible. Use an abrasive paper to rub over the surface.

To dissolve minute particles that are not seen by the eye, use a chemical neutraliser. Immediately apply a coat of one of the pigmented rust-binding metal primers. These compounds neutralise the rust and turn it to iron phosphate, leaving a plastic film on the surface.

When the primer is dry, normal paint can be applied.

RUSTED NUTS AND BOLTS
There are few things more annoying than trying to undo a rusty nut, bolt or a hinge that has locked tight. Dismantling fluid poured on and left for a while usually clears the trouble. This problem can be lessened in future by smearing Vaseline on all screws and bolt threads before inserting.

A screw that has rusted in a wall can sometimes be removed after tightening it a little before unscrewing. If this fails, a soldering iron applied to the screw head can cause sufficient expansion to break the rust grip.

A rusted countersunk screw that will not budge with a screwdriver is really a problem. It cannot be gripped in any way to turn it. However, a twist drill of about the estimated diameter of the screw can be used to drill into the screw head.

Eventually the head will break away and the batten or whatever else the screw is holding in place can then be slipped free and the remaining part of the screw gripped and turned with a suitable wrench.

EXTERIOR METALWORK
Gutters and downpipes can be treated with rust binding primer where the trouble cannot be reached for fuller treatment. Remember that plastic gutters and downpipes are now available and these should be used where existing metal types have to be replaced.

Clean rusty metal window frames with a wire brush followed by emery paper. This should be followed with a coat of rust-inhibiting primer and then the normal paint top coats.

Electricity

An electric current flows, rather like the flow of water in a pipe, but electricity needs a complete circuit to flow round. The flow is measured in amps, it's pressure in volts, and its power (the work it can do) in watts.

Two wires, at least, must be connected to an appliance to provide a circuit. Often there are three, including an earth wire.

If electricity needs a complete circuit for the current to flow, to prevent it flowing when not required, the circuit must be broken. This is the purpose of a switch. A switch turns an appliance on or off, so the circuit is always under control.

A fuse protects the circuit from damage if a fault develops in the wiring, or in an appliance. Like a switch it breaks the circuit and stops the current flowing.

However, unlike the hand operated switch, it works automatically by melting if an excessive current passes through the circuit. When a fuse blows it indicates that something is wrong. Every circuit must have a fuse of the correct rating.

All the electrical fuse boxes and meters and main switches in your home are located in accessible places such as a cellar, garage, in the hall, under the stairs, or, possibly, in a special meter box outside the house.

The electricity board's service cable brings the electricity supply into your house. It usually contains two wires – live and neutral. Often a terminal is provided on the latter, which is connected to earth and to which all the earth wires in the home are linked.

Your main fuse box contains a fuse which isolates your electrics from the public supply, so if your electrics develop a fault or overload it will not affect anyone else. You must never tamper with this fuse box. It is the property of the electricity board and is sealed.

A meter registers the amount of electricity you have used. The meter

A basic ring circuit.

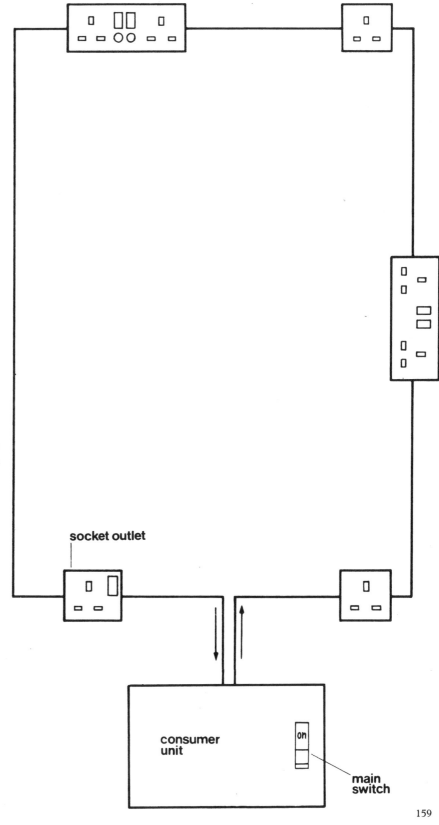

socket outlet

consumer unit

on

main switch

may be a single black or brown unit, or two meters (one for the cheaper off-peak supply for storage heaters), or a White Meter (for cheaper central heating and hot water). The consumer's installation (the part of the installation which is your responsibility) begins at the meter. It is for you to ensure that the earth connection is effective. A qualified electrician should check the earth connection periodically.

The main circuit in a house is split into a number of sub-circuits by distribution fuses. There is one fuse for each circuit (older installations have two fuses per circuit).

If you have an older-type fuse box ask the electricity board to modify it or install a new one which conforms to modern safety standards.

The cables to separate circuits each contain two supply wires and an earth wire. The cables may be run in tubes embedded in walls, or modern plastic cables can sometimes be embedded without further protection.

The main switch on the circuit fuse box is for switching off the current before replacing a fuse or carrying out any other electrical work. The main switches and fuses should be labelled so that they are immediately identifiable.

The earth connection in the home is for safety. Appliances provided with an earth wire should have the earth wire properly connected. If an appliance is faulty, but properly earthed, the current will take the path of least resistance through the earth wire and not through someone's body to earth. If you touched an unearthed faulty appliance while in contact with a water pipe or water in a bath, or even while standing on a concrete floor or a damp surface, the shock would probably be fatal. You would also get a severe, possibly fatal shock if you touched the bare connections in the plug or appliance.

COLOUR CODING
Government regulations specify a new colour coding for three-core flexes attached to all new household electrical appliances. These colours have been standardised throughout Europe.

Under the regulations, the earth wire (which was green) is now green with a yellow stripe. The live wire (which was red) is now brown. The neutral wire (which was black) is light blue. Both the old and new types will be in existence for a while so learn the new code as well as the old to avoid making wrong connections.

Cables of wiring systems of old and many new homes will still be red, black and green, so when connecting new flex into permanent connections like a ceiling rose for a light, connect brown to red, blue to black, green/yellow to green (or bare earth wire).

HOW TO WIRE A PLUG
Trim back 2in. of the outer sheath on the flex, without cutting the insulation around individual wires. Push the flex in under the clamp provided in the plug and tighten the clamp on the beginning of the uncut sheath.

Cut the individual wires so that they are just the right length to go through the terminal holes, or around the terminal screws.

Strip off just enough insulation to make the connection and no more. The green or green/yellow is the earth and is connected to the largest pin in the plug – marked E. The red or brown lead is connected to the pin marked L (for live) or R (for Red). And the black or light blue lead is connected to the pin marked N (for Neutral) or B (for Black).

If an appliance has a two-core (two-wire) flex it may be connected to a 3-pin plug as described above, but leaving the larger, earth pin

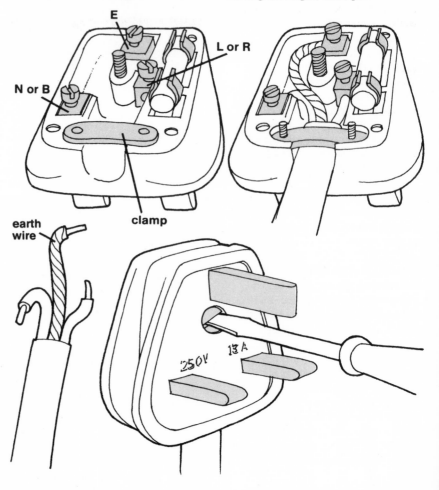

unconnected. Never connect a three-core flex to a two pin plug.

Clamp the wires firmly in the terminal connections.

Before replacing the plug cover, make sure that there are no stray whiskers of bare wire, and that the nuts or screws holding the wires are tight.

Make sure that the outer sheath of flex is secured under the clamp where the lead enters the plug. This will prevent the wires being pulled away from the terminals. Replace the cover and tighten the screws or nuts holding the plug together.

REPLACING AN ELECTRIC FIRE ELEMENT

When an electric fire fails, the usual cause is the element (the bar or bars). Replacing a burnt out element is quite simple but ensure that you replace it with one of the correct type.

First, though, check that the trouble is not more basic. A fuse may have blown or the milled nuts at either end of the element and which hold it in place may be loose. Turn off the fire, unplug it and tighten the nuts.

If this fails you will have to remove the element. First release the guard by removing the retaining screws (if fitted) and squeezing it in the centre to free it from the holes in the casing.

One of the element-retaining brackets has a spring-loaded slot, designed so that, when the nuts are loosened, the element can be eased out.

The reverse procedure is adopted to fit the new element. Push back the spring loaded bracket and locate the fixing pins on either side of the element into the holes in the brackets. Finally, replace the milled nuts and the guard.

WIRING A LAMP HOLDER

Turn off the supply at the mains. Do not just switch off at the light switch.

Unscrew the cap and remove the lampholder.

If the existing flex is in good condition, prepare the ends of the flex by removing about $\frac{1}{4}$ inch of covering.

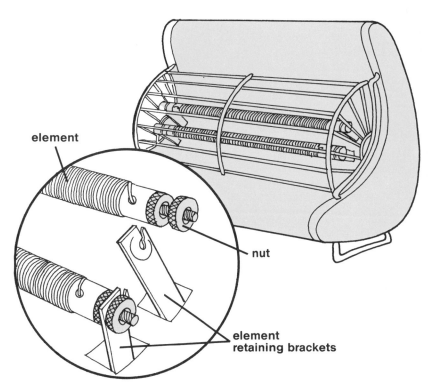

element

nut

element retaining brackets

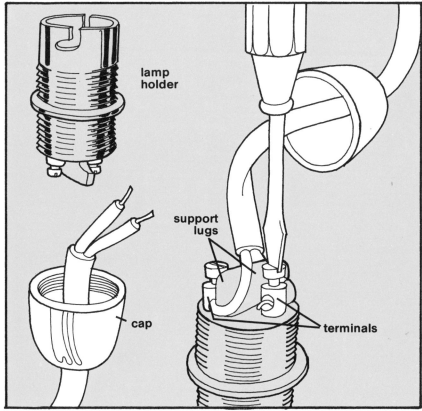

lamp holder

support lugs

cap

terminals

Twist the ends neatly. Use a new piece of flex if the existing flex is frayed, perished or baked hard.

Thread the flex through the lamp-holder cap.

Loosen the small screws in the lampshade terminals, insert the wires, and tighten the screws firmly. Make sure that there are no stray ends of flex spreading out from the terminal.

Hook the flex under the support lugs in the lampholder and screw down the cap firmly. It is important to use the support lugs to avoid straining the connections.

REPLACING A FUSE

Circuit fuses: The usual kind in older installations is the re-wirable type. They are usually rated at 5 amps or 15 amps.

If a fuse blows, turn off the main switch. This may be on the fuse box itself, or possibly in a separate switchbox nearby. Also switch off the faulty appliance or lamp, unplug it, or remove the bulb; otherwise the new fuse might also blow when fitted. Check the wiring of the appliance to see if you can see the fault.

To find the blown fuse take out and inspect each fuse. Usually it is clear which fuse has blown – not only will the fuse wire be broken, but often there will be scorch marks around the fuse carrier.

Replace the old wire with a fresh piece of the correct rating which should be marked on the carrier (a supply of fuse wire should always be kept near the fuse box). Do not stretch or strain the wire when tightening the screws.

Replace the fuse carrier, close the box and then turn on the main switch. If the fuse blows again, or you are in doubt, send for a registered electrician. Get the faulty appliance or light fitting repaired.

Cartridge fuses Your main fuses may be of the cartridge type which are available in different ratings. It is often difficult to find out which one has blown as you cannot see the wire

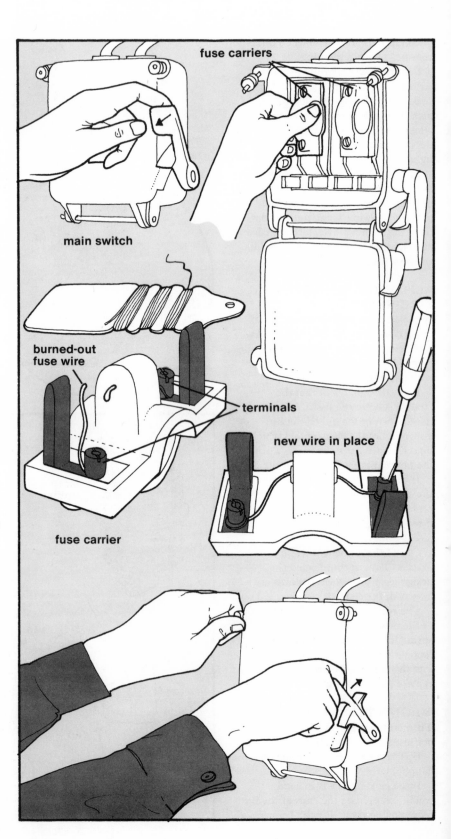

fuse carriers

main switch

burned-out fuse wire

terminals

new wire in place

fuse carrier

inside, but they are easy to replace.

Turn off the main switch on the fuse box. Try to ascertain the cause of the fuse blowing and take the same precautions as before to prevent it blowing again.

Take out each fuse holder in turn and test the cartridges to see which one has blown. This can be done with the aid of a metal-case torch.

Switch on the torch. Unscrew the bottom cap and place the fuse so that one end touches the metal case of the battery and the other makes contact with the metal of the torch case. If the torch comes on again, the fuse is intact.

If a torch is not available, test by replacing each fuse with another fuse of the same rating.

Replace the fuse carrier, close the box, and switch on the main switch. If the fuse blows again call an electrician. Whenever in doubt get qualified help. Get the faulty appliance or fitting repaired.

Ring Circuit plug fuses Flat pinned plugs contain their own 13 amp cartridge fuses (or 3 amp for appliances rated 700 watts or less).

Always use the correct fuse for the flex. New appliances will be fitted with the correct flex; the watts will be indicated on the maker's rating plate on the appliance and will enable you to select the correct fuse to use.

These fuses are simple to replace – they are located in spring clips inside the plug. Just lever the old fuse out and insert the new one.

It is almost impossible to tell whether a fuse has blown simply by looking at it, but it can be tested with a torch as before.

Appliances with motors – vacuum cleaners and spin dryers, for instance, might need a large fuse even though their rating is less than 700 watts. This is because the starting current required for the motor is higher in the first few moments of running.

Things you should not do.

SOME THINGS TO REMEMBER

Take good care of flexes. Renew them as soon as they show signs of wear.

Use three pin sockets and plugs where possible, especially in rooms with concrete or tiled floors, or where there is a water supply, or a pipe carrying water.

Never overload a socket by using several appliances from it. It is far better to have a double socket outlet fitted.

Always replace flex with a new unbroken length. Never make joins in a length of flex.

Never secure flex to walls or ceilings without proper conduits or lay it under a carpet.

Never use twisted, unsheathed flex for power appliances.

Never fit socket outlets or take portable appliances into the bathroom.

Bathroom heaters must be out of reach of anyone using the bath as must the essential pullcord switch. Have these installed by a registered electrician.

Try not to knock socket outlets with chair legs or vacuum cleaners. Fixing the sockets a little way up the wall, say 6 inches above floor level, helps to prevent this.

Never touch a fire element until the plug is out and the element is cold.

Never touch a plug, switch or socket with wet hands.

The Electricity Council can be contacted for advice and information on domestic electricity.

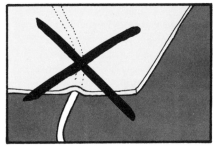

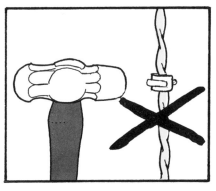

Window Maintenance and Repair

Provided that wooden window frames are well looked after they will give a lifetime of service.

A good, sound film of paint is essential at all times. So if the frames are in a poor condition then put matters right now.

Paint will adhere only to a clean, dry surface. If necessary, remove all areas of defective paint and thoroughly clean the bare wood. Slight defects can be overcome by scraping and glasspapering.

Where the paintwork is really rotten, strip it off, using either a blowlamp or chemical stripper and a scraper. Chemical stripper must be throughly washed off and the surface allowed to dry out before painting.

Before using a coat of primer, make sure the bare wood is completely dry. Do not, for example, start work immediately after a rainy spell.

Apply suitable undercoat and finally top coats of gloss according to manufacturer's instructions.

Any gaps between the window frame and the wall can be sealed with a non-hardening mastic which will not shrink. Use a mastic gun to work the mastic in to a depth of about ½in.

For added protection, cover the mastic with a small timber moulding fixed with rustless 1in. round nails.

Defective paint spots on steel windows should be scraped, wire brushed, and cleaned with emery paper. Then apply a metal primer followed, as before, with undercoat and top coats.

Eventually, the build-up of paint may prevent proper closing of the window. If so, strip back to bare metal with a blowlamp and scraper before priming and painting again. Protect the glass from direct heat.

If wood casements warp they may bind. Try planing the sticking edge without removing the casement.

Where wood or metal casements are in a really poor condition – beyond simple repair, fix new units. The old windows can be replaced with any suitable modern unit.

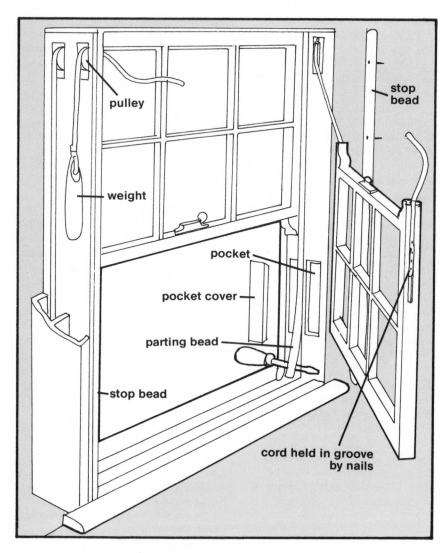

How a sash cord works.

Double glazing could be considered if you can afford it. There is more information on double glazing on page 126.

REPLACING SASH CORDS

Older houses often have vertical sliding sashes with balanced weights or cords. These are often in a poor state with worn frames and pulleys and broken or badly worn sash cords.

Broken sash cords are easily removed and replaced by new ones. First, remove the stop bead on the inside (this is pinned in place) and swing out the lower sash.

Remove the parting bead from its groove and swing out the upper sash.

Remove the broad nails which secure the cords in a short groove.

The pocket cover near the bottom of the box frame is normally secured by a screw. Remove the screw and the cover.

Remove the sash cord from its weight after taking it out of the pocket.

Before fitting the replacement cord,

164

stretch it by looping it round a post and pulling it.

To fit the new cord, tie a string to one end with a nail secured to the free end of the string. Thread the nail and string over the pulley and allow it to drop. It will draw the sash cord down the box frame. Cut the new cord to the same length as the old one and replace the weight in position.

Use galvanized broad-head nails to nail the free end to the sash. Replace the weight, pocket cover and beading.

Exactly the same method is used for the upper sash. The lower sash must be removed first though.

REPLACING OLD WINDOWS

To remove an old timber window frame, cut through the metal lugs, screws or nails holding it to the wall.

Locate these by slipping a thin knife blade between the frame and the wall. Cut through the nail or lug with a padsaw. It may be necessary to chisel away some of the wood to allow the padsaw to gain access to the nail or lug. Remove the frame by striking it with a mallet or by levering it out with a crowbar or similar implement.

To fit a replacement frame, choose a size which is slightly less all round than the 'hole' in the wall.

Manufacturers supply a vast range of standard frames. Their sizes are often in metric measure but usually have imperial equivalents indicated.

The simplest way to fit a new frame is, first, to drive wedges into a mortar joint on the walls on either side of the position of the frame. Obviously the mortar will have to be raked out of the joints first. Soak the wedges in preservative before fitting them and indicate on the brickwork their positions – when the frame is placed in position they will be covered up.

It will probably be necessary to use packing pieces to hold the new frame in place.

Drill through the frames into the wedges so that screws can be inserted to secure the frame.

holding wedges

new frame screwed to wedges

WINDOW SILLS

Most windows have timber sills of either hardwood or softwood. An unprotected sill will deteriorate rapidly. Softwood will rot and hardwoods (such as oak) which tend to have an open grain will become clogged by dirt and grime.

Paint can only be applied to sound timber.

Scrape or plane off any decayed timber to leave a clean, healthy surface before applying a coat of primer. Any rotten wood must be cut out and, if excessive, fresh timber inserted by gluing and pinning it in place. Then a coat of paint primer can be applied.

Keep the drip groove beneath the sill free from dirt at all times so that rainwater will drain away.

If a sill is really rotten, consider

For making a concrete replacement sill, chisel out the existing sill. Drive in four or five 6in. nails at even spaces into the bottom of the window frame. These should project well into the new sill. They provide reinforcement for the concrete. (a)

Screw a wood batten to the wall to provide anchorage for a timber shutter box in which to place the concrete. The tops of the timber pieces forming the shuttering should correspond with the intended top of the sill. Stretch a line of cord along the base of the shuttering inside the box to form a drip groove. (b)

For the concrete use a mix of 1 part fine shingle, 2 parts clean, sharp sand and 1 part cement. Pack the mix down hard in the shuttering. It should not be too sloppy – aim for a buttery consistency. (c)

When the concrete has set, remove the shuttering and the cord line and then allow to dry thoroughly before painting. (d)

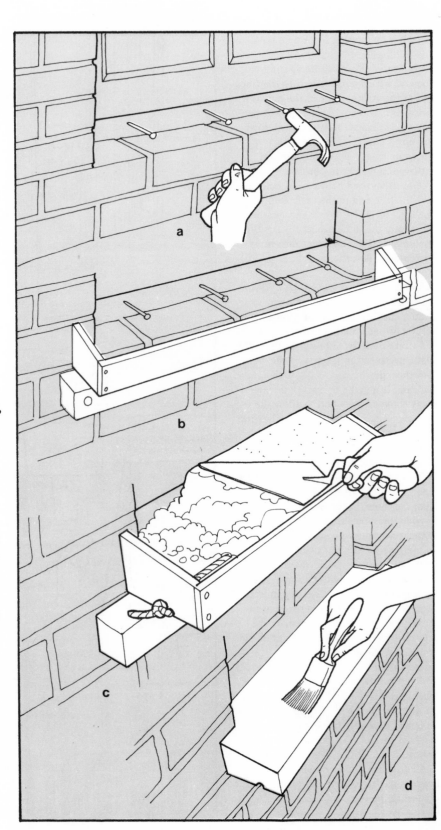

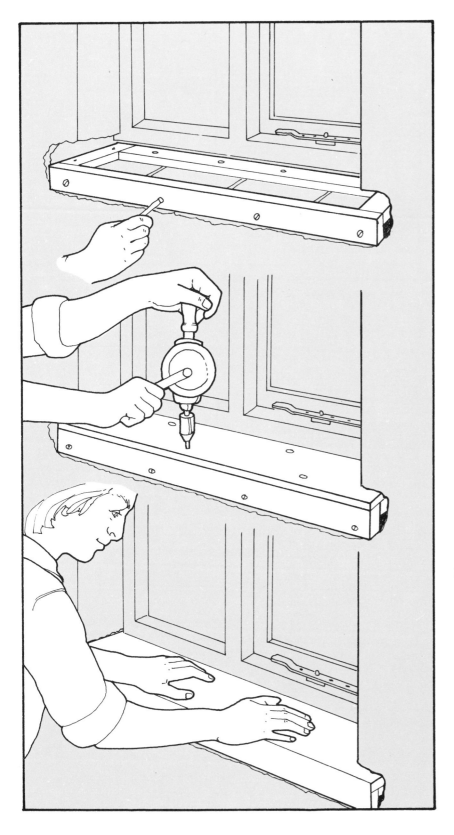

replacing it with concrete. Whereas timber is expensive and sometimes of suspect quality, a concrete sill is economical to construct and will last for many years if properly maintained.
Interior sills Conventional wood painted sills are difficult to maintain at their best. They are constantly being marked by normal household stains from over-filled flower pots, to carelessly placed drinks. They also collect dust, and moisture from condensation dripping down windows. In no time a fresh coat of paint starts to look shabby.

Replacement sills can be made with 18mm. resin bonded plywood, set on battens and faced with laminate. Thereafter a quick wipe over will keep the sill looking as new.

See page 115 for details of working with laminate.

Remove the old sill and screw 2in. × 1in. battens to the brickwork.

Cut plywood or chipboard to size and screw it to the battens with countersunk screws. Drill starter holes for the screws. The back edge must be well sealed to prevent damp penetration. Use a mastic compound.

Cut the laminate to size and stick it down. Apply a slightly oversize lipping piece to the front edge and trim back before fixing the sill laminate. If excess condensation is likely, use a waterproof resin adhesive to stick laminate to the sill.

A NEW PANE OF GLASS

If you have never cut glass before or you do not own a glass cutter ask your supplier to do the cutting for you. Measure the frame first. The new pane of glass must be $\frac{1}{8}$in. smaller than the width and length of the frame. Check that the diagonals are equal in case the frame is out of square.

Your supplier will also advise on the type of putty you need (it varies with metal and wood window frames) and the type of glass. Different types are needed for, say, a greenhouse.

If you need a circular piece of glass, make a cardboard template of the shape for your supplier to cut to.

The glass in wood frames is held in place by special pins called sprigs. Glass in metal frames is held by special clips; the existing ones can be used again if you are careful not to damage them.

Wear a pair of old leather gloves to lever out the broken glass from the rebates, starting at the top. Difficult pieces will be released when the old putty is cut out with a sharp chisel.

Remove the old sprigs which held the glass in place. Clean off all remaining traces of putty. Paint the frame immediately with a priming paint. (a)

Press a strip of putty with your thumb and forefinger around the entire rebate. Dipping your hands in water, at intervals, will prevent the putty sticking to them. (b)

Press the new glass into place applying pressure only on the edges – never in the middle. (c)

Use the edge of the chisel to tap new $\frac{5}{8}$in. sprigs at 6in. intervals around the rebate. Then apply another strip of putty as before. Use a putty knife to angle the putty to match surrounding windows. (d)

Trim off surplus putty visible from the room side of the glass. Allow to harden for a week before painting. (e)

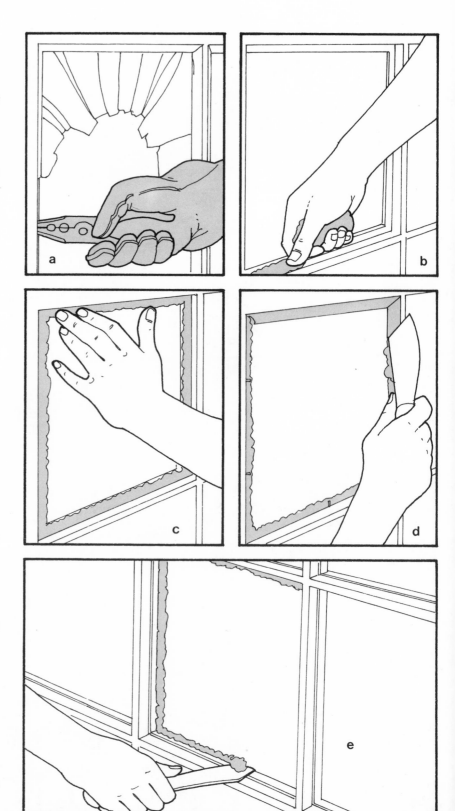

The Menace of Woodworm

Woodworm and dry rot are the main enemies of timber. Regular checks must be made on all the timber in and around the house – especially those out-of-sight areas in lofts and cellars where damage can spread unnoticed for months or years.

Several species of woodworm are likely to attack the house timbers. Eggs are laid in any small crevice or crack. Each egg hatches a larva which bores through the wood until it reaches a point just short of the surface. The larva has grown on its journey by feeding off the wood and it is now ready to enter the chrysalis stage where it remains before emerging at the surface as a beetle. As it emerges, fine dust is driven out, surrounding the tell-tale small hole in the wood surface.

So, when looking for woodworm, these are the signs you will be hoping *not* to see.

The beetle then continues the cycle. It mates and the female lays more eggs in crevices. It is because the beetles can fly that the damage can spring up in areas all over a loft or elsewhere.

It can take as long as three years for the larvae to reach the beetle stage though the beetle itself dies soon after laying its eggs.

Most people have heard of the furniture beetle since this is most common in furniture and structural timber. It is about $\frac{1}{8}$in. long. It is likely to attack softwood, plywood made with animal glue and furniture made of softwood or dry hardwood.

The spring and summer months are the best times to treat the trouble with insecticide since at this time of year, the beetle emerges to lay more eggs.

Death watch beetle attacks mainly old oak. It can be located by the ticking noise it makes. If it is allowed to remain in the wood it will eventually do so much damage that a structure can collapse.

A rarer species is the powder post beetle which attacks the sapwood of hardwoods. This can launch its attack in a timber yard and from there be carried to joineries in hardwoods which are then made into furniture or other things. The beetle emerges in May.

The house longhorn beetle is the most likely enemy to be found in the house roof. This is about $\frac{1}{2}$in. long. The hole it makes on emerging from the wood is oval in shape and a minimum of $\frac{1}{8}$in. wide. These are larger than the holes made by most other types of beetle.

Strangely, this type is most common in Surrey – being comparatively rare in other parts of the country. Under Building Regulations all structural timbers in certain parts of the country must be treated to prevent infestation. Any bad attack should be reported to the Building Research Establishment at Bucknalls Lane, Garston, Watford, Hertfordshire.

Since the larvae lives in the wood for about four years, there are few flight holes to reveal its presence; so detection is difficult.

TREATMENT

Having identified the likely type of beetle attack, what can be done?

It is possible that, despite finding a number of holes, there may no longer be any larvae present in a structure. Provided the timber has not been weakened in the attack, no drastic steps need be taken. Just squirt some suitable insecticide into the holes in the surface, not forgetting cracks and joints – just in case.

Always buy a reputable brand of insecticide. There are spray-on, injection, or brush-on types available but remember, no insecticide can be applied to painted or varnished surfaces.

For minor attacks apply a generous brush coat of insecticide, taking special care with crevices or cracks. This will make sure that any larvae near the surface are killed – as well as any newly laid eggs.

Complete the treatment by making a few small holes and injecting insecticide into each one.

Wear gloves when handling insecticides and extinguish any naked lights – insecticides are flammable and give off fumes. So, if treating a loft or cellar, use a torch if an electricity supply is not provided.

Although, as was said earlier, summer is the best time for treatment since this is when the beetles emerge to lay eggs, if you see the tell-tale signs at any other time of the year then start treatment immediately. Repeat the treatment again in the spring and continue to do so for several years if a severe attack is discovered.

Should no new signs of attack be noticed at the end of a year then you can be fairly certain that the trouble has ceased.

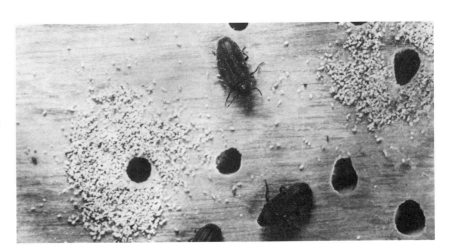

Dry and Wet Rot

Preventing rot is much better than curing it. Paint gives excellent protection – provided the coat remains unbroken and the timber is in a sound condition when the paint is applied.

Numerous preservatives are available. There are water soluble chemicals which are odourless and often colourless and can be painted over when dry. But rain will wash them away if they are not painted.

Solvent types are quicker drying and so can be painted over more quickly. They are not affected by rain.

Creosote is a cheaper type of preservative; it resists rain, is non-corrosive for nails and so is ideal for applying to garden fences. However, the fumes it gives off will damage plants near it so be careful when using it.

Dry rot is far more serious than beetle attacks and must be treated immediately it is discovered, since it spreads rapidly.

It is, in fact, a moisture carrying fungus which raises the moisture content of timber. The fungus consists of microscopic spores produced from mature fruiting bodies developed on decaying timber.

The spores are carried in the air and thus may be distributed over a wide area. Should they fall on timber with a moisture content higher than 20% they germinate, and mycellium (a cotton wool-like substance) develops fruiting bodies which liberate more spores into the air. And so the cycle continues.

The mycelium can penetrate crevices in masonry to reach timber. The timber, in time, will become brittle and cracked and will become a darker colour.

The main attacking fungus is *Merulis lacrymans*. Its white strands grow and form yellow and grey patches. The fruiting bodies form later and produce rust coloured spores.

Another fungus is 'cellar' fungus. This has black strands. The correct name for this type is *Coniophora cerebella*. The popular name arises from the fact that it is found in wet

conditions – typical of cellars – or where a roof has been leaking.

There are other types of fungi which are classed as wet rot because they do not spread from the immediate area of damp. Decay with these is most active where timber has been damp for a while and where there is poor ventilation.

Dry rot is usually hidden from view – under ground floor timber, in roof rafters, or in eaves that have been boxed in. These are the places to look.

A musty smell often indicates trouble, so take up a few floorboards – especially near skirtings – and use your nose. Stick a knife into the wood in a few places – if it goes in easily there could be trouble.

Examine anywhere where there are water pipes – especially areas like under closed-in baths.

Check that airbricks are not obstructed and that the damp proof course has not been covered with piles of earth or similar material.

Provided the rot is in a comparatively minor stage, you can treat it yourself. Cut out all affected timber and burn it immediately. Since the cause of the rot will still be present make sure it cannot start up again by providing permanent ventilation. The

Signs of wet rot round a kitchen window. Note the wrinkled and flaking paint.

rot can infiltrate brickwork and concrete so sterilise any of these adjoining the trouble spot with heat from a blowlamp.

Fix new timber to replace any cut out. Coat the new timber immediately with preservative, or buy pressure treated timber in which preservative sinks right into the wood during the process, which is not possible to achieve simply with a brush coating. Your timber yard should be able to supply you with pressure treated timber, though it will cost a bit more and may have to be specially ordered.

If a brush coating is used, then be generous with the preservative. Apply it when the timber is dry. Coat any parts exposed after cutting, and be especially careful to give a good coating to any areas in contact with brickwork.

Very serious attacks of rot should be handled professionally. The British Wood Preserving Association, 150 Southampton Row, London WC1B 5AL, will give you a list of firms who will guarantee their work for twenty years.

Tiles for Walls and Floors

CERAMIC TILES

Although they provide a hardwearing and long lasting floor-covering or wallcovering, the odd one may get cracked.

Individual tiles can be replaced without disturbing the surrounding areas, or old tiles that have become crazed can be replaced with decorative tiles or tile-prints (see page 176).

Lift out any loose undamaged tiles, scrape off the old adhesive and refix with ceramic tile adhesive. Check before fixing that the new tile will lie flush with the surface. If it projects, chip away the old backing material (probably a sand and cement mix) from the wall or floor.

The grout line between wall tiles inevitably becomes discoloured. Rake out the old grout and refill the joints with new material. New grout cement is bought in powder form and mixed with water to a thick, creamy consistency.

Wall tiles can be given a colour change by painting with gloss paint.

If necessary, use a chisel and hammer to chip the old mortar or adhesive from the wall before re-fixing a loose tile.

If the new tile is likely to be splashed by water use a waterproof adhesive.

An old, worn screwdriver is ideal for raking out discoloured grout.

Use a damp sponge to spread the new grout cement over a square yard of the tiles at a time. Do not mix more grout than can be used in half an hour or it will set in the mixing container. Do not mix fresh grout on top of any that has started to set – the fresh material will also start to set immediately.

Before changing the colour of tiles with gloss paint, rub down the surface with coarse emery paper to provide a key for the paint. Defective grout between tiles must be replaced before painting.

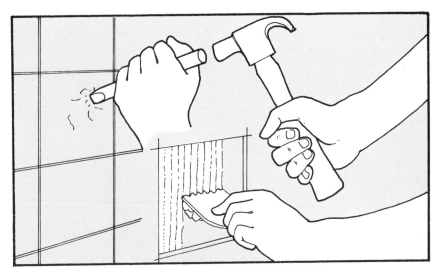

VINYL TILES

It is always worth while buying a few extra tiles at the outset in case any have to be replaced at a later date. It is sometimes difficult to find individual tiles of a particular design or colour if they are a few years old.

Never simply re-lay floor tiles that have lifted. The lifting indicates that the original adhesive was the wrong type or that the floor is damp. Any damp must be remedied before a new tile is laid, otherwise the problem will re-occur.

Originally, the tiles may have been laid on felt paper or hardboard. If it was felt paper then this will inevitably be torn off when the damaged tile is removed; if so it must be replaced. The new tile, though the same make, may be a slightly different colour. This could be because a protective coat of sealer was applied to the original tiles. Sealer is available from d-i-y shops. To obtain a uniform colour, may necessitate sanding off the old sealer from the entire floor before re-coating.

If ceramic floor tiles are not laid on an even bed of adhesive, they will be cracked by chair legs, or other pressure exerted on hollow spots. Remove a damaged tile (see page 171) and replace using correct adhesive. Alternatively, fix as for quarry tiles (page 174).

A partly lifted vinyl tile can be pulled off, taking care not to disturb surrounding tiles.

Remove remaining fragments with a scraper or a broad, worn chisel, working from the centre outwards.

Spread adhesive on the floor. Warm the tile in an oven to make it pliable. It can then be arched and lowered into position.

To mark out a border tile, a spare tile of the same dimensions is needed. (A) Lay the replacement tile (B) over the last full tile in the row. Position the spare tile with its edge against the skirting and draw a pencil line where its other edge meets the replacement tile.
Cut along the pencil line and fit the replacement tile.

Cutting around obstacles involves a difficult marking-out procedure. A simpler method is to make a cardboard pattern of the required shape and transfer this to the replacement tile. A 'Mimic' tool can be employed for tracing awkward shapes.

Use a sharp knife (such as a Stanley type) to cut slits along the back edge of the tile so that it can be slotted into position. The slits will not be noticed behind the obstacle.

Make a cardboard pattern for L-shapes at corners.

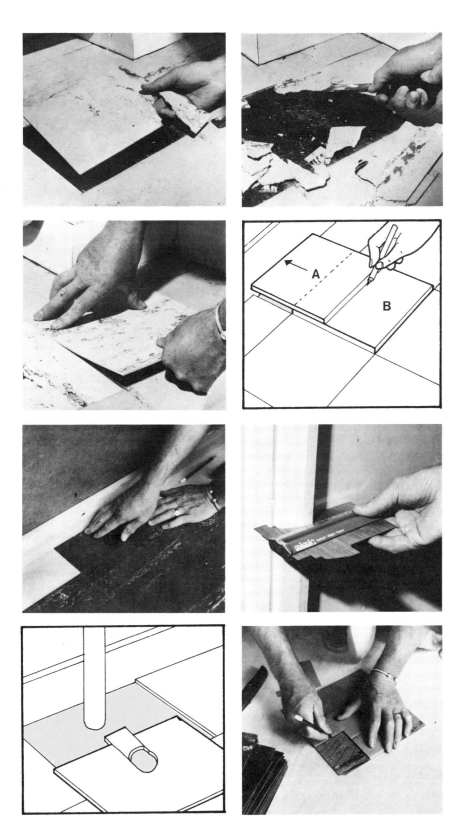

QUARRY TILES

These are difficult to cut. Awkward shapes are best cut into several smaller, convenient shapes and laid jigsaw-fashion around obstacles.

Replacement tiles and adhesive are available from builders' merchants.

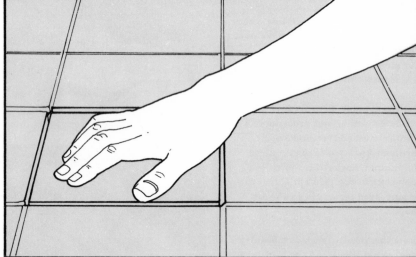

Craze the complete surface of the damaged tile. Then, using a cold chisel and a hammer, remove the tile, working from the centre outwards.

Check that the new tile lies just below the surface of the surrounding tiles. If it does not, then chisel away the old mortar (probably a sand and cement mix) from the floor.

Spread a mix of one part cement to 3 parts sand on the floor and press the new tile into place. Remove surplus material which squelches to the surface.

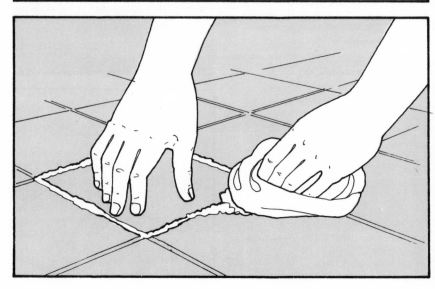

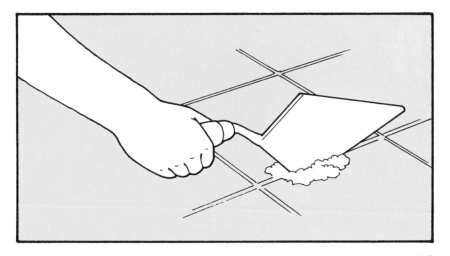

After 24 hours, fill the joints with a mix of 1 part cement to 4 parts sand. Use a trowel to force it well into the joints.

Your supplier may agree to cut a tile for you for a small charge. This is worth paying since the tiles can crack easily if cut incorrectly. If you have to do it yourself, mark the cut line on the back of the tile. Place the tile on the edge of a brick and tap along with a cold chisel and club hammer.

Tap the tile against the edge of the brick to break it along the line. Awkward shapes must be nibbled off with pincers as for ceramic tiles.

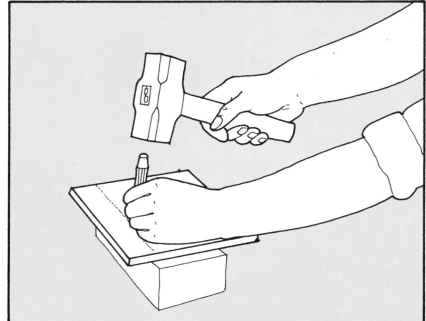

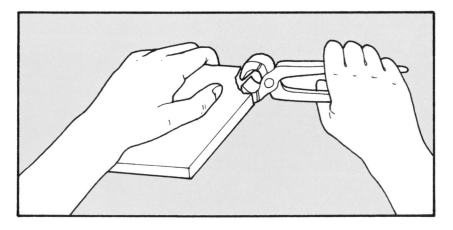

Fireplaces

Fumes and heat from an open fire can cause tiles to become crazed or the pointing between the bricks to deteriorate.

Make sure you can obtain a matching tile before removing a damaged one. This can be a problem with older fireplaces.

A possible alternative to replacement is to cover the defective tile with a Sellotape tile print. These are available in a variety of designs and pictures, but do not use them where tiles get excessively hot near the fire opening. Alternatively fit a non-matching decorative tile.

Where damage is extensive, the whole fireplace can be covered with new, thin decorative ceramic tiles.

A crazed ceramic tile can be covered with a suitable decorative tile print. These are just pressed into place after peeling away the paper backing.

Where crazing is extensive, to give a new look, fix modern ceramic tiles over the existing ones, using the special adhesive supplied with the tiles. (a)

To remove a single, damaged tile, first drill through the centre with a masonry bit fitted to a brace or power drill. (b)

Use a cold chisel and club hammer to chip away the tile from the centre outwards. Be careful not to damage surrounding tiles and always wear protective goggles. (c)

Replace the new tile using ceramic tile adhesive. Use a thick enough layer to leave the tile flush with the surface of the others. (d)

Use a damp cloth to remove any adhesive that squelches to the surface. Special grouting cement is available to fill in the joints. Press this well into the joints using a damp sponge. (e)

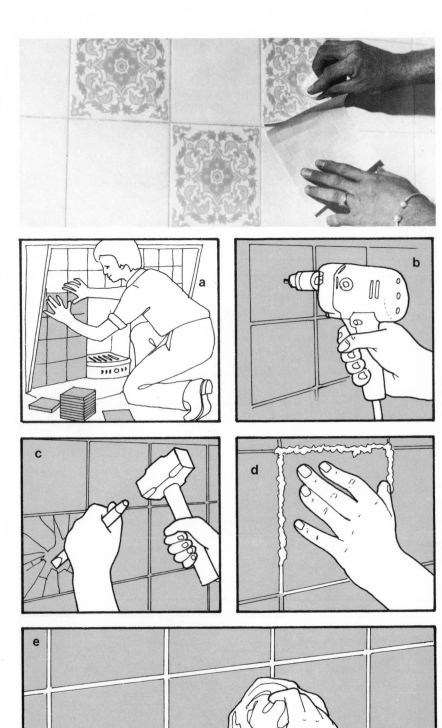

BRICK FIREPLACES

If a brick fireplace needs repointing, the mortar used depends on whether the fireplace is used for an open fire or whether it is purely decorative. If still in use, make a mix of 1 part Portland cement, 3 parts lime and ten parts heat resistant sand (called silver sand).

If purely decorative, then you can use the normal brickwork mortar mix (see caption below).

It is possible to add a coloured dye, available from builders' merchants, to the mortar mix to give a more decorative effect. In this case, though, you would have to repoint all the joints between the bricks in order to achieve a uniform overall effect.

Replacing a brick Usually it is the hearth surround that suffers the most wear and tear. Consequently loose bricks are usually found here. Corners are especially prone to damage.

Remove the loose or damaged brick using a bolster chisel and club hammer. Chip through the mortar joints to form a clean, square-cut cavity. (a)

Wet the brick with clean water before applying a mortar mix (3 parts sand to 1 part cement) to the bricks with a trowel. (b)

Use the handle of a trowel to tap the brick into place. Any of the cement that squelches to the surface should be cleaned back to leave a ¼in. recess in the joints. When the cement has set the joint can be repointed. (c)

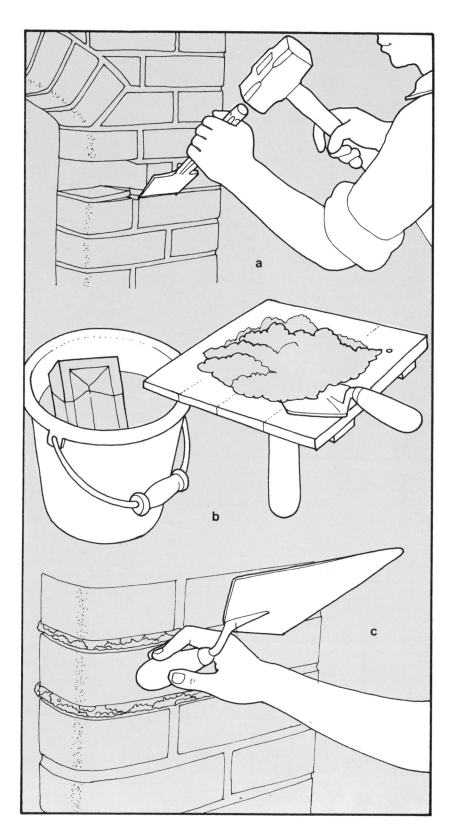

STONE FIREPLACES
The replacement of loose or broken stones is covered in the illustrations and captions on this page.

Remove the loose stone by chipping away the existing cement mortar. Clean out the cavity. (a)

Wet the stone with clean water and butter on a mortar mix (as for bricks). (b)

Replace the stone, using wood wedges to hold it in line with the existing stones. (c)

When the cement has set, remove the wedges and re-point. (d)

MARBLE FIREPLACES

It is possible to replace a broken piece of marble with an epoxy resin adhesive.

If very small fragments of the broken piece are lost, the gaps can be filled with the adhesive. Follow adhesive manufacturer's instructions closely. Usually the cavity from which the piece came and the back of the broken piece have to be dusted down with a stiff brush and rubbed with fine glasspaper to make a key for the adhesive.

Apply the adhesive to both surfaces and then press the broken piece back into place. Hold it in position until it has set, using adhesive tape. (a)

Fill in chips with epoxy resin adhesive. If necessary, add a vegetable dye (available from builder's merchants) to match up with the colour of the marble. (b)

When set, wash the repair, using clean water to remove all traces of adhesive. Finally, polish the area with a fine carborundum stone. (c)

FIREBACKS

A fireback protects the chimney structural brickwork from being damaged by heat and smoke. Provided a fireback is only slightly cracked, repairs can be made with plastic fireclay.

The cracks must be raked out thoroughly to remove all dust particles. Use a trowel and wire brush. Soak the cracks thoroughly with water. Work the fireclay well into the cracks and remove excess clay before it dries.

Where damage is more extensive a new fireback has to be fitted. The old fireback can be chipped away with a club hammer and cold chisel.

A new fireback often has to be fitted in two sections. They are normally supplied as a complete unit so ask your supplier to separate the lower and top sections for you.

When the two sections are fitted in the fireplace, the joint between them should be filled with fire cement using a trowel. The throat of the chimney may then have to be built up using a sand and cement mortar.

Minor cracks can be repaired with plastic fireclay. The crack is cleaned out thoroughly, dampened with water, and the fireclay forced into the cavity and smoothed level. (a)

Extensive damage will mean fitting a new fireback. First, remove the broken back section, using a club hammer and brick bolster. When the upper and lower sections have been taken out, remove the loose infill that forms the backing. (b)

Fit the lower half of the new fireback accurately in position. Fill the recess behind the lower half using a mix of 1 part cement, 1 part lime and 10 parts sand. (c)

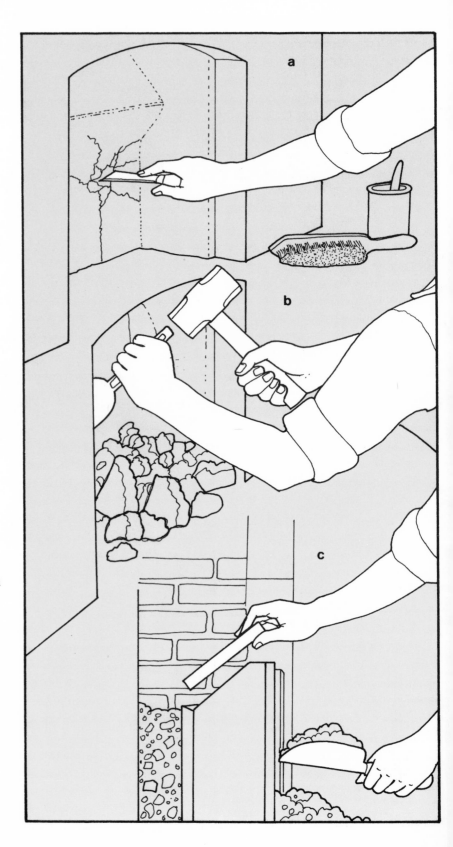

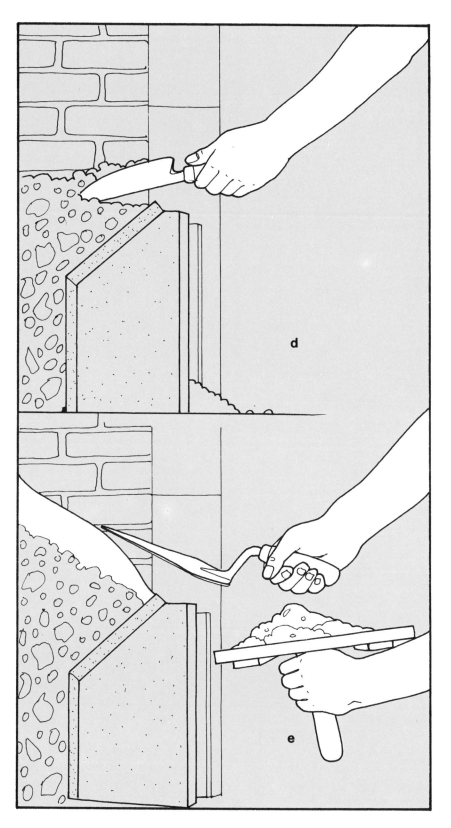

Fit the top section in place and fill the cavity behind it in the same way. (d)

Use a rendering mix of 1 part cement to 4 parts sand to angle the top of the fireback to meet the chimney brickwork and form the 'throat' to the flue. (e)

Looking After Gates

If a gate will not close properly or is sagging, try tightening the hinge screws. If they will not tighten, remove the hinge, fill the screw holes with wooden plugs and replace screws.

Alternatively, use thicker screws, enlarging the holes in the hinges with a drill and countersink bit.

If the hinges themselves are faulty, fit new ones.

WOODEN GATES

Examine the joints in a wooden gate to see if they are loose or have come apart. If they have, then take the gate off its hinges, prise all the joints apart and clean out all the old paint and glue. Apply preservative to all areas. Reassemble the gate using waterproof glue in the joints. Before the glue sets, check that the gate is square.

To reposition a sagging gate post, you must first dig it out. Inspect the base for rot. Cut back to sound timber if necessary. Apply a liberal coat of preservative.

Fix the post vertically in position and fill the hole round it with rubble and concrete. If necessary, insert a concrete spur to bolt the post to.

If the gate jams and the problem is minor, try planing off a small amount from the upper part of the stile to a bevel before repainting. (a)

Poor joints can be reinforced with galvanised metal brackets available from d-i-y shops. (b)

If a new gate post has to be fitted, dig a hole at least 18in. deep. Refix the post and pack out the hole with rubble topped by 6in. of concrete (mix as for fence posts). (c)

A damaged panelled garage door can best be prepared by screwing an exterior quality plywood panel over the entire lower section and into the outer framework of the door. It is important to see that the back of the panel is primed before fixing and that all edges of the panel are primed thoroughly before painting. (d)

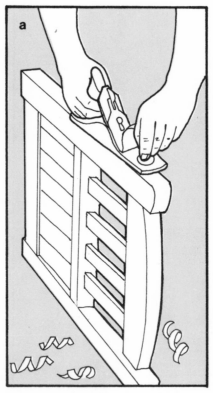

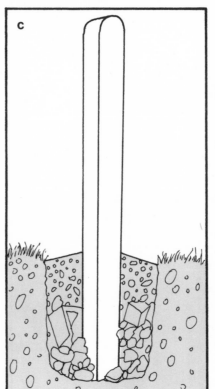

IRON GATES

Rust is the biggest enemy of iron gates. Make regular checks to ensure that the paint film is unbroken. Even small cracks are an open invitation to rust.

Iron gates often have cracks where moisture becomes trapped and sets up corrosion.

Deal with any rust spots immediately, by scraping the corrosion back to bright metal (it need not gleam). Tackle minor spots with emery paper, or use a wire brush followed by abrasive paper.

It must be remembered that paint alone is not a complete protection against rust; a metal primer is needed underneath.

Before priming, clean the surface with white spirit. Apply the priming coat at once or rusting will start again immediately.

A blowlamp and scraper or shave hook is a useful and speedy method for cleaning rust from an iron gate.

Brush primer well into any rivets, bolts, nails or screwheads. Give all metal edges a second coat (after the first has dried) as they are susceptible to knocks.

If using a wire brush to clear away rust, it is advisable to protect the eyes from flying particles by wearing goggles.

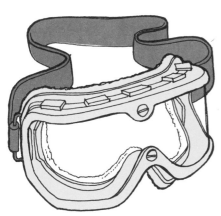

Looking After Fences

One popular type of fence is a close-board type consisting of feather-edged pales (vertical boards) fixed to horizontal arris rails. The arris rails are slotted into sockets in the posts and the pales overlap each other. The height of this type of fence can be anything you like.

Interwoven and interlocking panels are cheaper than the close board fences. Here the wide ready-made panels are simply fixed to the posts with nails. The interwoven type does have gaps in the woven sections but still provides a reasonable amount of privacy.

Interlocking panels ensure complete privacy.

Palisade fencing is a traditional boundary fence. It is ideal as a backing for flower beds since it allows plenty of sunlight and fresh air through. The pales, again, are fixed to the arris rails, which, in turn, are secured to the posts.

Ranch-style fences are becoming more and more popular as simple boundary fences, especially between front gardens of neighbouring houses. Consisting simply of a couple of horizontal timbers fixed to evenly spaced posts (often only about 2 or 3ft. high), their attraction is ease of maintenance as well as their appearance.

Rustic fences consist of a series of criss-crossed rustic poles and give a garden a rural atmosphere.

Trellis is usually used as a capping section along a solid fence. It is lightweight and cheap and is especially useful for supporting climbing plants.

Ranch-style plastic fences in various heights have several advantages over wooden types. They will not rot and are virtually maintenance-free. Normally a quick wipe over with a damp sponge will keep them shining white.

INSTALLING A FENCE

Unless special care is taken to install a new fence, you can be sure that it will not be long before you have to do some maintenance work on it.

The first thing to do is to mark out, with a string line, the path that the fence has to follow.

Place a wooden peg into the ground at either end of the boundary and then tie a piece of string between them, pulling it tight.

The holes for the posts now can be dug. The spacings will vary according to the type and height of the fence. Manufacturers of individual fences will give you guidance – though in some cases, such as 6ft. long panel types, the posts will obviously be set 6ft. apart.

The most difficult part of installing a fence is digging the holes for the posts. The easiest way out is to hire a post hole borer from a local hire shop. These are turned into the ground rather like a corkscrew. After each few turns, the borer is withdrawn and the earth collected on the blades is deposited nearby. This is continued until the hole is the right depth.

And this depth is another point on which you will need individual advice from manufacturers. However, as a general rule, if the fence is under 5ft. high, then a 2ft. deep hole is required. Above 5ft. the hole should be 2ft. 6in. at least.

The kind and size of posts is often decided for you since many fences are supplied in kit form. However, if you select a type which leaves you the choice then you can opt for one of two things:

For appearance sake, most people prefer to use all-timber posts. However, these will rot in the ground eventually (though with preservative treatment this risk can be considerably reduced). The alternative is to buy concrete spurs from a builders' merchant and use these in the ground with the timber posts bolted to them 1ft. or so clear of the soil.

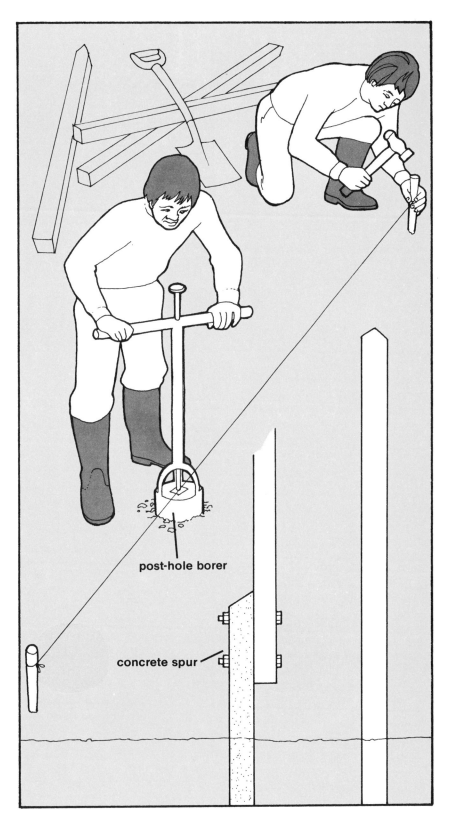

post-hole borer

concrete spur

The thickness of posts varies with the fence type. Normally, for fences up to 5ft. high, 4in. square posts are needed. Above this height 5in. × 4in. posts are needed. If possible, choose Western red cedar as the timber for posts; this is particularly durable.

Earlier, mention was made of preservative treatment. The best way to protect the bottom of a post from rotting in the ground is to soak it overnight, before fixing, by standing it in a bucket of preservative. Creosote is a common preservative, though there are several other proprietary types available. This method will allow the preservative really to soak into the timber – something that does not happen with a straightforward brush application. Since fumes from creosote will damage plant life, a non-bituminous preservative is preferable in certain situations. Solignum is one example.

Fixing the posts A post can be fixed in the ground in one of several ways. It is not sufficient to insert a post in the ground and ram earth around it. After only a short while the soil would become softened by rain and the post would lean one way or the other.

Even a complete filling of the hole round the post with concrete has its disadvantages. The timber, in time, will shrink away from the concrete leaving gaps for rainwater to run into and eventually cause rot. And, of course, should you ever want to remove the fence to install a new type, removing the posts will be a real problem.

Soak the bottom of the posts overnight in preservative.

Check that the post is upright with a spirit level.

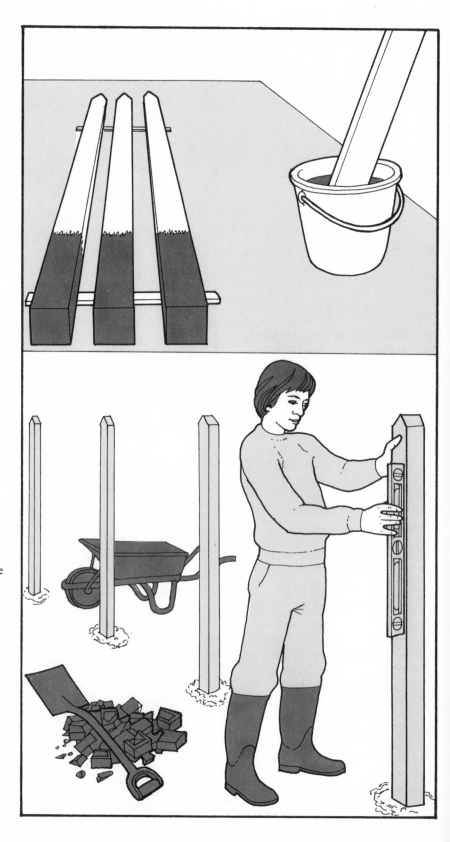

The best method is to pack out the bottom of the hole with pieces of brick, rubble and other hardcore. This will allow good drainage. Put in the post and the hole can then be filled with alternate layers of earth and rubble, finishing with a layer of concrete.

Check that the post is upright with a spirit level – it must be truly vertical.

You can, of course, choose concrete posts. They will not rot but they do have the disadvantage of being unattractive to look at.

If you do want to use them, you can, for economy, make concrete posts yourself using a simple timber mould. The method of casting these is to make a wooden frame of two sides (to the correct post length and thickness) and with end pieces attached. Nail this framework together and also nail several small timber battens across the top opening.

A concrete mix of 1 part Portland cement: $1\frac{1}{2}$ parts sand and 3 parts of coarse aggregate is needed. To reinforce each post, a mild steel rod can be used down the centre.

If holes are needed through the posts for fixing wire fencing to them, insert oiled steel pins through the concrete when wet. These can be withdrawn after the concrete has set.

If wood fencing panels are to be joined to the posts, then wallplugs set into the posts during casting will allow wood fillets to be screwed to them to support the fence panels.

A simple timber mould for making a concrete post.

Constructing the rest of the fence

If the fence is a type supported by arris rails, then these should be located in the sockets of the posts as the posts are fixed in the ground.

Erect all the posts and rails before fixing the fencing itself. If pales are being used, then the first one must be fixed absolutely vertically or the whole lot will be out of line.

This is also important with close board fencing and palisade fencing.

At the bottom of the fence, a gravel board is needed to help prevent rot setting up in the bottom edges of the fencing. A gravel board is simply a horizontal board secured to the fence posts.

Although fixing methods vary with panel fences, in general the posts will be set with 6ft. gaps between them for 6ft. panels and the panels nailed to the posts. Always use galvanized or aluminium alloy nails which will not rust.

The tops of the posts should be shaped to allow rainwater to drain away. So cut them to a bevel shape. Obviously it is much easier to do this before a post is fixed.

An alternative method is to cap the posts with a piece of zinc or aluminium, nailed in place.

If the fence was not pre-treated with preservative, then see to this as soon as the fence is up. More information on preservatives is given on page 186.

The top of a fence post can rot through rainwater collecting on it. Cut the top of the post at an angle to allow water to drain away. Remember that it is easier to do this before setting the post into the ground.

Alternatively, cap the post with zinc or lead. Use these methods on an old post that is rotting from the top. Cut back to sound timber first, though.

FENCE MAINTENANCE

Garden fences have to withstand a regular buffeting from the elements. If they are not fixed firmly, the wind can blow them down; if they are not protected with preservative, they will inevitably rot.

A regular inspection of fences is essential. If damage is spotted early on, it can usually be dealt with effectively and cheaply by making a simple repair. The longer it is left, the worse it will become and eventually replacement may be the only course – at a price.

The simplest form of maintenance is to apply wood preservative or creosote to a fence. This will protect it from rot, woodboring insects and fungus.

Check manufacturer's instructions to find out how often the treatment should be repeated. Usually it must be repeated every other year.

Unlike other preservatives, creosote will darken the colour of the wood. Choose a creosote which has a British Standard number on the container and apply it when the timber is dry – creosote will not penetrate damp timber.

DAMAGED OR ROTTEN FENCE POSTS

If a fence post has rotted at the bottom and the damage does not extend too far up, cut out the rotted section and refix the post to a concrete spur available from a builders' merchant.

If damage is extensive, the whole post will have to be dug out. This can often be hard work. Buy a replacement post of the same size – usually they are 4in. square or 5in. × 4in.

Before attempting to remove the post, take off one fence board from either side of the post and remove also the gravel boards on either side. You may have to cut through the arris rails in order to free these from the post.

Wedge the fence temporarily in position on either side of the post.

Dig out the earth around a post that needs renewing. If the post cannot be removed easily, it will be necessary to rig up a lever using an old post, bricks, ropes and nails. The fulcrum can also be on the side of the post nearest the man, in which case he would push down on it.

Fit the new post in a hole at least 2ft. deep. Fill it with rubble, well rammed down for the first 6in., then pack at least 1ft. of concrete (dryish) mix before covering the top with soil. The mix should be 1 part cement to 4 parts all-in aggregate. Check with a spirit level that the post is upright both at the front and side.
Refix the arris rails, fence boards and gravel boards.

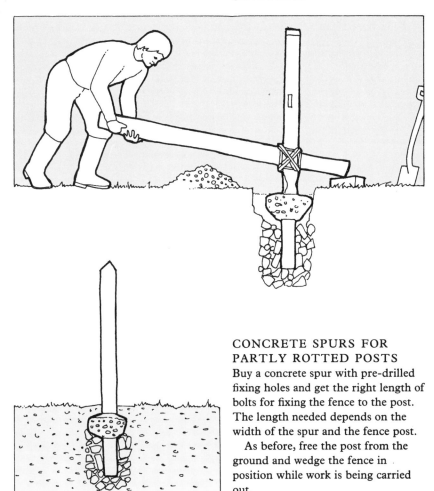

CONCRETE SPURS FOR PARTLY ROTTED POSTS

Buy a concrete spur with pre-drilled fixing holes and get the right length of bolts for fixing the fence to the post. The length needed depends on the width of the spur and the fence post.

As before, free the post from the ground and wedge the fence in position while work is being carried out.

Dig out the old post stump. Place the concrete spur in the hole; this must be at least 2ft. deep. Check with a spirit level that the spur is upright. Pack out the hole with bricks and rubble to keep the spur in position. (a)

Fill the top of the hole with concrete (using the same mix as for fence posts). When the concrete has set, fix the post in place and tighten the bolts firmly. Finally refix the fence. (b)

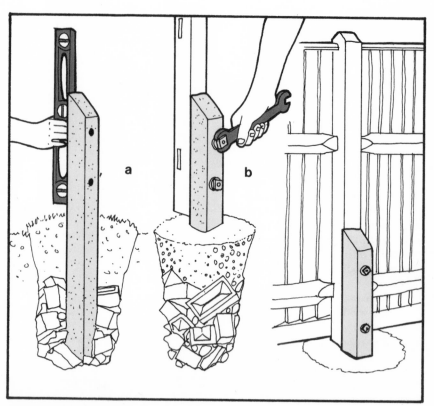

FEATHER EDGED BOARDS
Where boards have not been treated with preservative they are likely to warp and split.

Isolated boards can be removed and new lengths be inserted without removing the whole section of fence between two posts.

If a board is in reasonable condition and has just worked loose, there is no need to buy a new length.

Use aluminium alloy nails for re-fixing.

Remove the damaged board by punching the fixing nails through into the arris rail. Use a nail punch and hammer. If the nails can be extracted with a claw hammer or pincers use one of these. Often the nails will have rusted making extraction impossible. (a)

Repeat this operation by punching the nails securing the thick, outer edge of the adjacent board through into the arris rail. (b)

Fit the new board by sliding its thin edge under the thick edge of the adjacent board. Board edges usually overlap by about ½in. Nail through the overlapping edges into the arris rail. (c)

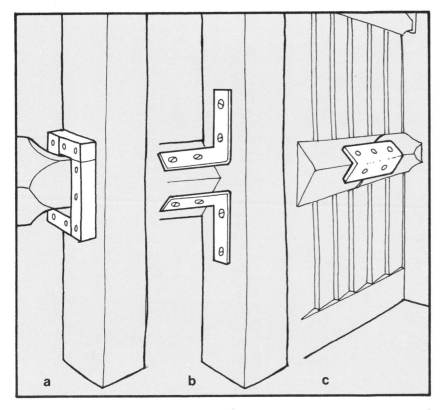

A broken end can be re-secured by making a frame of 1in. square battens around the recess in the post. Screw the battens to the post. See that they are well treated with a wood preservative before fixing – especially the end grain. (a)

Proprietary extension brackets are simple to fit if the end of a rail breaks. (b)

Repair brackets are made also for splits which occur in the middle of a rail. (c)

If buying a completely new rail, it should be at least 3in. longer than the space between the posts. The extra amount allows for the tenons which go inside the posts. (d)

If a fence post is loose, it can be pushed out of position temporarily to enable both ends of the new rail to be slotted into the recesses. If posts are solid in the ground, fit one of the rail ends into the recess; fit the other end using one of the methods already described. (e)

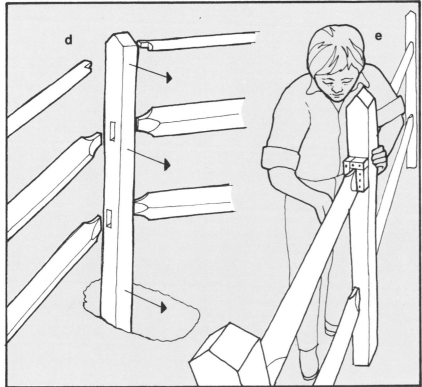

ARRIS RAILS
The arris rails which stretch between the posts are slotted into recesses in the post ends. The ends of the rails are shaped where they enter the post. Often this shaped end breaks off when the rest of the rail is in good condition. Here, a simple repair can be made to avoid having to buy a new rail.

If a complete rail needs renewing, it is best to shape the ends of the rails into tenons so that they can slot into the posts as before, provided the posts are loosened first.

GRAVEL BOARDS
At the base of a fence there is often a wide piece of timber – about 6in. × 1in. – which is called the gravel board. This prevents damp rising up and damaging the fence boards.

The gravel board must be kept clear of a build up of soil and plants.

If the board gets damaged or shows signs of rotting, replace it immediately. It may be slotted into a recess in the fence posts or be nailed to wood blocks.

Having removed the old gravel board, dig a small trench. This makes it easier to manoeuvre the new board into position.

Fix a 2in. × 2in. batten to each fence post. Screw them in place keeping their tops in line with the bottom of the boards. These battens are then ready to receive the gravel boards.

Nail the gravel board to the wood battens. It should be flush with the front of the fence. When the positioning is correct, fill in the trench.

Where concrete posts are encountered, drive pegs into the ground alongside the posts. At least 1ft. of each peg must be buried. Fix the gravel boards to the pegs.

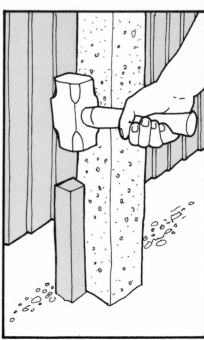

Simple Furniture Repairs

It is surprising how often an uneven chair leg, a burn mark or a crack is allowed to remain for a long time to spoil the appearance of an otherwise attractive piece of furniture.

Many basic repairs are well within the scope of the ordinary handyman.

Even when a solid piece of furniture is looking really shabby, it need not necessarily be thrown on the scrap heap. It can be given a facelift to modernise it and keep it in service. Decorative coverings such as laminate, mirror tiles and veneers are not difficult to apply.

UNEVEN LEGS

If a chair has one leg longer than the other three, it is a simple matter to measure the even legs and saw a little off the long leg. After sawing, clean up the cut edges with fine glasspaper.

Where one leg is shorter than the others there is a choice. Either the three longer legs can be sawn down to match the length of the odd one or the odd

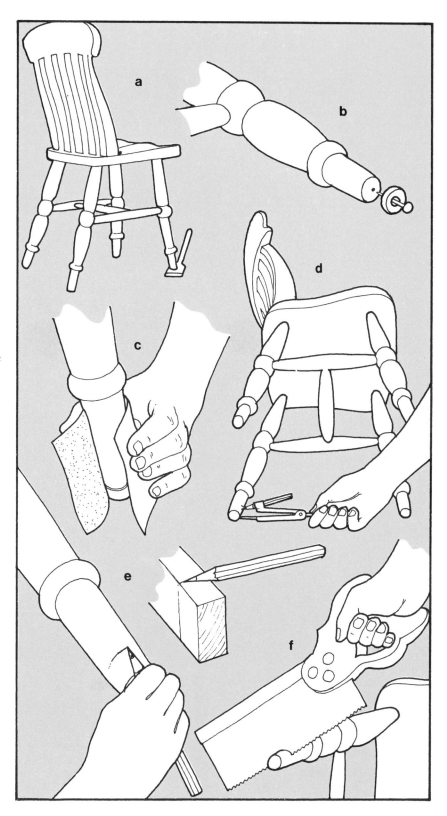

With the chair standing on a level surface, slip different-size pieces of wood under the shorter leg until the chair no longer wobbles. (a)

Trim the piece of wood to suit the shape of the leg, and screw it in place with a countersunk screw. Drill pilot holes for the screw in both the chair leg and the wood block to prevent the screw causing splits as it sinks in. (b)

Fill the joint between the new piece and the leg with wood filler. Allow it to set before rubbing it smooth with the grain and painting. (c)

Alternatively, use compasses to transfer the thickness of the block to the other three legs. (d)

Draw a guide line for the saw around all four faces of each leg. (e)

Saw down to the guide lines. Smooth edges with fine glasspaper. (f)

one can be built up with a wood block to match the others.

The latter will be less noticeable where a piece of furniture is to be painted, for there will be no problem about matching the wood block to suit the grain and colour of the leg.

A SPLIT LEG

Misuse of furniture on castors can cause the legs to split. Castors are usually screwed into a housing which, in turn, is located in a hole drilled in the underside of the leg. The housing is held in place by spikes that bite into the wood. After unscrewing the castor the housing can be prised out with a screwdriver.

SCRATCHES

Hairline scratches can often be made less noticeable by rubbing shoe polish of the same shade into the surface.

Deeper scratches that have penetrated through the protective coating on the wood can be smoothed out with burnishing cream.

Wedge the crack apart so that woodworking adhesive can be squirted inside. (a)

Use G cramps to hold the legs in position while the glue sets. Clean off glue that squelches to the surface. (b)

Remove the cramps, knock back the spiked housing, screw on the castor. (c)

Fill deeper scratches with shellac varnish stain of the correct colour. This should be thinned with methylated spirit according to the manufacturer's instructions. Apply several coats with a small brush until the varnish is just proud of the surface. Then rub down the dry varnish with fine wet or dry abrasive paper. Finally use metal polish to bring the shine back to the surface. (d)

Rub down minor scratches with fine wet or dry abrasive paper until the scratch is removed. (e)

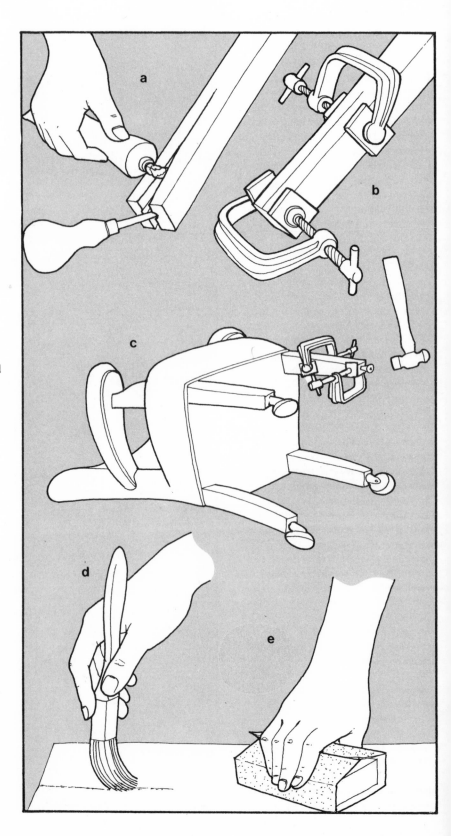

HEAT AND WATER MARKS

Furniture tops with a shellac or cellulose finish are liable to be stained by heat or water marks. Provided the mark has not penetrated through the protective coating to the wood, it can be removed with a mild abrasive such as burnishing cream.

HANDI-VENEER

Handi-veneer is a simple way of giving a new timber grained surface to an old piece of furniture. This has adhesive already on the back. It is fixed in position using a warm iron.

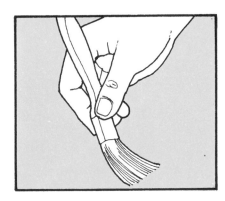

Use a sharp knife to scrape away the scorch mark completely. Rub the area with fine glasspaper.

Where the surface was previously covered with a clear finishing liquid (varnish, polish, etc.) apply transparent French polish according to the manufacturer's instructions. Several applications will be needed. Use fine glasspaper to rub down the area carefully. Finally, apply metal polish to bring back the shine.

Use burnishing cream to remove heat and water marks. Use a soft cloth and work in the direction of the grain. Fill cracks with plastic woodfiller. Allow to set and then glasspaper lightly until flush with the surface.

Apply a varnish stain which matches the colour of the wood. Finish with a clear finish where one was previously used.

Cut Handi-veneer to size with scissors; peel off the protective paper backing. (a)

Smooth it into place with heat from a warm electric iron. (b)

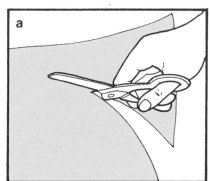

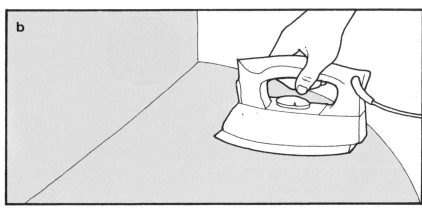

Adhesives for Everyday Use

Choosing the right glue to stick two things together can be a somewhat confusing business nowadays. Yet, if you know exactly what you are looking for, the extensive selection available will be very much in your favour.

Not so long ago there was very little choice and therefore repairs, whilst not exactly carried out on a hit or miss basis were not always successful.

If you use the right type of modern glue and the two items do not adhere, or soon fall apart, then the explanation will probably be that you did not follow the directions properly.

For example, you will always find that the directions say that the surfaces of the materials being joined should be clean, dry and free from grease and dust. This is not something that can be done by a quick wipe with a rag or by blowing dust from the surface.

It means clean them with soap and water, white spirit or whatever is appropriate for the materials in question.

You will find, too, that some glues will stick only to roughened surfaces, and others will work only on smooth, non-absorbent ones.

Do not take lightly warnings about using naked lights nearby or about providing adequate ventilation. Many glues have flammable bases and others give off vapours which can be harmful if inhaled for a long time.

ANIMAL GLUES
These glues are made from the skin and bones of animals and will stick leather, paper and wood. Two types are available, a cold setting type and a Scotch glue.

The latter has to be heated for use. When it cools it sets, and in a cold atmosphere, it can cool too quickly – before you have time to use it, for it starts setting immediately it is taken away from the heat. When using it to glue joints, it is essential to apply cramps for a longer period than with other types of adhesive.

One other disadvantage of Scotch glue is that it is not waterproof, but it is extremely valuable for work such as sticking down wood veneers.

Cold-setting animal glues are made in liquid form and take longer to set than Scotch glue. More time is available, therefore, to position the pieces being joined.

PVA
This type of adhesive is often specified for use in the manufacturers' instructions in a whole variety of products that come in kit form.

The name in full, is polyvinylacetate. The adhesive comes ready to use on wood, paper, fabrics, card and leather.

In woodwork, the adhesive (a white liquid) is applied to one half of the joint only before cramps are applied.

SYNTHETIC RESIN ADHESIVE
This is usually supplied in powder form for mixing with water.

Used for woodwork, these adhesives are resistant to water, acid and heat and will not stain the wood. The glue is stronger than the wood it sticks together so that once it has set, a joint cannot be dismantled or pulled apart without damaging the wood.

How long the glue takes to set depends on the temperature in the workshop or room. The hotter it is, the shorter is the setting time. The type of hardener used can also vary the setting time. Check this point before buying.

Cramps must be applied to hold the parts in place whilst the adhesive sets. When all the joints have been glued, the pieces can be cramped together.

EPOXY RESIN
An expensive adhesive which is supplied in two parts, which are mixed together. One part is resin, the other is hardener.

There are many brands available. Although it sticks virtually anything to anything, is really unnecessary in many cases where an effective cheaper substitute will do.

The big advantage with epoxy resin adhesive is that non-porous materials – rigid plastics, glass and metal – can be joined together effectively.

It will resist such things as boiling water, acids and heat and is usually supplied in two tubes – resin and a hardener – to be mixed in equal proportions. Heat, applied gently, will reduce the setting time.

CONTACT ADHESIVES
Made of synthetic rubber and resin glue, they must be applied to both surfaces being joined. When they become touch dry the two surfaces are brought together and a strong bond is formed immediately.

Obviously, since the positions of the two parts being joined cannot be adjusted after sticking, their positioning must be absolutely right first time. Nowadays you can get non-drip contact adhesives, which are to be recommended as they are easier to work with and do allow some time for adjustment. Contact adhesives are suitable for joining together plastic laminate and wood, rubber, leather, fabrics, cork, etc.

GENERAL PURPOSE ADHESIVES
It is always worth while keeping a tube of one of the vast army of general purpose glues in the house. They stick together a whole variety of materials – paper, leather, fabrics, pvc, plastics, china, glass and so on. Two things they will not stick are expanded polystyrene and polythene. The latter can only be joined by heat welding, so never waste time attempting to do the job with an adhesive.

THIN FILM ADHESIVE (CYANOACRYLATE)
This is ideal for making invisible repairs to china and glass. A secure bond will result after about 20 seconds of finger pressure. The article should not be placed in water afterwards. *Warning:* Take care not to get the adhesive onto the hands as it sticks to skin immediately.

Resurfacing a Path with Cold-laid Macadam

One of the speediest methods of improving the appearance of a path or a drive is to use a cold-laid macadam, such as Colascrete.

An alternative method is to use Colas, a black, treacly liquid in conjunction with coloured stone chippings.

An average size garden path should take no more than one good morning's work to re-surface, using either of these materials.

Colascrete is sometimes used by itself and sometimes it is spread over a layer of Colas. The sub-floor is the deciding factor.

If economy is important (assuming that either system is acceptable to you) which of the two systems is adopted depends on the dimensions of the area to be treated. Colas on its own is certainly more economical for larger areas.

Both these treatments can be used on a variety of surfaces – ash, gravel, concrete, clinker, and so on. The basic techniques are the same for both materials.

USING COLAS

Taking the Colas and stone chippings system first, the first decision to be made is the quantities of materials to order. This is related directly to the conditions of the surface to be treated.

Should you be dealing with an old, concrete sub-floor, then the Colas can be spread out much further than on a loose surface.

As a guide you can use one gallon of Colas to cover about 5 square yards on concrete. For loose surfaces, one gallon can be used to cover only $1\frac{1}{3}$ square yards.

These figures are based on minimum and maximum spreading. You will have to use your own judgement as to how much to use on reasonably firm surfaces that fall somewhere between concrete and loose ash.

Some time before the work is going to be tackled, you should start to prepare the site so that it will be ready in time.

Preparation really means getting rid of any grass, weeds, or moss.

This must be done thoroughly, or some months after the macadam is laid, the more persistent weeds could grow up through the new surface.

Use a proprietary weedkiller – any gardening shop should stock a selection of brands – and allow it plenty of time to do its job. Tar-oil winter wash will get rid of moss. Follow manufacturer's directions closely.

Another thing to bear in mind is that the ground should be shaped to allow for drainage. In other words the centre should be higher than the sides, or there should be a slight tilt where this is practicable. Nothing is worse than a new drive that is dotted with puddles during rainy spells.

Immediately prior to using the macadam, sweep away any loose material such as leaves, from the surface.

If there are drains or manhole covers in the work area, then cover these to make sure they do not become clogged or blocked with the new material. They can be masked with pieces of plywood, weighted down at the edges with bricks and stones.

Next the Colas must be transferred from the container – a drum – to a one gallon watering can.

Then, in order to make sure that the correct quantity is spread over the area evenly, three things should be done.

First, the site can be marked out roughly into small plots of equal size according to the distribution coverage decided upon – for example, one gallon to three square yards.

Second, as it is not easy to control the flow of liquid pouring from the spout of the watering can, an old dessert spoon tied securely to the spout of the can so that the liquid will gush out on to its concave side will give much more even distribution.

It must be an old spoon as it will not be usable for its normal purposes afterwards!

If two people can work together, then so much the better. Whilst one is

brushing out the Colas with a yard broom to leave an even surface film, the other one can be distributing the stone chippings. In any case the chippings should be laid within twenty minutes of spreading the Colas. In this period, the liquid will remain tacky enough for the chippings to adhere to it.

The chippings can be scattered with a shovel though a few extra handfuls will probably be needed here and there to cover any bare or thinly covered patches.

In general, 50kg. (about 1 cubic foot) of chippings will cover an area of about 7sq. yds.

The newly laid chippings must be compacted immediately by rolling. It is advisable to keep a bucket of water handy so the roller can be kept wet at all times because, if the roller is used dry, it will continually be picking up a coating of tacky stones.

A thorough rolling will knit nearly all the stones and Colas together. Any odd, loose stones can be swept away later using a light broom. Extra rolling at this stage, though not essential, will add to the performance and appearance of the surface.

USING COLASCRETE

On many drives, there is a place which, because of its location, is subject to much more wear than any other. The places to note are the entrance itself, any sharp bends where car brakes will be regularly applied, or under trees where the surface remains damp for long periods.

Should there be any deep depressions or even potholes in the surface, Colascrete will be needed to fill them. This is a much more solid material and comes in bags. Use a shovel to transfer it from the bag to the hole and spread it out level with a rake. Compact it thoroughly with a garden roller.

To lay Colascrete, follow the same preparation techniques as for Colas some time before the day that the new surface is to be laid.

All weeds and plants must be

Fill potholes with Colascrete.

Rake level and compact with roller.

Spray on Colas from an old watering can and brush out with an old yard broom.

removed, the surface shaped to facilitate drainage, manhole covers and drains masked and the area swept clean.

Colas liquid, as was said earlier, often has to be used prior to spreading the Colascrete. Whether or not you have to use it depends on the surface being covered.

If the existing surface is of loose material – or concrete – then it must be used. Otherwise you can omit it.

Over concrete, use one gallon to eight square yards. On other surfaces use one gallon to five square yards.

Brush out the liquid, working in one direction only. Allow about twenty minutes for it to set.

At the end of the drying period, the liquid will have changed in colour from brown to black.

Use a knife to slit open the polythene bags containing the Colascrete. Empty the contents on to the ground. Try to shake the material over a square yard or so – not in a heap. This makes spreading it out to the required thickness an easier task.

Use a rake to spread the material to a thickness of about ¾in. over a convenient section. As far as possible, avoiding standing on the fresh material as you are spreading it as it will stick to your shoes.

As soon as each section is raked, it can be compacted by rolling. As before, keep the roller wet to avoid it picking up.

Doubtlessly, you will leave depressions at first through over-rolling some areas. Should this happen,

add more material to make up the depressions to surface level before re-rolling. Continue in this way until the whole area is complete.

A few days later, the area should be given another roll. At this stage, you may choose to scatter some decorative chippings which will break up the overall colour of the drive.

Colours of Colascrete are red, green, or black.

The decorative chippings come in small polythene bags from your Colascrete supplier. Just scatter these in handsful over the surface prior to the final rolling, which will bed them in.

As a guide to the quantity of Colascrete needed – you will require about 2cwt. to cover 40 sq. ft. to a thickness of about ½in. when rolled.

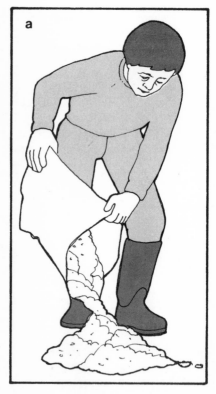

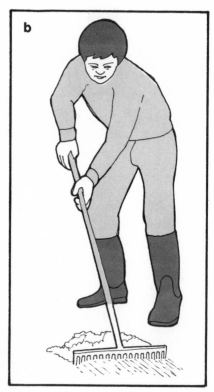

Emptying Colascrete from bag. (a)

Raking level. (b)

Compacting with a roller. (c)

Scattering decorative chippings before final roll. (d)

The Use of Ladders and Scaffolds

Any home maintenance job is easier if it can be done in comfort. This means that all the necessary tools should be easily to hand and the work area should be within easy reach.

There are few difficulties in arranging this when a job can be done with your feet planted firmly on the ground but problems do arise once you have to scale the heights.

Few people enjoy working at a height. It is never particularly easy to concentrate fully on what you are doing while half your thinking is devoted to keeping your balance.

This applies even if you are standing on a small step stool. Many people are aware of the alarming statistics concerning injuries in the home from falls, sometimes of only a few inches. The rate is high and it could happen to you if you do not put safety first.

So let us look at the various means available which enable us to work in comfort.

LADDERS

If you own a ladder then you must ensure that it is kept in good condition. A wooden ladder, provided it is made of well-seasoned wood and is stored, horizontally, under cover, will give a lifetime's service.

Irrespective of how it is stored, inside or outside, a coat of exterior grade varnish will prevent it from rotting.

Never paint a ladder – it will not be possible to see if rot develops. Through clear varnish, the condition of the wood is always evident.

Before use, no matter how good the ladder looks, examine it carefully for damage.

If you buy or hire a ladder, you have to decide which is the best type for your particular needs.

This depends on several factors. First, the correct height. Work out the highest point at which you are likely to stand on the ladder and buy a ladder that will extend 3ft. 6in. above this point. You might also take into account that, should you move house,

you might need a bit more height in the future.

Ladders come in one, two or three sections. The three section ladders are easiest to store since they fold down to a smaller length.

Their disadvantage is that they are awkward to erect unless you get the knack by using them constantly.

You might be better off going for a two-section one, but the best way to find out is to go to the nearest large

stockist where you can try your hand with different types.

Ladders are generally of wood or aluminium. The latter are much lighter and need no maintenance.

Should you buy an aluminium ladder wipe it all over before use. There will often be a coating of grease on it and this could mark paintwork.

Always erect a ladder on a firm base. Should the erection site be on earth, or other soft ground provide a platform of

Erecting a ladder.

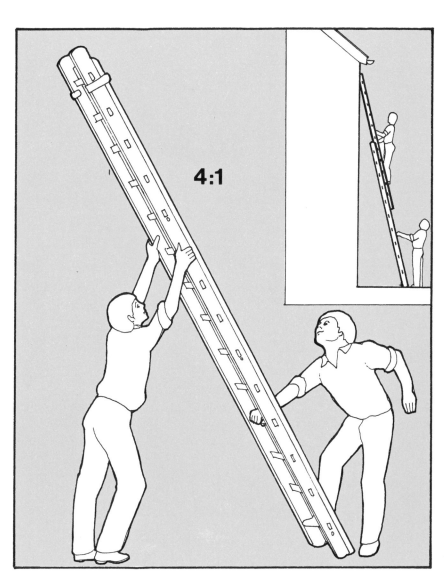

4:1

boards to prevent the legs from sinking in.

To stop the legs slipping backwards a batten can be screwed to the board as a stop ledge.

On firm ground get someone to stand at the foot of the ladder – not on it – so that they can steady the ladder.

If help is not available, tie the bottom rung to any firm, permanent support – a downpipe, for example – or use a weight such as a sandbag.

Correct footwear is conducive to easier and more comfortable working from a ladder. Plimsoles are not suitable – the rungs will soon make your feet ache. Always wear shoes, not boots; the latter are clumsy and locating the rungs is not easy when wearing them.

Make sure that your shoes are not muddy as your feet could easily slip off the rungs.

When erecting a tall ladder for work on a roof or gutter, it is useful for the beginner if a helper is on hand.

Get the helper to hold one end of the ladder firm whilst you raise the other end.

Position it, vertically against the house wall. Now pull out the base so that the correct angle can be achieved. The distance between the house wall and the base of the ladder should be one quarter of the ladder's height.

Make sure that at least three rungs of the ladder extend above the level of the gutter or whatever height you are working at.

Tie the ladder to a ring bolt screwed to the fascia and this will prevent it from sliding sideways.

Never lean a ladder against a plastic guttering as it is not strong enough to withstand this sort of weight.

There are various proprietary aids and gadgets which make working from a ladder much easier. Standing on the rungs for long periods is uncomfortable, whether or not the correct footwear is worn, but you can use a ladder platform. The 'arms' of this device lock on to the rungs,

leaving a small step for you to stand on.

As an alternative, ladder cripples (brackets) can be fixed to two ladders to support a scaffold board thus providing a continuous working surface.

Painting the underside of an overhanging roof would mean reaching backwards if a ladder stay were not used. And reaching backwards in this way is only advisable for a circus trapeze artiste, not a handyman.

A ladder stay locks on to the top rungs of the ladder and the other end rests against the house wall, so that the ladder is held firmly a couple of feet away from the wall.

You will certainly need an S-hook to hold your paint can or a container for the tools needed for the job you are doing.

Never lean out sideways to reach a work area. Only work in areas that are within comfortable reach.

When you have to move the ladder to a new work position, never slide it along with the top resting against the wall. This could damage pebble-dashing or paintwork. Lift the ladder clear of the wall before repositioning.

To make sure that the ladder never

has a chance of rubbing or damaging fresh work, start painting on the right hand side of a window or wall if you are right handed. Left handed people should work from left to right.

Where you have to work above a window opening and the ladder has nothing to rest against, tie a stout batten to the ladder parallel to the top rungs. The batten should be wider than the window so that it rests against the walls at either side of the window frame.

SCAFFOLDS
No matter how safely secured a ladder is, there are many people who start feeling jittery as their feet leave the bottom rung.

In the past, these people had little alternative but to call in professional help for high-up work. Not only has this become very expensive, but it is also frustrating for the man who enjoys maintaining his home and knows that an unreliable professional might well skimp awkward pieces of work.

A stout batten tied to the ladder helps when decorating over a window.

For this group of people there are scaffolding kits available, generally known as tower platforms. Several manufacturers produce their own type.

Before you start thinking in terms of tubular bars joined together in a complicated arrangement with nuts, bolts and anchor plates – the sort of thing that can be seen on a construction site – let me reassure you that the home handyman tower platforms are much more simple.

Indeed if they were as complicated and time consuming to assemble and dismantle, I would not recommend them to the amateur.

To whet your appetite, let me tell you at the outset that even if you have never used one of them before, then it will take you no more than ten minutes to erect a 16ft. high scaffolding that is completely safe to use. And if you had another pair of hands to help you, that time could be cut in half comfortably.

The great advantage of these kits is that all your high-level jobs can be carried out in ground level conditions. This mean that you will feel secure and can concentrate all your thoughts on your work.

Furthermore you will not get tired so quickly as when working from a ladder. There is no need to be continually going up and down and repositioning the ladder for new work areas.

As I have said earlier, there are several types of these kits made. Basically, however, they are all similar. I use a Junior Kwiktower kit which is fairly representative of all other models.

The tower is comprised of a series of tubular steel frames which interlock and are built up gradually to whatever height is required.

Each frame consists of two vertical uprights joined by two horizontal bars. At the top of each upright is a spigot (a bottle neck). At the other end is the full diameter of the tube socket.

A straightforward tower.

To join up the frames, all one has to do is to locate the sockets of successive frames on to the spigots of the frame below.

Thus the first frame is placed at ground level with the spigots pointing upwards. The sockets of the next frame slide over the spigots of the previous one and are pushed down firmly to anchor it.

That is all there is to it. No tricky fixings in sight. Frames, incidentally, are either 2ft. or 4ft. wide.

Before running through the exact assembly technique, it is worth listing all the various accessories. Some are essential to a basic tower; others bring out the full versatility of the towers.

The basic essential is a horizontal brace. This is a long tubular bar with rings on both ends. The rings are of a slightly larger diameter than the frame members.

The brace is used to prevent the tower 'doing the splits'. It is secured diagonally to the first two frames set at ground level. The rings simply slide over the tubular uprights.

When the required height of a tower has been reached, an enclosed working platform has to be assembled. To achieve this, there are handrails and guard rails which are similar to the brace and are fixed in the same way.

The working platform itself is comprised of thick boards which butt up to each other. On the underside are wood strips which lock up against the tubes to keep the platform in place.

Depending on how and where a platform is to be used, there is a choice of five different bases or feet. Where a tower is being used on level ground, socket bases are fixed to the base frames.

If a platform is being arranged that will run continuously alongside a wall giving a long, low level platform, then trestle feet are fitted.

Such is the width of the frames that, in many cases, whereas two of the feet may be resting on a flat concrete path

running alongside the house, the other feet may be on uneven ground. For this and all similar situations, such as where one or more feet are resting on steps, there are adjustable bases. These can be altered to take up any unevenness in the ground.

Mobility is the key factor of these tower platforms. To enable them to be repositioned conveniently for a new work area, there are castors.

Finally, there are rubber feet, should

you want to convert some of the frames into a workbench.

Now for the assembly method in more detail. First of all the correct bases – trestle, adjustable, castors or whatever, have to be selected for the ground conditions.

Let us take a typical example and discuss a situation where two of the legs are on firm ground and two are on uneven ground. As we have just seen, adjustable legs are needed.

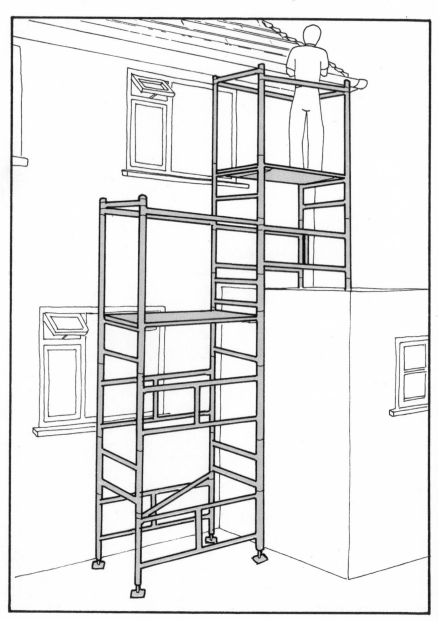

Cantilevering over a roof.

These are placed on their approximate positions on the ground. The first two frames are located on the feet (spigots uppermost). The horizontal brace is now slotted diagonally to join up these two base frames.

The next two frames are added at right angles to the base frames. It is at this point that any adjustments to the bases have to be made.

One of the most important things

about a tower is that it must be built up perfectly level. So a spirit level is needed to check it.

Provided, these base frames are level, the frames placed above them will automatically be level.

By laying the spirit level on the horizontal crossbars of the second frames just placed in position, and adjusting the bases as necessary, a true level can be found quickly. From there on more frames are added until

Decorating a stairwell.

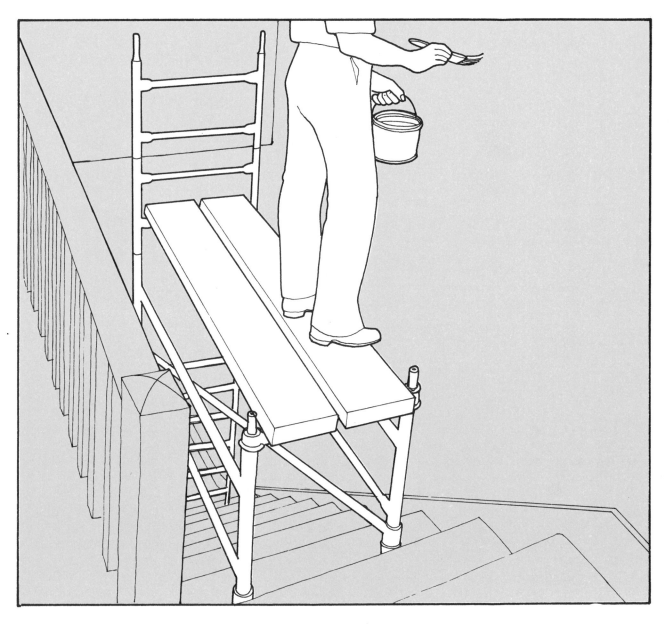

the required working height is reached.

A safe foothold can be provided, during construction, by laying a couple of the working platform boards in position whilst you slot on more frames.

At this point a word of warning about ascending tower platforms. At no time should you attempt to climb up the outside of a tower as it could topple over. You must climb up on the inside only, using the bars of the frames as handgrips and footholds. There are a sufficient number of these to make almost anyone feel as nimble as a monkey.

Never lean a ladder against a tower to reach the working platform either.

Some manufacturers make special clip-on ladders which are fixed inside the framework, making it far easier for the less agile to climb up or down.

At the working platform height, the various safety bars – hand and guard rails – can be fixed. The working platform boards then can be put in position.

Although the towers provide the safest way of working at height, the erection procedures must be followed closely to avoid the possibility of accidents.

If the tower is to be used on grass or other soft surface, a firm base must be laid to prevent the legs sinking in. A suitable base can be provided by laying down stout boards as bearers.

In all cases individual manufacturers' instructions and recommendations for use must be read and followed closely.

Moving a tower to a new work position is more convenient where castors are fitted – provided that the ground is even. It does not take a great deal of effort to push a tower along.

There are usually restrictions on how high a tower can be when castors are fitted. Incidentally, no one should even be allowed to remain on the tower during repositioning and no tools or equipment should be left on the platform. These could easily be dislodged and fall on your head.

Always make sure that the castors' locking device is in operation before scaling a tower.

Some towers can be pulled along on level ground without castors – but again there are manufacturers' height restrictions.

Once a tower reaches a certain height (specified in the instructions), it has to be tied to a building or other permanent support.

Apart from high towers for dealing with top windows, gutters and so on, other tower arrangements can be formed for dealing with interior ceilings and for similar purposes.

There are two ways of obtaining a tower. You can buy or you can hire one. In either case you must specify the number of frames you need and any accessories – castors, adjustable legs and so on, but if you buy, manufacturers will send a leaflet setting out the parts needed to build up a tower to various heights.

You only have to buy the amount you need. If you only want a low level job for interior work, you will not need many frames.

The components for towers are not cheap. However, if a group of people, club, association or neighbours get together the expenses could be shared.

A 16ft. tower is not likely to be needed very often by one person. It could be used only once a year which would mean it lying redundant the rest of the time. With a group scheme, much fuller use is assured.

On the other hand, as I mentioned earlier, the tower components are very versatile. You can use frames to make such things as a temporary workbench or children's climbing frame (at low level of course) when they are not being used for the tower.

Adding more frames.

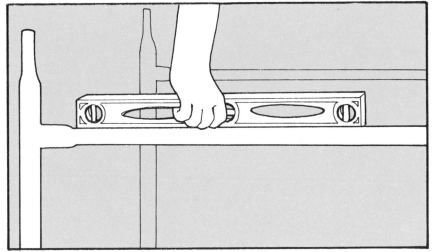

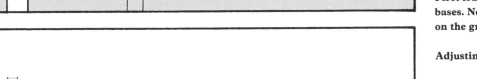

Checking with a spirit level.

First frames positioned on adjustable bases. Note the timber base provided on the grass.

Adjusting a base.

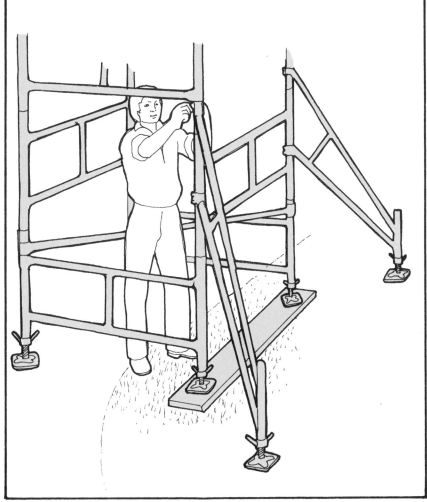

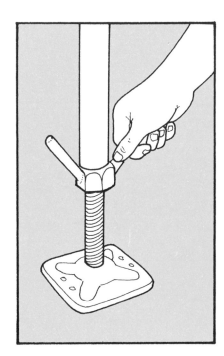

Using Man-made Boards

Hardboard, chipboard and plywood are names that nearly everyone has encountered. It is quite usual to hear someone recommending the use of chipboard 'to knock up some cupboards' or plywood 'to make some shelves' but unless you have had some practical experience there may be some uncertainty about buying and working with these materials.

Since they cover large areas with one sheet, these materials are used for much that the handyman does.

Indeed there are many occasions where, by employing them, a much better end product will result, with far less work. So, let us take a close look at each of these man-made materials individually.

HARDBOARD
Hardboard is made from reconstructed wood fibres minus the knots.

There are a dozen different types in the group, all serving specific purposes.

Standard hardboard can be used for a variety of jobs – for wall and ceiling panelling, covering floors, panelling a softwood framework when making cupboards, fitted wardrobes and so on.

Medium grade hardboard can be used for the interior uses outlined above, though exterior grades are also available. They are thicker boards and therefore more rigid, but less dense than the standard type.

Hardboards with a melamine facing are called plastic-faced. Various colours and patterns are available, making them ideal for use in the kitchen for working surfaces and for splashbacks.

If you need to line the walls in the kitchen or bathroom, or enclose the bath behind panelling, you could use an enamelled board. Again, there is a whole range of colours from which to choose and an increasing range of interesting decorative patterns. Surface textures offered are gloss and matt.

If you like the idea of an embossed surface, then have a look at some moulded hardboards. There is a reasonable selection of pattern types available making them suitable for pelmets, panelling and other decorative uses.

For a woodgrain effect, choose hardboard with the prefix 'woodgrain'. There is a good choice of grain types. The obvious application for these is in furniture making.

Most of us have seen pegboard used in a variety of ingenious ways. Pegboard is hardboard covered with holes of various diameters – either uniform or irregular – and in various pattern arrangements.

Clips fit into the holes on which you can hang up kitchen utensils or tools so that they can be selected at a glance.

Insulating board is another hardboard type. This is a thermal insulating material with a wide range of decorative finishes. There are three types:

Fibre insulating boards are lightweight and porous to give a good heat insulation.

These come in plain, or textured surfaces and are available in the form of large sheets, planks or tiles.

Acoustic board is the second type, which will increase sound absorption. It is, in fact, a treated insulating board and comes in the form of tiles or board.

Should you wish to insulate and decorate at the same time, choose a third type – surfaced insulating boards. The surfaces are available in a wide range of materials – paper, textiles, sheet plastics, veneers.

The thickness and size of the sheets of hardboard varies with type. The types listed here vary in thickness between $\frac{1}{8}$in., $\frac{3}{16}$in., $\frac{1}{4}$in. and $\frac{1}{2}$in. Some are available in three of the sizes, others in only one.

All are sold in large sheets, 2ft. × 2ft. being the smallest size; 4ft. × 12ft. is the largest in some cases; in other types, moulded and plastic faced for examples, 4ft. × 8ft. is the maximum.

Insulating boards are thicker. The acoustic board is available only in two sizes – $\frac{1}{2}$in. and $\frac{3}{4}$in. The other types can be bought 1in. thick. Overall dimensions are basically the same as above. Tiles come in 1ft., 1ft. 4in. and 2ft. squares.

You can regard hardboard, more or less, as a piece of natural timber when it comes to working with it. Your normal woodworking tools will be suitable.

A couple of points to watch though: a fine tooth saw should be used to cut the cleanest edge, and, when dealing with a decorative faced board, it is always best to score along the intended saw line with a sharp knife. This avoids the possibility of the saw chipping the decorative surface. You will find that a rough edge is usually left after sawing. This can be cleaned off with glasspaper.

Earlier, when outlining the various ways that hardboard can be used, panelling over a softwood framework was mentioned. You can fix the hardboard with nails, screws or woodworking adhesive.

The method chosen depends on the job and is based on requirements such as the desired strength and appearance of the item.

Where standard hardboard is being used to cover a floor, fix it with hardboard pins. Adhesive can be used also if desired.

To avoid the possibility of hardboards buckling in use, conditioning may be necessary, see page 143. Insulating boards and medium hardboards should be left standing on edge in the room where they are to be used for 48 hours before fixing. Do not stack the boards butted up to each other; keep them separated so that the air will flow around all surfaces freely.

Many people, in order to give the ground floor of their home an open plan look, remove one or more doors. The resultant gap – left as a rectangle – is hardly attractive. However, an arch can be built into the opening by bending hardboard to the appropriate shape and fitting it into the frame.

Various methods are used to bend hardboard. A large radius bend can be made by pinning one end of a standard sheet to a support framework and gradually working around to the other end of the sheet, pinning it to the framework as you proceed.

Hardboard can be finished with paint or a clear sealer. The latter is especially suitable where the board is being used as a decorative surface covering over poor floorboards.

The surface of hardboard is smooth and tough, and will be further toughened and protected by applying a couple of coats of sealer. Wax polish provides additional protection.

If you choose a paint finish, start off with a coat of hardboard primer or emulsion lightly diluted with water. If the hardboard is being used outside the home, a coat of aluminium-based primer may be more durable.

After the priming coat, complete the job with normal undercoat and top coat.

CHIPBOARD

Chipboard is perhaps the most versatile of all the man-made boards. Its applications are so numerous that a use could be found for it in every part of the house. Most people use it for furniture making and, in fact, much of the factory produced furniture of today uses chipboard as its base.

The obvious advantage of making your own built-in furniture is that you do not have to compromise between what is available and what you want, at least as far as dimensions are concerned.

It is most irritating when you want to buy a fitted unit to slot neatly into a vacant alcove and you cannot find anything of the right dimensions, so you purchase the nearest possible size and learn to live with the ugly gaps that are left between the sides of the unit and the walls. This is never a satisfactory arrangement.

There are a great many types of chipboard available to perform

different functions. There are surface finished grades that are prepared all ready for painting, boards with decorative surface finishes of plastic, wood veneer or metal, or melamine boards bonded to vinyl, textile covering on a paper backing, hessian and so on. There are also special fire-retardant and water resistant grades.

Chipboard is a homogeneous material with no grain. It is made from wood particles which, after being coated with a resin adhesive, are subjected to intense pressure and heat.

There are two main density types – the density of a board governs its strength – and these are called standard and flooring grade boards. The latter type is heavier. The standard type is used in furniture making and general building work.

Care must be taken to select the right grade of chipboard for particular

purposes. Though it is sufficiently strong for most applications, it does not have the same strength as solid timber.

Good do-it-yourself shops and timber merchants will stock a selection of chipboard types. Certainly the standard grade will be readily available.

The standard board size is 8ft. × 4ft. in thicknesses of 18mm. ($\frac{3}{4}$in.) and 12mm. ($\frac{1}{2}$in.).

Proprietary brands of chipboard, such as Contiboard and Handiboard are readily available. These have decorative surfaces over a chipboard core.

Using a straight-edge to check that an edge of a chipboard sheet is even.

Working with chipboard is enjoyable since the boards are easy to cut and join. A unit of furniture, therefore, can be built relatively quickly.

The first essential is to take great care at the marking out stage. Always follow the golden rule 'mark twice and cut once'.

Do not assume that the edge of a sheet of chipboard is true or that corners are at right angles, important requirements if a finished item is to be square.

Use a straight-edge to ascertain if there are any bumps in the edge of the sheets. If there are, level them off with a plane. Once a true edge has been established, use this to take measurements from.

Your marking pencil should have a fine point – if the lead is thick it will give rise to inaccuracies. Even better than a pencil is a marking knife. Use a straight-edge to join up lines.

When you cut a length off a sheet it is unlikely that the saw will have left a true-cut edge, even though it appears to have followed the marked guide lines exactly. Always keep checking to ensure that an edge is true and corners are at right angles.

Incidentally, never fall into the trap of assuming that from a 4ft. wide sheet of any board (or natural timber) that you will be able to cut four pieces, each 1ft. wide. This is not so. You will end up with three pieces each 1ft. wide but the fourth piece will only be about 11$\frac{3}{4}$in. wide. The lost $\frac{1}{4}$in. is accounted for by the saw cuts.

The resin in chipboard tends to wear out saws more quickly than would natural timber. Should you have a tungsten carbide tipped general purpose saw in your kit, this is the ideal tool to use. If you work with hand tools, then use a fine tooth saw as this will produce a cleaner cut.

A couple of important points to note when using a power saw: the distance that the edge of the circular saw blade is above the board, determines the cleanness of the cut made.

Should the blade project too much – or too little – then the bottom or top surface of the board, respectively, will be chipped. The ideal projection is somewhere between $\frac{1}{8}$in. and $\frac{1}{4}$in. Should chipping still occur between these points, then increase the speed of the saw or reduce the rate at which the board is fed into the cutting blade.

Boards with a plastic laminate covering should be cut with a tungsten carbide tipped power saw. The brittle surface is less likely to be chipped if a slow rate of feed is used and a smaller diameter saw blade is fitted.

If the cut edges have to be planed smooth, then a normal hand plane or a Stanley Surform will do the trick.

Never plane the surface of chipboard.

Should you intend to cover the cut edge with an edge lipping material, then planing beforehand is advisable.

However, should you intend an edge to remain uncovered or painted, then it is preferable to finish by sanding the edges.

Depending on the degree of smoothness aimed at, use 120 to 200 grit grade sandpaper.

The points of the nails should project through the board.

Spread PVA woodworking adhesive to give a strong joint. Place the boards together and knock the nails home.

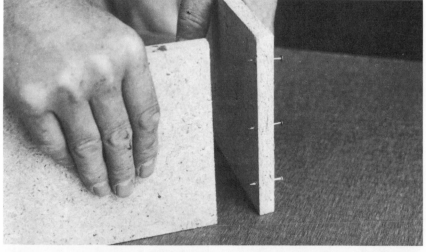

Jointing chipboard Provided that clean saw cuts are made, chipboard sections can be glued together very effectively. Liberally coat the mating edges with adhesive before positioning the sections in their correct positions. Clamps must be applied until the adhesive has set.

The adhesive to use is a pva type or a synthetic resin glue.

Where a piece of furniture or anything else is likely to have to withstand a lot of wear and tear, then a stronger joint should be made, using either nails or screws in addition to the adhesive.

When using nails, first knock them into one of the two boards to be joined. They should be in a straight line with their points just projecting through the other side of the board.

Apply glue to the mating edges according to manufacturer's instructions. Next, bring the two boards together in their correct position. Drive home the nails and apply clamps until the glue has set.

Plane inwards from the corners to the middle to avoid chipping the corners.

PLYWOOD

Plywood is constructed from various timbers including birch, pine and beech.

Veneers of these timbers are cut from the log and are joined together with the grain of each sheet running at right angles to the one below it. Resin adhesive is used to join the veneers.

Special adhesive grades are used dependent on whether the plywood is to be used for inside work (interior grade) or for outside work (exterior grade).

The layers of veneer are called plies; hence a board containing three plies is called three-ply, five plies are called five-ply; over this number the board is called multi-ply.

When buying plywood, the species, overall dimensions, thickness, grade and construction, must all be stated.

The species refers to the timber used. The overall dimensions are the length and the width – many sizes are available from 4ft. × 4ft. to 5ft. × 12ft.

Thicknesses go from 3mm. to 25mm. The grade refers to whether it is for interior or exterior use. The construction means the number of plies.

The timber grade you use depends on the way that the plywood will be finished. Finnish birch plywood, for example, is available in various qualities – as are all the plywood types.

If a standard paint coat is to be used, then B quality should be specified. Should a high class paint finish, or staining, or clear sealing, be required then ask for BB quality.

There are other grades for lesser used finishing techniques which will not generally concern the average handyman.

There are no special problems to overcome when working with plywood. It can be cut, drilled, and shaped in much the same way as natural timber.

A clean cut will be made with a fine tooth saw. For shaped cuts, use the conventional bowsaw, padsaw, or fretsaw. If using power equipment, then a jigsaw or bandsaw will make a clean cut.

All plywood can be drilled without fear of splitting the grain, but always drill through into a softwood back held firmly into place to ensure a clean hole.

The only point to remember, when planing edges, is to work inwards from the corners to the middle. If you plane towards the corners, chipping could result at the corners themselves.

Sheets of plywood can be joined with glue and screws or special detachable jointing blocks.

Plywood can be bent quite easily without having to condition the sheet as with hardboard. Use thin sheets only and bend them in the direction of the face grain. Should a thick curved panel be required, then use two or more thinner boards to achieve the desired thickness.

Putting Up Shelves

Every house needs shelves – lots of them. There are books, ornaments, glasses, chinaware, photographs and a hundred and one other things in most homes that need to be displayed or simply stored.

So the home handyman is faced with the age old job of putting up a shelf. It is a relatively simple task but then so are many other jobs – if you have the know-how.

The following stages are involved: selecting the materials and cutting them to size, drilling the wall to receive the fixing screws, fitting suitable wallplugs and, finally, fixing the shelf.

Obviously you can choose a proprietary shelving system – there are many available on the market – but this will still involve you in having to screw into the wall and will cost more.

For economy and freedom of design, it is preferable to make your own shelves from scratch, using softwood bearers to support a shelf of man-made material – chipboard or plywood.

The bearers have to be screwed to the wall, so the first thing to do is to make certain that it is safe to drill into the bricks, remembering that electric cables and plumbing pipes may be below the surface.

To drill a hole in the wall, you will need a drill – either hand or power operated – and a masonry drill bit. The bit fits into the chuck (the nose) of the drill. The bits come in various sizes, indicated by a number.

When the hole is drilled, a wallplug must be inserted to hold the screw.

The wallplug and the screw must be the same size as the masonry bit used. Thus, you would select, say, a No. 8 bit, a No. 8 drill and a No. 8 screw. The number eight refers to the diameter of the screw – not its length. Many diameters are available but for the purpose of fixing shelving bearers, a number eight is usually used.

No. 8 screws are made in various lengths; for shelf bearers, 1½in. to 3in. will cover most needs. The length used is determined by the thickness of the

bearers and the load that the shelf has to carry.

For example, a shelf intended to carry heavy kitchen pots and pans would need thick softwood bearers (say 2in. × 1in.) and long screws (say 2½in. to 3in.). A display shelf intended for lightweight ornaments might have 1in. × ½in. bearers fixed with 1½in. long screws.

Brick walls are covered by a layer of plaster and this is not strong enough to hold a screw. The threaded part of the screw has to go right into the brickwork behind the plaster.

Since a screw will not grip on to brickwork, the wallplug has to be inserted into the pre-drilled hole.

Wallplugs come in two main materials – fibre and plastic. Both are available in sizes relative to the screw size to be used. The round fibre plug is a traditional wallplug suitable for most fixing jobs. Plastic plugs are available in several different types ranging from the simple round plastic plug to nylon versions with ribbed barrels and projecting wings to ensure a really tight grip when the screw is inserted into place.

Incidentally, since the hole in the wall should be the same length as the screw to be inserted, you will have to know when to stop drilling into the wall. A good idea for, say a 3in. deep hole is to tie a piece of cotton to the drill bit at 3in. from its tip. When the cotton reaches the surface of the wall, the whole will be 3in. deep in the wall.

In modern houses, many internal walls are hollow. They are constructed of plasterboard fixed to a wood framework. Often the thickness of the plasterboard is only 10mm. Since their are no bricks behind it, a screw cannot be inserted.

For this situation, there are special cavity wall fixings.
SPRING TOGGLES These have 'wings' which open after being passed through a hole drilled in the plasterboard. The screw at the front is then tightened causing the wings to grip on to the back of the plasterboard.

These devices can never be removed after fixing.
GRAVITY TOGGLES These have a hinged section which again is fed through a pre-drilled hole in the plasterboard. The hinged section drops down at right angles and grips the plasterboard at the back when the screw at the front is tightened. Thus the hinged section acts as an anchor. These devices cannot be removed.
RAWLNUTS Should an irregular size hole be drilled, these are useful. They have a rubber sleeve which expands as the screw is tightened and shapes itself to the contours of the

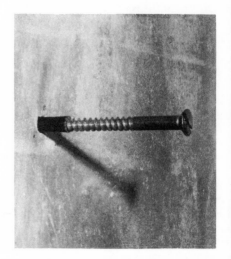

Rawlplug.

Rawlnut.

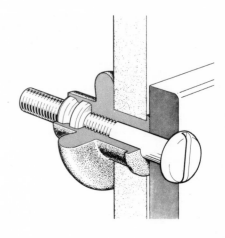

cavity. These can be removed and re-used.

RAWLANCHORS These have thick metal arms which spread out behind the plasterboard as the screw is tightened at the front.

FIXING A SHELF IN A RECESS
To make a shelf for a recess, you need two softwood bearers plus the shelf material (chipboard, plywood, etc.). The length of the bearers should be about ½in. less than the depth of the shelf so that they will be set back from the front of the shelf and will not show.

Drill holes through the bearers at both the front and the back of each bearer.

Place one bearer in position on the wall using a spirit level to make sure it is horizontal. Use a pointed implement to transfer the hole positions on to the wall.

Drill the holes in the wall and insert the wallplugs and the screws to secure the bearer.

Use the spirit level again to draw a line across the recess on the line of the shelf to ensure that the second bearer is at the same level as the first one.

Fix the second bearer and then secure the shelf in place by screwing through it into the bearers.

For wide recesses or shelves to carry a heavy load, a long bearer should be screwed to the back wall between the two side bearers to support the centre of the shelf.

Marking screw holes through the first bearer.

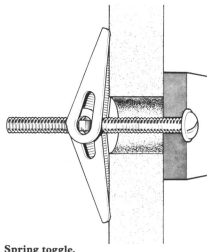

Spring toggle.

Gravity toggle.

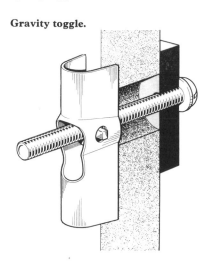

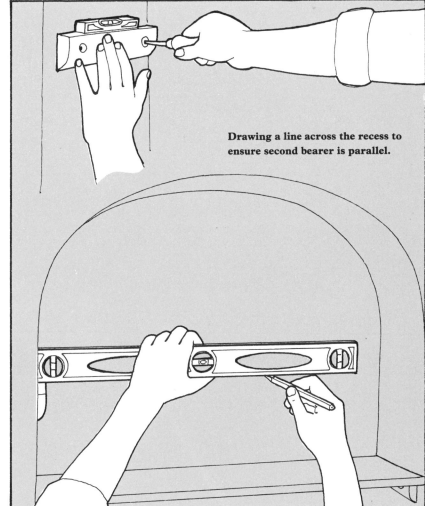

Drawing a line across the recess to ensure second bearer is parallel.

Plumbing and Central Heating

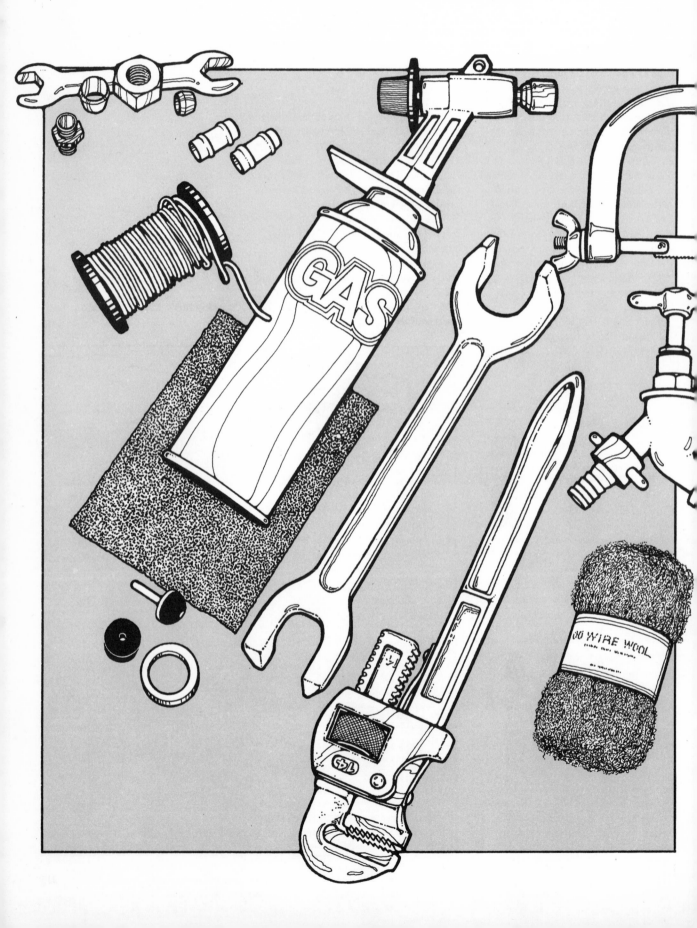

Water Supply

Some domestic plumbing arrangements are more complicated than others but, generally speaking, basic layouts follow a traditional pattern.

One of the most important things to know is where vital stopcocks and stopvalves are positioned. Even if you are not prepared to make minor plumbing repairs yourself, it is essential to know which stopcock or stop-valve to turn off in the event of an emergency.

Some parts of a plumbing installation are not visible. For example, take the stopcock of the pipe which carries the water into the house. This is often buried under the pavement outside the house – but not always. It could be under the footpath which leads to the front door or, in some old houses, it could be buried somewhere in the garden. Normally, you will find the stopcock under the pavement.

INTERNAL STOP-VALVE
In modern houses it should not normally be necessary for a householder to use this stopcock. Usually the pipe which supplies the water to the house has a stop-valve fitted *inside* the house, as a rule near an entrance. Many older houses, however, lack this internal refinement, so to turn off the water the occupants have to rely upon the outside stopcock.

Even if you have a stop-valve inside the house, it is obviously an advantage to be able to turn off the water from the outside stopcock. This applies particularly when the inside stop-valve needs a new washer.

Few houses, comparatively speaking, have a key to operate the outside stopcock and they are not always easy to obtain.

The stopcock is usually buried about 30 inches below ground level, *fig. 1*. This is to protect it from frost. These stopcocks normally close in a clockwise direction. They are sometimes enclosed in a box or a length of drainpipe.

There is a hinged cover at the top at ground level which should at all times be kept clear of soil, weeds and anything else which may make the cover

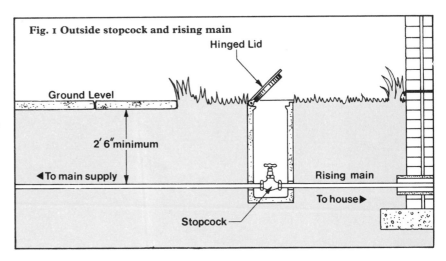

Fig. 1 Outside stopcock and rising main
Hinged Lid
Ground Level
2′ 6″ minimum
◄ To main supply
Rising main
To house ►
Stopcock

difficult to open. Keep the hinged flap clean and put a spot of oil on it occasionally. .

DRAINCOCKS
The stop-valve inside the house, *fig. 2*, should have a draincock fitted near it, *fig. 3*. In most cases both stop-valve and draincock are combined in one fitting, *fig. 4*.

A draincock will have a hose connection so that the rising main can be drained if it has to be repaired, or as a frost precaution if the property is to be left empty during the winter months.

The stop-valve should turn freely at all times. So it is a good idea to make a regular check that it will do so. Turn the water on and off two or three times when you make this check.

Fortunately, the washer on this stop-valve does not wear out very often. However, they do not last for ever so you will need to know how to rewasher your valve. For this see the section on rewashering taps.

RISING MAIN
The pipe which carries the water into the house is called the rising main. It climbs up through the house and supplies the cold water storage cistern normally situated in the loft. This pipe should at all times be protected against frost (see chapter on frost precautions).

The water in the storage cistern should never be used for drinking

purposes. This is because it can easily become contaminated by insects crawling into the cistern. Drinking water should come direct from the main – that is, normally, from the kitchen tap. The diameter of the rising main pipe is ½ in (15 mm).

After supplying the kitchen tap with water, the rising main pipe normally continues its journey through the house up into the loft. There it feeds the cold water storage cistern, *fig. 5*, which supplies water to various other parts of the plumbing system to be described later.

The only other tapping likely to be taken off the rising main before it reaches the loft is a branch pipe for an outside tap.

There are, of course, alternatives to having the cold water storage cistern situated in the loft. Sometimes a cistern is installed in the bathroom or in a cupboard on the landing.

While this sort of arrangement will mean that the cistern is less likely to be affected by frost, it may also mean, for one thing, that the w.c. cistern which it supplies will refill very slowly. For another thing, it may make it impossible to work a shower properly owing to insufficient water pressure or head, as it is called. This problem I will deal with later.

SUPPLY PIPES
Water is supplied to the cold water

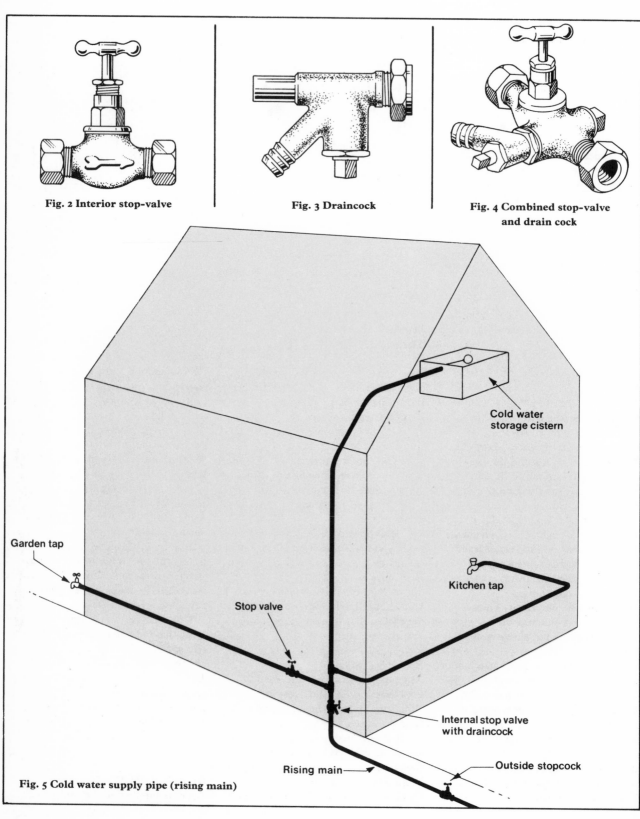

Fig. 2 Interior stop-valve

Fig. 3 Draincock

Fig. 4 Combined stop-valve and drain cock

Cold water storage cistern

Garden tap

Kitchen tap

Stop valve

Internal stop valve with draincock

Rising main

Outside stopcock

Fig. 5 Cold water supply pipe (rising main)

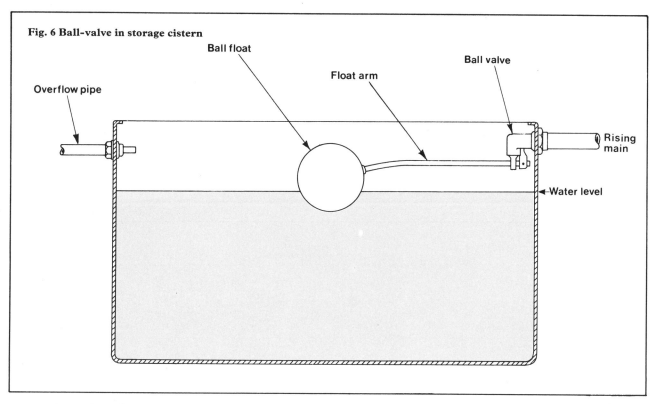

Fig. 6 Ball-valve in storage cistern

Ball float

Float arm

Ball valve

Overflow pipe

Rising main

Water level

storage cistern through a ball-valve fitted in the cistern, at the end of the rising main, *fig. 6*. The cistern supplies cold water to the bath, the bathroom basin and the toilet cistern. It also provides a cold water supply to the hot water cylinder or tank, *fig. 7*.

You will find at least a couple of supply pipes leading from points about 2 in from the base of the cold water storage cistern. These are normally $\frac{3}{4}$ in (22 mm) in diameter. One leads to the hot water cylinder and the other supplies the bath and bathroom basin taps and w.c. cistern.

Each of these pipes should be fitted with a gateway valve, *fig. 8*. These valves enable supplies to the cold water system and to the hot water system to be turned off independently. This is a great advantage when repairs are necessary as only the circuit affected needs to be isolated from the water supply.

It is a sound idea to make sure both these stop-valves – and the one on the rising main – turn easily. Give them a

couple of turns occasionally and apply a little grease at the same time.

DIRECT AND INDIRECT

To recap. The rising main feeds the tap over the kitchen sink, possibly a tap in the garden and the cold water storage cistern. All other points are normally supplied from that cistern. This is an *indirect* cold water system.

In some older houses, a *direct* cold water system may be found. In this case the rising main feeds not only the tap over the kitchen sink, but branches are also taken from it to the bath, bathroom basin and w.c. cistern.

The direct method is not usually found in modern installations. In some older houses both systems are sometimes used. For example, one w.c. may be supplied direct from the rising main, while the second w.c. may be connected to a cold water storage cistern.

There is a way to find out if the system is direct or indirect. Turn off the stop-valve on the rising main. If this stops water flowing to all the cold

water taps and w.c. cisterns, the system is direct. If only the flow to the kitchen tap stops, you have an indirect system.

TYPES OF CISTERN

The most unusual type of cold water cistern is a galvanised steel one, at least in older homes. These cisterns are liable to rust unless their interiors are protected by a special type of paint or by other means which are explained in the chapter on corrosion.

Fortunately, there are other types of cistern available. Undoubtedly the least troublesome are the polythene and glass fibre types.

These, of course, cannot corrode or be damaged by frost and they are extremely tough though light in weight. Some polythene cisterns are even flexible enough to be bent and passed through small trap doors into the loft.

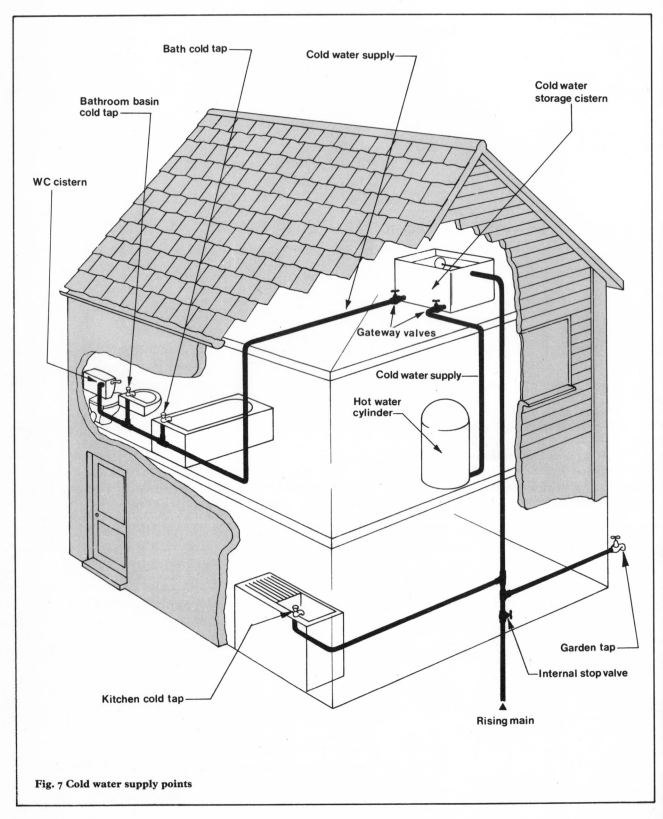

Fig. 7 Cold water supply points

Fig. 8 Gateway valve

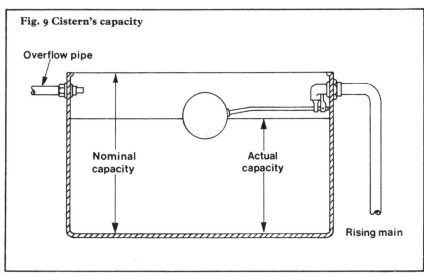

Fig. 9 Cistern's capacity

Overflow pipe

Nominal capacity

Actual capacity

Rising main

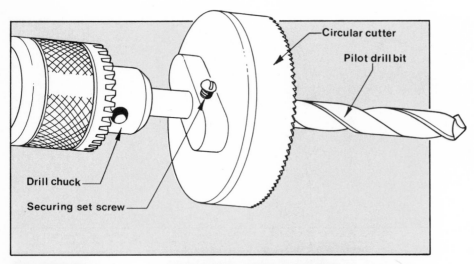

Circular cutter

Pilot drill bit

Drill chuck

Securing set screw

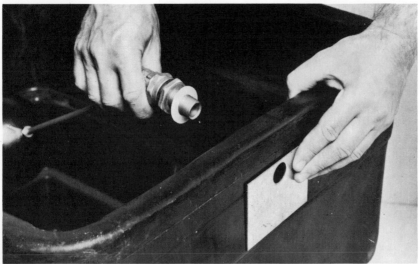

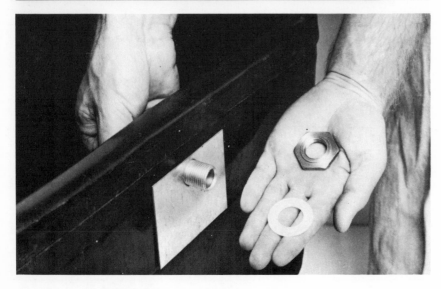

Fig. 10 Tank cutter

Fig. 11 Offering the stem of the float valve to the tank hole

Fig. 12 Offering the nut and plastic washer to the float valve stem

Fig. 13 Securing the nut to the stem

Fig. 14 Offering the tank connector to the float stem

Fig. 15 The tank connector fitted

Fig. 16 Copper rising main connected

(Photographs by courtesy of and Copyright Summerhill Heating Services Ltd)

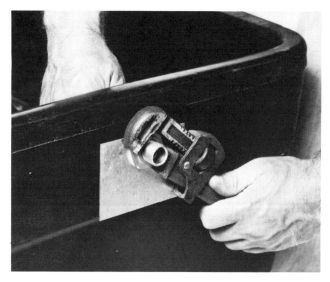

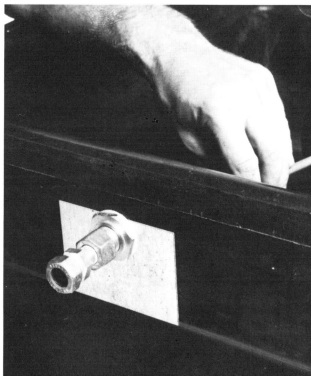

CAPACITIES

Most probably your cistern will be a galvanised type and its *actual* capacity will be 50 gallons. This is the normal maximum size stipulated by water boards in some parts of the country for a cistern which supplies hot and cold water systems. In other areas an 80

gallon capacity is the maximum requirement.

The quantities referred to represent the *actual* capacity of a cistern – to the point where the overflow pipe is filled, or rather just below it, *fig. 9*. If you see a cistern advertised as having a *nominal* capacity of, say, 60 gallons,

this would be the amount it could carry if filled to its brim. Its *actual* capacity would be 50 gallons. A cistern with a *nominal* capacity of 100 gallons will have an *actual* capacity of 84 gallons.

These figures will be of interest to you if it becomes necessary to buy a

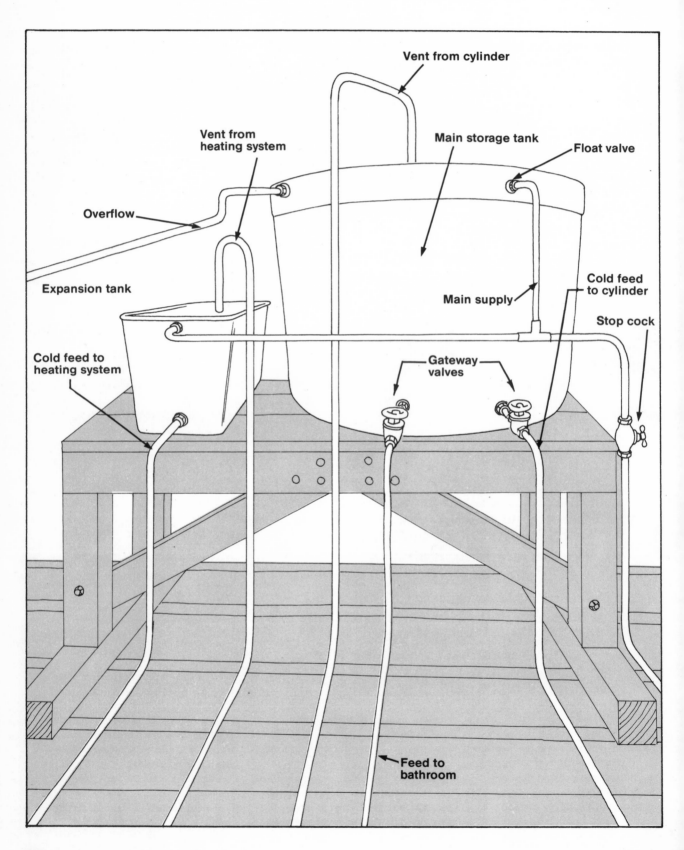

Fig. 17 The installation of a cistern on a firm platform base, showing pipe connections for feed and supply

new one. You can get a good idea of an existing cistern's capacity by measuring it.

A galvanised cistern measuring 30 inches long by 24 inches wide by 24 inches deep will have a nominal capacity of 60 gallons (50 gallons actual).

INSTALLING A CISTERN

An advantage of the round polythene cisterns is that they are fairly simple for a d-i-y man to install. It is not a difficult job to cut holes in a cistern of this type for the supply pipe connections.

The recommended distance from the base of a cistern for the supply pipe hole is 2 inches. The reason for leaving a space is to prevent grit and other foreign matter washed in from the main finding its way into the pipes.

Obviously, the greater the distance is, the more the capacity of the cistern will be reduced, but there will be less risk of debris entering the pipes.

In most cases it will be easier to cut the holes and fit the connectors *before* the cistern is taken into the loft.

BALL-VALVE HOLE

Near the top of the cistern a hole has to be made for the ball-valve. In most cases the centre of the hole will be $1\frac{1}{2}$ in from the top of the cistern, but its position may be dictated by a backplate which is fitted by some makers to support the ball-valve's weight.

This plate has a flange positioned against the cistern's flange which runs around its top. The tapping for the ball-valve is indicated by the position of the hole in the backplate.

The holes can be cut with a hole saw or a centre bit hole cutter or, better still, a hole saw attachment fixed in an electric drill.

To fix the pipes and ball-valve to the cistern, flange nuts are used.

A polythene or rubber washer should be fitted between the cistern and flange nut on the outside of the cistern.

FIRM BASE

It is essential that polythene cisterns

should stand on a firm and flat platform, *fig. 17*. The joists in the loft are not by themselves sufficient support.

Before attempting to replace a cistern, check that all the pipes involved are long enough to reach the holes in the new cistern. If not, they can be lengthened or shortened as described in the chapter on Pipes and Joints.

This is a point worth watching if you are planning to install a shower. In this case you may have to raise the level of the cistern to provide greater water pressure to the shower. And if you do this, make certain the cistern can be safely supported. Although these modern cisterns are light to handle, one gallon of water weighs 10 lb! The weight of the whole thing is therefore considerable, so a very strong timber framework must be made.

OVERFLOW PIPE

The overflow pipe position is very important. Its distance from the top of the cistern must be at least twice the pipe's diameter. Also, the bore of the pipe must be larger than that of the inlet – at least $\frac{3}{4}$in.

Note, too, that the height of the overflow pipe above the water must be at least one inch, or not less than the internal diameter of the pipe – whichever is the greater.

Make sure the overflow pipe has a slight fall to prevent water lying in it and possibly freezing.

The cistern should be covered with a lid to prevent insects entering and debris falling into it. Some polythene cisterns are supplied complete with lids.

Although the measurements quoted here are in imperial sizes, the plumbing industry has now 'gone metric'. We no longer talk of $\frac{1}{2}$ in pipe but 15 mm. The apparent discrepancy in the two measurements is explained on page 257, Pipes and Joints.

Ball-Valves

Most homes have at least two ball-valves – one in the w.c. cistern and the other in the cold water storage cistern. Ball-valves are simply a means of admitting water to a cistern to a pre-determined level – an inlet, in other words. They are self-operating and work only when a w.c. cistern is flushed or when water is drawn off, through a tap, from a storage cistern.

All ball-valves work on a similar principle although there are various types. A float – usually a hollow ball – operates a float arm (a rod). This opens (or closes) the ball-valve as the water in the cistern falls (or rises).

For example, when the w.c. is flushed and the cistern empties (or when water from the storage cistern is run off through a tap) the valve opens. This allows water to enter and fill the cistern to the level required.

When that level is reached, the valve closes again so that no more water can enter. The level of the water can be changed by adjusting the float arm, but more of that later.

PORTSMOUTH VALVES

Perhaps the most common type of ball-valve in use is the Portsmouth, fig. 18. This is a simple valve comprising a brass body containing a plug with (or without) a cap which screws on to its end. The body has a nozzle inlet through which the water enters.

The plug section is slotted and has a washer fitted at one end. The plug fits loosely in the valve body. The body has an opening through which the end of the float arm passes and fits into the slot in the plug. The float arm is held steady by a split pin.

As water rises in the cistern, the float arm rises and pivots on the split pin. This action pushes the washer end of the plug against the valve seating.

This closes the valve and prevents more water entering the cistern.

When water is drawn off, the water level falls, the float descends and pivots its arm in the other direction, pulling the plug from the valve seating and allowing water to enter.

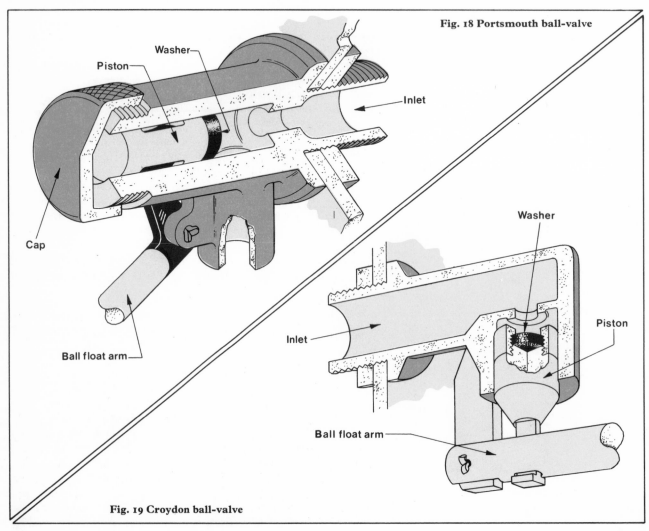

Fig. 18 Portsmouth ball-valve

Fig. 19 Croydon ball-valve

CROYDON VALVE

Another type of ball-valve is the Croydon, *fig. 19*, which works on a similar principle. Unlike the Portsmouth plug, which moves *horizontally*, the Croydon plug operates *vertically* within the valve body – down when the water falls and up when it rises.

These are the two most common types of valve, but there are others with which I will deal later.

Both the Portsmouth and the Croydon are likely to develop a fault from which most householders have suffered – a steady drip, or a flood of water, from the overflow (warning) pipe.

Various things can cause this trouble: a worn washer on the ball-valve, a fault in the ball float, or a worn valve seating. Or it may be that the valve is a type designed for a water pressure lower than that of the supply to which it is fitted.

STOPPING AN OVERFLOW

Before dealing with the cause of an overflow, the first essential is to stop the water flowing. Worry about repairs *after* this has been done.

If the cistern overflows in a roof space, it can cause considerable damage to ceilings and floor coverings, so no time should be lost.

First, open up all the taps and turn off the main stop-valve in the house. That will stop the overflow almost at once.

If there is no indoor stop-valve, the water will have to be turned off from outside the house, but open up all the taps *before* doing this.

Once the water in the cistern has fallen to its normal level (usually 2 or 3 inches below the overflow pipe) the taps can be turned off. But keep the stop-valve turned off meantime.

BALL FLOAT TROUBLES

You can now look around for the cause of the trouble. Examine the ball float first. This may be a copper type made in two halves soldered together.

Sometimes corrosion forms on the soldered seam and this in time can lead

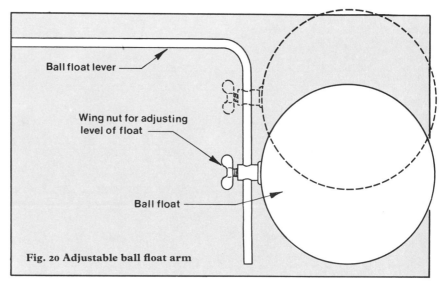

Fig. 20 Adjustable ball float arm

Ball float lever

Wing nut for adjusting level of float

Ball float

to a leak. The weight of the water will cause the ball float to sink. This, of course, means that the valve will be open all the time, and water will flow into the cistern continuously – above the level at which it would normally stop flowing – and cause an overflow.

As the overflow pipe usually leads out through an exterior wall of the house, it can flow harmlessly on to the ground below. In some situations, however, this can cause flooding problems if the pipe discharges, for example, near the door of an outside cupboard or coal shed. This is a point to watch, so find out exactly where the overflow pipes are located.

Another point to note is that although an overflow pipe can carry away a fair amount of water, it is intended as a *warning* pipe. There can be no guarantee that the pipe will be able to cope with a continuous flow of water from a ball-valve which is operated under mains pressure.

If the pipe cannot cope, the water will quickly flow over the sides of the cistern and cause flooding.

TEMPORARY REPAIR

If a fault is found in a ball float it is not worth the effort of making a repair. Unscrew it from the float arm and replace it with, preferably, a polythene type which will not corrode.

If a float develops a hole or crack when no replacement is immediately available, it is possible to make a makeshift repair.

Unscrew the float and empty it of water. Screw it back on the arm and enclose it in a plastic bag, tying the bag tightly by its neck around the float arm.

While on the subject of ball floats, it should be mentioned that the level of water in a cistern can be adjusted by bending a metal (not plastic) float arm upwards or downwards. If you bend it upwards the water level will rise. Bend it downwards to lower the water level. If you are not used to doing this, it is advisable to unscrew the float (to avoid damaging it) before you bend the arm.

Some plastic floats, incidentally, can be bought complete with a plastic float arm fitted with an adjustable screw, *fig. 20*. This enables you to raise or lower the float easily.

BALL-VALVE FAULTS

If the ball float is not responsible for the cistern overflowing, take a look at the ball-valve. Sometimes a ball-valve jams in either the open or closed position. Ball-valves are especially prone to this trouble in hard water areas.

To free the plug, move the float arm up and down several times. This may

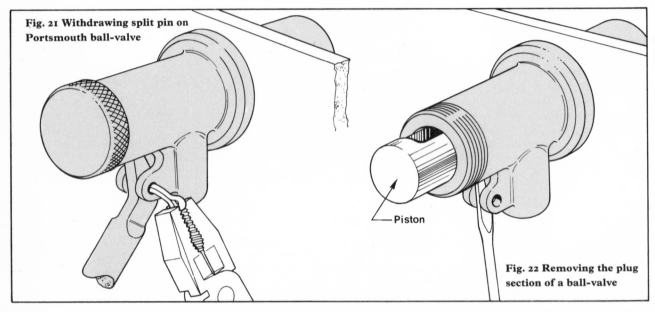

Fig. 21 Withdrawing split pin on Portsmouth ball-valve

— Piston

Fig. 22 Removing the plug section of a ball-valve

cure the trouble temporarily, but for a more permanent solution the ball-valve should be dismantled, cleaned and greased with Vaseline.

A steady drip from the overflow pipe is a sign that the ball-valve needs re-washering. As this involves dismantling, we can treat this job and that of cleaning the ball-valve as a combined operation.

REWASHERING

To rewasher a Portsmouth type ball-valve, you will need a $\frac{1}{2}$ in ball-valve washer. Turn off the water at the stopcock or stop-valve as described. Unscrew the cap (if there is one) on the body of the valve. Now close the ends of the split pin on which the float arm pivots. Do this with pliers – carefully or the pin may snap if it is corroded. Then withdraw the split pin, *fig. 21*.

Put a screwdriver blade in the slot on the valve body and push the plug section of the valve out of the open end, *fig. 22*. Make sure you don't drop it in the cistern!

The plug is in two parts, one of which is the washer retaining cap. This should be unscrewed with pliers, but be careful not to damage the valve body.

If you find the cap difficult to un-screw, an alternative is to pick out the old washer with a penknife. The new washer can then be persuaded to go under the lip of the cap, but make sure it fits firmly on the seating.

While the valve is dismantled, clean the plug inside and out with a fine grade of emery paper, grease it with Vaseline and reassemble in the body of the valve.

Croydon ball-valves are rewashered in a similar way to Portsmouth types, but if you have a Croydon valve fitted and it gives trouble, it is well worth considering replacing it with a modern diaphragm type.

DIAPHRAGM BALL-VALVES

If, after replacing the float arm, the overflow trouble persists, the seating of the ball-valve may be damaged. To reseat the valve you need a special reseating tool.

The expense of this tool and the effort involved is hardly worth while. It is better to get a new ball-valve, preferably a diaphragm pattern, *fig. 23*, which is less likely to leak or jam than a Portsmouth or Croydon type.

A diaphragm valve has a replaceable nylon nozzle which is closed by a

rubber diaphragm. This is operated by a plunger which passes through the backplate of the valve. The plunger is pressed against the diaphragm by the float arm as it pivots upwards when the water rises in the cistern.

Diaphragm valves rarely go wrong, but occasionally the diaphragm may jam against the nozzle. This will reduce the flow of water to a mere trickle.

Fortunately, these valves are simple to take apart. If the valve jams, un-screw by hand the knurled cap, *fig. 24*, and pick the diaphragm from the nozzle with a penknife. After cleaning and reassembling, the valve should work normally again.

WATER PRESSURES

Ball-valves are designed for low, medium or high water pressures. This is indicated by the diameter of the nozzle orifice.

If a low pressure valve is fitted to a pipe which is under mains pressure, this can cause a leak from the overflow pipe. The majority of ball-valves fitted to cold water storage cisterns are under high pressure and it is unlikely that the low pressure valve will have been fitted in error.

Ball-valves fitted to w.c. cisterns may be under low *or* high pressure. Most w.c.s, however, will be supplied by the storage cistern and will therefore be under low pressure.

If a high pressure valve were used in such an installation the w.c. cistern would fill very slowly. In persistent cases of slow filling a full-way valve may have to be fitted.

As a rule, ball-valves are stamped HP or LP (high pressure or low pressure). Diameters of nozzles are: high pressure, $\frac{1}{8}$ in; medium pressure $\frac{3}{16}$ in; low pressure, $\frac{1}{4}$ in; full-way, $\frac{3}{8}$ in or $\frac{1}{2}$ in.

NOISY VALVES

One of the greatest annoyances some ball-valves cause is noise when they are operating. Much of this is caused by ripples forming on the surface of the water as water flows in to the cistern. This causes the ball float to vibrate and the rest of the plumbing system involved magnifies the noise and at times causes water hammer (hammering in the pipes).

Many existing ball-valves are fitted with plastic silencer tubes screwed to the valve outlet, *fig. 25*. Through this tube the inflowing water discharges – below the water surface – thus reducing the ripples.

Unfortunately, from the point of view of noise, anyway, these tubes have been banned by the British Waterworks Association. The reason for this is the possible danger of contaminated water from a storage cistern being siphoned back to contaminate the main water supply.

At the time of writing, there has been no move to ban existing silencer tubes, but they should not be fitted in new installations.

OVERHEAD OUTLETS

Manufacturers have produced alternative ways of silencing the incoming rush of water and no doubt will continue to improve upon these methods.

Some diaphragm ball-valves are now designed with an overhead outlet, *fig. 26*. In one case, at least, this outlet can be adjusted so that the spray

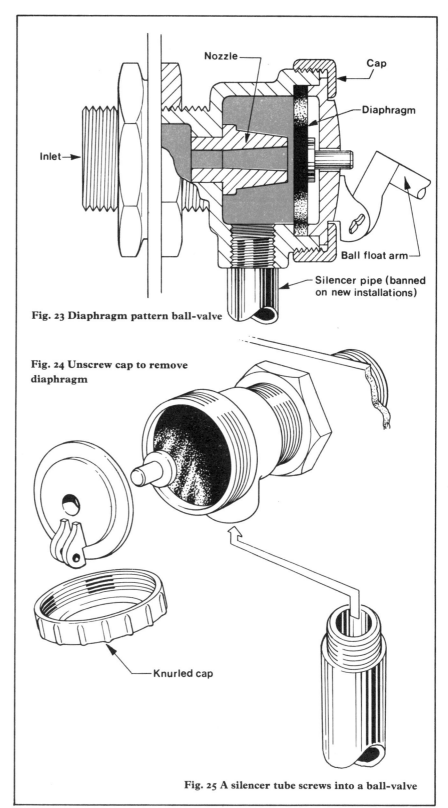

Fig. 23 Diaphragm pattern ball-valve

Fig. 24 Unscrew cap to remove diaphragm

Fig. 25 A silencer tube screws into a ball-valve

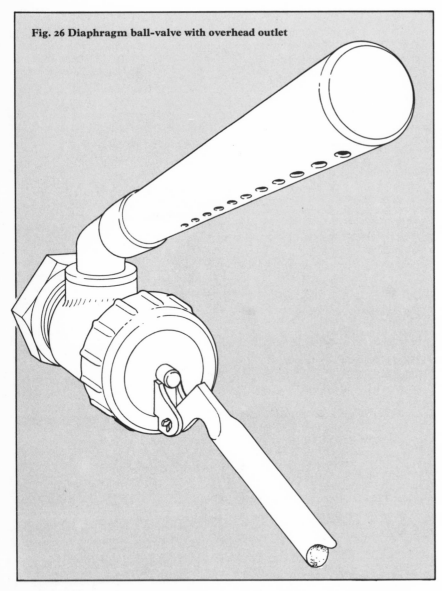

Fig. 26 Diaphragm ball-valve with overhead outlet

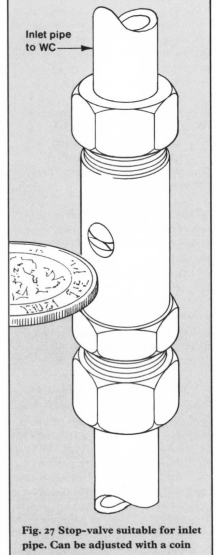

Inlet pipe to WC →

Fig. 27 Stop-valve suitable for inlet pipe. Can be adjusted with a coin

of incoming water hits the side of the cistern instead of the water surface.

There are other ways in which a noisy water supply can be quietened. The pipe attached to the ball-valve, for instance, should be firmly anchored to a permanent support such as the roof timbers.

EQUILIBRIUM VALVES
If your cistern suffers from severe water hammer, or if the water pressure is variable, it may be worth while fitting an equilibrium valve. Although

more costly than ordinary ball-valves, these types have a smooth, quiet action.

An equilibrium valve has a channel drilled in its plug which lets water pass through to another water chamber behind it. So there is equal pressure behind and in front of the plug. In other ball-valves, water pressure is constantly trying to force the valve open from one side only.

When a ball-valve on a w.c. cistern needs attention, it usually means that the bath and the bathroom basin taps

are also deprived of water when it is turned off at the stop-valve. To avoid this, it is worth fitting a simple stop-valve in the pipe to the w.c. ball-valve, *fig. 27.* (A suitable valve is the Mark-fram control valve. Another is the Nevastop.)

This can be fixed anywhere along this pipe, but preferably near the w.c. cistern. It needs only a screwdriver or coin to turn it off or on and can be fitted easily by using compression joints. These are dealt with under Pipes and Joints, page 249.

Hot Water Systems

Once the layout of the cold water supply system is understood, you will find it easier to appreciate the workings of the hot water system. Although the hot and cold water systems work partly in conjunction with each other, I have omitted most of the cold water pipes in *figs. 28* and *29* so that the hot water system can be more readily understood. In *fig. 30*, however, I have combined both hot and cold systems in one diagram, illustrating an indirect hot water system.

I must emphasise that the arrangements shown in these diagrams are *basic* layouts. Variations may be found in some systems, especially in older houses where the plumbing has been

extended or altered from time to time.

In older houses some pipes may appear to serve no purpose whatever! It may be that they form part of an old plumbing system now bypassed by a later design.

The safest course to follow in these circumstances is to leave well alone until you can get advice from an expert. Plumbing in some ways is rather like electricity. It's perfectly safe to carry out alterations and repairs yourself provided you know exactly what is involved!

TWO SYSTEMS
I will now describe a basic hot water system, which is not to be confused

with a central heating system. For the moment I will deal solely with a supply of water for washing, bathing and similar purposes, heated by a boiler.

There are two types of hot water systems – direct and indirect.

A typical *direct* system comprises a hot water cylinder which is fed with water from the cold water storage cistern in the loft, *fig. 28*.

The water flows down what is called the return pipe from the *bottom* of the hot water cylinder to the *bottom* of the boiler. There the water is heated and rises up the flow pipe from the *top* of the boiler to the *top* of the cylinder.

As it enters the cylinder, the hot water pushes the cold water down the

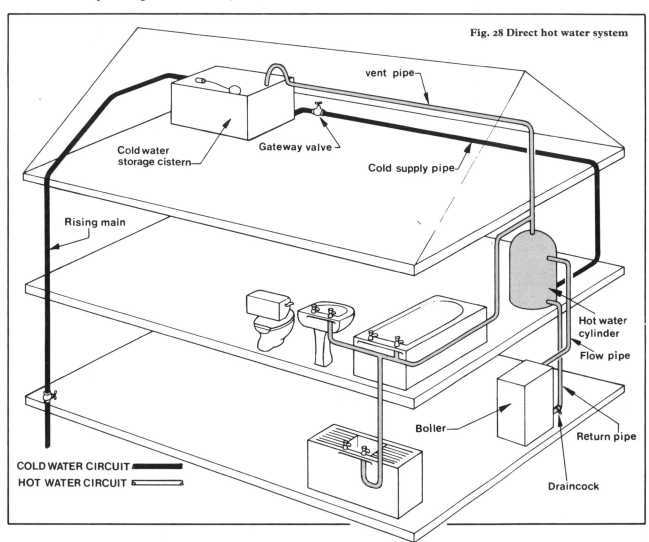

Fig. 28 Direct hot water system

Cold water storage cistern

vent pipe

Gateway valve

Cold supply pipe

Rising main

Hot water cylinder

Flow pipe

Boiler

Return pipe

Draincock

COLD WATER CIRCUIT
HOT WATER CIRCUIT

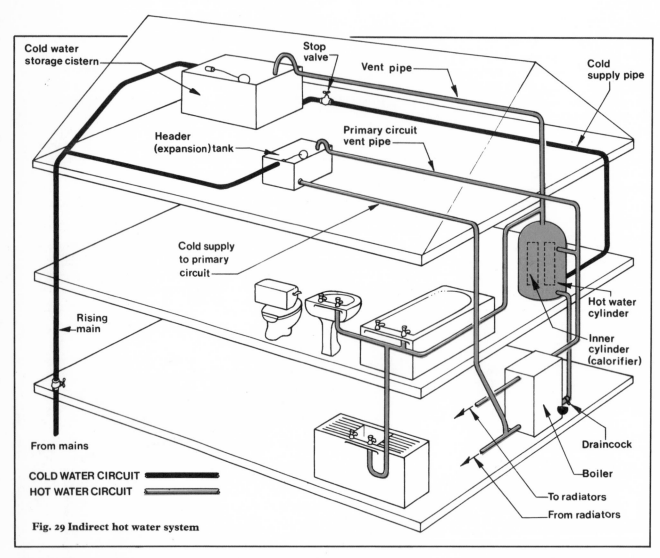

Cold water storage cistern

Stop valve

Vent pipe

Cold supply pipe

Header (expansion) tank

Primary circuit vent pipe

Cold supply to primary circuit

Hot water cylinder

Rising main

Inner cylinder (calorifier)

From mains

Draincock

COLD WATER CIRCUIT

HOT WATER CIRCUIT

Boiler

To radiators

From radiators

Fig. 29 Indirect hot water system

return pipe to the boiler to be heated.

This circulation or cycle continues until all the water in the boiler and cylinder circuit is hot.

BOILING POINT
If the boiler were allowed to burn continuously without any water being run off from the hot water taps, the water would boil. You may have noticed your boiler makes a noise rather like a boiling kettle when the water is very hot. This is a sign that the water is near, or has reached, boiling point.

Boilers should never be allowed to boil. The water can usually be cooled down sufficiently by running some off from the hot water taps. However,

there is a safety device built into hot water systems which safeguards them against boiling. This is the vent pipe.

This pipe runs from the top of the cylinder up to the cold water storage cistern. The pipe is open at its top end and is normally bent over the cistern. If the water in the cylinder boils, it is pushed up the vent pipe to discharge into the cold water storage cistern.

Supplies of heated water to the hot water taps come from a branch pipe which is connected, just above the hot water cylinder, to the vent pipe.

A draincock should be fitted at the lowest point of the system. It is usually on the return pipe near the boiler. The draincock enables the whole system to

be emptied if necessary.

The direct method of heating water is a very common one and the principles involved in it are similar whether the hot water is stored in a cylinder or in a rectangular galvanised steel tank. And the same principles apply to any method of heating – solid fuel, gas, oil or electricity.

INDIRECT SYSTEM
Two separate circuits are used in an *indirect* system, *fig. 29*. One, called the primary, is from the boiler to a small cylinder, or calorifier, fitted in the main hot water cylinder. Water cannot be drawn off the primary circuit (unless the system is drained off). Therefore

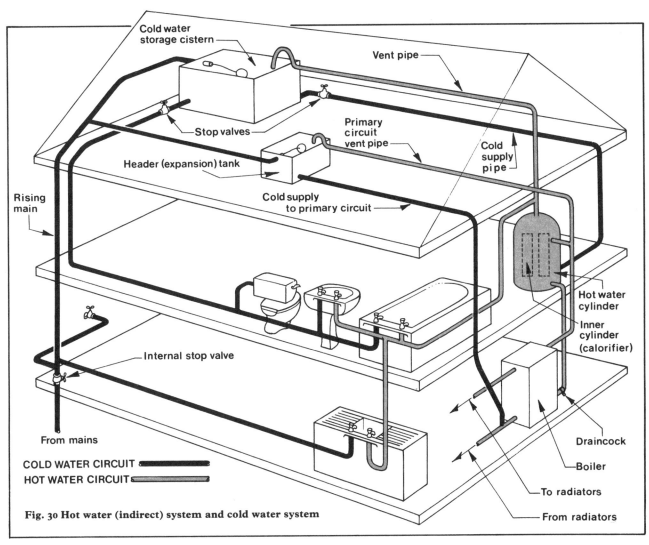

Cold water
storage cistern

Vent pipe

Primary
circuit
vent pipe

Cold
supply
pipe

Stop valves

Header (expansion) tank

Cold supply
to primary circuit

Rising
main

Hot water
cylinder

Inner
cylinder
(calorifier)

Internal stop valve

From mains

COLD WATER CIRCUIT
HOT WATER CIRCUIT

Draincock

Boiler

To radiators

From radiators

Fig. 30 Hot water (indirect) system and cold water system

the same water is used over and over again.

Water in the *main* cylinder is heated indirectly by the inner cylinder and is supplied to the hot taps.

The inner cylinder normally gets its own supply of cold water from a small header or expansion tank. This is needed only to replace losses caused by evaporation or for renewing the water supply to the inner cylinder if the whole system is drained off.

The header tank's capacity is usually around ten gallons and it has its own vent pipe. Some types of indirect cylinder, however, do not need a header tank.

If radiators are added to an indirect

system they are supplied by the primary circuit.

It is essential in most cases that an indirect hot water system should be used if any form of central heating is installed in the system.

How can you tell which system is installed in your house? Look at the connections on the cylinder. On an indirect cylinder both the primary connections are male. *Figures 31* and *32* show two types of indirect cylinder to illustrate this point.

The secondary and cold water connections are female. On a direct cylinder all the connections are female, *fig. 33*.

ADVANTAGE

A big advantage of an indirect system is comparative freedom from scale in hard water areas or from corrosion in soft water areas. (Scale and corrosion are dealt with in a separate chapter).

HEADER TANK

One purpose of a header tank in an indirect system is to allow for expansion of the primary circuit when it has been heated. Expansion can cause the volume of water in the circuit to be increased by several gallons.

Therefore, the ball-valve in the header tank should be adjusted so that it cuts off the supply when only 2 or 3 inches of water are in the tank. When expansion takes place, the water will rise above the level of the ball float but should not rise up to the level of the ball-valve.

Incidentally, as this ball-valve will not need to operate very often, to replace water lost through evaporation, it may jam when it is in either the open or closed position. A careful eye should therefore be kept on it.

To be on the safe side, it is better to change the ball-valve, if it is a Portsmouth or Croydon type, to a modern diaphragm valve which was described earlier in the chapter on ball-valves.

AIR LOCKS

One of the most common problems in hot water systems is an air lock. Sometimes you may find that hot water will flow from a tap evenly at first, but soon it will be reduced to a mere trickle, or

the water may stop flowing entirely.

There can be several reasons for air locks forming, some of which I will outline. First, though, the cure.

Fit one end of a length of garden hose to the tap which has the air lock and the other end to the cold water tap in the kitchen, *fig. 34.* When both taps are fully turned on, the pressure from the main should force the air bubbles out of the pipe and up through the vent pipe.

MAINS PRESSURE NEEDED

The kitchen tap is the one to use because normally it will be the only one which is under mains pressure. The pressure at the taps supplied by the cold water storage cistern will not usually be great enough to shift the air bubble.

If an air lock forms in a pipe supplying a bath tap, it is unlikely that

your hose pipe will fit the tap. The solution here is to connect the hose to the bathroom basin tap instead. Both taps are fed by the same supply pipe so the air lock can be dispersed from either.

One possible cause of an air lock is that the diameter of the pipe supplying cold water to the hot water cylinder, *fig. 35,* is too small. It should be at least $\frac{3}{4}$ in in diameter. A $\frac{1}{2}$ in pipe fitted here in error can cause air locks.

Other possible causes of air locks include:

1. A $\frac{1}{2}$ in diameter stop-valve fitted in error on the cold water supply pipe to the hot water cylinder. The remedy for this is to change the stop-valve to a $\frac{3}{4}$ in type.

2. The stop-valve is partly closed. It should, of course, be kept fully open or its diameter will, in effect, be reduced.

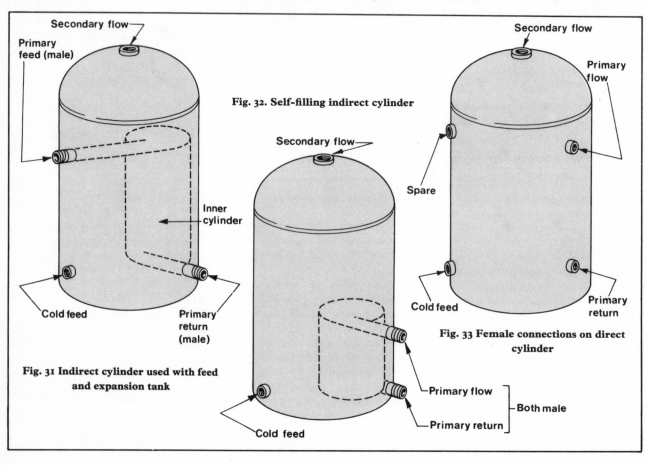

Fig. 32. Self-filling indirect cylinder

Fig. 31 Indirect cylinder used with feed and expansion tank

Fig. 33 Female connections on direct cylinder

3. The cold water storage cistern is too small to supply enough water for both the bath taps. The water level in the cistern may drop to below the draw-off point before the bath is filled.

Check that the *actual* capacity of the cold water cistern is at least 50 gallons.

4. Check that the draw-off point for the hot water cylinder is no more than 2 in from the base of the cold water storage cistern (*X* in *fig. 35*). If the distance is greater than 2 in, the capacity of the cistern will be reduced accordingly.

5. Hot water supply pipes are exactly horizontal or rise slightly.

In a correctly designed system, these pipes should, of course, *fall* slightly, *fig. 36*, from the point at which they are connected to the vent pipe, to the point where they rise to be connected to the hot water taps. The vent pipe is there to let any trapped air escape, so any air bubbles which form in the pipes should be able to reach the vent pipe easily.

6. If the hot water system has to be drained entirely for any reason, the whole of the hot water circuit will be filled with air.

REFILLING
To prevent air locks forming when refilling the system, connect a hosepipe to the draincock beside the boiler and to the cold tap in the kitchen. Turn both the taps on and the cistern will fill upwards, the water driving the air out of the system in front of it.

There are other causes of an inadequate flow from hot water taps which can be due to a badly designed system. For example, if the boiler is not standing absolutely level an air bubble can form in the boiler itself. This can cause loud banging sounds in the system.

Trouble can also arise if the flow and return connections between boiler and cylinder are not correctly made. The correct method of making these connections is shown in *fig. 30*.

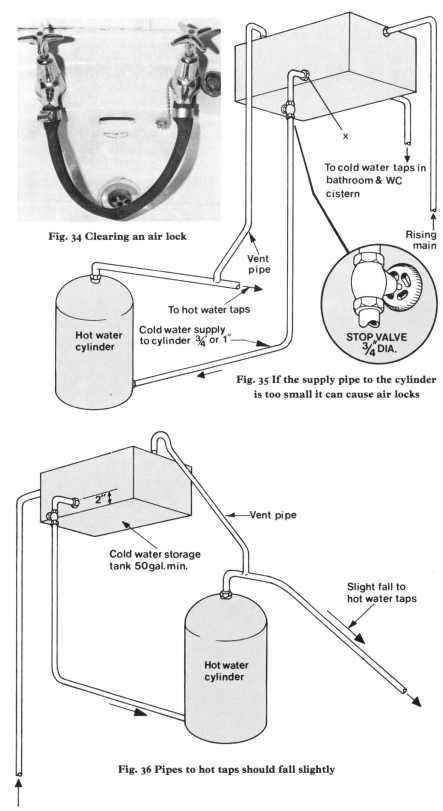

Fig. 34 Clearing an air lock

Vent pipe

To hot water taps

To cold water taps in bathroom & WC cistern

Rising main

x

Hot water cylinder

Cold water supply to cylinder ¾" or 1"

STOP VALVE ¾" DIA.

Fig. 35 If the supply pipe to the cylinder is too small it can cause air locks

Vent pipe

2"

Cold water storage tank 50 gal. min.

Slight fall to hot water taps

Hot water cylinder

Fig. 36 Pipes to hot taps should fall slightly

Toilet Cistern Troubles

One room in the house which is often more likely to develop plumbing troubles than any other room is the lavatory. And the piece of equipment frequently responsible is the flushing cistern.

It may be noisy, its ball-valve may jam or it may refuse to flush the first time it is pulled. These are the most common problems which can arise.

First a brief outline of how flushing cisterns work. They are normally supplied with water from the cold water storage cistern in the loft, but some are supplied direct from the main.

BALL-VALVE INLET

In each case, the water enters the cistern through a ball-valve inlet as in the cold water storage cistern. Occasionally the toilet cistern may overflow due to the ball-valve jamming or its washer becoming worn out. If that happens, the treatment is the same as that described in Ball-valves, page 225.

Turn off the water from the internal stop-valve. If there isn't one, you will have to drain off the main storage cistern after turning off the water from the external stopcock. Flush the toilet cistern to empty it, then proceed as described on page 225.

While you are at it, clean out any rust flakes or other debris from the base of the flushing cistern.

FLUSHING PROBLEMS

A most annoying and embarrassing situation is a flushing cistern which won't flush the first time. Equally irritating is a cistern which continues to discharge after the flushing process is completed.

Let's take first the old-fashioned high level type, the Burlington pattern flushing cistern, *fig. 37*. Its base contains a well in which stands a heavy bell. The bell is joined to a lever which pivots on a support fixed in the cistern. The chain is attached to the other end of the lever.

Pull the chain and the bell is raised. Release the chain and the bell falls. Its weight traps water in the well, forcing the water level in the bell to rise, and some water flows over a stand pipe into the flush pipe.

The stand or siphon pipe is connected to the flush pipe and rises under the bell to a point above the normal water level.

VACUUM

When this water passes through the flush pipe it creates a partial vacuum. The air pushes water in the cistern under the bell down through the flush pipe and flushes the toilet pan.

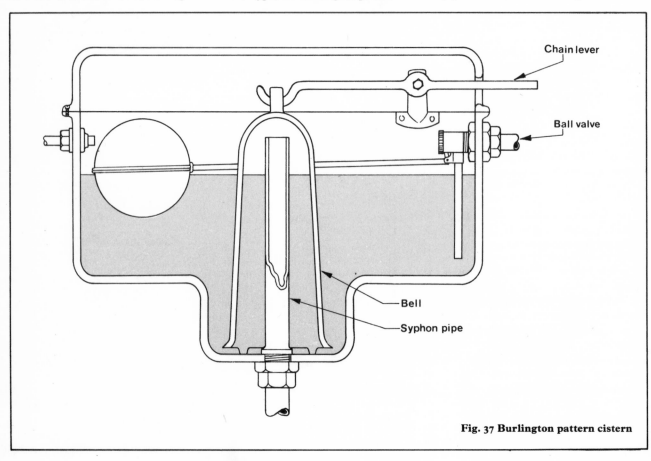

Chain lever

Ball valve

Bell

Syphon pipe

Fig. 37 Burlington pattern cistern

The flow of water continues until air gets under the bell and breaks what is called siphonic action.

It will be seen that this is not a complicated cistern, but it can be a very noisy one. Not a great deal can go wrong with a Burlington, but after a time grit and other rubbish may collect in the well of the cistern. This causes water to continue to flow down the flush pipe after the flushing operation is completed.

The cure, of course, is to clean the cistern out – if you can get at its bottom, that is! Access can usually be obtained by lifting off the lid.

Occasionally this type of cistern will give trouble after a new ball-valve has been fitted. The flow of water into the cistern is then usually so rapid compared with when the old valve was operated, that air is not able to reach the rim of the bell. The result is again

continuous siphonage.

To cure this, it should be sufficient partly to close the stop-valve on the inlet pipe. If no stop-valve is fitted, this should be done.

CORROSION

Burlington pattern cisterns are also subject to corrosion inside and out. They can be wire brushed to remove loose rust and treated with a chemical rust remover to get rid of the rest.

The interior of the cistern can then be painted, when dry, with bituminous paint and the exterior with ordinary paint.

However, if the cistern gets into a state such as I have described, you may feel that all the repair and maintenance necessary is hardly worth the effort, and you will probably consider having the cistern replaced with a modern direct action type.

If it is desired to keep a new cistern at a high level, you can get one which has a well bottom. These are specially designed as replacement cisterns for the Burlington models.

A far better solution, though, is to have a modern, low-level suite fitted. This type is much easier to get at when things go wrong.

LOW-LEVEL CISTERN

Now let's see what faults can arise with low-level direct action cisterns. First, a look at how these cisterns work, however.

Most of them have a flat base and a siphon pipe which is connected direct to the flush pipe. The siphon pipe rises above the level of the water. It is joined to an open-ended dome below the water which terminates just above the base of the cistern. The design may vary according to the model.

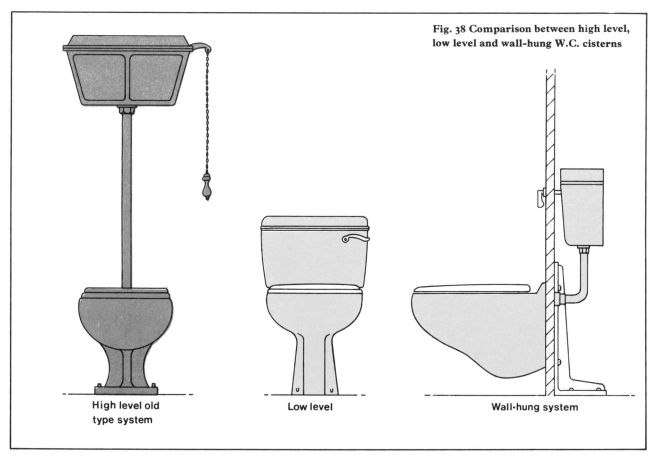

Fig. 38 Comparison between high level, low level and wall-hung W.C. cisterns

High level old type system

Low level

Wall-hung system

When the lever is pulled to flush the toilet, a disc with one or more holes in it rises in the dome. A diaphragm or flap valve covers these holes and does not allow any water to pass the disc. This action causes water to be thrown over the bend in the siphon pipe into the flush pipe.

As the water falls, it mixes with air and makes a partial vacuum. The water pressure now increases behind the flap valve and forces it away from the disc. Water flows through the holes and the cistern empties.

THE FLAP VALVE

It is failure of the flap valve which is usually to blame when the cistern refuses to flush at the first pull or even after several attempts.

Renewing the flap valve is not a difficult job, but it is not really one I would recommend for anyone who has no plumbing experience. Once you have seen the job done, however, you will probably say, 'nothing to it'.

New flap valves can be obtained from plumbers' or builders' merchants. They are made in various sizes, but you can safely choose the largest size. As they are made of thin plastic they can be easily trimmed to size with scissors if too large. It is a good plan to keep one or two spares handy once you know the size required.

To replace a faulty flap valve, first turn off the water at the internal stop-valve or tie up the ball float arm, *fig. 39*. This will prevent more water entering the cistern. Flush the cistern to empty it of water.

The next job is to unscrew the nut which holds the flush pipe in position, *fig. 40*. Have a bowl or bucket handy to catch what water there is left in the cistern after flushing.

Immediately above this nut is a larger one just below the cistern. Unscrew this next and use a wrench with jaws that open wide. After removing this nut you can then lift out the siphoning mechanism complete.

Now disconnect the rod or hook which is joined to the operating lever,

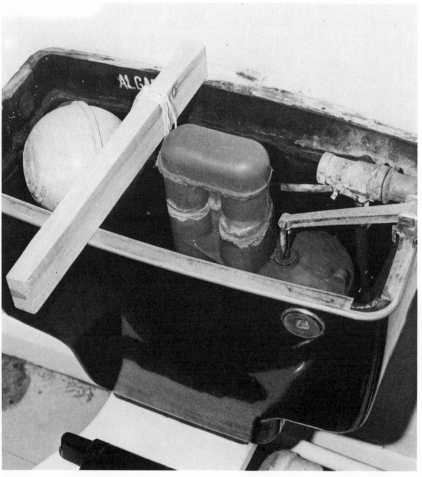

Fig. 39 Ball float arm tied up

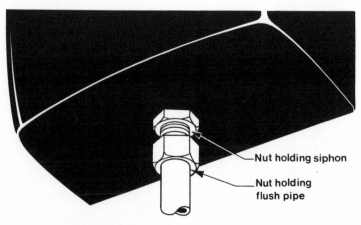

Nut holding siphon

Nut holding flush pipe

Fig. 40 Remove these nuts to release siphoning mechanism

fig. 41. Pull up the disc and the rod which operates it and you will see the old flap valve, or what is left of it.

TRIM TO SIZE
Remove this and replace it with your new plastic flap valve and trim it to the same size as the disc it is to cover. The valve must not foul the sides of the siphon.

(Means of access to the disc and flap valve will vary according to the make of cistern. Some siphons are in two parts which are bolted together near the base. Make sure you know the order in which to put back all the bits and pieces.)

Before reassembling all the components in reverse order, clean out the cistern and the siphon. All sorts of rubbish tends to collect in the bottom of a w.c. cistern and if any of it gets under the siphon, it can cause water to trickle continuously down the flush pipe after the cistern has been flushed. In other words, continuous siphonage takes place, as already described.

WATER LEVEL
Before you put the lid back on the cistern, restore the water supply, flush the pan and note the level to which the water has risen in the cistern when the ball-valve closes and water stops flowing in.

This level should be about $\frac{1}{2}$ in below the overflow pipe outlet. If it is lower than this, you may find that when the cistern is flushed the pan is not completely cleared.

This is an irritating fault sometimes caused because the flush is inadequate. Also, if the water level is too low, the cistern may fail to flush at the first pull.

You can control the water level either by bending the float arm (if a metal type) up or down or by adjusting the screw on the arm as described earlier.

Another reason for an inadequate flush can be that something is obstructing the flush pipe at the point where it is connected to the toilet pan. Or there may be an obstruction around the rim of the pan. The only way you can check this is by holding a small hand mirror in the pan under the rim.

When a flushing cistern is working properly, the water should run around each side of the pan in two cascades and meet in the centre of the front.

Sometimes a toilet cistern is suspected of having sprung a leak when its exterior surface is covered in moisture which, in severe cases, may drip to the floor.

Usually this is due to condensation and the answer to the problem is to increase ventilation in the room and to introduce some form of dry heat – a heated towel rail, for example, or a radiant heater fixed high up on the wall.

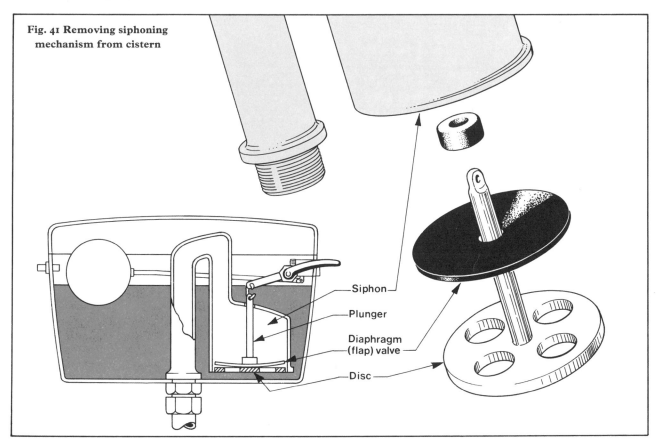

Fig. 41 Removing siphoning mechanism from cistern

Siphon

Plunger

Diaphragm (flap) valve

Disc

Taps Old and New

Rewashering a tap is a job every house-holder should be able to do. It is a simple operation, especially if the taps are modern types.

There is a wide variety of taps, but generally speaking most of them are based on two patterns. One is the bib tap, *fig. 48*; the other is the pillar tap, *fig. 49.*

Bib taps used to be the type fitted at kitchen sinks and are still fitted in some cases. These have a horizontal inlet. Pillar taps have a vertical inlet and are more likely to be found in bathrooms and wash basins. The procedure for rewashering is similar in each case.

An indication that a tap needs a new washer is, of course, a steady drip which persists even when the tap is tightly turned off. But there may be other causes to account for the drip.

WASHER SIZES

If you suspect that the washer is faulty on a cold water tap, get a new washer before dismantling. For cold water taps on a kitchen sink or bathroom basin you normally need a $\frac{1}{2}$ in washer, but for bath taps the size is $\frac{3}{4}$ in (a garden tap is usually fitted with a $\frac{1}{2}$ in washer).

I suggest that once you know the sizes of the washers required, you keep a small supply by you, or better still, buy the washers complete with jumpers, *fig. 50.*

The reason I suggest this is because old washers are sometimes very difficult to remove from their jumpers. The majority of washers on sale now are suitable for both hot and cold water taps, but check this when you buy them.

For rewashering taps you need two wrenches – one for holding the body of the tap and the other for turning the headgear. One wrench should prefer-ably have slim jaws so that they can fit under the easyclean cover.

TURN OFF THE WATER

First turn off the water supply to the tap. If it is a mains tap, turn off the

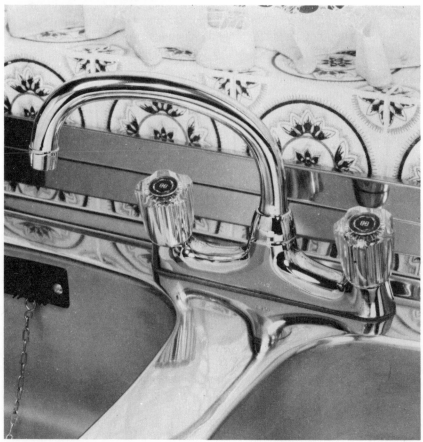

There is a wide range of taps available for modern plumbing installations

Fig. 42 Bath mixer taps

Fig. 43 Mixer taps for a double sink unit

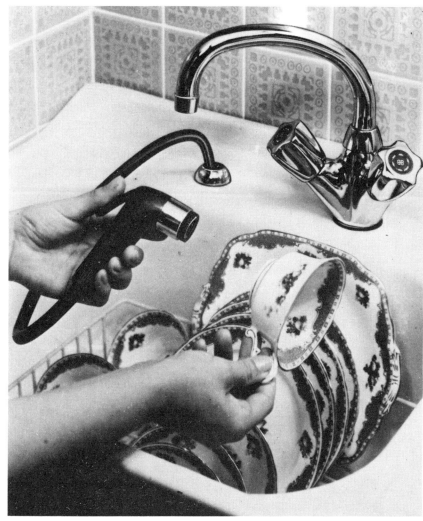

Fig. 44 Sink mixer with hot water spray attachment

Fig. 45 Wall mounted Bibcock

Fig. 46 Pillar tap for sink

Fig. 47 Wash basin tap

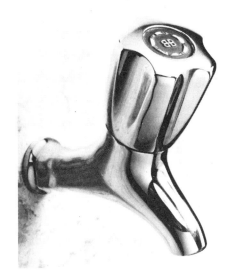

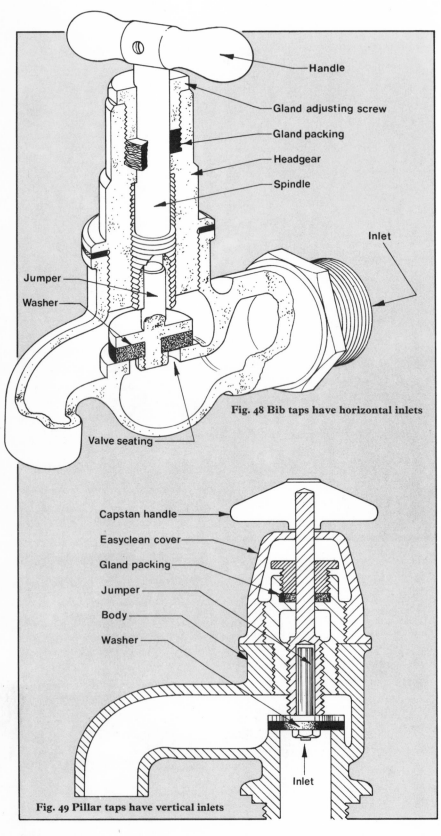

Handle

Gland adjusting screw

Gland packing

Headgear

Spindle

Inlet

Jumper

Washer

Valve seating

Fig. 48 Bib taps have horizontal inlets

Capstan handle

Easyclean cover

Gland packing

Jumper

Body

Washer

Inlet

Fig. 49 Pillar taps have vertical inlets

internal stop-valve on the rising main or the stopcock in the pavement as described earlier.

For the bathroom or other taps which are fed from the storage cistern, turn off the stop-valve on the supply pipe.

If there is no stop-valve on the supply pipe, you will have to drain all the water from the cold water storage cistern.

To do this, tie up the ball float arm so that the ball-valve closes and no more water can enter the cistern. Then open the bathroom cold taps and run off all the water in the cold water cistern.

If the tap to be rewashered is a hot water tap, you will still have to follow this procedure if there are no stop-valves on the supply pipes.

Having emptied the cold water cistern, turn on the hot water tap which is to be rewashered and let the water flow. You will probably find you will lose very little hot water.

The reason for this is that the hot water cylinder is emptied from its *top*. Once the water in it has fallen below the level of its discharge pipe, water will cease to flow.

Now turn on the tap as far as it will go. If there is an easyclean cover on the tap, this should be raised first.

STUBBORN COVERS
Here you will probably meet your first snag, especially if the cover hasn't been unscrewed for years. Sometimes you can unscrew the cover by hand, but stubborn covers will have to be shifted with a wrench.

If you have to use a wrench, protect the chromium plating of the tap by padding the jaws. In very stubborn cases it helps to apply a little oil between the easyclean cover and the tap spindle, *fig. 51.*

Another way to move an easyclean cover is to pour boiling water over it. Then try to shift it wearing a glove. As the metal expands with the heat, any scale deposits will be loosened and the cover should be easier to turn.

Once the cover is raised, *fig. 52a*, you

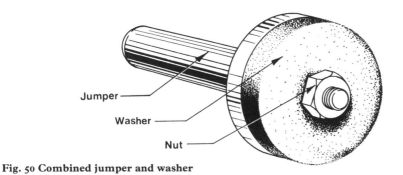

Fig. 50 Combined jumper and washer

Fig. 51 Oiling a tap spindle helps to remove a stubborn cover

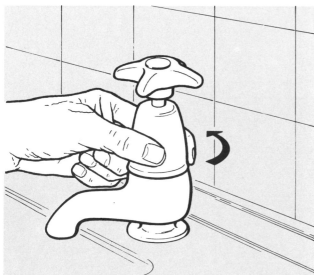

Fig. 52a Unscrewing an easyclean cover

Fig. 52b Removing the headgear

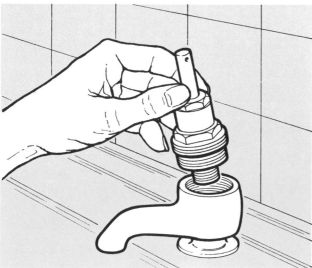

Fig. 52c Headgear of tap removed

Fig. 52d Jumper and washer removed from tap

Fig. 53 Tap with capstan handle

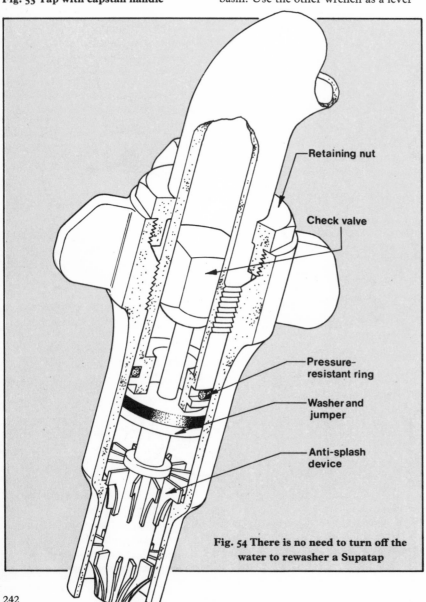

Retaining nut

Check valve

Pressure-resistant ring

Washer and jumper

Anti-splash device

Fig. 54 There is no need to turn off the water to rewasher a Supatap

can get at the headgear with the slim-jawed wrench, *fig. 52b*. Use the other wrench (padded) to grip the tap's body. Turn the headgear anti-clockwise to unscrew it. It lifts right out of the body of the tap, *fig. 52c*.

The headgear may also be difficult to shift. Sometimes a little drop of oil will help here too, but if it has become badly corroded with scale, considerable force may be needed to move it.

Be careful here not to exert too much force or you may wrench the tap away from its seating in the sink or basin. Use the other wrench as a lever to counter the muscle power.

With the headgear removed, the jumper of a cold water tap with the old washer attached, *fig. 52d*, will probably be seen sitting on the valve seating near the bottom of the body. (See also hot water taps section.)

If you intend only to renew the washer and not the jumper, unscrew the small nut which holds it to the jumper, release the washer, fit the new one and replace the nut. If it is impossible to shift the nut (it too may be scaled up) fit a new combined jumper and washer.

Replace this in the tap, screw back the headgear, tightly, and replace the easyclean cover (not too tightly).

Turn on the water (or release the arm of the ball float in the cistern) and your tap should now turn off without dripping.

CAPSTAN HANDLES

Before moving on to other types of tap, there are one or two points worth noting if this is your first attempt at rewashering. I suggested earlier that one of your wrenches should have slim jaws so that it can slip under the easy-clean cover.

This is not really essential if the handle of the tap is a capstan type, *fig. 53*. Capstan handles are secured by a small grub screw. Unscrew and remove this and the handle should come off the spindle by simply lifting it upwards.

Here again, however, you may have difficulty in shifting it. One answer is to protect the handle with a thick cloth and tap it gently from below with a hammer (a soft faced hammer is useful here). Be ready to grasp the handle or it may fly off and damage the sink or basin.

If this doesn't work, turn the tap on full, then insert an adjustable spanner on the spindle just above the easyclean cover. Turn the tap off. As you do so, the handle will be forced upwards and off. Don't use too much force or the cover may be damaged.

Having removed the handle and

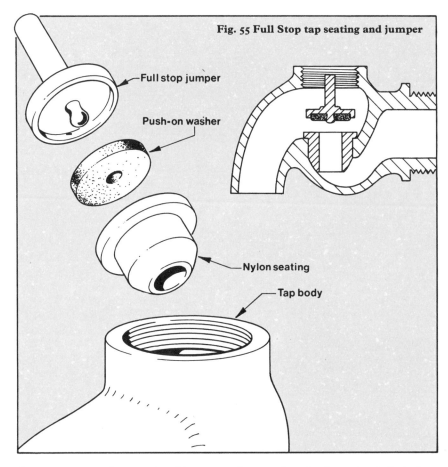

Fig. 55 Full Stop tap seating and jumper

Full stop jumper

Push-on washer

Nylon seating

Tap body

the cover, you are less restricted in your choice of wrench to shift the headgear of the tap.

Before replacing the cover and the headgear, grease the screw threads with Vaseline. Never overtighten a component.

REWASHERING SUPATAPS

Modern taps are different in appearance to the old patterns, but generally the rewashering procedure is similar. One exception to this, however, is the Supatap, *fig. 54*.

To rewasher this type of tap there is no need to turn off the water. First undo the retaining nut. Then turn the tap on and continue until the nozzle comes off. Don't be alarmed when the water starts to flow. This will soon stop when the check valve drops to seal the outlet.

If you then turn the nozzle upside down and tap it, the anti-splash device will fall out. Release the jumper and washer from the device; replace with a new jumper and washer combined.

Replace the anti-splash device in the nozzle and note that the nozzle is connected to the other part of the tap with a *left-hand* thread.

Water will flow again as the nozzle is replaced. When the nozzle is almost closed, tighten the retaining nut and close the tap fully.

Some taps have a combined handle and easyclean cover with a 'hot' and 'cold' indicator recessed in the cover. These indicators can be levered out gently with a penknife. Underneath will be a screw which holds the cover in position.

Undo the screw to remove the cover and the tap mechanism will be revealed. This should be similar to an ordinary tap.

HOT WATER TAPS

Rewashering a hot water tap is an operation similar to that with a cold water tap, but there is one difference. When the headgear is removed, the jumper and washer will probably still be in it instead of resting on the valve seating. Although you may be able to turn the jumper, it won't come away from the tap.

This is because it is pegged into the tap to ensure that, when the tap is turned on, the jumper and washer can be raised inside. Hot water pressure from the storage cylinder is normally too low to raise a jumper from the valve seating.

In these circumstances, the nut holding the washer to the jumper *must* be removed. Here you will probably have to apply a little oil to the nut and then give it time to soak through.

If the nut defies all efforts to shift it, the only thing to do is to prise the jumper out of the body of the tap with a screwdriver and replace it with a new jumper and washer combined.

PEGGING

Unfortunately, prising the jumper out will break the pegging, so the only way to ensure the new jumper will stay in the headgear of the tap is to burr the jumper so that it grips in the headgear.

This, however, should not be attempted until every effort has been made to unscrew the nut holding the old washer.

WORN SEATING

If a tap still drips after a new washer has been fitted, the valve seating of the tap may have become worn through constant use and age. There *are* reseating tools available, but the effort of doing the job is hardly worth while when you can buy a simple device to overcome the problem.

This is the Full Stop nylon washer and seating set combined, *fig. 55*, and costs only a few pence from ironmongers and some d-i-y shops.

All you do is drop the assembly into the base of the tap where the jumper

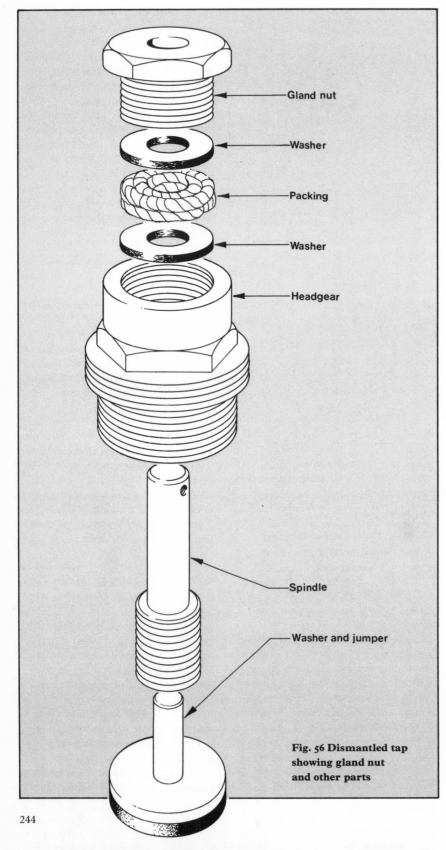

Gland nut

Washer

Packing

Washer

Headgear

Spindle

Washer and jumper

**Fig. 56 Dismantled tap
showing gland nut
and other parts**

of a cold tap normally rests. Make sure
you get the correct size: there is one
for kitchen and basin taps and another
for bath taps.

LOOSE TAPS

Sometimes water will leak out of the
top of a tap around the easyclean cover.
This is a sign that the gland of the
valve needs repacking or tightening.

The tap may turn too loosely in the
hand when this fault develops. You
may even be able to spin the tap with
very little effort. Sometimes there will
be the noise of water hammer as the
tap is turned off.

To cure this, all that is necessary in
some cases is to tighten the gland nut,
fig. 56, about half a turn in a clockwise
direction. Don't overdo it.

To get at the nut, you will have to
remove the easyclean cover and take
off the handle as described earlier. If
there is no easyclean cover, the job is
simpler, of course. There is no need to
turn off the water to make this slight
adjustment.

GLAND PACKING

There is, naturally, a limit to the
number of adjustments that can be
made to the gland nut. After a time,
the gland will require repacking. If this
is necessary, the water will have to be
turned off.

Take off the handle and easyclean
cover, then unscrew the gland nut and
remove it and the fibre washer that lies
beneath, *fig. 56*. Note that this is a
different washer to those I have been
talking about earlier.

Underneath the washer you should
find the packing material which is
usually hemp, but may be string or
wool. Dig all this out (there may not be
much left!) and beneath it you should
find another fibre washer. Remove this
too and renew it.

Repack the gland with hemp or wool
smeared with Vaseline, pressing it
down firmly, *fig. 57*. Renew and
position the top washer and replace the
gland nut – fingertight plus about half
a turn.

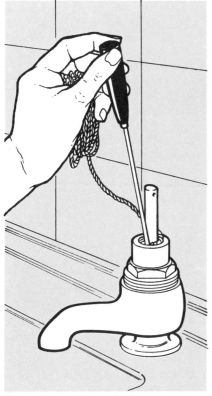

Fig. 57 Repacking a gland nut

Before replacing the handle and the cover, test the tap and adjust the gland nut as required. (You can turn the tap on by gripping the spindle with pliers.)

REWASHERING STOP-VALVES

As stop-valves inside the house are operated less frequently than other taps in the house, they don't need re-washering very often. Most internal stop-valves will resemble the one shown in *fig. 2*.

If one of these is fitted on the rising main pipe and needs rewashering, the main stopcock outside the house will have to be turned off first. If a stop-valve on a supply pipe other than the rising main needs attention, turn off the water at the internal stop-valve on the rising main.

If you do not have a key to turn off the outside stopcock, you will have to get the local water board to do it, unless you make one as shown in *fig. 58*. But that, too, will depend on the type of stopcock fitted.

If your outside stopcock is as shown

in *fig. 59*, then you will need a proper turnkey.

To rewasher the rising main stop-valve, first drain the water from the rising main pipe by turning on the kitchen cold water tap and the drain-cock incorporated with the stop-valve. (See *figs. 3* and *4*.)

If there isn't a draincock, have a bowl ready to catch any surplus water which runs out of the stop-valve.

The procedure now is similar to rewashering an ordinary tap except that there will be no easyclean cover to worry about.

If you rewasher a stop-valve on a pipe other than the rising main, this part of the plumbing circuit will need to be drained by running the appropriate taps until no more water flows.

Sometimes stop-valves leak past their gland packing like other taps. The treatment here is similar to that with ordinary taps.

Check these valves regularly to ensure that they turn easily and don't become stuck. If they are stiff to turn, you can oil them occasionally.

Some internal stop-valves are called full-way gate valves, and they are usually to be found on pipes supplied by a storage cistern.

These valves normally need no maintenance apart from a slight adjustment of the gland packing nut – a rare requirement.

CHOOSING TAPS

Fortunately, taps have a long life and renewals are not often necessary. The appearance of a tap, however, has a great aesthetic value and modern taps are designed to please both in performance and in appearance.

There is an enormous variety of taps available these days and selection is not easy. So what should you look for when choosing new ones?

First of all, try the tap and make sure it turns smoothly and doesn't stick. Does it feel comfortable in the hand? If you are satisfied on these points the tap should be suitable

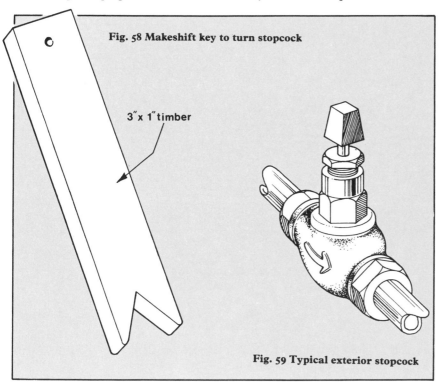

Fig. 58 Makeshift key to turn stopcock

3″ x 1″ timber

Fig. 59 Typical exterior stopcock

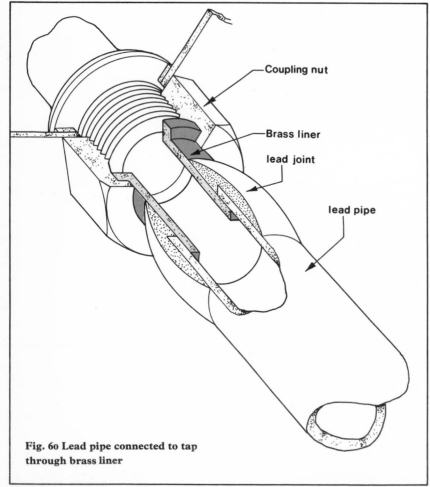

Fig. 60 Lead pipe connected to tap through brass liner

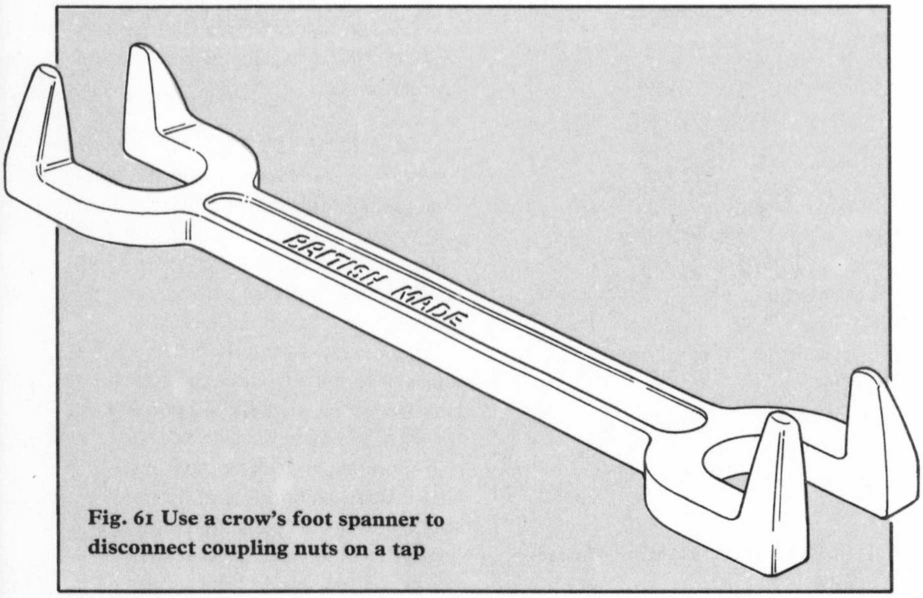

- Coupling nut
- Brass liner
- lead joint
- lead pipe

Fig. 61 Use a crow's foot spanner to disconnect coupling nuts on a tap

provided, of course, it is the right *type* for the situation.

If you are buying mixer taps, however, there is one very important thing to remember. A mixer should be designed to operate satisfactorily if, as is probable, the hot and cold water supplies are at different pressures. If the taps are not so designed, it is difficult to control the temperature of the water.

FITTING NEW TAPS
The job of replacing worn out or ugly taps is, frankly, one I would hesitate to recommend the unhandy handyman to attempt. Getting at the fitting can itself be a problem, and when removing old taps it is quite easy to damage a basin or sink.

So think twice before you attempt the job. Even if you think you can remove the old taps, make sure you know exactly how to fit the new ones. You may not be able to get hold of a plumber if you need one urgently to finish the job for you.

There are, however, many householders who have done this job themselves successfully, so if you feel confident, have a go.

The first thing to do, of course, is to cut off the water supply in one of the

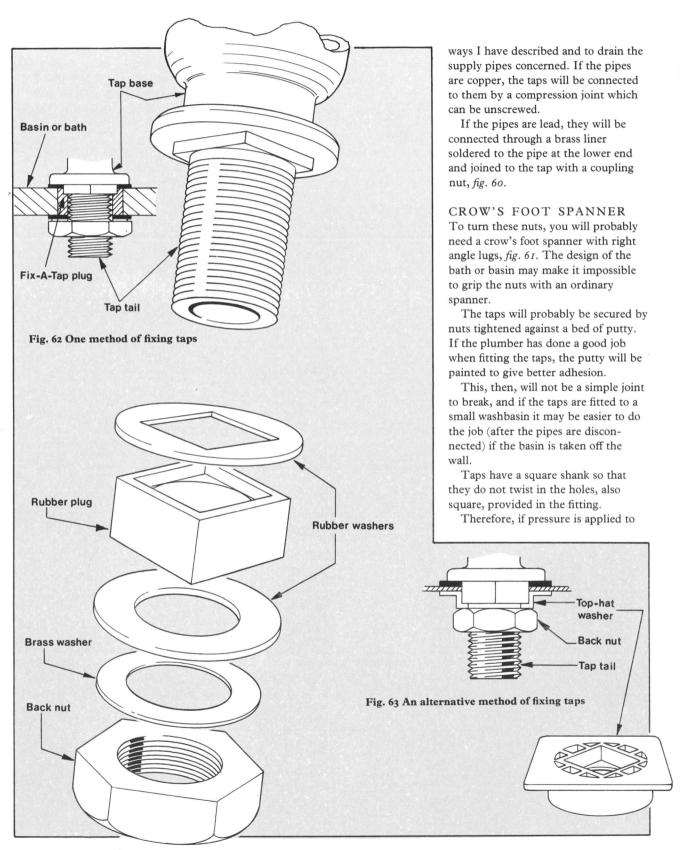

ways I have described and to drain the supply pipes concerned. If the pipes are copper, the taps will be connected to them by a compression joint which can be unscrewed.

If the pipes are lead, they will be connected through a brass liner soldered to the pipe at the lower end and joined to the tap with a coupling nut, *fig. 60*.

CROW'S FOOT SPANNER
To turn these nuts, you will probably need a crow's foot spanner with right angle lugs, *fig. 61*. The design of the bath or basin may make it impossible to grip the nuts with an ordinary spanner.

The taps will probably be secured by nuts tightened against a bed of putty. If the plumber has done a good job when fitting the taps, the putty will be painted to give better adhesion.

This, then, will not be a simple joint to break, and if the taps are fitted to a small washbasin it may be easier to do the job (after the pipes are disconnected) if the basin is taken off the wall.

Taps have a square shank so that they do not twist in the holes, also square, provided in the fitting.

Therefore, if pressure is applied to

Tap base

Basin or bath

Fix-A-Tap plug

Tap tail

Fig. 62 One method of fixing taps

Rubber plug

Rubber washers

Brass washer

Back nut

Top-hat washer

Back nut

Tap tail

Fig. 63 An alternative method of fixing taps

the coupling nuts without equal counter pressure being applied to the tap's body, the fitting may crack as the tap tries to turn in its hole.

To avoid this happening, remove the easyclean cover from the tap and apply the necessary counter pressure to the headgear with one hand, while unscrewing the coupling nut with the other.

PUTTY BED

To fix a new tap, first dab some enamel paint around the hole in the fitting. Then arrange a bed of metal casement putty around the flange of the tap and insert it in its hole.

Use a jointing compound to smear around the tap's threads and tighten up the coupling nut. Put some of the compound on the other end of the connection and refit the supply pipe.

Now this may sound fairly straightforward, but you may find it difficult to make a joint with putty good enough to fix the tap firmly in its hole. The hole will be larger than the shank of the tap, thus giving a loose fit. Only practice can enable you to make a good job of the jointing.

THE EASY WAY

There is, however, an easier way of doing the job. You can buy what is known as a Fix-a-Tap set. All you do is to fit a Fix-a-Tap plug over the tap's shank and insert it in the hole in the fitting, *fig. 62*. The plug is then cut so that it protrudes slightly from the underside of the basin.

When the coupling nut is tightened, the protruding part of the plug is forced back into the hole. The result – a firm joint which can be taken apart at any time and reassembled.

You should be able to buy Fix-a-Tap sets, and the Full Stop fitting mentioned earlier, but if you have difficulty write to:

Nicholls & Clarke Ltd., 3 Shoreditch High Street, London, E1 (for Fix-a-Tap) and

Robert McArd & Co. Ltd., Crown Works, Denton, Lancs. (for Full Stop).

For thin basins and sinks you can use a special top-hat washer to ensure that the tap fits tightly in its hole, *fig. 63*. For ceramic basins, however, the Fix-a-Tap method is preferred.

Pipes and Joints

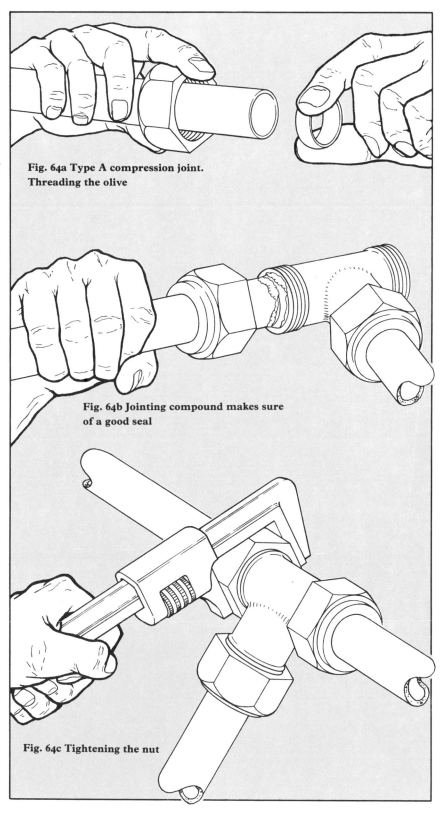

Fig. 64a Type A compression joint. Threading the olive

Fig. 64b Jointing compound makes sure of a good seal

Fig. 64c Tightening the nut

In the chapter on taps I mentioned a compression joint used to connect a tap to its supply pipe. Although for simple plumbing maintenance it is not vital to understand all the joints, pipes and fittings used in a domestic system, a little knowhow can be useful if, for example, you need to extend or replace existing pipework.

For ordinary domestic use, light gauge copper tubing is suitable and can be used as both hot water and cold water pipes. It can be cut simply, is available in small diameters and can be bent to shape without the need of costly tools.

As to joints, the simplest, I think, are non-manipulative (Type A) compression joints and fittings. A typical joint of this type is illustrated in *fig. 64a*.

COUPLING NUTS

These fittings can easily be disconnected at any time and reassembled. Threaded components are connected by coupling nuts. These screw down on to soft copper collars called olives or rings.

As the nuts are tightened, they crush the olives and make a watertight seal, but to make certain of this the connection can be smeared with a jointing compound.

A compression joint should be tight but should never be over-tightened. The drill is to twirl the coupling nut by hand as far as possible and then give it up to one full revolution of the spanner to tighten it up. If a joint weeps slightly, tighten it by degrees until it stops.

What sort of jobs would the average householder undertake which could involve the use of joints? One example is the fitting of an extension pipe to an existing one, the two pipes being the same diameter. If it is to be a straight run of pipe, you will need a simple compression coupling, *fig. 64a*.

The only tools needed for this job, apart from a spanner, are a hacksaw or tube cutter and two wrenches.

To extend the pipe, cut off the

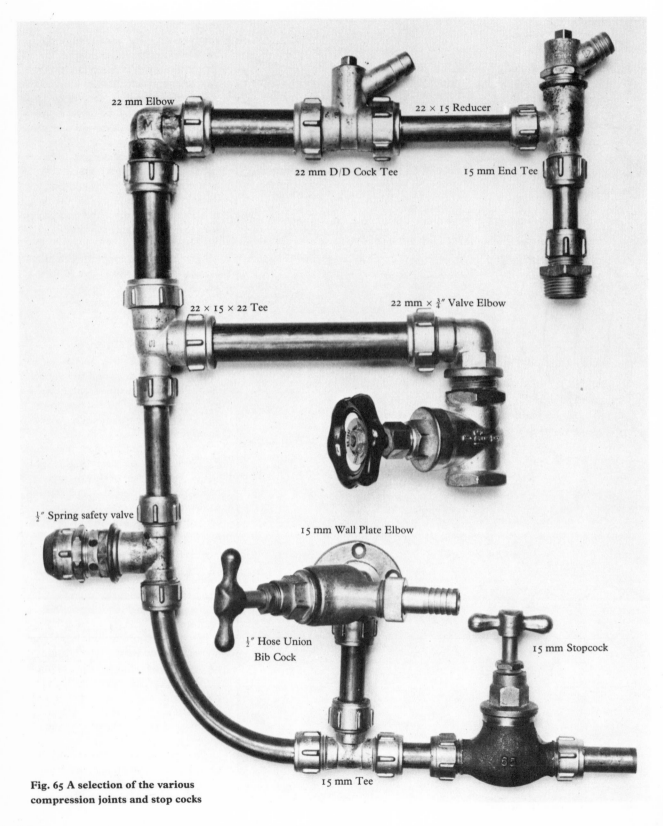

22 mm Elbow

22 × 15 Reducer

22 mm D/D Cock Tee

15 mm End Tee

22 × 15 × 22 Tee

22 mm × $\frac{3}{4}$″ Valve Elbow

$\frac{1}{2}$″ Spring safety valve

15 mm Wall Plate Elbow

$\frac{1}{2}$″ Hose Union
Bib Cock

15 mm Stopcock

15 mm Tee

**Fig. 65 A selection of the various
compression joints and stop cocks**

supply of water and drain the pipe. Cut
the pipe squarely if using a hacksaw –
after measuring carefully, of course –
and remove the internal burrs from
the pipe with a file or penknife, *figs. 69*
and *71*. If you use a tube cutter, *fig. 70*,
this may be fitted with a reamer which
will remove the burrs.

Loosen the nut on the compression
joint and insert one end of the cut pipe
into it as far as it will go, *fig. 64b*.
Tighten the nut with the wrench,
fig. 64c.

Repeat the performance with the
other end of the cut pipe and your
compression joint is made.

FITTING A STOP-VALVE

A compression joint can also be used
to fit an internal stop-valve on a supply
pipe.

First turn off the water supply and
drain the pipe. Measure the distance
between the shoulders, or stops, on
the inside of the threaded ends of the
compression joint and cut out the
correct amount of piping.

Take great care when cutting the
pipe. Cut out too little rather than too
much; you can trim a little off, but
you can't put any back on!

If you *should* make a mistake and cut
the pipe too short, you can, of course,
fit a compression coupling joint to fill
the gap, but this would be an unnecessary expense to incur simply
through carelessness.

Burr off the ends of the cut pipe,
slip on the coupling nuts and then the
olives to each end of the pipe and insert
the pipe into the valve as far as it will
go. You will feel it hit the stops when
it is in to its full extent.

Note that the arrow on the stop-
valve should always point in the
direction of the water flow.

Screw the nuts on to the stop-valve
and tighten them up over the olives.

TYPE B FITTINGS

The compression joints mentioned
above are *non*-manipulative joints.
Manipulative fittings are slightly
different and are designed mainly for

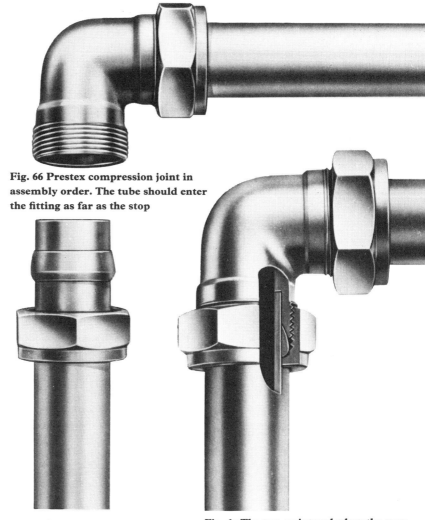

**Fig. 66 Prestex compression joint in
assembly order. The tube should enter
the fitting as far as the stop**

**Fig. 67 The two-point seal when the cone
is compressed**

Fig. 68 A steel drift to open up the end of a pipe

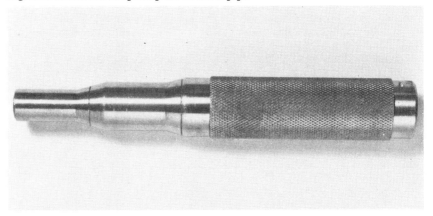

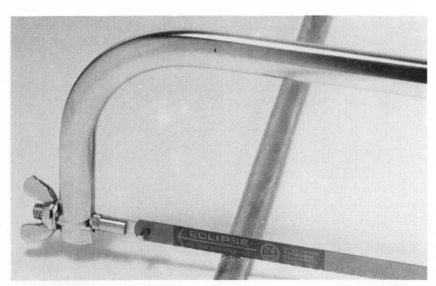

Fig. 69 Cutting a pipe with a hacksaw

Fig. 70 Tube cutter

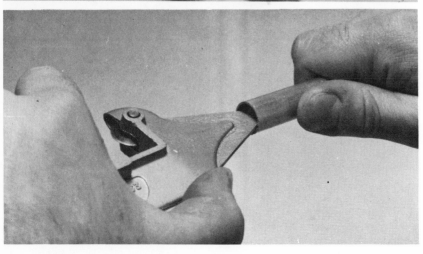

Fig. 71 Removing burrs

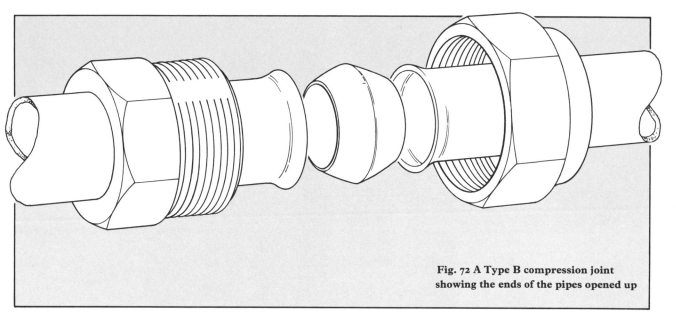

Fig. 72 A Type B compression joint
showing the ends of the pipes opened up

work underground where the joint will
be inaccessible. Once this type of joint
has been formed, it cannot be pulled
apart.

Manipulative compression joints are
known as Type B fittings. When using
these joints, the shape of the end of the
pipe has to be altered so that it can be
gripped by the fitting.

One way to do this is to open up the
end of the pipe by hammering a steel
drift, *fig. 68*, into it.

To make a Type B joint, the holding
nut is removed from the body of the
joint and slipped over the end of the
pipe before it is manipulated.

The next step depends on the
method used. A steel drift is used to
manipulate Prestex, Conex and Kontite
joints. For Kingley fittings you use a
swaging tool.

So, depending on which fitting has
been chosen, either open the end of the
pipe with the steel drift, or put the
swaging tool in the end and turn its
handle. Grip the pipe firmly while
turning.

In the case of the Kingley fitting, the
swaged (or ridged) end of the pipe is
now pushed into the fitting as far as
possible, and the nut tightened against
the swage.

In the other method, the flared end

Fig. 73 Cleaning up the end of a pipe with wire wool
before making a capillary joint

of the pipe is positioned on the
shoulder of the joint's body and the
nut tightened.

CAPILLARY JOINTS

Another type of joint more likely to be
of interest to a handyman than Type B
fittings is the soldered capillary joint.
This, of course, involves the use of a
blowlamp or blowtorch.

If this is the sort of joint you prefer,
it should be borne in mind that the
flame from a blowtorch can be quite

fierce! When working in confined
spaces it is only too easy to let the
attention wander and direct the flame
on to combustible material such as
timber framework, rafters or skirting.
So take care if you use this method.

Personally, I would suggest a blowtorch rather than a blowlamp for a
beginner.

An integral ring joint is the simplest
form of capillary joint for a d-i-y man
to make. This has a ring of solder
inside.

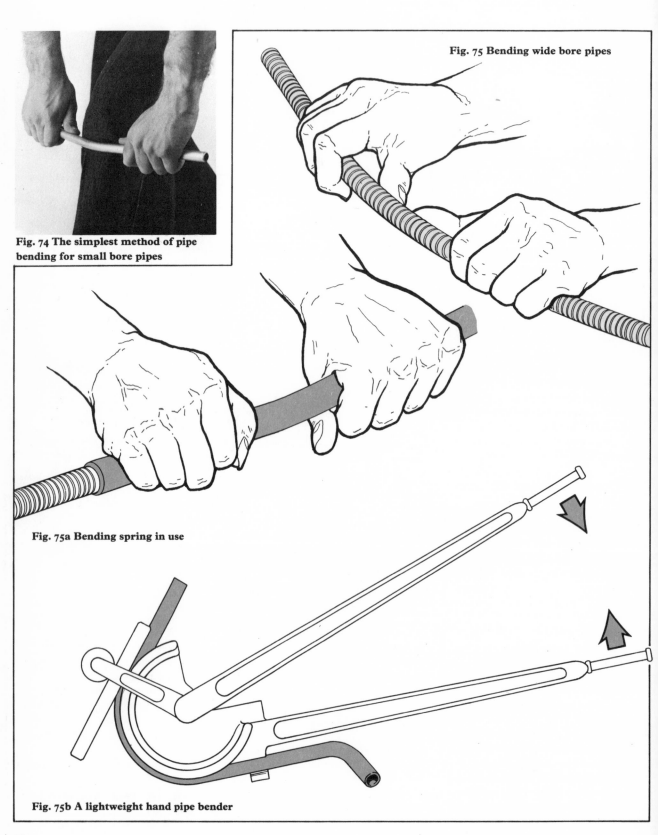

Fig. 74 The simplest method of pipe bending for small bore pipes

Fig. 75 Bending wide bore pipes

Fig. 75a Bending spring in use

Fig. 75b A lightweight hand pipe bender

An example is shown in *fig. 76*. These are sometimes called Yorkshire joints.

To make this type of joint you cut the pipe as before and remove the burrs from its ends. You then have to clean the outside of the pipe and the inside of the capillary fitting with fine grade emery paper.

RING OF SOLDER

Now apply some flux to both the cleaned areas and slip the pipe into the fitting *as far as possible*. Direct the flame of the blowtorch on to the fitting until the solder starts to run.

When you can see an even ring of solder all the way round the end of the fitting, the joint is complete and should now be left to cool off.

There are other types of capillary joint, including the Endfeed, *fig. 77*, and Konsilet fittings. In these, the solder is fed into the mouth of the fitting using solder wire.

After cleaning the fitting and the pipe, and inserting it into the fitting as before, you direct the flame of the blowtorch onto the body of the fitting and gradually move it towards the mouth.

At this point, you then apply solder wire to the mouth until the ring of solder is complete as before.

STAINLESS STEEL TUBE

Although copper pipe is widely used in domestic plumbing systems, there are alternatives.

One is stainless steel tube which has been more widely used in the past few years. This material is harder than copper and is not so easy for an amateur to bend by hand.

However, its rigidity means that it requires less support than copper pipe and it can withstand greater water pressure.

It is possible to use Type A compression joints with stainless steel tube and it can be cut in the same way as copper. You cannot, however, use Type B compression joints with this material. Soldered capillary joints can

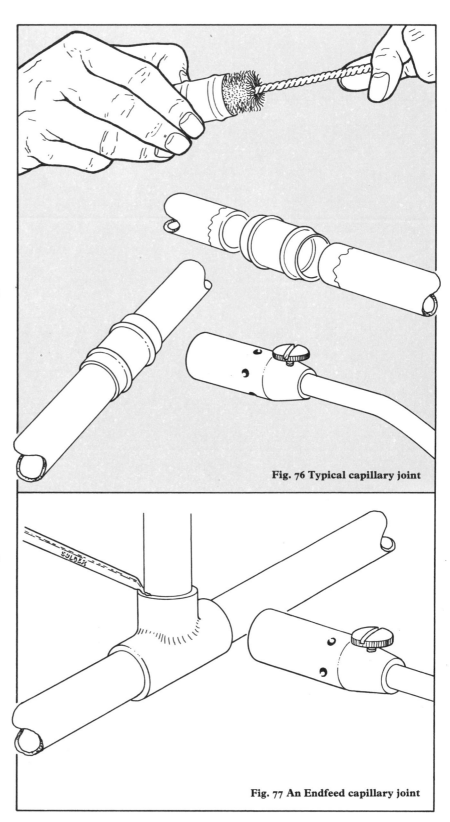

Fig. 76 Typical capillary joint

Fig. 77 An Endfeed capillary joint

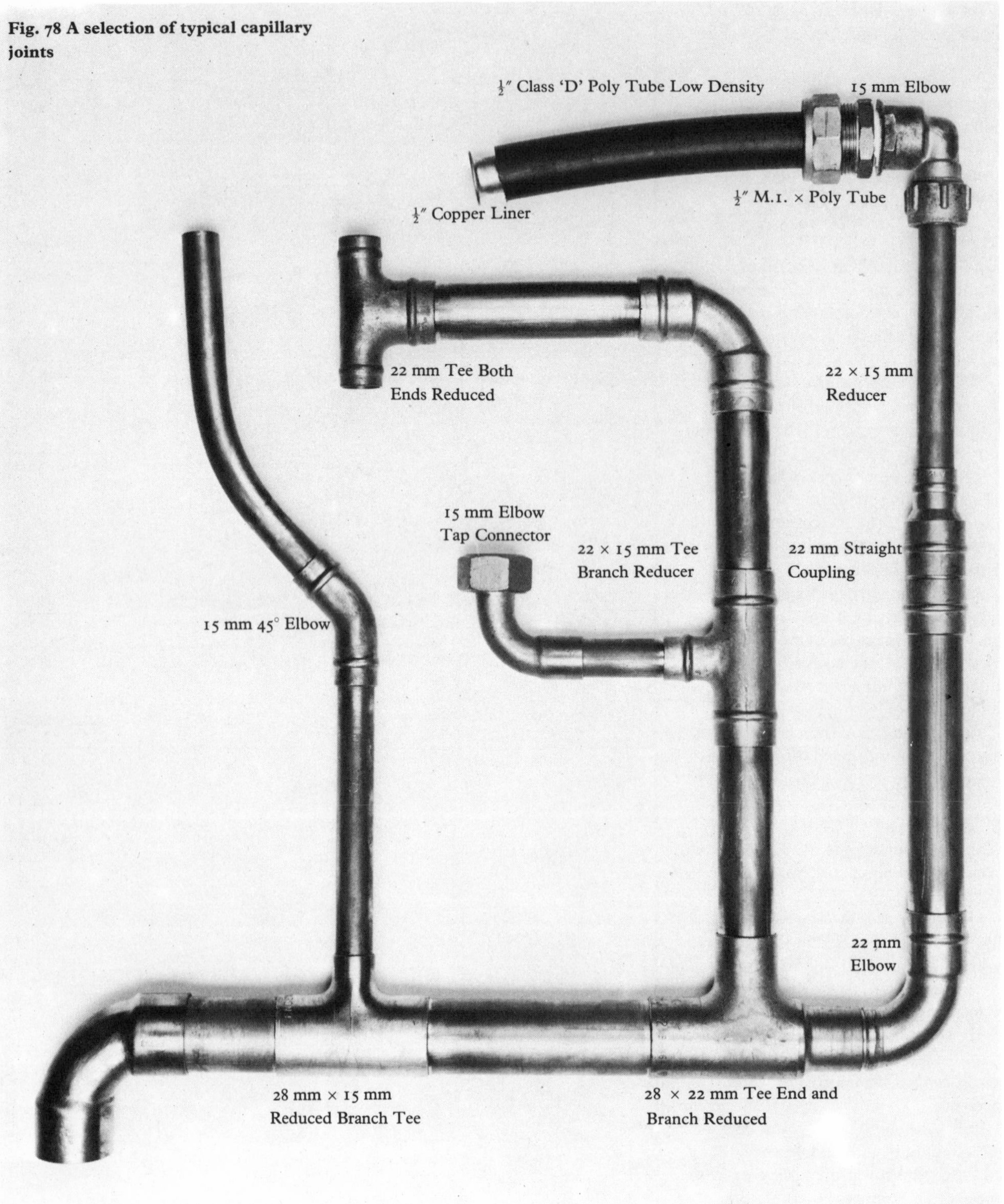

Fig. 78 A selection of typical capillary joints

½″ Class 'D' Poly Tube Low Density   15 mm Elbow

½″ Copper Liner   ½″ M.I. × Poly Tube

22 mm Tee Both
Ends Reduced   22 × 15 mm
                                               Reducer

15 mm Elbow
Tap Connector

22 × 15 mm Tee   22 mm Straight
Branch Reducer   Coupling

15 mm 45° Elbow

22 mm
Elbow

28 mm × 15 mm   28 × 22 mm Tee End and
Reduced Branch Tee   Branch Reduced

Conversion Table. Inches to millimetres

in	mm	in	mm	in	mm
$\frac{1}{32}$	0.794	$\frac{9}{32}$	7.144	$\frac{5}{8}$	15.875
$\frac{1}{16}$	1.588	$\frac{5}{16}$	7.938	$\frac{11}{16}$	17.463
$\frac{3}{32}$	2.381	$\frac{11}{32}$	8.731	$\frac{3}{4}$	19.050
$\frac{1}{8}$	3.175	$\frac{3}{8}$	9.525	$\frac{13}{16}$	20.638
$\frac{11}{64}$	4.336	$\frac{7}{16}$	11.113	$\frac{7}{8}$	22.225
$\frac{3}{16}$	4.763	$\frac{1}{2}$	12.700	$\frac{15}{16}$	23.813
$\frac{1}{4}$	6.350	$\frac{9}{16}$	14.288	1 in	25.400

Note: metric-sized pipes are measured across their *outside* diameters. Imperial-sized pipes are measured across their *internal* diameters. E.g. the equivalent of a $\frac{1}{2}$ in pipe in metric size is 15 mm.

be used, but a special flux which is based on phosphoric acid is required.

POLYTHENE TUBE

Polythene tube can be used for cold water pipes, but not for hot because it softens when heated and will melt at about 230° Fahrenheit. Possible uses for it in a domestic plumbing system include waste pipes, cold water pipes in the loft and to supply taps at the end of a garden.

This material comes in normal gauge and heavy gauge. Most water boards insist on heavy gauge if the pipe concerned is to be under mains pressure, so this is a point to check with your board before changing over any part of the system's pipework to polythene.

Non-manipulative compression joints can be used for joining, but when ordering the joints, state the tube's internal diameter and its gauge. For many joints you will need a size larger than the size of the tube.

RIGID PVC

Another type of pipe more widely used nowadays in *cold* water plumbing is rigid pvc, which is self-supporting. Its rigidity makes it difficult to bend, however, and it is easier to avoid bends by using elbow or similar joints instead, where necessary.

One point to watch when using this tube is to avoid running it close to hot water pipes. Keep the cold water and hot water pipes at least 3 in apart.

METRICATION

Like other industries, plumbing has been affected by the gradual change-over to metrication. The main concern of home plumbers in this respect is the altered sizes of pipes and joint fittings. These are now sold in metric sizes.

One question likely to be asked by home plumbers is: how can an imperial-sized pipe be extended if the compression joints now available are in metric sizes? No great problem is involved, however.

To take pipe sizes. Probably the only ones likely to be used by a handyman are $\frac{1}{2}$ in, $\frac{3}{4}$ in and 1 in. The metric equivalents of these sizes are 15 mm, 22 mm and 28 mm.

There is very little difference in size between 15 mm and $\frac{1}{2}$ in pipes in actual measurement. The reason that they are similar is because they are not measured in the same way.

NO NEED FOR ADAPTORS

For imperial measurements the quoted size refers to the *internal* diameter of the pipe, whereas metric measurements refer to the *external* diameter; hence the apparent discrepancy in measurement.

Therefore, both sizes can be used with 15 mm compression joints without the need for adaptors. The same thing applies to 1 in and 28 mm size pipes.

The $\frac{3}{4}$ in and its 22 mm metric equivalent are not quite the same size. Nevertheless, you can use 22 mm compression fittings with $\frac{3}{4}$ in pipe provided you use $\frac{3}{4}$ in cap nuts and olives (rings) instead of the metric-size cap nuts and rings.

CONVERSIONS

Capillary soldered fittings, however, can cause problems when metric-size pipes need to be fitted to imperial sizes. Capillary fittings are more exact than compression types and the two sizes (imperial and metric) are not interchangeable.

However, the problems are not insoluble. You can buy conversion items which have *inlets* in the old imperial sizes and *outlets* in the new metric sizes.

That is one solution. Another is to fit a compression joint at the point where the new size pipe is to connect to the old. For any subsequent joints along the run of new pipe, metric capillary joints can be used.

You will find that there is an enormous variety of compression and capillary fittings available – bends, straight couplings, elbows, tees and so on.

If you plan to carry out a lot of pipework, I suggest you send for catalogues to the following manufacturers. You will find them extremely useful.

Compression fittings: Conex Sanbra Ltd., Great Bridge, Tipton, Staffs. DY4 7JU. Peglers Ltd., St Catherine's Avenue, Doncaster, Yorks. DN4 8DF.
Capillary fittings: Yorkshire Imperial Metals Ltd., Stourton 10, Leeds, LS 1RD. Kay & Co. (Engineers) Ltd., Exchange Street, Bolton, Lancs. King's Langley Engineering Co. Ltd., King's Langley, Herts.

Frost Precautions

As a nation we are now becoming more conscious of the vital need to insulate our homes to conserve heat and thus save money on fuel.

That is a good thing, for a well insulated house will also go far to protect the plumbing system against frost damage – provided that the heat which is circulated can reach vulnerable pipes and plumbing equipment.

Let us suppose you have taken precautions to insulate your home. In the loft you have probably laid vermiculite or other granules or spread glass fibre blanket material between the the joists. By doing this, you have ensured that valuable heat will not rise through the first floor ceiling into the loft and be finally dissipated through air spaces in the roof itself.

But what of the plumbing which is up in the loft? Are all the pipes and the cold water storage cistern thoroughly lagged to prevent icy draughts from freezing them up in severe weather? That, oddly enough, is something a great many people overlook.

WATCH THOSE BENDS

All plumbing materials in the roof space should be adequately lagged. Bends in pipes should receive particular attention, especially those which are situated in remote corners of the loft far away from any warmth which may reach the area from below.

The cold water storage cistern should be lagged unless it is a polythene type. It should not be necessary to lag these cisterns but they, like any other type (galvanised steel or asbestos cement), should have a dustproof cover.

This is necessary not only as a precaution against freeze-ups, but, as mentioned earlier, to prevent the water from being contaminated by insects and debris which may drop into it from the roof.

EXPANSION PIPE

Make sure that the expansion pipe over the cistern is also lagged. A hole can be made in the cover on the cistern so that any water which runs from this

Fig. 79 Blanket-type lagging for the loft

Fig. 80 Lagging jacket for the hot water tank

pipe can enter it. If you fit a plastic funnel in the hole the water will not splash on to the cover.

When insulating the floor of a loft, by the way, do not lay insulation material *under* the storage cistern and don't lag the base of it. By leaving these parts uninsulated, a little warm air from below will then be able to rise and help to prevent the base of the cistern freezing up.

When lagging the cistern, don't overlook any stop-valves which may be fitted to the outlet pipes. Lag these thoroughly, leaving just the handles visible.

BOARDING THE LOFT

Insulating the plumbing system in a loft is not a comfortable job, but it is one which no householder should neglect. You can make the job easier by screwing boards across the rafters, where necessary, so that you can walk about without fear of slipping a foot through the ceiling of the room below!

A good place to start boarding is on the route from the trap door to the cold water storage cistern. You never know when you may have to dash into the loft and attend to a faulty ball-valve.

Not all the area in the roof space normally needs to be boarded over; catwalks as in *fig. 81* will probably suffice. Much will depend, of course, on the layout of the pipes.

Incidentally, I suggest screwing the boards down rather than nailing them. If you use screws, any cables and pipes hidden under the boards will be more easily accessible in future. If any pipes are buried under the boards, make a note of what they are for quick future reference.

OVERFLOW PIPE

While lagging the pipes in the loft, don't overlook the overflow pipe from the cold water storage cistern. If this should freeze up, and the ball-valve should happen to stick in the open position, the result could be disastrous. This open-ended pipe is an invitation to icy blasts to whistle up it

Fig. 81 Boards over the rafters in the loft provide easy access to the plumbing

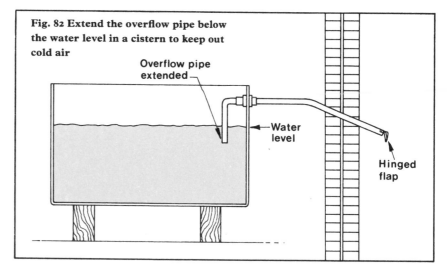

Fig. 82 Extend the overflow pipe below the water level in a cistern to keep out cold air

Overflow pipe extended

Water level

Hinged flap

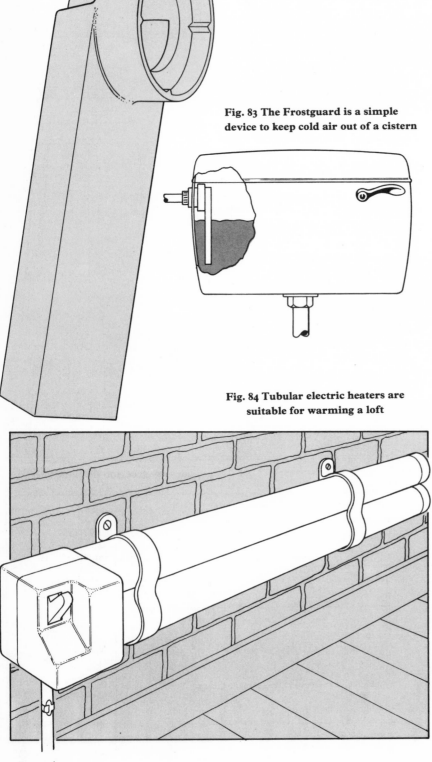

Fig. 83 The Frostguard is a simple device to keep cold air out of a cistern

Fig. 84 Tubular electric heaters are suitable for warming a loft

and freeze the water in the cistern, but open ended it has to be.

There are a couple of ways of avoiding a freeze-up. One is to arrange the pipe so that its internal end is continued into the cistern and terminates below the level of the water, *fig. 82*.

Any draughts entering the overflow pipe will then meet a barrier of water.

Another method is to fit a small hinged flap (if you can get one) to the *external* end of the overflow pipe, *fig. 82*. As cold blasts of air hit the flap from outside, they keep it in the closed position.

If you choose this method, keep a watchful eye on the flap and make sure it is kept free of dirt and corrosion. Otherwise it may jam open and become temporarily useless until released.

DANGER
Another reason I don't favour this method is because there is always the danger of the cistern overflowing and causing icicles to form on the overflow pipe. If this ice jammed the flap in the closed position, the pipe would not be able to do its job if the cistern overflowed again. Flooding in the house would be the result.

An alternative method to extending the overflow pipe into the cold water cistern is to fit a Frostguard. This simple device, shown in *fig. 83*, simply screws on to the *internal* end of the pipe.

USING HEATERS
When you are satisfied that everything has been lagged in the loft, you will have done much to ensure a winter free of worry from frost damage in one area at least. But it is by no means certain that your lagging precautions will prove effective against a *very* severe frost.

All that lagging can do is to keep frost at bay for a time; it cannot, in itself, provide extra warmth for the plumbing installation.

Therefore, a wise householder will consider introducing some form of heating in the loft, especially if the house is an old one and the roof is not lined.

I think the only suitable and safe form of heating for this purpose is electricity, and I suggest one or more tubular heaters, *fig. 84*. These operate at black heat, rather like a radiator.

A radiant fire is not to be recommended for this purpose. Neither is a paraffin heater, no matter how safe it is thought to be.

Tubular heaters are sold in various lengths and operate at a rate of about 60 watts to 1 ft. A 6 ft length (360 watts) is suitable for many requirements, but more heat than this will be needed in most lofts.

These heaters, by the way, should never be run off a lighting circuit as this could cause an overload. Operate them from earthed socket outlets which have been correctly wired.

Another suitable way to provide warmth in the loft is to use a fan heater. This will warm up a loft rapidly.

WARNING
Having said that, I must, however, add a warning when using any sort of loft heating. This is a place where all sorts of things get thrown up from below. It is the easiest thing in the world to toss up an unwanted rug or carpet so that it becomes accidentally draped over a fire up there.

Later, when the fire is turned on, possibly from a switch on the landing, the carpet may well have been forgotten. The heater can then overheat and cause a fire in the loft. This will probably not be noticed until it is too late to prevent extensive damage being done.

One more thought on loft insulation before we move on to the rest of the plumbing system. If you want to keep the loft at a reasonable temperature, consider insulating the rafters instead of the floor. If you can see daylight through the tiles of an unlined roof, that is one spot where your precious warmth will make its escape.

One suitable form of roof insulation

is waterproof paper or sheet aluminium foil pinned to the rafters with generous overlaps at the joints.

When all the plumbing in the loft has been insulated, the danger of frost damage to the system will have been reduced but not dispelled altogether. There are other parts which are vulnerable and this is especially true where older houses are concerned.

CHECK THE WHOLE SYSTEM
It is worth carrying out a check of the complete installation, starting from the stopcock outside the house.

As this will be (or should be) buried at least 30 inches below ground level, it is unlikely to be affected by frost unless the cover of the stopcock is loose or inadequate, or the ground level has been lowered since the stopcock was installed, which again is unlikely.

You won't be able to get at the stopcock to lag it, of course, so the only alternative is to drop some vermiculite granules (loose fill insulation) down the hole until only the top of the stopcock is exposed, so that it can be turned off when required.

THE RISING MAIN
From that point, the rising main pipe should already be protected by 30 inches of earth until it emerges inside the house.

Commonsense will tell you whether this pipe needs lagging at this point. If the pipe rises in a warm kitchen against an *internal* wall (as it should), no lagging should be necessary to protect it against frost, but lagging is advisable if the pipe rises against an *external* wall.

CONDENSATION
There is, however, one other very sound argument for lagging the rising main pipe in a kitchen. Have you ever noticed how wet this pipe becomes as a result of condensation? You can prevent this by lagging the pipe thoroughly so that no part of it is exposed.

Fig. 85 Fix plastic foam lagging material with adhesive tape

This is especially important if the pipe is fixed close to an external wall. Get the lagging material *behind* the pipe as well as in front to insulate it.

All these remarks apply equally to other pipe runs in the house which may be affected by condensation. Incidentally, it will be found that painted pipes are sometimes less affected by condensation than unpainted ones.

The appearance of a pipe in the kitchen or elsewhere is a consideration, of course, and some ordinary lagging material is not exactly a joy to the eye! Less unattractive – and certainly very effective – are lengths of foam plastic lagging material which are simply slipped over the pipes, *fig. 85*, and secured with adhesive tape.

This form of insulation will not only help to protect a cold water pipe, but can also be used to lag hot water supply pipes in order to reduce heat losses.

INTERNAL TOILETS
Another spot vulnerable to frost is, of course, an internal toilet cistern and its supply pipe. In a house which is

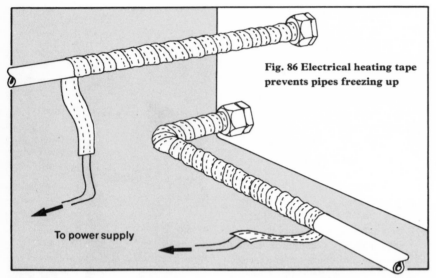

Fig. 86 Electrical heating tape prevents pipes freezing up

To power supply

constantly warm the danger of a freeze-up here may be remote, but in a cold house the danger is very real.

The overflow pipe of the toilet cistern can, as stated earlier, admit icy draughts, and although these cisterns are fitted with covers, in a severe winter the water in them could freeze.

The problem can again be overcome by turning the overflow pipe's internal end into the cistern below the water line or by fitting a Frostguard as suggested for the cold water storage cistern.

If you fit a Frostguard, by the way, make sure that the water level does not then rise above its normal line, and ensure also that you can fit it without it fouling any part of the mechanism in the cistern.

OUTSIDE TOILETS
Outside toilets pose special problems. Many are very draughty places, sometimes with no light and with great gaps between the foot of the door and the doorstep.

There is little point in carrying out anti-freeze precautions in such a toilet until it has been thoroughly draught-proofed. Even when that is done, the fact that the room is unlikely to be heated will make its plumbing system vulnerable to frost.

So try to introduce some heat – even

the heat from a 100 watt bulb placed near the cistern's ball-valve will be a help – but avoid radiant fires and paraffin heaters because of the fire risk.

There are more advanced methods of protecting exposed pipes from frost apart from lagging. One which is very popular is electrical heating tape. This is simply wound around the pipes, *fig. 86*. This tape can be plugged into a socket outlet and turned on whenever a frost is forecast.

INSULATION MATERIAL
Most insulation material is available from builders' merchants.

For wrapping round cold water storage cisterns you can get glass fibre blanket or expanded polystyrene tank lagging sets.

Insulation jackets are available for hot water cylinders, and pipe lagging material is sold in various forms.

OTHER PRECAUTIONS
There are other precautions which should be taken whenever frosty weather is likely. Briefly, they are:

1. If you have any dripping taps, get them attended to before winter sets in.

2. Don't leave a tap to run all night during frosty weather in the hope that this will prevent it freezing up. There is a danger during severe frost of the

water freezing in the waste pipe outside.

If this happens and the tap is allowed to run on, the whole of the waste pipe could eventually become frozen up. The result – a flood of water in the room where the tap is left running.

3. When leaving the house unoccupied for a few days during a cold spell, drain the whole of the plumbing system. Then flush the toilet cistern and put a handful of salt in the pan.

Remember, when you return, to refill the system before lighting the boiler! And make sure the system *is* filled before doing so.

These precautions are perhaps not strictly necessary in a house with a well-appointed central heating system which is automatically controlled. But the plumbing system should nevertheless be adequately lagged.

BURST PIPE
If, after taking all possible frost precautions, a cold water pipe bursts, the first thing to do is to stop the supply of water to the circuit involved. Do this *before* you look for the burst.

Should the burst occur in the rising main, turn off the internal stop-valve or the stopcock in the pavement.

If there is a burst in a supply pipe leading from the cold water cistern, turn off the stop-valve on that pipe.

If the supply pipe to the hot water cylinder bursts, the stop-valve in this case may also be near the cistern or possibly in the airing cupboard near the cylinder.

PLUG THE OUTLET
If no stop-valves are fitted on the pipes leading from the cistern, the outlet to the supply pipe affected can be plugged from inside the cistern with a thick cloth wrapped around a length of broomstick. Then tie up the ball-valve of the cistern so that no more water can pass into it.

The kitchen cold water tap can still be used in this case provided, of course, that it is supplied direct from the main.

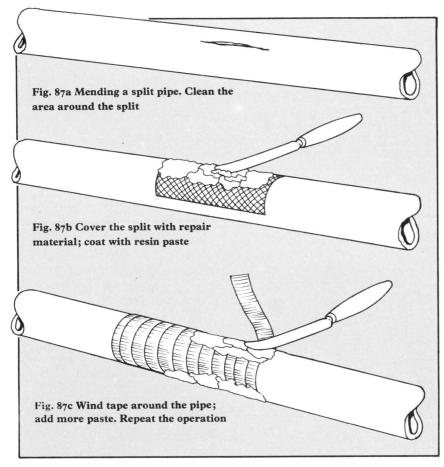

Fig. 87a Mending a split pipe. Clean the area around the split

Fig. 87b Cover the split with repair material; coat with resin paste

Fig. 87c Wind tape around the pipe; add more paste. Repeat the operation

If the stopcock in the pavement, or the internal stop-valve on the cold water supply pipe to the hot water cylinder, is turned off, you should also, as a precaution, turn off the boiler or, in the case of a solid fuel type of boiler, remove the fuel with a shovel.

In an emergency such as this, knowing your plumbing system is half the battle. As soon as water starts to drip from a leaking or burst pipe, you may be able to stop this turning into a flood if you can quickly locate the fault and isolate that part of the system. But first, concentrate on cutting off the water supply.

I repeat what I said earlier: get to understand your system thoroughly. A good time to do this is in the summer when the boiler is not operating. Then there will be no fear of it exploding if you accidentally drain it of its supply of water.

MENDING LEAKS

Having found the leak, what you do next depends on the type of pipe involved. The water may be coming from a compression joint in a run of copper pipe which has simply been forced apart by the frost. If this is the case, then you are lucky! A turn of the nut with a spanner may do the trick.

If, however, you have lead pipes and one of these has split, the correct method of repair is to cut out the affected length and replace it with a new length.

This, however, involves making wiped soldered joints which I consider are not strictly do-it-yourself jobs, although I hasten to add that many a d-i-y man *has* tackled the job successfully.

TEMPORARY REPAIRS

With the advent of synthetic resins, however, it is possible to make temporary repairs to split pipes which will at least enable them to be used until the job can be done properly. In some cases, the repair may well last for years.

Isopon and Plastic Padding are two types of repair kit you can get easily. It is a good plan to keep one handy.

Figures 87a to *87c* illustrate how a repair can be made.

Clean the pipe around the split and remove any paint. Bridge the split with glass fibre mat. Apply the resin (mixed with hardener) over the area; wind glass fibre tape round the pipe. Brush on another layer of resin/hardener mix. Repeat the process if necessary.

The method may vary according to the product used.

If a pipe has frozen up but has not burst, locating the frozen section will obviously be a little more difficult, but it needs to be found quickly before the freeze-up spreads to other sections of the pipe.

By turning on various taps you should be able to locate it fairly soon. One of the most likely places is in the loft and it could be that the rising main is the one affected.

When you have located the trouble, try applying some cloths, dipped in hot water and then squeezed out, to the suspect pipe. You may not need to treat more than one or two spots on the pipe as it will itself conduct the applied warmth along its length.

WATCH THE BENDS

Other pipes which are most likely to freeze up will be the supply pipes leading from the cold water storage cistern, especially if they should happen to run near the eaves.

Go for any bends in the pipes. This is where ice can form and quite often these bends are situated in awkward spots difficult to reach comfortably.

These bends are also a problem to lag thoroughly, so if you spot an exposed section of pipe where the lagging has, perhaps, slipped, this may be where the freeze-up has occurred.

For reaching awkward corners try

using a hair drier or a fan heater with the warm air directed at the suspect spot.

Quite often a warm (not hot) water bottle laid on the pipe will do the trick, too.

For pipe runs which are exposed to draughts, normal lagging may not be enough to prevent them freezing up. It is these, especially, which will benefit from the electrical heating tapes I have already mentioned.

If these are not readily available, Hotfoil Ltd., Heathmill Road, Womborne, Wolverhampton, can tell you all about them.

KEEP THE BOILER BURNING

When the weather is frosty, never put the boiler out at night because you fear that it might explode. Even if you have no central heating and use the boiler simply to heat water for normal domestic use, the heat the boiler distributes helps to keep the temperature of the house above freezing level.

All the pipes between the boiler and the hot water cylinder will be kept warm and will themselves act as miniature radiators. If your cold water storage cistern is positioned immediately above the hot water cylinder – an

excellent arrangement – this will receive its quota of warmth from the vent pipe.

The danger of a boiler explosion is more real if the boiler is used after being left unlit during a long period in frosty weather and the plumbing system has been frozen up.

Ice can form in the cold water supply pipe to the hot water cylinder, in the hot water system's vent pipe, or even in the flow and return pipes which run between the cylinder and the boiler, *fig. 88*.

Ice in any of these pipes will seal the hot water system which should normally be open and under pressure from the atmosphere. Therefore, when the boiler is relit, the water in it will not be able to circulate and expand. So pressure in the boiler increases until finally it is released by the whole system exploding!

CYLINDER COLLAPSE

This, luckily, does not happen very often, but there is another danger which arises more frequently in cold weather – cylinder collapse. This can happen on a freezing night if the boiler is allowed to go out and the hot water system cools down.

Ice can then collect in the vent pipe and in the pipe which supplies cold water to the cylinder. This causes the system to be sealed off as before, but now the system is cooling down.

As it does this, the water contracts. This causes a vacuum to form in the system and the cylinder (which is not designed to stand up to external pressure) will collapse. This collapse may take place when a hot water tap is turned on.

So be warned. Don't let the boiler go out in freezing weather.

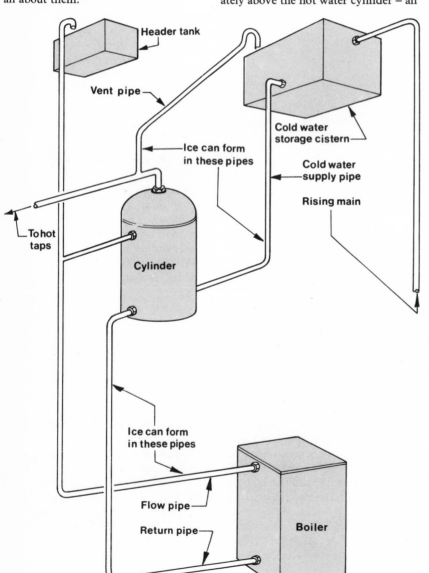

Fig. 88 Pipes vulnerable to frost

Clearing a Blockage

One of the most irritating things that can happen to a housewife is a blockage in the waste pipe of the kitchen sink. This is often caused by something becoming stuck in the trap underneath. This may be a build-up of tea leaves, pieces of vegetable or congealed fat – or a combination of all three.

In many instances these blockages can be cleared quickly by using a rubber suction cup, *fig. 91*. Run water into the sink, seal off the overflow outlet to exclude air and then pump the suction cup rapidly up and down over the plughole.

If this doesn't work, the blockage may be too solid to shift in this way. But repeat the treatment a few times before admitting defeat. Then examine the trap under the sink.

If this is a bottle trap, *fig. 100*, unscrew its bottom section. If it is a U

Fig. 91 A suction cup is useful for clearing sink blockages

trap, *fig. 99*, unscrew the inspection plug in the bend.

Place a bucket or bowl under trap. Poke a length of springy wire into the hole in both directions.

If you manage to remove the obstruction, flush through with boiling water before replacing the bottle trap section or inspection plug.

BLOCKED BEND

If you don't find the object, it may be lodged in the bend of the waste pipe where it passes through the wall to the outside gully. Try poking a cane up the pipe from outside or try to reach the blockage from the inspection plug on the trap.

It is a good plan to check the trap under the sink about once a year.

Bath and basin blockages normally respond to the plunger treatment.

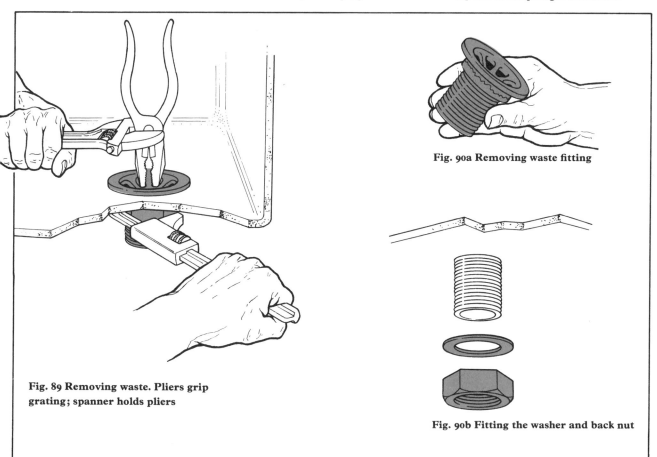

Fig. 89 Removing waste. Pliers grip grating; spanner holds pliers

Fig. 90a Removing waste fitting

Fig. 90b Fitting the washer and back nut

Fig. 92 Gullies should be cleaned out regularly

It is usually very difficult to get at a bath trap and the operation may involve removing the bath side panel. It is therefore worth persevering with the plunger treatment before going to this extreme.

SEALING A WASTE

Occasionally a waste fitting on a sink or bath will leak. To remedy this, first disconnect the trap underneath. Then get someone to hold the grating of the fitting steady, *fig. 89*, while you un-screw the back nut underneath with a wrench.

Take the waste fitting out of the outlet hole, *fig. 90a*, remove the old washer and clean up the fitting. Re-move all dirt and old putty and make sure you get the outlet thoroughly dry.

If the threads on the waste fitting are worn or damaged, renew the part. Apply some putty underneath the flange, put the fitting in the outlet and add putty to the washer. Replace the washer and the back nut, *fig. 90b*.

Get someone to hold the grating steady from above while you tighten up the back nut from underneath. Remove any surplus putty from the flange and underneath the back nut.

TOILET BLOCKAGE

The plunger treatment is sometimes also effective when there is a blockage in a w.c. pan. But if a block of toilet paper becomes wedged in the pan or the pipe it can be a difficult thing to shift. It may be possible, however, to dislodge it with a flexible cane.

In some houses, inspection plates are fitted at the soil pipe connection on an outside wall. These can be checked if a blockage of this sort cannot be cured by any other means.

A blockage in a w.c. on the ground floor may be due to an obstruction in the drainage system underground.

Fig. 93 A simple cover keeps rubbish out of gullies

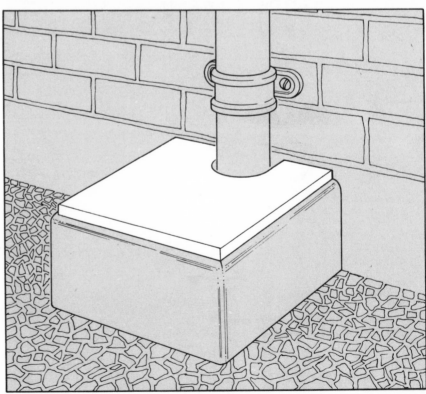

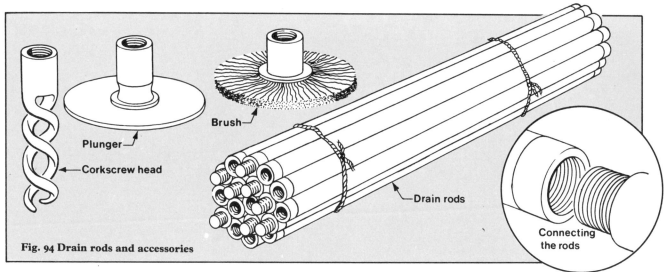

Plunger — **Corkscrew head**

Brush —

Drain rods

Connecting the rods

Fig. 94 Drain rods and accessories

This, of course, will involve an inspection of the manholes.

Gullies, *fig. 92*, are plumbing items which are often neglected. Consequently the grids can become choked up with leaves and other debris which gets blown into them. The result is that when soapy water is released from the sink, it does not flow to the gully and thence to the drains. So it overflows into the garden.

CLEAN THE GRIDS
The grids of gullies should be cleared of rubbish regularly and be cleaned and sterilised. This is a most unpleasant job but for the sake of hygiene it must be done.

Getting an old metal grid thoroughly cleaned and sterilised can be done by placing it in a fire for a few minutes. A better idea, though, is to replace it with a plastic type which is simple to keep clean.

There should, of course, be a concrete curb built around these gullies which helps to keep out a lot of the rubbish blown about in a garden. But it can't keep it all out, so the answer is to build a simple cover for it as in *fig. 93*.

UNDERGROUND BLOCKAGES
If water will not run away in a gully after the grid has been cleared of rubbish, the underground drainage system

may be blocked up. This could also be the case if a ground floor w.c. pan fills nearly to the brim and is very slow to clear.

To find out where in the drainage system the fault lies, lift the cover off the inspection chambers or manholes and see where the water is lying. When you spot a dry chamber the blockage will be above that point (nearer the house).

To clear the obstruction, a set of drain rods will be needed. These can be screwed together like a chimney sweep's rods and can be fitted with various attachments, *fig. 94*. Some plant hire firms or builders' merchants hire them out.

A rubber plunger head is one attachment used for this purpose. Being flexible, it is capable of shifting soft obstructions.

Screw a few rods together and feed the plunger into the drain, twisting the rods in a *clockwise direction* as you do so, otherwise you may unscrew the rods and leave the leading rod and the plunger attachment stuck in the drain.

If the plunger fails to shift the obstruction, try a corkscrew head attachment but use it gently or you could fracture a pipe.

When finally the blockage is cleared, flush out the section thoroughly with a hosepipe while using the plunger disc to shift any remaining sediment.

FRACTURED PIPE
If, after all your efforts, the blockage cannot be cleared, the trouble may turn out to be a fractured pipe. An indication of its position can be obtained by counting the number of rods used in order to meet the obstruction.

This may well be under an impossible place to get at like a concrete path. In any case, all defects in the drainage system should be notified to the public health inspector. Repairs of this nature are normally best left to an expert. They should, in any case, be supervised by the health inspector's department, and tested and approved by him.

A knowledge of how a domestic drainage system works above ground, at least, is a valuable asset to any householder. There is much he can do to keep the system in working order.

TWO-PIPE SYSTEM
Take a look at *fig. 95*. If you can recognise your drainage system from the diagram, yours is what is known as a two-pipe installation. It may surprise you to learn that this system is now obsolete! However, don't despair. The majority of homes have similar installations.

A brief description is necessary. First there is the soil pipe to which the w.c. is directly connected, and which runs underground to empty into the sewer. Its other end should terminate at least 3 ft above the top windows; it acts as a vent pipe to allow the sewer gases to escape.

Every soil pipe should have a cage on its top to prevent it becoming blocked up with wind-blown rubbish and birds' nests.

Other pipes used in this system carry the rest of the house water to the sewer. These pipes discharge into open gullies.

HOPPER

In the typical system illustrated in *fig. 95*, both the bath and bathroom wash basin empty into a hopper on the wall outside. The hopper connects to a downpipe, which discharges into a gully at ground level.

In some systems the kitchen sink waste empties into the same gully via a short length of downpipe, but in other systems it has its own gully.

All the gullies mentioned are connected to the main house drain which leads to the public sewer.

In some old drainage installations both the house waste *and* the rainwater pipes are discharged into the same sewer, but in new buildings these are now normally separated.

In some even more primitive arrangements rainwater is disposed of via soakaways in the garden, but this practice is fast dying out.

DRAINS

Now to the drains themselves. Those which carry domestic waste to the sewer may be salt glazed earthenware or cast iron or, in modern buildings, pitch fibre or plastic.

Drains are laid in straight runs so that blockages can be cleared easily. However, if they have to change direction, or if a branch pipe joins the main drain, a manhole is provided at this point to permit access for clearing blockages, *fig. 96*.

In many areas the authorities lay down that the manhole should be provided near the boundary of the house at the point where the main drain falls to the sewer. To prevent gas from

the sewer building up in the house drains, this manhole is provided with an interceptor trap, *fig. 97*.

The rodding eye of this trap enables

any blockages which may occur between the manhole and the fall to the sewer to be cleared.

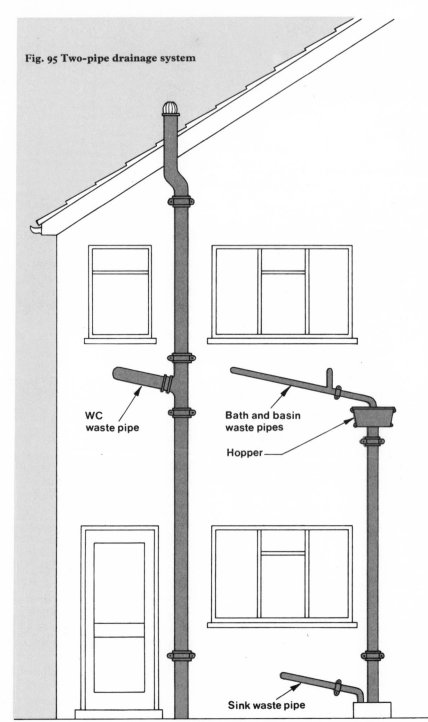

Fig. 95 Two-pipe drainage system

WC waste pipe

Bath and basin waste pipes

Hopper

Sink waste pipe

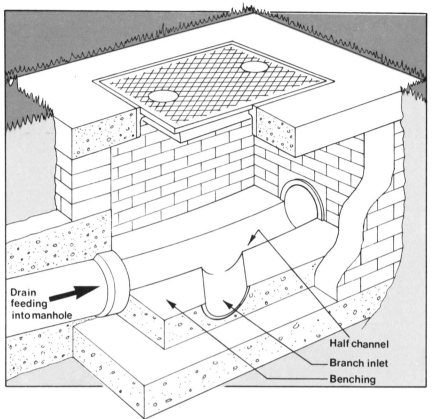

Fig. 96 Typical manhole

- Drain feeding into manhole
- Half channel
- Branch inlet
- Benching

Fig. 97 Manhole with interceptor trap

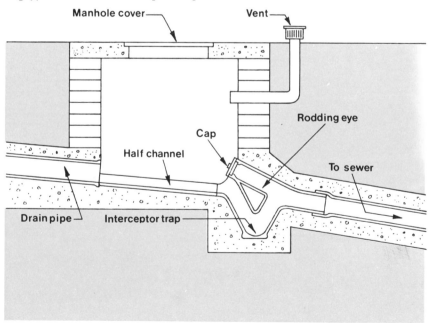

- Manhole cover
- Vent
- Rodding eye
- Cap
- Half channel
- To sewer
- Drain pipe
- Interceptor trap

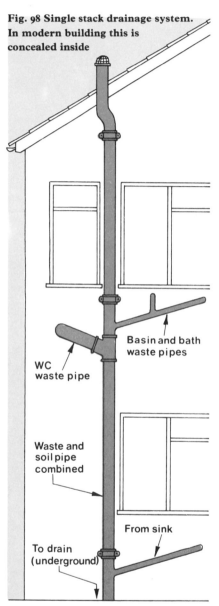

Fig. 98 Single stack drainage system. In modern building this is concealed inside

- Basin and bath waste pipes
- WC waste pipe
- Waste and soil pipe combined
- From sink
- To drain (underground)

VENTILATION

To ventilate the house drains, a short vent pipe is connected to the manhole. This is known as the disconnecting manhole and it may serve more than one house.

The domestic waste is carried from the inlet to the outlet section of a manhole by half channels encased in benching. This benching is simply smooth finished concrete which assists the flow of waste water through to the sewer.

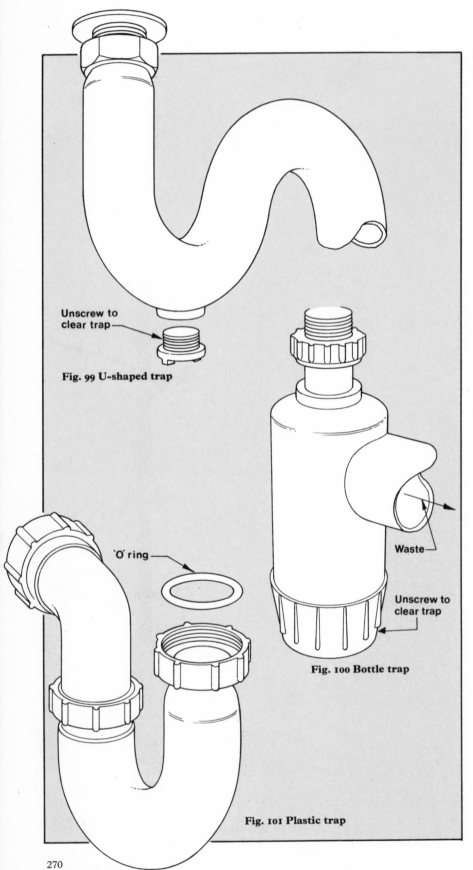

Fig. 99 U-shaped trap

'O' ring

Fig. 101 Plastic trap

Waste

Unscrew to
clear trap

Fig. 100 Bottle trap

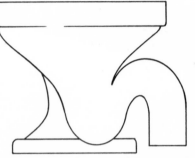

Fig. 102 S trap for ground floor w.c.

Fig. 103 P trap for upstairs w.c.

Manholes in some areas where there
are modern developments have been
replaced by a different method. This
comprises a series of rodding points
and involves the use of plastic drain
pipes. Access to these points is provided by an inspection chamber or
concrete cover.

SINGLE STACK
That is really all you need to know
about your drainage system, but before
leaving the subject, a word about
drainage systems in new properties.

Under the Building Regulations, new
houses are provided with what is called
the single stack or one-pipe system,
fig. 98. The difference in the new and
the old systems will be appreciated if
figs. 95 and *98* are compared.

This new system is built inside the

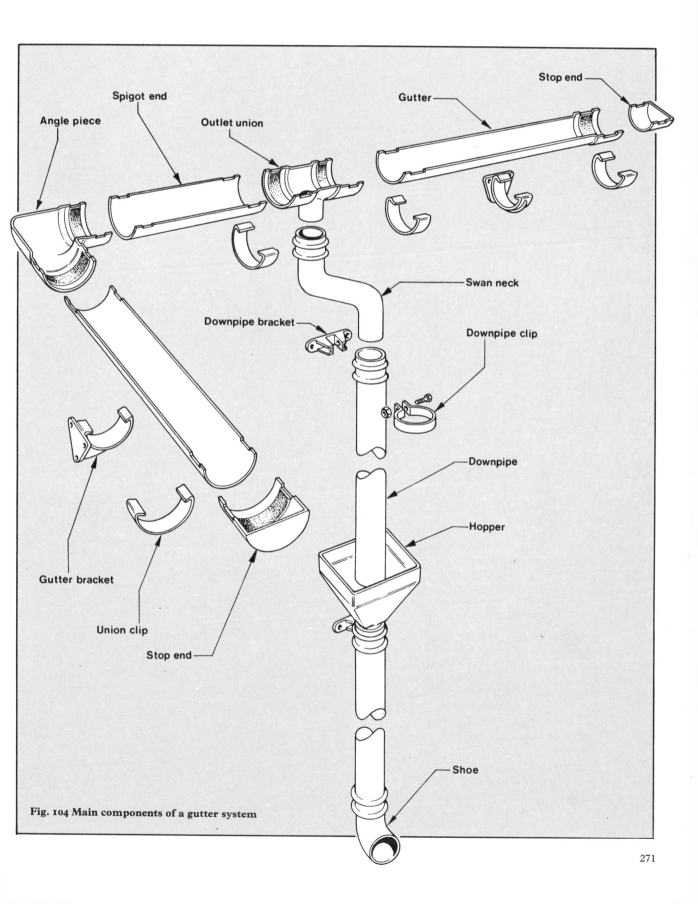

Fig. 104 Main components of a gutter system

house and all the wastes from sinks, basins, w.c.s and baths empty into the soil pipe (one-pipe). This pipe connects directly with the main drains of the house. It is vented above the level of the eaves and is served by the manholes already mentioned.

In some of these modern installations anti-siphonage vent pipes connect to the waste pipe of all the fittings (bath, sink, basin and w.c.) and to the soil pipe itself.

The purpose of the anti-siphonage pipe is to stop the water seal in a waste trap being sucked out by the force of the waste matter passing through the pipe from a fitting (perhaps a bathroom basin) on a floor above.

In some modern buildings, the waste traps of fittings are provided with deep seal traps as an alternative to the above system. In many of the modern single stack drainage systems, plastic is used instead of cast iron.

GULLIES AND TRAPS

We saw earlier how waste traps can give access to waste pipes in order to clear blockages. These traps are permanently filled with water to prevent odours rising from the drains and entering the waste pipes and permeating the atmosphere in the house by escaping through the w.c. pan and basin plug holes.

Many basin and sink traps are U shaped, *fig. 99*; others are bottle traps, *fig. 100*. In a plastic pipe system they may be shown in *fig. 101*.

In a ground floor w.c. it is usual to fit an S trap, *fig. 102*, but in an upstairs floor w.c., a P trap is usually installed, *fig. 103*.

NEW WASHER ON TRAP

Another simple plumbing job to be added to the d-i-y man's list is that of fitting a new washer on a leaking waste trap.

First put a bucket under the trap to catch the flow of water from it. Then unscrew the connecting nut as required. The leak may be at the top of the trap where it joins the sink, or at the bottom.

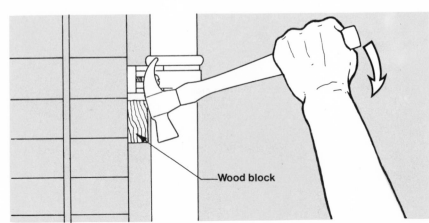

Fig. 105 Releasing downpipe bracket

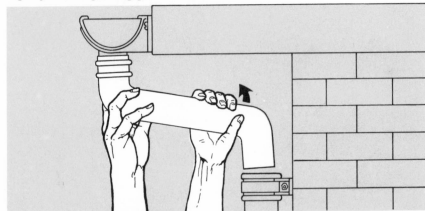

Fig. 106 Releasing a swan neck

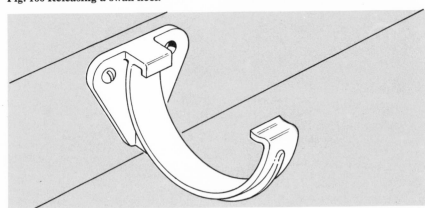

Fig. 107 Gutter bracket for screwing to fascia

Figs. 99 and *100* show two types of trap – the U shape and the bottle trap. After removing the faulty washer, take it with you as a pattern when you buy the new one. After renewing, turn on the tap and check that the leak has stopped.

GUTTERS

If he can work from a ladder, a d-i-y plumber should be able to maintain his gutters and downpipes in good working order.

Most gutters are now either cast-iron or pvc. While cast-iron types are extremely robust, they are liable to corrode if neglected. Therefore they should be examined regularly for signs of rust.

If a cast-iron gutter leaks at one or two points, this will probably be caused by corrosion which has eaten right through the material. Small holes can be repaired with an epoxy resin filler – Plastic Padding or Isopon, for example – after wire brushing the gutter to remove the rust (wear safety spectacles when you are doing this job or protect the eyes in some other way). But if a gutter is badly worn, it is better to replace the section affected by a new length.

Once corrosion starts in one length of gutter, it is quite likely that the remainder of the lengths will be similarly affected before long. If this is so, it is worth replacing the whole of the system with modern pvc materials.

Figure 104 gives an idea of how a gutter and its downpipes are constructed. Rainwater runs down the roof into the gutters which are fixed to fascia boards at the eaves. The gutters fall slightly to an outlet. This carries the water through the downpipe to the drainage system.

START AT THE TOP

There are various spots in the system which can become clogged up with leaves and other rubbish. So clearing them out should be made a regular task. Begin at the highest point and work downwards. Clean not only the gutters themselves, but all the outlets, swan necks, hopper heads and downpipes.

While doing this job, a lot of muck may pass through the downpipes into the gullies through the grids, so put a bowl or basin under the shoe of each downpipe to prevent the rubbish entering the drainage system. It is advisable to wear gloves on this job, especially if the gutters have sharp metal edges.

If the gutter is blocked, remove the debris but avoid letting it fall into outlets and thence to the downpipes.

CLEARING OBSTRUCTION

To clear an obstruction in a downpipe, tie a thick old rag securely to a cane and see if it can be pushed through the pipe. If this is not effective, you may have to disconnect the downpipes.

The pipes are fixed to the wall with brackets and clips. Use a claw hammer held against a block of wood to withdraw the nails from the bracket lugs, *fig. 105.*

The obstruction should be easy to remove once the length of downpipe is released. Flush the pipe through with a hose afterwards. Then refit the pipe. You will probably have to put new wooden wall plugs in the holes into which the nails can bite.

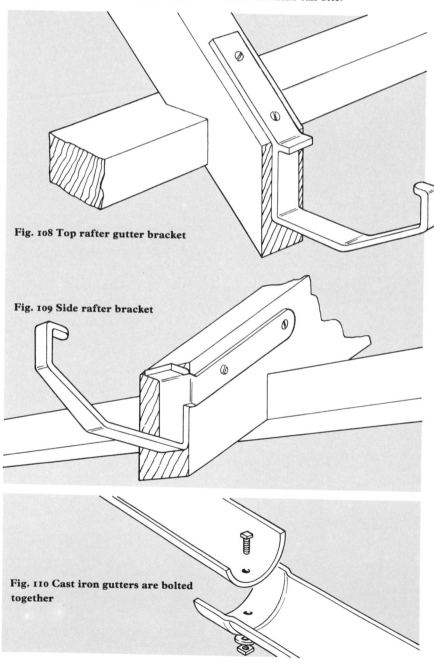

Fig. 108 Top rafter gutter bracket

Fig. 109 Side rafter bracket

Fig. 110 Cast iron gutters are bolted together

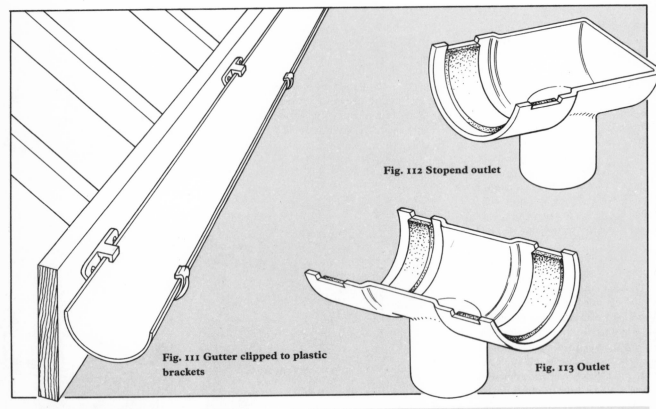

Fig. 112 Stopend outlet

Fig. 111 Gutter clipped to plastic brackets

Fig. 113 Outlet

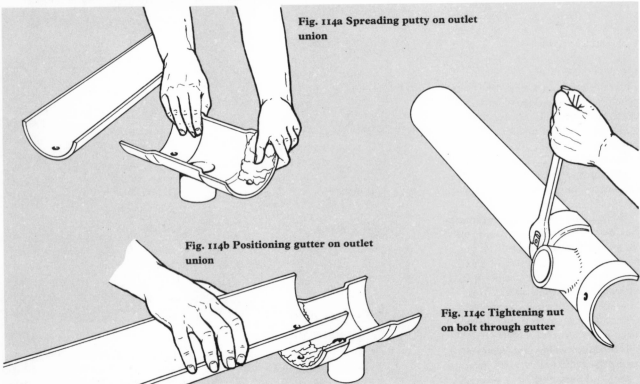

Fig. 114a Spreading putty on outlet union

Fig. 114b Positioning gutter on outlet union

Fig. 114c Tightening nut on bolt through gutter

The joints of the pipes may be loose after taking them apart. If so, apply mastic to the joint and coat it with bituminous paint.

Swan necks, *fig. 104*, are also likely to become clogged with debris. To free a swan neck from a downpipe, push its lower part upwards to release it from the pipe. Then dismantle its other end from the gutter itself, *fig. 106*.

You will need two hands for this job so be careful you don't overbalance. Two pairs of hands, in fact, are better than one for jobs like this.

REMOVE RUST

Clean the section out thoroughly after dislodging the obstacle and remove any loose rust. Cast iron swan necks should be reconnected to the downpipe first, then to the gutter. If, however, the section is made of plastic, fix it in the reverse way.

When you have removed all the debris, tip some water in the gutter at its highest point and see if it runs away quickly. If the gutter has sagged at any point, water will tend to build up there and may cause the gutter to overflow.

Faults of this nature should receive immediate attention or the wall will become soaked with water and, in a solid wall especially, may cause internal damp problems.

SAGGING GUTTERS

There are two ways to cure a slight sag in a gutter. You can try raising the length of gutter concerned by fixing a new gutter bracket to support it where it sags, or the section between it and the downpipe can be lowered but not by more than 1 in. This movement is restricted to prevent the joints between the gutter sections being forced apart.

There are two main types of gutter bracket, *figs. 107* and *108*. If yours are rafter brackets, you will have to remove a slate or tile to get at the fixing rafters. The other type screws to the fascia.

If the brackets are cast-iron types, they will probably be bolted to the gutters, *fig. 110*. Plastic brackets are simply clipped over the gutters, *fig. 111*.

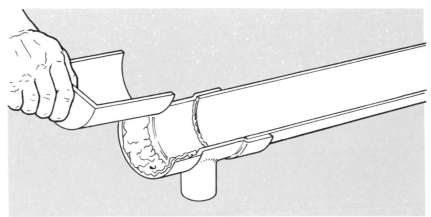

Fig. 115 Joining the end piece to the outlet union

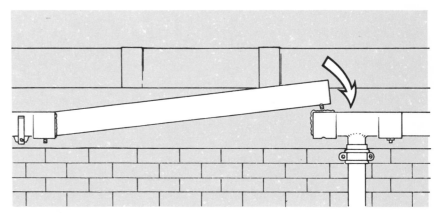

Fig. 116 Positioning a section of gutter

NEW LENGTH OF GUTTER

To replace a length of cast-iron gutter, first clean out any debris and remove the swan neck or, if there isn't one, the downpipe. Next, the nut holding the gutter to the bracket should be undone, but this will most probably need to be oiled first to help release it. If it won't budge, you may have to cut right through the nut with a small hacksaw and renew it.

When the section has been released from its brackets, lift it carefully and lower it to the ground. It will be heavy and brittle (if old), so don't try to go it alone!

Cut the new gutter, if necessary, to length with a hacksaw, using the old length as a guide. If there are any joints, allow for overlaps. Drill a $\frac{5}{16}$ in (8 mm) diameter hole for the bolt.

The outlet union (which may be a stopend or intermediate type), *figs. 112* and *113*, will come away with the section of gutter. Clean this up (or renew if necessary) and spread a layer of metal casement putty on the inside edge, *fig. 114a*. Press the new length of gutter into the putty – aligning the holes on both gutter and union, *fig. 114b*.

Press a bolt into the hole, add a washer and nut and tighten up, *fig. 114c*. Clean off all excess putty.

Cut off a new end piece and drill bolt holes as before. Line the stopend (new or old) with putty, bolt it to the end piece and join to the outlet union, *fig. 115*.

PAINT IT

Before fixing the new section of gutter, paint it inside with bituminous paint. Renew the gutter brackets if necessary,

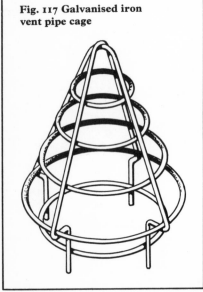

Fig. 117 Galvanised iron vent pipe cage

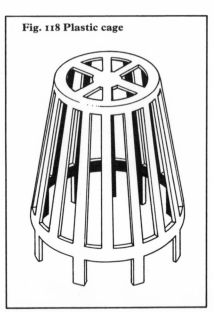

Fig. 118 Plastic cage

rest the section of new gutter on them and adjust it until it meets the section next to it, *fig. 116*. Spread putty at the end of the new section and bolt to the existing section.

Gutters are made in 6 ft lengths (1.8 metres). Diameters are 3 in, 4 in and 4½ in (75, 100 and 115 mm). Make sure you get the right size.

SOIL PIPE CAGE

A point to check when cleaning or fixing gutters is whether the soil pipe is fitted with a cage to prevent birds nesting on top of the pipe and perhaps causing a blockage. If there isn't one, measure the internal diameter of the pipe and get one of the right size from a builders' merchant.

The cages are made in galvanised iron or plastic, *figs. 117* and *118*. They

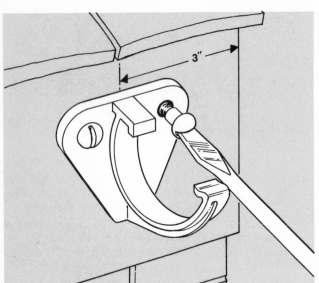

Fig. 119 Fixing first gutter bracket to fascia

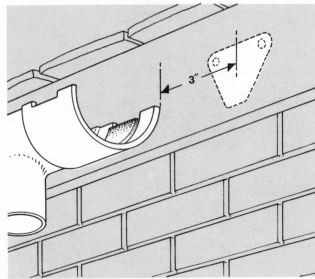

Fig. 120 Making a mark for end bracket

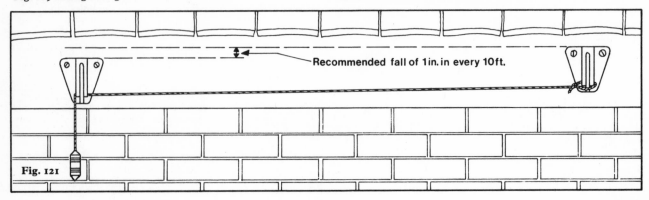

Recommended fall of 1 in. in every 10 ft.

Fig. 121

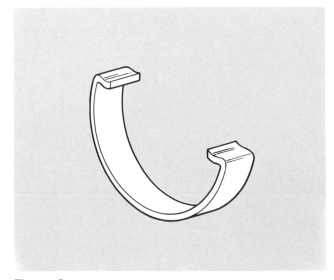

Fig. 122 Gutter strap

Fig. 123 Secure a ladder to a ring bolt screwed to the fascia

are easily fitted by squeezing the prongs and pushing the cage into the top of the pipe as far as possible.

PLASTIC RAINWATER FITTINGS

There are several manufacturers of plastic rainwater fittings. If you plan to replace your gutter system with plastic materials, it is a good idea to get pamphlets from a dealer or from the manufacturers themselves. These include Marley and Osma Ltd. (Marley Plumbing, Dickley Lane, Lenham, Maidstone, Kent. Osma Plastics Ltd., Rigby Lane, Dawley Road, Hayes, Middx.)

You will find instructions and illustrations on how to fit the components and these should be followed implicitly.

A gutter should slope (fall) gradually from its closed end down to the outlet pipe (downpipe). The recommended fall is 1 in in 10 ft.

Methods of fixing plastic gutters vary according to make. Here is a brief outline of the procedure but watch for variations in the pamphlet supplied. The pamphlet should also give directions on welding and jointing where this is applicable.

Having taken down the old gutter,

clean the fascia board and paint it if necessary. When the paint is dry, fix your first bracket 3 in from the top end (the one at the opposite end to the downpipe, *fig. 119*). At the other end, hold the stopend outlet where it is to be positioned and make a pencil mark 3 in from it for the final bracket, *fig. 120*.

STRING LINE

Run a string line attached to the bracket at the other end and tie a weight to it such as a plumb bob. Hold the bracket against the fascia and let the string line hang over it, *fig. 121*. Check that the line is horizontal by using a spirit level. Then fix the bracket slightly lower so the water will flow towards the downpipe.

Fix the rest of the brackets in position at the distances recommended. Make sure all the joints have brackets near them for support. Fix the outlet and the gutter lengths, linking them with jointing pieces.

There may be variations in the types of jointing pieces, but generally they are gutter straps, *fig. 122*, which clip on to hold the spigot and socket of the gutter in a watertight joint.

The lengths of downpipe are fitted from the top downwards and you add

the necessary supports according to the manufacturer's instructions.

SCAFFOLDING IS SAFER

Fixing gutters really needs two pairs of hands, as I said earlier, and it is much easier to work from some form of scaffolding rather than from ladders. If you have to use a ladder, make sure it is anchored firmly by tying it to a ring bolt screwed into the fascia board, *fig. 123*.

Don't lean a ladder against a plastic gutter. Being smooth surfaced, a ladder can slip on these gutters very easily. For another thing, plastic gutters are flexible, which means that they are not really suitable as ladder supports.

Plastic gutters should not be painted. In fact, they are most difficult to paint because the release agent used in the mould to shape the gutters adheres to their surface for some time afterwards and it is not easy to get paint to 'take' on their surfaces.

If, however, you want to paint them so that they match the rest of the exterior decorations, don't do so for at least a year. This will give the release agent time to be washed off by the rain. Then paint them with two coats of gloss paint. Do *not* use primer or undercoat.

Outside Taps

One tap in the house which does a lion's share of the work is the cold water tap at the kitchen sink. Even when the garden needs watering or the car requires hosing down, it is frequently this tap which is used, frequently at an inconvenient time for the housewife!

Fitting an outside tap is the obvious solution and it is a job within the scope of a handyman, provided he has at least some idea of how a pipe should be cut and can take accurate measurements.

My advice is to make certain you know exactly what is involved before you attempt this job because it will mean cutting the rising main pipe. If a hash is made of this part of the operation, then you will be in trouble!

When the job is being done, the domestic water supply will have to be turned off, so make sure your cold water storage cistern is full and, as a safeguard, first draw off some drinking water from the kitchen tap for cooking and other purposes.

TURN OFF THE WATER
Let's assume that your rising main pipe is either copper or stainless steel and that it emerges from the floor or the wall under the kitchen sink. A few inches above the floor there should be a stop-valve and draincock (they may be combined) fitted to the rising main pipe. If this is so, you can turn the water off at this point. Otherwise use the stopcock buried in the pavement outside.

The rising main pipe above the stop-valve may then go direct to the kitchen tap, or there may be a tee-jointed branch pipe, *fig. 124.*

A new branch pipe to your outside tap should be taken from a point *above* the existing stop-valve, but *below* the branch pipe supplying the kitchen tap, *fig. 125.*

You may therefore be restricted in your choice of position for the branch to the outside tap. But remember not to fit the branch too low down. Allow plenty of room for buckets or watering cans to be held under the tap outside.

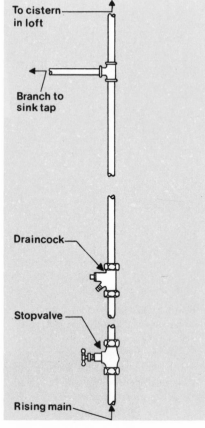

Fig. 124 Branch to sink tap

The branch pipe to the garden should slope *slightly* downwards so that it can be drained completely in frosty weather.

MATERIALS
Measure up carefully for the amount of pipe needed. Allow a little extra as a precaution and for any bends to be made. I will assume that compression joints will be used as these are simpler for an amateur who is working in a confined space.

Apart from $\frac{1}{2}$ in (15 mm) copper pipe, you will need

One tee connector ($\frac{1}{2}$ in or 15 mm), *fig. 125.*

One stop-valve (may be referred to at the shop as a stopcock) 15 mm × 15 mm, *fig. 125.*

One wall plate elbow with compression joint inlet and threaded female outlet (to accept tap), *fig. 126.*

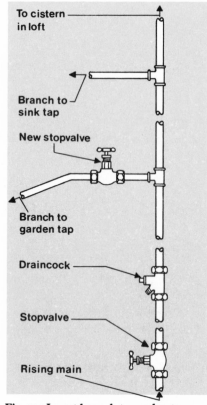

Fig. 125 Insert branch to garden tap below branch to sink tap but above the stopvalve

One hose union bib tap.

I suggest you buy all the fittings at the same place, explaining what they are needed for. You can then try them out and see that everything fits neatly together. If possible, I suggest you buy a bib tap which will incline forwards. This prevents grazing your hands on the wall when operating the tap.

If you are pushed for time, it is better to do the job in two parts. The first thing to do after cutting off the water supply and draining the rising main pipe through the draincock is to fit the tee connector.

CUT THE PIPE
Hold the connector against the rising main pipe and carefully mark off the section of the pipe to be cut out to make way for the tee, ie. the distance between the shoulders on the inside

of the connector. Be very careful not to cut away too much pipe.

As you will be working in a confined space, it may be easier to cut the pipe with a small hacksaw rather than with a tube cutter (as described on pages 251 and 252). Cut the pipe squarely and trim off all the burrs.

Remove the nuts and olives (rings) from the tee connector and slip them over the cut ends of the pipe. One end of the pipe may have to be sprung slightly to get it into the connector. Tighten up the nuts over the olives and the tee joint is almost complete.

You will now need to cut off a short length of copper pipe from your new length and join it to the branch outlet (the remaining hole) of the connector. Tighten up as before.

FIT THE STOP-VALVE
The new stop-valve is now fitted to the other end of the short length of pipe in the same way. Take care to ensure that the arrow on the stop-valve is pointing *away* from the rising main but *towards* the garden tap. If the valve is fitted incorrectly, no water will be able to flow through to the tap outside!

Fig. 126 Wall plate elbow

Now you can turn this stop-valve off. This completes the first part of the job. The water can now be turned on again to bring the house supply back to normal. Water cannot now flow through the new stop-valve, and the rest of the operation can be completed at any time.

The next thing to do is drill a hole through the brick wall for the pipe to the tap. For this you will need a long masonry drill to be fitted in a power drill. If you have a solid wall, this will be about 9 in thick. A cavity wall, of course, will be about 11 in thick, including the cavity.

You need a hole big enough to take a $\frac{1}{2}$ in (15 mm) pipe. The job *can* be done with a cold chisel and hammer, but it is not a method I would choose.

If the pipe has to change direction to enter the hole in the wall, you can use an elbow bend compression fitting, to avoid bending the pipe. This is the easiest way to do the job.

Cut off another short length of pipe and fit one end of it into the vacant end of the stop-valve and its other end into the compression bend. Now cut off enough pipe to run from the com-

pression bend to the wall plate elbow outside.

BEND THE PIPE
Note that this pipe will have to be bent slightly *downwards* towards the garden tap. You can, of course, use another compression bend to achieve this change of direction, but it is less expensive to bend the pipe using a $\frac{1}{2}$ in bending spring.

Grease the spring, then drop it into the pipe to the spot where the pipe is to be bent. Bend the pipe over your knee. As you do this, the spring inside the pipe will act as a support and prevent the pipe from becoming flattened.

When the bend is complete, insert a metal rod into the ring on the bending spring to act as a tommy bar. Turn the spring clockwise and pull it out of the pipe.

Now push the pipe into the hole in the wall and connect it to the compression bend inside or, if no bend is needed inside, direct to the stop-valve.

WALL PLATE ELBOW
The position of the wall plate elbow

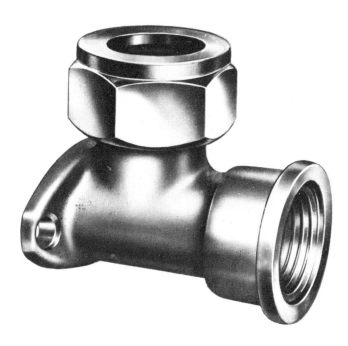

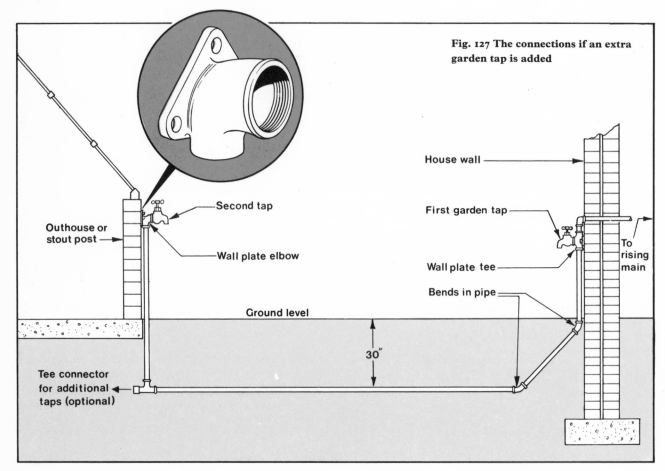

Fig. 127 The connections if an extra garden tap is added

Second tap

Wall plate elbow

Outhouse or stout post

House wall

First garden tap

To rising main

Wall plate tee

Bends in pipe

Ground level

30"

Tee connector for additional taps (optional)

can now be determined. Holes should be drilled in the wall and plugged for the fixing screws. Now join the pipe to the elbow, *fig. 127*.

To make sure of a watertight joint, bind ptfe plastic thread sealing tape around the thread of the tap before screwing it into the wall plate elbow.

Your garden tap is now complete and you can turn on the new stop-valve. If the outside tap should drip or is hard to turn, you may find that some bits of brass filings have found their way inside. This is common in some new taps.

If so, remove the headgear of the tap, as described on page 242, and see if any filings are in the bottom of the body or elsewhere.

They may prevent the water being turned off completely. Unscrew the tap from the wall plate and clean it out as necessary.

Before replacing the headgear in the tap's body, apply Vaseline to the thread. This will make it easier to remove if and when it needs a new washer.

In the winter the water supply to the garden tap should be turned off at the new stop-valve and the garden tap drained as a frost precaution.

EXTENSION TAP
Having got a water supply freely available on an outside wall you may want another tap fitted near the top of the garden. This is now no problem. If you decide to do this, instead of fitting a wall plate elbow to the wall as described, fit a wall plate tee. The pipe to the second tap can be joined to the bottom outlet.

It is best to use polythene tube instead of copper pipe to supply the second tap, and it should be buried

about 30 in below ground level to protect it from gardening tools thrust into the soil.

Similar compression joints to those used for the first tap will be suitable for polythene tube. You can get special inserts which are designed to stop the tube collapsing as the nuts on the compression joints are tightened.

With polythene tube, you usually have to get compression fittings a size larger than those used to join copper pipes. So if you use $\frac{1}{2}$ in (15 mm) polythene tube you will require $\frac{3}{4}$ in (22 mm) fittings.

ADAPTORS
You can get polythene adaptors which will greatly simplify the process of changing over from copper to polythene.

These have a plain end which fits into an existing compression joint. The

**Fig. 128 A patio swimming pool
installation in the author's garden**

other end is an enlarged joint to take
the polythene tube. The fitting is
joined to the bottom of a wall plate tee
and your polythene tube is connected
to it.

When you have made the connection
at the tee, bury the length of polythene
tube in a trench 30 in deep. Near its
other end fix a timber post in the
ground to which the second tap can be
attached. Use hardwood for the post
and protect it against the weather by
treating with preservative.

Screw a wall plate elbow to the post
and your second tap to the elbow,
fig. 127.

You will have to bend the polythene
tube in two places – where it is first
buried and where it rises to join the
second tap.

To bend the tube, you will need
water kept at boiling point. Immerse
for a few minutes and bend as required.
Once the tube has cooled off, the bend
should remain.

Remember to drain the pipe and
turn off the water supply when the cold
weather arrives. You won't get the
water out of the pipe which is underground, of course, but as the pipe is
polythene, no harm can arise even if
the water in it should freeze up.

Scale and Corrosion

One great disadvantage of a direct hot water system (see also chapter on hot water systems) is that it is more prone to scale problems than an indirect system – especially in hard water areas.

When scale forms, the flow pipe becomes furred up near the boiler. This restricts the circulation of the water. If steps are not taken to prevent this happening, back circulation will eventually take place.

The hot water will force its way back up the return pipe, *fig. 129*. This will cause all sorts of gurgling and banging noises which will be especially noticeable when the boiler fire is burning well.

When a system produces these noises, it can be dangerous and should be descaled as soon as possible. Before the noises are heard, it may be noticed that the boiler will be taking longer to fill the cylinder with heated water.

UNWANTED INSULATION
When scale forms in a hot water system it acts as an insulator and a type of insulator you can well do without! When scale forms inside a boiler it actually insulates the water against the heat produced by the boiler fire. This is why the water in the cylinder takes longer to heat up.

The remedy for this is *not* to stoke up the boiler to increase the heat. By doing this, you will cause the system to overheat and thus produce even more scale. Then the noises will increase in volume as the water tries to force its way through the pipes. Overheating can eventually cause the boiler to leak.

Fortunately, it is possible for a d-i-y man to descale his own hot water installation by introducing chemicals which will remove the layers of scale (the insulators). You can buy descaling kits just as you can the small packets of descaler which are designed to remove scale from kettles.

Contact your local plumbing and heating merchants for details of manufacturers and where you can obtain a kit. Full instructions are supplied.

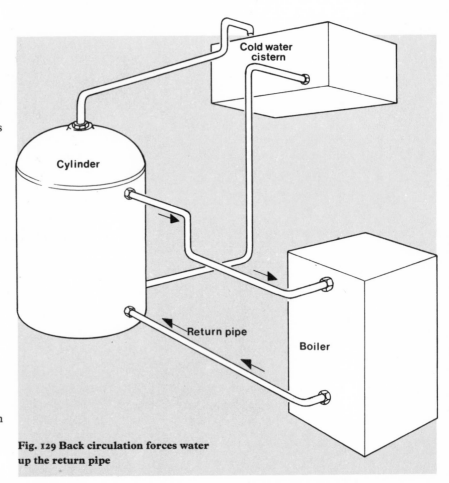

Fig. 129 Back circulation forces water up the return pipe

The chemicals are put into the system via the cold water storage cistern or through the draincock on the boiler.

PRECAUTIONS
There are one or two things you can do to avoid the system becoming scaled up to the extent described. First and foremost, don't let the water boil in the boiler. Although many older types of boiler which use solid fuel cannot be temperature controlled, in time you get to know the 'feel' of the thing and can judge when the water is getting near boiling point.

When in doubt, you can do the obvious thing – run some of the hot water off before it boils. This may be wasteful, but it is kinder to your system in the long run.

If you have a boiler fitted with a temperature control, there is no prob-lem. The temperature of the water has to reach about 160°F (71°C) before scale starts to form to any appreciable extent, so if the temperature can be kept at no higher than 140°F (60°C), the risk of scale is considerably reduced. The thermostat on the immersion heater should also be set at 140°F (60°C) for the same reason.

ADDITIVES
Another thing you can do is to introduce chemical additives into the water. These will have the effect of stabilising the chemicals which are responsible for scale forming.

A well-known one is Micromet, made by Albright & Wilson Ltd. This is a simple device consisting of a polythene mesh basket, *fig. 130*. This is suspended in the cold water storage cistern. Although it prevents scale in the *hot* water system, it must be hung

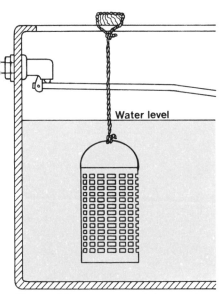

Fig. 130 Micromet crystals in container to prevent scale

in the *cold* water cistern which supplies that system.

The basket is submerged in the water near the ball-valve inlet, but clear of both the ball float arm and the bottom of the cistern.

The life of the Micromet is six months. The makers will send you a reminder every six months that a refill is due.

This device does not soften water and it is not intended for use in closed-circuit central heating systems.

Another problem can arise in *soft* water areas. Iron and galvanised parts of a system may corrode causing tap water to become rusty and leave stains on the sanitary ware. You can use Micromet for this purpose also. It controls this type of corrosion and eliminates rust-coloured water.

INDIRECT SYSTEM

The most drastic cure for scale is to replace a direct hot water system with an indirect one, which would be less likely to scale up.

The reason for this is that a given volume of water contains only a certain quantity of the chemicals which can cause scale to form. Therefore, once these have been deposited in the primary circuit of an indirect system

(when it is first fitted) no more scale can form. The water is used over and over again, and only small losses which are caused by evaporation have to be replaced.

The secondary circuit of an indirect system (the one which supplies the domestic hot water) will not normally become hot enough to cause much scale to form.

CORROSION

Electrolytic corrosion can occur in galvanised steel cold water cisterns and hot water tanks if copper and galvanised steel are both used in the same plumbing installations. We don't need to worry too much how it occurs, but briefly the cause is this.

When, say, the steel of a cistern is galvanised to protect it against corrosion, it is coated with zinc. Some types of water are charged with a large amount of carbon dioxide which can act as an electrolyte (a sort of electric conductor).

An electric current flows between the zinc on the cistern and the copper pipes. This causes the zinc to dissolve, leaving the steel exposed. Rust will then form on the cistern.

PAINT THE CISTERN

This can be prevented by painting the inside of a *cold* water storage cistern with bituminous paint. This paint must be tasteless and have no smell. (This method cannot be used on a galvanised steel hot water tank.) The paint will stop the water coming into contact with the galvanising on the cistern and causing corrosion.

Have a look at the cold water cistern up in the loft, or wherever it is. If you find traces of rust inside it, but the outer sides of the cistern are in good

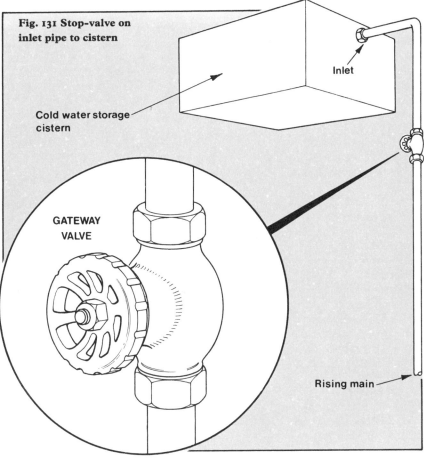

Fig. 131 Stop-valve on inlet pipe to cistern

Cold water storage cistern

Inlet

GATEWAY VALVE

Rising main

283

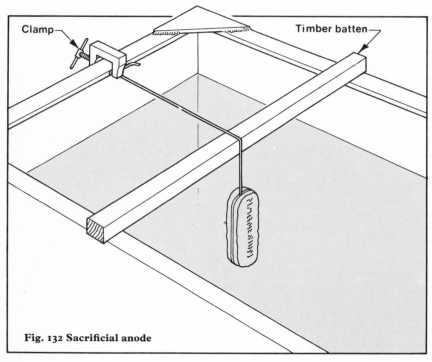

Clamp

Timber batten

Fig. 132 Sacrificial anode

order, then you can extend its life by coating it with this type of paint.

First you will have to shut off the water supply to the cistern, drain and wait until it is thoroughly dry. You may be able to speed up the drying process by using a hair drier.

Tie up the ball-valve to make sure no water can seep past the stop-valve.

REMOVE THE RUST
The first job is to get all the rust off by wire brushing (protect your eyes) and by using abrasive paper. As you remove the rust you may find that the surface of the cistern is pitted in places. These areas should all be filled in with a resin filler (Isopon or Plastic Padding, for example).

Then give the cistern two good coats of the bituminous paint, making sure the first is dry before the second is applied. This is obviously a job which cannot be done in a few minutes. Most of the plumbing system will be out of action while it is being done.

However, if there is a stop-valve fitted on the inlet pipe (the rising main) to the cistern, *fig. 131*, it will not mean that the whole of the cold water supply

to the house will have to be cut off. Water will still be available from the cold water tap at the kitchen sink.

Treating a cistern as described should add a few more years to its life, but if the rust is too widespread and the cistern shows signs of leaking, then it should be scrapped and replaced, preferably with a type that cannot rust.

SACRIFICIAL ANODES
There is a good way of preventing corrosion in a plumbing system. This involves fitting a sacrificial magnesium anode in the hot water tank and cold water cistern.

This is simply a lump of magnesium which has a higher electrical potential than zinc. When it is fitted into a cistern or tank it must make good electrical contact with the metal.

The electrolytic action will then occur between the zinc on the cistern and the anode (which is made of metal) itself. This will cause the anode to dissolve, or be sacrificed, thus protecting the galvanising on the cistern.

You can buy these sacrificial anodes easily. A well-known one is called the Mapel Tank-Saver and there is a

different type for cold water cisterns and for hot water tanks.

The cold water type is hung in the water and the copper wire attached to it is fixed to the edge of the cistern by clamping it, *fig. 132*. First, though, the metal part of the cistern where the wire is to be fixed must be scraped clean to ensure perfect electrical contact.

HOT WATER TYPE
Fitting a Tank-Saver to a hot water tank, *fig. 133*, is slightly more complicated. To begin with, first drain the tank from the draincock next to the boiler. Then remove the cover of the tank.

Drill a $\frac{1}{4}$ in diameter hole in the centre of the cover and screw the Tank-Saver in place. Make sure of a good electrical contact by scraping the metal thoroughly around the hole.

There are other types of anode available, including the Metalife Solid which is simply stood in the base of either a hot water tank or cold water cistern.

You should be able to buy or order these anodes through a plumbers' or builders' merchant.

MAKING REPAIRS
Repairs can be made to galvanised steel cisterns and tanks and copper cylinders using glass fibre matting and polyester resin repair kits. The tank, cistern or cylinder must be drained first, of course, and thoroughly dried. All rust must be removed as already described. Take great care that all the rust dust is removed – preferably by a vacuum cleaner.

Cold water cisterns can be repaired from the inside; hot water cylinders from the outside. To mend a hole in a cold water cistern, cover the hole from the outside with a piece of card taped on to the cistern so that the repair material cannot fall through the hole, *fig. 134*. The inner side of the card can be covered with wax to prevent the resin adhering to it, or waxed paper can be inserted between the card and the cistern.

Three pieces of glass fibre matting are now needed, each one big enough to overlap the area under repair by about 1 in all round.

After mixing the hardener with the resin, according to the manufacturer's directions, apply a coat of it about $\frac{1}{8}$ in thick to the area and bed a piece of matting into it.

Apply another coat of resin and add a second layer of matting. Repeat the operation and leave the repair to harden. Use the same process to make a repair to a hot water cylinder from the outside.

Read the instructions in your kit carefully and if they vary from the method outlined, follow them implicitly.

There are many other repair jobs which can be tackled around the house using one of these kits. In the plumbing field, these include burst or leaking pipes, cracked radiators, chipped metal baths and cracked basins.

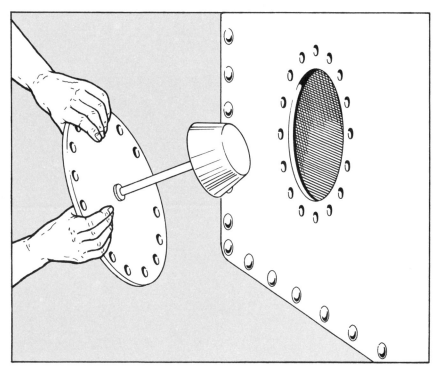

Fig. 133 Tank-Saver fitted to cover of hot water tank

Fig. 134 The stages of corrosion in a tank

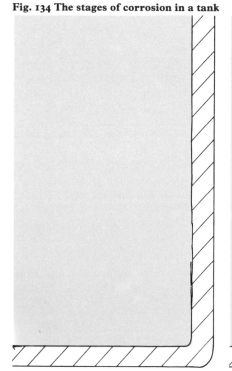
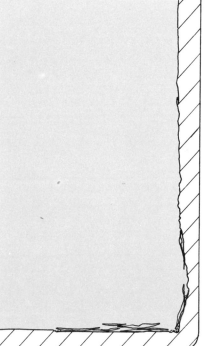
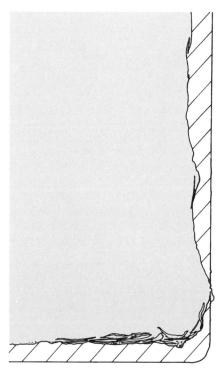

Condensation

Two rooms in a house which suffer more from condensation than any other are the bathroom and kitchen. This is due to the high volume of water vapour produced by cooking, washing up, bathing, washing and so on. What can be done to reduce the condensation?

The answer is to increase ventilation, provide steady controlled warmth, insulate thoroughly and do everything you can to cut down the volume of water vapour produced.

It sounds very simple but unfortunately it isn't as easy as it sounds. There are many ifs and buts.

Both the bathroom and kitchen have cold surfaces wherever you look. In the bathroom there is the bath, the basin, possibly exposed pipes, a w.c. cistern, probably wall tiles and glass. In the kitchen we have the sink, plastic laminate worktops, possibly exposed pipes, washing machine, fridge and various other appliances, plus no doubt partly tiled walls.

When warm air which is filled with moisture hits these surfaces when they are cold, it immediately cools down below what is known as its dew point. The water the air contained then turns into droplets rather like early morning dew on the grass.

WARMTH

Steady warmth of the correct kind will help to ensure that all the cold surfaces I have mentioned, and others besides, will not cool off below dew point.

One of the best forms of heating for this purpose is an electric convector or fan heater, or an oil-filled radiator. Don't use portable oil or gas heaters which are not fitted with flues as they generate vapour and will cause even more condensation, excellent though they may be for other heating purposes. A heated electric towel rail in a bathroom will also help to keep condensation down.

Heating alone, however, is by no means the complete answer to the problem. Some ways have to be found to make sure that whatever moisture-laden air there is in the room can

Fig. 135 Extractor fans ensure proper ventilation

Fig. 136 Fit a cooker hood to dispel cooking odours and vapour

Fig. 137 Another type of extractor fan

escape and be replaced by drier air from other parts of the house.

AIR EXTRACTORS

The best way to ensure that is to fit an electric air extractor, *fig. 135*, in the window of the room concerned. You need a type which can be switched on when moisture is being produced.

Fitting a cooker hood, *fig. 136*, which is ventilated to the air outside, will dispel the vapour caused by a cooker.

There is not a great deal that can be done to reduce the amount of vapour produced by normal domestic activities. As you may well argue, no-one produces steam or vapour deliberately! There are small things, however, that may be overlooked which would undoubtedly help to keep the condensation at least at a tolerable level.

BATHROOM CONDENSATION

In the bathroom, for example, do you run several gallons of hot water into the bath before adding cold water? If you do, this will cause a heavy volume of vapour (steam, if you prefer) to form, so try the reverse method. Run a couple of inches of cold water

first, then turn on the hot tap and note the difference in the amount of steam which rises from the bath. This method also helps to protect the bath surface.

If, for any reason, you are unable to fit an electric towel rail in the bathroom, get a radiant-type electric heater fixed really high up on the wall. It must be out of reach of anyone in contact with the bath and be operated by a pull cord switch.

If you can turn the heater on some time – say half an hour – before running the bath water, this will take the chill off the cold surfaces in the room and reduce condensation.

I have said elsewhere that the temperature of 140°F (60°C) is adequate for domestic hot water. If the temperature can be kept at this level, less condensation will be produced when the hot water is run off at any point.

INSULATION

Insulating the house thoroughly will also be a great help in keeping condensation at bay. Although the subject is too complex to be covered adequately in this book, I would emphasise the importance of insulation for this purpose.

Apart from reducing the amount of heat lost through walls, ceilings, windows and so on, adequate insulation of the areas immediately above both the kitchen and the bathroom, and the addition of expanded foam polystyrene tiles on the ceilings of these rooms, will do much to cut down the formation of vapour.

Cavity infill for cavity walls is one of the most effective ways of insulating the whole house, but unfortunately this

is not a job you can do yourself. You need a contractor armed with the right equipment to inject the special insulation materials.

Solid walls are more of a problem and cannot, of course, be treated in this way, but covering them with sheet polystyrene before hanging your wall-coverings will keep the walls warmer and prevent a lot of the condensation which might otherwise form on them.

And while talking of wallcoverings, a vinyl type has a higher insulation value than ordinary wallpaper (even washable types) and are much easier to strip, by the way, when redecorating.

DOUBLE GLAZING

It has often been claimed that double glazing will cure condensation, but this is far from true in most cases. Much depends on the type of double glazing installed. If factory sealed units of a reliable make are used, no condensation should form between the outer and the inner panes of glass. But it can form on the inside of inner panes in some cases if the room gets cold.

With the cheaper forms of double glazing there is no guarantee that condensation will not appear on the insides of the panes if the unit is not sealed, and if any moist air in the room can get to them.

Properly installed, however, any efficiently sealed double glazing unit will *reduce* condensation on the glass and will, of course, cut the amount of heat lost through the panes. But a tubular heater or radiator fixed underneath a window will probably be more effective in preventing the glass from becoming steamed up.

Showers

No bathroom can be described as fashionable or really up to date if it does not contain a shower. No longer is a shower considered a luxury. Indeed, in these days when economy is one of our main concerns, a shower is a most useful appliance which has several advantages over the traditional bath.

Apart from the fact that a shower is hygienic and convenient, it uses considerably less water than a bath – a fact which, perhaps, is not generally recognised. A shower is quicker to take than a bath and the space needed to accommodate it is far less.

There are types of shower small enough to be fitted into an area 2 ft 6 in square. It will be seen, therefore, that a shower need not necessarily be installed in a bathroom upstairs.

Given certain essentials, which I'll deal with in a moment, a shower can be fitted in a spare room, in a corner of another room (perhaps a bedroom), or even in a hall or on a landing. It would normally be no problem to disguise its presence by erecting a simple enclosure for it – a challenge, in fact, to a handyman's ingenuity!

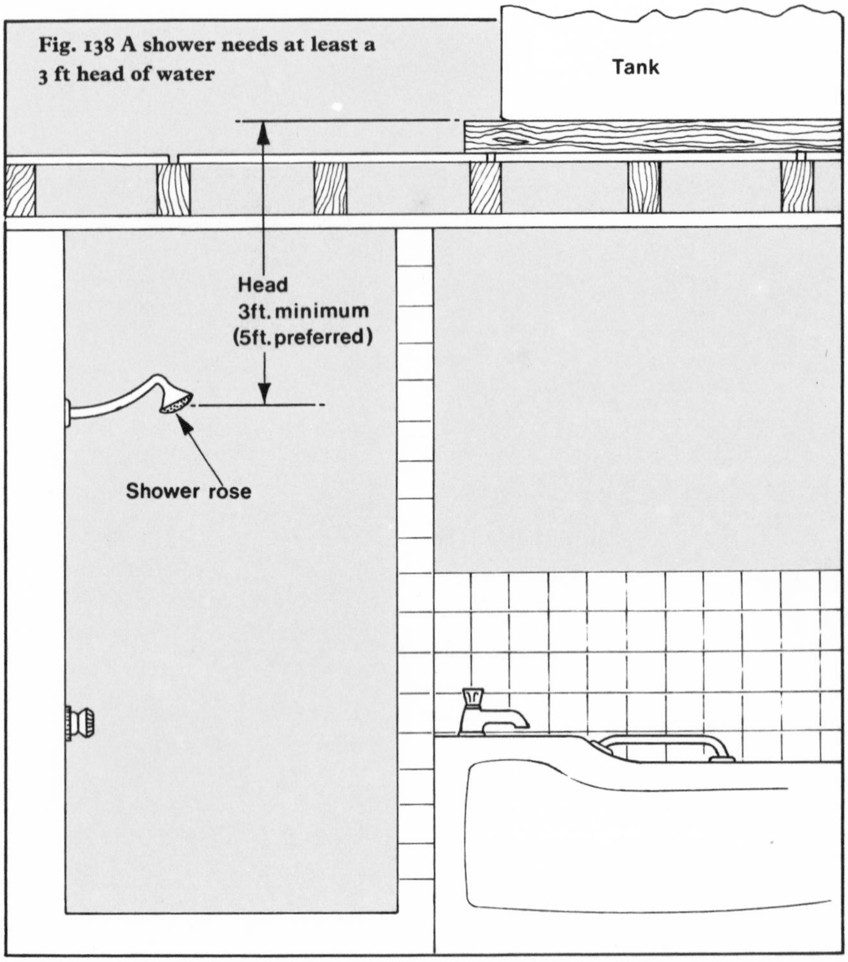

WATER PRESSURE

An essential requirement for a shower is sufficient water pressure or head at the outlet, *fig. 138*. If this pressure is not adequate, the shower will be a disappointment.

To get an adequate head, the base of the cold water storage cistern, which will normally provide the water supply, should be at least 3 ft above the level of the shower outlet, and 4 ft or 5 ft would be better still.

It is not important at what level the *hot* water cylinder or tank is positioned. It can be higher, lower or on the same level.

Ideally, too, the cold water side of the shower should be fed by a separate pipe from the cistern. The reason for this is that no water from it can then be drawn off the pipe. If there are other draw-off points, the pressure to the shower will fall when these are used and the temperature of the water will

Fig. 138 A shower needs at least a 3 ft head of water

Tank

Head
3ft. minimum
(5ft. preferred)

Shower rose

increase suddenly. There will then be a danger of the occupant of the shower being scalded!

The same remarks apply to the hot water supply. If water can be drawn off this supply pipe from elsewhere, the hot water pressure will fall and the occupant will receive a freezing cold shower.

Regulations do not normally allow cold water supplies direct from the main to be mixed with hot water supplied by a gravity system. The cold water supply should come from the cold water storage cistern.

SPECIAL FITTINGS

There is, however, one way in which this problem can sometimes be overcome. There are special fittings available in which the hot and cold water

supplies are channelled separately to the point where the water is discharged and are mixed just below the sprinkler. So long as the hot water pressure is sufficient, a shower can be fitted in this way and it will not contravene the regulations.

If the cistern is not high enough to ensure adequate pressure, it may be possible to fix it at a higher level by building a raised platform for it. If you decide to do this, however, bear in mind that the platform will have to carry a great weight!

To do this will involve lengthening the pipes leading to and from the cistern, but this can be done by using simple compression fittings. The alternative way to increase the water pressure is to fit a pump, but this will increase the cost considerably.

WATER HEATERS

If it is not possible to run a shower off your cold water system, there is an alternative method which may be acceptable. This involves fitting a gas or electric instantaneous water heater.

The heater has to be a special approved type of appliance. Not all heaters are satisfactory for this purpose so you should make careful inquiries, not only from the shower supplier, but from the local gas or electricity board as well.

These appliances must also be acceptable to local water authorities and bylaws governing their acceptance or otherwise may vary from area to area.

So make careful inquiries before launching into the purchase of this type of equipment.

These heaters are connected direct to the main, the heater control valve and sprinkler combining in one unit.

MIXING VALVES

The mixture of hot and cold water needed for a shower can be obtained by fitting a mixing valve. This will equalise the pressures of the hot and cold water supplies.

Mixing fittings can be separated into two categories. The first is simply a pair of hot and cold taps whose outlets are joined together by a mixing chamber. The required temperature is reached by adjusting the taps.

The other is a mixing valve. This combines the two taps in one and is operated by a single control. With this type, the required temperature is chosen manually by moving a pointer round a scale which is usually marked hot, warm, tepid and cold.

THERMOSTATIC VALVES

Some mixing valves are thermostatic. Showers fitted with a thermostat can adjust the water temperature automatically when it runs too hot or cold. This is the type of valve which should be used if separate supply pipes are not run to the shower from the cistern and cylinder.

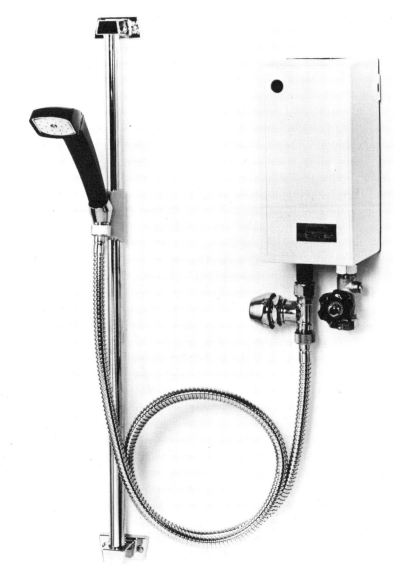

Fig. 139 A compact shower unit with its own water heater

The non-thermostatic type is a screw-down valve and has an indicator for 'hot', 'tepid', 'cold' and 'shut'. These valves are operated by a single control which turns through cold before the tepid and hot settings are reached. This is a British Standards stipulation. The best models of this type of valve have washers, and sometimes seatings, which can be renewed.

SHOWER HEADS

There are two types of shower head (the final outlet for the water) available. One is referred to as a rose, *fig. 144*, like that on a watering can, even though some models may not look exactly like one. However, they all work on the same principle, and the water is expelled through a number of small holes.

The rose type of shower head will normally operate from a slightly lower head of water than the other type – the sprayer.

The sprayer types are fitted with somewhat larger holes to discharge the

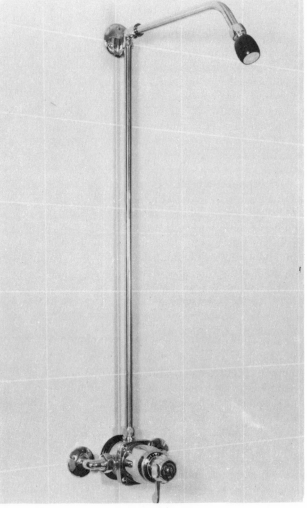

Fig. 140 Pipes are concealed with this type of shower fitting

Fig. 141 Thermostatic shower unit with exposed pipework

water, but are more economical in the amount of water they use. The larger holes, of course, make the sprayer easier to clean, and it is less likely to become clogged up than a rose type.

On some models the size and volume of the spray produced can be varied by changing the end cap. With some types of shower head the pipes can be concealed, *fig. 149.*

TYPES OF SHOWER

A shower can be fitted in some circumstances so as to be used in conjunction with a bath. In other cases, the bath is dispensed with and the shower occupies part of its space; or the shower can be fitted as a separate unit, space permitting of course. The method chosen will obviously depend on the amount of room available.

If the shower is to be separate from the bath, or is to replace it, the first requirement is a shower tray, *fig. 145.* These trays are made in a number of materials including enamelled iron, glass fibre and stainless steel. Some are finished with ceramic tiles.

The shower cubicle can be purchased complete with plinth, tray, a curtain for the open side, shower head and mixing valve. These cubicles can

be positioned more or less anywhere in the house where connections for the hot and cold water supply pipes and the waste can be conveniently made.

If you choose a cabinet of this type, get one with a top provided, as this will prevent the vapour escaping and causing condensation in the room.

An alternative is to build the shower in a corner using the existing walls for two of its sides. An angled tube can then be fitted to both walls to carry a curtain wide enough to be draped along its full length. You can get plastic shower curtains in many colours and patterns to match the decor of the room.

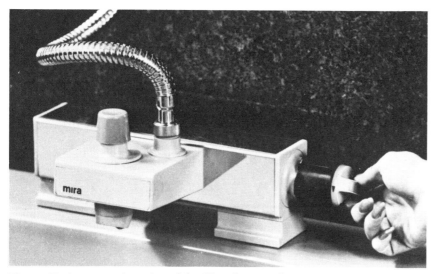

Fig. 142 Bath-mounted version of the Mira shower selector

If a shower is to be fitted above the bath, and the bath used for standing in instead of a tray, make sure that the curtain is long enough to fall inside the bath to prevent splashing. The usual place to fit the shower is at the end where the bath taps are positioned.

KEEP PIPE RUNS SHORT

When installing a shower of any sort, keep the length of pipe runs to a minimum. This will prevent a big build up of hot water in the pipes which will cool rapidly while the shower is not being used.

Not a great deal of plumbing work is involved in fitting a shower. If one is to be fixed over the bath, a thermo-

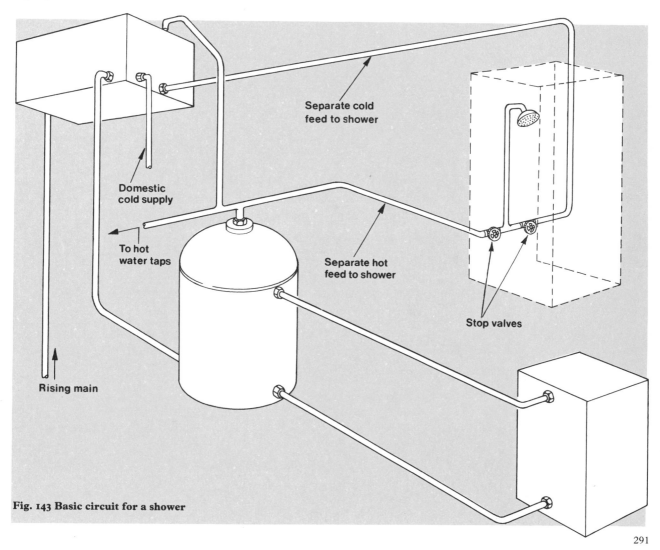

Fig. 143 Basic circuit for a shower

Separate cold feed to shower

Domestic cold supply

To hot water taps

Separate hot feed to shower

Stop valves

Rising main

Fig. 144 Rose-type shower head
Fig. 145 Shower tray

Fig. 146 Simple but strong wooden framework for supporting a bath

Fig. 147 The wall plate for the shower mixer is screwed to the wall

static mixing valve can be combined with the bath taps.

If the shower is to be separate, $\frac{1}{2}$ in copper or stainless steel supply pipes can be used and connected to the mixing valve. Non-manipulative compression joints can be used to join the the pipes and fittings.

When fixing the supply pipes to the mixing valve, make sure the joints are watertight. Wrap ptfe plastic thread sealing tape around the male threads of the fittings before screwing the connections up tight.

Figure 143 shows the basic connections for a simple shower.

The waste disposal can prove a problem in some circumstances. If, however, the shower is to be fitted in a

bathroom, or other room on the ground floor, the waste pipe can pass through a hole made in the wall and discharge into the most convenient gully.

Where a shower is to be fitted in an upstairs bathroom in an old house, the waste pipe can be taken through the wall and discharge into the hopper head.

As shown on page 269, however, many homes are now fitted with a single stack drainage system. In these houses, all the waste from bath, bathroom basin, w.c. and sink is discharged into a single waste pipe. So if you fit a shower, its waste will also have to be discharged into this pipe.

Here you should consult the local council health inspector before trying

to make the connections as it may be contrary to the local bylaws.

If your shower is to be independent of the bath you will need a $1\frac{1}{2}$ in waste and a P trap. Some shower trays are fitted with an overflow outlet; others don't have one.

In the latter type, no stopper should be fitted to the waste outlet. To fix the waste, pass it through the outlet hole provided in the tray and bed its flange in a mastic jointing compound.

Underneath the tray, push some more jointing compound up between the threads of the waste and the underside of the outlet hole, put the washer on and screw up the back nut. Then fit the P trap to the waste and the waste pipe to the trap.

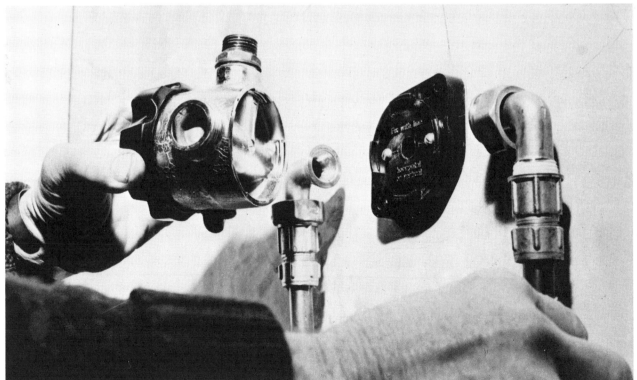

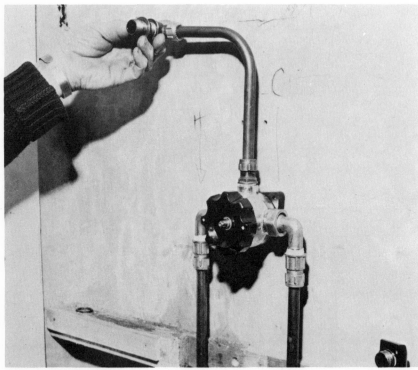

Fig. 148 The mixer pipe has a right angle connector for the flexible cord attachment

Fig. 149 Concealing the pipework with a waterproof panel

Fig. 150 The concealing plate is set in the hole over the mixing valve

Fig. 151 The black flow control is slotted over the spindle, followed by the temperature control

Fig. 152 Marking out the position of the hand spray mounting

Fig. 153 The finished shower installation

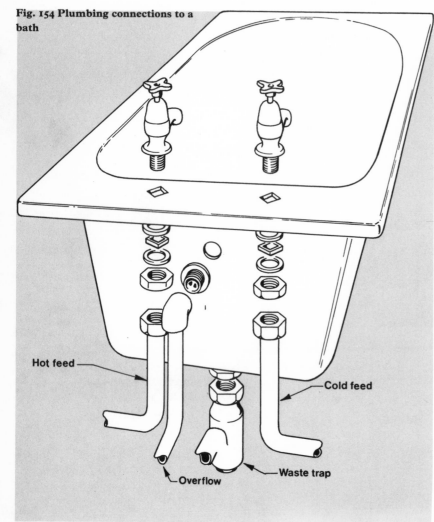

Fig. 154 Plumbing connections to a bath

Hot feed

Cold feed

Overflow

Waste trap

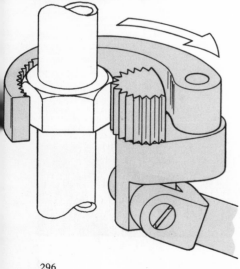

Fig. 155 A tool like this is useful for working in confined spaces

Dismantling an old bath and installing a new one would appear to be a formidable task to many people. Certainly this is by no means a simple job, and one that calls for at least some practice in unscrewing awkward nuts which may be badly corroded and in a confined space.

It is therefore advisable to think seriously before tackling the job. Take a long, cool look at your existing bath. Remove the panel and see whether access to the taps and waste is going to be feasible. The chances are that you will have to work in inadequate light while lying on your side or, at best, on your back. *Figure 154* shows a typical bath plumbing arrangement.

If you think you can cope, make sure at the beginning that you have, or can borrow or hire, the proper tools for the job. Those nuts will probably take considerable effort to shift, so you will need a strong bath or a basin crow's foot spanner or wrench *fig. 156*.

This tool can be used vertically (as you will probably have to use it) or horizontally. There is one size which is designed for coping with the taps' back nut and another, larger, version for dealing with wastes and traps. You will need both unless it can be found by prior experimenting that an ordinary wrench will do both jobs.

After removing the bath panel and the frame to which it is fitted, you will be able to see the plumbing connections.

DISCONNECT THE TRAP
The first job is to unscrew the nut which connects the trap to the outlet of the bath, *fig. 156*. The overflow may also be attached to this trap and will have to be disconnected.

You will now have to turn off the water before going any further. If the hot and cold water to the bath is supplied from the cold water storage cistern, there will be no need to turn off the main stopcock on the rising main. Simply turn off the gate valves or tie up the ball-valve. This will ensure that the supply of cold water to the kitchen sink will not be interrupted.

In a well-designed hot water system, there should be no need to put out the boiler fire. Better still, though, tackle the job in the summer months when the boiler is out. The light will be better for working in at this time of the year in any case.

Next, turn on the hot and cold water taps at the bathroom basin and the hot tap at the kitchen sink. This will drain the cold water storage cistern and the supply pipes.

DISCONNECT THE TAPS
Now undo the nuts which connect the taps to the supply pipes, *fig. 157*. This

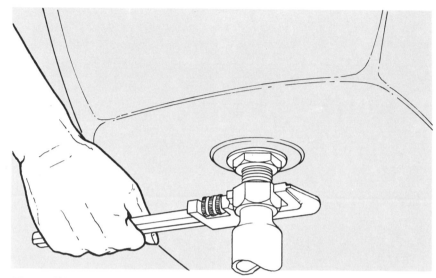

Fig. 156 Disconnecting bath waste trap

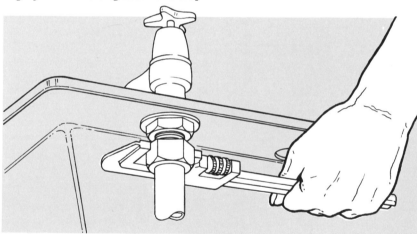

Fig. 157 Disconnecting bath pipes from taps

is easier said than done and you may need to use penetrating oil first.

The bath can then be removed. You will need help at this stage as the old type of bath is very heavy and cumbersome. The taps can now be removed from the bath.

If there is going to be a delay before the new bath is fitted, the taps can be reconnected temporarily to the supply pipes and the water turned on again.

Cast iron baths can be broken up in the bathroom with a club hammer, but it is advisable to smother the bath with a blanket or something similar to prevent chunks of the thing flying around and causing damage – possibly to you!

FIXING THE NEW BATH

Methods of fixing a new bath vary according to make. If you have chosen one of the modern plastic baths, this will be supplied with a specially-made cradle to support it. This should be fitted according to the accompanying instructions.

Enamelled steel or cast iron baths usually have four lugs which are screwed to the underside. The feet are then screwed into the lugs and the back nuts tightened up. To do this, you will have to roll the bath on its side and put a block or other support under it so you can get at the lugs comfortably.

When the feet have been attached and the bath lifted into position, you

Fig. 158 Set taps in mastic compound

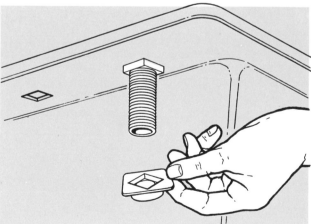

Fig. 159 Adding a top hat washer to the tail of a bath tap

can fit the taps. These can be set in a bed of mastic sealing compound, *fig. 158*. If you plan to use the old taps again, it is a good idea to first examine their washers and renew them if necessary.

Put a thick rubber or polythene washer (known as a top hat) on the thread of the tap before adding and

tightening up the back nuts, *fig. 159*. Before fitting the pipes to the tails of the taps, wrap some ptfe tape around the threads to make sure the joint will be watertight. If the tails of the new taps are shorter than the old ones, you can get a small adaptor which will lengthen them by $\frac{1}{2}$ in.

Now fit the bath waste, *fig. 160a*,

bedding it into a mastic sealing compound and again insert a thick washer between the bath and the back nuts, *fig. 160b*.

That completes the operation. But before you fit the bath panel, turn the water supply on again and release the tied-up ball float arm in the cistern. Turn on both the bath taps and check that the connections are not leaking and that the water runs away down the waste.

ADD THE PANEL

When buying your new bath, you probably ordered a bath panel to go with it. In case you didn't, and for those who want to make a panel for their existing bath, here's one way to do it, *fig. 161*.

You will need a timber frame to which the panel can be fixed. Battens of 2 in × 1 in timber will be satisfactory. One should be fitted firmly to the floor and another parallel with it will run along the top. Fit upright battens at each end and spacing battens about

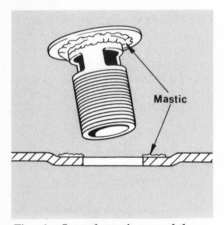

Fig. 160a Spread mastic around the waste outlet

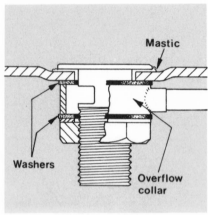

Fig. 160b Spread more mastic under the waste outlet; add rubber washers

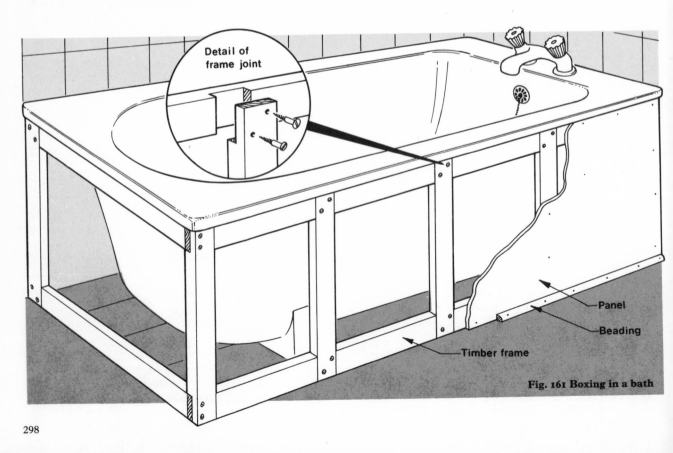

Fig. 161 Boxing in a bath

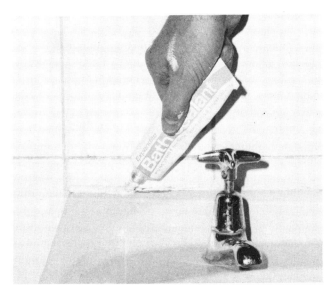

Fig. 162 A rubber-based sealer can be used to fill the gap between bath and wall

Fig. 163 Quadrant ceramic tiles can also be used to fill the gap

1 ft apart between them.

This frame will need anchoring to the wall and how this is done will depend on where the walls are.

The frame can then be covered with ordinary hardboard and then painted, or you may prefer to fit plastic-faced hardboard. The facing materials should be fixed with rustless screws and their heads covered with plastic domes.

Alternatively, ordinary hardboard can be covered with flexible plastic sheeting such as Con-Tact or Fablon. Either will provide an easy-to-clean surface which can be renewed when required.

FILLING THE GAP

After you have fitted your new bath, you may find that a gap may gradually develop between it and the wall tiles. There are a couple of ways you can fill this gap.

The first method is to fill it with a rubber-based sealer which is flexible to allow for any movement of the bath. Make sure that the gap is free of dirt and grease and, of course, thoroughly dry.

Squeeze the sealer into the gap with a steady movement, working forwards, *fig. 162*. If any parts of the sealer are uneven, they can be levelled with a

Fig. 164 A modern bidet

moistened finger. Any uneven edges can be trimmed with a knife or razor blade.

Another way to seal the gap is to fix quadrant tiles along it, *fig. 163*. These are normally supplied in packs and instructions are included. Make sure you use the adhesive recommended by the manufacturer.

BIDETS

The bidet is far more popular in this country than it used to be and can be regarded as a beneficial accessory to health and hygiene.

Some local authorities have special bylaws concerning the installation of a bidet, so these should be checked first before any arrangements are made to

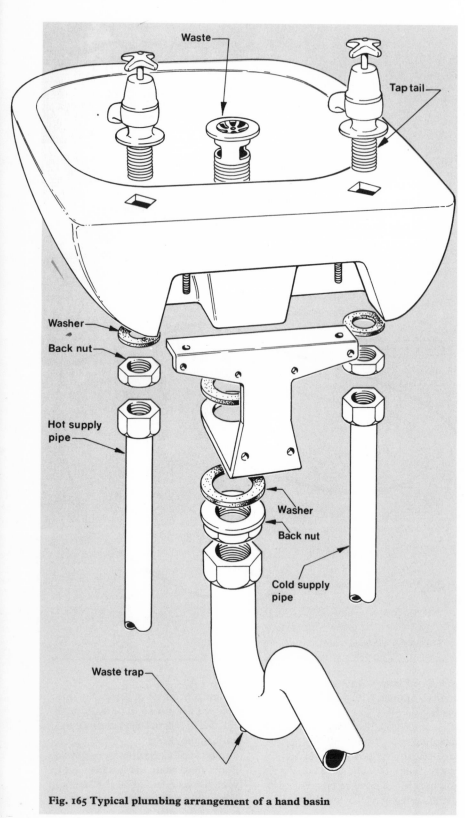

Waste

Tap tail

Washer

Back nut

Hot supply
pipe

Washer

Back nut

Cold supply
pipe

Waste trap

Fig. 165 Typical plumbing arrangement of a hand basin

have one fitted.

Some bidets are 'all rim supplied': the rim seat is warmed by hot water which fills the bowl for washing. Alternatively, the supply of water can be diverted through a douche which may have a spray or jet nozzle.

Other types of bidet have an 'over rim' supply. These are simpler types which have no douche but simply the bowl for washing purposes. This is supplied in the same way as an ordinary washbasin.

To avoid back siphonage, most water boards have special regulations for the fitting of bidets with douche facilities. The regulations mentioned below do not apply to bidets with an over rim supply.

Generally speaking, requirements are (a) that bidets are supplied with cold water from the cistern and not from the main, (b) both hot and cold water supplies should be drawn direct from the source and there should be no branch pipes teed off to any other fitting.

WASHBASINS

If you are competent enough to fit a new bath, the job of fixing a new washbasin will not daunt you. One point to watch is that many washbasins are supplied with safety brackets for fitting. These should be used whenever possible to ensure stability. Do not rely on the plumbing connections alone for support.

Before fitting a wall basin, make sure the wall has sufficient load bearing strength to support it.

Another important point is that when fitting the waste into the basin, the slot in the overflow must line up with the opening which is incorporated in the basin, *fig. 165*.

The pipework will be similar in most respects to that for a bath. Arrangements of pipes vary, but a likely installation is shown in *fig. 165*.

If you choose a pedestal-type basin, the pedestal will hide much of the pipework. A good arrangement is to run the hot and cold water supply pipes up through the bathroom floor. The waste pipe should, if possible, pass through the wall behind the basin, but much will depend on the situation.

The taps can be fixed with Fix-a-Tap sets described earlier and compression joints can be used for the pipe connections.

Some basins are supplied without brackets, their weight being supported partly by the pedestal and partly by the pipes.

To fix the basin, put it on its pedestal and mark the position on the wall. Prop up the basin securely, remove the pedestal and connect the pipes. Slide the pedestal underneath and bed the basin to the pedestal with Plumber's Mait compound.

Figs. 166 and 167 Two modern bath designs

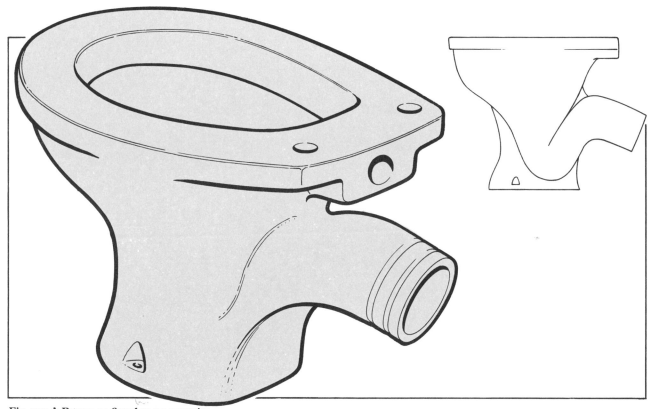

Fig. 171 A P trap as fitted to an upstairs toilet

Opposite

Fig. 168 A corner-mounted seat bath for the elderly or infirm

Fig. 169 A modern basin design

Fig. 170 Layout for basin and bidet

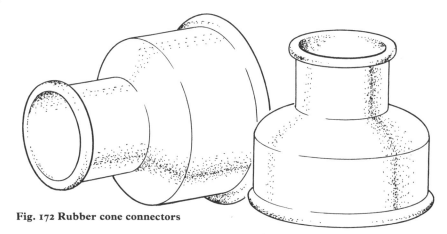

Fig. 172 Rubber cone connectors

CRACKED W.C. PANS

Never attempt to mend a cracked toilet pan. Even if the crack is merely superficial, any repair that may be made will mean that the pan is no longer a hygienic piece of equipment. Renewing the pan is the only safe remedy.

This job may appear daunting to the inexperienced eye and with good cause, especially if the toilet is on the ground floor. The main problem here is how to disconnect the cement joint between trap and the drain socket without it sustaining damage.

If the toilet is upstairs, however, it will most probably be connected to a soil pipe by means of a mastic joint. This is less of a problem so I will deal with this one first.

FLEXIBLE JOINT

The w.c. will discharge into the soil pipe probably through a P trap up-stairs, *fig. 171*. A flexible joint (mastic) is used in these cases to allow for any possible movement of the floorboards. If the joint were solid cement, as may be found on a ground floor w.c., the pan could easily crack if there was any noticeable movement.

303

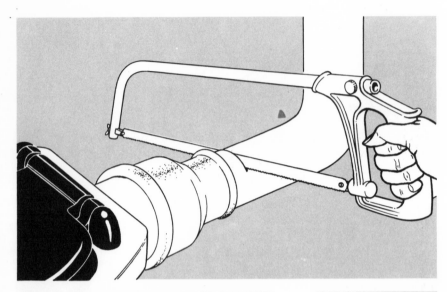

Fig. 173 Cutting a flush pipe with a hacksaw

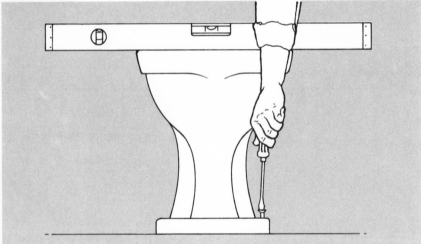

Fig. 174 Make sure the pan is level before screwing it down

Fig. 175 Multikwik connector

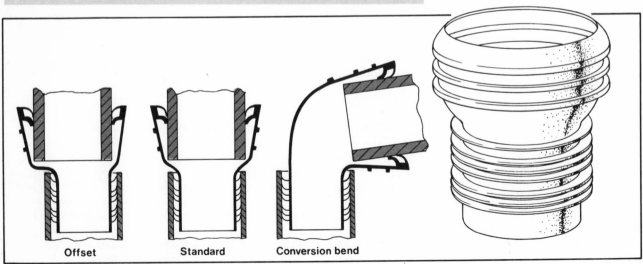

Offset   Standard   Conversion bend

To remove the old pan, first tie up the ball float arm in the cistern, flush and then disconnect and remove the flush pipe. If the joint holding this pipe is a rubber cone connector, *fig. 172*, simply roll this back and pull out the pipe.

If the joint is made with cement or putty, cut through the pipe with a hacksaw as close as you can get to the joint at the pan, *fig. 173*. If the pipe is lead or copper, I suggest it should be replaced with a plastic type.

Unscrew the nut under the cistern which connects the other end of the flush pipe.

You will now have to bale out the water lying in the trap. Then, with a sharp blow from a hammer, break the pan at the top of its bend. It will then be disconnected from the trap. You can then unscrew or lever the pan from the floor and remove it.

Take great care to prevent any rubble from now on falling into the soil pipe. Insert a thick wad of cloth so it fits tightly but can be easily removed. Carefully chip out all the remaining pieces of the old pan. Wipe the rim of the collar clean and remove the rag from the soil pipe.

GET THE PAN LEVEL

Now put the new pan in position and make certain it is absolutely level before screwing it to the floor, *fig. 174*. Use brass screws and don't overtighten them. You can fit washers or grommets under the screw heads to prevent damage to the pan.

Use a non-setting mastic such as Plumber's Mait to make the joint between the pan and the soil pipe. Bind Sylglas tape around the outlet, fill the area between the outlet and socket with mastic, then add another couple of turns of tape.

Alternatively, you can use a plastic connector called a Multikwik, *fig. 175*, between the w.c. outlet and a cast iron soil pipe or stoneware drain.

Now fit the flush pipe to the pan with a rubber connector, *fig. 176*, and connect its other end to the cistern.

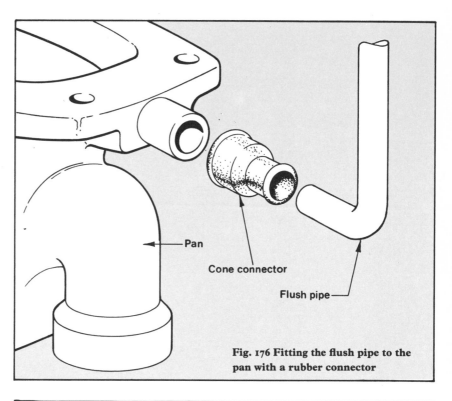

Pan

Cone connector

Flush pipe

Fig. 176 Fitting the flush pipe to the pan with a rubber connector

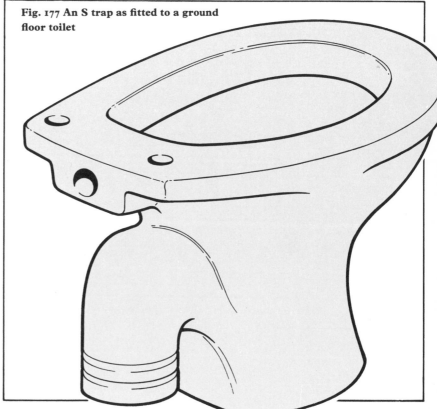

Fig. 177 An S trap as fitted to a ground floor toilet

GROUND FLOOR PANS

Removing a ground floor toilet pan is similar in most respects, but take great care when removing bits of the w.c. outlet not to damage the drain socket. The w.c. on the ground floor normally discharges through an S trap, *fig. 177*.

The new pan would formerly have been set in a bed of sand and cement mix, but the practice is now to screw the pan to the floor to avoid possible stresses.

If you decide to use a sand and cement bed, press the pan down into it, *fig. 178*, and check with a spirit level to make sure the pan is horizontal.

Now a cement joint has to be made between the outlet of the pan and the drain socket, *fig. 179*. Avoid getting any of the cement into the drain by putting some damp newspaper into the socket first. Make sure the joint has set hard before fitting the flush pipe. You can use a quick setting cement so that the pan won't be out of action for too long.

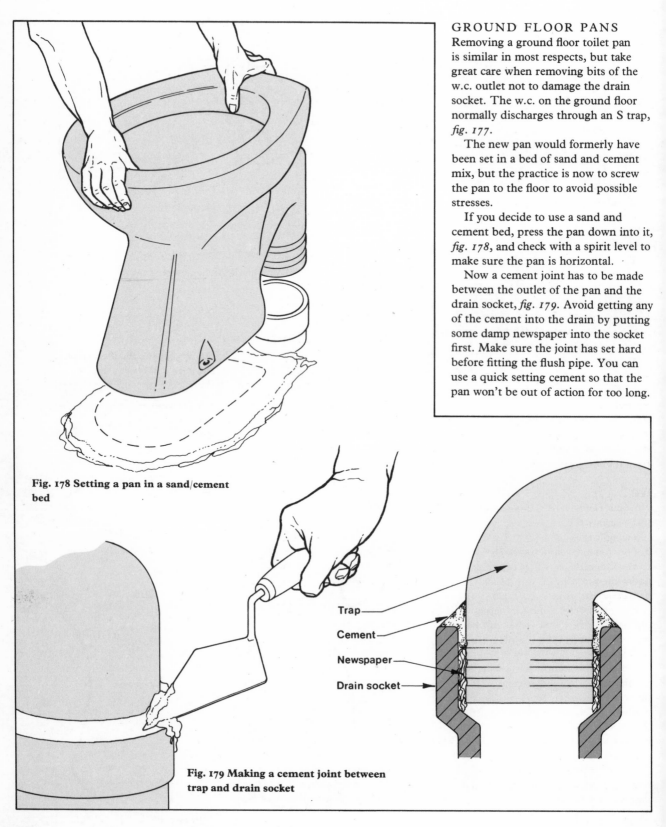

Fig. 178 Setting a pan in a sand/cement bed

Trap

Cement

Newspaper

Drain socket

Fig. 179 Making a cement joint between trap and drain socket

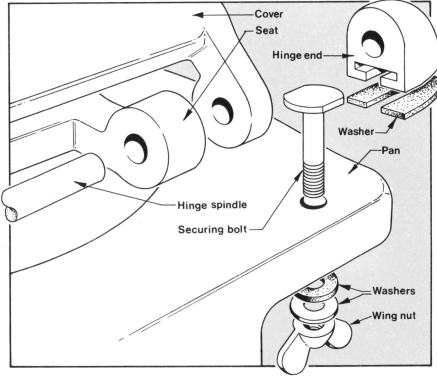

Fig. 180 One type of lavatory seat fixing

Cover
Seat
Hinge end
Washer
Pan
Hinge spindle
Securing bolt
Washers
Wing nut

TYPES OF W.C.

There are two main types of w.c. – siphonic and washdown.

In siphonic types the waste matter is removed by suction from a strong siphonic action. With washdown types, the waste is cleared by the volume and force of the flushed water.

Some siphonic pans are fitted with a single trap; others have double traps. The single types have a trappage shaped to retard the flushed water slightly until it completely refills the bowl of the trap. As the water moves towards the outlet, the siphonic action draws the contents of the pan into the soil pipe.

When a double trap siphonic pan is flushed, air is drawn from the pocket between the two seals by the flush water as it passes a special fitting. This causes atmospheric pressure to force the contents of the pan through both traps and into the soil pipe.

The traps are then resealed and the sides of the pan cleaned by water flowing from the rim.

An important point to watch when a new w.c. pan is contemplated is not to mix components made by different manufacturers. The flushing apparatus should be a suitable type for the installation concerned and should be bought with the pan as a complete unit or matched up, if that is possible.

NEW SEAT

When a lavatory seat or its lid becomes damaged, no attempt should be made to repair it; it should be renewed.

First measure up the size of the bolt holes at the back of the pan. Measure also the distance between the holes. The supplier of your new seat will need this information.

Seats are usually sold in units complete with lids, but you can sometimes buy them separately. Fitting instructions are usually supplied.

The units are simply bolted through the holes in the pan, *fig. 180*, and tightened with wing or ordinary nuts screwed down on to washers. Take great care not to overtighten the wing nuts. They should be only fingertight.

Fixing may vary slightly with make.

Central Heating

Although the subject of central heating is too broad and complex to be covered adequately in the space available here, many aspects of it fall within the sphere of plumbing.

Therefore, without going into great detail, I will try to give an outline of what a central heating system involves and pass on a few general hints regarding maintenance, installation and minor alterations.

First, how do central heating systems work? Their aim, of course, is to circulate warm air or hot water, or both, throughout the house from a central source of heat which is usually a boiler.

TYPES OF BOILER

There are basically three types of boiler – gas fired, oil fired or solid fuel. Apart from circulating heated water to radiators, some boilers also supply the hot water for domestic use. Most boilers used in domestic installations are free standing, but some open fires which burn solid fuel have a back boiler built in behind the fire.

Although boilers which are designed for central heating purposes are larger than those which supply the hot water for normal domestic use, they operate in much the same way. Some can be adjusted so that in summertime they heat only the domestic hot water and not the radiators which warm the rooms.

In gas fired boilers there are a number of burners that are lit by a pilot flame which should be on all the time.

A time switch is fitted to turn on the supply of gas automatically. This supply is controlled either by the boiler itself or by thermostats fitted in the rooms.

Where gas boilers are fitted in a room, some form of ventilation is needed to permit efficient combustion. Many gas boilers also require a flue. A chimney serves this purpose in many cases.

There is another boiler known as the balanced flue type. This is basically similar in principle to the conventional flued boiler, but some have fan assistance.

OIL FIRED BOILERS

There are various types of oil fired boilers. In one type – the *vaporising* boiler – the oil is fed into a pot. There it is heated, vaporised and burnt.

The oil in a *pressure jet boiler* is reduced to a fine spray and ignited by electricity.

Two other types – the *Dynaflame* and *Wallflame* – are fitted with electric motors which rotate jets that supply the oil. The oil is thrown against the burner ring where it is then reduced to small droplets.

Do not tinker with the controls of a boiler. This is a job for a trained engineer. If your central heating system is installed by a reputable company, they will make arrangements with you to have the system serviced at regular intervals.

I realise that many people have installed their own central heating and carry out their own maintenance. This is fine if you know what is involved. I have heard of many self-installed systems which work smoothly, but I have also heard of others which give constant trouble! So if you are thinking of installing your own system, do give it careful thought beforehand.

CONTROLS

Improvements are made constantly to the various controls used in a domestic central heating installation. Basically these controls can be divided into time and temperature types.

It is the time control which determines when the system is to be on or off. The most basic type is a time switch which has a dial marked off in 24 hourly sections. Around the dial are small levers which can be set manually to give either one or two on–off periods in the 24 hours as required.

A more advanced type is a programmer fitted with an electric clock. This type of control enables you to operate a programme for the hot water systems and the central heating.

TEMPERATURE CONTROLS

The simplest of these is a boiler thermostat which can usually be adjusted manually to vary the temperature of the water.

A room thermostat, *fig. 186*, however, gives better control of temperature. Some types are fitted with a clock and have a separate temperature setting for day and night.

In most cases a room thermostat is satisfactory for controlling the temperature of the water in the installation from a central point. But in larger installations, where the system may be divided into two or more zones, more than one thermostat will be needed. Under this arrangement, each thermostat will operate a separate circuit.

If a single room thermostat is to control the whole central heating system, it should be positioned so that it cannot give a false reading because of draughts or local heat. For example, don't stand a portable electric fire immediately beneath it!

OTHER CONTROLS

Most radiators are fitted with *lockshield* valves, *fig. 187*, which are operated by hand. These are for controlling the heat output of the radiators but are not the ideal means of controlling the actual temperature of the room. They are, however, invaluable for adjusting a system after it has been installed.

Where radiators are fitted with *thermostatic* valves, *fig. 187*, these will automatically control the room temperature at a predetermined level.

Mixing valves are also used to control water temperatures They mix some of the cooler water as it returns to the boiler with the hot water leaving. They also control the temperature of all the radiators connected to the system without any adjustment of the thermostat on the boiler being made.

WARM AIR SYSTEMS

Although the majority of central heating systems use radiators to circulate the heated water and thus heat the rooms, warm air systems use a

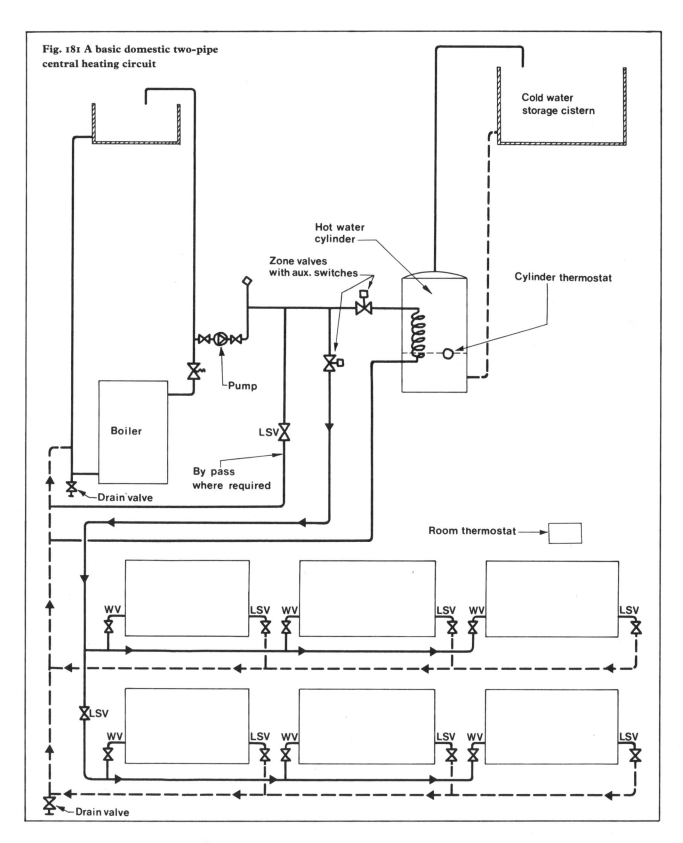

Fig. 181 A basic domestic two-pipe central heating circuit

Cold water storage cistern

Hot water cylinder

Zone valves with aux. switches

Cylinder thermostat

Pump

Boiler

LSV

By pass where required

Drain valve

Room thermostat

WV   LSV   WV   LSV   WV   LSV

LSV

WV   LSV   WV   LSV   WV   LSV

Drain valve

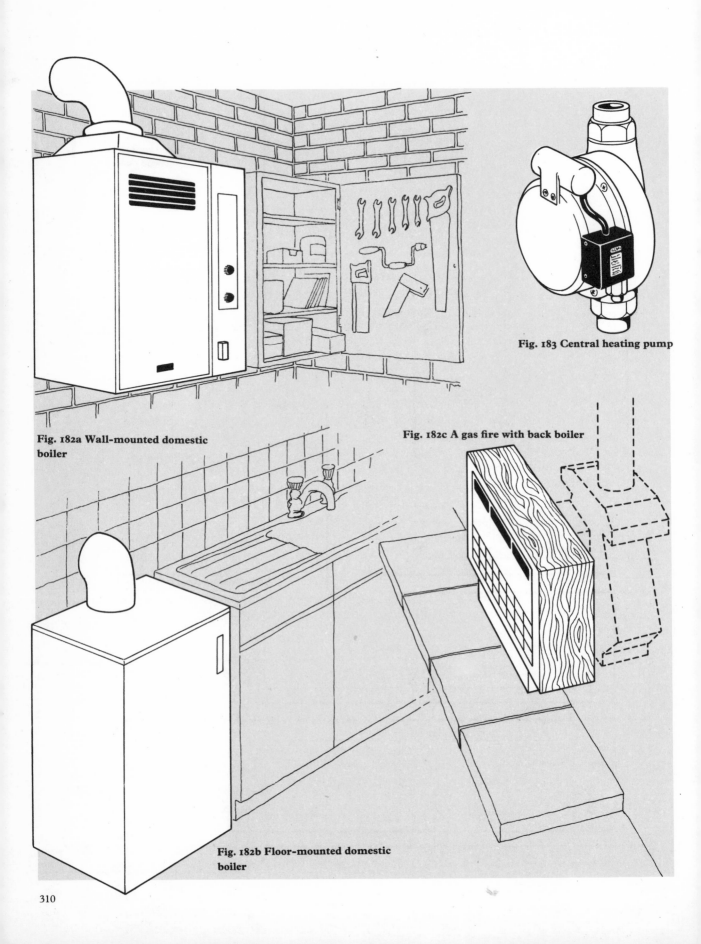

Fig. 183 Central heating pump

Fig. 182a Wall-mounted domestic boiler

Fig. 182c A gas fire with back boiler

Fig. 182b Floor-mounted domestic boiler

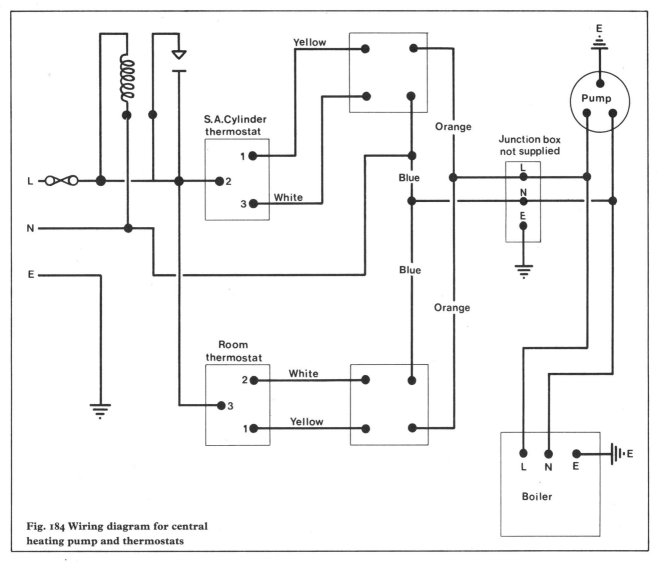

Fig. 184 Wiring diagram for central heating pump and thermostats

number of ducts through which air is circulated after being heated by electricity, gas, solid fuel or oil. In these systems the domestic hot water is usually supplied to the taps by an immersion heater or a separate boiler.

There are systems in which hot water rises from the boiler, passes through the radiators, and then, as it cools, returns by the force of gravity. These are known as gravity systems.

Usually, however, a pump is fitted near the boiler to circulate the water through the pipes and radiators. These are called forced circulation systems.

BOILER NOISES

Hissing – This can be a sign that the pipes, boiler and cylinder have become scaled up. See chapter on scale.

Another cause is overheating the water. Various things can be responsible for this: the flue may be blocked; a thermostat or the pump, *fig. 183*, may not be working properly; or there may not be enough water circulating in the system. The latter can be caused by the ball-valve in the feed and expansion tank becoming jammed.

If overheating occurs, shut off the gas or oil supply, or in the case of a solid fuel boiler, rake the burning fuel

into the ash pan and carry it outside. Then open the door of the boiler and let it cool down. Leave damper open.

If the pump can still be run while the boiler is switched off, let it pump water around to cool the system.

You can usually tell if a thermostat is doing its job properly. It should click when turned in either direction.

If the ball-valve in the expansion tank has jammed, it may need a new washer or simply dismantling and cleaning. See pages 225 and 226.

If the pump is switched on but no water is circulating, an air lock may be causing the trouble. Open the vent

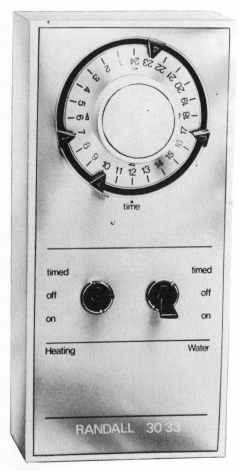

Fig. 185a Time switch controller for
pump and hot water

Fig. 185b Fully automatic programmed
control

Fig. 185c Time clock especially suitable
for single change-over circuits

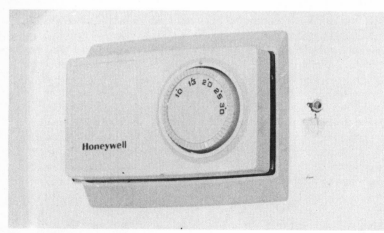

Fig. 186 Room thermostat

valve of the pump, *fig. 183*, and bleed
the air off. Close the valve when the
water begins to flow again.

As a guide to temperature, that of
the water flowing from the boiler
should be about 44·5°F (7°C) higher
than the water in the bottom pipe. You
can test the temperature by fixing a
thermometer first on the bottom pipe
and then on the upper one.

Adjustment of the flow regulator on
the pump should be left to a service
engineer.

ROOM TEMPERATURES
Well-designed central heating systems
keep room temperatures at a com-

fortable level by the use of room or radiator thermostats. Once these are adjusted to a satisfactory level, it should not be necessary to alter them.

No two people in a house have the same idea of a suitable temperature for a room, so a compromise figure will usually have to be agreed upon. The following temperatures are regarded as generally acceptable:

Bedroom 55°F (13°C); living room 70°F (21°C); bathroom 65°F (18·5°C); hall, kitchen and toilet 60°F (15·5°C).

DRAINING A SYSTEM
Before attempting to drain off a central heating system, make sure the fuel supply to the boiler is disconnected and that the ignition system is switched off. This should be done several hours beforehand to give the water time to cool down.

You will need a hose long enough to stretch from the draincock by the boiler to a drain outside.

First tie up the ball float arm of the feed and expansion tank. Fit the hose to the draincock and take the other end to the drain. Undo the draincock, *fig. 188*, and wait for the system to empty. Then close the draincock and release the ball float arm in the tank.

Let the system refill slowly. This will allow any air in it to escape through the vent.

AIR LOCKS IN RADIATORS
A common problem with central heating radiators is that sometimes they do not heat up as they should. Often the top of a radiator will be cool while the rest of it is warm. Air locks are a probable cause.

If this often happens, it is a good idea to fit an air eliminator, which works automatically, but the occasional air lock can usually be cleared quite simply.

A hollow key with a square-shaped end is usually required. This is inserted in the radiator, *fig. 189*, when the water is warm, and turned anti-clockwise to open the vent valve.

Some water may escape as the valve is opened, so hold a container underneath.

When the air stops coming out of the radiator and water begins to flow, tighten up the valve again. You may have to repeat the operation before a cure is effected.

The air eliminator has a valve containing a gland which is porous. This permits the air but not the water to escape.

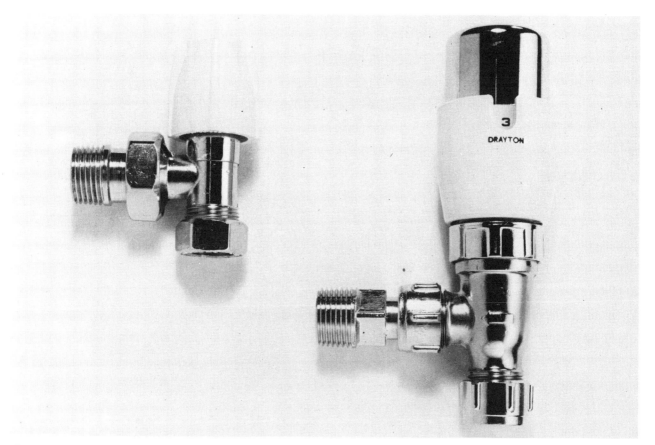

Fig. 187 Lockshield valve and thermostatic valve

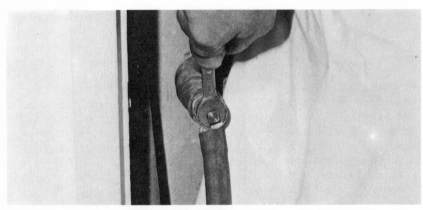

Fig. 188 To drain a central heating system, fit a hosepipe to the boiler draincock. Take the other end to a drain outside. Open the draincock with a spanner

Fig. 189 Clearing an air lock on a radiator

Fig. 190 Circulating pump with isolating valves fitted at each side for easy removal of pump

DRAIN THE SYSTEM

To fit an eliminator, the system will first have to be drained. Then undo the vent valve with the key as for an air lock, but this time remove the valve.

The eliminator is then screwed into the same hole. First, however, to ensure that the joint will be watertight, wrap some ptfe tape around the threads, *fig. 191.*

When you have screwed up the device fingertight, the system can be refilled.

If, after fitting the eliminator, you still find that a large amount of air needs to be released from the radiator, undo the adjusting screw of the device and hold a container beneath it to catch any water.

Take out the screw and gland.

Now press the valve with a screwdriver and bleed the system. Replace the screw and gland and turn the screw fingertight.

Bleeding the system is a job which should be done two or three times during the winter months whether air locks occur or not. When air gets into a radiator, it impairs its performance and there is always a possibility that internal corrosion may occur.

Bleed the ground floor radiators first.

LEAKS FROM JOINTS

Pipes and radiators in a central heating system expand and contract according to the temperature of the water. This can cause irritating leaks at the joints.

If a leak occurs around a compression joint, simply wipe the joint dry and tighten up its nut with a spanner.

When there is a leak at a capillary joint, however, enough water needs to be drained from the system to clear the water from the pipe.

Heat the joint with a blowtorch or blowlamp (mind the wall!) until you can release the pipe. Clean it up and apply flux to the end. Put the pipe back in the joint and solder around it until the joint is sealed.

Fig. 191 For a watertight joint, wrap plastic tape around the thread of an air eliminator

CARE OF THE BOILER

If you have a solid fuel boiler, clean out the ashes and top up with fuel regularly to keep the boiler burning steadily rather than fiercely.

Don't allow the boiler fire to die right down before adding more fuel to it. The boiler flue should be cleaned twice a year. Don't neglect the elbow of the flue near the base where deposits can settle. Give it a good clean out regularly.

During very cold weather, the boiler should not be allowed to go out. If it *has* to be left cold for more than a few hours, drain the system completely and empty the boiler of fuel.

Do remember to refill the system before lighting the boiler!

Gas boilers are fitted with pilot lights and the majority contain a safety device which cuts off the supply of gas automatically if the pilot light should go out.

If at any time you should suspect a gas leak, turn off the gas at the main cock which is fitted near or on the meter. Don't try to find the leak by testing with a naked flame! Telephone your local gas board at once.

OIL STORAGE TANKS

If you have an oil-fired boiler, the oil storage tank should be maintained regularly. There are small things you can do to ensure that it works smoothly.

It is important to keep the filter clean. Turn off the stopcock, remove the filter bowl and clean the element with petrol. Reassemble it when dry.

Keep the cap of the filter pipe oiled so it can be removed easily.

The vent pipe must be kept clear of obstructions. You can fit wire mesh over it to keep out leaves or other debris. If the vent pipe does become obstructed, clear it with a length of stiff wire.

Sludge can form in the storage tank. This should be drained off about once a year by opening up the draincock to let the sludge run out. Stop draining when pure oil begins to flow.

Exposure to the elements may cause the sides of the tank to rust. Any rust should be removed by wire brushing and abrasive paper. Then coat the tank with a rust inhibitor followed by a coat of bituminous paint.

Do this regularly and pay particular attention to the welded seams.

FLUES

Most gas, solid fuel and oil-fired boilers need a flue. For the best results, this should be as straight as possible. Sharp bends should be avoided as they hinder the flow of gases and allow debris and soot to collect.

If oil or solid fuel appliances are used, the height of the flue becomes especially important to ensure adequate draught. Generally speaking, a tall chimney will provide more draught than a short one.

Height of the chimney is, of course, less important for gas appliances. Here the flue acts as a channel or duct to carry the combustion products out into the open air.

An ordinary brick chimney by itself is not always suitable for this purpose. This is because very little heat escapes up chimneys when modern gas appliances are used.

Consequently, as the gases pass through a relatively cold chimney, they cool down to such an extent that condensation can form. This in turn can lead to damp walls.

In these situations, the flue is usually lined and the best method is to have a flexible stainless steel liner inserted in the chimney, *fig. 192*. Your heating

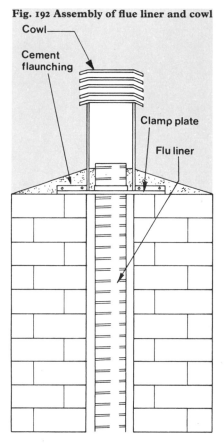

Fig. 192 Assembly of flue liner and cowl

Cowl

Cement flaunching

Clamp plate

Flu liner

supplier should be able to arrange this for you if it is necessary.

A terminal is normally fitted to the top of the chimney to stop birds nesting and to keep out the rain. Examples of gas and oil terminals can be seen at your suppliers.

RADIATOR POSITIONS

While it is important that any central heating system should be carefully designed to give maximum efficiency, the positioning of radiators does not always get the attention it deserves.

To lessen the affects of cold draughts entering, radiators should, if at all possible, be positioned underneath windows – preferably running along their full length. If this is not convenient, place the radiator on a wall adjacent to the window.

Don't position a radiator opposite windows. This could make the draughts even more noticeable.

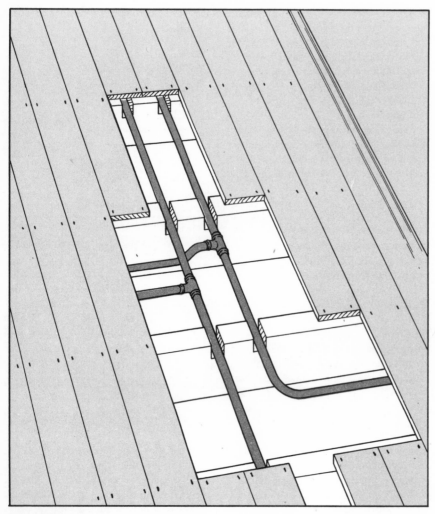

Fig. 193 Pipe layout recessed into joists

The best type to use in this situation is a fan convector radiator. This will distribute warm air across the window area and help to counter the effect of the incoming draughts.

If radiators have to be fixed on outside walls, some of their heat may be lost *through* the walls. This can be prevented to a degree by insulating the internal wall surface, perhaps by hanging sheet foam polystyrene under a heavy vinyl wallcovering.

Alternatives are to attach insulation boards and to decorate over them, or use aluminium foil. This treatment is more suitable for solid walls. For cavity walls, of course, specialist applied cavity infill is the best solution.

OBSTACLES

A point to remember about a radiator is that a great deal of the heat it generates is the convected type. A smaller proportion of radiant heat is produced.

Single-panel radiators produce more radiant heat than two- or three-panel radiators. Often, however, the full benefit of this heat is not obtained because large items of furniture are placed in its path. If this can be avoided, so much the better.

D-I-Y-KITS

For the do-it-yourself enthusiast who wants to install his own central heating, various firms produce kits

designed especially for this purpose. Many of these companies also offer design services to cover all aspects of the work.

I need hardly add that to do this job and make a success of it, you need preferably at least some plumbing experience. Equally essential is a sound understanding of what is involved.

It is worth paying the fee that most firms charge for their design services. There are many things to be considered such as correct balancing of the system, the outputs and inputs of various appliances and the complicated business of U values and heat losses.

These things are all taken care of by reputable firms who provide such design services. All you have to worry about is the physical job of installation! This, of course, is an involved subject beyond the scope of this book, but here are some general hints which I hope will prove useful.

If you deal with a reputable firm you should get full instructions on how to assemble all the components.

ORDER OF WORK

Advance knowledge, however, is always useful. Some firms advertise very comprehensive catalogues which contain many helpful illustrations or photos of the various bits and pieces. It is well worthwhile following the advertisements and sending for one or two of these catalogues.

If you order a kit to assemble yourself, check it over carefully when it arrives and familiarise yourself with all the parts. As I said, the kit should contain full instructions for assembly, but here is a general guide to the order in which the various jobs are usually done, though much will, of course, depend on the system.

1. Fit the radiator valve unions, plugs and air cocks.

2. Fix the radiator brackets to the wall.

3. Fix the radiators on the brackets and then add the radiator valves.

4. Assemble the boiler.

5. Fix the fittings to the hot water

cylinder and position it.

6. Attach the fittings (outlet, overflow and ball-valve) to the feed and expansion tank.

7. Mark out the runs for the pipes. Drill holes in the walls for the pipes as necessary.

8. Run in the pipes.

9. Fix the pump.

10. Connect the boiler to the chimney.

11. Connect up the oil or gas supply to the appliance. The gas board should make a check at this final stage.

FITTING THE BOILER

The boiler must stand on a perfectly flat and level base and the centre of the flue outlet must line up with the centre of the flue itself.

Make sure that all joints, especially those on the boiler, are absolutely watertight.

When fixing the fittings on to the hot water cylinder, avoid overtightening them and don't confuse the connections. Note that the male threads are the primary connections and are connected to the boiler. The female threads are those for the domestic hot water connections.

Use ptfe tape on the male threads to ensure that the connections will be watertight.

USE WASHERS

When you come to drill holes in the feed and expansion tank for the various fittings (ball-valve, overflow and cold feed), don't use jointing compound if the tank is a plastic type. Here you should use polythene washers.

To make holes in walls for the pipes a masonry bit used in a power drill and driven at a low speed is better than using a hammer and chisel – and less noisy.

There are two important points to note when running in the pipes. Keep the primary pipes rising steadily throughout their journey and ensure that vent pipes rise continuously from the point where they are connected.

Bending pipes is dealt with else-

Fig. 194 Flue terminal

where. Avoid making too many bends in one length of pipe. For one thing, the pipe will look unsightly; for another, it will be difficult to manoeuvre into its final position. Although it works out more expensive, it is better to use compression fittings to achieve neat changes in pipe direction.

FILLING THE SYSTEM

When the proud moment comes to fill the system, do this slowly so that you can detect and remedy leaks before any damage is done.

If you have had to lift floorboards in order to lay pipes, it is advisable not to replace the boards until the system has been filled and checked. Then I suggest you replace the boards with screws instead of nails so that future access will be easier.

The gate valve on the domestic cold supply pipe should be opened a couple of turns to enable the cylinder to fill gradually.

As soon as water begins to flow from the hot taps, turn them off. The cold water cistern can then refill.

Now turn on the cold supply pipe to the feed and expansion tank and make sure all the radiator valves are open.

Keep a weather eye open for leaks in the pipework while the system is being filled.

BLEEDING

When the system is full you will need to bleed the radiators, boiler and pump which may be filled with air.

When you are sure the system is free of leaks, drain it and flush through a couple of times before finally filling it.

The next job will be to fire the boiler, but first make certain that all the controls and valves on the radiators are open.

Set all thermostats as required and make sure that the pump is working. Here you should pay particular attention to the instructions supplied.

Now the system can be balanced. Before this is done, however, the lock-shield valves on the radiators should be partly closed. Balance the radiators when they are hot.

While doing this, the room thermostat should be set at maximum and the pump adjusted to give the flow required.

CORROSION

There are a number of factors which can cause corrosion in a central heating system. One example is the use of different metals for the components and pipework.

Gases are produced in most systems and can cause air locks. They also create deposits which collect in the pipes and radiators. These can restrict the circulation of water.

These deposits are in themselves a form of rust and are magnetic. Consequently they are attracted by the circulating pump because of a magnetic field which the electric motors of the pump produce. If this is allowed to get out of hand, pump failure is possible.

This can be avoided by introducing a chemical inhibitor into the system, and this is a point worth discussing with your supplier at the outset.

COMMON PROBLEMS

Corrosion in one form or another is a common cause of trouble in central heating systems. In a *direct* hot water system, corrosion can, of course, occur very soon after installation. In an *indirect* system, the process is considerably slower, but it can happen.

Air is an essential element in the process of corrosion. As a direct system is constantly filled with fresh aerated water, this can corrode rapidly.

An indirect system has a closed heating circuit. Once it is filled, the same water is used over and over again (unless the system is drained, of course). The system's water, therefore, becomes stale once the air in it dissolves.

It would seem, then, that with an indirect system corrosion cannot take place. Unfortunately, though, it is possible because air can enter the system in other ways – at the feed and expansion tank and through tiny leaks at pipe joints. These are too small to let any water out but are big enough to let the air get in.

SYMPTOMS

If the system is not protected by a chemical corrosion inhibitor, the corrosion will sooner or later cause various problems. These include: radiators running cold and requiring frequent venting, small leaks in the radiators and pump failure.

After a time it may be found that the radiators are not warm all over. If this is discovered after the system is vented, it may be that the radiators are clogged with sludge, which is also due to corrosion. This sludge will eventually find its way around the system to the pump and cause it to fail.

The chemical inhibitors can be introduced into the system via the feed and expansion tank to prevent this happening. Two well-known inhibitors are Fernox and Radicon. Your supplier should be able to suggest one that is suitable.

HUMIDIFIERS

After their central heating has been installed many people find that the atmosphere in the house becomes too dry for comfort. They complain of sore, dry throats, headaches and possibly sinus troubles.

Sometimes even the furniture is affected; the adhesive at the timber joints dries out. Pianos have even been known to become unplayable. The better the central heating system, the more prevalent this sort of trouble is likely to be.

The answer is to fit a humidifier which will ensure that moisture in the air will be kept at the proper level.

Atmospheric moisture is determined by the relative humidity. For example, in a centrally-heated room which has no humidifier and a temperature of 70°F, the relative humidity will be around 20%. The recommended humidity is nearer 55%.

Some form of humidification is needed to provide the necessary water vapour and the figure of 55%.

Some people stand saucers of water in the room to moisten the air, but this is not the solution to the dry air problem. A proper humidifier is needed which has the appropriate output for the situation.

CALCULATIONS

To get the exact amount of humidification, various calculations need to be made. These involve the size and layout of the room, the air temperature and that of surfaces, plus the number of air changes made per hour in the room. To get it right you need expert advice.

There are two sorts of humidification, background and positive. The former prevents dry air absorbing moisture from the surroundings. It cannot, however, restore the humidity to the recommended level of 55%.

Positive humidification, however, *can* add the correct amount of moisture to the dry air.

To achieve this, you need an electric type of humidifier which is capable of producing a minimum of half-a-pint of water vapour every hour. It should be fitted with an automatic humidistat (this is rather like a thermostat) and a means of adjusting the output of vapour.

There are several types on the market and there is a specialist company which can give you advice on the subject – The Humidifier Advisory Service, Felvic House, 21 Napier Road, Bromley, Kent BR2 9JA.

If your property lacks a modern plumbing system, you may be able to get a home improvement grant towards the cost of installing up-to-date amenities. Much will, of course, depend on your council, on the property itself and on the local bylaws.

At the time of writing, three types of grant are available:

1. Standard grants for the provision of standard amenities (a bath or shower; washbasins; sink; a hot and cold water supply to a fixed bath or shower, washbasin or sink; a w.c.).

2. Improvement grants to improve the standard of existing properties, or to convert them into flats. These grants do not apply to modern houses or properties which are well equipped and in good repair.

3. Special grants at the discretion of local councils for standard amenities to be shared in houses in multiple occupation, if there is no immediate likelihood of converting the property into permanent separate dwellings.

To find out more about home improvement grants, apply to your local council. Whatever you do, don't start work on a project in anticipation of getting a grant. Any scheme you may have in mind *must* be approved by the council first. They will not entertain an application for a grant if the work has already begun.

There are hundreds of terms used in the plumbing industry and many variations of some of them. For example, the term stopcock is used in many cases when in others it might be called a stop-valve or stoptap.

So far as the householder is concerned, he need not concern himself about the variations of these terms, so long as he can make his requirements understood when making purchases.

Here are a few terms which may be encountered, with a brief definition of each.

Air lock Pocket of air trapped in pipe. Tap splutters and may stop running.

Backnut Nut on stem of fitting (a tap, for example) for fixing to basin or other fixture.

Ball valve Valve which controls the flow of water into a cistern or tank.

Bib tap Tap with horizontal inlet. Sometimes referred to as a bib cock.

Bird's mouth End of an overflow pipe shaped like a bird's beak.

B.Th.U. British Thermal Unit. Amount of heat needed to raise 1 lb of water through one degree Fahrenheit.

Crow's foot Basin wrench or spanner. Can be used vertically or horizontally.

Downpipe Rainwater pipe.

Drift Tool for opening out the end of a copper tube. Also called swaging tool and flaring tool.

Elbow Fitting which enables a change to be made in pipe direction.

Flashing Strip of lead, copper or zinc which covers a joint between a roof covering and another part of the building.

Interceptor Trap on drain to stop sewer gases entering.

Jumper Combined disc and spindle to which tap or stop valve washer is fixed.

Mandrel Cylindrical length of hardwood to shape lead pipes.

Pillar tap Tap with a vertical inlet.

Rising main Pipe which carries the water from the main into a house and up to the cold water storage cistern.

Seal Water in a trap under a sink, basin, bath or w.c. which prevents the passage of foul air.

Spigot Plain end of a pipe or gutter which is fitted into the enlarged end (faucet) of the following section.

Stopcock Device fixed in a pipe to regulate the flow of water.

Stop-valve A valve fitted in a pipe to control the flow of water.

Note: both stopcock and stop-valve serve the same purpose. They are described variously in different parts of the country.

Swan neck A pipe bend (offset). The pipe continues on a parallel course.

Trap Fitting or part of an appliance which stops the passage of foul air.

Water hammer Knocking noises in pipes caused by high water pressure. Indicates a fault in the system.

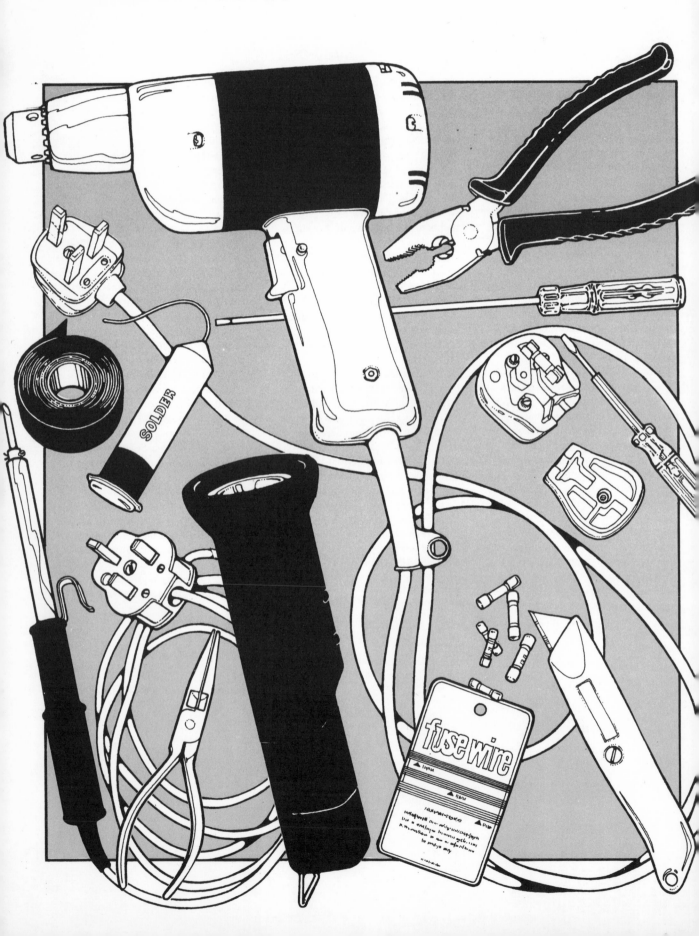

Wiring up a plug and mending a fuse are basic electrical jobs most house-holders have to do. Although these jobs are fairly elementary, knowing how to do them correctly and safely is essential.

Sooner or later, also, some other parts of the domestic electrical system may need maintenance, or the need may arise for an extra light or a socket outlet. It is then that a basic grasp of how a house is wired becomes a valuable asset.

A word or two of warning. Electricity is a very dangerous thing. So don't attempt any rewiring job unless you are convinced you know exactly what you are doing.

Most important, and I repeat this warning several times, always remember to turn off the current at the fuseboard or consumer unit before interfering with any wire, accessory or appliance which is connected to the system. Fires and accidents are caused every day by carelessness in handling electrical appliances. Make sure you do not become a victim through neglecting to take simple precautions.

Fig. 1 A selection of modern switches and sockets

Source of Supply

For simple wiring-up jobs and routine maintenance of a household's electrical system, it is usually sufficient to know what goes on on the consumer's (that is, your own) side of the installation. However, a basic understanding of the principles of electrical supply from the electricity company can be helpful.

Let us, then, take a brief look at the methods used to supply electricity to domestic premises without becoming involved in theory and too many technicalities.

SERVICE CABLES

Electricity is supplied from a power station to a house through two wires called conductors. One is red; the other is black. The red one is called the Live; the black is known as the Neutral. These wires are the service cables.

Current is supplied by the live wire. After it has entered the house, lighted the lamps and fed power to your various fires and other appliances, the current returns to the power station. This time it is the black (neutral) wire which carries the current.

The red wire is live at, usually, 240 volts. The black wire is connected to earth on its journey back to the power station.

The supply cable to the house leads into the electricity board's sealed fuses, through the meter which records the amount of electricity you use, to a main switch on your consumer unit or fuseboard.

The meter is situated near the consumer unit or fuseboard. This measures the electricity used in kilowatt hours.

A kilowatt is another way of saying 1,000 watts. If you use a 1,000 watt appliance for one hour, then you will consume 1 kilowatt hour of electricity in that period. One kilowatt hour (or 1 kWh as it is usually expressed) is the standard unit of electrical consumption.

THE COST

As your electricity bill will show, the cost of electricity used in a domestic property is calculated at so much a unit. If you know the cost of a unit and the wattage of an appliance, you can work out how much it costs to run the appliance, but you will need to be good at arithmetic to arrive at an accurate figure!

Prices will vary according to the tariff you are on. You may have two meters, one for Economy 7 and the other for the General Tariff. As an example, here is the type of bill which would show two meter readings:

Economy 7
Present, 24673
Previous, 23512
Units consumed, 1161
General Tariff
Present, 40436
Previous, 39626
Units consumed, 810

Of the two separate totals of units the 1161 are charged at 1.69p, giving a total of £19.62. The 810 units are charged at 4.52p, giving a total of £36.61. In addition, there is a standing charge of £6.45, giving a total bill of £62.68.

Most people, of course, will be only too familiar with electricity bills, but for the uninitiated, that is a general guide as to how they are made out.

It pays to keep a close eye on the amount you are charged for electricity as mistakes are made occasionally.

THE METER

However, if your bill should jump alarmingly in one quarter, don't immediately assume that the meter is inaccurate. As a matter of fact, they rarely go wrong.

It is unlikely, too, that the board's representative who reads the meter will make a mistake. If you were out when he called and supplied your own reading of the meter, a mistake could easily be yours. Later I will tell you how to read a meter.

So it is advisable, when a bill for electricity seems abnormally high, to check all possibilities before complaining to the board that you have been overcharged.

If you do suspect your meter is not working properly, turn off all your electrical appliances. Now look at the meter. Just below the dials is a circular disc. This is designed to revolve *only* when electricity is being consumed.

The speed at which the disc revolves depends on how many appliances are switched on at one time and upon their rating (how many kilowatts they consume).

An electric clock, for instance, uses hardly any electricity and you may find it difficult to detect a movement of the meter disc when a clock is the only appliance switched on in the house. But watch the meter disc and see the difference in the rate at which the disc turns when you switch on, say, a 2,000 watt fire or perhaps an immersion heater (which is usually 3,000 watts).

If, after turning off all your appliances (and lights too, of course) the meter disc is still revolving, there is something wrong. But before you call in the board to investigate, make absolutely sure an appliance has not been overlooked.

I emphasise this because I once heard of an instance where this sort of thing happened. After exhaustive checks had been made to find out why a meter disc continued to turn after all the appliances had been turned off, an electric heater was finally found switched on in the loft. It had been turned on at the beginning of a cold spell in the autumn and had burned away merrily until discovered the following spring!

Apart from the fact that this was misleading and indicated a fault, think of the waste of electricity! There could always be the danger of fire from an unseen heater as well.

CONSUMER UNIT

The meter is connected to the consumer unit by two wires (one red, the other black). These are called the meter tails and I shall refer to these again later on.

Apart from these wires, there is one

more wire – a very important one – involved in the installation. This is the earth or safety wire.

All installations must be earthed to comply with the regulations. This is done by linking all the installation's earth wires to a common earthing point at the consumer unit. This, in turn, is linked by the board to a special earthing terminal usually provided by the board.

In some areas it is not possible to bond the installation to a suitable point, so an earth leakage circuit breaker is fitted instead. This device, *fig. 2*, disconnects the electrical supply when a fault causes a current flow in the earth circuit.

The service cable is protected by a fuse which is accommodated in a box and sealed by the electricity board. This seal must never be broken by a householder, only by the board.

Fortunately, this fuse rarely blows. If it does, ring the board, but do be sure before you do so that the fault is not in your own circuits or in any plug fuse or appliance.

That is really all you need to know about the supply of electricity into your home. However, to appreciate what goes on on the consumer side of an installation, you need to know more.

So what happens after the supply has reached the consumer unit? Before we go into that, study this list of accessories and terms used in the electrical industry. It will help you to understand your circuits more fully.

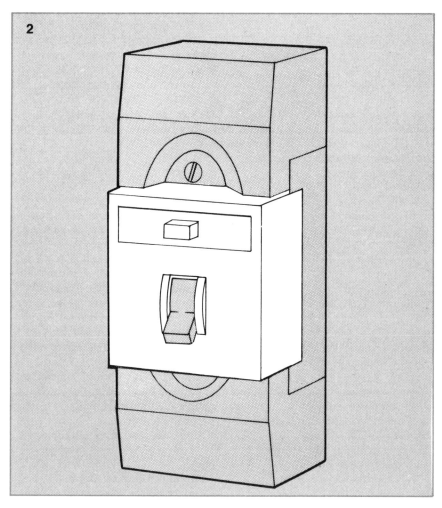

Fig. 2 Earth leakage circuit breaker

Accessories and Terms

Adaptor: Enables more than one appliance to be used from one socket outlet. Do not use too many; there is always the danger of overloading the circuit.

Alternating current: A current which changes its direction at regular intervals. Known as a.c., this is the type of current supplied to domestic premises.

Architrave box: Narrow steel box to house narrow switches. Also acts as a connection box for cables and flex wires to wall light fittings.

Backplate: Metal or plastic plate fixed behind open backed rose or switch to stop cables touching the wall or ceiling. Also *pattress*.

Blank or **blanking plate:** Covers (blanks off) a socket outlet no longer required or an outlet box used to join cables.

Block connector: Used to join cables in a wall box, or for connecting cables to flex.

Box, steel, knockout: Houses a socket outlet or fused connection unit. Is sunk in the wall to contain circuit cables.

Cartridge fuse link: Fuse element for 13 amp plugs and consumer unit fuses (alternative to fuse wire in consumer unit).

Conductors: Insulated wires in cable or flexible cords. Usually one live, one neutral; sometimes also an earth wire.

Connection unit: Outlet fitted with a fuse. Used to connect fixed appliance to ring circuit. Formerly called fused spur unit or box.

Consumer unit: Modern compact version of a fuseboard with a number of fuseways housing circuit fuses.

Core: A cable or flex conductor enclosed in insulation material. See *sheath*.

Direct current: A current which does not change direction (i.e., is continuous), as supplied by a storage battery. Also called d.c.

Earth continuity conductor: Uninsulated earth wire. The third wire of two-core and earth cable or of three-core flex. Known as e.c.c.

Flex connector: See *block connector*.

Flexible cord: Usually called flex. Lead from appliance to the source of power (i.e., socket outlet). Has one, two or three cores each containing strands of wire. See chapter on cables.

Joint box: Junction box with knockout sections permitting cables to enter and be joined to its terminals.

Knockout box: See box (steel). Also available in plastic for surface-mounted accessories.

Line: See *Live conductor*.

Live conductor: One pole of an a.c. (alternating current) two-wire electrical system. Also called line or phase. The other pole is the *neutral*. Somewhat similar to the positive of a d.c. (direct current) system.

Miniature circuit breakers: In many countries of the world the rewireable fuse is not allowed to be used. The main reason for this decision is safety. The problem with a rewireable fuse is strangely enough that it can be rewired. Not only by the correct size and type of fuse wire but, either inadvertently or deliberately, by heavier fuse wire, paperclips, pins, silver paper.

This action will prevent the 'nuisance' of the fuse blowing in the middle of a favourite television programme, but since in the event of a fault 'something's got to give', it could then be the wiring or the whole fuse-holder which could explode.

The cartridge fuse, although technically superior to the rewireable, has the same dangerous disadvantages.

The miniature circuit breaker (MCB) is an electromechanical device which in the event of an overload or short circuit opens. It cannot be easily tampered with and a great advantage is that in the event of the MCB opening or tripping it can simply be switched on again. No more fiddling with fuse wire and screwdrivers.

If the fault persists it will trip again and cannot be held onto a faulty circuit.

Neutral conductor: One pole of a two-wire electrical system. Resembles the negative pole of a d.c. system. See also *Live Conductor*.

Pattress: Similar to *backplate*.

Phase: Another name for live or line.

Plaster depth box: Steel box to house a plateswitch on wall.

Plateswitch: Modern term for wall switch set in slim front plate.

Rose: Accessory which screws to ceiling to house lighting cables and flex wires.

Sheath: Outer covering of cable or flexible cord.

Socket outlet: Modern version of the old 'power point'. Houses a fused plug.

Spur: Branch of a ring circuit cable which supplies fused connection units or remote socket outlets.

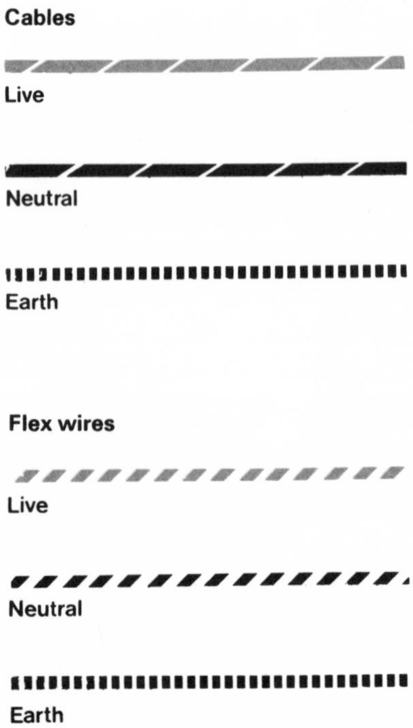

Cables

Live

Neutral

Earth

Flex wires

Live

Neutral

Earth

3

Fig. 3   Code for cables

Circuits

After the electricity supply is fed into the consumer unit, it is then distributed through the various circuits and fuses to lighting points and socket outlets (sometimes wrongly called power points).

In a typical consumer unit are a number of fuseholders housed in fuseways, *fig. 4*. The number can be anything from two to ten. Each of these holders accommodates a circuit fuse. These fuses supply and protect the various house circuits – heating, lighting, cooker, immersion heater and so on.

Each circuit is supplied by its own fuse; *no fuse may supply more than one circuit.*

Fig. 4 Connections in a typical eight-way consumer unit

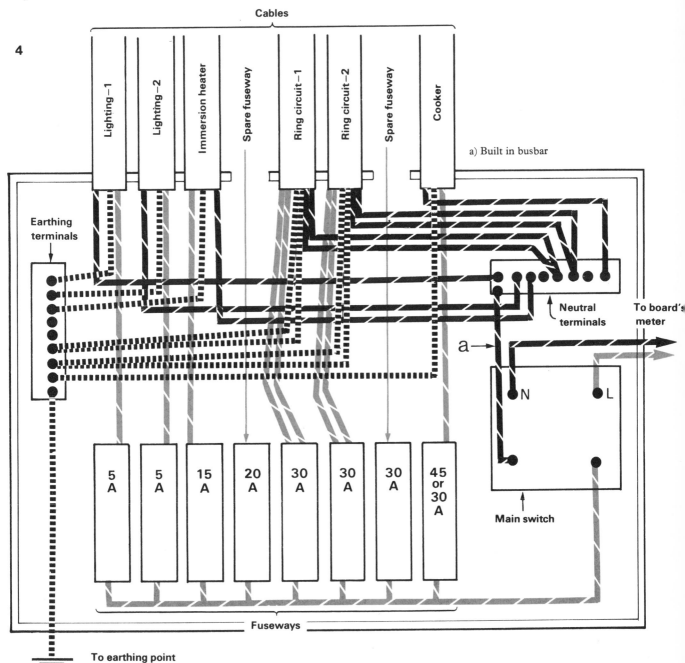

TYPES OF FUSE

There are two types of circuit fuse used in a domestic system, *fig. 6.* One type is rewirable and consists of fuse wire as the fuse element. The other is the cartridge type. In principle the cartridge fuse is similar to a 13 amp fuse used in a plug, but is bigger.

Cartridge type fuses cannot be rewired. They must be replaced if they 'blow'. No attempt to repair them should be made.

Each circuit fuse is designed to carry a maximum amount of current. This current is called the load. Each fuse has its own rating which determines the load it can carry. Generally speaking, these ratings are:

5 amp for lighting circuits; 15 amp for special circuits such as immersion heaters; 30 amp for ring or power circuits; 45 amp for large cooker and heating circuits.

FUSE COLOUR CODES

The fuses in modern consumer units are colour coded so that they can be instantly recognisable. The colours used are:

5 amp, white; 15 amp, blue; 30 amp, red; 45 amp, green.

There are also 20 amp fuses (colour coded yellow) which are used for special circuits.

In older installations, the fuse carriers may have the current ratings stamped on them in figures instead of being coded with coloured dots.

Fig. 5 Fuse box showing the amperage of the different fuses

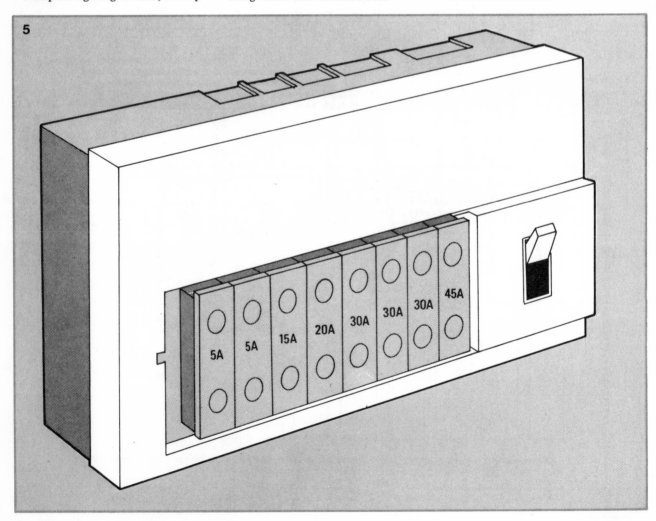

It pays to examine your consumer unit to become familiar with the fuses. If they are not easily identifiable, make a sketch of them on a postcard. Give each one a number and list its function (lighting, ring circuit, immersion heater etc.) against the appropriate number. Hang the card near the fuseways where you can find it quickly in an emergency.

If the fuses are rewirable types, keep a card of fuse wire handy. It is sold wound on small cards with a supply for each of the three main fuse ratings – 5, 15 and 30 amp.

If the fuses are cartridge types, always keep a supply of spares handy. Fuses have a habit of blowing when all the shops are shut!

Each consumer unit (I will stop referring to fuseboards from now on) has a main switch. When turned off, this switch isolates all the circuits connected to the consumer unit.

This switch should always be turned off when inspecting or mending a fuse, and when making any alteration to the wiring system. If ever you read a book or article which says, 'Turn the current off at the main switch', that is the switch you should look for.

EARTHING TERMINALS

Now for a few more details about the consumer unit itself. If you look at *fig. 4*, you will see on the left the earthing terminal strip or block. The number of individual terminals on the

Fig. 6   Circuit fuses: rewirable and cartridge types

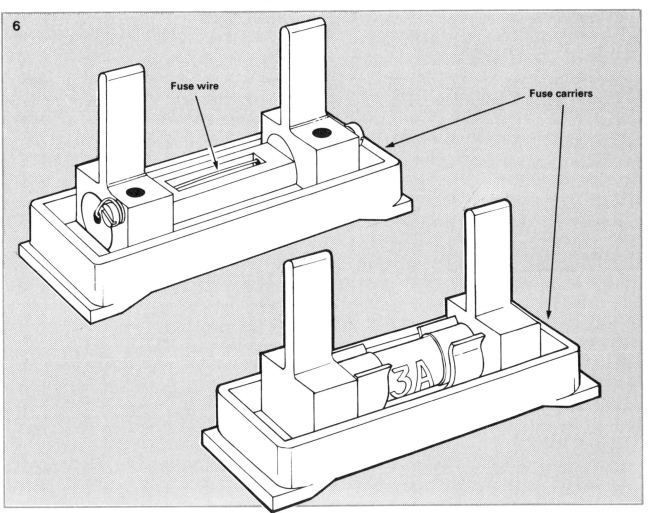

6

Fuse wire

Fuse carriers

3A

strip will, of course, vary according to the size and the make of the unit.

The terminal at the bottom of the strip is the one usually used by the electrician when the wiring of the installation is carried out. But this may not always be the case.

From this terminal runs the earth lead to whatever central earthing point the installer may have used to earth the installation.

The rest of the terminals on the strip are used to accommodate the earthing wires (conductors) of the various circuit cables running throughout the house.

NEUTRAL TERMINALS

On the right of *fig. 4* is the neutral terminal strip or block. This also has a number of individual terminals. It is to these that all the neutral conductors of the house cables are connected.

The live conductors of the cables are connected to the individual fuseways as shown in *fig. 4*. You will see that the conductors of the ring circuit cables are joined to a terminal or fuseway where another conductor has already been connected. This will be explained later.

Note that the positions of the earthing terminal strip and of the neutral terminal strip in a consumer unit can vary according to make.

CABLE LAYOUT

To make a neat wiring job, and to make it easier to locate cables, all three types of conductor should be arranged in the unit in logical order. The highest rated fuseway is now normally the one next to the main switch (farthest right in *fig. 4*) and the lowest rated is on the far left.

When wiring up a consumer unit, the earth and neutral terminals are normally used in the same order as the live fuseways are positioned. This has been done as far as it is possible in *fig. 4*.

The live terminal on the main switch is linked by a busbar to the fuseways, and the neutral terminal is similarly linked to the neutral terminal slip. These links are all part and parcel of the unit's construction and are built-in fitments.

The two leads (live and neutral) which run to the board's meter are called the meter tails and are connected to the meter by the electricity board when they have approved the installation. This must only be done by the board.

If you ever have to install a consumer unit, you will be required to supply and connect these two tails to the unit's main terminals, so that they are ready for the board to connect to the meter.

The tails should normally be about one metre in length, but if for any reason the consumer unit is not positioned near the meter (as is the normal procedure) the tails will, of course, need to be longer.

Cables and Flexes

Although there are many types of cables and flexible cords (usually called flex), for general wiring purposes the householder needs to be concerned with only a few.

First, however, it is important to be quite clear on the difference between cable and flex. A cable is used for fixed wiring; flex is used to connect a portable appliance to a plug; a lampholder to a ceiling rose; or a fixed appliance to its fused outlet.

Cable should never be used instead of flex, and flex must not be used as a substitute for cable. This is a very important rule.

CORE COLOURS

Another point – an important one – to remember is the colour of the cores (insulated conductors). Although the colours of three-core flexible cords were changed some time ago, house wiring *cable* core colours were *not* changed.

The colours are:

CABLES: Live is red; neutral is black; earth is green.

FLEXIBLE CORDS: Live is now brown; neutral is blue; earth is green with yellow stripes.

The *old* colours were: Live (red); neutral (black); earth (green). On older appliances you will probably find the flex wires are in the old colours.

The *sizes* of both cables and flex have been changed to metric measurements. *Table A* gives some cables sizes and *Table B* gives the sizes of some flexible cords. *Figure 7* shows some examples of cables and flexible cords.

As a general rule, it is necessary for a householder to remember only two or three sizes of cable. These are $1 \cdot 0 \text{ mm.}^2$ (or $1 \cdot 5 \text{ mm.}^2$) for lighting circuits; and $2 \cdot 5 \text{ mm.}^2$ for ring circuits, 20 amp storage heater circuits and immersion heaters. For cooker circuits 6 mm.^2 or 10 mm.^2 cables are used.

Fig. 7   Examples of cables and flexible cords
a) Mineral insulated copper clad (m.i.c.c.)
b) PVC armoured
c) PVC sheathed and insulated (house wiring cable)
d) As above, but seven-strand if 4.0 mm^2 or above
e) PVC sheathed and insulated twin flat
f) PVC parallel twin (figure of eight)
g) Cotton braided circular
h) PVC twisted twin

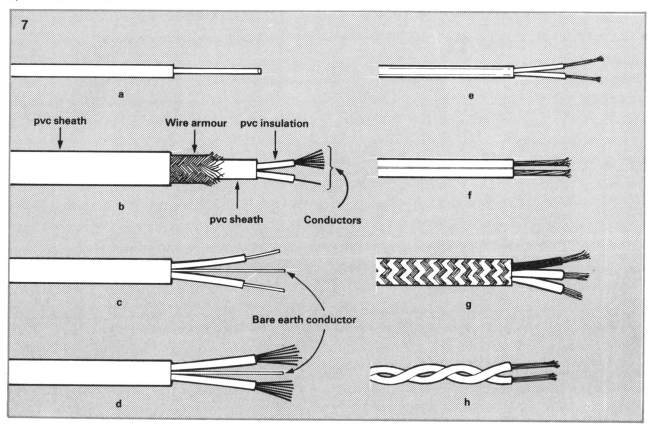

For interior house wiring, pvc sheathed cable is normally used. It is available in single core (one conductor); twin core; twin core and earth; and three core.

For outside wiring, there are two types of cable especially suitable. One is m.i.c.c. (mineral insulated copper clad). The other is armoured pvc insulated twin-core cable. See separate chapter on outside wiring.

TABLE A
Cables

Cable size	Max. current rating (amps)	Circuit fuse
1·0 mm.²	12	5 amps
1·5 mm.²	15	15 amps
2·5 mm.²	21	30 amps

TABLE B
Flexible cords

Cord size	No. of wires	Current rating
0·5 mm.²	16	3.0 amps
0·75 mm.²	24	6·0 amps
1·0 mm.²	32	10·0 amps
1·5 mm.²	30	15·0 amps

The main uses for the various sizes of flexible cords include:

Lighting, 0·5 mm.²

Lighting and small appliances, 0·75 mm.²

Appliances rated up to 2 kW, 1·0 mm.²

Appliances rated up to 3 kW, 1·5 mm.²

It will be seen from *Table B* that flexible cords have a number of fine wires (strands) which combine to make up the conductors. The reason for this is to make the flex as flexible as possible.

Cables used to have a number of strands, too, but most of them are now single strand. Many houses, however, are still wired in the old multi-strand cables.

For circuits such as cooker circuits which carry heavy current, seven-strand cables are the ones which are used.

WIRING HINTS

If a lot of wiring is planned, it will pay you to buy a proper cable stripper. These are available at modest prices. Take care, if you use a knife to remove the sheath or the insulation material from a cable or flexible cord, not to cut the conductor wires.

The best way to join cables is to use a joint box (sometimes called a junction box) where the ends of the conductors can be safely anchored under its terminals. A joint box suitable for lighting circuit cables is shown in *fig. 72*.

Fig. 8   Typical cable stripping tools

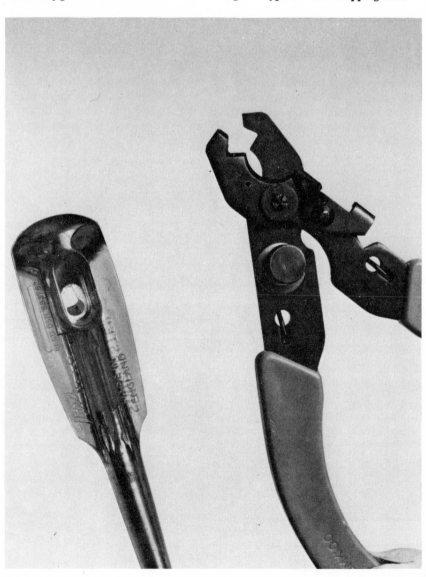

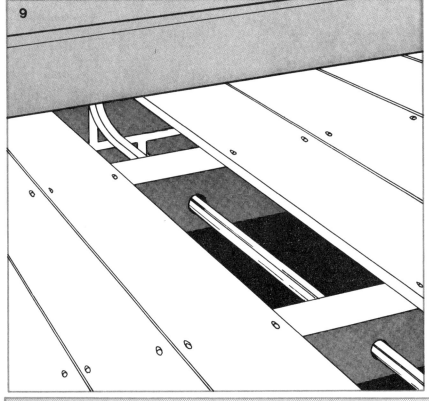

PVC (polyvinyl chloride) sheathed cable can be buried under wall plaster. There is no need for further protection.

Where cables cross timber joists under floorboards they should pass through holes drilled not less than 2 in. below the tops of the joists.

Cables should not be laid in grooves cut in the tops of the joists. The danger here is that nails driven through the floorboards could penetrate the cables.

Do not use insulating or self-adhesive tape to join flexible cords or cables. Proper flex connectors and cable connectors (*fig. 10*) are available which ensure a sound and safe connection.

Fig. 9   Cables should pass through holes in the joists

Fig. 10   Flex connectors

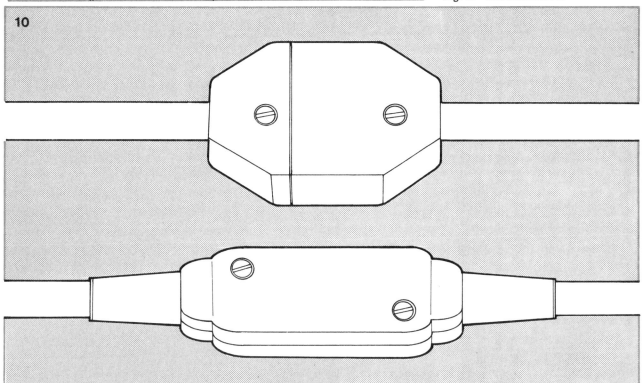

Mending Fuses

A common fault which occurs in a house wiring system is the failure of an electric light. Being suddenly left in pitch darkness can be unnerving, even dangerous, so always keep a candle or a torch where it can be found quickly.

When a light fails, the normal reaction is to replace the lamp. But in these days of power cuts, especially, it is a good idea to check first if any lights are showing from neighbouring houses.

If they are ON, then try your other lights *on the same floor*. The reason for specifying the same floor is that the house probably has two or even three lighting circuits – one for each floor is the common practice.

CHECK THE MAIN FUSE

If the lights on the same floor do not work, the lighting circuit fuse in the consumer unit may have blown. Turn off the main switch in the consumer unit and check the appropriate lighting fuse by pulling it from its holder to inspect it.

In rewirable types, the fuse wire element will be broken if the fuse has blown. Here's how to mend it.

Release the two screws and remove the broken fuse wire – *all of it*. From your card of fuse wire, thread the 5 amp wire through the hole in the fuse holder at one end and tighten the wire under the screw (clockwise). Trim any surplus wire around the screw.

Cut the fuse wire to the length you require and fix this end under the other screw. Do not stretch the wire or allow it to become too slack. *Figure 6, page 327* shows this type of fuse.

If the fuses are cartridge types, they should simply be renewed if suspect. They can be tested as shown in *fig. 11*.

After repairing or renewing the fuse, replace it in its holder and turn on the main switch. If the fuse blows again immediately the light is switched on, there is a fault somewhere which needs investigation. This could be a broken or disconnected flex wire at the bulb holder.

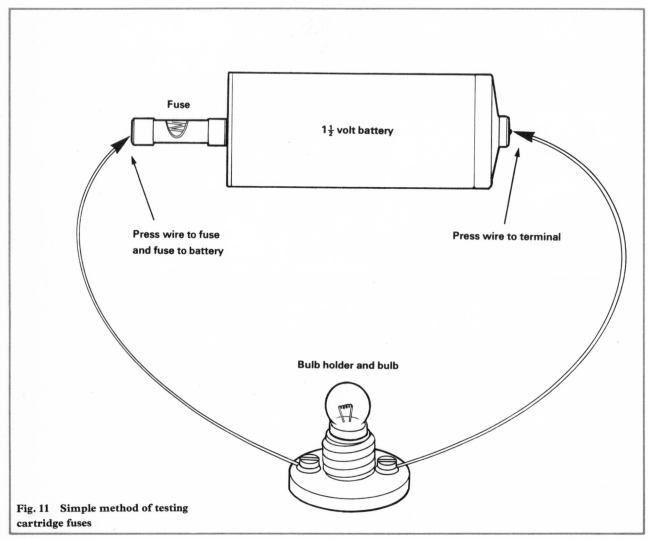

Fuse

1½ volt battery

Press wire to fuse and fuse to battery

Press wire to terminal

Bulb holder and bulb

Fig. 11 Simple method of testing cartridge fuses

If the lighting fuse has not blown, and the bulb is in order but still does not light up, check to see if the ring circuit is working. You can do this by switching on an appliance which you know is in order. If that fails to work also, then the electricity board's main fuse may have blown. Telephone the board only when you have eliminated all possible causes of the fault on your side of the installation.

To reduce the risk of being left in the dark when a lighting circuit fuse blows, it is a good idea to have a standard or other type of lamp plugged into a socket outlet on the ring circuit in as many rooms as you may find to be practicable.

FUSES TO USE

When acquiring an appliance, make sure you know its wattage and the correct fuse to use in the plug. The following is a rough guide to the rating of fuse to use for appliances in common use. If in doubt, always ask in the shop or follow the manufacturer's instructions.

Appliance	Approx. wattage range	Fuse needed	
		Flat pin plug	Round pin plug
Blanket	150 or less	3 amp	2 amp
Coffee maker	250 to 750	3 amp	5 amp
	over 750	13 amp	5 amp
Cooker	to 3kW	13 amp	15 amp
	(fuses of larger cookers wired in circuit)		
Drill	150 to 450	3 amp	5 amp
Food mixer	to 300	3 amp	5 amp
Heater (radiant)	to 3kW	13 amp	15 amp
„ (convector)	? to 3kW	13 amp	15 amp
„ (fan)	2 to 3kW	13 amp	15 amp
Hair drier	to 720	3 amp	5 amp
„ „	over 720	13 amp	15 amp
Iron	750 to 1,200	13 amp	5 amp
Kettle	750 to 1kW	13 amp	5 amp
„	1kW to 3kW	13 amp	15 amp
*Refrigerator	120	13 amp	5 amp
Spin drier	200	3 amp	5 amp
*Vacuum cleaner	150	3 amp	5 amp
„ „	to 750	13 amp	5 amp
Washing machine (motor 300 watts; heater 2½kW)		13 amp	15 amp

*Refrigerators and some vacuum cleaners draw a large amount of current when starting up and so require a plug fuse of a slightly higher rating than is usual for their wattages.

Jobs Around the House

There are quite a few simple wiring jobs which need to be done regularly in any household. Several of them are outlined here.

Always make sure before you start that you have all the tools and materials you are likely to need. Don't follow a make-do-and-mend policy. It simply does not pay where electricity is concerned. Take your time over wiring connections and don't be tempted to experiment.

Always use the correct size cable or flex for the job, not just any odd bit of wire that may be lying around. Remember, electricity can be lethal, so **TAKE CARE.**

NEW FLEX FOR AN IRON

Friction often causes the flexible cord of an electric iron to become worn and therefore potentially dangerous. If the sheath of the flex is worn near either end, it may not be necessary to replace

the whole length. If the sheath is worn nearer the middle, however, the complete flex should be replaced without delay.

If it is not renewed, before long the insulation of the conductors will also become worn and the wires will be exposed.

Fig. 12   Tools for the home electrician

Fig. 13   How an electric iron is wired

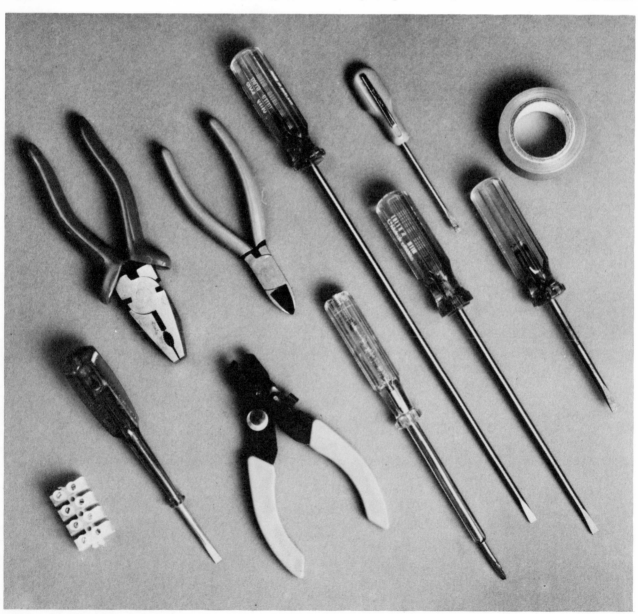

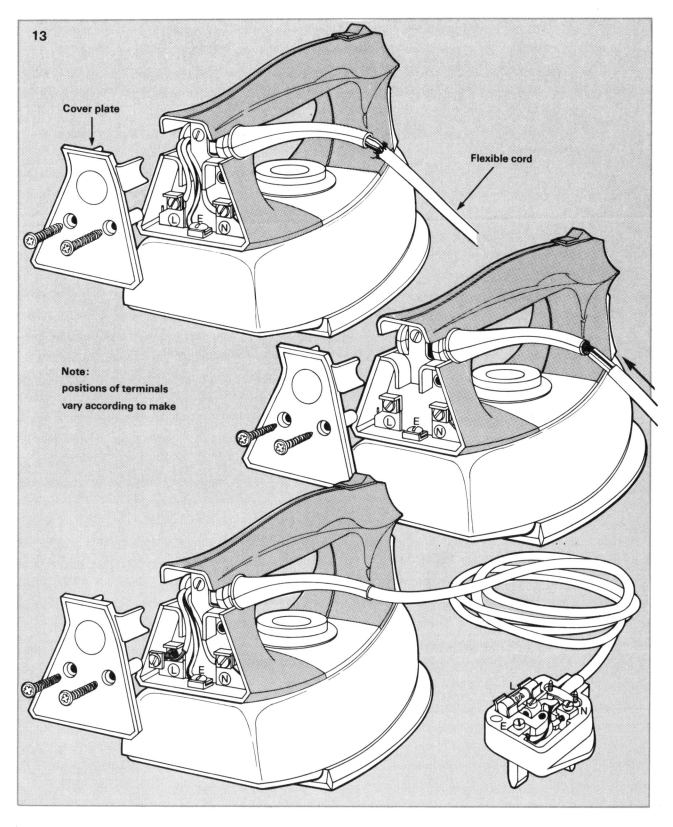

13

Cover plate

Flexible cord

Note:
positions of terminals
vary according to make

Replacing the flexible cord is not difficult, but it is most important to make a sketch of the wiring arrangements of the iron before disconnecting the conductors from their terminals.

In most cases, these terminals will be located under a cover at the back of the iron (*fig. 13*). The arrangement, however, will depend on the make. So first take off the cover and make your sketch.

Then release the three conductors from their terminals and pull the old flex through the grommet. Make sure no loose strands of the flex are left on or around the terminals as these could cause a short circuit.

Insert one end of the new flex (you will need about 9 ft. of unkinkable flex) into the grommet. Strip off a suitable length of sheath. Then prepare the ends of the three conductors. You can use the old flex as a guide to determine how much wire to leave exposed.

The blue core of the flex goes to the neutral (N) terminal; the brown core to the live (L) terminal; and the green/yellow core to the earth (E) terminal.

(On an old iron, red, black and green were the colours used for live, neutral and earth respectively, but as stated earlier, these colours were changed some time ago to fall in line with world standards.)

Make a final check that the connections have been properly made. The ends of the conductors must be firmly anchored under the terminals.

The sheath should now be anchored in the same way as it was originally. Replace the terminal cover. Then connect a fused plug fitted with a 13 amp fuse to the other end of the flex. If you have no ring circuit and use round pin plugs, fit a 5 amp type.

WIRING UP PLUGS

Fitting a plug to the end of a flexible cord is not a difficult job, but care must be taken to ensure that the wires are fitted to the correct terminals. This may sound obvious, but it is very easy to make a mistake.

To wire up a three-pin fused plug, first take off the cover by removing the centre screw located at the back of the plug. Release the cord grip (if there is one) by removing the other two screws on the back of the plug.

Fig. 14   Connections for a 13 amp plug with pillar type terminals

Fig. 15   13 amp plug with clamp-type terminals

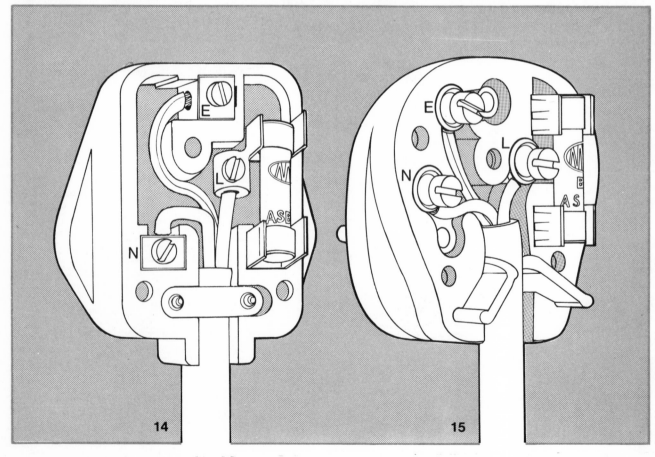

Now take out the cartridge fuse by levering it gently from its sockets. On plugs with pillar type terminals this probably will not be necessary.

Remove about 1½ in. of the outer sheath from the flexible cord and ½ in. of insulation material from the ends of the three conductors. Connect the conductors as in *figs 14 and 15*.

It is important that all the strands of each conductor are twisted together as a stray strand could foul the wrong terminal.

If the terminals are the clamp type, wind the bare ends of the conductors in a clockwise direction under the terminal washers. Tighten the screws.

Pillar type terminals are those shown in *fig. 14*. The clamp types are illustrated in *fig. 15*.

To get a firm fixing in pillar type terminals, double back the ends of the conductors on themselves, insert in the terminal holes and tighten the small screws on top of the terminals.

Now anchor the flex by replacing the cord grip and tightening its screws. Before replacing the cartridge fuse, check that it is of the correct value for the appliance.

For appliances which are rated up to 720 watts, choose a 3 amp fuse. If the appliance is rated at between 720 and 3,000 watts (3 kilowatts), insert a 13 amp fuse. A table of fuses for various appliances is given on page 333.

Arrange the conductors neatly in the plug (slots are usually provided), replace the cover and tighten the centre screw on the back.

Some modern plugs have an alternative method to the cord grip for anchoring the flex.

READING THE METER

Every householder should be able to read his or her electric meter. For one thing it helps you to keep a close watch on the amount of electricity you are consuming. For another, you may be asked by your board to provide a reading yourself if you should be out when the man calls to read the meter.

A typical meter is shown in *fig. 16*. When taking a reading, ignore the small dial marked 1/10kWh. The other dials are then read from left to right, although there seems to be two schools of thought about this.

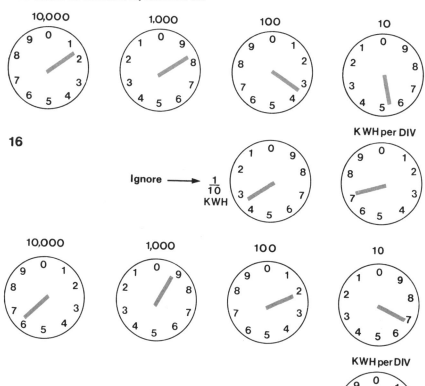

Fig. 16   Ignore the dial marked 1/10 kWh when reading a meter

Fig. 16a   Note carefully the positions of the pointers

16

16a

Some say read from right to left, putting the second figure down on the left of the first and so on. Personally, I feel that there is always the possibility of obtaining a reading in reverse by using this method! However, you have a choice.

Using the left to right method, note that the digit to read is the one which the dial pointer has just *passed*, not necessarily the digit which is nearest the pointer.

Deduct the previous reading shown on your last bill for electricity from the reading you have taken. The answer will be the number of units consumed since the meter was last read. This, of course, can be done at any time if you want to check consumption over a given period.

Some meters have no 10,000 dial, but the method of reading is the same. The reading of the meter in *fig. 16* is 18,357.

ERRORS TO AVOID

It is possible to take an incorrect reading of a meter by failing to note carefully the positions of the pointers. To illustrate my point, look at *fig. 16a*.

At a quick glance it would appear that the reading is 69,273. On closer examination, however, we see that although the 10,000 dial pointer has passed figure 6, the 1,000 pointer is between 9 and 0 and has not, therefore, completed its revolution.

The correct reading is 59,273, which makes a considerable difference!

FITTING A KETTLE ELEMENT

To fix a new element in an electric kettle, first unscrew the shroud ring, *fig. 17*. This may be tight, so you may need a wrench to shift it. Avoid damaging the chrome of the kettle by protecting it with a thick cloth.

Next, remove the washer immediately behind the ring. Push the flange towards the kettle and lift out the element through the top. Remove all traces of the old washer and scale from both sides of the element hole.

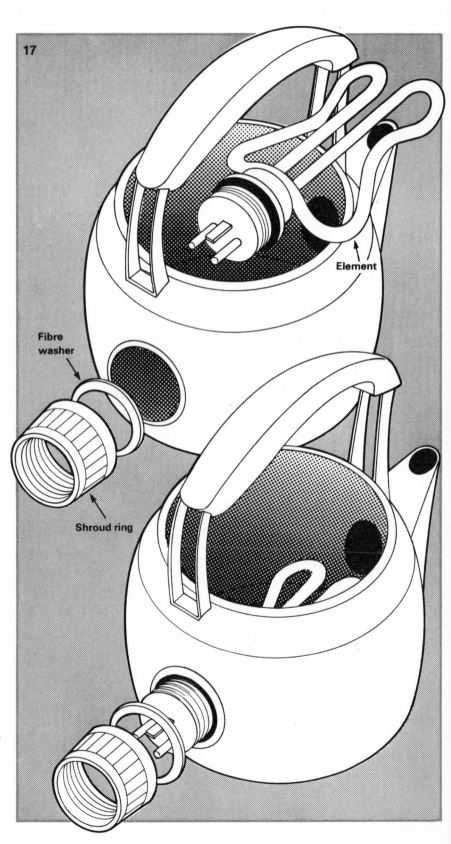

17

Element

Fibre washer

Shroud ring

Fig. 17 Remove the shroud ring and washers to renew a kettle element

There are several types of element, so unless you know exactly the one you want, take the old one to the shop as a guide. With the new element buy a fibre washer and a rubber washer.

Put the rubber washer on the flange of the new element. This washer is the one which goes inside the kettle. Pass the element through the hole into the kettle the right way up. Pull the flange through the hole and position the element.

Watch for leaks Now fit the fibre washer on the flange and screw the shroud ring on tightly so no water can leak out.

If the kettle leaks slightly when filled, try tightening the shroud still more. Be careful if you use a wrench

not to overdo it and damage the rubber washer inside.

Make sure the water covers the element before you push the connector in and switch on.

Sometimes when a kettle boils dry it damages the connector and the flex. If this happens, the best thing to do is to buy a kit which contains an element, washers and a connector with the flex already wired into it.

REPLACING LAMPHOLDERS
Sometimes bayonet type lampholders become damaged and need replacing. Or the contact plungers, *fig. 18*, can lose their tension. The plungers are the two pins whose ends make contact with the lamp.

Fig. 18 Contact plungers in a lamp holder can lose their tension

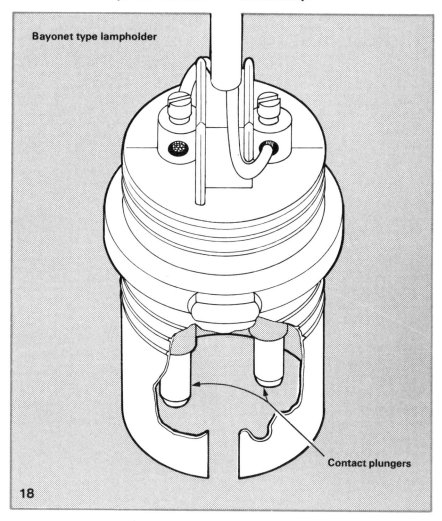

Bayonet type lampholder

Contact plungers

18

339

Before attempting to replace the holder, turn the current off at the main switch.

Take out the lamp, remove the shade and unscrew the shield or cover, *fig. 19.* Disconnect the flex from the two terminals. If the shade or the fitting is metal, there should be an earth wire fitted. This, too, will have to be disconnected.

Now take off the cover from the new lampholder and pass the flex through it. Connect the flex to the terminals and make sure the screws are tightened firmly.

Arrange the flexible conductors neatly around the pillar of the holder. Screw the cover on to the holder and replace the shade.

The shade is normally held in place by a skirt or a plastic ring. Take care not to get the ring or skirt on a cross thread and do not overtighten. If you do, the ring or skirt will be very difficult to remove next time. Put the lamp in, restore the current and switch on to test.

WORN FLEX

If the flex is worn, this too should be renewed. But if the damage is confined to the end of the flex, it may be sufficient simply to cut an inch or so from the worn end.

With ceiling lights this obviously will depend on the total length of the flex and how close the fitting is to the ceiling.

If, however, the whole length needs to be renewed, it will be necessary to unscrew the cover of the ceiling rose. This may be a difficult thing to do and it may be necessary to break the rose in order to get it off. This will mean fitting a new rose and to do this you will have to disturb the cables themselves.

So before you break the rose, do make sure you are experienced enough to carry out the work involved.

When the cover of the rose is removed you will see the cables leading through a hole in the ceiling. Don't disturb them if you are merely

connecting a new length of flex. Simply remove the old flex from its two terminals and connect the new flex, making sure you tighten the terminals firmly. *Figure 21* shows one arrangement of cables and flex at a ceiling rose. Your rose may not necessarily look like this, so make sure you connect the flex to the proper terminals.

If you have to replace the old rose, make a careful note of the cable and flex connections before you disconnect any wires. After loosening the terminals and releasing the wires, unscrew the fixing screws holding the base of the rose to the ceiling and withdraw it.

Thread the cable ends through the base of the new rose and connect their

ends to the proper terminals. Note that the red cable or cables (there will probably be more than one in a terminal) go to the live terminal and the black cable or cables to the neutral terminal.

In some installations the apparent confusion of wires at a ceiling rose has to be seen to be believed, so I repeat, make sure you know which wires go where before you disconnect any of them.

EARTHING

To conform with the wiring regulations, an earth wire (a single length of green sleeved pvc sheathed cable) should be run from the earthing terminal of the

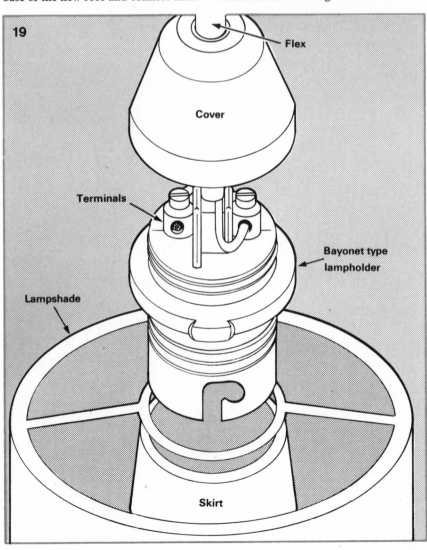

Fig. 20 The component parts of a
ceiling rose

21

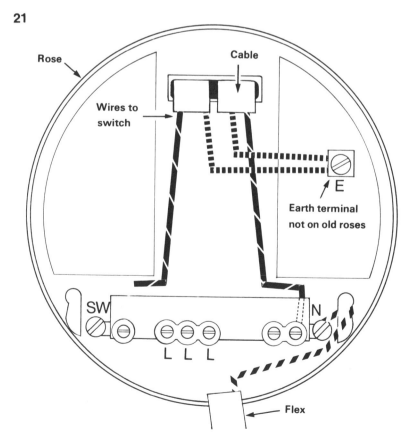

Rose

Cable

Wires to
switch

E

Earth terminal
not on old roses

SW

N

L L L

Flex

Fig. 19 Unscrew the cover to reveal a
lampholder's flex terminals

Fig. 21 Electrical connections at one
type of ceiling rose

new rose back to the earthing terminal strip on the consumer unit.

If, however, yours is an old installation which is likely to be completely rewired in the near future, this earth wire can be omitted until the work is done. But if the lighting fitting is a metal one, the earth wire must be fitted.

With all the cables fixed to the terminals securely, screw the base of the new rose to the ceiling. Fit the flex wires as described. Always choose a heat resistant flex if this has to be renewed.

TESTING APPLIANCES

Most of the electrical appliances sold today are reliably made and will give good service provided they are looked after properly. In most cases it is unwise to attempt what may turn out to be complicated repairs. This applies particularly to the larger appliances such as washing machines and refrigerators, but it is also unwise to meddle with smaller appliances unless you know exactly what it is you are doing.

It is true that many do-it-yourself enthusiasts do most, if not all their appliance repairs, but it is not a practice I would recommend for beginners.

When portable appliances stop operating for no apparent reason, however, there are some simple tests which can be made.

The first thing to do is to switch the appliance off at its own switch and at the switch at the socket outlet. If there is no switch at the outlet, pull out the plug. If the plug is a fused type, the fuse may have blown. This can be tested as shown in *fig. 11*.

If the fuse is in order, examine the flexible lead from the appliance. If this also is in order, try another appliance (which you know is in good order) in the socket outlet. If this works, there is something wrong with the original appliance and it should be sent for servicing.

LIFTING FLOORBOARDS

If you have to lift any floorboards to do a wiring job, you will need several tools: a hammer, a couple of electrician's bolster chisels, a cold chisel about 1 ft. long, a tenon saw, handsaw and a nail punch.

Look for a board which does not run the full length of the room, but butts up to another length of floorboard. Use the bolster chisels to prise the board up, *fig. 22*, and the batten to keep the board in a raised position, *fig. 23*.

Move the bolsters along the board in order to ease it up. Get someone to raise the end of the board, then move the cold chisel along underneath it as far as possible.

Let go of the board and press its end downwards. The rest of the board should then come up, the cold chisel acting as a fulcrum.

Repeat the process until you can finally pull the floorboard from under the skirting board. (Skirtings are usually fixed after the floorboards have been laid.) Remove the nails from the floorboard and any still in the joists.

Fig. 22   Use a bolster chisel to prise up a floorboard

Fig. 23   Use a wooden batten to keep the free end of the board raised

WATCH OUT FOR CABLES

Floorboards that run the entire length of the room will have to be cut. Great care must be taken when doing this so as not to cut through cables or gas and water pipes. Make sure, therefore, that the current is turned off at the main switch before you start.

Begin by drawing a line across the board in front of the nail holes which secure it to the joist at one end. You will now need a pad saw. Make a starter hole for the saw by drilling holes closely together to form a sufficiently wide gap into which the blade of the saw can be slipped. The thin blade is ideal for cutting across a floorboard since it is designed to work in confined areas. Insert a batten under the cut end of the board to keep it raised. Saw through the other end of the board on top of the joist. Then lift it clear. Support it, when refitted, by a batten, screwed firmly, to the joist.

T & G BOARDS

If the boards are tongued and grooved, the tongue on the board to be lifted, and that on the one next to it, will first have to be cut off with a handsaw. Here, too, special care should be taken

Fig. 24 Cut through the tongue of a tongued and grooved board with a pad or hand saw

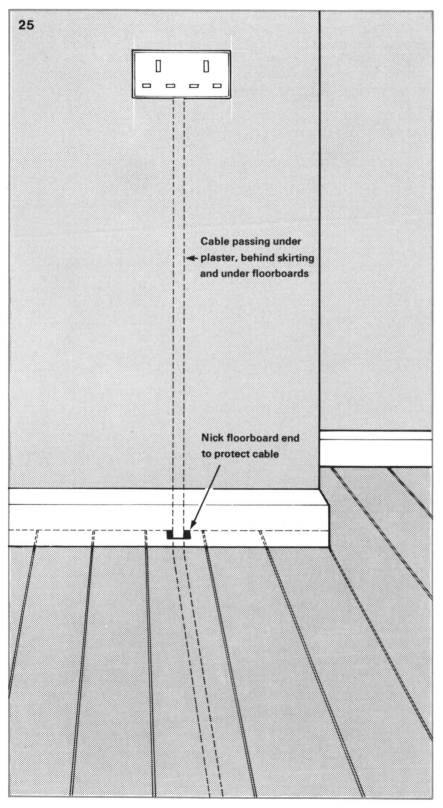

25

Cable passing under
← plaster, behind skirting
and under floorboards

Nick floorboard end
to protect cable

to avoid cutting pipes or cables.

It is a good idea to replace floorboards with screws rather than nails so that the cables will be accessible.

One more tip. As floorboards usually extend under skirtings, any cable rising up the wall from the area under the boards could be damaged by the end of the board. This can be avoided by nicking the end of the board to form a small channel for the cable to pass through, *fig. 25*.

Fig. 25   Nick the ends of floorboards to protect cables

Fixing Electric Bells

Any handyman can tackle the job of fixing an electric bell. Nowadays you can buy all the necessary parts in a complete kit except, of course, the battery.

The simplest circuit, *fig. 26*, consists of a bell or buzzer which works when a bell push fixed at the front door is pushed; a suitable length of two-core insulated bell wire; a 4½ volt battery; insulated staples to fix the wire; and fixing screws to fit the push and bell.

To install such a circuit, fix the bell in the selected spot. Drill a hole in the door frame for the wires which go to the back of the bell push. Before fixing the bell push to the frame of the door, fix the two ends of the bell wire to its

terminals. One of these wires will need to be cut and its other end fixed to one terminal of the bell. The rest of that length of wire runs from the other bell terminal to a terminal on the battery (it does not matter which).

The other (uncut) length of wire from the bell push runs to the other terminal on the battery.

When the push is operated, the circuit will be complete. Current will flow through it and the bell will ring.

The battery can be housed in a home-made wooden box positioned near the bell or stood on a convenient shelf – perhaps in a cupboard. You can, of course, buy bells which

themselves house the battery, thus reducing the amount of wiring which will be visible.

The bell wire can be anchored to skirtings and door frames using insulated staples.

EXTENSION BELL

If a bell is clearly audible in one part of the house but not in another, an extension bell can be fitted to overcome this problem. *Figures 27a* and *27b* show how two bells can be wired up.

For the best results, the bells should be similar types (i.e., their characteristics should be the same). Too long a wire to the extension bell should be avoided as this will mean

Fig. 26 Simple battery bell circuit

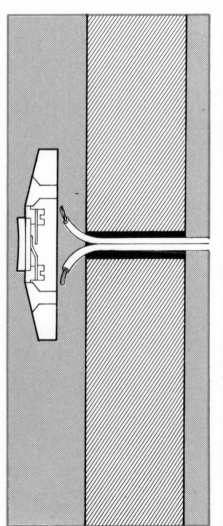

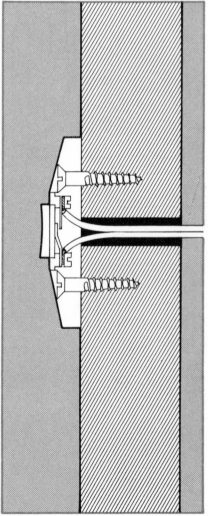

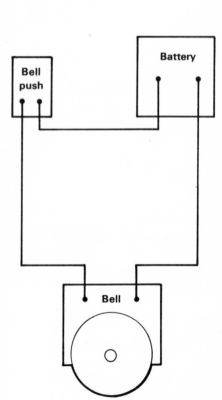

its resistance to the current will be high.

In *fig. 27a*, the bells are wired in series. In *fig. 27b* they are wired in parallel.

No detailed explanation of the difference between parallel and series wiring is necessary. All you need to do is to follow the diagrams.

Some experimenting, however, may be necessary to get both the bells to work satisfactorily, so if one method of wiring will not work, try the other.

Problems sometimes arise with the parallel method of connection. One is that one of the bells may cause the amount of current supplied to the other to be reduced. The answer to this

one is to increase the voltage slightly with a stronger battery or to adjust the contact setting screw of the bell. The position of this screw may vary according to the make of bell, but *fig. 28* showing the contact screw of an ordinary trembler type of bell will give you a clue.

If an extra bell is wired in series you may again require a stronger battery to drive the extra current needed around the circuit. A suitable type of battery for this purpose is a six volt lantern battery.

I suggest that you experiment first with both methods of connecting before you finally fix the bell and the wire in position.

Fig. 27a   Bell circuit wired in series

Fig. 27b   Bell circuit wired in parallel

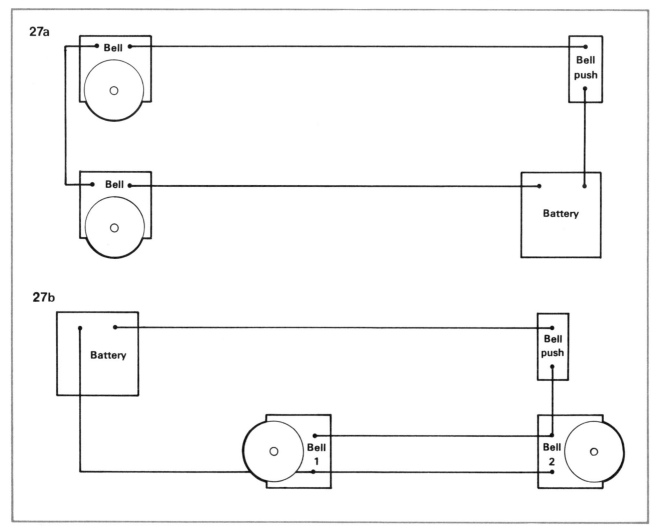

OFF THE MAINS

For operating door bells or chimes from the mains a double-wound transformer with its secondary winding earthed is essential. Transformers sold especially for bell circuits incorporate this safety device as a built-in feature. Make sure this is the type you buy.

There are two windings to a transformer – the primary and the secondary. The primary (input) is connected to the mains, and the secondary (output) to low voltage appliances such as bells, *fig. 29*. Transformers sold for operating bells or chimes have various tappings on the output side. These enable you to choose the voltage you require.

The tappings may be four, eight and 12 volts *or* three, five and eight volts, according to type. The most suitable should be chosen after experimenting.

WIRING UP

To wire up a bell or chimes from the mains you need two-core and earth pvc-sheathed house wiring cable, size 1·0 mm.² or 1·5 mm.². Position the transformer near the consumer unit. Run a length of the cable from a spare 5 amp fuseway in the consumer unit to the primary terminals of the transformer.

Then run a length of bell wire from the secondary terminals of the transformer to the bell push and to the bell or chimes (as for the battery operated circuit already described.)

If there is no fuseway to spare in the consumer unit, or this method of wiring is not convenient, there are other ways of wiring bells from the mains. These are described on page 389.

Fig. 28   A contact screw of a bell is adjustable

Fig. 29   Transformer connections for bell circuit

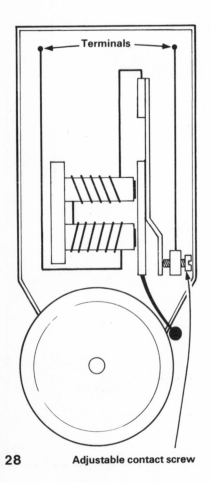

28   **Adjustable contact screw**

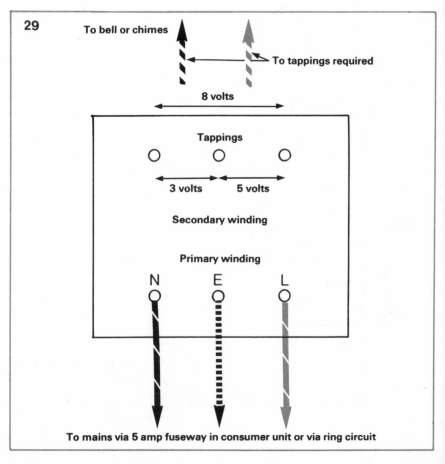

Watts, Volts and Amps

There are three terms in particular used in the electrical trade with which householders should become familiar.

Watts is the term heard most often, perhaps. This is the measurement of the amount of electricity used at a given moment by an appliance.

Volts, the second term, represents the measurement of pressure which forces current to flow along a conductor.

The amount of flow of electricity along a conductor is measured in *amperes*, usually abbreviated to amps.

Earlier on, I said it was important to know the wattage of an appliance. This is usually indicated on a metal plate or label on the appliance – it can often be found on the back. This may appear, for example, as 2,000 watts (2 kilowatts).

On the same label, the voltage of the appliance is sometimes marked also. This will almost certainly be 240 volts, as this is now the standard voltage in most parts of Britain.

SIMPLE DIVISION

It is sometimes helpful to know how many amps a plug, cable or socket outlet can cope with, and you can find this out easily if you know the wattage of the appliance and the voltage of the mains supply.

All you have to do is to divide the wattage by the voltage. For example, to find out the amperage of a plug required for a 2,400 watt appliance, divide 2,400 by 240. The result is ten amps.

In this case a 13 amp rectangular-pin plug is suitable – the type used in socket outlets on a ring circuit. The plug should, in this case, be fitted with a 13 amp fuse.

If the wattage of an appliance is, say, only 480 watts, only a 3 amp fuse needs to be fitted in the plug: 480 divided by 240 volts equals two amps.

It will be seen that the higher the wattage, the greater will be the power expended by the appliance.

RESISTANCE

There is one other term widely used by electricians – resistance. All appliances and circuits offer resistance to the flow of electricity. The resistance of an appliance or cable is measured in ohms.

The three units – volts, ohms and amps – are co-related. If, therefore, any two of them are known, the third can easily be calculated by the use of three simple formulae:

Volts = amps × ohms.
Ohms = volts divided by amps.
Amps = volts divided by ohms.

Fig. 30 A typical voltage plate for an electrical appliance

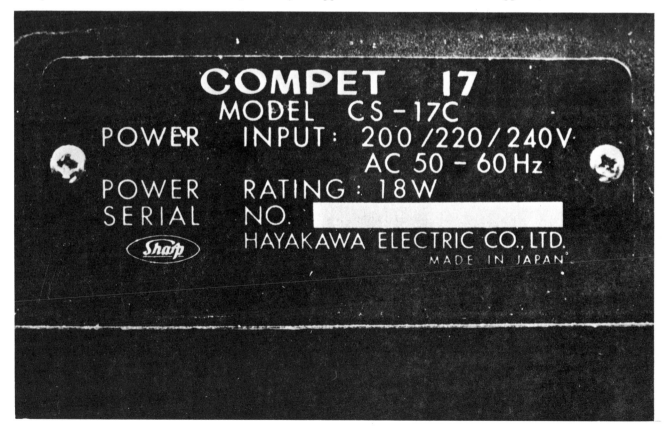

Plugs and Connections

Most of the plugs used in domestic wiring systems nowadays have three pins. Two-pin plugs are still used but only for appliances which are double insulated and for some lighting fittings. The two-pin type of plug, *fig. 31*, of course, has no earth terminal.

All appliances which are sold with a three-core flexible lead should be connected to a three-pin plug.

Three-pin plugs are made in two types. First, the modern plug which is fitted with a fuse and has rectangular (flat) pins, *fig. 32*. These are all made in a 13 amp size, but 3 amp as well as 13 amp fuses can be fitted into them.

Round pin plugs, *fig. 31*, are produced in three sizes – 15, 5 and 2 amps. These are *not* fitted with fuses. In installations where these plugs are used, the circuit fuse in the consumer unit is the only fuse for the circuit to which the plug is connected.

EXTENSIONS

There are various connectors which can be used to fit an extension lead to an appliance. If you want to use an

Fig. 31   Two-pin non-fused plug

Fig. 32   Modern 13 amp fused plug

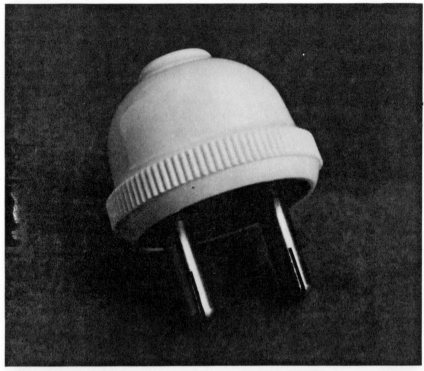

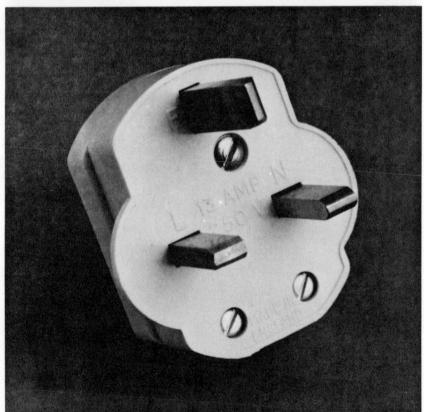

350

extension flex with an appliance fitted with a three-pin plug, the flex has to be connected to a socket at one end and to a plug at the other. Sockets are available in 15, 13 and 5 amp sizes.

One way to increase the length of a flexible lead is to use a flex connector (not to be confused with a block connector). This has a shrouded socket and a non-reversible three-pin plug, *fig. 33*. There are also connectors with only two pins, *fig. 34*. These *are* reversible, which means that the wires can be connected to either of its terminals in safety.

CORRECT CONNECTION
The socket section of a flex connector should always be fitted to the lead from the socket outlet or bulbholder. The plug section of the connector should be connected to the lead from the appliance.

This is most important because if it is not done, the plug pins will be live if the connector is accidentally pulled apart while the plug is still switched on and therefore dangerous.

It is important, too, that all connections in these accessories are firmly made. Should the connector or

Fig. 33   Flex connector with non-reversible plug

Fig. 34   Other types of flex connector

the plug become warm, make certain that there are no loose connections at the terminals. If, after checking, you find that the plug still gets hot, it could be overloaded, so check that the plug is the right type for the purpose.

Never use a connector or a plug which is chipped or cracked. Replace it as soon as possible.

EARTHING APPLIANCES

Every electrical appliance must be adequately earthed unless it is double insulated. Appliances which are double insulated normally carry a label in the box to this effect.

If you buy a recognised make of appliance, there is little danger that it will not be thoroughly insulated if it claims to be double insulated, but always make sure that it does.

There is an easy way to check the safety of this type of appliance if it has a metal casing. All you need are a torch battery and bulb, and a couple of

crocodile clips. Wire these up as shown in *fig. 35*.

When you want to test the earthing efficiency of an appliance, disconnect it from the mains. Fit one clip to, or hold it to, the metal of the appliance. Fix the other clip to the earth pin of the plug. If the appliance is adequately earthed, the bulb will glow brightly.

If there is only a dim glow from the bulb, and the battery is known to be in order, the appliance is inadequately earthed. There is, however, always a chance that there may be a fracture in the flexible lead, so check this.

As a further check, touch the clip to each of the other two pins of the plug in turn. There should be no light from the bulb. If there is light, the appliance is dangerous and certainly needs expert attention.

You can, of course, dispense with the crocodile clips and simply hold one wire to the appliance and the other to the pin on the plug.

Fig. 35 Testing the earthing efficiency of a power drill

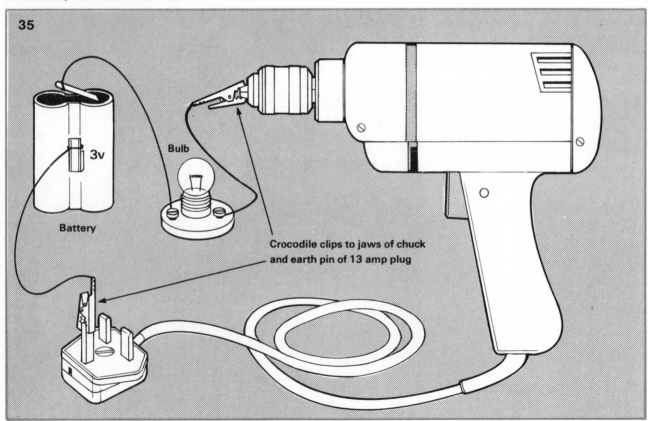

35

3v

Bulb

Battery

Crocodile clips to jaws of chuck and earth pin of 13 amp plug

Fluorescent Lamps

Tubular fluorescent lamps have a longer life than ordinary lamps of the same wattage. Another of their advantages is that they cost less to run. They are available in various lengths and wattages.

Their length can range from as little as 6 in. to 8 ft. and their wattages from four to 125.

When choosing fluorescent lamps, allow ten watts per square metre, or about one watt to a square foot, for the floor area to be illuminated.

These lamps normally have a life of at least 5,000 hours. They should be replaced when the light becomes dim, when they are difficult to start or when their ends begin to become black, *fig. 36.*

Fluorescent lamps should not be allowed to flicker; this can damage the controls. Also, avoid switching them off unnecessarily. It is better to allow them to stay on for brief periods, such as when leaving the room for a few minutes, because each time they are switched on their electrodes shed some of their oxide coating.

As the majority of fluorescent lamps are fitted with metal casings, they should be earthed. Many houses, of course, will not have an earth wire in the cable running to the lighting point. In these cases, an earth wire should be run from the lighting point back to the earthing terminal strip of the consumer unit.

There are two types of fluorescent

lamp. One works in conjunction with a starter switch and a choke; the other has no starter switch and is known as a quick start or instant start type.

The advantage of those with a switch start is that they last longer, but if you want immediate light, then the quick start type is the one to choose.

Another advantage of the quick start lamp is that it is noiseless. With the other type, there is a slight hum from the choke. One possible cure for this is to have the choke fitted away from the tube – perhaps on a joist and enclosed in a box.

FAULTS

The odd thing about fluorescent lamps is that they rarely fail suddenly or entirely. And provided the fault is in the tube itself and not in a component, some sort of life is apparent in the lamp.

There are, however, a number of things which can go wrong with this type of lamp.

For example, if a lamp seems to be dead, the circuit fuse or the fuse in the fitting may have blown; there could be a break in the circuit wiring some-where; or, in the case of a switch-start type, the lampholder may be at fault (i.e., faulty contact).

If the lamp refuses to start when switched on, you may notice that the electrodes are glowing at each end. The colour of the glow can give you a clue to the fault.

If the electrodes glow white on a switch start tube, the starter is probably faulty. If they glow red, then the tube has reached the end of its useful life and should be replaced.

This sort of fault on a quick start type of tube may be due to an inadequate earth connection, or the wrong type of tube may have been fitted.

Sometimes a tube will make a number of efforts to start but fail to do so. On a single tube this could be due to a fault in the starter. If the model is a twin tube type, the lampholder connections may be crossed.

Sometimes, when a new tube is fitted, it will light but with a shimmering effect. This is usually nothing to worry about; the tube will soon settle down and work normally.

There are a number of possible faults which can cause a lamp to flicker on and off. It could be due to low mains voltage, a faulty starter switch, the lamp itself may be faulty, or it may have reached the end of its useful life.

If the flicker is slow and very noticeable, then the lamp needs renewing.

Fig. 36 Fluorescent lamps should be replaced when the ends turn black

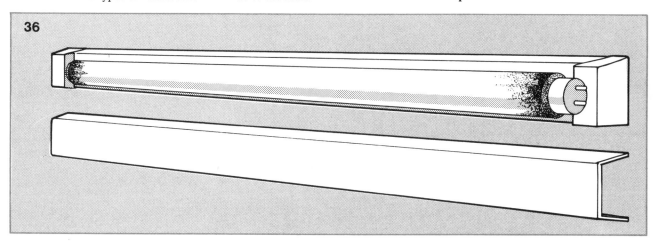

36

Caring for Heaters

To get the best results from an electric heater, the appliance needs regular maintenance. Basically, there are two ways in which the heating element of a radiant type heater is mounted.

Reflector types, *fig. 37*, have a thin element wound around a rod or tube. This element is fitted in front of a metal reflector which reflects the heat back into the room.

In a fire bar type of heater, the element wire is in the form of a coil set in the grooves of a slab of fire clay, *fig. 38*.

All fires of this type should be fitted with a wire guard in front of the element.

An electric heater should never be connected to a lighting point or to a plug which has only two pins.

Take care always that the flexible lead does not cross in front of the heater.

Reflectors should be cleaned regularly with metal polish, not with the scouring type of polish or powder. The heater should be unplugged from its socket outlet before it is cleaned and must be completely dry before being used again.

Convector-type heaters are prone to gather dust around their elements. Some types can be cleaned by turning them upside down and using a vacuum

Fig. 37   Radiant heater, reflector-type

Fig. 38   Fire bar radiant heater

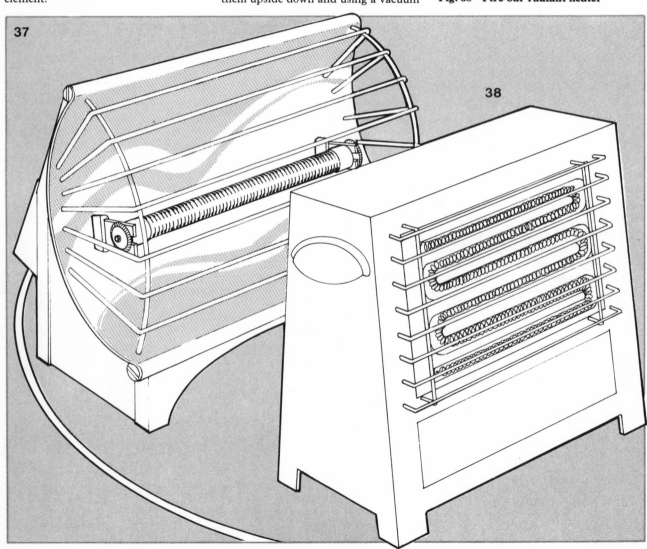

cleaner. But be very careful, if you do this, not to damage the heating element.

SIMPLE REPAIRS

With an ordinary reflector type of heater there is not a great deal which can go wrong. A damaged or broken flex lead is one common fault and that is easily rectified.

A more common fault, perhaps, is the failure of the element. These are usually the pencil rod types, *fig. 39*, and may be fitted to the fire in three ways: they may simply fit into spring clips; they may be held by nuts; or they may have dagger-type end caps which are fitted into spring-loaded contacts.

To replace a pencil rod element, first remove the guard. This can be done easily as a rule by pressure from the fingers. Then undo the screws which hold the shields covering the ends of the element. Release the element from its fixture. The way this is done will depend upon the make of heater.

Put your new element in (and do make sure you have the correct type), screw back the end shields and replace the guard.

Most other types of electric heater have their working parts enclosed and are best left to the expert for repairs.

Fig. 39   There are various types of electric fire elements. Make sure you buy a replacement similar to the one you are discarding

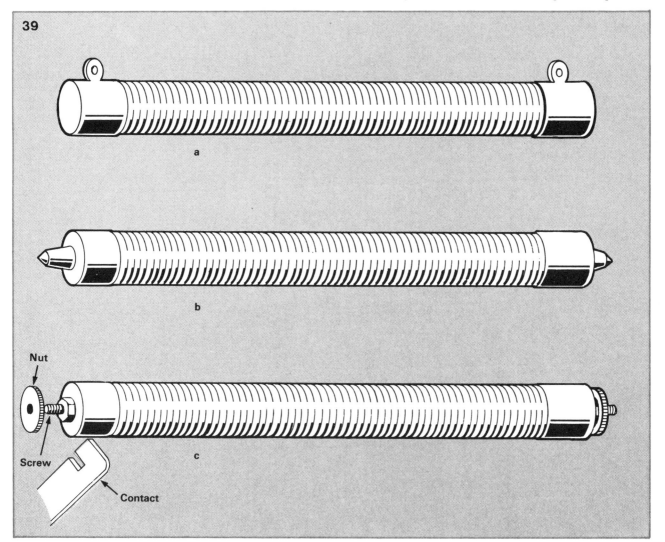

Ring Circuits

Before ring circuits came into being, every power point, as it used to be called, in a domestic wiring system had its own circuit.

In an old installation, therefore, this meant that a house with, say, six power points had six power (heating) circuits originating at the fuseboard!

All these individual circuits were in addition to separate circuits for lighting, cookers and immersion and other types of water heaters. The result – confusion at the fuseboard!

This arrangement also meant that if the occupier of the house decided that extra power points were necessary, separate circuits had to be installed for each.

Some houses are still wired in this way, using round pin socket outlets, and having an old-fashioned fuseboard or a multiplicity of fuse units instead of a modern consumer unit.

My advice to anyone who has a confusion of wires and fuse units such as this is to get the house rewired with modern equipment so that all the circuits originate in one neat consumer unit.

Many householders have installed their own ring circuits; others have rewired their homes completely. But to do either of these things, you need to be familiar with all the necessary cables, accessories and circuits before you begin.

Fig. 40   Confusion at the fuseboard with an old type installation!

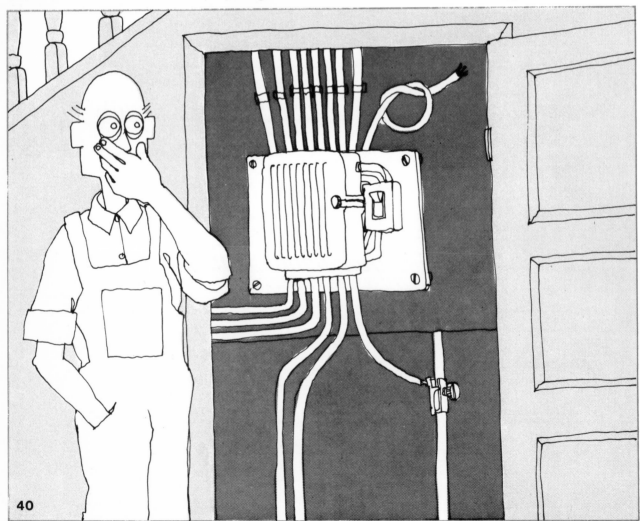

40

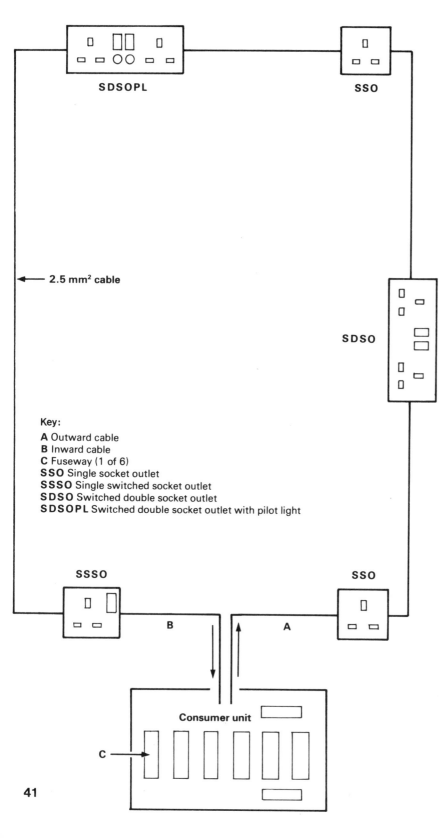

Key:
A Outward cable
B Inward cable
C Fuseway (1 of 6)
SSO Single socket outlet
SSSO Single switched socket outlet
SDSO Switched double socket outlet
SDSOPL Switched double socket outlet with pilot light

Describing such operations in complete detail is beyond the scope of this book; but I hope that the explanation of circuits given here, plus hints on various wiring jobs, will help readers to understand how a ring circuit installation works. Once this understanding is complete, carrying out the installation job itself becomes a practical possibility.

BASIC CIRCUIT

First, let me describe a basic ring circuit, *fig. 41*. A ring circuit is so-called because its cables, in effect if not in design, follow a circular route.

The cable starts its journey from the consumer unit and eventually it returns to it. On its journey throughout the house it is looped into and out of all the 13 amp socket outlets connected to the circuit.

At the consumer unit, the live (red) conductor of the cable is fitted to a fuseway terminal; the neutral (black) conductor to the neutral terminal strip; and the earth conductor (bare wire fitted with a green sleeve) to the earthing terminal strip.

Fig. 41 Basic ring circuit

41

Figure 42 illustrates how our basic ring circuit shown in *fig. 41* is wired up.

After the cable has completed its journey to all the socket outlets en route, its three conductors return to the consumer unit. There the live conductor is fitted to the same fuseway from which it started its journey. The neutral conductor returns to the neutral terminal strip and the earth conductor to the earthing terminal strip.

If you refer back to *fig. 4* page 325 and what I said earlier, you will now see why more than one wire in the consumer unit is connected to a terminal.

Virtually an unlimited number of socket outlets can be connected to a ring circuit though the number which can be used at the same time will be limited. The number shown in *fig. 41* has been limited for the sake of simplicity.

Provided the area of the floor (ground or first) where the ring circuit is to be installed is not greater than 1,080 square feet, only one ring circuit will be needed. If, however, the area is greater than that, an extra ring circuit will be necessary for each additional 1,080 square feet or part of that figure.

CAPACITY

One ring circuit is usually enough to suit requirements for small houses and flats. However, it is better to install two circuits in houses, or large bungalows, because this will double the capacity of the installation.

For example, a single ring circuit has a capacity of about seven kilowatts. This means that no more than three two kilowatt (2,000 watts) electric heaters and one kilowatt (1,000 watts) heater – or their equivalent – can be in use at the same time. If other appliances are switched on while these are in use,

Fig. 42   Connections for basic ring circuit in fig. 41

Fig. 43   Basic ring circuit with two spurs

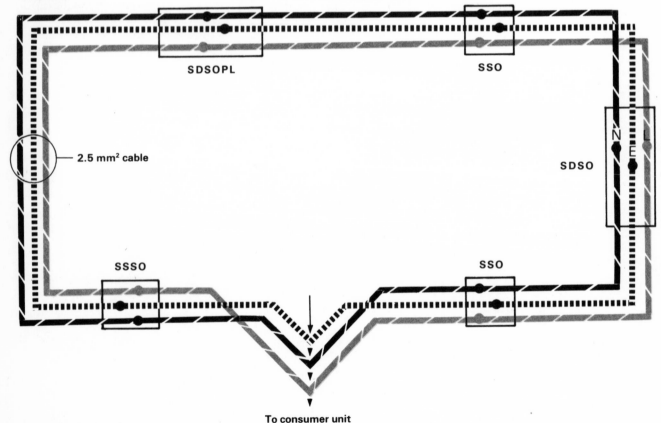

SDSOPL

SSO

2.5 mm² cable

SDSO

N L
E

SSSO

SSO

To consumer unit

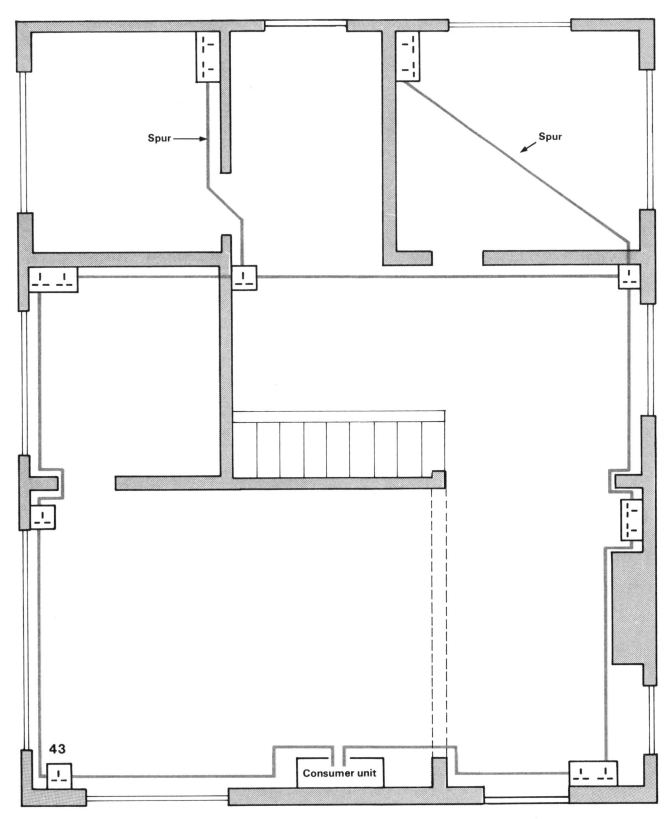

Spur

Spur

43

Consumer unit

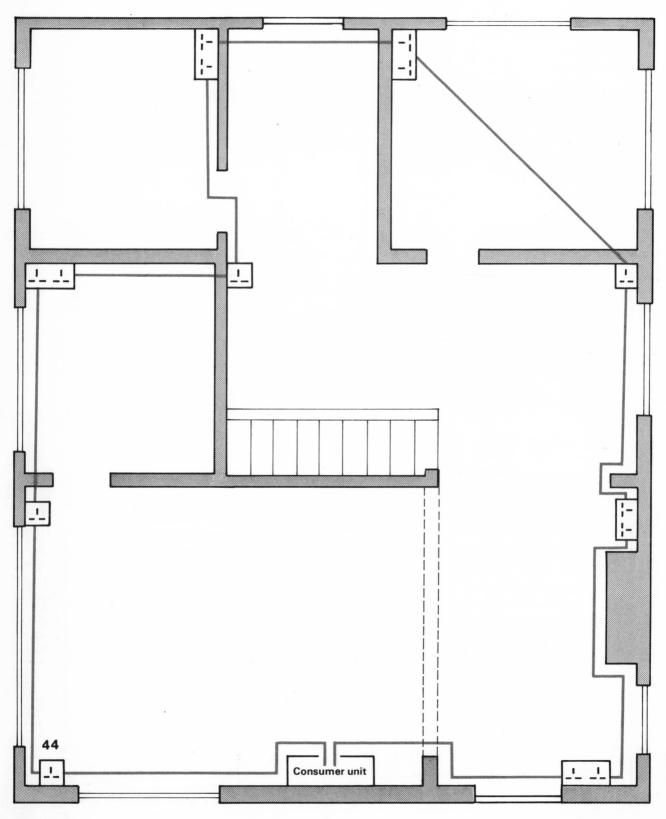

44

Consumer unit

the circuit may become overloaded and the circuit fuse in the consumer unit will blow.

The total capacity of two separate ring circuits, therefore, is roughly 14 kilowatts. This means, of course, that seven two kilowatt heaters (or their equivalent) can be in use at the same time, *provided that this load is evenly distributed between the two circuits.* Remember they are separate circuits, each fitted with its own individual circuit fuse.

Many houses are wired for two ring circuits – normally one for the ground floor and another for the first floor. This method of allocating one circuit to each floor makes it easy to remember which socket outlets are on each circuit, thus reducing the possibility that trouble may be caused by overloading either of them.

SPURS

Most ring circuits have a number of spurs connected to them. A spur is a single cable (a branch, if you like) which feeds socket outlets situated in remote parts of the house; for example, in the hall, in the far corner of a room – or in a garage attached to the house.

The use of spurs can save cable. In *fig. 43* a circuit is illustrated using two spurs. *Figure 44* shows a similar circuit wired without spurs.

Each spur can feed only two single socket outlets *or* one double (twin) socket outlet (*figs 45* and *46*). Not more than half the total number of socket outlets on the ring circuit *and* on the spurs can be fed from spurs. If the total number of socket outlets (including those on spurs) is 28, for example, no more than 14 of these should be fed from spurs.

Fig. 44   Basic ring circuit; no spurs

Fig. 45   Single wall-mounted unswitched socket outlet

Fig. 46   Twin wall mounted switched socket outlet

CONNECTING SPURS

There are various ways in which spurs can be connected to a ring circuit. They can be taken direct from the terminals of a socket outlet; or a joint box can be inserted in the ring cable, *fig. 47*, and the spur taken from that; or a separate cable can be run from the ring circuit fuseway in the consumer unit.

Incidentally, if the joint box method is used, the cable should not be cut but simply stripped of its insulation at a suitable point and its conductors should then be laid in the terminals of the joint box.

Although the main purpose of spurs is to supply socket outlets in more remote positions, they are also used to feed a fixed (not portable) appliance such as a wall fire, for example. In these cases, a fused switched connection unit (formerly called a spur box), *fig. 48*, is used instead of a socket outlet at the end of the spur cable. The fused connection unit is

Fig. 47   Spur connected to 30 amp joint box

Fig. 48   Switched fused connection unit

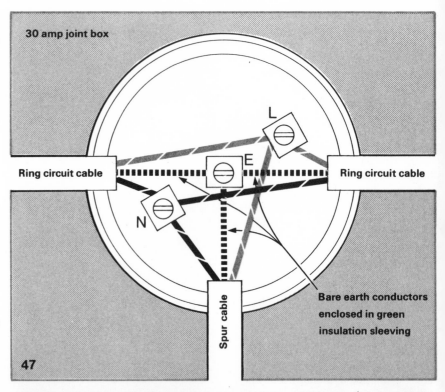

30 amp joint box

Ring circuit cable

Ring circuit cable

Spur cable

Bare earth conductors enclosed in green insulation sleeving

47

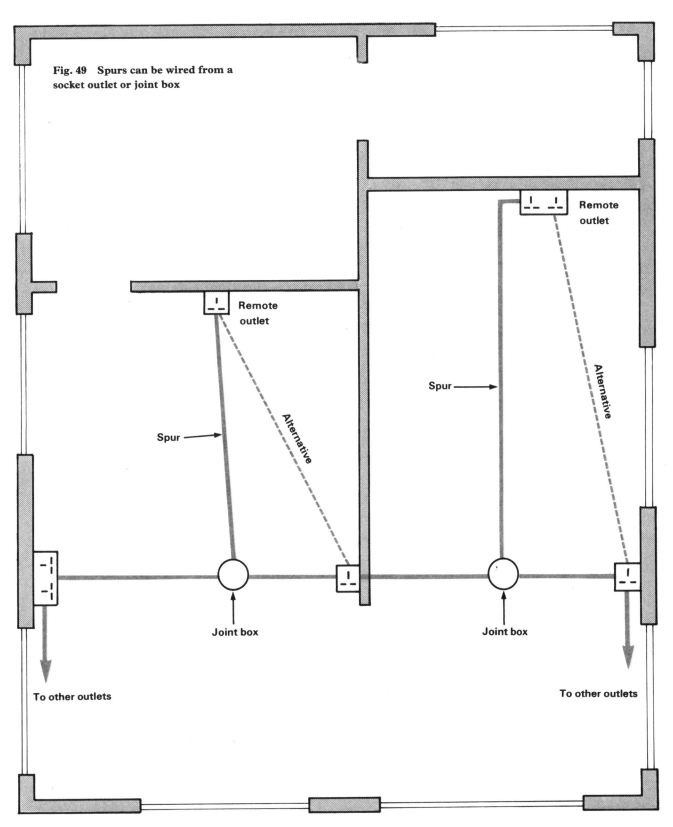

Fig. 49   Spurs can be wired from a socket outlet or joint box

positioned near the fixed appliance and joined to it as shown in *fig. 50*.

It is an advantage if the fused connection unit is a type which has not only a switch to master-control the appliance, but a pilot light also, to indicate whether it is switched on or off.

The fuse in a connection unit is similar to that in a 13 amp fused plug. It can be either a 3 amp or 13 amp type fuse, according to the wattage of the fixed appliance. The fuse is housed in the front of the unit and is held by a small screw. It is essential to fit a fuse of the correct rating.

THE CABLE

The size of the cable now used in a ring circuit is the metric single strand 2·5 mm.^{2}. The most common type of cable now used in domestic installations is pvc sheathed twin and earth. Some houses, however, are wired in TRS (tough rubber sheathed) cable of the same size.

Many existing ring circuits, of course, are wired in the old imperial size cable which had seven strands and was known as 7/029 (see separate chapter on cables). The new metric size cable can be used with the old type when extending a ring circuit.

Fig. 50   Fused connection unit wired from joint box

Fig. 51   Ring circuit with three spurs

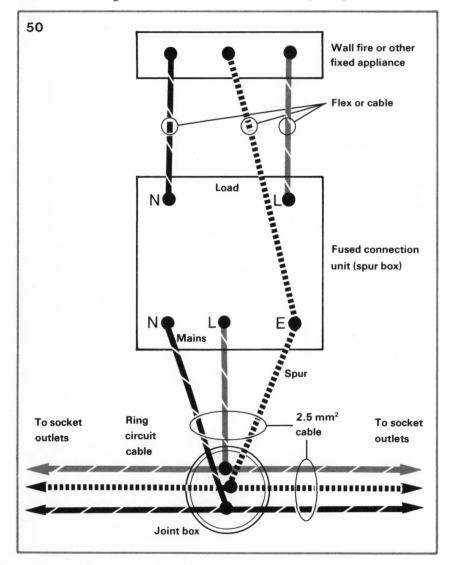

50

Wall fire or other fixed appliance

Flex or cable

N Load L

Fused connection unit (spur box)

N L E

Mains

Spur

To socket outlets

Ring circuit cable

2.5 mm² cable

To socket outlets

Joint box

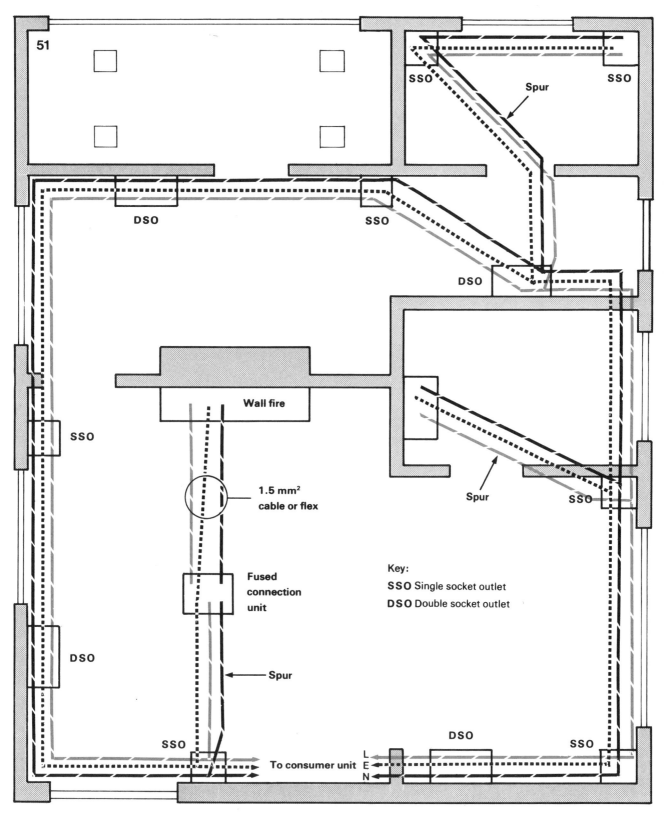

51

SSO

Spur

SSO

DSO

SSO

DSO

Spur

SSO

SSO

Wall fire

1.5 mm² cable or flex

Spur

Fused connection unit

Key:

SSO Single socket outlet

DSO Double socket outlet

DSO

Spur

SSO

To consumer unit

L
E
N

DSO

SSO

SOCKET OUTLETS

Some socket outlets used are not fitted with a switch. The tendency now, however, is to install more of the switched type and fewer of the unswitched. Other types used are not only switched, but have a pilot light also, *fig. 52*.

Double (or twin) socket outlets have the obvious advantage of providing two outlets adjacent to each other. This eliminates the need for plug adaptors, *fig. 53*, to a large extent, when a socket is required for more than one appliance.

For example, a standard lamp can occupy one socket and an electric heater the other; or a TV set can be connected to one outlet and a radiogram to the other.

When a house is being rewired, it is wise to have as many double socket outlets installed as possible. The double types are also available with switches and/or pilot lights if they are required.

Your ring circuit, of course, can consist of all single socket outlets, all twin outlets or a mixture of both. Remember, though, that a spur can feed only two single outlets or one double outlet.

ADDING AN OUTLET

One of the biggest faults in some houses (even modern properties) is the inadequate number of socket outlets provided. Adding an extra outlet to a ring circuit is a job a handyman can do. If, though, you have never attempted any wiring work before, make sure you understand what the operation involves.

There are various ways in which an extra outlet can be added. One method is to run a spur from the nearest, or most convenient, existing outlet to the position required. If you decide to do this, first turn off the main switch at the consumer unit and undo the screws on the front plate of the nearest existing socket outlet. Pull the outlet gently away from its wall box and examine the cables to make sure the

outlet is not itself a spur.

If there are two red, two black and two earth (green or possibly bare) conductors in the box, the outlet is probably not a spur. I say 'probably' because it could be the first single

socket outlet of two on a spur.

The way to check this is to examine also the nearest two socket outlets on either side of it or, better still, trace the route of the cable.

If there is only one set of conductors

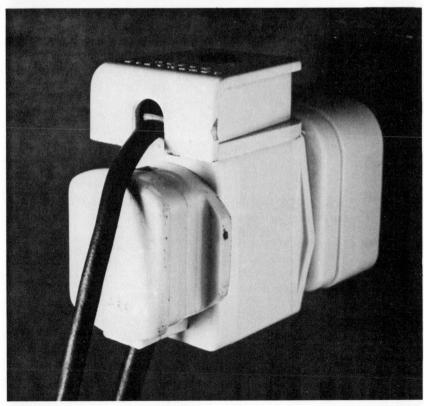

Fig. 52   Twin flush switched socket
outlet with pilot light

Fig. 53   Two-way plug adaptor

Fig. 54   Socket outlet on a spur

Fig. 55   Socket outlet on a ring circuit

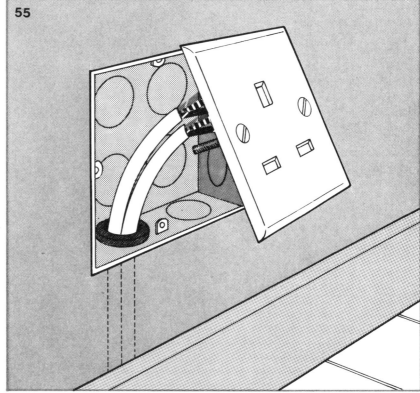

on the existing outlet, then this will be a spur and should not be used for this purpose.

If the outlet is not a spur, you can now replace the examined outlets and restore the current on the circuit until you are ready to start work.

WHAT YOU NEED

Buy a suitable socket outlet and, if the new outlet is to be a flush type, also buy a matching steel box to accommodate it. If your existing outlets are surface mounted types, you will want to match the new with the old. You will therefore need a matching backplate for the outlet, *fig. 56*, but for the purpose of this book we will assume you are using the flush type.

Also you will require a couple of $\frac{3}{4}$ in. grommets (plastic or rubber) to fit in the knockout holes of the wall box, *fig. 58*, to protect the cable; a suitable length of 2·5 mm.^{2} pvc sheathed twin and earth cable; and a short length of green sleeve insulation. This insulation sleeving is to slip over the bare end of the earth conductor in the steel box to prevent the bare wire fouling another terminal if it should at some time work loose.

As it will be necessary to channel out a groove for the cable on the plastered wall from the old outlet to the new, the best time to do this job is before redecorating. Alternatively, it may be possible to run the new cable under the floorboards or behind the skirting board, *fig. 60*. Much will, of course, depend on circumstances. If you plan to redecorate in the near future, the cable can be fixed temporarily on the surface of the wall.

FIXING THE WALL BOX

Mark out the position of the new socket outlet by holding the steel box to the wall and make a pencil mark around it. Score the lines with a sharp handyman's knife to break the plaster surface. Then with an old but sharp chisel, tap out the plaster back to the brickwork. Avoid damaging the

58

Fig. 56   Backplate for single socket outlet for surface mounting

Fig. 57   Wall box for single socket outlet

Fig. 58   Grommets for a knock-out box

Fig. 59   Step-by-step stages for the installation of a recessed socket outlet

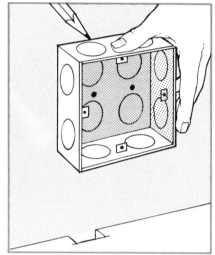

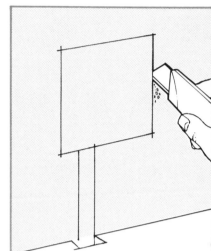

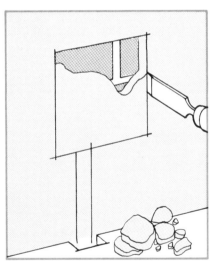

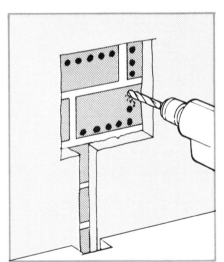

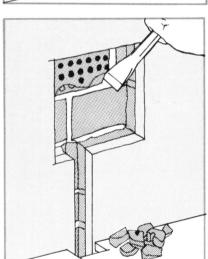

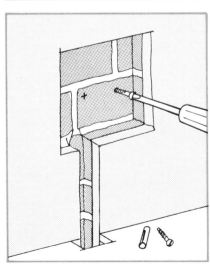

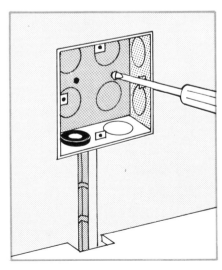

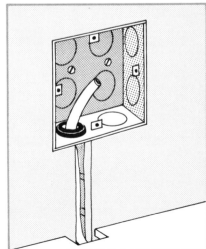

surrounding plaster as much as possible.

Another method is to drill a series of small holes within the marked off area, to produce a honeycomb effect, and remove surplus plaster with the chisel.

You will require a hole about 1¾ in. deep, so a certain amount of brickwork will also need to be removed. It helps to drill a series of holes with a masonry drill first and remove the surplus brickwork with a cold chisel. Make sure the hole is deep enough by trying the box in it at intervals.

GET IT LEVEL

When the box fits snugly, hold it firmly in place, make certain it is level,

and make a mark on the wall for the fixing screws at the back of the box using a sharp tool through the fixing holes of the box. Drill and plug the holes for the screws and drive them partly in. Check again that the box is level and then withdraw the screws.

The box will have a number of knock-out holes, some of which may be marked M (for metric size). Remove a suitably positioned knockout using an old nail punch and hammer, or just the hammer. The knockout can be finally pushed out, *fig. 61.*

Insert a grommet in the hole knocked out and thread about 5 in. of cable (no more) into the box, *fig. 62.*

Fig. 60 Adding an outlet; alternative cable routes

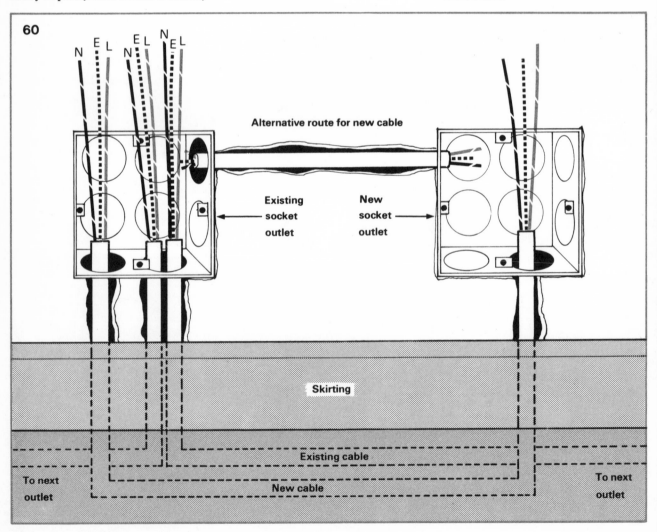

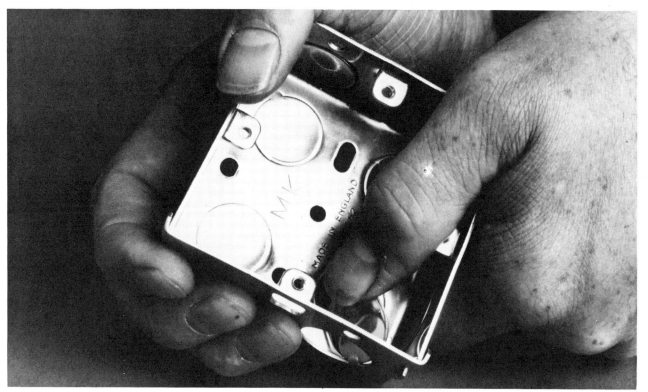

Fig. 61   Pushing out a knockout

Fig. 62   Ring circuit cables ready to connect to an outlet

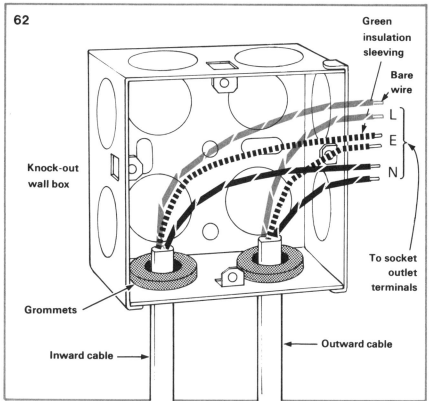

Green
insulation
sleeving

Bare
wire

L

E

N

Knock-out
wall box

To socket
outlet
terminals

Grommets

Inward cable

Outward cable

CABLE CHANNEL

If the new cable is to be buried under the plaster, mark out its route by drawing two parallel lines the width of the cable apart. Score the lines with a sharp knife to break the plaster.

The plaster can then be removed in the same way as for the outlet's wall box, starting from the new outlet position.

Another way to do this is to drill a series of holes along the route and chase out the plaster with a simple little tool called a Cintride router, *fig. 63*. This can be fitted into an electric drill run at a slow speed.

Unless the plaster is very thin, it should not be necessary to remove any brickwork, but if it is, this can be done by drilling several holes with a masonry drill and removing the surplus brick with a cold chisel. Make sure that the channel is deep enough all along its route, for nothing looks worse than a cable bulging even slightly from a wall.

Stop well short of the existing socket outlet, *turn off the current*, and then complete the channel.

Turning off the current is a safety precaution which should be taken from the outset if you are not sure where existing cables are situated.

Fig. 63 A Cintride router for chasing out wall plaster

Fig. 64 Ring circuit cables rising behind skirting

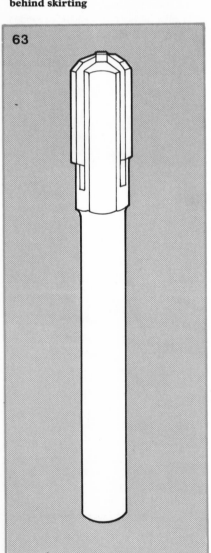

63

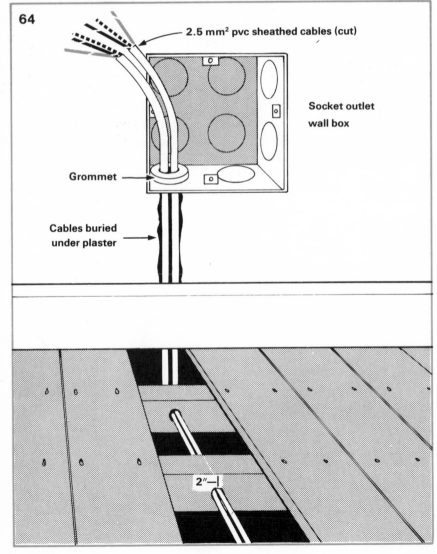

64

2.5 mm² pvc sheathed cables (cut)

Socket outlet wall box

Grommet

Cables buried under plaster

2"—|

65

Fig. 65   Earthing terminal

EXISTING CABLES

Now release the fixing screws of the existing socket outlet, pull it gently from its box and unscrew the terminals to free the conductors.

You will probably find that the cable comes up from below into the steel box, *fig. 64*. As I said earlier, there should be two black, two red and two green conductors, twisted together in pairs, in the box. These are the neutral (black); live (red); and earth (green). Leave these in their twisted state. They will be the old imperial size, seven strand conductors. If, however, yours is a modern installation, you will find the conductors are single strand (metric size).

Your new cable will, of course, also be single strand and the conductors will be difficult to twist around old seven-strand wires. Don't try it! Let the end of each new conductor enter the terminal *beside* the twisted wires, but do make sure that the terminal screw bites firmly on to all the conductor ends when you wire up.

The next step is to remove the existing wall box to knock a hole in it (a knockout) for the extra cable. (It is sometimes possible to remove a knockout from a box while it is still in position in the wall, but it is not very easy. Also, it usually involves damaging the surrounding plaster).

The old box should be fixed with screws at the back, but it may be simply cemented in the wall.

You will probably have to chip away a fair bit of plaster to get the old box out and it may become distorted in the process. Have a spare one handy in case you need it.

Fit a grommet in the knockout hole.

If the house is wired in metal conduit, there may not be an earth wire. Metal conduit can act as the earthing conductor. However, your new socket outlet must be earthed. So fit an earthing terminal, *fig. 65*, to your old wall box if one is not already fitted.

At this stage your new cable can be finally cut to size. Fit it into the channel but do not plaster over it yet.

The cable may have to be temporarily wedged in place with thin pieces of wood. This size of cable is tough stuff with a mind of its own and will probably jump out of the channel if not wedged!

Thread about 5 in. of cable into a knocked out hole in the existing box and remove about 4 in. of outer sheath. You may find it easier to do this before finally threading the cable into the box.

JOINING UP

Strip about 1 in. of insulation material from the red and black conductors. The earth conductor will be bare. Slip a short length of green insulation sleeving over it, leaving about 1 in. of its end bare.

Arrange your new conductors neatly with the old ones (black next to black; red with red; green with green) so that they can conveniently enter the terminals.

Take the two (twisted) old red wires and single (new) red wire to the terminal marked L for live. Connect the black wires to terminal N for neutral; and the greens to terminal E for earth. Tighten the terminals; make sure the ends of the conductors are firmly secured by the terminal screws. Then replace the socket outlet.

If your house is wired in conduit, run a short length of single core bare wire covered with green sleeving from the earth terminal you fitted on the old wall box to the earth terminal on the new socket outlet. This will ensure good earth continuity to the new outlet.

The new socket outlet is wired up in the same way except, of course, that there is only one set of conductors.

When both socket outlets are wired up and the cable temporarily in place, turn the current on and try both outlets with an appliance you know is working.

If all is well, the channel can then be made good with a plaster filler, but to be on the safe side, turn the current off again before doing so. If the cable is reluctant to stay in position in its channel, try fixing it with a few spots of contact adhesive.

USING A JOINT BOX

Another method of increasing the number of socket outlets is to break into the wiring of the ring circuit at a suitable point and add a spur cable. Again, make sure you do not break into an existing spur for this purpose.

To add the spur cable, you will need a 30 amp joint box, *fig. 66*, which can be fitted on a short length of timber fixed between joists, or to other suitable timber fixture within reach of the cable.

The terminal box has three terminals – for live, neutral and earth conductors – and knockouts to permit cable entry.

The middle terminal is used for the earth conductors. It does not matter which of the other terminals is used for live or neutral so long as you are consistent!

Remove suitable knockouts for the ring circuit conductors – one for their entry; another for their exit. Remove one other knockout for the spur cable. Screw the box in position.

Prepare one end of your new cable as for entry into a socket outlet. Don't cut the ring circuit cable if you can avoid doing so. Simply strip the sheath and the insulation at a suitable point so that there is enough bare wire of

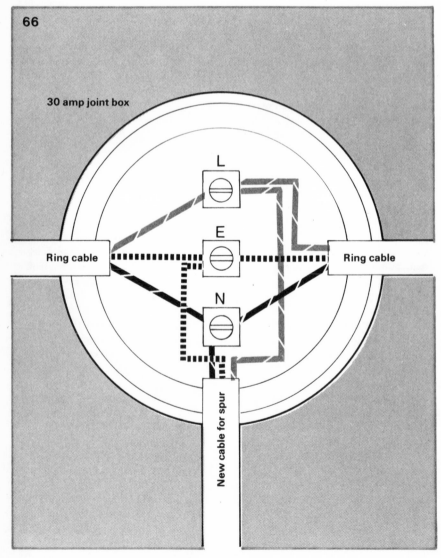

66

30 amp joint box

L

E

N

Ring cable

Ring cable

New cable for spur

Fig. 66   Joint box used to supply a ring circuit spur

each conductor to lay in the terminals of the joint box under the terminal screws.

Tighten the terminal screws and replace the joint box cover.

The other end of the new cable is then taken to the new socket outlet which is fixed as already described.

EXTENDING THE RING
If you want to add more than one socket outlet to a ring circuit, this can be done by opening up the ring at a suitable point and extending it.

This is subject to my earlier remarks regarding the size of the floor area;

i.e., you need more than one ring circuit if that area is greater than 1,080 sq. ft.

To add the outlets, all you do is disconnect either the inward or the outward cable at a socket outlet. Take this cable to the first of the new socket outlets A, via a joint box if too short.

The first outlet, in turn, is linked to the next outlet and so on likewise until the last of the new socket outlets is reached. This outlet is then linked to the original socket outlet where the ring was broken into. Thus, the continuity of the ring is maintained. *Figure 67* is simply an example.

Fig. 67 Three outlets added to a ring circuit

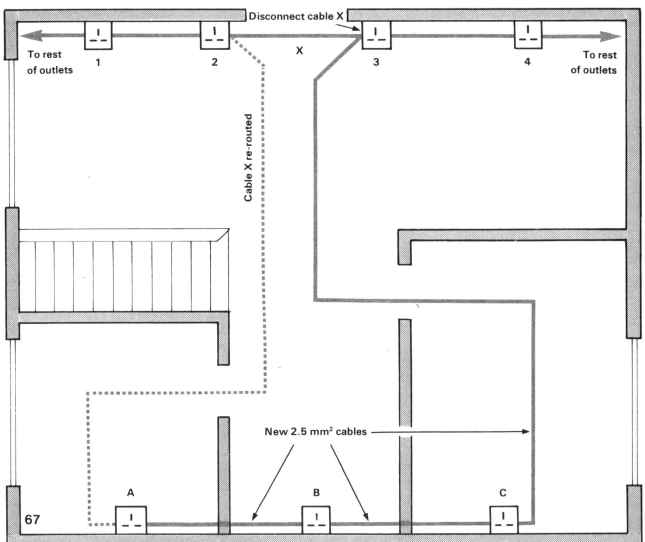

SOLID FLOORS

Many modern houses have solid ground floors which can present problems when running cables after the house is built. Obviously, they cannot be buried under a concrete floor at a later stage.

One way out of the difficulty is to drop the ends of the cables down through the ceiling to the floor below immediately above the position planned for the new socket outlet. The cables can then either be buried under the wall plaster as described earlier, or can be run on the surface of the wall.

This method will, of course, take a lot of cable as the cables will, in all probability, first have to be taken from the consumer unit on the ground floor, up to the first floor (under the floorboards) and down again.

A possible alternative is to take out the skirting board and replace it with special trunking designed to house cables. This is available in metal and plastic.

The solid floor problem can be overcome if you want to add only one or two outlets by using the method of burying the cables in the wall plaster and looping out of existing outlets as described.

FIXING WALL BOXES

Instead of fixing a metal type flush wall box to house an outlet or other accessory, you may be tempted to think of an easier way of doing the job than cutting out a hole in the plaster and brickwork to accommodate it.

In this case, the best plan is to use a surface-type box with its appropriate surface type accessories. Whatever you decide to do, don't be tempted to fix a wall box in the skirting board. This is against the regulations and can be very dangerous.

Equally, if not more, dangerous is the practice of fitting a socket outlet to a skirting or to a wall without using any sort of box. This should never be done.

The danger is that, although the brickwork may be non-combustible, there is always the possibility of condensation running down the wall or damp creeping up it and finding its way to the terminals of the outlet.

The regulations lay down that cores of sheathed cable from which the sheath has been removed should be enclosed in non-combustible material.

The boxes sold to accommodate either flush or surface type accessories comply with these requirements.

Lighting Circuits

A lighting wiring system is usually regarded as complicated. In fact, basically, this is not so; it is the number of wires which are gathered together at each point which make it seem so.

Like a ring circuit, a lighting circuit starts from the consumer unit. It runs to all the lighting points on that circuit and finishes at the last one. Unlike the ring circuit cable, the lighting cable does *not* return to the consumer unit, *fig. 69*.

Each cable contains three conductors – live, neutral and earth. Old installations have no earth wire, but this is now compulsory in new wiring. The regulation, however, is not retrospective; it applies only to new wiring.

The cable used in a lighting circuit can be either $1.0\,\text{mm}^2$ or $1.5\,\text{mm}^2$ flat twin core and earth pvc sheathed.

TWO SYSTEMS

There are two basic ways of wiring a domestic lighting circuit – the looping in system or the joint box system. There are some installations which use a bit of each.

Generally speaking, the looping in method is the more popular. The other method is for surface wiring where the looping system is not suitable. Wall lights are one example. They have no facilities for looping in and, of course, no ceiling roses.

LOOPING IN

With the looping in method the cable runs from the consumer unit to each ceiling rose in turn. The cable conductors loop into and out of each rose terminal until the last rose is reached. This is where the cable terminates.

Fig. 68 Live and neutral connections at a rose

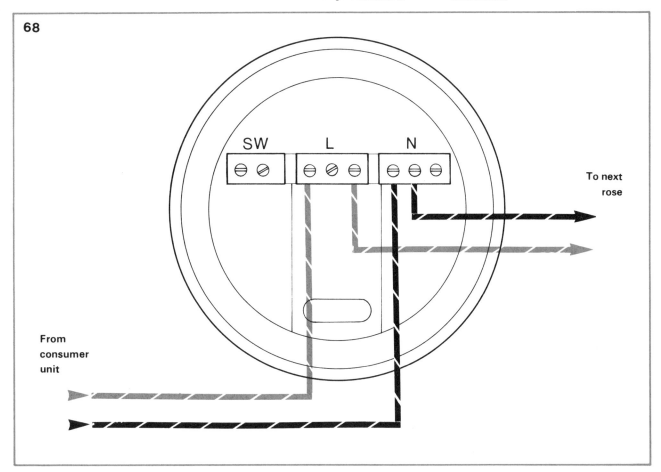

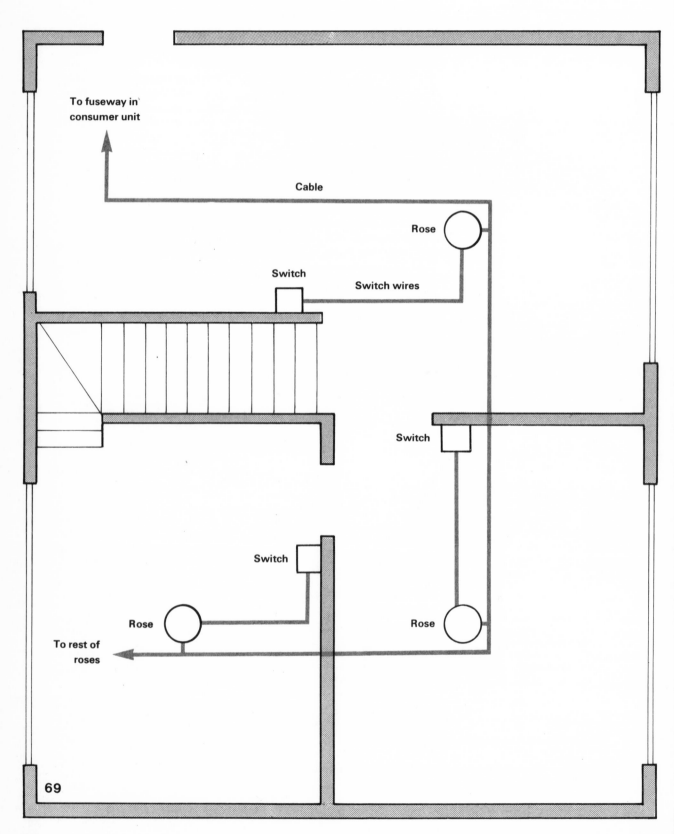

To fuseway in
consumer unit

Cable

Rose

Switch

Switch wires

Switch

Switch

Rose

Rose

To rest of
roses

69

Fig. 69 Basic lighting circuit

(It is partly the looping in and out of these conductors which gives the impression of confusion at a ceiling rose.)

Also, a length of cable runs from each rose down to the switch on the wall. *Figure 68* illustrates the basic principle. Switch and earth wires have been omitted to make it clearer. *Figure 70* shows the basic wiring details at a ceiling rose.

In most existing installations (apart from brand new property) the wiring will appear as shown – i.e., no earth

Fig. 70 Basic wiring of rose (earth wire omitted)

wire. The earth connections in *fig. 70* have been omitted purely for clarity's sake.

Although the wire from the SW (switch wire) terminal on the rose to the switch is black it is, in fact, the switch return wire and is therefore on the *live* side of the circuit. It is common practice to use the black conductor of a length of twin pvc cable for this purpose.

Therefore, it is never safe to assume that a black wire in a lighting circuit is not live!

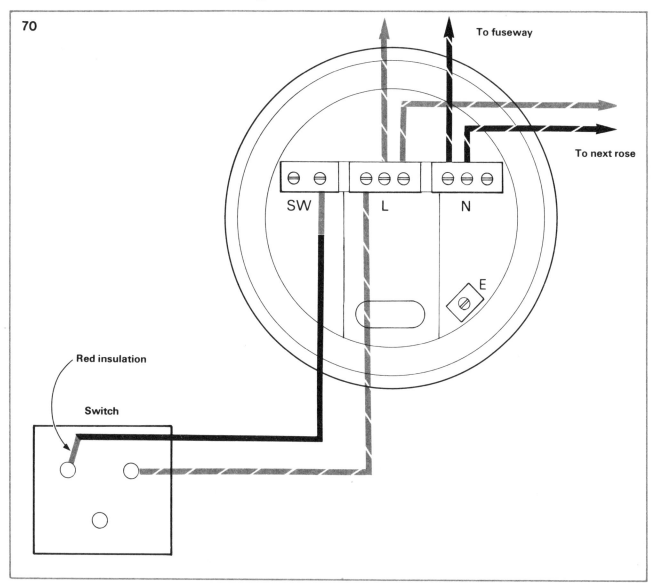

Ideally, the end of the black switch wire should be enclosed in a short length of insulation sleeving so as to identify it as the switch wire. This, unfortunately, is not always done as it should be.

Figure 71 shows the full wiring at a loop-in ceiling rose and illustrates the remarks made about the switch return wire.

Fig. 71 Elaboration of fig. 70

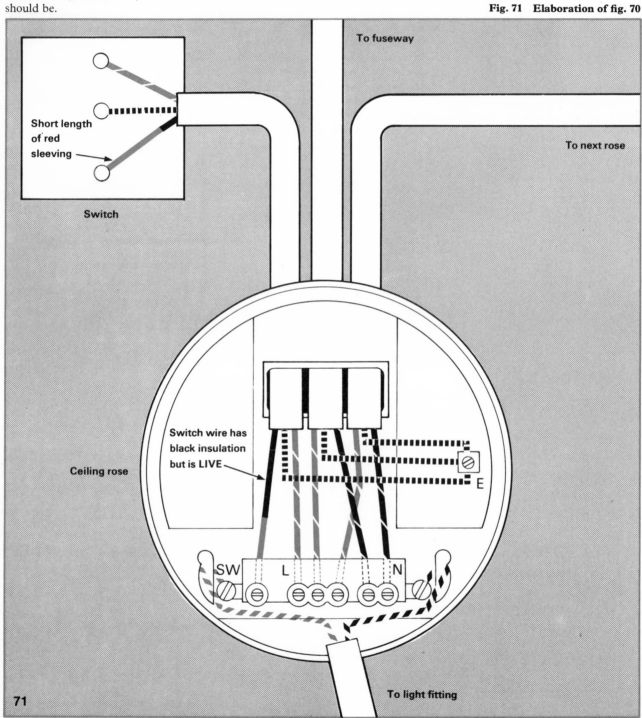

Short length
of red
sleeving

Switch

To fuseway

To next rose

Switch wire has
black insulation
but is LIVE

E

Ceiling rose

SW   L   N

71

To light fitting

JOINT BOX METHOD

This method resembles the looping in system in some respects, but the feed cables from the fuseway in the consumer unit are looped in and out of joint boxes instead of ceiling roses, *fig. 72.*

If your house is wired in the joint box system, you will find a number of small plastic joint boxes above the

Fig. 72 Joint box connections in a lighting circuit

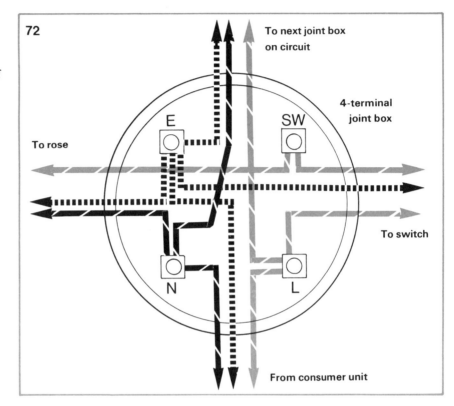

Fig. 73 Joint box for lighting circuits

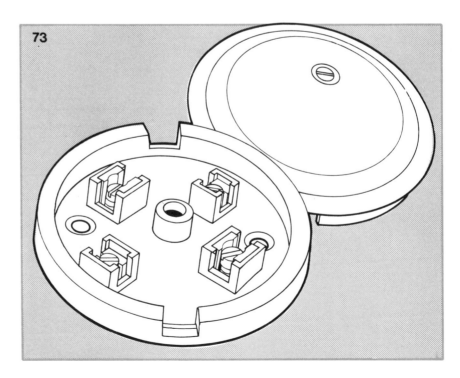

spots where the cables run down the wall under the plaster to the switches: that is, between joists in the roof space and under the floorboards.

The joint boxes normally have four terminals, *fig. 73*. In an old wiring system, where there is no earth wire, the box may supply two lights, the fourth terminal sometimes being utilised for the switch wire of another light situated nearby.

Some old-type ceiling roses used with the joint box method have only two terminals. This is because no looping into a rose is necessary, each light having its own joint box.

ADDING A LIGHT

Before contemplating the addition of a lighting point to a circuit, it is essential to examine the wiring system thoroughly. If it is a jumble of wires, don't attempt any alterations unless you are absolutely sure what you are doing.

Electrical shops are only too familiar with customers who start a rewiring job but are unable to finish it because they 'don't know where the wires go.' And how can the poor shopkeeper help when he cannot possibly guess which wiring system has been used?

A quick way to establish which method of wiring has been used is to examine a ceiling rose. Turn off the current at the main switch in the consumer unit and unscrew the rose cover.

If the rose has only two terminals, yours is the joint box method and you can confirm this by locating the various joint boxes as described. Three terminals or more indicate that the looping in system has been used.

CONNECTIONS

To add a lighting point to the looping-in system, a twin-core and earth pvc sheathed cable should be run from the nearest convenient existing ceiling rose to the new point, *fig. 74*.

Connect the red conductor to the live (L) terminal and the black conductor to the neutral (N) terminal of the existing rose. If this rose has only three terminals, you will have to terminate the earth conductor in the backplate or pattress and wrap insulating tape around its end to prevent it fouling a terminal. Label it Earth Wire.

For the new rose, buy a loop-in type with an earthing terminal. Connect the other end of the earth conductor to the terminal, but slip a short length of green insulating sleeving over its exposed portion. Then take the red and black conductors to the L and N terminals respectively.

Fig. 74   Wiring up a new rose

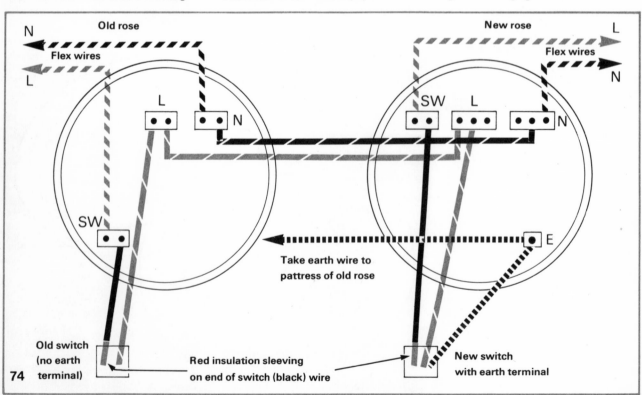

Fig. 75 Modern flush switch

Fig. 76 Plaster depth wall box

SWITCH CONNECTIONS

A length of similar cable is needed to run from the new rose to its switch. The red conductor goes to the L terminal of the rose and the black conductor (the switch wire) to the unoccupied terminal (SW).

The other ends of these conductors go to the switch. Slip a short length of red sleeving insulation over the end of the black wire in the switch box to identify it as the switch wire, or simply label it Switch Wire.

FITTING THE FLEX

That completes the wiring of the cables. Now you need to fit the flex wires. The best type of flex to buy for this purpose is heat resisting circular flex, size 0·75 mm.²

Connect the flex connectors to the rose terminals N and SW, *fig. 71*. Choose a heat resisting type of lampholder which is suitable for the circular flex.

The type of switch used will obviously be chosen so as not to clash with the appearance of the others on the circuit. If there is a choice, I suggest a modern flush type, *fig. 75*, which is mounted on a metal wall box you sink into the plaster.

These boxes are about ⅝ in. deep and most of them now have an earthing terminal, *fig. 76*. Some also have adjustable lugs so that a switch can be aligned if the box is mounted slightly out of square.

The hole for the switch box can be made as described for a socket outlet on page 368, but to a shallower depth, of course. The cable to the switch goes through a grommet in a knockout in the metal box. Make sure about 1 in. of the cable's outer sheath enters the wall box.

FITTING THE ROSE

To fit a modern loop-in type of rose, take off the cover and make a hole for the cable by removing a plastic knockout from the base of the rose.

Being fully enclosed, modern roses do not need to be mounted on a pattress. They can be screwed direct to the ceiling joists or to a length of timber firmly fixed between the joists. Older type roses which have no backs must be mounted on a pattress, *fig. 77.*

JOINT BOX METHOD

To add a light to a joint box system is simple. Fix your new joint box in a suitable position. From an adjacent existing box run a suitable length of 1.0mm.² pvc two core and earth pvc sheathed cable to the new box. Connect the live and neutral conductors to their appropriate terminals in each box.

If there is no earth wire used in the existing box, the end of the earthing conductor of your new cable can simply be left in the box, but enclose its exposed portion in the box in insulating tape so that it does not foul the terminals.

In your new box, the other end of the earth conductor should be taken to the earth terminal. Add a length of green insulation sleeving to its bare end for identification purposes.

TWO CIRCUITS

It is desirable that a house should have at least two lighting circuits. No one circuit should supply more than eight (but preferably six) lighting points.

Although the maximum load of a 5 amp lighting circuit is 1,200 watts (equal to twelve 100 watt lamps), some allowance has to be made for fluorescent lamps as for this purpose

they are rated at double their quoted rating.

Allowance should also be made for wall lights fitted with two or three lamps, and for any extra lights which may be added to the circuit later on.

When assessing lighting points, the loading of each lamp is taken as 100 watts (even if it is rated below this figure). Each lamp over 100 watts, however, is taken at its actual rating.

For example, if you have only one circuit for lighting, and it supplies four 100 watt, four 60 watt (say for two wall lights), and two 150 watt lamps, the total load is reckoned at 1,100 watts (the 60 watt lamps counting as 100 each).

A system such as this would require eight lighting points, the maximum for a lighting circuit. By having all these points on one circuit, the house would be in darkness if the lighting circuit fuse blew.

USING THE RING CIRCUIT

One answer to this problem, if a second lighting circuit is not possible, is to make use of the ring circuit, not only for operating table and standard lamps, but for the wall lights also.

If, however, two lighting circuits are feasible, it is a good idea to have one for the ground floor and one for the first floor. A third circuit could be used to supply lights for the garage, shed or greenhouse.

DANGER SPOT

A potentially dangerous situation can arise where the landing and hall lights run off the same circuit. When the circuit fuse blows, this area can suddenly be plunged into total darkness. When these lights are controlled by two-way switches (one on the landing, the other in the hall), they run off the same circuit.

One solution to this problem is to fit a separate light on the landing run from a different lighting circuit, or have a table lamp in the hall operating off the ring circuit.

Either method is enough to relieve

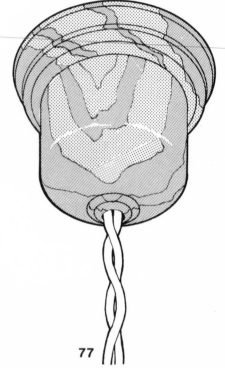

77

Fig. 77   Ceiling rose and pattress

Fig. 78   Block connectors

total darkness and perhaps prevent a nasty accident.

WALL LIGHTS
The normal method for wiring wall lights is to use the lighting circuit and there are various ways in which this can be done. With a modern circuit properly wired, there should be few problems. Some older houses, however, are wired haphazardly. Additions have been made over the years and the result is often a confused mass of wires.

In my view, a beginner with electrics would be unwise to attempt wiring wall lights from a circuit such as this. No amount of guidance on paper will be of value where an existing circuit defies all the known rules! On-the-spot expert guidance is needed in cases like this.

Personally, if I wanted to fix one or two wall lights in a room, I would do the job just prior to redecorating and I would make use of the ring circuit to do so. For a greater number of lights, however, the lighting circuit should be used.

ALTERNATIVE
Although ring circuits are not intended to supply an entire lighting circuit, they can, within reason, be used to supply the odd wall light or two, or an ordinary light in a remote spot.

One good reason for selecting the ring circuit method for supplying wall lights is that it provides an alternative source of light when a circuit fuse blows on a lighting circuit. Apart from that, the method is fairly straight-forward and does not involve a lot of wiring under floorboards or in a perhaps inaccessible loft space.

First, though, a few words in general about wall lights. Many of these are supplied complete with flex, to which is attached a small block connector, *fig. 78*. This enables the light fitting to be connected to the cable conductors.

Most wall light fittings have a built-in switch, but wall lights should be operated also from a master switch. If they are not, the fitting and its flex will always be live.

Fig. 79   Wall lights operated from a master switch

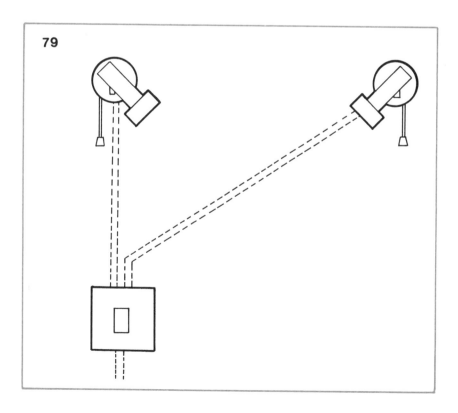

79

FIXING METHODS

There are wide variations in the design of wall lights, particularly in the way in which they are fixed to the wall. In most cases a metal knockout box (sunk into the wall) is needed to accommodate the joint between the circuit cable and the flex of the fitting.

Other types require a conduit knockout box, *fig. 80*; spotlights are one example. But for many types of fitting a narrow architrave metal box, *fig. 81*, is now used.

There are some fittings which do not need a box, such as the Slidona types made by Maclamp. These are fitted with a backplate which is in two parts, *fig. 80*.

The part which contains the cable terminals is fixed to the wall. The other part (attached to the fitting) simply slides into the front part after the connections have been made.

When buying wall lights, study the method of fixing and choose the best one for the situation you have in mind.

TWO METHODS

There are two ways in which the ring circuit can be used to supply wall lights. The simplest is the 13 amp plug and sheathed flexible cord method,

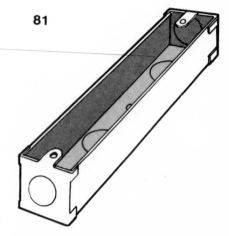

81

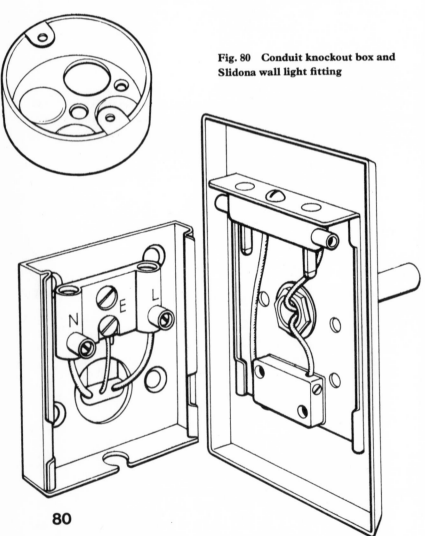

Fig. 80 Conduit knockout box and Slidona wall light fitting

80

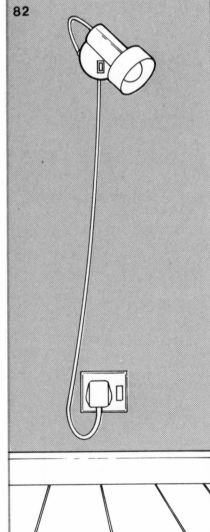

82

Fig. 81   Architrave wall box

Fig. 82   Wall light supplied by ring circuit plug

Fig. 83   Fixed wiring for wall lights

fig. 82. This can be used for such fittings as spotlights, bedhead lights and pin-up lights such as those made by Conelight.

The sheathed flexible cord is fixed to the wall surface. One end of it goes to the 13 amp plug; the other runs direct into the lampholder of the fitting.

The plug should contain a 3 amp fuse and the socket outlet should be a switched type. This can then act as a master switch for the wall light.

The disadvantages of this method, of course, are that only one wall light can be operated from each plug and

socket outlet, and surface wiring (the flexible cord) will be visible. It should not be buried under plaster.

FIXED WIRING METHOD

The other method is shown in *fig. 83.* This is called the fixed wiring method. It involves breaking into the ring circuit at a suitable point. One of the easiest places to do this is at the terminals of a socket outlet which is not a spur already supplying socket outlets. See Adding an Outlet on page 366 onwards.

From the socket outlet terminals, run a short length of 2·5 mm.² twin and

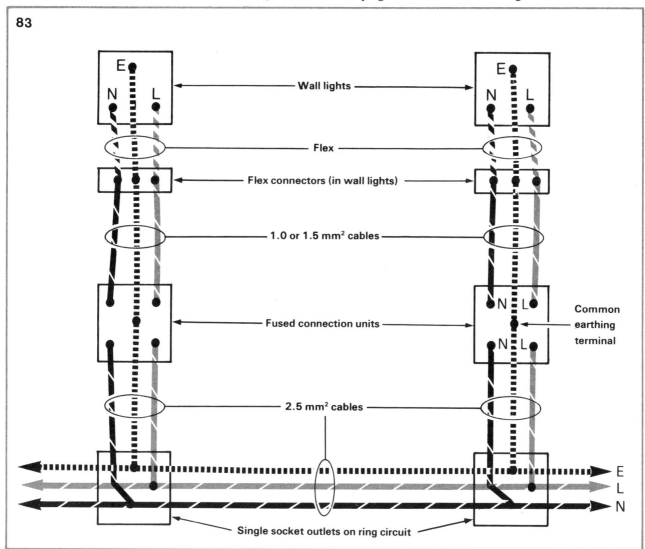

83

Wall lights

Flex

Flex connectors (in wall lights)

1.0 or 1.5 mm² cables

Fused connection units

Common earthing terminal

2.5 mm² cables

E
L
N

Single socket outlets on ring circuit

earth pvc sheathed cable to a switched fuse connection unit. This used to be called a fused spur unit or fused spur box.

From this unit run a length of similar cable, but size 1·0 mm.² or 1·5 mm.², to the wall light. It does not matter which of these two size cables you choose. The fused connection unit's switch can be used as the master switch for the lights and as their local switch if they have no built-in switches.

Terminal connections for these units may vary slightly according to make. Generally speaking, there is one common earth terminal to which the circuit earth continuity conductor is connected. The earth continuity conductor of the 1·0 mm.² or 1·5 mm.² cable is also connected to this terminal.

One set of live (L) and neutral (N) terminals on the unit is sometimes marked MAINS. To these go the live and neutral conductors of the cable

from the socket outlet on the ring circuit.

The other set of L and N terminals is sometimes marked LOAD. To these terminals go the live and neutral conductors of the 1·0 mm.² or 1·5 mm.² cable to the wall light fitting.

Some connection units are fitted with a hole in the front plate. This is the outlet for the flex from a fixed appliance. You don't need this type for wall lights as the flex from the light will be housed in the wall box and connected to the cable there.

The design you need is shown in *fig. 85*.

The fused connection unit is fixed to a metal knockout box in the same way as described for a socket outlet earlier on.

Do not attempt to wire up wall lights *direct* from the terminals of a socket outlet (or from elsewhere on the ring circuit) without using a fused

Fig. 84 Two wall lights supplied from ring circuits

Fig. 85 Switched fused connection unit with pilot light

Fig. 86 Fused connection unit wired in a bell circuit

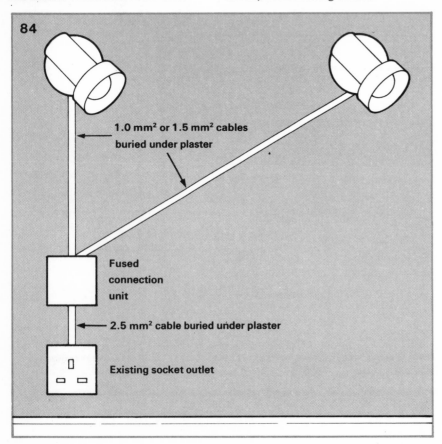

84

1.0 mm² or 1.5 mm² cables buried under plaster

Fused connection unit

2.5 mm² cable buried under plaster

Existing socket outlet

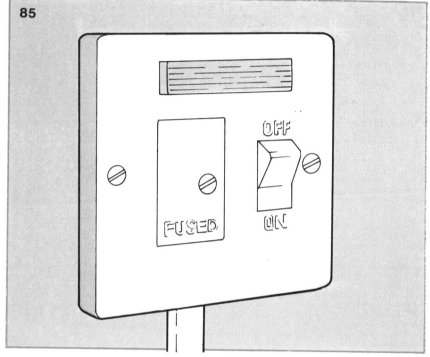

85

connection unit. This unit should be fitted with a 3 amp fuse which protects the wall light circuit.

More than one wall light can be wired from one unit, but if this is done, the master switch on the unit will control all the lights. So unless the lights have their own switches, all the lights will be off or on at the same time. One way to keep wiring to a minimum is shown in *fig. 84.*

BELLS FROM THE MAINS
While on the subject of fused connection units, let me return for a moment to house bells, already dealt with on page 346.

A fused connection unit can also be used if you want to wire up an electric bell from the mains. The transformer is simply connected to the fused connection unit and the unit to the ring circuit as described above and illustrated in *fig. 86.*

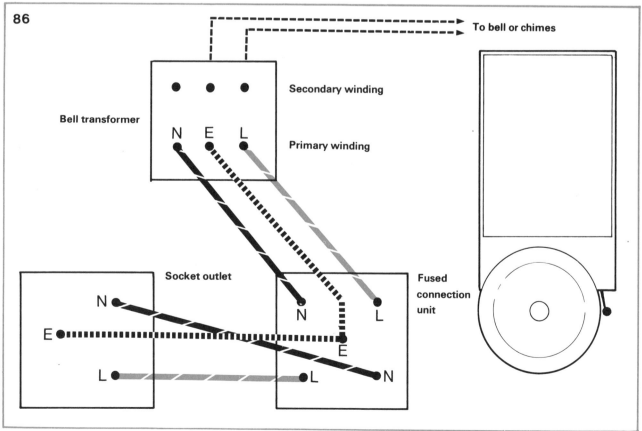

86

Switches

Old-type switches fitted in rooms with a modern decor are an eyesore. Today's switches are neat, attractive and unobtrusive.

If your wiring installation is old but sound, replacing ancient switches with up-to-date flush types is a job well worth doing.

Probably the ugliest arrangement is an old tumbler switch, *fig. 87*, mounted on a block of wood screwed to the wall or perhaps fixed to a wooden box which is sunk flush into the wall plaster.

OBSOLETE

These methods of mounting switches are obsolete. If you want to replace a tumbler switch mounted as described, here is how to do it – after turning off the current, of course.

If the switch wire running from the ceiling is buried in the wall, the new switch can be either a flush or a surface mounted type, *figs. 88* and *89*. But if the switch wires run in a length of conduit fixed on the wall surface, the new switch will have to be a surface mounted type.

The alternative is to hack away the plaster and possibly some of the brickwork so that both the switch wires and the conduit can be buried under the wall surface.

If the conduit is to stay on the wall surface, the switch will have to be mounted on a suitable size plastic pattress box, *fig. 90*. A hole will need to be made in the top of the box to accept the conduit.

After removing the old switch and its wooden mounting block or box, examine the ends of the cable. If the installation is very old, the ends of the conductors may be coated in verdigris. Clean these up or, if there is enough wire to spare, nip off the ends and prepare clean ends for the terminals of the switch.

If the cable is housed in conduit under the wall plaster, fit a plastic or rubber bush on the end of the conduit to protect the sheath of the cable from chafing.

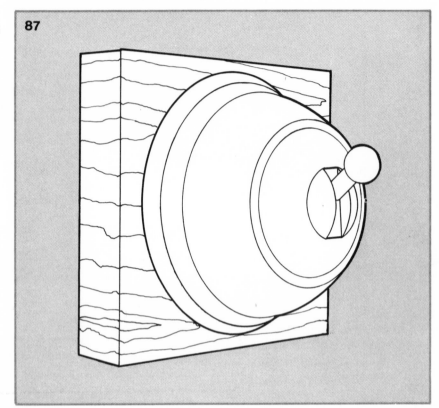

87

88

MOUNTING THE SWITCH

If your new switch is to be flush-mounted, get a plaster-depth steel knockout box which is fitted with an earthing terminal. Cut a hole for the box in the wall and fix as described for a socket outlet on page 369 but to the correct depth.

For surface mounting, the plastic pattress box should be fitted with an earthing terminal. Part of the base of this box is thin plastic, which is knocked out to make a hole for the cable.

Place the box over the old switch position and fix it to the wall with screws into plugs. Make sure it is level. Take care to get the switch the right way up. Most of them are marked TOP on the casing which contains the switch mechanics.

Connect the conductors to their terminals. In an old installation there will be no earth wire at the old switch to connect to the earthing terminal on your new switch box.

Strictly speaking, an earth continuity conductor should be run back from the switch box to the consumer unit or other convenient earthing terminal on the circuit. If this is not possible, the earthing terminal on the new switch pattress can be left empty until the lighting circuit is completely rewired.

TWO-WAY SWITCHES

If you want to incorporate two-way switching in your lighting circuit, for example, in a hall, you will need two-way switches which are fitted with three terminals plus, of course, wall boxes or pattresses fitted with an earthing terminal.

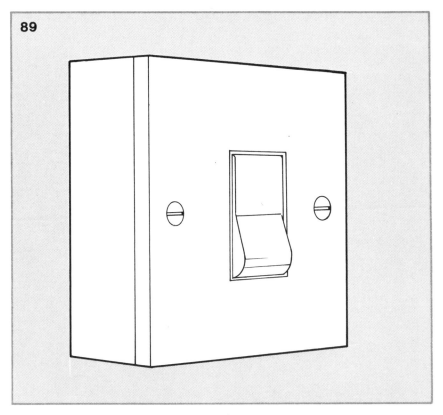

89

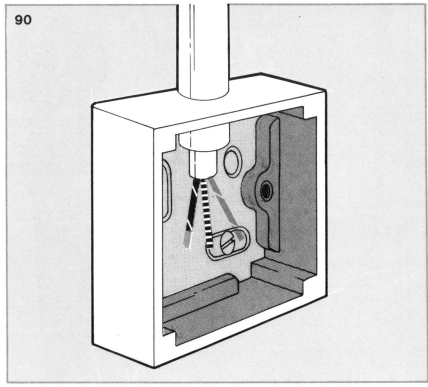

90

Fig. 87   **Tumbler type switch**

Fig. 88   **Modern flush switch**

Fig. 89   **Surface mounted switch**

Fig. 90   **Pattress box for switch**

In a two-way switching system, a light can be switched off or on from two positions. For example, one switch could be fitted just inside the front door and the other at the opposite end of the hall.

STRAPPING WIRES

Both switches are connected by what are known as strapping wires. All the cables used in such an installation should be 1·5 mm.², but if your old switch is wired in the imperial size seven strand cable, this can remain.

The metric size cable can be used with it in any circuit, provided its size is similar.

The new two-way switches will have one terminal marked Common. The other two terminals are usually marked L1 and L2.

The switch wire to the old switch should be taken to the L1 terminal of the new switch. The wire running from the live terminal of the ceiling rose to the old switch should be connected to the L2 terminal on the new switch, *fig. 91*.

If you have an earth wire at the old switch, which is unlikely, this should now be taken to your earthing terminal on the switch wall box or pattress.

All you have to do now is to link the first new switch with the second using three core and earth cable. This is simple, as *fig. 91* shows. L1 is strapped to L1; L2 to L2; and earth to earth. The other wire of the cable joins the two Common terminals of the switches.

Fig. 91   Wiring two-way switches

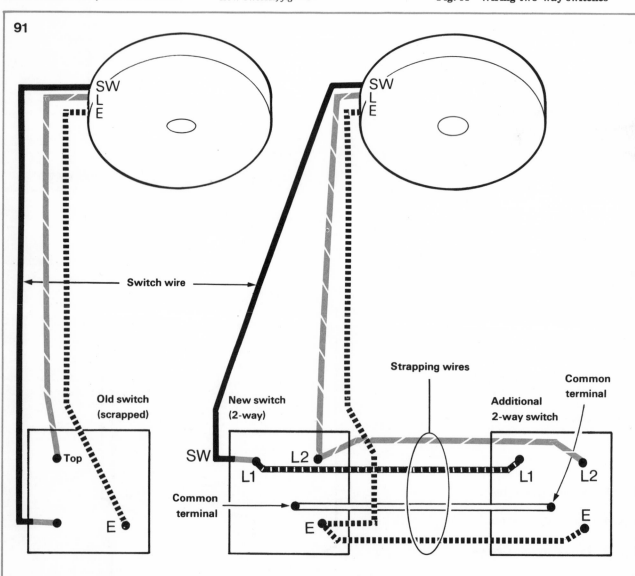

CONTROLS

When buying switches, you may be asked whether you want dolly or rocker operated types. This refers merely to the type of finger control on the front plate of the switch.

A rocker switch, *fig. 93*, operates with a rocking action as it responds to the touch. The more common dolly control, *fig. 92*, simply moves up and down in the more conventional way. Both types will, of course, fit any wall box designed to accommodate switches for domestic use.

Take care when fitting one-way switches to get the switch the right way ·up. Most have the word TOP clearly marked. If the switch is mounted upside down, the dolly will be down when the light is off and up when the light is on. This could be dangerous!

For example, when putting in a new lamp, one's first reaction is to push the dolly up to switch off the current. If the switch were reversed, the action of pushing the dolly up would be to turn the current on.

A SHOCK

Therefore, the lampholder would be live and potentially dangerous. Even if your fingers did not come in contact with the lampholder contacts, the fact that the bulb would light up immediately it was inserted would in itself be a minor shock to some people.

With two-way switches fitted with dolly controls, each dolly's position will depend on the position of the other: when one is up, the other is down. Therefore, to be on the safe side when inserting a new lamp, turn the current off at the main switch.

Fig. 92 Dolly operated switch

Fig. 93 Rocker operated switch

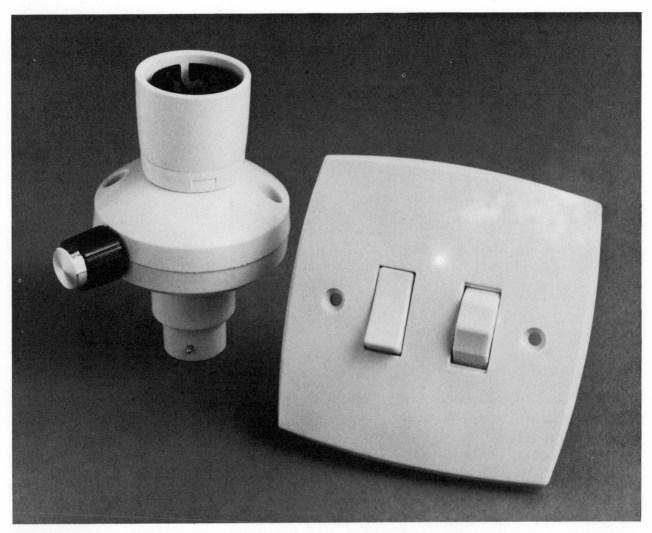

DIMMER SWITCHES

Uses for a dimmer switch, *fig. 94*, in the home are many and varied. Three popular situations are in a child's bedroom (where it can be a substitute for the old-fashioned nightlight); for viewing television in a subdued light; or in the sick room.

There are several types on the market and it is very easy to make an unwise choice. Shop around until you find a type which can be substituted for an ordinary switch *without involving any extra wiring*. Make sure, too, that you choose one in which the printed circuit at the back is completely enclosed so that no live parts are exposed.

If your existing switch is fitted in a plaster-depth box, check that the dimmer is shallow enough to fit it. Some types need a deeper wall box such as that which houses a socket outlet.

DANGER POINT

Some dimmer switches can reduce the amount of light to nothing and yet still remain switched on. This can be dangerous, because if you decide to change the bulb with the dimmer still switched on, you could get a shock. The circuit would still be live.

There is one dimmer (the Myked) which avoids this danger. The light cannot be dimmed beyond a tiny red glow – a valuable reminder that the light is still switched on.

Most dimmers are easy to fit, but follow the maker's instructions carefully.

Dimmers usually have only two terminals – one is for the live feed; the other is for the switch return wire. So you can fit this type of dimmer in place of an ordinary switch without changing the method of wiring.

The fixing holes of dimmer switches will fit a standard plastic surface or metal flush wall box. If your box is not quite deep enough, you can get a mounting piece which fits between the surface plate of the dimmer and the wall box, *fig. 96*.

Turn off the current at the consumer unit before you start to fix the dimmer. Remove the fixing screws from the front of the old switch. Disconnect the two conductors and connect them to the terminals of the dimmer. Screw the dimmer to its box and restore the current.

Don't attempt to fit an ordinary dimmer switch to a fluorescent lighting circuit. Special types of dimmers are available for this purpose.

CEILING SWITCHES
A number of circumstances can call for the installation of a ceiling switch in place of an existing wall switch. Two examples which come to mind are a

bathroom fitted with a wall switch, or a room which has been converted to a bathroom and also has a wall switch controlling the ceiling light.

The job is reasonably simple. Turn off the current from the main switch, of course, and remove the old switch. Disconnect the ends of the cables from their terminals.

The cable may run down the wall in conduit. If it does, go up to the attic or the next floor, locate the cable and pull it up.

Make a hole in the ceiling for the new switch position, cut the cable to the length required, and make sure you don't cut it too short!

Pass the cable through the ceiling hole and through the backplate of the ceiling switch. Most modern ceiling switches have their own backplate and therefore need no pattress. The connections are similar to those made at a ceiling rose.

If the switch cable is plastered in the wall instead of being enclosed in conduit, it will have to stay there and be cut from the top. You may then find that the remainder of the cable is not long enough to reach the new ceiling switch.

In this case, simply take the cable to a new joint box fitted at a convenient point, *fig. 95*. Then run a new length of cable from the joint box to the new ceiling switch.

The cable to use is 1·0mm.² or 1·5mm.² twin and earth pvc sheathed.

95 New joint box — Switch wire — Switch cable cut — From rose or existing joint box — To new ceiling switch — SW — E — L — Leave blank

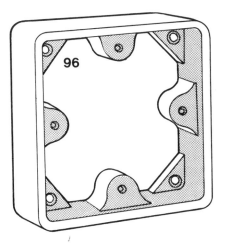

395

Be Safe!

SAFETY IN THE BATHROOM

Electrical appliances are now used to such a large extent in bathrooms that these rooms can be potential killers. Many accidents happen in bathrooms every year, some of them fatal.

Most of the accidents are caused by using appliances which should never be allowed in the room, such as portable heaters and hair driers.

A primary rule to remember if you want to avoid such accidents is that every piece of electrical apparatus fixed in the bathroom should be properly fitted and correctly used.

Here are a few points worth noting to make your bathroom safe.

1: Fix radiant fires high up on a wall so that they are well out of reach of a person under a shower or in the bath.

2: Make sure that every electrical fitting is firmly fixed and cannot be removed without the use of tools.

3: See that all heaters and light switches are fitted with pull-cord switches. If this isn't possible the switches should be fitted on the wall *outside* the bathroom door.

4: Cord operated ceiling switches for towel rails or heaters should contain a pilot light so that you can tell at a glance whether they are on or off.

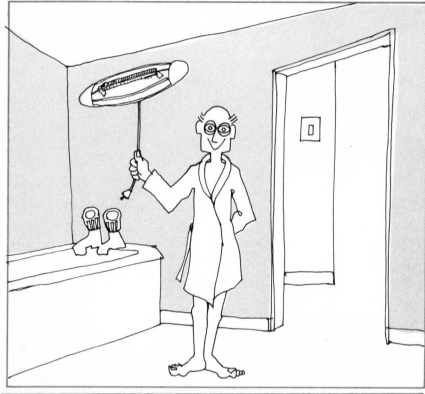

5: If an open reflector type of fire is used, make certain it can be controlled by a separate switch as well as by its own cord-operated switch. The separate (master) switch should, of course, be fitted outside the bathroom.

6: Electric shavers (except battery types) must be used from a properly fitted shaver socket. This must be supplied from a special unit fitted with an isolating transformer. Many strip lights which have a shaver socket are not fitted with a transformer. These must not be used in a bathroom.

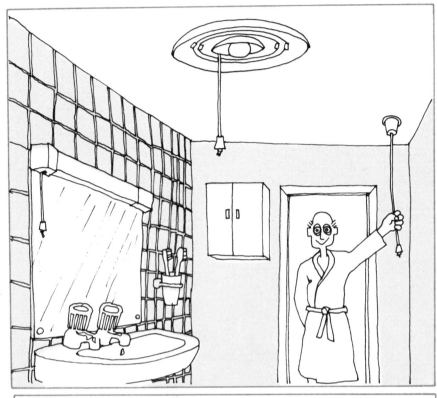

7: Make sure all lights which have a built-in switch are also controlled by a separate switch. Examples are heat/lighting units and strip lights fitted on mirrors.

8: Many people convert a spare bedroom or other room into a bathroom. If you do this, the electrical installation will need to be altered to conform with wiring regulations. This involves removing all socket outlets (or old power points); moving wall switches to outside the bathroom; and using ceiling cord-operated switches. Also, a pendant type of light fitting suspended by flex should be changed and a ceiling type fitting used instead. Steam in a bathroom can damage flex very quickly.

9: Ensure that the lamp bulb cannot be changed by a person who is standing in the bath or under the shower.

10: *Never* use a portable appliance in a bathroom.

11: No switch should be within reach of a person in the bath or under the shower except an insulated cord-operated switch.

12: Never take a television set or radio connected to the mains into the bathroom.

Storage Heaters

The most common form of electric central heating is supplied by storage heaters, *fig. 97*. They operate during off-peak periods, being normally switched on from 11 p.m. to 7 a.m.

During these hours the heaters are charged with heat under a white meter or other off-peak electricity tariff. Electricity is cheaper during these hours, under these special tariffs, than throughout the day when demand for power is high.

Although the heaters give out some heat during their charging period, most of their stored heat is discharged from 7 a.m. to 11 p.m. – the period when you need it most.

Heat output is highest at 7 a.m. when the off-peak period normally ends. During the day, the heat output gradually reduces.

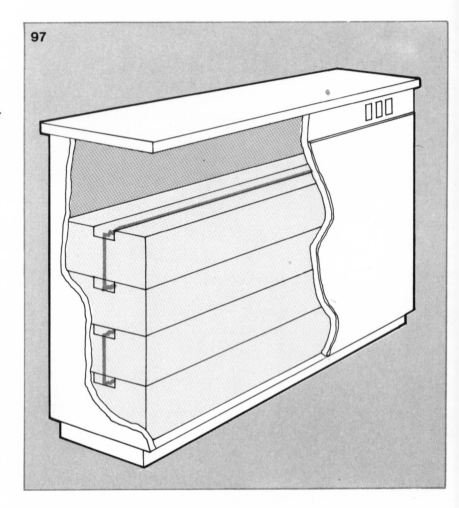

Fig. 97   Storage heater

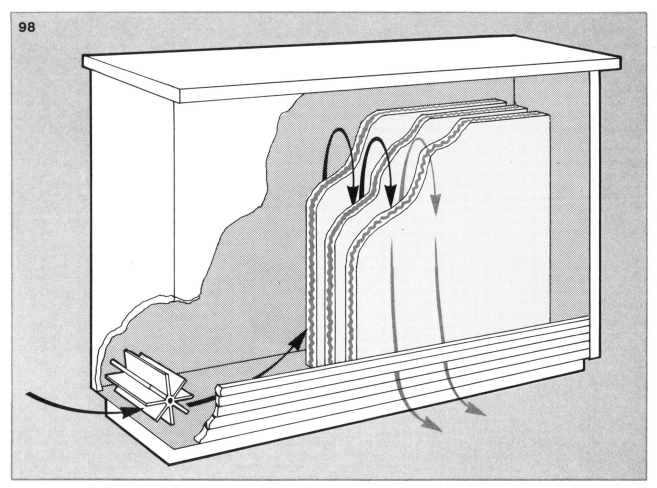

98

Storage radiators are the most popular type of heater used for this purpose. An alternative is the storage *fan heater*, *fig. 98*. This is not to be confused with the ordinary type of portable fan heater, of course.

Both types of storage heater come in various sizes (loadings) – storage radiators from $1\frac{1}{2}$ kilowatts to about $3\frac{1}{3}$ kilowatts, and storage fan heaters from 3 kilowatts to round about 8 kilowatts.

OUTPUT

A point to note about these loading figures is that they do not represent the actual amount of heat discharged (output). For example, the largest type of storage radiator ($3\frac{1}{3}$ kilowatts) will produce heat at the rate of roughly 1 kW continuously for most of the day

before it gradually begins to reduce its output.

Although it is not possible for you to alter the heat *output*, the amount of heat stored *can* be controlled by an input controller fitted on the heater. This, of course, will to a degree affect the amount of heat which is discharged during the day.

As its name suggests, a storage fan heater is fitted with a fan which drives warm air out into a room through a grille. These heaters are dearer than storage radiators and are normally used only if you want to control the amount of heat generated or to choose the time when the heat is to be discharged. This can be done by using the heater's fan switch. Alternatively, it can be done by having a thermostat or time switch incorporated in the fan circuit.

Fig. 98   Fan type storage heater

WIRING STORAGE RADS

Installing storage radiators is a job a competent home electrician can do himself. Wiring up for storage fan heaters, however, is slightly more complicated as two circuits are needed: one is for the heater itself; the other is for the fan.

To take storage radiators first, an important point to remember is that each radiator should preferably have its own separate circuit.

As these heaters are on continuously and run at a reduced tariff rate, they must have a consumer unit to themselves. They are not normally connected to the ordinary consumer unit which supplies the ring circuit and other circuits.

HOW MANY?

If you decide to go in for this type of heating, the first thing to decide is not only how many heaters you need *now*, but whether you are likely to need more later on. Your requirements will dictate the size of the consumer unit.

For example, if you need two storage radiators (or fan heaters) now, the smallest size consumer unit required will be a two-way. But if you also want to run your immersion heater off the same cheaper tariff (discuss this with your electricity board), then you will need a three-way unit.

That will give you two fuseways for the storage heaters and one for the immersion heater. This obviously makes no provision for fitting additional storage heaters later on. Therefore, while you are doing the job, it is well worth while putting in a larger consumer unit now to provide spare fuseways for use later on. You can get units fitted with up to ten fuseways for this purpose.

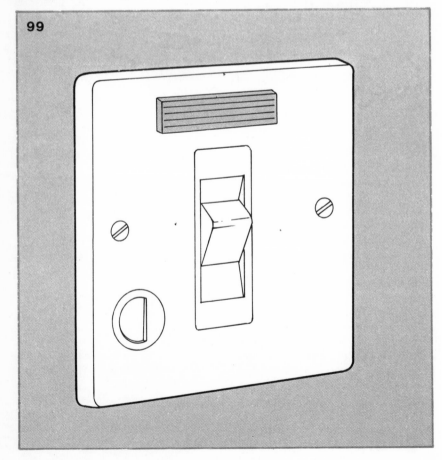

99

Fig. 99   Double pole switch (20 amp)

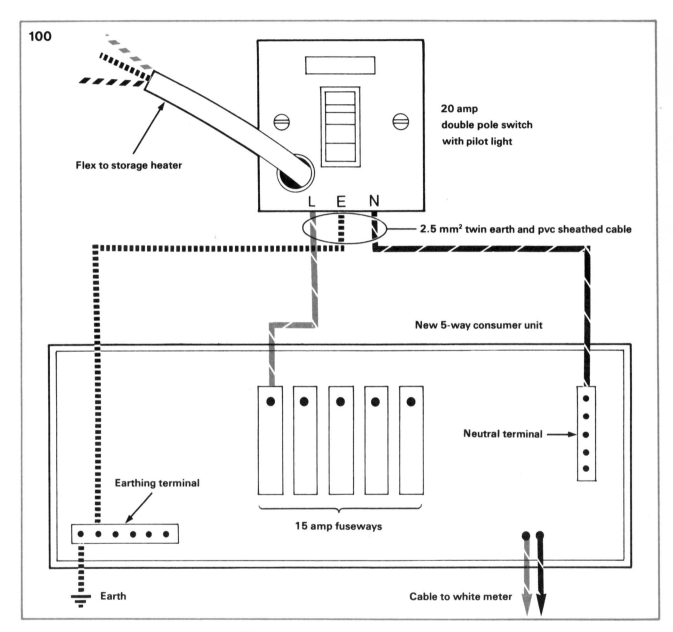

100

Flex to storage heater

20 amp
double pole switch
with pilot light

L E N

2.5 mm² twin earth and pvc sheathed cable

New 5-way consumer unit

Neutral terminal

Earthing terminal

15 amp fuseways

Earth

Cable to white meter

**Fig. 100 Five-way consumer unit
wired for one storage heater**

WIRING UP
To wire up for a storage radiator, you
use 2·5 mm.² twin and earth pvc
sheathed cable (the same as is used in
ring circuits). The rating of the fuse in
the consumer unit should be 15 amps.

The best circuit outlet to use for
connecting the heaters up is a 20 amp
double pole switch. You will need one
for each heater. This switch is suitable
for all sizes of storage radiators with
loadings of 4·8 kilowatts or less.

The double pole switch is fitted into
a flush metal or plastic surface pattress
type of wall box as used for 13 amp
socket outlets. The switch should be
the type provided with a cord outlet,
fig. 99. This provides an entry for the
flexible cord which runs from the
heater to the switch.

Figure 100 shows a five-way
consumer unit wired up for one storage
heater. Additional heaters are wired in
the same way.

Fig. 101 Wherever warm, dry air exists, a humidifier is desirable to prevent damage to woodwork and furniture

STORAGE FAN HEATERS

The heater section of a storage fan heater is wired similarly to a storage radiator. A 2·5 mm.² twin and earth pvc sheathed cable runs from a 15 amp fuseway in your separate consumer unit, but in this case it terminates at a 25 amp twin double pole switch, *fig. 102*, fixed near the heater. Each heater should have its own 25 amp switch, *fig. 103*.

Fig. 102 25 amp double pole switch
Fig. 103 25 amp double pole switch wired to consumer unit for storage fan heater

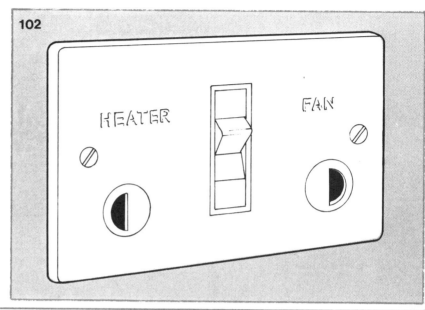

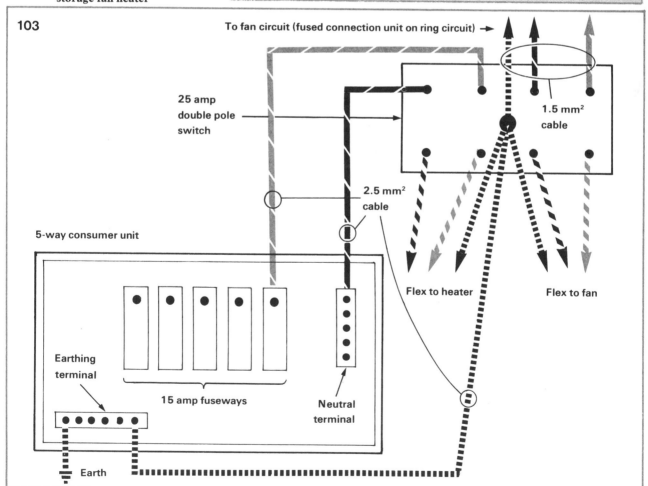

407

To feed the *fan* with current, you can use your ring circuit. From there you take a 1·0 mm.² twin and earth pvc sheathed cable to the 25 amp twin switch. This cable has to be joined to the ring circuit via a fused connection unit which should be fitted with a 3 amp fuse.

One way to do this job is to fit the fused connection unit next to a convenient 13 amp socket outlet. From the terminals of that outlet, you loop out to the fused connection unit using 2·5 mm.² twin and earth pvc sheathed cable, *fig. 104*.

(Alternatively, you can loop out of the lighting circuit to feed the fan but not, of course, the heater itself.)

The 25 amp twin switch serves a double purpose. One side of it controls the heater; the other operates the fan. It has two cord outlets – one is for the flex to the heater; the other is for the flex to the fan.

This switch is for isolating purposes only and is a linked type operated by one dolly. This switches both the heater and the fan off and on together. The heater itself, of course, has its own built-in switches for fan and heater.

Fig. 104   Heater's fan supplied by ring circuit

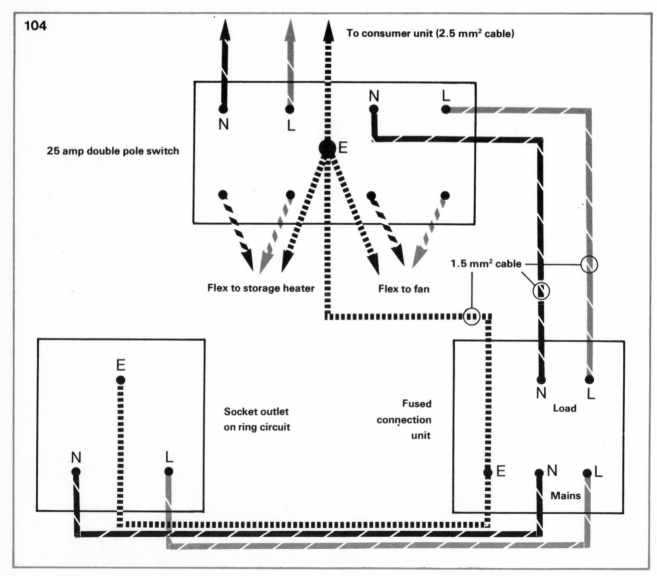

104

To consumer unit (2.5 mm² cable)

N   L

25 amp double pole switch

N   L

E

Flex to storage heater   Flex to fan

1.5 mm² cable

Socket outlet on ring circuit

Fused connection unit

N   L

Load

E

N   L

E   N   L

Mains

Appliances

Many electrical appliances used in the home can be easily connected to the wiring system by means of a plug fitted to a length of flexible cord. These are called portable appliances and examples include irons, vacuum cleaners, drills, some heaters, hair dryers and so on.

Fixed appliances, however, usually connect to the wiring system by other methods. Some involve installing a new circuit or extending an existing circuit. These appliances include cookers, immersion heaters, towel rails and storage heaters.

To take the cooker as an example. The only appliance which can be connected to a cooker circuit is, in fact, the cooker. On the other hand, its circuit can supply *both* sections of a split level cooker. This type of cooker is operated from a single control panel.

Normal-size cookers are wired in 4·0 mm.² two core and earth pvc sheathed cable. The circuit is 30 amps.

Large cookers which have a loading higher than 12kW have a 45 amp circuit, however. The size of cable used in this case is 10·0 mm.². For this type of cooker you need a 45 amp fuse fitted to the consumer unit.

The cable of a normal-size cooker runs from a 30 amp fuseway in the ordinary domestic consumer unit to the cooker's control unit. These units usually consist of a double pole switch for the cooker and a 13 amp three-pin socket outlet for an electric kettle, *fig. 105*.

A double pole switch breaks the current not only in the live conductor, but in the neutral conductor as well.

The units can be flush-mounted or surface-mounted types and you can get them with or without pilot lights.

The control unit for the cooker can be fitted up to 6 ft. away from the cooker itself. The cable which connects the cooker to the control unit is the same size and type as that used from the consumer unit to the control unit, 4·0 mm.² or 10·0 mm.².

This cable can be buried under the wall plaster and terminated at a cable connector box positioned low on the kitchen wall.

Fig. 105 Double pole switch for cooker

TWO TYPES OF BOX

There are two versions of cable connector box. One is a terminal box, *fig. 106*, in which the fixed portion of the cable and the lead on the cooker are connected up. This allows the cooker to be moved without interfering with the wiring.

The other type is called a through box, *fig. 107*. This type has a cable grip which avoids cutting the cable to make a joint between the fixed portion of cable and the lead on the cooker.

It is possible to supply both units of a split level cooker – the oven and the hob – from one circuit, and to control both with one switch. However, neither of the units should be positioned more than 6 ft. away from the control unit.

You can run separate cables to each from the control unit provided that they are the same size as the circuit cable.

Small table cookers which have a loading of less than 3 kW can be operated from a fused 13 amp plug and socket outlet on a ring circuit.

IMMERSION HEATERS

Generally speaking, immersion heaters should not be supplied from a ring circuit but from a separate 15 amp circuit. The reason for this is that an immersion heater is considered to be an appliance with a continuous load of 3 kW. This is regardless of whether you keep it switched on all the time or not.

As the capacity of a ring circuit is only 7·2 kilowatts, to add an immersion heater to it would reduce that capacity by 3 kW.

The heaters are normally supplied by a 2·5 mm.² two core and earth pvc sheathed cable. This runs from a 15 amp fuseway in the consumer unit to a 20 amp double pole switch with a pilot light, *fig. 108*. The switch should be positioned near the heater and have a flex outlet.

The wiring from the switch to the heater should be three-core 20 amp butyl rubber heat-resisting flex.

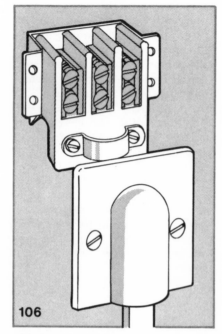

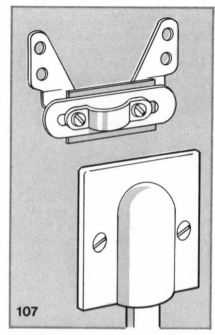

Fig. 106   Cooker terminal box

Fig. 107   Cooker through box with cable grip

Fig. 108   Double pole switch with pilot light

109

Fig. 109   Clock connector

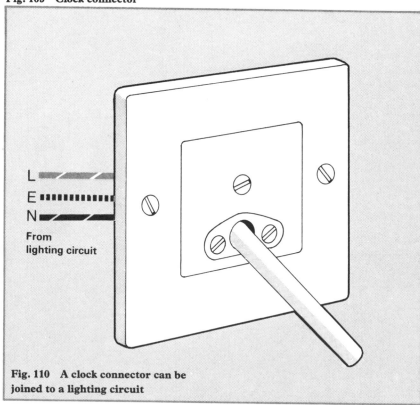

L
E
N

From
lighting circuit

**Fig. 110   A clock connector can be
joined to a lighting circuit**

IN THE BATHROOM

Fixed appliances fitted in a bathroom
such as towel rails or oil-filled radiators
should be supplied from fused
connection units – not from socket
outlets – which are wired from the
ring circuit.

The connection units, which should
contain pilot lights, are fitted near the
appliances but out of reach of anyone
who is in contact with the bath or
shower.

CLOCKS OFF THE MAINS

Electric clocks run off the mains have
to be supplied from a special socket
outlet called a clock connector, *fig. 109*.
These connectors comprise a fused
plug and a socket outlet – in two
sections.

The plug section is secured by a
captive nut. This prevents it being
accidentally removed from the outlet
and thus stopping the clock.

The plug is fitted with a fuse which
may have a 1, 2 or 3 amp rating, but is
now normally 3 amp. The connectors
are made in flush or surface types and
you can also get a type which can be
accommodated in a metal plaster-
depth wall box such as that used to
house a plateswitch.

An electric clock consumes very
little current and can therefore be
safely supplied by a lighting circuit.
It is, however, also possible to use the
ring circuit as the source of supply.

MORE THAN ONE CIRCUIT

If a number of clocks are to be
supplied from the mains, it is better
that they do not all run off the same
circuit. If more than one circuit is used,
not all the clocks will be out of action
if a circuit fault develops. This could
be awkward.

If you decide to utilise the lighting
circuit, the cable to install is $1 \cdot 0 \, \text{mm}^2$
two core and earth pvc sheathed. This
cable can run from the live and neutral
terminals of a lighting joint box or
loop out from a ceiling rose to the
socket outlet section of the clock
connector, *fig. 110*.

In *fig. 110* an earth conductor is shown, but as old lighting installations are unlikely to have an earth conductor, it can, in this case, be disregarded.

Most electric clocks are, in fact, double insulated, so no earth connection is normally needed. However, some clock connectors are fitted with an earthing terminal.

If the cable to the outlet has an earthing conductor, the mounting wall box for the clock connector should be fitted with an earthing terminal to accommodate the conductor.

USE OF RING CIRCUIT

If you decide to use the ring circuit as the source of supply for an electric clock, you can loop into a 30 amp joint box on the ring and run from it a length of 2·5 mm.² two core and earth pvc sheathed cable to the connector, *fig. 111*.

This, however, could involve a long run of cable – an expensive item these days. A better idea, therefore, is to connect a *non*-switched fused connection unit fitted with a 3 amp fuse direct to the ring circuit. From the fused unit run a length of 1·0 mm.² two core and earth pvc sheathed cable to the clock connector.

The clock is connected to the plug section of the connector with two core circular sheathed flex. If the clock has a metal case and is not double insulated, three core flex will be needed as this has the necessary earthing conductor.

TELEVISION SETS

One appliance many people take for granted in the home is the television set. Often it is not treated with the respect it deserves.

There is, of course, very little you can do if the set should go wrong apart from calling in a qualified service engineer. In fact, television sets should never be interfered with by anyone who is not qualified to service them. They are complicated pieces of equipment carrying very high voltages and are therefore potentially dangerous.

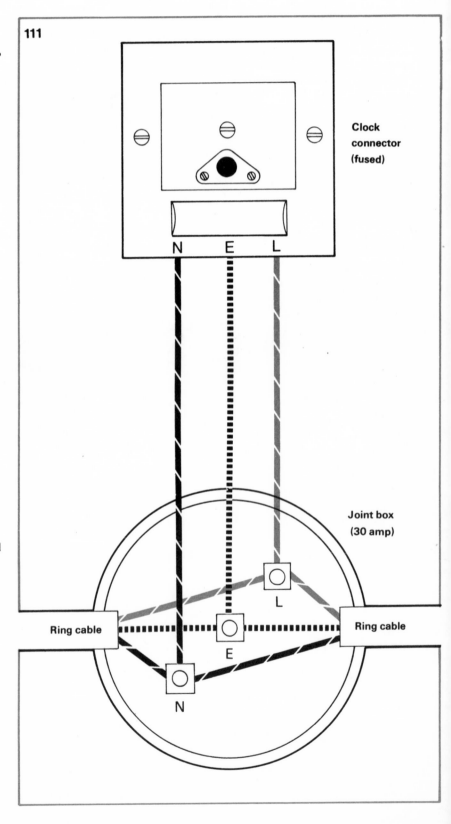

111

Clock connector (fused)

Joint box (30 amp)

Ring cable

Ring cable

What you *can* do is to take precautions when using the set. First and foremost, the socket outlet on the wall to which the set is plugged in, must be correctly wired up. If it isn't this could cause a fire.

In most cases, of course, the outlet will be properly wired and safe to use. If, however, your installation is at all suspect, have it attended to before

connecting a TV set (or any other appliance for that matter) to it.

If you have to install a new socket outlet on the ring circuit to supply a TV set, make sure you have got all the conductors connected up properly. I cannot repeat this too often: the red conductors go to the live (L) terminals; the black to the neutral (N) terminals; and the earth (green) conductors to the earthing (E) terminals. I repeat these connections in *fig. 112*.

Although this may seem obvious, it is vitally important. If, for example, the black and red conductors were reversed in the outlet terminals, parts of the TV set and the flexible cord leading from it would become permanently *live*. This error could cause a fire even if the switch (if any) at the socket outlet and the switch on the set itself were turned off.

This is because the reversing of the cables would mean that the plug fuse and the outlet switch would both be in the neutral lead and not in the live lead as they should be. Switches should always be connected in the live lead.

To be on the safe side, it is better not to rely on the switches but to pull out the plug from its outlet whenever the set is not in use. This is the most efficient way of ensuring that the set or other appliance is completely isolated from the mains.

Whatever you do, it is in any case a good plan to use a switched socket outlet for a TV set. If you have to use an unswitched outlet, however, you can get a switched plug fitted with a pilot light. This at least will show you whether the set is off or on. But for complete isolation of the set, you will still have to pull out the plug.

Fig. 111 Ring circuit connections for clock connector

Fig. 112 Socket outlet wiring on the ring circuit for a TV set

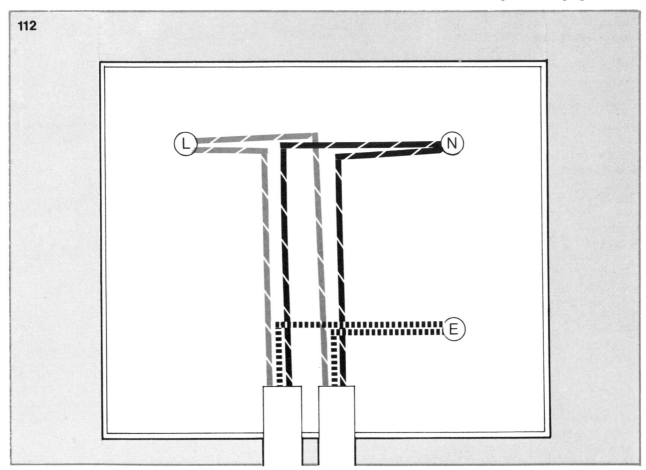

112

EARTHING

Like many electrical appliances, the majority of TV sets have no earth connection and are fitted with a two core flexible lead, the earth pin of the three-pin plug being left unoccupied.

Never connect your set to a plug which has only two pins, nor to the type of plug which is sometimes used in a lampholder. This could cause the chassis of the set to become live and therefore dangerous if the back of the set were removed while the current was switched on.

Also, if the control knobs happened to become damaged and any metal part of them became exposed to the touch, this part, too, could become live.

ELECTRIC BLANKETS

Electrical appliances which have been responsible for a large number of fires and accidents in the home are electric blankets.

Nowadays, these appliances conform to a very high safety standard, and many of the fires caused are due to misuse by the owner of the blanket. It is therefore essential that the instructions supplied by the manufacturer should be followed to the letter.

Never attempt repairs to an electric blanket. Get it serviced regularly by experts and leave it with them to put right if the appliance goes wrong. Care of the blanket will cut repairs to a minimum.

Safety measures you should take when using electric blankets include:

1: Keep the switch well out of reach of children.

2: Under blankets should not be kept switched on when a person is in the bed.

3: Don't fold blankets up when not in use as this can bend and possibly fracture the heating cable.

4: Keep the instructions safely with the blanket so that anyone unfamiliar with it can read them before use.

5: Avoid buying a blanket which is not made by an established and recognised company.

HEAT/LIGHT UNITS

There are a number of electrical appliances on the market today which supply both heat and light and are known generally as heat-light units. You often find them fitted in bathrooms and kitchens in place of the usual ceiling light, but there are types which are designed to be used in other rooms.

Many of them have a heating unit with a loading of 750 watts and a light rated at 100 watts – a total of 850 watts.

These units are often connected to the lighting circuit, but they should not be. The reason is that there is a risk of overloading such a circuit with so highly rated an appliance.

A lighting circuit is rated at 5 amps and its maximum load should not exceed 1,200 watts. This is the equivalent of twelve 100 watt lamps.

As I said in chapter 10, each lamp rated up to 100 watts is, for the purpose of specifying the number of lamps for a circuit, assessed at 100 watts regardless of whether its actual wattage is 100 or below. Every lamp over 100 watts, however, is assessed at its true rating.

Therefore, if you fit a heat/light unit of 850 watts, you leave a margin of only 350 watts in reserve for other lights on the circuit.

OVERLOADING

Let's see what could happen in a typical family residence, with only one lighting circuit, one winter's evening where a heat/light unit of this size is fitted in the bathroom.

Mother decides to take a bath and switches on the unit: watts in use, 850.

Daughter sits reading in the lounge under a standard lamp fitted with a 100 watt bulb. Total watts in use, now 950.

Two wall lights burn also in the lounge. Although these may be only 60 watt lamps, they are assessed at 100 each. Watts now in use, 1,150.

So far so good, but supposing father decides to go into the kitchen and

switches on the fluorescent light? If this has a 100 watt tube, it will be assessed at 200 watts. So the total of watts rises to 1,350 and the circuit then becomes overloaded, in theory anyway.

At this stage, the circuit *may* not, in practice, be overloaded because if we had used the true rating of the two wall lights and the fluorescent tube, the actual wattage being consumed would be 1,170 – 30 watts below the permitted 1,200 which it the total for the circuit.

MARGIN TOO SMALL

However, this margin of only 30 watts is not sufficient to take into account the possibility of one more light being switched on, say in the toilet or in a bedroom, even momentarily. If that happened, then the circuit would definitely be overloaded and the circuit fuse would blow.

This can be disturbing at the best of times, especially if all the lights are on the same circuit and therefore all fail simultaneously. It could be dangerous to anyone taking a bath, for example, and even more dangerous for anyone using a power tool supplied off the ring circuit.

Although the fusing of the lights would not affect the working of the power tool, the shock of being plunged into sudden darkness could cause a nasty accident to the person using the tool.

No doubt many of these heat/light units have been used off a lighting circuit, but it is a practice to be deplored. One person living alone (perhaps even two) might remember to keep other lights turned off while the unit is in use, but it is asking too much to expect a family to do so at all times.

Therefore it is better to play safe and avoid fitting such a unit of so high a wattage in place of an ordinary lamp.

There are, fortunately, alternative methods of wiring such a unit. It can be supplied either from a separate 5 amp circuit run from the consumer

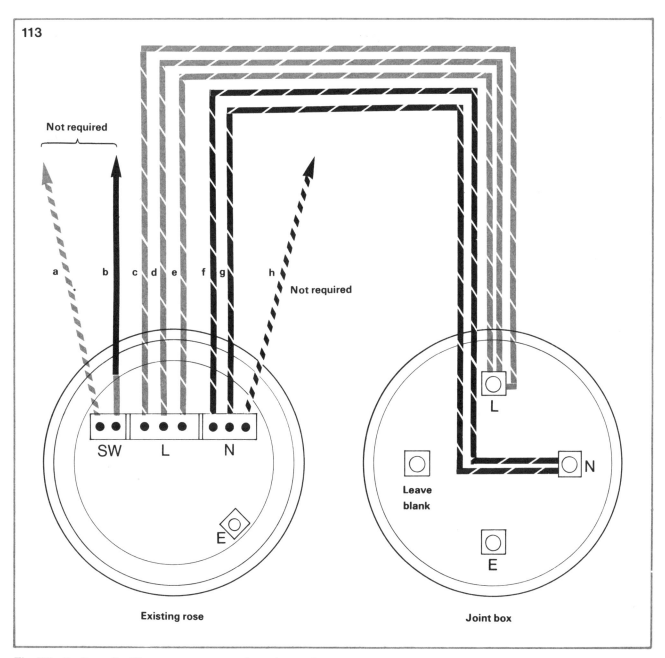

113

Not required

a b c d e f g h

Not required

SW   L   N

E

Existing rose

L

N

Leave
blank

E

Joint box

**Fig. 113 Sealing off ceiling rose
wires in a joint box**
a) Flex live wire
b) Switch wire
c) Live feed
d) Live switch wire
e) Live loop to next rose
f) Neutral feed
g) Neutral feed to next rose
h) Flex neutral wire (not required)

unit, or from a fused connection unit
joined to the ring circuit.

If you plan to fit the unit in place
of an existing light, the cables at the
ceiling point, will no longer be needed
as they will be connected to the lighting
circuit. They will have to be disconnected from the ceiling rose and
terminated (sealed off) at a joint box
fixed at a point above the ceiling,

on the joists, *fig. 113*.

DISCONNECTING
While doing this, great care will have
to be taken to be absolutely sure that
the connections are not accidentally
changed. There may well be a
confusion of cables at the lighting
point. It is impossible to say exactly
what the wiring arrangements will look

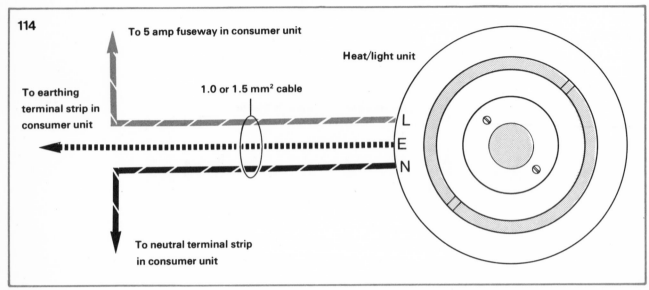

114

To 5 amp fuseway in consumer unit

Heat/light unit

To earthing terminal strip in consumer unit

1.0 or 1.5 mm² cable

L
E
N

To neutral terminal strip in consumer unit

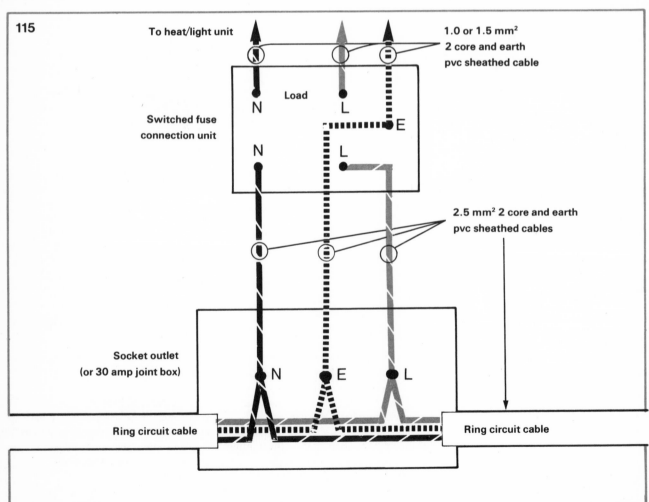

115

To heat/light unit

1.0 or 1.5 mm² 2 core and earth pvc sheathed cable

Load

N   L

Switched fuse connection unit

E

N   L

2.5 mm² 2 core and earth pvc sheathed cables

Socket outlet (or 30 amp joint box)

N   E   L

Ring circuit cable

Ring circuit cable

Fig. 114 Heat/light unit supplied from consumer unit

Fig. 115 Heat/light unit supplied from ring circuit

like, so if you cannot understand the cable layout, postpone the job until you can get expert advice. And do remember to cut off the current at the main switch before you remove the rose cover in order to make your initial inspection.

One way to avoid mixing up the cables, once they have been identified, is to disconnect one conductor at a time and label it accordingly. There will almost certainly be more than one conductor at the live and neutral terminals. Make sure that these are kept together on the same terminal when they are eventually transferred to your joint box.

The earthing terminal in *fig. 113* on the old rose has been purposely left blank, as has the one in the joint box. The reason for this is that old installations are unlikely to have earthing conductors at lighting points.

If, of course, your installation has an earthing conductor at this point, it should be transferred to the joint box earthing terminal.

NOT REQUIRED
The old switch wires and the flex wires at the lighting point will not be required for the heat/light fitting and should be disconnected. Be very careful when looking for the switch wire not to remove the wrong wire.

The switch return wire, as it is called, will probably be one conductor (the black one) of a two-core cable, the red conductor of this cable going to the live terminal on the rose. But although it is black, remember that it will, in fact, be live!

As I said on page 380, the switch wire should carry a short length of red insulation sleeving to identify it (at the switch terminal), but rarely is this done.

Figure 114 illustrates how the unit can be connected up if you decide to run a new circuit from the consumer unit.

Figure 115 shows how to join the unit up to a ring circuit using a fused connection unit. This unit should be fitted with a 13 amp fuse, unless the instructions specify otherwise.

Wiring Outside

If you want a lighting point or socket outlets in the garden shed, garage or greenhouse, special equipment must be used to meet the wiring regulations.

A special type of cable is run from the house but this should be separate from the house circuits. This cable can run underground, but it must be buried at least 18 inches below ground level, *fig. 116*. Alternatively, the cable can run overhead or along a wall.

It must not run along a fence.

The cable has to be controlled by its own main switch. This is fitted near the electric meter in the house.

The installation in a shed (or whatever) has to be controlled by an isolating switch which is fixed in the shed.

This switch can cut off current at the shed, thus isolating the circuit and the appliances from the mains.

Fig. 116   Outside cables can run under the ground

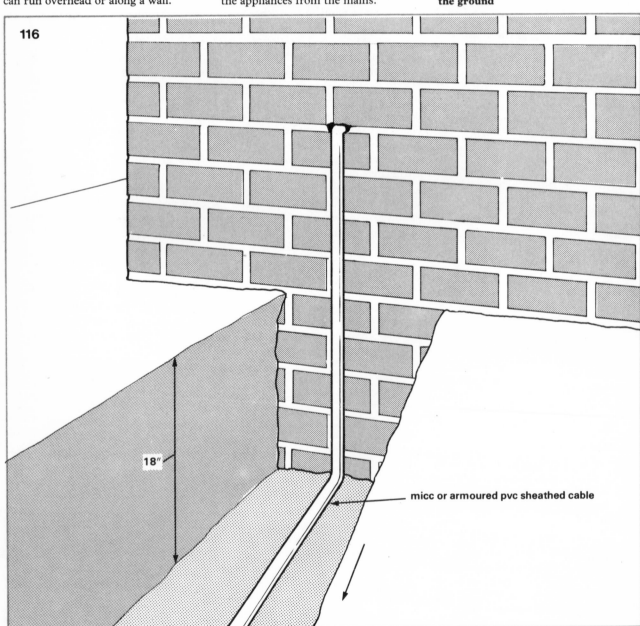

116

18"

micc or armoured pvc sheathed cable

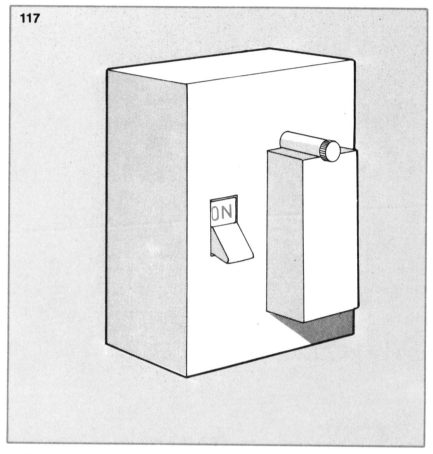

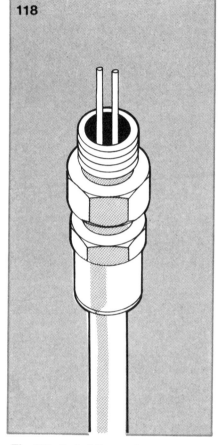

You have a choice of main switches: a switch-fuse unit (a combined main switch and fuse), *fig. 117*, or the main switch of a separate consumer unit.

A switch-fuse unit can supply only one circuit for lighting and power, but is enough for modest needs. A consumer unit, of course, can supply several circuits, according to its size.

CHOICE OF CABLE

Two types of cable can be used underground (a) mineral insulated copper clad (m.i.c.c.) or (b) pvc armoured pvc sheathed. See separate chapter on cables.

These cables have only two cores – live and neutral – but no earth wire.

The copper sheath of (a) and the armoured core of (b) themselves act as the earthing conductors. If you order m.i.c.c. cable, stipulate that it must have a pvc covering.

For most purposes, the 2·5 mm.² size cable will be adequate. If, however, the load demand is above 4·8 kW (4,800 watts), or the cable is longer than 70 ft., use 4·0 mm.² cable.

You can lay these cables in a trench without giving them any other protection, but if you indulge in double digging or trenching in the garden, bury them deeper than 18 inches.

TERMINATIONS

Holes will have to be cut in the walls of the house and of the shed for the cables to pass through. Whether you use pvc armoured pvc or m.i.c.c. cable, its ends should terminate in screwed glands, *fig. 118*. You can get the cable with these already fitted. If you use m.i.c.c. cable, this will need glands *and* seals. The seals can be fitted at the shop.

Fig. 117   Switch/fuse unit (MEM)

Fig. 118   Ends of outside cables terminate in screwed glands

To terminate the cable at the house end, you need a metal knockout box of the same type as that used to house a flush socket outlet. Remove a suitable knockout and pass the house end of the cable, with glands fitted, into it. This box is fitted just inside the house.

Screw a conduit locknut on to the end of the gland. This ensures good earthing continuity. From the knockout box run a cable of the same size, but twin and earth pvc sheathed, to your main switch in the house, *fig. 119*.

The joints in the metal box (between this cable and the outside cable) can be made using a special terminal block, *fig. 120*. After making the joint, fit a blanking plate, *fig. 121*, over the box.

Make sure, by the way, that this box has an earthing terminal. From that terminal run a short green insulating wire to the earthing terminal of the terminal block in the box, *fig. 120*.

Fig. 119 Cables joined at terminal block in wall box

Fig. 120 MK terminal block

Fig. 121 MK blanking plate

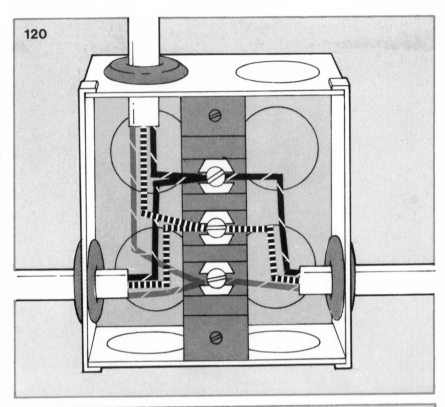

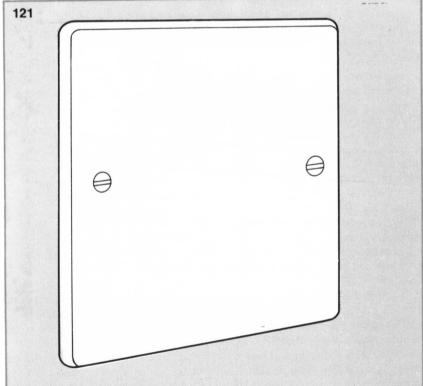

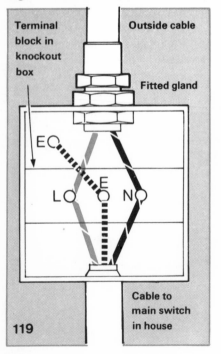

Terminal block in knockout box

Outside cable

Fitted gland

E

L   E   N

Cable to main switch in house

119

The other end of the outside cable should run direct into the isolating main switch in the shed. So fix the isolating switch near the spot where the cable enters the shed.

If this is not possible, use a metal knockout box and the same method of jointing as for the house end of the cable.

ALTERNATIVE
For a shed, you will probably need only a light and perhaps a couple of socket outlets. If so, you can forget about a main switch at the shed end. Instead, you can use a 20 amp double pole switch (plateswitch type) and a fused connection unit fitted with a 13 amp fuse.

These can be mounted on a dual . pattress box and linked with a short length of 2·5 mm.² twin and earth pvc sheathed cable. The connections are shown in *fig. 122.*

Fig. 122 Double pole switch and fused connection unit for power and lighting in outbuilding

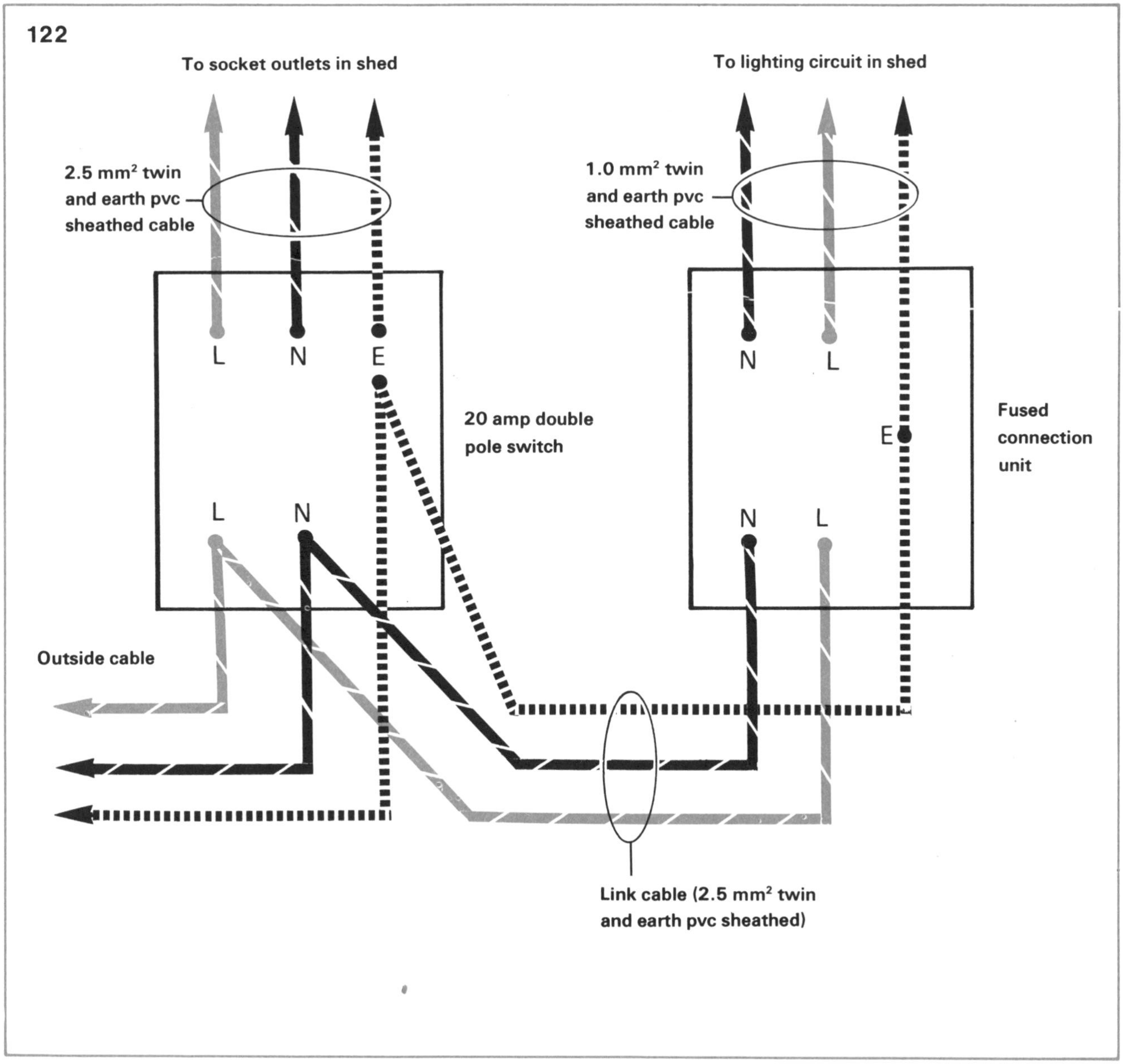

122

To socket outlets in shed

To lighting circuit in shed

2.5 mm² twin and earth pvc sheathed cable

1.0 mm² twin and earth pvc sheathed cable

L   N   E

N   L

20 amp double pole switch

Fused connection unit

E

L   N

N   L

Outside cable

Link cable (2.5 mm² twin and earth pvc sheathed)

OVERHEAD WIRING

If it is not possible to bury the cable underground, you can use the overhead method of wiring, *fig. 123*. The cable required in this case is 2·5 mm.² twin and earth pvc sheathed, as used in house wiring. But if your power requirements exceed 4·8 kilowatts, or 20 amps, use a larger cable.

Provided the shed to be wired is situated not more than 10 ft. away from the house, the cable will not need any extra support. The cable should be fixed at least 12 ft. from the ground.

If the distance between the shed and the house is greater than 10 ft., you should hang the cable from a suspension wire. This is called a catenary and is strung between the two buildings.

For this you need a length of galvanized stranded wire and eye bolts for fixing it.

The cable should be fixed to the suspension wire at intervals of about

Fig. 123 Overhead wiring method for outside lighting or power

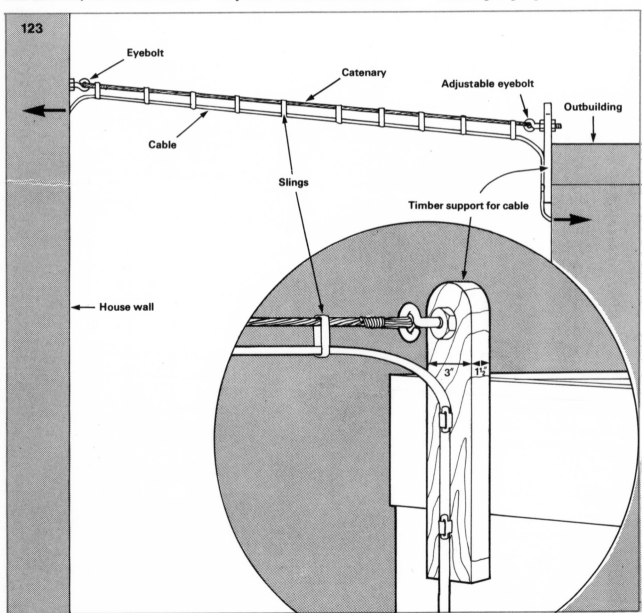

9 in. You can do this by using plastic slings available from electrical accessory shops.

Fix the suspension wire at one end with an adjustable eye bolt and a straining eye bolt at the other. The suspension wire should be connected to earth (the earthing terminal of the main isolating switch in the shed.)

In no circumstances, however, can the suspension wire be used as the earth continuity conductor for the outdoor circuit. The conductor which should be used for this purpose, of course, is the bare earth wire in the cable itself.

USING CONDUIT

Another method of wiring is to run the overhead cable in conduit. This should be a continuous length of heavy gauge steel. The conduit should be long enough to enter both the house wall and the wall of the shed. If you

Fig. 124 Using conduit for overhead cable. It is best if the conduit goes through the wall. If it has to run down, make an elbow joint (inset)

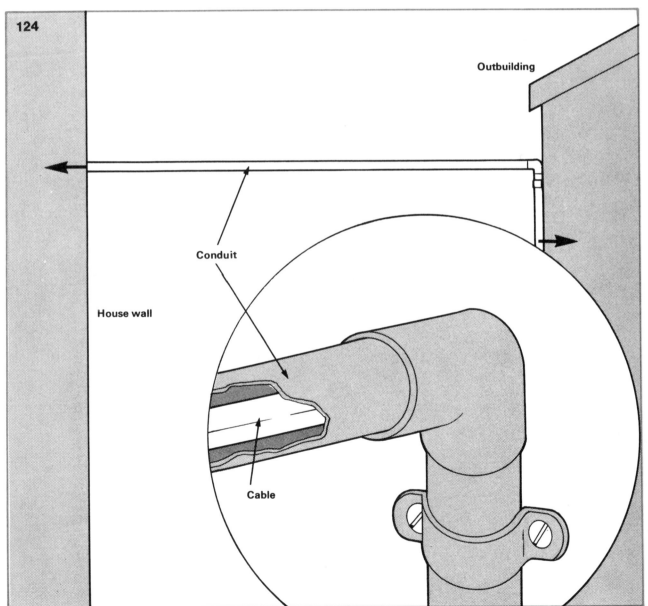

124

Outbuilding

Conduit

House wall

Cable

use metal conduit, this must be connected to earth (bonded, as it is called).

To do this, fix an earthing clip, *fig. 125*, on one end of the conduit. To the clip connect a green insulating cable. This runs to the earthing terminal of your isolating switch in the shed.

At the house end, connect two lengths (about one metre each) of 6·0 mm.² single core pvc sheathed cable to the switch/fuse unit or main switch of your new, separate consumer unit. Connect the red conductor to the live terminal and the black to the neutral.

Leave these wires for the electricity board to connect to the mains. They will do this after you have filled in an application form and arranged with them a date for the circuit to be tested, approved (we hope) and connected.

If you are at all doubtful about your ability to carry out outside wiring (or, indeed, any form of house wiring), get expert advice.

As I have emphasised, electricity is potentially dangerous, especially if mishandled, so make sure you know exactly what you are undertaking *before* you start.

Many of the accessories and cables mentioned in these pages can be obtained from department stores and electrical shops. For some materials, however, you may have to go to an electrical contractor.

Whatever you do, always buy materials made by a reputable firm. Don't be tempted by cut price items. They may be adequate for a time, but you cannot be certain.

By doing your own electrical jobs you are saving money, so you can afford to buy the best available.

Fig. 125   Earthing clip

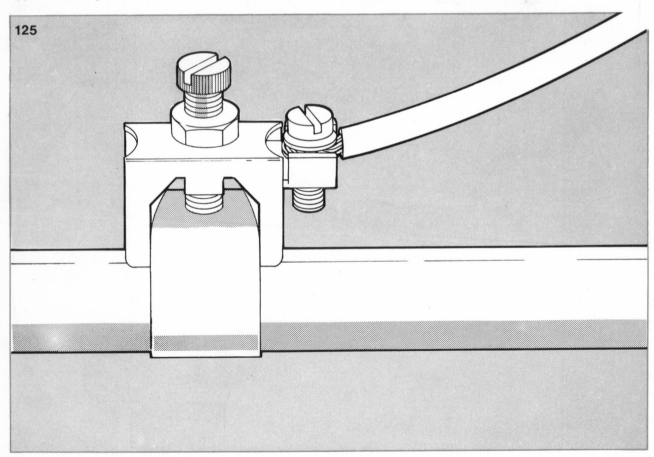

125

Some Attractive Ideas in Concrete

With the use of a little imagination, concrete can be used in many attractive ways. These two pages, and the two which follow, are intended to show some of the things which can be done, and the ideas can be adapted to fit in with your own particular setting.

For patio gardening, concrete is the ideal material as it can be cast into many different shapes. The screen (top right) is supplied in sections ready to to erect. As an extension of the stone wall, it adds a touch of decoration and lets air and light through for the patio plants.

Large concrete plant containers (bottom right) can be made very easily by the home handyman, using sand moulds. They can be cast in a variety of shapes and have a comparatively smooth finish, as in the ones shown in the picture, for a fairly formal setting. The picture (far right, bottom) shows a different approach, where the finish of the containers is left deliberately rough to blend in with the stonework of the house.

In the picture (far right, top) something rather more advanced has been carried out most successfully. The double waterfall has been cast in concrete sections which are then joined together, and the water trickles down into a concrete-lined pool surrounded by decorative paving and cobbles. The plants in their cast concrete containers complete the picture.

The picture on the left shows a well-worked-out combination of concrete with stonework. The square slabs set in loose chippings makes a change from a completely paved path. Concrete and brick has been used successfully together for the patio (top right) and again in the picture below it. An openwork screen such as this makes a pleasant change from a low hedge for dividing the garden. The brick surround to the small pool, gives a change in texture and colour from the concrete slab paving.

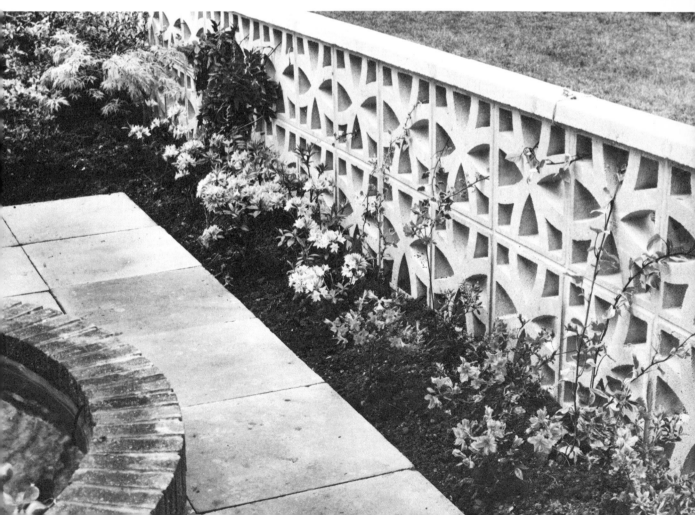

If you have never used concrete before, it as well to know what happens when the ingredients are mixed together with water. How quickly does the concrete become rock hard? That is one of the basic questions that a beginner will want answered.

To appreciate what to expect, it is useful to know about the ingredients themselves.

MATERIALS FOR PRODUCING CONCRETE

A concrete mix consists of Portland cement, sand and aggregate (stones or other inert material) to which water is added. Let us look at each one of these ingredients separately.

Portland cement is the basic cement used in concrete. Portland is not a brand name, it is a type. It is suitable for all jobs that the home handyman is likely to tackle.

Made to a British Standard, it is either grey or white in colour.

Your local builder's merchant will stock ordinary (grey) Portland cement in 50 kilogram bags. This new metric size is about the same as the 1 cwt bag that it has replaced. White Portland cement is also sold in 25 kilogram ($\frac{1}{2}$ cwt) bags.

A word here about the weight of these bags. In case you have no conception of how heavy 50 kilograms is, be warned; you will need help to lift a bag of cement of this size.

All the cement should be dry, fresh, and must not contain any lumps which cannot be broken into fine powder under light hand pressure.

Concrete aggregates are available from builders' merchants as well. Many stockists supply the aggregate in plastic bags. The small extra cost is probably worth while since the bags are much easier to store than loose material.

There are three types: coarse aggregate, fine aggregate and combined aggregates.

Coarse aggregate is comprised of gravel, crushed gravel or stone. The particles are graded in sizes from about 5 mm ($\frac{3}{16}$ in) across, up to a maximum of 10 mm ($\frac{3}{8}$ in) or 20 mm ($\frac{3}{4}$ in).

Fine aggregate really is coarse sand. Not the sort of stuff you would expect to find on your favourite beach.

Combined aggregates are sometimes called all-in ballast. Since these are a mixture of coarse aggregate and sand, they make mixing concrete a little bit easier.

Be careful here as the builder's merchant could offer 'as-dug' ballast which means exactly what it says. It is sold in the state that it is dug from the ground. It is not at all suitable for concreting. If you specify to your supplier what the concrete is to be used for, he should sell you washed ballast.

Concrete, therefore, consists of particles of stone stuck together with a paste of Portland cement and water. The paste hardens as it dries, gaining strength as it does so, gradually bonding the stones into a durable, structural material.

You will find that correctly mixed concrete is 'plastic'. It can be placed in its required position and compacted into a mould prepared for it. From then on, it gradually becomes more difficult to handle as it starts to harden. At the end of less than a couple of hours, it will be stiff and unworkable.

If you are working under a hot sun, an hour will be the deadline in which to get the concrete placed and compacted after mixing.

Since there is no way that the hardening process, once it has started, can be halted, it is important to mix up a quantity of concrete that can be placed in the time allowed. Incidentally, concrete should not be left exposed to dry out quickly under a hot sun. If it is not allowed to dry out in its own time, it will become weak.

You may hear about things called admixtures which can, in one way or another, affect the drying properties of fresh concrete or mortar mixes. Generally speaking these should not be used by the handyman. Precise measuring and thorough mixing are essential to avoid damaging the concrete in some way.

In special circumstances, however, they are obviously beneficial. That is to say, for example, if you have to finish a job quickly or you need more time than usual to place the concrete after mixing. You can speed-up the setting rate if work has to be done at a time of year when severe frosts are likely, or the concrete cannot be protected until it has set normally in its own time.

The setting process can be slowed as well if extra time is needed to place it after mixing.

CONCRETE MIXES

Two concrete mixes will cater for all the concrete work that the handyman is likely to tackle in the house and garden.

The Cement and Concrete Association recommend the mixes given in Table 1.

Mix A: This is suitable for foundations, floor slabs, *in situ* paving and other uses where a thickness of 75 mm (3 in) or more is needed.

Mix B: This is stronger and is more suitable for small units or for thinner sections of less than 75 mm.

Combined Aggregates: Where combined aggregates are used, use 1 part cement to 5 parts combined aggregate for Mix A.

Use 1 part cement to $3\frac{3}{4}$ parts combined aggregate for Mix B.

In both the mixes, damp sand is quoted. The sand supplied to you will nearly always be damp. If dry sand is used, however, reduce the proportion of sand in Mix A to 2 parts. In Mix B, reduce the proportion of sand to $1\frac{1}{2}$ parts.

ESTIMATING MATERIALS NEEDED

Before going down to the builder's merchant to order the materials, you will have to know how much concrete will be needed to complete the job.

An overall figure is no use by itself however. The individual number of bags of cement and the cubic metres (m^3) of sand and coarse aggregate needed to make up the mix will have to be calculated.

This is not as difficult as it may sound. Since materials must now be ordered in metric terms, anyone who still cannot calculate easily in metric will find Table 2 especially useful.

First of all work out the area to be covered by, say, the path or base, working in either square metres (m^2), square feet (ft^2), or square yards (yd^2). Also establish the thickness or depth of concrete that is required.

Locate the area on the left-hand scales then read straight across to the sloping line that corresponds with the desired thickness. Then read straight down the chart to the volume scales to find out how much you need.

The dark area on the right of the chart relates to when the amount of concrete needed to make buying the more expensive ready-mix concrete (see pages 440-1) is a viable proposition.

An allowance should be made for wastage. When ordering separate ingredients to mix yourself, allow 10 per cent extra for cement and round up the aggregate quantities to the next half or whole cubic metre.

Example: An area of $25\,m^2$ ($30\,yd^2$ or $270\,ft^2$) is to be covered with a 100 mm (4 in) thick slab. Therefore, $2·5\,m^3$ ($3·25\,yd^3$) of concrete is needed. An allowance of 10 per cent means that ready-mix is worth considering.

If mixing your own, for a 100 mm (4 in) thickness, Mix A will be used. On the mix A scales, you can see that 15 bags of cement, $1·25\,m^3$ of sand and $2\,m^3$ of coarse aggregate are needed.

With a 10 per cent allowance for waste, the figures are rounded up to 17 bags of cement, $1·5\,m^3$ of sand and $2·5\,m^3$ of coarse aggregate (or $3\,m^3$ of combined aggregates).

HARDCORE

Assembling a sufficient amount of hardcore and reinforcing materials for foundations can be an exhausting and frustrating business. What seemed to be a healthy collection of bricks and rubble lying at the bottom of the garden can prove to be quite inadequate when spread over the area of a path or a garage base.

So how do you go about assembling a stock? Basically, it is a matter of anticipating the need for a supply well in advance. For instance, if you know that you will have to make a path or a garage base in a year's time, then start hunting for hardcore now.

Anyone who moves into a new house will doubtlessly be provided with the nucleus of a stock by the builders. Inevitably a varied collection of stones, bricks and other rubble remains on the site. This is especially true where the house purchaser is left with a barren site to convert into a garden.

Those people with established gardens usually will have to start from scratch. Neighbours might be able to assist, so they should be your starting point. Often, someone in the same road has to hire a skip to dispose of a mountain of unwanted hardstuff. Hiring the skip is a costly business, so someone in this situation would no doubt be only too pleased to allow you to trundle back and forth with a wheelbarrow to remove the 'collection'.

Failing a ready-made supply such as this, it becomes largely a matter of keeping your eyes open. It is surprising how many stones and other oddments are unearthed during normal garden work. So keep a bucket handy in which all this raw material can be collected.

In some parts of the country, stones are in abundance in the soil. Elsewhere a morning's work may realise only a handful of insignificant bits and pieces. The garden itself is not the only source of supply. A house can be fruitful, especially where any alterations are being made that involve structural work.

Table 1   Concrete Mixes

Note that cement quantities are in 50 kg (1 cwt) bags.

Mix A	Portland cement	Damp sand	Coarse aggregate	Yield (approx.)
Proportion by volume	1	2·5	4	5
Bags of cement	1 bag	$0·085\,m^3$ ($3\,ft^3$)	$0.140\,m^3$ ($5\,ft^3$)	$0·17\,m^3$ ($6\,ft^3$)
Per cubic metre (m^3) of concrete	6 bags	$0·5\,m^3$	$0·8\,m^3$	$1\,m^3$
Per cubic yard (yd^3) of concrete	5 bags	$15\,ft^3$	$24\,ft^3$	$1\,yd^3$
Mix B				
Proportion by volume	1	2	3	4
Bags of cement	1 bag	$0·07\,m^3$ ($2·5\,ft^3$)	$0·11\,m^3$ ($3·75\,ft^3$)	$0·14\,m^3$ ($5\,ft^3$)
Per cubic metre of concrete	7 bags	$0·5\,m^3$	$0·75\,m^3$	$1\,m^3$
Per cubic yard of concrete	5·5 bags	$14\,ft^3$	$21\,ft^3$	$1\,yd^3$

Table 2   Estimating Work Quantities of Concrete Mixes

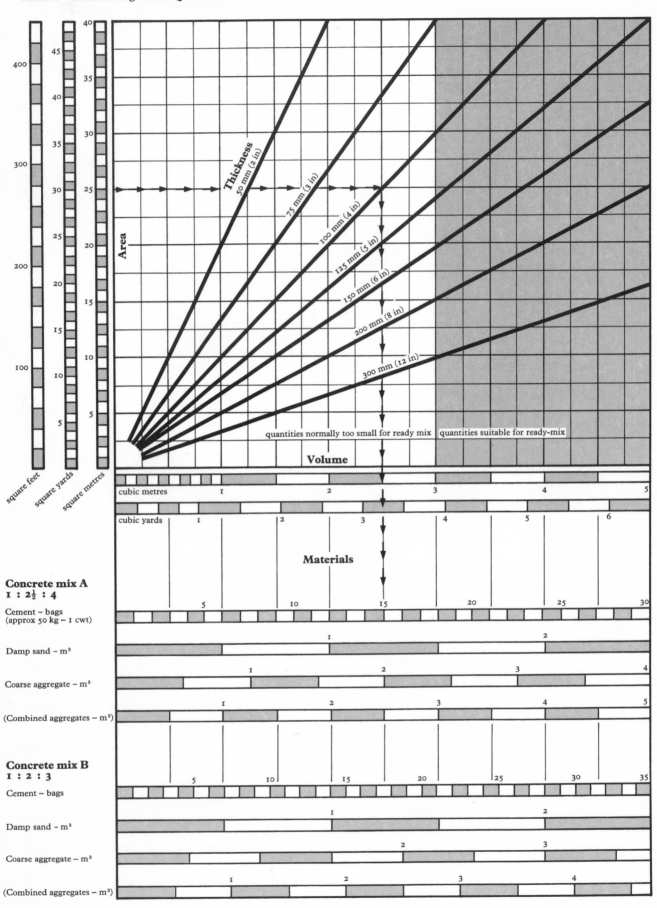

square feet

square yards

square metres

Thickness

Area

50 mm (2 in)

75 mm (3 in)

100 mm (4 in)

125 mm (5 in)

150 mm (6 in)

200 mm (8 in)

300 mm (12 in)

quantities normally too small for ready mix | quantities suitable for ready-mix

Volume

cubic metres

cubic yards

Materials

Concrete mix A
1 : 2½ : 4

Cement – bags
(approx 50 kg – 1 cwt)

Damp sand – m³

Coarse aggregate – m³

(Combined aggregates – m³)

Concrete mix B
1 : 2 : 3

Cement – bags

Damp sand – m³

Coarse aggregate – m³

(Combined aggregates – m³)

You may find that a fireplace is being knocked out, somewhere nearby. Should a neighbour be doing the work, then, no doubt, you could get involved in helping him with a club hammer – your reward being the spoils of the day's labours.

Probably the best thing to do is to put the word around that you are in need of hardcore. Sunday morning at the local could be a good bet.

Do not however think solely on the lines of stone and brick. Metal objects are every bit as valuable to the collector.

Old drainpipes, pipes or rods left over from plumbing alterations, bicycle frames, discarded doll's prams and other metal toys that are no longer required because they are irreparably broken. These are the sorts of things that normally are just left to rust away

at the back of the garden shed – since they are not easy to dispose of through the normal refuse channels. An hour's exercise with a sledge hammer will reduce the scrap to small, convenient shapes.

When these sources of supply are non-existent or have been exhausted, you can always take to the road. A 'collection' box left in the boot of the car as a permanent fixture can become a receptacle for any odds and ends of hardcore or scrap metal that are found on picnics or other family outings. It might even prove a useful way of keeping the children amused for an hour or so during the day – 'hunt the hardcore'.

Incidentally, be a little discerning about using part bricks in hard core.

Reasonable size part bricks should be

kept to one side. These can often be used to form a small, decorative wall enclosing a flower bed or a raised flower garden. Old bricks that have mellowed are far more acceptable and often more pleasing to the eye than new bricks which are brightly coloured.

The pile of hard core you are collecting should be built up on a hard foundation. If the pile is built on earth, there is a danger of it becoming a breeding ground for weeds over a period of time.

TOOLS

Much of the equipment needed for concrete work will be found in most households already. Should the need arise for you to buy any equipment, then pay as much as you can afford for good quality tools.

Fig. 1 Buckets

Fig. 2 Shovel – two are required

Fig. 3 Spade

Fig. 4 Fork

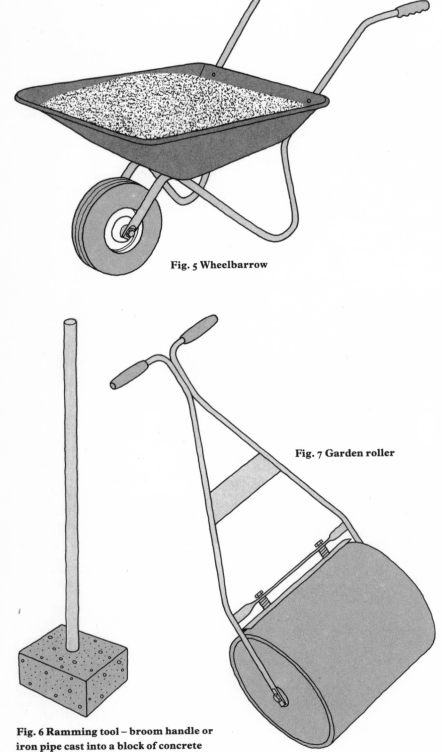

Fig. 5 Wheelbarrow

Fig. 7 Garden roller

Fig. 6 Ramming tool – broom handle or iron pipe cast into a block of concrete

Buying low-priced equipment is a false economy. It will probably need to be replaced – often much sooner than later.

If you use good quality equipment correctly and take the time to clean it and store it properly after use, it will last you a lifetime.

Cleaning after use applies especially to any tools or equipment used in concrete work. Buckets, spades and wheelbarrows and anything else needed to transport or work the concrete must be washed thoroughly after use, and also dried off. 'After use', does not literally mean after each shovelful of concrete has been heaved into the wheelbarrow. It refers to the termination of a work session.

The washing and drying routine is not essential for a short tea break for example, but it should not be neglected before a lunch break. If concrete is allowed to set on any of the equipment, it will have to be chipped away using a cold chisel and a club hammer.

So, the golden rule is that all traces of concrete must be washed off and all equipment dried to prevent a caking of dried concrete and rust forming on metal tools.

There is another aspect about keeping concrete equipment clean. Concrete is heavy stuff to shift around, so it is pointless to allow a layer of concrete to build up on, say, a shovel; this can double its weight and make it much more tiring to lift, which is the last thing you want.

The following is a list of tools needed to cover most of the jobs that a handyman is likely to tackle. Individual descriptions of some of the tools are given later when their use is described in various processes.

Buckets: The handiest size is about two gallons. Heavy-duty types will be needed if they are to be used to carry the concrete from the mixing area to the site. If the buckets are to be used only for measuring out individual materials, then strong polythene types will be perfectly acceptable.

Shovels: Square-end types are

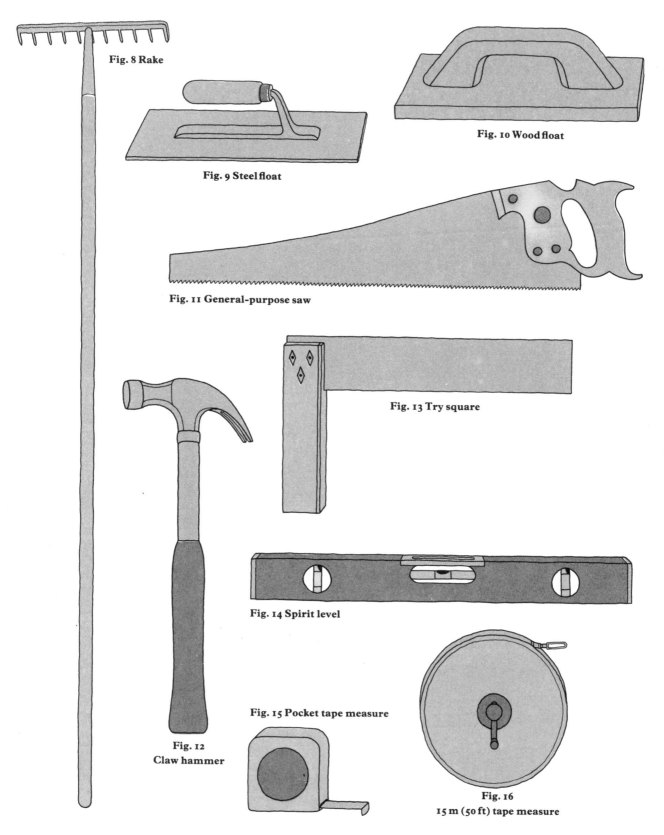

Fig. 8 Rake

Fig. 9 Steel float

Fig. 10 Wood float

Fig. 11 General-purpose saw

Fig. 13 Try square

Fig. 14 Spirit level

Fig. 15 Pocket tape measure

Fig. 12
Claw hammer

Fig. 16
15 m (50 ft) tape measure

needed for mixing and shifting the concrete. When mixing concrete from separate ingredients it is important to keep one shovel solely for cement and one for the other ingredients.

Spade and Fork: These are necessary for digging out foundations, clearing the site, and so on.

Garden roller: Needed for compacting foundations and soil. In the absence of a roller, an ideal 'ramming' tool can be made by casting a broom handle or a piece of iron pipe into a block of concrete measuring about 200 mm × 150 mm × 100 mm (8 in × 6 in × 4 in). This will be as heavy as most people will be able to wield.

Wheelbarrow: For transporting the mixed concrete from the mixing area to the site. Make sure that the wheelbar-

row you use is of sufficient strength to withstand the weight. A light model, normally used for collecting weeds and grass cuttings is not strong enough for this work.

Rake: After placing the concrete on to the site, a rake is needed to spread it out evenly.

Steel Trowel or Steel Float: For smooth finishing the surface of the concrete.

Wood Float: To finish the surface of the concrete to a texture.

General-purpose Saw and a Claw Hammer: For making the formwork in which the concrete is placed to set.

Try Square: For checking right angles. Also needed to make a boning rod (see below).

Spirit Level: A reasonably long, say

460 mm (18 in) model, is preferable. It is used for setting formwork to levels.

Pocket Tape Measure: For setting out small areas of formwork.

String: For setting out.

Builder's Square: Also for setting out, see page 453.

Timber Straight-edge: For setting out the fall of an area of concrete. For example, to ensure that a path slopes away from a house wall to carry off rainwater.

Mixing Platform: If needed, can be made from waterproof plywood or similar material of sufficient size and thickness, or from timber pieces nailed together.

Boning Rods: Three boning rods are needed to ascertain the level of an area. Make your own rods from pieces

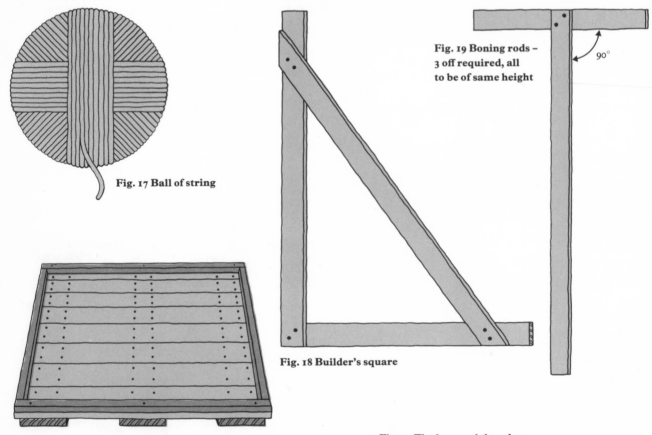

Fig. 17 Ball of string

Fig. 18 Builder's square

Fig. 19 Boning rods – 3 off required, all to be of same height

90°

Fig. 20 Mixing platform

Fig. 21 Timber straight-edge

of softwood as shown in Fig. 19. Nail or screw the cross-piece at right angles to the stem section. All three rods must be exactly the same height or the levels of an intended path will not be predetermined correctly. Use a try square to check the cross-piece is at a right angle.

Tamping Beam: A length of softwood with handles – used for compacting the placed concrete.

Punner: For compacting concrete in foundations. A few square pieces of timber nailed to an old broom handle will suffice.

Brooms: Soft and stiff types to brush finished concrete to leave different surface textures.

Watering Can with a Fine Rose: For adding water when mixing concrete.

MIXING CONCRETE

Anyone who has ever spent their lunch hour break away from the office as a spectator at a nearby building site could have gathered a false impression about concrete mixing.

Watching a site worker knocking up a pile of concrete can give the feeling that it is not too difficult or laborious a job. Be warned, that building site worker is used to it, you are not.

Mixing up concrete is hard work. There is no way that anyone can say in advance how much concrete an individual will be able to knock up and lay before getting too tired. Some may want to work for only an hour at a stretch, others will want to carry on for the best part of the day.

It is important to mix up only

relatively small batches – say about a couple of wheelbarrow loads at a time. Then, if there is a sudden interruption – like an unexpected visitor, or a long telephone call – a huge pile of concrete will not start setting in the sun. If rain clouds do appear on the horizon, use up all the concrete that you have already mixed, and then wait until the rainclouds have passed.

The first essential is to clear an area where you can mix up the concrete. This must be clean, level and firm.

The ideal, of course, is a few square yards close to the site for the path or the shed foundations. The close proximity of the mixing area to the site is important to minimise the extra work involved in transferring each mixed batch of concrete by wheelbarrow to the

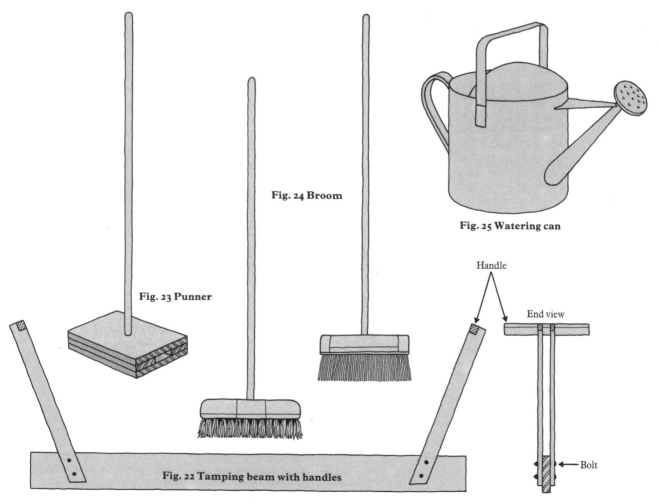

Fig. 23 Punner

Fig. 24 Broom

Fig. 25 Watering can

Handle

End view

Bolt

Fig. 22 Tamping beam with handles

site. There is enough hard work involved without adding to it by poor planning. Besides, if the route passes across a lawn, you will have to provide a line of planks to prevent the wheels of the laden wheelbarrow from sinking into the lawn and leaving unsightly ruts, a problem accentuated after a spell of rain when the ground is more soft than usual.

If the route is uphill then the fully-laden barrow will take a lot of pushing – especially towards the end of the day or a work session when fatigue has started to be noticeable.

Making a Mixing Base: If there is not a convenient mixing area near the site, one should be made. A piece of 25 mm (1 in) thick waterproof plywood, about 1·2 m (4 ft) square, makes an ideal base (Fig. 20); though a few boards held together with battens nailed to the undersides and running in the opposite direction will make a suitable substitute. Use long nails to secure the battens to the boards. Knock them in from the top face so that their points project at least 13 mm (½ in) through the battens. The points can then be knocked down at right angles so that they clench on to the battens and will not be pulled through.

Whatever material is used to make the platform, the addition of some side pieces – 25 mm thick × 25 or 50 mm wide softwood battens – are useful to prevent any of the mix running away when the water is added.

Protection of Drains: It is most important that any nearby drains are covered to prevent any of the concrete mix from inadvertently running down them. This can happen easily during the mixing process if a little too much water is added to the mix. And any concrete that sets in drains could spell real trouble later on.

Tools Required: The mixing tools needed are two buckets, two shovels and a watering can fitted with a fine rose.

Maintaining Uniform Consistency of Mix: It is of no importance whether the buckets used are of plastic or metal, but it is essential that they are the same size. This way you will know that if the concrete mix required demands one part of cement, two parts of sand and three parts of coarse aggregate, then you will need one bucketful of cement, two bucketsfull of sand and three buckets-full of coarse aggregate. All the buckets must, of course, be filled to the same level.

Clearly, using the quantities listed above will produce only a certain amount of concrete – a uniform concrete mix of a certain volume.

If it is your intention to work with only small amounts, then this might be a suitable amount to mix up each time. Certainly, if the work is being carried out at intervals of perhaps half an hour in the evening, it will be. If you want to mix up a larger 'pile' each time, then double or treble the proportions of materials used.

For example, if you are doubling the quantities, use 2 buckets of cement, 4 buckets of sand and 6 buckets of coarse aggregate. Or, to treble the quantity, use 3 buckets of cement, 6 buckets of sand and 9 buckets of coarse aggregate.

The important thing is to attain uniform consistency of the volume of the ingredients. Provided that you are able to use it before it sets, then you can mix up as much as you like in one go. Whatever you do, do not lose count of the number of buckets used for each ingredient.

Despite the fact that there are three ingredients, only two buckets are needed – one to be used solely for cement and the other one to be used for the sand and the coarse aggregate. This

second bucket can be used also to fetch fresh water from a tap to add to the mix via the watering can.

Two spades are needed for the same reason. One must be used solely for cement – lifting it directly from its bag on to the mix. This way there is no chance of the spade becoming wet. The second spade can be used for mixing only – and heaving the mix into the wheelbarrow if need be.

Amount of Water Required for the Mix: Now comes another of those difficult questions which beginners always ask and which is extremely difficult to give a written answer to. It is the sort of thing that I would prefer to explain through demonstration.

The question is, how much water should be added to the mix? How will I know the exact amount to add to the dry ingredients?

Well, before answering that, I must stress the absolute necessity of using clean water to mix concrete. If the water contains any organic matter – which it certainly will if it is taken from a pond – then it will prevent the concrete from setting correctly.

Now for the amount to use. Basically there is no way that you can measure it out in the same way as the other ingredients are measured. As a rough guide to the sort of quantity required, a mix of one bucket of cement, two buckets of sand and three buckets of coarse aggregate would need about half a bucket of water to bring it to the right sort of consistency.

Now for this term consistency in relation to concrete. Consistency relates to how sloppy the concrete is after mixing.

The ideal consistency is a buttery mixture which is neither too dry nor too wet.

If this description is not entirely clear, then play it safe until you get more experience and aim at producing a drier rather than a wetter mix. Provided that the mix is workable, then the drier it is, the better its performance will be.

Should the water start to run out of the concrete when a shovelful is emptied on to the ground, then it is far too wet. As the water drains away it will take with it some of the chemicals that make the concrete set hard.

It is no use crossing your fingers and hoping for the best in this situation. When the concrete dries out it will almost certainly crack up.

Mixing the Dry Materials: Now to the actual mixing. Initially, pour out the buckets of aggregate to form a flattish circle on the mixing site or the boards. On top of this add the correct number of buckets of sand. Into the hole in the middle of the circle, pour the cement (Fig. 26).

Then mix all the ingredients thoroughly.

Start at the perimeter of the circle and turn over the ingredients (Fig. 27). At first, when turning the ingredients where they are spread thinly around the edges, the work will be quite easy. As you work inwards, however, towards the cement in the centre, it will become increasingly more difficult to lift and turn the spade over to disperse the ingredients.

For this reason a lot of people prefer to spread the mix over a wider area to form a thin layer perhaps only about 50 mm (2 in) thick. This can be easier to mix up.

It is of little consequence how you go about the mixing provided that, when the going gets tough, the temptation to skimp the job is resisted.

When the ingredients have been well mixed, the heap will have taken on an overall grey appearance. Some larger stones from the coarse aggregate may not be covered by a complete grey coat but this is of little importance.

Now, form the ingredients into a crater, before adding the water.

Adding the Water: There is some disagreement about the best method of adding the water. Expert opinion is

Fig. 26 Pour the cement into the hole in the middle of the aggregate

Fig. 27 Turn over the ingredients

Fig. 28 Add a little water

divided as to whether it should be poured on straight from a bucket or whether it should be sprinkled on from a watering can.

Personally, for the beginner, I favour the watering can. This in fact is the method recommended by the Cement and Concrete Association. It gives greater control over the amount of water added and prevents some draining away and getting everywhere – except into the mix.

As more experience is gained, if the individual feels happier using a bucket, then there is no reason to avoid this.

So, sprinkle about one half of the total water into the hole in the centre of the crater. If the walls of the crater have been made evenly, the water will not escape. If a friend should be willing to do the sprinkling for you, so much the better.

Sprinkle some of the dry material from the perimeter into the water and, as it gets soaked up, start to mix the ingredients together.

Gradually add all the water by forming the crater again, sprinkling a little water into it and then mix as before.

Keep turning over the mix, occasionally chopping it with the spade as though you are slicing an onion until it is of the correct buttery consistency throughout.

It is absolutely essential to ensure that all the ingredients are mixed thoroughly after adding the water.

The mix can now be loaded into the wheelbarrow and transferred to the site to be placed and compacted as soon as possible.

READYMIX CONCRETE

Readymix concrete is available in most areas – your yellow pages directory will give a list of suppliers.

Readymix certainly saves a lot of time and effort and you are assured of getting a consistent mix but it has its disadvantages as well.

Whether or not you decide to use it or mix your own concrete depends on several factors.

The basic factor is the amount of concrete needed – this will determine whether it is really viable to use readymix. Since most companies have a minimum charge based on a given quantity, frequently about $3\,\text{m}^3$ ($4\,\text{yd}^3$), readymix becomes uneconomic for small jobs.

So, for a start, you will have to telephone around a list of suppliers to

Fig. 29 Spreading readymix concrete with shovels

find out what is the minimum load that they will deliver. You might even find a company that will entertain loads as little as $1\,\text{m}^3$ ($1\frac{1}{3}\,\text{yd}^3$).

Many people who have had experience of hand mixing or of hiring a mechanical mixer for the job would prefer to pay out the extra money for readymix – the difference may not be that big at the end of the day, depending on the job.

But you must remember that a lorry will be delivering a huge load of wet concrete to you all in one go. And this

has to be placed and compacted in a couple of hours – even less on a hot day. To give you an idea of the pile of concrete that you will have to deal with quite rapidly, a 3 m³ load weighs about seven tons – and that is an awful lot of shifting to get through in a short time.

Should the lorry have direct access to the site, things will be much more convenient and simpler. The lorry driver will be able to tip the complete load directly on to the site where it can be spread out immediately with a shovel and rake to a rough level.

The lorry delivering the concrete will be a twenty tonner which may be far too heavy for your driveway to support. It is also possible that your garden gates will not have a wide enough gap for the lorry to drive through. If access is impossible, then the load will have to be discharged as near as possible to the site. From that point, as many friends as you can assemble will have to get busy with wheelbarrows to transport it quickly for placing.

Should help not be available, then you could have the concrete delivered in batches on successive days, or on Saturdays, or whenever you are ready for it. This will work out to be more expensive, however. One load of 4 m³ (5·2 yd³) will cost less than two loads of 2 m³ (2·6 yd³) or four loads of 1 m³ (1⅓ yd³).

Many readymix concrete suppliers will deliver your order within a couple of days and at prearranged times.

Ordering Readymix Concrete:
When ordering, you will need to tell the supplier, the quantity of concrete required and its purpose. The last detail will help to establish the correct mix.

The strength of each mix available is often described by using a numerical grading system. For a greenhouse base, your supplier might, for example, recommend grade 15. For a drive, he might recommend grade 25, depending on the intended thickness and the type of vehicle that is likely to be using the drive.

It is also possible to get warm

concrete from suppliers. This will set more quickly – very beneficial if work has to be done at a time of the year when frost, which could damage the concrete, is likely.

Other considerations are whether the load is to be dumped all in one spot, all in one go, or whether you will want it to be distributed over the site.

These factors, of course, determine the amount of time that the lorry will remain at your home – usually of course, extra waiting will involve extra expense.

A final point to remember is the weather. Find out what policy the supplier adopts if it turns out to be raining on delivery morning. Obviously, you will not want to work in heavy rain; this could harm the concrete.

Although, since you will be ordering locally, it is unlikely to be pouring where you are but dry at the supplier's yard; but it could happen and the lorry could suddenly, unexpectedly, arrive after you have sent your helpers away to their homes.

So make sure that you can cancel your order in bad weather or for any other reason – illness, for example. Most firms, however, automatically stop delivering in rainy weather.

Finally, the site and all the necessary tools should be ready when the lorry arrives.

DRY MIX
Bags of dry mixed ingredients are available under various brand names, Marleymix and Readymix Drypack are examples. In these bags, you will find cement, sand and aggregate all ready to be mixed with water.

There are normally two basic mixes. One to make fine concrete and the other to make coarse concrete. The former is intended for thinner sections – footpaths rather than driveways, for example; the latter can be for bases, driveways and similar surfaces which require strength. Fine mixes contain 10 mm aggregate; coarse mixes contain aggregates up to 20 mm.

The obvious question that arises, of course, is : why not use these dry mixes to save all the bother of buying separate ingredients ? The answer is economy. These bags of dry-mixed materials cost considerably more than buying separate ingredients.

On smaller jobs requiring a small amount of concrete, they are a good investment. Indeed, by the time you have spent petrol money collecting a minimal amount of sand, cement and aggregate from your local builder's merchant, you could be much better off financially buying a bag of dry mix.

There is another factor in favour of buying dry mix and that is that there will not be much left over at the end of the job. If you bought a bag of cement, it is possible that a good deal of it will still be left at the completion of the job. And, if there is not an immediate use for it, then there will be all the problems of storing it.

On larger jobs, where a fair number of bags is required, dry mix is certainly uneconomical. A large bag of dry mix makes about 0·02 m³ (0·75 ft³) of concrete. There are smaller bags available.

Factors which have to be weighed against economy and which, in borderline cases, could sway your decision in favour of dry mix rather than mixing your own, are access, storage, and whether or not the job is to be done in stages.

If a delivery lorry is going to dump sand and aggregate in a pile outside your gate leaving you to trundle back and forth with a wheelbarrow – or buckets – to transport it to the back garden, then you may well decide to pay the extra money for the convenience of dry mix.

If there is nowhere to store heaps of sand and aggregate, then the dry mix bags will certainly be more convenient.

Finally, if the work is going to be done on 'an hour this week, an hour next week' basis, then you may also consider that you will be better off with dry mix.

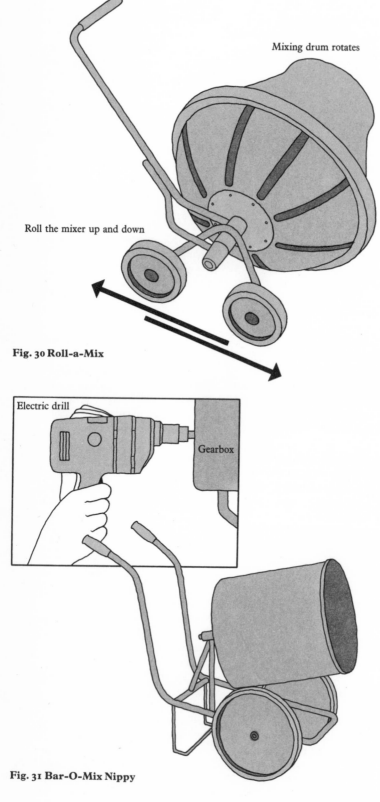

Mixing drum rotates

Roll the mixer up and down

Fig. 30 Roll-a-Mix

Electric drill

Gearbox

Fig. 31 Bar-O-Mix Nippy

MIXERS

Much of the spadework required for hand mixing can be avoided by using a mixer. Whether you buy or hire a mixer depends on the amount of work you are doing.

There are various types available starting with a lightweight type which will mix about $0.02 \, m^3$ ($0.75 \, ft^3$) in a couple of minutes. This type, called a Roll-a-mix (Fig. 30) is, in essence, a mixing drum on a trolley. You shovel in the ingredients and roll the mixer up and down to mix them as thoroughly as possible.

A slightly more sophisticated version is the Bar-O-Mix Nippy (Fig. 31). This is operated by attaching it to an ordinary electric drill. The drill is connected to a gearbox from where a belt runs to, and turns the mixing drum.

You can dispense with the mechanical operation and turn the drum manually if, for example, an electricity supply for the drill cannot be arranged. Since the drum is mounted on a trolley arrangement, the mixed concrete can be pushed to the site for placing.

There are other forms of small mixers. One, for example, is operated by oil and petrol, having a four-stroke engine.

If there is an enormous amount of concreting to be done, then it would probably be worthwhile buying a diesel mixer (Fig. 32). A diesel mixer can produce more than $0.08 \, m^3$ ($3 \, ft^3$) of concrete in one mix and enable the mix to be deposited on to the site much more easily.

When I say buy a mixer, I am thinking in terms of a second-hand one. If a really big job is likely to take at least eight weeks to complete, it would be much more expensive to hire one for that period. At the end of the job, don't forget that, when the mixer is returned to the hire shop, there is nothing to show for it.

Look at it this way. In the past I have hired a mixer, which for a week was fairly costly, but for eight weeks proved to be a considerable outlay, even with a reasonable discount.

Now, at the start of the job, I could probably have bought a second-hand diesel mixer for about £50 which, at the end of eight weeks, must have been worth most of what I had paid for it. Of course, you would have to be careful not to buy a poor mixer which could break down after a short period of use, and you would have to have somewhere to store it if you do not sell it.

Fig. 32 Diesel mixer

COLOURED CEMENTS
A wide range of colours can be introduced into concrete using coloured cements. Thus a path can be formed in an attractive shade to harmonise with any surrounding brickwork or stonework.

Cements of various colours are available from builders' merchants and garden centres.

If you design a path in a colour you must take into account the effect that

time will have on its appearance. The initial brightness of a coloured cement softens and mellows after a while so this must be considered if the object is to harmonise the colour with the surrounding area.

If a path is to be left with either a straightforward smooth or textured surface then it does not really matter what colour is chosen, it is simply a matter of personal taste.

However, should you intend to

expose the aggregate to leave a stony finished effect, or you intend to use cobblestones set in mortar over the concrete, then the colour of the stones will have to be considered in relation to the cement colour.

Here, again, the combination of the differing colours of stones and cements offer a whole host of alternative effects.

Many coloured cements cost only a little more than ordinary types.

It is most important to keep all materials and working conditions clean when using coloured cements – which must also be kept clear from cements of other colours. Uniformity of mixing is especially important, otherwise a patchy effect could result.

USING CONCRETE

Whether you are transporting large or small loads in a wheelbarrow or a bucket to the site, make sure that all the concrete is emptied out each time. Any left behind could gradually accumulate and go hard. Either tip the concrete from the barrow into a heap on the site (or into the foundation trenches) or shovel it out in stages. It is not important how this is done since, in any case, it will have to be raked out evenly after it has been tipped.

It is advisable to support the side of a trench with a platform of, say, thick plywood, to withstand the weight of the barrow, or the earth could well cave in when you are unloading the concrete.

Make certain that the concrete is pushed well into any crevices or cracks in trenches or between corners of formwork timbers. Use a piece of timber or even your boot to do this.

Spread out each layer with a rake before fetching another load. Since the

Fig. 33 On wide drives and bases, it is useful to fit 'handles' to the tamping beam so that it can be manoeuvred more easily (see also Fig. 22)

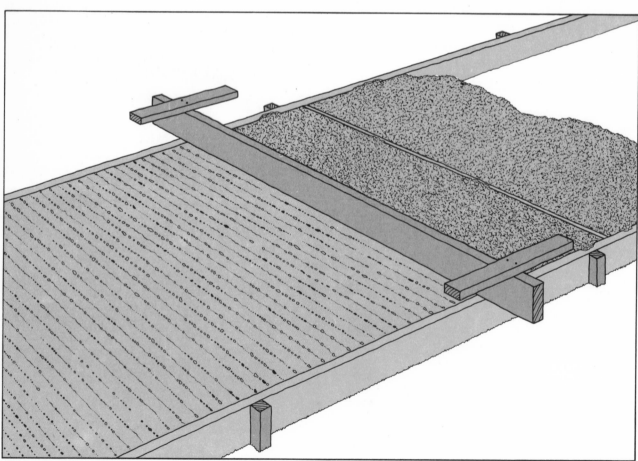

concrete will have to be compacted tightly, initially rake it out slightly higher than the level of the side forms. Thus, when it is compacted, it will not drop below the finished intended height.

As a guide, for an intended 100 mm (4 in) thick layer, rake the concrete to about 13 mm ($\frac{1}{2}$ in) above the side forms.

Where trench foundations are being filled, place the concrete in layers about 230 mm (9 in) deep before compacting.

After each layer has been thoroughly compacted, add another layer.

The object of tamping concrete after it has been placed is to make certain that no hollows or air pockets remain under the surface. If these are present, the concrete will be less strong and durable.

The tamper should be long enough to span the formwork with about 150 mm (6 in) to spare on both sides (Fig. 33).

On a path, one person will probably be able to cope with the tamping by themselves by standing on the uncon-creted section as they work down the path. Here, though, you would be able to concrete only about one yard at a time since this would be the maximum distance that you will be able to reach without kneeling on the fresh concrete.

On wider paths or garage bases, or similar areas, a helper will certainly be needed on the other end of the tamper.

The tamper should be used with a chopping action by dropping it on to the formwork. Progress in stages of about half the thickness of the tamping board. If, for example, the tamping board is of 25 mm (1 in) thick timber, progress with 13 mm ($\frac{1}{2}$ in) chops. Complete each concreted section working with a steady, rhythmic action.

When the tamping is finished, the surface of the concrete will have a rippled or corrugated appearance which has to be levelled off. Do this by placing the tamper across the formwork and using a sawing action to flatten off any high spots, and fill the low spots.

If necessary, add more concrete to fill up any depressions. The object is to leave a flat surface which is flush with the tops of the forms.

Fig. 34 Using a punner

Obviously, when filling a trench in layers of about 23 cm (9 in) thick, it will not be possible to use the type of tamper suitable for working across formwork as Fig. 33. Here you will have to use either a punner (Fig. 34), or the end of a stout piece of timber.

Since the pegs that were driven into the ground to give a reference for the correct height levels are needed right up to the final compaction stage, do not tamp on top of them otherwise they will be driven deeper into the ground.

FINISHES

Dependent on whether the concrete is forming a path or a garage floor, or whatever, different surface finishes can be formed. For example, a garage or shed floor will inevitably have to be swept clean from time to time – which is clearly a much easier operation when carried out on a smooth surface.

However, on a path or steps, a rippled or rough surface is more appropriate since it makes things a lot safer under-foot for the elderly and for the very young in icy weather.

For a smooth, durable, easy to sweep floor, a steel trowel or steel float finish is called for. This is not an easy task for an inexperienced person who has to deal with a large area and wants a high-quality finish. However, a reasonably smooth result can be achieved with a little practice.

The fresh concrete should be finished with a wood float first of all. Then, after a break to allow the concrete to harden sufficiently without being fully set, the steel trowel is used.

I must emphasise, here, that if first rate results are essential, it would be worth while calling in professional help.

If you decide to stop at the wood float stage, you will have produced a semi-smooth surface. By using the float correctly – in a semi-circular movement

Fig. 35 Brush across the concrete in lines with a stiff bass broom to leave a deeper texture

Fig. 36 Protecting fresh concrete with a cover

– a slight, though attractive texture will result. A similar effect, though the texture will be more random, and slightly more prominent, is achieved by tapping the concrete with the back of a clean spade.

Other finishes fall into the rough surface category. If a rippled surface is needed, you can finish off at the tamping stage. If only a slightly rippled effect is required, use the tamper on the right angles to the centre line of the concrete. Maintain a steady, sawing rhythm with the tamper.

If a slightly smoother appearance is required, brush the concrete with a soft broom. The degree of roughness resulting will depend on when the brushing is done. It all depends on how much the concrete has set. With experience you will know the sort of finish that you can anticipate. So, experiment on a small area until you get the desired effect.

If a drive or a path is on a slope, a deeper texture finish is desirable. Use a stiff bass-broom, brushing across the concrete in lines (Fig. 35). Do this when the concrete is fresh.

Should you prefer to see an exposed aggregate surface, which can be very attractive, use a soft brush to finish.

Leave the concrete to set sufficiently so that the stone particles cannot be dislodged.

Now, using the brush in conjunction with a watering can, spray on water and brush out, gradually working over the whole area. The object is to brush away the slurry of cement and water to leave the stones fractionally above the surface. Aim to leave a consistent finish.

Protection: The wet concrete needs to be protected from both accidental damage and from the elements. By damage, I am thinking in terms of footprints sunk in the new surface. This is much more likely where there are children or animals about.

So after each section of, say, 1 or 1·5 m (3 or 4 ft) of concrete is placed, cover it with any suitable material which will act as a deterrent. Scraps of wire netting, a few planks stretched across the formwork, this is the sort of thing to use. Indentations are very hard to fill in successfully; they nearly always remain identifiable.

I should emphasise here, that protective coverings that could themselves mark the surface should be laid only when the concrete has hardened sufficiently not to be damaged by them.

Extreme elements – sun and frost can damage concrete when it is fresh. If work is carried out on a hot summer's day, the fresh concrete can dry out far too quickly. The result could be cracks in the surface.

Suitable protective coverings include plastic sheeting, hessian or sacking (Fig. 36).

If plastic sheeting is used, make sure that the edges are well weighted down with bricks or stones. If you forget, then the wind will get underneath the edges and blow the sheeting away.

Where hessian or sacking is used, make sure that this is kept damp for about three days.

When frost attacks concrete that is setting, it leaves the material loose and crumbly. Remember, as well, that 'unexpected' frosts are a reasonably regular occurrence right into May.

The ideal protective method is to use a layer of straw over the concrete and cover this with plastic sheeting. Make sure that there are no loose edges where cold winds can blow underneath.

If sacking or hessian is used, again fasten down the edges. Obviously, if they are being used as a frost protection, they will not be watered as before.

COBBLESTONES

Cobblestones provide a finish which has a charming 'period' flavour especially suited to courtyard settings of 'olde worlde' gardens or patios.

Producing a cobbled area is a slow process since each stone has to be placed by hand into a fresh layer of mortar.

A builder's merchant will be able to supply suitably large stones – about 75 mm (3 in) is the ideal size.

Fig. 37 Press down cobblestones with a wood float

Having laid a concrete base (using Mix A) at least 75 mm thick, a small quantity of mortar (use one part cement to three parts sand) should be made up and placed over the base. The sand must be builder's sand and not coarse sand.

No guidance can be given as to the exact amount of mortar to mix up each time and place over the base since much depends on individual working speeds. The best practice is to start with a little and build up to larger quantities as you get more experience.

The important thing is to place the mortar within about an hour of laying the main base. This will ensure that the stones are well bedded down into the base. Dependent on the area being covered help could be essential if the time limit is to be met.

As each layer of mortar is spread,

press each stone individually into the mix so that a little over half its depth lies below the surface. Obviously, there is no hard and fast rule about the arrangement of the stones. Just butt up edges as close as possible.

After each area is complete, level off the tops of the stones by pressing down with a wood float (Fig. 37). At this stage, do not waste time removing any mortar which finds its way on to the projecting surfaces of the stones.

Complete the whole area and then leave it for about three hours. The mortar then can be removed by washing and brushing.

PATH LAYING

Once the line that a path is to take has been established, a couple of helpers with an hour or so to spare will be needed to assist with the job of establishing a level site. Puddles of water that collect after a rainfall on to a finished path are a sure sign of negligence at the levelling stage.

Before summoning the helpers, collect together the essential equipment needed – three T-shaped boning rods of equal length, three pegs and a mallet. At either end of the site, hammer a peg into the ground in the middle of the path. The peg tops represent the intended surface level. Bear in mind any damp proof course of a building nearby; the level of the path should not raise the ground to within 150 mm (6 in) of any adjoining damp proof course. This will not, of course, be a problem with a path running away from the house, but it may well be where the path adjoins a house wall.

The helpers can now be called in. Get one to stand at the far end of the path with the boning rod resting on the first peg. The person who will be doing the sighting should take up a similar position at the other end of the path. The third person who will be levelling the intermediate peg should be positioned midway down the path (Fig. 38). The person doing the sighting, by peering along the boning rods will be able to gauge how far the intermediate

peg should be driven into the ground in order to bring the cross-pieces of the three boning rods into line.

When the three boning rods are exactly in line, a correct level has been established.

Depending on the thickness of the concrete to be used, the ground might have to be lowered a little. Usually, though, any extra digging at this stage will be minimal. The three pegs sunk into the ground will serve as a yardstick for the amount of extra earth that has to be removed. The base must allow for a covering of, say, 75 mm (3 in) of

concrete to finish level with the tops of the pegs.

Fill any soft areas of the ground with hardcore and roll the whole length of the path to ensure thorough compaction.

Fig. 38 The person levelling the intermediate peg should be positioned midway down the path. The 'sighter' will gauge how far the intermediate peg should be driven into the ground

Laying the Formwork: If the path is to be laid in a straight line, then stretch a length of string between the start and finish points on each side of the path (Fig. 39). When the string lines are pulled taut, they will indicate exact straight lines as a guide for fixing the formwork.

The timber formwork can now be laid following the line of the strings. Remember that the width of the timber should be equal to the required depth of the concrete.

Drive pegs into the ground and nail them to the formwork every few metres so that, when the concrete is poured in, the formwork will remain in the correct position.

Pieces of stone or brick, about half the depth of the timber will give extra stability if placed against the inside edges of the formwork. These will eventually be covered by the concrete.

Fig. 39 Stretching a length of string as a guide for the formwork

Fig. 40 Drive pegs into the ground

Fig. 41 Nail the pegs to the formwork

Fig. 42a Checking formwork for level

Fig. 43 A curve in the formwork made
with a series of saw cuts

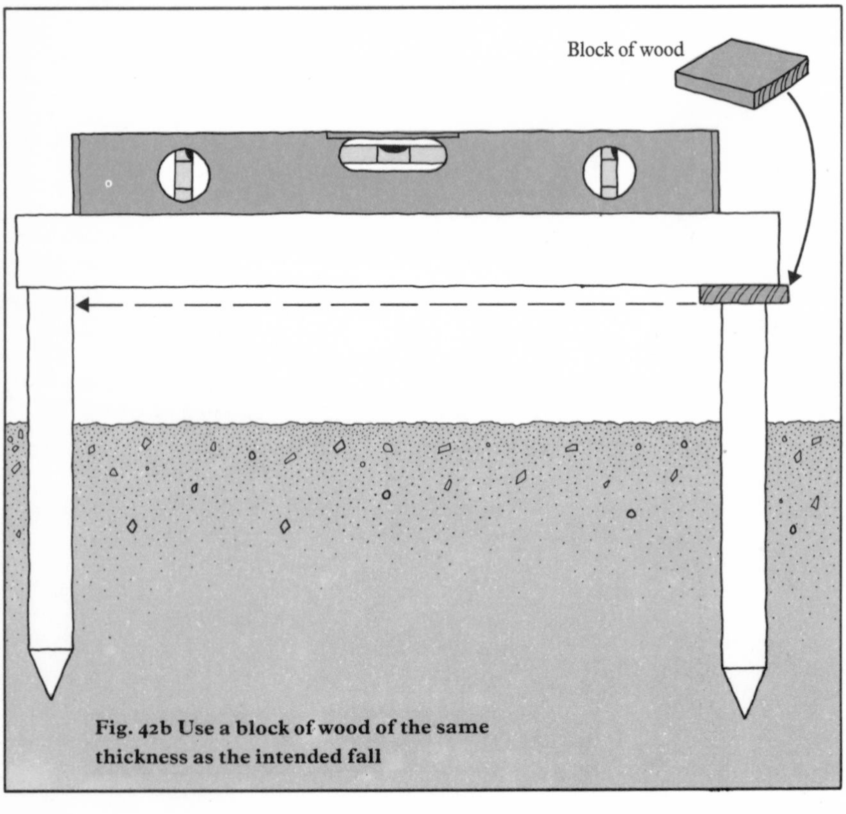

Block of wood

Fig. 42b Use a block of wood of the same
thickness as the intended fall

**Allowing for Slope and Crossfall of
Path:** Ideally, the path should slope
very slightly to one side to ensure that
rainwater drains away. Indeed, if a path
is laid against a house wall, a slight slope
is essential so that water drains away
from the house.

The required slope, usually called a
crossfall, depends on the width of the
path. It must be steep enough for
speedy drainage, but not so steep that it
is immediately obvious to the eye.
Somewhere around a 13 mm slope in 1
metre or 1 in in 6 ft is adequate.

Obtaining a correct crossfall (extreme
accuracy is not essential) is achieved by
setting one side of the formwork lower
than the other. To check the forms for
level, place a block of wood (of the same
thickness as the intended fall) on the
lower side of the formwork, and use the
spirit level with the aid of a piece of
spare timber as shown in Figs. 42a and
42b. Repeat this check at regular
intervals down the length of the path.

If a curved path is being laid, the
formwork can be bent to the required
shape simply by making a series of saw
cuts into the timber to half its thickness
(Fig. 43).

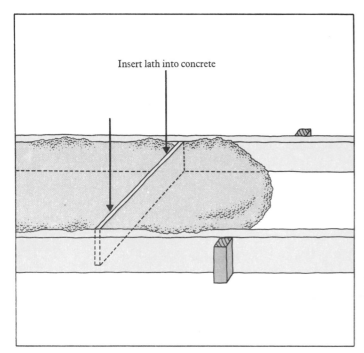

Insert lath into concrete

Laying Paths in Sections: To prevent the possibility of the path cracking, it is necessary to lay a path in sections – each about 2·5 m (8 ft) long. The work can be completed in a continuous run by inserting thin, softwood laths across the end of each section (Fig. 44), leaving the laths permanently in place, or an alternative sectional method can be used.

In this case a larger batten should be placed across each section and be removed when the concrete has set eventually. The next section is then laid, leaving butt joints between each section.

If hard core is not used to form the base, the concrete can be laid on bare earth, well compacted. It is advisable always to dampen the ground with water before placing concrete.

Mix up enough concrete to complete one bay at a time. Should the weather show signs of turning nasty, the bay can be completed and covered, and work finished for the day, and resumed when dry weather returns.

Fig. 44 Inserting a thin lath at the end of a section

Fig. 45 Rest the tamper on the formwork

Fig. 46 Using a lengthwise tamper on alternate bays when a wall prevents normal tamping

Spread out the concrete with a shovel, working it well into place; then rake it down to a height of about 6 mm ($\frac{1}{4}$ in) above the top of the formwork.

Even if the path is narrow, a helper makes life a lot easier when compacting the concrete. With the tamping beam, or a length of timber about 300 mm (1 ft) wider than the path, resting on the side forms, work it across the surface, first with a chopping motion and then with a sawing motion (Fig. 47). If a continuous sectional method is used, make sure that the concrete on both sides of the lath is well compacted (Fig. 48).

For butt joint laying, when the work session for the day is completed, lay a stout batten across the edge of the concrete to make a vertical joint (Fig. 49). When work is resumed, a simple butt-joint is formed, after removing the batten (Fig. 50).

SETTING OUT A SITE

Having settled on the area to be occupied by a garage base or a terrace, the important thing is to ensure that the corners of the marked out site are at right angles.

To do this you need a builder's square. This you can make yourself; there is nothing difficult about it; it is a straightforward hammer and nails job.

The only requirements are three lengths of softwood; one 5 ft long, one 4 ft long and one 3 ft long – or, if working in the metric system, the three lengths can be 1·666 m, 1·333 m and 1 m.

Join them up to form a triangle as shown in Fig. 51. The sides must be kept to the proportions of 3:4:5. If this is so, then the angle between the two shorter sides is certain to be at a right angle (90°). Geometric principles guarantee this.

You can make a smaller square if it is more convenient. The important thing is to make certain that the 3:4:5 proportions are correctly maintained. Use a straight-edge to check the square when complete.

Next, several bits and pieces are needed: a builder's tape measure,

Fig. 47 Stronger handles are needed when tamping a wide drive using thicker timber

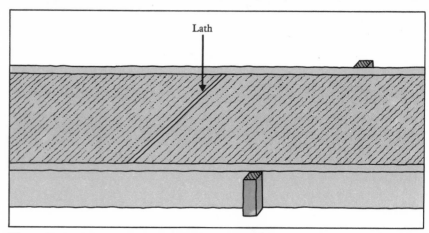

Fig. 48 Compact the concrete on both sides of the lath

Fig. 49 At the end of the day, make a vertical stop end

452

Fig. 50 Form a butt joint when work is resumed

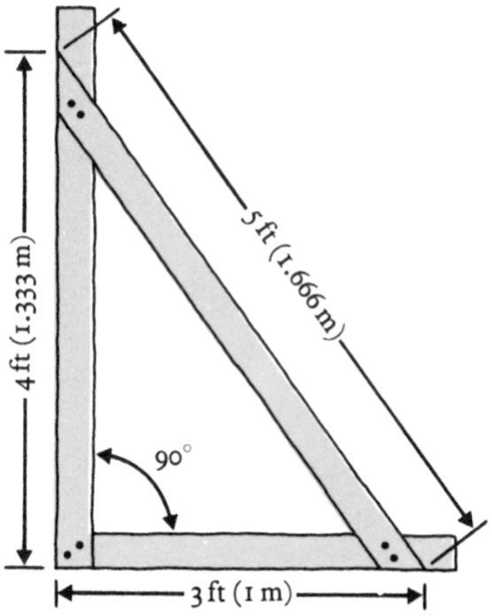

pegs, sufficient string (this will depend on the size of the site being marked out), and a club hammer.

The site for a simple rectangular base should be set out as follows: Locate one side and corner A of the proposed rectangle (Fig. 53) using a known reference point – a nearby building or a wall boundary can be used. (For setting levels of the formwork, a damp-proof course in an existing building is a handy reference point.)

Side 1 can now be pegged out and joined with string. Line 2 can now be set out between pegs (corners A and C). Check with the builder's square that corner A is at 90°. Locate B from A by measuring along line 1. Peg out line 3 using the builder's square to check for a right-angled corner at B. To position the pegs for line 4, measure from line 1 outside corners A and B.

Having pegged out the area and joined up all pegs with string, double check all corners and measure all sides for length. Measure the diagonals to ensure that they are exactly the same in length.

Fig. 51 The angle between the shorter sides of the builder's square must be at 90°

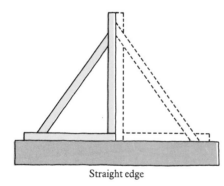

Straight edge

Fig. 52 Check the square with a straight-edge

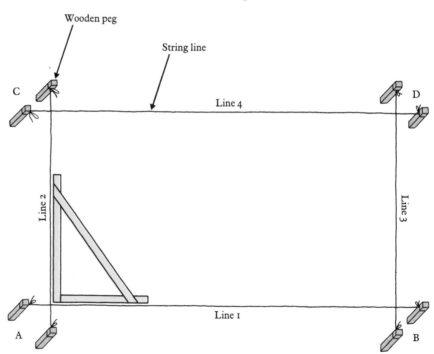

Fig. 53 Marking out a site for a rectangular base

LEVELS

To check levels using a damp-proof course as the reference point, follow the set-up shown in Fig. 54. Drive one peg into the ground until its top is level with the damp-proof course. Repeat this procedure by driving in another peg along the intended line of the path. Bridge the two pegs with a straight-edge and check with a spirit level. Any adjustments needed should be made to the outside peg – not to the peg nearest the damp-proof course (d.p.c.). Remember, however, that the finished level of the path should be at least 150 mm (6 in) below the d.p.c.

Water levelling, using a length of transparent tubing, is an extremely accurate alternative method. With this method of levelling, make sure that all air bubbles have escaped from the tube, otherwise faulty readings will be obtained.

Again, drive a wooden peg into the ground adjacent to the wall until its top is level with the d.p.c. line. Tie one end of the tube temporarily to the peg. Tie the other end to a second peg. Now, adjust the position of the tube nearest the wall until the water inside is level with the d.p.c. line. The water line inside the other end of the tube should now be marked on the peg that it is tied to. The two water levels will now be exactly the same.

MAKING A SMALL BASE

Prepare the site by skimming off the topsoil and digging out any roots. Then, having compacted the soil by rolling or tamping, fill any soft spots with pieces of hardcore. Repeat the compacting process over any such filled areas. Where the base is to be laid over an existing base of asphalt, gravel or old concrete, level the surface, again filling holes or soft areas before compacting.

Prepare an area 150 mm (6 in) oversize all round the intended size of the complete base. This will provide a good surface for pegging down the formwork.

Having set out the site, position the formwork using 25 mm (1 in) thick

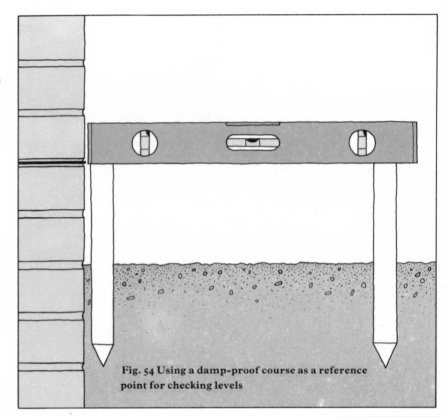

Fig. 54 **Using a damp-proof course as a reference point for checking levels**

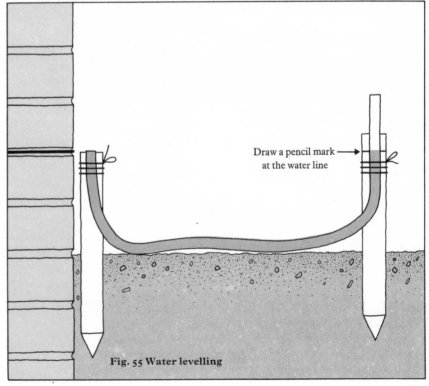

Draw a pencil mark at the water line

Fig. 55 **Water levelling**

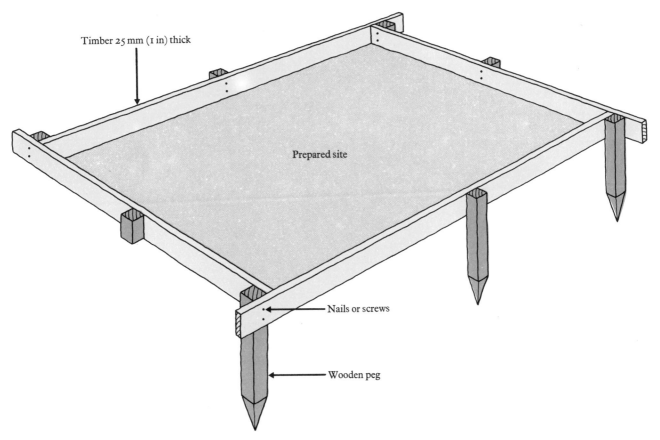

Timber 25 mm (1 in) thick

Prepared site

Nails or screws

Wooden peg

Fig. 56 The formwork in position

lengths of timber of the required size for the finished depth of concrete. There is no need to cut the formwork timbers to the exact length. Provided that the timbers form right angles at corners and are well secured with nails or screws to the pegs driven into the ground, this is sufficient (Fig. 56).

For this sort of job, use Mix A (see page 431). Spread the concrete with a rake until it is about 13 mm ($\frac{1}{2}$ in) above the level of the formwork. It can then be compacted. Allow it to cure for four days in warm weather; one week in normal conditions; ten days during cold weather.

The formwork can now be removed and the floor put into use. Never remove the formwork before the curing period has ended; the edges and the corners of the concrete will still be weak.

LARGER BASES
Basically, the same techniques used for a smaller base are followed. The preparation of the site may, however, involve more work if the subsoil is soft clay or is not consistent over the whole area. Here, dig out another 75 mm (3 in) of soil to allow for a layer of hardcore. Compact this well.

Although it could effect small bases also, it is advisable with larger areas to check the positions of underground drains in case any need to be relaid away from the concrete area. Your local authority will advise you on this aspect. Concrete Mix A is suitable for a larger base.

Points to watch
A number of other points to watch are as follows:

Where new concrete adjoins an existing building, make sure that there is no risk of an existing damp proof course being bridged.

The surface of the new concrete should be at least 150 mm (6 in) below the d.p.c. level.

Between the existing building and the edges of the new concrete, interpose thick bituminous felt strip in the joint as a damp preventative.

Should the new concrete slab be intended as, for example, a workshop floor, it is important that it is damp proof. A damp-proof membrane can be inserted at construction stage using 1000 gauge plastic sheeting.

Having prepared the sub-floor, spread a layer of sand over any sharp material such as stones. This will prevent the sheeting from being pressed against the sharp edges and becoming torn. It might even be necessary to sand the whole area to prevent this possibility.

Lay the sheet over the base and the formwork – allow for plenty of sheeting to cover the formwork on all sides. If sheets have to be joined to cover the site, then overlap edges with a double fold at least 150 mm (6 in) wide and concrete over them.

In general, for larger bases, a 100 mm (4 in) thickness of concrete is adequate. Should the sub-floor be soft clay, it is best to increase it to 125 mm (5 in).

Up to a certain size, a base can be laid in a continuous layer of concrete. Over this size, the concrete will have to be laid in sections. Provided that the slab is no longer than about 4 m (13 ft) in any direction, or the length is not more than twice the width, a continuous layer can be used. On a large area, a ratio of $1\frac{1}{2}$ to 1 (length to width) is safest.

On bases over this size, divide the area into two or more equal size slabs and form a joint between them. To make the joint, use a 13 mm ($\frac{1}{2}$ in) thick softwood board of a depth equal to the thickness of the concrete. As a support for this, use a strip of the formwork timber, in turn supported by pegs driven into the ground.

Concrete up to the exposed side of the board and to within a few inches of the support strip and the pegs on the other side. Remove the support board and pegs; fill in the few inches up to the joint board and compact the concrete thoroughly on both sides of the board.

CONCRETE DRIVE

The same techniques are used as for larger bases. Mix A again is suitable. The thickness specified for larger bases (dependent on the subsoil) is required; this will be sufficient to support normal cars. However, if the drive will be used for heavier vehicles, add another 50 mm (2 in) of thickness.

Fig. 57 Forming a joint. A softwood lath is supported by a thicker, 25 mm (1 in) timber board

Fig. 58 Removing the support board

To allow for drainage, a drive should slope approximately 1 in 60 to one side. If the drive slopes down towards a garage then, to avoid the garage floor becoming regularly dotted with puddles, aim to leave the end of the new drive slightly below the garage floor. The last couple of feet should slope away from the garage, with provision for a run-off to one side.

Joints will almost certainly have to be made. Make them at 3 m (10 ft) intervals along the drive at right angles to the centre line of the concrete.

The drive can be used by cars after a seven-day curing period has elapsed. In cold weather allow 14 days before use. In any weather allow a 14 day curing period before a heavy vehicle uses the drive.

STEPS

All too often in gardens where there are one or more levels, the steps linking them are of really poor construction. They might be crumbling in places; an individual step can be loose and act like a see-saw under foot pressure; or they can simply be comprised of an irregular collection of treads and risers formed from a variety of materials.

These faults can be a great hazard to anyone descending the steps – especially older people and young children who may not be too steady on their feet and can become disorientated very easily.

Garden steps must be well constructed and always kept in a good condition. Uniform treads and risers are an absolute must from both the safety and asthetic viewpoints. The question of steepness can be overcome simply by constructing an S-shape staircase, enabling users to descend or ascend in comfort.

Pre-cast Blocks and Paving Slabs: A simple method of making an attractive staircase is to use pre-cast blocks and paving slabs. The slabs form the treads and the blocks form the risers (Fig. 59).

How many steps should be used in a bank? Obviously, unless you have a set design in mind, use the least number possible to economise on both time and money. Since safety comes before beauty, the maximum height for the risers should be about 200 mm (8 in). The treads should be at least 300 mm (1 ft) wide.

Bearing this in mind, it is for you to

measure the difference between the top and bottom levels of the bank. The number of steps needed can then be calculated. Provided maximum and minimum depths are not exceeded, the width and depth of each tread is a matter of personal taste when using paving slabs.

The standard sizes of pre-cast blocks limit the possible heights of the risers. However, since these are available in various depths of around 50 to 150 mm (2 to 6 in), it can be seen that, including 10 mm ($\frac{3}{8}$ in) for the mortar joints the choices are reasonably varied. For example, if a 125 mm (5 in) riser is required, two 50 mm (2 in) blocks plus the necessary $\frac{3}{8}$ in mortar joints will give, as near as makes no difference, the exact maximum height.

Having arranged the soil roughly to suit the required shape of the staircase, work can begin on marking out on the ground the position of the bottom slab. A sketch is useful to show the positions of the steps and risers.

The blocks forming the first riser can be bedded either on paving slabs or on the ground, using a mix of one part cement to three parts builder's sand.

Stagger the blocks in brickwork fashion (Fig. 60). After bedding them

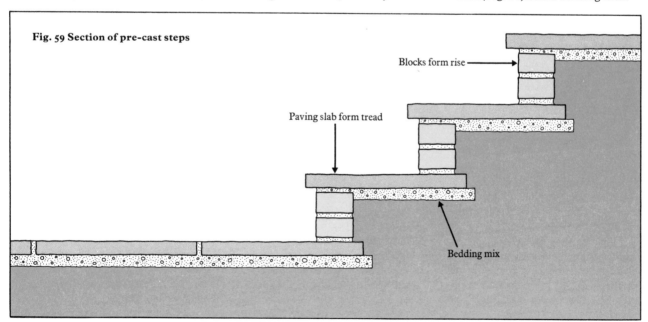

Fig. 59 Section of pre-cast steps

Blocks form rise

Paving slab form tread

Bedding mix

Fig. 60 Stagger the blocks in brickwork fashion

Fig. 61 Lay the treads on a level base

on to a 10 mm ($\frac{3}{8}$ in) – nominal – layer of mortar, tap them into place with the handle of the trowel and clean up the joints by removing any excess mortar that squelches out. The treads must be laid on a level base (Fig. 61) – again bedded on a mix of one part cement to three parts builder's sand. The treads should project over the edges of the blocks by about 25 mm (1 in). After that it is a matter of laying the remaining treads and risers in the same fashion.

For the sake of appearance and uniformity, the blocks forming each riser should be laid in the same bonding pattern (Fig. 62).

PLANTING BOWLS

The big advantage of having one or more planting bowls on a patio – or elsewhere in the garden for that matter – is that they provide the opportunity to alter the visual impact of an area quickly.

Very often, when flowers are at their best – blooming with colour – they could be out of sight at the end of the garden. Those nearest to you could, at that time be wilting and dying – hardly the most pleasant sight and one which you can easily rectify.

If some of the flowers were in concrete planting bowls, their positions could be changed so that the full benefit of the plants in bloom could always be gained.

A concrete bowl can be cast on a sand mould – a heap of soft sand (ask your supplier for builder's sand) – so that the desired shape, circular or oval, can be achieved.

The tools and materials required, apart from sand and cement, are a sheet of hardboard or plywood, narrow saw, pencil, a plant pot, 13 mm ($\frac{1}{2}$ in) mesh galvanized wire net, trowel, short bristle brush, a file or other shaping tool.

A word of warning at the outset. A

large concrete bowl filled with earth is extremely weighty so, if you are likely to be faced with the problem of moving the bowl by yourself, then do not make anything over about 600 mm (2 ft) in diameter at first. If you feel confident, having shoved it around, in handling a larger bowl, then make one of a larger diameter for your second effort.

Making the Pattern: The first thing to do is to make a pattern using the sheet of hardboard. Draw, then cut a curve in the sheet which represents the interior shape of the bowl. This can be of whatever depth or diameter that you prefer.

Place the hardboard pattern over the heap of sand. Shape the heap to match the curve of the pattern (Fig. 64).

A second line should be drawn on the pattern about 75 mm (3 in) away from the first to represent the outer shape of the bowl (Fig. 64).

Check with the pattern that the sand

Fig. 62 Lay the blocks in the same bonding pattern

mould is the correct shape all round by positioning the pattern over the mould and turning it through 360°.

Moist sand is much firmer than dry stuff, so add a little water if the mould crumbles easily on the surface.

Now, remove the pattern and cut along the second pencil line to remove the 75 mm (3 in) strip from the pattern. Replace the pattern over the sand mould and there will be a 75 mm gap all round. This gap represents the thickness of the bowl (Fig. 65).

Preparing the Materials: The mortar mix should comprise one part cement to three parts sand. The consistency to aim for is paste-like; so go easy when adding the water, it is preferable to be left with a mix that is on the dry side rather than one that is too sloppy.

At this stage it is best if you have cut the wire mesh into convenient sized pieces of about 150 to 225 mm (6 to 9 in)

Fig. 63 Home-made planting bowl

square. They act as reinforcing material and so must be bedded into the wet mortar mix.

Making the Bowl: Cover the sand mould with mortar, pressed down smoothly with a float. Apply a layer of about 38 mm (1½ in) thick.

Since a drain hole must be provided in the base of the finished bowl, place a suitable flower pot on the top of the sand mould (before this area is touched by the cement). Draw the cement around the flower pot (Fig. 66).

The reinforcing mesh should now be pressed into the surface of the wet mortar (Fig. 67). Cover the complete area of the bowl with the mesh.

Spread more layers of mortar over the mesh until an even 75 mm thick layer is built up and the plant pot at the top is completely covered. The pattern placed over the mould will indicate if the correct thickness of cement has been applied (Fig. 68).

If you are not experienced enough to be able to achieve a smooth finish with a float, then an effective roughened texture can be applied by drawing a short-bristle brush across the surface.

As always, protect the mortar from the elements whilst it is setting, see page 446.

When the mortar has set, lift the bowl away from the mould. Remove the plant pot by striking it hard (Fig. 69), when a large drain hole will be left in the base.

It will probably be necessary to 'clean-up' any rough edges with a file or other suitable shaping tool. Scrub out the inside of the bowl with clean water. After a couple of weeks of further drying time, the bowl can be filled with earth and plants added.

FISH PONDS

A fish pond is something that most people consider having in the garden at some time or other. A water feature of any kind adds a delightful attraction to any setting.

It need not be anything too lavish – even a small scale feature provides the

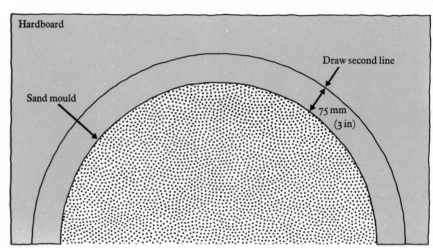

Fig. 64 Draw a second line on the pattern following the curve

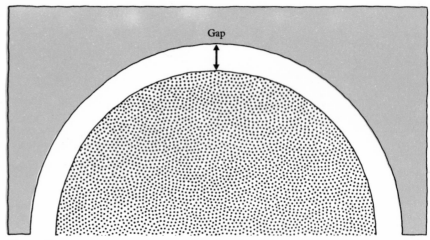

Fig. 65 The gap represents the thickness of the bowl

Fig. 66 Drawing the cement around the flower pot

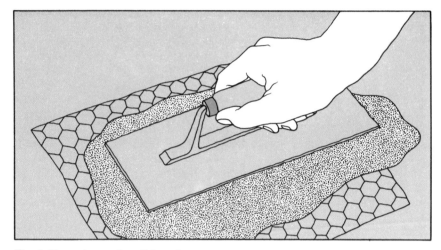

Fig. 67 Press the mesh well into the concrete

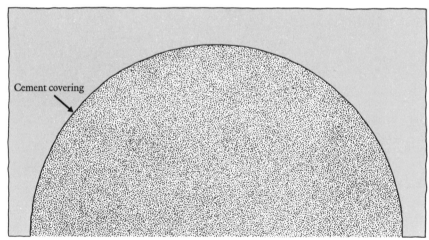

Cement covering

Fig. 68 Place the pattern over the cement mould

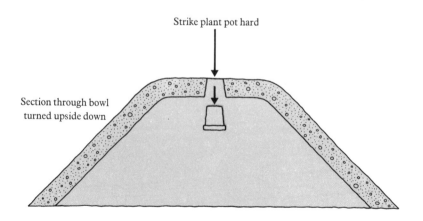

Strike plant pot hard

Section through bowl
turned upside down

Fig. 69 Removing the plant pot. This drawing, and Fig. 66, show an alternative shape for the bowl

opportunity to introduce a whole range of water lilies and other beautiful ornamental water plants both in the pond and around the edges.

Fish, of course, add colour, beauty, movement – and interest. They make a pond an idyllic spot to sit beside and laze away summer afternoons.

Years ago, using concrete was the only way to install a pond. The age of plastics meant that plastic liners and pre-formed fibre glass ponds became more in fashion. Now, though, these products have become very expensive so concrete has returned to favour for those who have to think about economy – which means most people.

Positioning and Design of the Pond: Before rushing out into the garden, spade in hand, to start excavating, there are many things to consider about the positioning and design of the pond.

The type of garden and the way that it is laid out, bear a direct relationship to the possible size and shape.

Many people think immediately in terms of a fancy shaped pond – heart shape, Maltese cross, and so on. The intention should be to get the largest possible quantity of water into the allocated space – no matter what its size. Heart shapes or similar are all right – especially in a garden where the layout is rather informal with irregular herbaceous borders.

But if the garden is laid out with a square or rectangular lawn with perfectly straight, manicured edges to the borders, and a perfectly straight path, then a conventional shape pond will be more appropriate. A square or circular shape will blend into the formal surroundings more easily.

The size of the pond depends on the size of the garden. Obviously a 'swimming pool' will look ostentatious in the extreme in a smallish garden, whereas a 'postage stamp' will look feeble in a large garden.

It's worth bearing in mind, if you envisage the larger varieties of lilies in the pond, that the area of the pond should exceed 7.4 m² (80 ft²) or thereabouts.

The position of the pond in the garden is very important. Water lilies and other aquatic plants thrive on plenty of light so an open, sunny site is desirable. It is advisable also to keep the pond away from sheltered areas – trees and bushes – for another reason : leaves and dirt, and insects are very likely to be blown in quantities into the water, thus clogging and fouling it. It is worth adding that a level site will make life a lot easier when constructing the pool.

A convenient water supply close to the pond is not necessary since, after the initial filling, only an occasional topping up will be needed and this can be done with a couple of buckets of water or the garden hose.

A small, informal pool, 2 m (6 ft) square and 150 mm (6 in) deep is a simple starting point for anyone not wanting anything too ambitious.

If precast paving slabs are to be used for the surround, the size of the pool may be lessened by the area taken up by the slabs, though this will not alter the dimensions greatly.

Excavating the Pond Site: The first job is the hardest – excavating the site, though, with a small area such as this, it is unlikely to take up more than a morning's digging. The excavation should be 250 mm (10 in) deep. This allows for a 100 mm (4 in) concrete base to be laid and a 150 mm (6 in) depth of water. In the same way, the width and the length of the hole should be extended beyond the intended 2m (6 ft) square surface area to allow for 150 mm (6 in) thick walls.

Follow the procedures laid down for checking levels given earlier, using pegs, a spirit level and a straight-edge.

Fig. 70 **Checking levels for garden pond**

Fig. 71 **Compacting the base**

462

Fig. 72 Brushing the perimeter to make a key for the concrete walls

Concreting the Pond Base: Mix up the required quantity of concrete using Mix B. Spread the mix over the floor of the pond and tamp it down with a length of timber.

It will probably take about three or four hours for the concrete to start to harden (in normal weather conditions). When this happens, a key has to be made for the concrete walls. This simply calls for the surface to be brushed or raked to roughen up the area that will be occupied by the walls. This is a crucial stage because how watertight the pool is depends to a large extent on the joint between the wall and the floor.

Positioning the Framework: A framework for the sides of the pool should be made up using 25 mm (1 in) thick timber to the shape shown in Fig. 73.

Allow 24 hours for the concrete to harden more before placing the frame into the excavation. It must be carefully positioned inside the 'wall' area. Thoroughly clean the joint surface around the outside.

To prevent the concrete from sticking to the frame, coat any parts of the timber that it will come in contact with using oil or limewash.

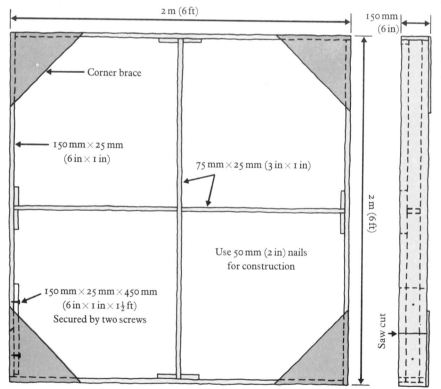

Fig. 73 Formwork for a small pond

Concreting the Walls of the Pond:
Next, mix up the required quantity of
concrete for the walls. Afterwards a
helper would be useful to ensure that
the framework remains in position
while the concrete is being poured in.

When the side walls are completely
filled in, tap the inner face of the timber
all round to ensure that the concrete is
thoroughly compacted.

Immediately, cover the pond with a
sheet of polythene (with bricks round
the edges to act as weights) and leave it
there for at least 24 hours so that the
concrete is cured.

Allow 48 hours before removing the
framework (Fig. 76). It can either be cut
out in sections or, if an inclined saw cut
was made in one side, it can be eased
out. The saw cut would have to have
been covered by a cleat – screwed in
position – during the concreting. See
Fig. 73.

Immediately the framework is
removed, the family, no doubt, will
move in to take over the most enjoyable
part of the job – filling the pond with
water. This is advantageous since the
water should be added quickly to help
cure the concrete. Since some of the
water will inevitably be absorbed by the
concrete in the first few days, the level
will probably drop a bit – so do not get
alarmed should this happen. Just top up
as necessary.

Finishing off the Pool: More than
likely the pond edges will be a bit
ragged. Here the advantage of pre-cast
slabs to form the surround can be seen.
If they are laid so that they project
slightly over the water, they will
obscure any untidyness (page 466). Lay
the slabs on a thin bed of mortar using 1
part of cement and 3 parts of builder's
sand.

For a really effective look, the floor of
the pool could be tiled.

Fig. 74 Placing the formwork in position

Fig. 75 Placing the concrete for the walls

Fig. 76 Removing the formwork

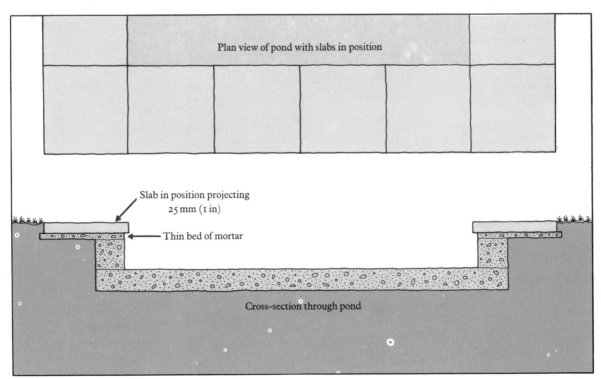

Plan view of pond with slabs in position

Slab in position projecting
25 mm (1 in)

Thin bed of mortar

Cross-section through pond

Fig. 77 Laying a surround of pre-cast slabs

Making an Informal Pool: An informal pool up to a maximum length of about 3 m (10 ft) is a slightly more difficult project. The excavation can be made as before, trimming the sides on a gentle slope to avoid having to reinforce the sides.

Anyone who is not certain that the projected shape will look right in the garden, should mark it out using a piece of rope first of all. View the shape from all parts of the garden – and from an upstairs room; an aerial view is often a great help.

To prevent absorption of water from the concrete, dampen the excavation with water. Use a watering can (Fig. 78), or a fine spray from a hose.

Mix the required quantity of concrete using Mix B. Spreading the mix on to the excavation requires the use of a trowel. An overall thickness of about 75 mm (3 in) is desirable. To remove the trowel marks and leave a smooth base, finish off with a steel float. Remember that a smooth finish is not easy to obtain

for an amateur. If this is important to you, then it may be worth getting professional help.

Cover the concrete with wet sacking or polythene to cure it. After 24 hours fill the pond with water to help the concrete to harden.

Precaution before Stocking Pool with Fish: The chemicals in cement could be harmful to fish and plants so it is important that the pool is seasoned before any 'life' is introduced.

Over a period of a month, the pool should be emptied and refilled three times. Each time the pond is emptied, the whole surface must be scrubbed thoroughly. Even at the end of this period, it is a worthwhile precaution to introduce a few minnows or tadpoles before stocking the pond with more valuable fish.

A quicker method is to treat the pond with a bituminous coating such as Aquaseal 40 or a liquid plastic paint such as Poolcote.

Fig. 78 Watering the excavation

Fig. 79 Placing and spreading the concrete

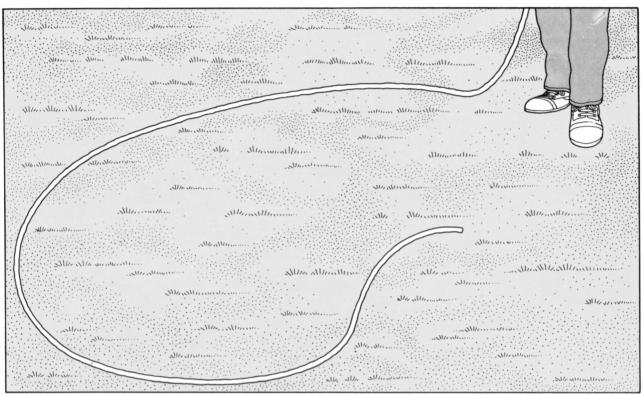

Fig. 80 Marking out the shape of an informal pool with rope

Fig. 81 Finishing with a steel float

FENCE POSTS

Anyone who has had the unenviable task of removing rotten timber fence posts, trying to dig out the stumps, and all the inconvenience of dismantling fence panels and re-erecting them, should consider installing concrete fence posts.

Builders' merchants stock fence posts of various types to suit different fencing arrangements. For example, there are posts with recesses into which the arris rails of a close-boarded fence can slot; vertical slots for pre-fabricated fence panels; or there are types with holes through them through which fence wire can be threaded.

In addition, you can buy concrete spurs which can replace only the lower part of a rotting fence post. With these, the lower portion of the post is sawn off to leave only sound timber. This joins on the spur which, in turn, is set in the ground. The post and the spur are joined together with bolts (Fig. 82).

The advantage here is economy. It's an ideal way of replacing a single, rotting post and retaining some of the expensive timber.

When erecting concrete fence posts, first fix the first and last posts in the run of fencing.

A string line run between these posts will establish the true line that the other posts must follow (Fig. 83).

Establish their correct positions – this is extremely important when using a fence with a predetermined length of panels – 1.8 m (6 ft) panels, for example.

Roughly speaking, about one third of a post's length should be buried in the ground. This depth can, of course, vary depending on the type of soil and required height of the posts.

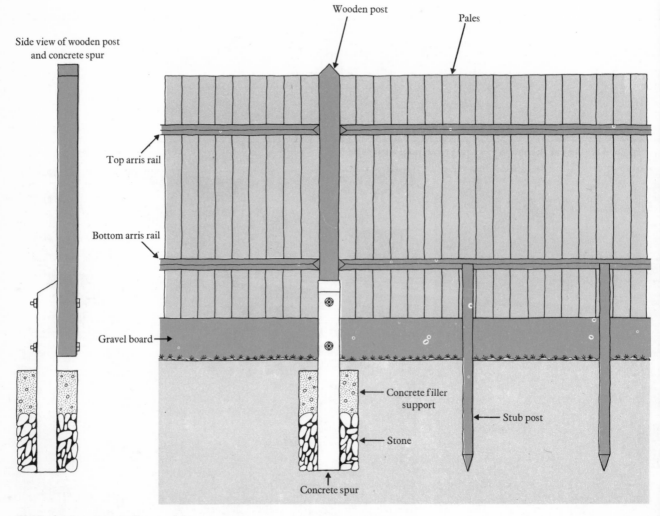

Side view of wooden post and concrete spur

Wooden post

Pales

Top arris rail

Bottom arris rail

Gravel board

Concrete filler support

Stone

Stub post

Concrete spur

Fig. 82 A concrete spur for repairing rotten fence post

Digging out post holes is not easy using ordinary digging equipment. The sensible solution is to hire a post-hole borer from a hire shop. If several posts are to be inserted, I would say that this is a must.

A post-hole borer is rather like a large corkscrew. It is twisted into the ground, with pauses every few inches to clean it. This is done by removing it from the ground to shake off the earth collected on the business end.

Insert a post in the hole and check it for height, alignment and also that it is truly vertical, using a plumb bob.

Use timber wedges or a few pieces of stone to wedge it in the upright position while you fill the hole with concrete Mix A to slightly below surface level.

Use a punner to ram down the concrete. Keep the post supported until the concrete hardens. This will take at least a week after which the fencing can be erected.

Dependent on the number of posts to be inserted, dry-mix concrete could be the most convenient.

Normally, gravel boards are run along the bottom of a fence, between the posts, so that the pales or fencing panels

rest on the top of the boards. This helps to support the fencing and prevents the pales from sagging in the middle of the bays, due to their unsupported weight causing the arris rails to bend.

The gravel board will also prevent rot starting in the bottom of a fence panel and working its way up the fence. Obviously, though, the timber gravel board itself will be susceptible to rot. So, there is an excellent reason for using concrete gravel boards: replacing timber nowadays is a costly business.

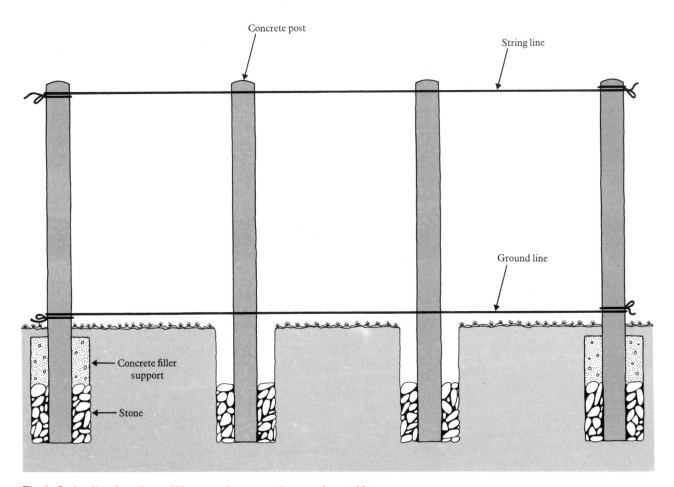

Fig. 83 String line for a fence. Where made-up panels are to be used between the concrete posts, correct spacing of the posts is very important

RAISED FLOWER BEDS

Now that a lot more thought is being given to garden design, homeowners are thinking well beyond the stage of a one-level garden combining a simple rectangular lawn with an herbaceous border. Flowers and colours on two or more levels add a new dimension to the garden and provide extra, interesting focal points.

There is another advantage too. That concerns the disabled – many of whom are gardening fanatics but are not able to grow flowers so easily from a wheelchair. For them, a raised flower bed is a boon – it can be designed to make access from a wheelchair comfortable. Experts recommend that a 600 mm (2 ft) average height is suitable for wheelchair users; for the ambulant disabled 860 mm (2 ft 10 in) is recommended. Width must obviously be restricted for accessibility. Here, 1·220 m (4 ft) with access from both sides is ideal.

Small pre-cast concrete walling units can be used to make a raised flower bed.

A good builder's merchant should be able to supply some small walling units, 900 mm long × 300 or 600 mm high (3 ft × 1 or 2 ft). Mostly these are faced with an aggregate finish. To provide a neat finish at external corners, walling units with their edges ready-mitred are available.

Provided that drainage is adequate, most ground surfaces will make a good base. It is essential, however, that the ground is firm and level. Time must be spent to make sure that this is so. If the ground is soft, then lay a concrete base. A lean mix of one part cement to about 8 parts coarse aggregate will be sufficient. A 75 mm (3 in) layer is the ideal.

The method used to ascertain a

Fig. 84 These Monowall units (Mono Concrete Ltd.) are suitable only for shallow-rooting plants

straight line for a fence is utilised here. A peg is knocked into the ground at either end of the intended line of the wall, and the two joined with a length of taut string.

The walling units should be bedded down on a mortar mix of one part cement to three parts builder's sand. A maximum thickness of 19 mm ($\frac{3}{4}$ in) should be aimed at. As each unit is positioned, check that it is truly horizontal and vertical using a spirit level and/or a plumb line. A 9 mm ($\frac{3}{8}$ in) mortar joint should be made between each unit.

When a corner is reached, check that the two units making the corner are at right angles to each other (Fig. 84). Then proceed as before.

When all the units are in position, fix a length of adhesive tape down the joints at the back of each unit. This will prevent contamination of the face of the units.

At this stage, the earth can be shovelled into the raised flower bed. However, a sensible precaution to prevent water seeping through the soil and attacking the joints, is to face the backs of the units with polythene sheeting.

Finally, clean up the decorative faces of the units with plenty of clean water and a hard bristle brush.

470

CONCRETE BLOCKS

Anyone contemplating building a straightforward garden boundary wall or even a garage or carport, or other building, should consider using concrete blocks. For the first-time builder, they are especially useful. Since they are much larger than bricks, there are less of them to lay and the results of your efforts will be seen more quickly. No great expertise is required to lay blocks and no specialist equipment is necessary.

Concrete blocks, 450 mm × 225 mm (18 in × 9 in) in size, in various thicknesses from 60 mm ($2\frac{1}{2}$ in) up to 225 mm (9 in), are available from builders' merchants. These dimensions are used to tie in with the standard dimensions of bricks; this makes the use of bricks and blocks in conjunction quite simple.

A standard block matches three vertical brick courses and two 'stretcher' bricks horizontally.

For small walls, surrounds and so on, modular co-ordinated blocks 400 mm × 200 mm (16 in × 8 in) and in thicknesses up to 200 mm are often used for a more attractive appearance.

If weather resistance is important, then dense concrete plain wall blocks should be used. These need not be covered by rendering to withstand the elements.

All lightweight load-bearing plain wall blocks are not weather resistant. They will need a weather resistant finish, such as rendering, to be applied.

Aerated lightweight blocks are very light and have a high insulation value. They are used increasingly for internal partitions or for the inner leaf of cavity walls. For exterior use, they must be protected from the weather with suitable material. Open textured lightweight blocks also have to be protected whether used internally or externally. Their appearance and cleanliness can suffer even in interior conditions.

As against the weather-resistant qualities, other aspects must be considered. For internal uses, light-weight and aerated blocks are much easier to work – an important factor when one considers that accurate cutting, and the chasing of service cables into the surface may be needed. These types are also more beneficial where insulation against noise and heat are considerations.

Facing blocks for exposed conditions come in various finishes. Standard sizes are 450 mm × 225 mm (18 in × 9 in) or 400 m × 200 mm (16 in × 8 in).

Since you may well be constructing a high wall or building, it is important to check with your local authority, before starting work, that there is no reason to prevent you going ahead.

Normal wall heights, up to 1·980 mm (6 ft 6 in), can be constructed following the guide lines given here. Should you want to build over this height, then get on-the-spot expert advice.

Where a wall is to be over 1·220 m (4 ft) high, piers should be built into the structure. This will give it stability. It also allows for economy since, in the main, thinner blocks can be used. There is more information on piers on page 474.

Expert advice is needed on sloping ground where the soil will be higher on one side of the blocks and the wall, or part of it, is to act as a retaining wall. On-the-spot, expert advice is needed because far too many differing situations exist for them to be covered here.

FOUNDATIONS

The techniques outlined earlier should be followed for building foundations. Use concrete Mix A.

The thickness of a wall dictates the width of the foundations. The foundation strip should be twice as wide as the wall along its entire length. This means, of course, that extra width must be allowed for at the positions of the piers.

The base of the foundation trench must be at least 356 mm (14 in) below ground level and the concrete itself must be at least 254 mm (10 in) thick.

If then one course of block-work is set below ground level, there is a reduced risk of the foundations being weakened later on by any digging or planting.

Where the ground slopes, 'step' the foundations. Each 'step' should equal the height of one course. Prepare the site by stripping top soil and removing roots and so on.

Fig. 85 A stepped foundation

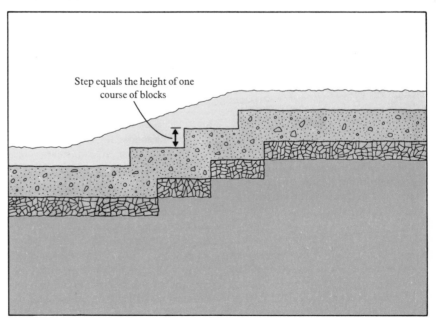

Step equals the height of one course of blocks

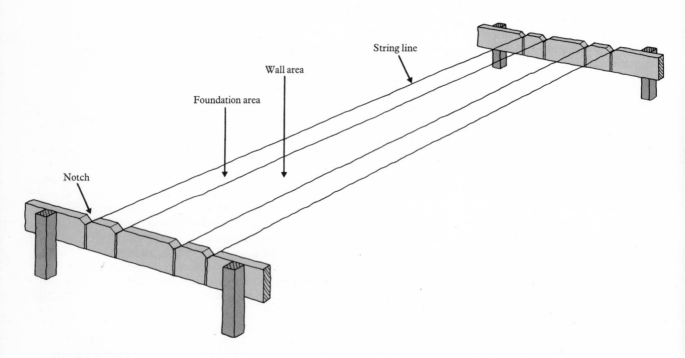

Fig. 86 Profile guides and string lines used to set out a site

As a guide for the line of both the foundation trench and the wall, use two profile guides. These can be made simply by fixing softwood strips to two pegs to form a 'goal posts' arrangement (Fig. 86). On the crossbars, cut notches with a saw at the positions of the wall line and the foundation line. Four notches will therefore be needed on each profile guide.

The profiles should be set up on extreme ends of the site and string lines stretched taut between the notches. The crossbar should straddle the centre line of the wall and be long enough so that the pegs on either side are driven into the ground well outside the foundation line.

BONDING

There is a choice of various bonding arrangements that can be used and these are shown in Figs. 87–92.

Normally, the stretcher bond system is used. This is the strongest con-

struction since the blocks in each course overlap those in the courses above and below to leave staggered joints.

To avoid having to cut any blocks to finish off at doorways, etc., half blocks can be obtained.

Cutting at corners can be avoided if standard size blocks are used, 200 mm or 225 mm. Here, the thickness of each block is half the length (400 mm or 450 mm) thus, as can be seen the bonding pattern is continued automatically onto the adjacent wall at a corner.

Cutting can also be avoided with stretcher bond by using piers at the corners. Expanded metal bonded ties (see page 475) span the joints between piers and the walls.

If thinner blocks are used, cutting will be necessary. A method of avoiding cutting at corners is to use quarter or third bonding. Cutting will still be necessary at door openings and so on, of course.

Mock Flemish or Mock English bonding involves quarter bonding. Here, whole and half blocks are used alternatively in each course; or there is a

separate course of whole blocks followed by a complete course of half blocks.

Stack bonding is the system used mostly with screen wall blocks; it leaves continuous vertical joints between the blocks since they are placed on top of each other without overlapping the block below.

When stack bonding is used, great care must be taken to make sure that the wall is stable. Horizontal reinforcement could be needed following the screen wall principle outlined on page 480.

CUTTING BLOCKS

Though cutting concrete blocks is not difficult, it can be time consuming to have to stop, measure the cutting line and actually cut a block. A little preparatory paperwork can minimise the amount of cutting and save a good deal of time in the long run.

When planning the number and arrangement of blocks needed, work in multiples of half block lengths (for stretcher bond) and full blocks for quarter or third bonding. Remember to

Fig. 87 Stretcher bond for concrete block wall. Each block thickness equals half block length. Half blocks are at the wall ends

Fig. 88 Mock Flemish bond. In each course, alternate whole and half blocks are used. Three-quarter blocks are at wall ends

Fig. 89 Thin stretcher bond. Cut block 'closers' at the corners

Fig. 90 Mock English bond: alternate courses of whole and half blocks changing at corners. Three-quarter blocks are at wall ends

Fig. 91 Quarter or one-third bond. Three-quarters or two-thirds cut blocks are at wall ends

Fig. 92 Stretcher bond with stackbonded corner piers and metal ties

Table 3   Maximum Height of Free-standing Concrete-block Walls

Block size	Thickness	Maximum height	Maximum number of courses
450 × 225 mm (18 × 9 in)	100 mm (4 in)	900 mm (3 ft)	4
	150 mm (6 in)	1·6 m (5 ft 4 in)	7
	225 mm (9 in)	2 m (6 ft 8 in)	9
400 × 200 mm (16 × 8 in)	100 mm (4 in)	1 m (3 ft 4 in)	5
	150 mm (6 in)	1·6 m (5 ft 3 in)	8
	200 mm (8 in)	2 m (6 ft 8 in)	10

Opposite

Fig. 93 Staggered panels to form lapped piers. Metal ties are used to lock the blocks together
Fig. 94 Separate panels are tied into a pier with expanded metal
Fig. 95 Wall laid to running bond with a stack-bonded side pier tied to the wall

In exposed locations and when constructing a boundary wall, piers must be used if the height of a wall is much more than 1·2 m (4 ft).

include any adjustments that may be needed at corners.

There is no necessity to include an allowance for the thickness of the mortar joints between blocks since the blocks are sold in nominal sizes which allow for a 10 mm ($\frac{3}{8}$ in) joint.

Use Table 3 for guidance in building piers. Generally speaking, a free-standing wall should not be higher than indicated in the table. This is assuming that the wall is laid to bond and has no piers. These dimensions apply to reasonably wind-sheltered garden walls.

Over these heights, depending on the thickness of the blocks used, lateral bracing is needed. An intersecting wall provides bracing but long, freestanding walls require piers.

Piers should be twice as thick as the walls between them. Spaces between piers must not be more than twice the wall height. If 100 mm (4 in) thick panels are used, piers should be spaced at not more than 2·4 m (8 ft) intervals.

PIERS FOR CONCRETE-BLOCK WALLS

The design of the pier, provided that it is correct, and assuming that it is well constructed, is a matter of choice. A lot

depends on the location of the wall and personal taste.

On a long run of wall, alternate panels can be set in front of the panels on either side (Fig. 93). A normal mortar joint is used between the faces of the overlapping blocks and expanded metal ties are used to lock the blocks together.

An alternative method can be used by stack bonding a pier and using expanded metal bonding ties with panels tied to it in a butt joint (Fig. 94).

On an unbraced bonded wall, the blocks of the piers can be stack bonded to make the correct pier thickness and, again, be tied with expanded metal bonding ties (Fig. 95).

A suitable mortar mix for most jobs is comprised of one part masonry cement to 4 to 5 parts builder's sand. Do not use Portland cement. This mix provides a mortar which is weaker than the blocks themselves. Later on should any stress be placed on the wall through settlement, any cracks will follow the line of least resistance, that is, through the joints and not through the blocks.

Any mortar cracks can be repaired with repointing. Should there be extensive cracking, either through the mortar joints or the blocks, then it is

essential to seek expert advice before remedial steps are taken.

Specially prepared blocklaying mortar is available in ready-mixed form. Do make sure, when ordering, that you specify blocklaying mortar.

Laying Blocks: Through all the work, check each block for vertical plumb against the blocks surrounding it. Make sure that the guidelines set between the profiles are followed.

Probably, at first, you will have difficulty in laying the correct thickness of mortar using the pointed bricklayer's trowel. After a while it will come naturally.

Should you use too little or too much mortar for the block to be tapped into its correct position, remove the block, clean off the mortar and try again.

Starting at the corners of a building (if constructing, for example, a garage) or the ends of a free-standing wall, build up about four courses at each corner. Between these courses lay the blocks one course at a time, continually checking with the string line and spirit level for level and plumb.

Spread a layer of mortar on the tops of the blocks in the course below and on

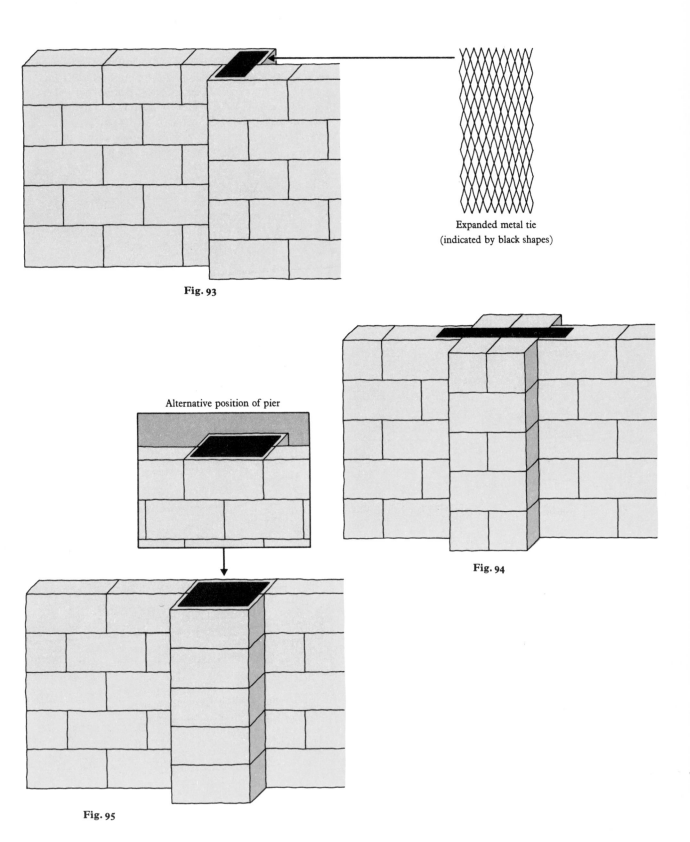

Expanded metal tie
(indicated by black shapes)

Fig. 93

Alternative position of pier

Fig. 94

Fig. 95

Fig. 96 A garage being built with tied corner piers

(a) Laying a corner pier
(b) Laying first course
(c) Starting intersecting wall
(d) Filling pier block cavities
(e) Expanded-metal ties at piers

(f) Continue working upwards and out from the piers
(g) Using a metal angle strap to fix a door frame
(h) Reinforcement at wall end as a door support. Cover reinforcement with concrete. Additional reinforcing steel to be tied to 'starter' bars

one side of the block being laid. Tap the block into place carefully and firmly to make sure that it is well bedded down.

If using coloured or textured blocks, be especially careful to avoid mortar getting on to their faces.

If the wall is to be higher than five courses – about 1·220 m (4 ft) – stop

a

b

c

d

work when this stage is reached to allow the mortar to set for a couple of days before proceeding. Protect the wall from rain and frost by covering it.

When piers are reached, use the expanded-metal strips to tie the blocks to the piers at every second course. Make sure that the metal is well anchored by bending it into the mortar thus forcing the mortar through the mesh. The long dimension of the diamond shape of the mesh should run at right angles to the joint.

Where pier blocks or hollow blocks are used at the end of a plain wall, fill the cavity in the block with concrete Mix B. This should be fluid enough to drop into the cavity to fill it completely. Use a rod to compact it.

Finishing Joints: Especially where textured or coloured blocks are used which are not to be covered by a cement rendering, the joints should be finished

e

f

g

h

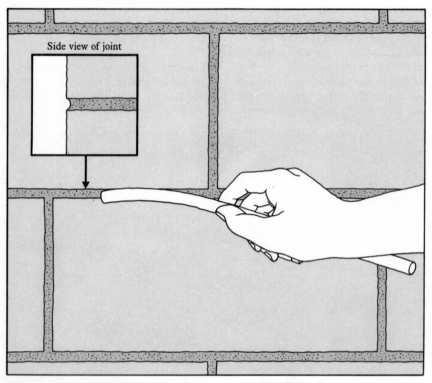

Side view of joint

Fig. 97 Forming a rubbed joint with a round steel bar

to give a neat appearance.

Though the mortar can be struck off flush with the surface of the blocks, an even more attractive finish can be made by using a 16 mm ($\frac{5}{8}$ in) diameter round steel bar to form a rubbed joint. To do this, strike off the mortar flush with the surface using the trowel, allow the mortar to set for a while and then compress the joints with the steel rod (Fig. 97). Complete all the horizontal joints before tackling the vertical ones.

Should you intend to render the wall, rake out the joints to a depth of about 13 mm ($\frac{1}{2}$ in) (slightly less with hollow blocks). This will provide a good key for the rendering.

While the mortar is curing, cover the wall with polythene sheeting or with sacking in cold weather, to protect it from the elements.

Reinforcement: Reinforcement was mentioned earlier. Here, I will repeat that on-the-spot expert opinion should be sought for high walls.

In low walls, reinforcement may be needed where, for example, piers are

used as gate posts. Here vertical reinforcement can be given by fixing stub starter bars of reinforcing rod in the footings and tying 50 × 50 mm (2 × 2 in) angle section (as used for fence posts) to it. The wall then can be started.

The starter bars must be bedded at least 250 mm (10 in) below the top of the pier so that it will be well covered up by the infill concrete.

SCREEN WALL BLOCKS
Screen wall blocks can be used in many ways in the garden – as the walls for a carport, or to hide a compost heap or an ugly storage area, or simply as a tall or small boundary or decorative wall.

A screen block wall is not intended for load-bearing applications but it will support a lightweight roof of a carport or a covered patio. Here, the sort of roof structure I have in mind is a framework of softwood timbers covered by corrugated plastic sheeting such as Novolux.

Where screen blocks are used as a wall alongside a flower border, the keen

gardener can be sure that plenty of light and air will be reaching his plants.

There's another aspect too, of course; since a block is identical from both sides, a wall will have two decorative faces making it ideal as a garden divider.

Screen wall blocks are manufactured by several companies and are stocked by most builders' merchants. Each manufacturer usually supplies specific instructions for using his own product plus recommendations for heights of walls, reinforcement required, and so on.

You will also be able to purchase matching pier blocks and coping units for a screen wall.

The screen blocks are available in various sizes. The most commonly used is 11$\frac{5}{8}$ in square × 3$\frac{5}{8}$ in thick (300 × 300 × 100 mm). These will be sold as 12 in × 12 in × 4 in blocks – the missing $\frac{3}{8}$ in on all dimensions is the built-in allowance for mortar joints between each block.

Matching 8 in × 8 in × 8 in pier blocks are available which are recessed to take the screen blocks, thus obviating the

Fig. 98 Starter bar for vertical reinforcement

1. Marker pegs on either side of foundation locate the centre line of a pier

2. Starter bar embedded in concrete foundation. Tie additional reinforcement to the bar

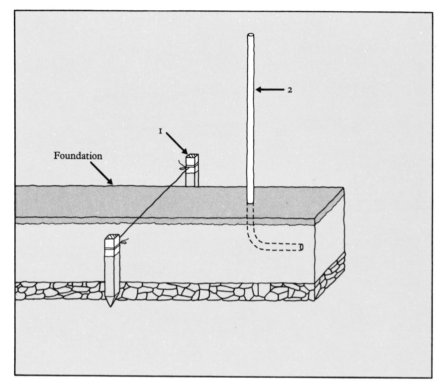

necessity to use metal bonding ties to secure blocks to piers.

If reinforcement has to be used, use expanded metal strips as for plain blocks. Use welded wire (available from builders' merchants) for horizontal reinforcement. Bed this well down into the mortar joints.

Laying Screen Wall Blocks:
Reinforcement details are given in Table 4 and will serve as a guide in the absence of specific manufacturer's instructions. The same basic methods used for laying plain blocks are followed.

Having laid and levelled the concrete foundations, any reinforcement (angle iron, etc.) should be inserted into the wet concrete. Insert other reinforcement lengths into the foundations at the appropriate spaces. A pilaster block can now be lowered on to a prepared mortar base and be filled with a fluid mortar mix.

Build up each pier until three pilaster blocks are laid on each one.

During construction of the piers,

check each pilaster block for alignment as it is laid on its $\frac{3}{8}$ in mortar joint.

Since the piers, or at least three courses, are built before any screen

blocks are laid, you must double and triple check that the piers are in line, otherwise the wall be out of true.

Spread a 300 mm (12 in) layer of

Table 4   Reinforcement Details for Screen Wall Blocks

Freestanding walls in private gardens	Reinforcement required
1·8 m (6 ft high × 3 m (10 ft) between piers	no reinforcement necessary
2·4 m (8 ft) high or over 1·2 m (4 ft) high in exposed locations × 3 m (10 ft) between piers	50 × 50 mm (2 × 2 in) angle steel vertical reinforcement in piers

Boundary walls and other free-standing walls	Reinforcement required
1·8 m (6 ft) high × 3 m (10 ft) between piers	50 × 50 mm angle iron in piers
2·4 m (8 ft) high × 3·6 m (12 ft) between piers	50 × 50 mm angle iron in piers, 60 mm (2¼ in) wide galvanised 'Brickforce' or equivalent reinforcement in horizontal mortar joints

mortar on the concrete base and in the groove of the pilaster block and then position the first screen block. Check that it is vertical and level using a spirit level.

Cover the edge of this first block and the extreme edge and base of the second block with mortar. Position the second block, again checking with a spirit level.

Continue in this way until the first course is complete. The accepted method of laying blocks – working from both ends to the centre – should be adopted.

Any reinforcement needed can be laid on the first course. From there on it is a question of building the wall up to the required height – remembering to check each block for vertical and to keep each course level and straight.

Finally, add the coping blocks and pier caps.

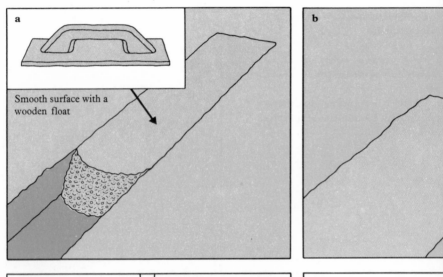

Smooth surface with a wooden float

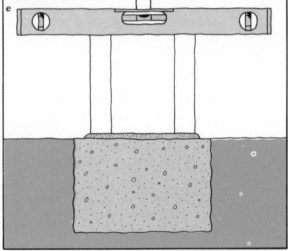

Fig. 99 Laying screen wall blocks

(a) **Laying foundations**
(b) **Inserting reinforcement angle iron before concrete sets**
(c) **Positioning first pilaster block on mortar**
(d) **Infilling with concrete**
(e) **Checking for level**
(f) **Sliding the first block into a pilaster groove**
(g) **Laying mortar on the edge of the second block**
(h) **Always lay a base of mortar for each block**
(i) **Checking blocks for vertical**
(j) **Checking for horizontal with a string line**
(k) **Fitting a cap**
(l) **The coping blocks are added last**

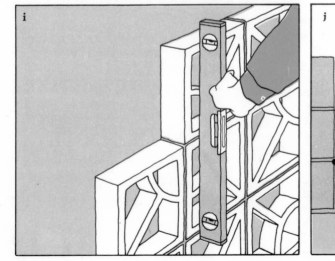

String line

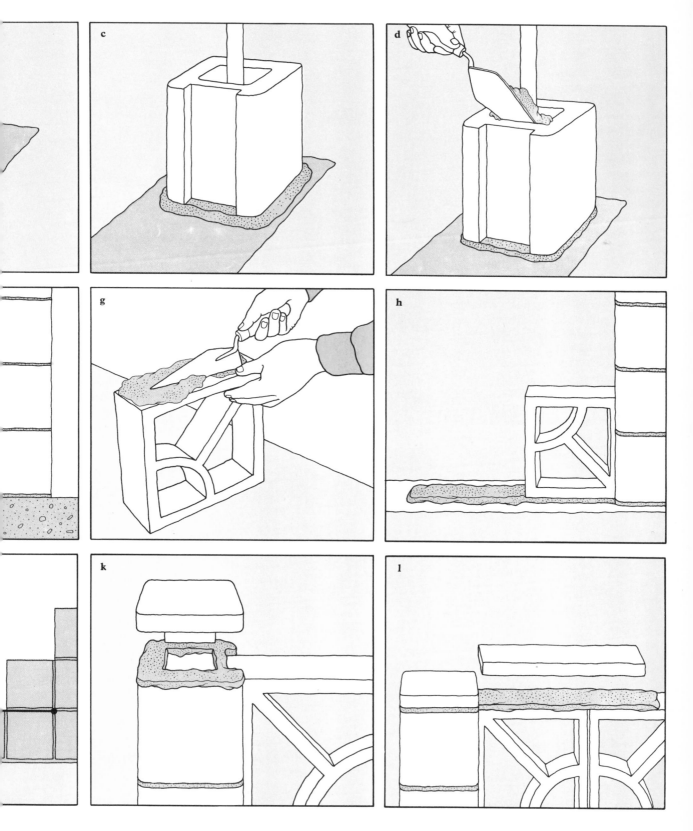

Bricks are Not Just for Building

Bricks are used for building houses and walls, but there are hundreds of other uses to which they can be put. The picture (top right) shows a wall, but a wall with a difference. A plain arch could have been made in it, leading from the stepping stones across the small pool to another part of the garden, but how much more effective and unusual is the complete circle. This would be a project to be attempted only by someone who has some experience of laying bricks, but is certainly not beyond the capabilities of the home handyman.

The bottom picture shows terraced flowerbeds constructed from old bricks. With new ones it would not have the natural look which it has here. Terracing like this is a good way of dealing with a change of level in a garden.

In the picture on the opposite page bricks have been used as a decorative border for a path of stone slabs and the circular flowerbed in the middle, with low-growing plants, gives it added interest.

A brick path can be laid in a number of ways. The picture above shows a herringbone pattern, while those used for the swimming pool surround (far right) are in a more traditional form. Bricks make attractive low retaining walls (top right) and in the picture (bottom right) a plant trough has been effectively matched with the walls of the house.

Anyone who has never tampered with bricks and mortar may develop a phobia about using them to tackle even the simplest job.

A good deal of this is due, undoubtedly, to the permanance of the intended structure, be it a dwarf wall or a house extension.

In brickwork, there is little room for error. Mistakes cannot be rectified easily; to put something right could mean going back to square one by demolishing the results of your efforts.

Most handymen, who stick to everyday jobs such as wallpapering and painting, know that an error is not too critical. Though frustrating, a length of badly hung wallpaper can be stripped off in a reasonably short space of time and a new length pasted and hung properly.

The mistake could be discovered and the remedy effected in half an hour.

Even a coat of paint that was applied a little too quickly the night before – to get the job finished – could look a sad sight in the morning. A wasted effort admittedly, but it can be rubbed down when hard and re-finished without too much trouble.

Most people, realising this, tend to stick to jobs that they know how to tackle.

I have deliberately started off this section on a slightly discouraging note for a very good reason. I want to drive home the point, at the outset, that care in planning and working with bricks is of the greatest importance. This applies at every stage of the work. Having stressed the point, let us look at the bright side.

Anyone who is prepared to take their time and do things properly will be able to work successfully with bricks.

There are no amazing skills involved that require a ten-year apprenticeship to acquire. In fact, brickbuilding can be categorised into three work stages.

One, laying foundations; two, mixing mortar; three, placing the bricks on top of each other using the mortar as a 'glue' to stick them together. That is all there is to it.

Of course, that is the theory. When you finally get to grips with the practical work, there are various dos and don'ts, and strict guidelines for you to follow.

Nowadays, more and more people are having to face up to the problem of brickwork for themselves. Not so long ago, only the keenest amateur would tackle his own brickbuilding. In those days, it was commonly accepted by most that this sort of work was best left to a professional bricklayer who would handle the whole job from start to finish.

I am not suggesting that you concentrate your first efforts on building a house of your own – though I do know of do-it-yourselfers who have achieved this end. They started out without having built so much as a coal bunker and managed to build a luxury bungalow or even a house – up to the highest professional standards.

PRACTICAL BRICKLAYING

The fact that you are bothering to read a book seeking guidance on bricklaying techniques implies that you have a belief in your own ability to do a job well. Any doubts you may have can be removed quickly with a little practice.

A corner of the garden can be set aside – only a few feet are necessary – where you can try your hand at tackling the real thing.

Doubtlessly you can lay your hands on a few old bricks, perhaps twenty or thirty. Then, whenever you have a couple of hours to spare, you can knock up a quantity of mortar and construct a small wall. If things go wrong, you can knock them down and start again until the technique comes naturally, as it almost certainly will.

Fig. 100

Fig. 100 First construct a small practice wall

Fig. 101 Chip mortar off old bricks with a bolster chisel and club hammer

Fig. 102 Plan the structure you intend to build carefully

If you are using old bricks, then there might be old mortar baked on to the sides. This must be chipped off with a bolster chisel and club hammer, otherwise you will have difficulty in getting all the mortar joints to be of uniform thickness and, indeed, getting the bricks to lie flush and plumb.

The Question of Clothing: At this stage, it is worth discussing clothes to wear. Most of us have a favourite set of working clothes which we feel most comfortable in. Working in comfort is an important element of all handyman activity.

Remember that bricklaying, like laying concrete and stonework, can be a messy business. Mortar is held on a hawk and transferred to the bricks with a trowel. This is a tricky operation. In the early stages, a beginner is liable to drop some. This is where your clothes can suffer, shoes especially. So keep a special set of clothes and shoes for all this sort of work.

The question of whether or not gloves should be worn is always open to discussion. One school of thought advises the amateur to wear them. An old leather pair are considered most suitable for resisting the sharp edges of the bricks. This opinion is based on the fact that anyone who is not used to handling bricks will, after a few hours work, find their hands becoming sore and blistered. This might not seem possible, but it is very likely to happen, especially to someone who five days a week is used to handling a pen or tapping a typewriter.

A clue to the sort of hammering your hands will take is the incredibly short length of time that an ordinary pair of woollen gloves will last before great holes are worn in them.

The other school of thought says an emphatic *no* to gloves. This opinion claims that gloves cause clumsiness in handling the bricks and mortar which, as professionals will tell you, is quite a delicate art.

Anyway the choice is yours. If you feel comfortable wearing gloves and your results are not affected adversely by them, then by all means try them. You will certainly prevent split fingers by using them.

Planning the Work: Before ordering materials and preparing the site it is worthwhile sitting down with a piece of paper and a pencil to get some idea of the size of the structure you intend building.

Say you progress to the stage of feeling confident about building a feature wall using coloured bricks. In the right proportions this will look very attractive and enhance the garden.

However, should it be too long, or too high, then it could be overpowering. A good idea of the finished effect can be achieved by making a scale drawing on graph paper before you start.

Finally, a word or two about weather conditions. Standing under a hot sun is guaranteed to reduce your work rate and the length of time that one is able to toil.

In Britain we have learnt never to plan according to expected weather conditions – the elements are a law unto themselves. However, if we are to have really hot days, then the midsummer months are more likely to produce them. So it would probably be wise to try and get things organised for a start in late April or early May. At this time of year, cool conditions can be expected.

There is a possibility that too much mortar will be made up and start to set before it can be used, but the individual will be able to gauge his own working speed to the quantity of mortar to be mixed; thus wastage will be avoided.

Finally, if you do choose to work in a heat wave, I would recommend a hat to keep the sun from the neck.

Fig. 101

Fig. 102

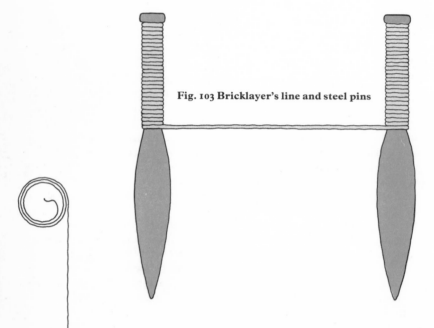

Fig. 103 Bricklayer's line and steel pins

Fig. 104 Plumbline and bob

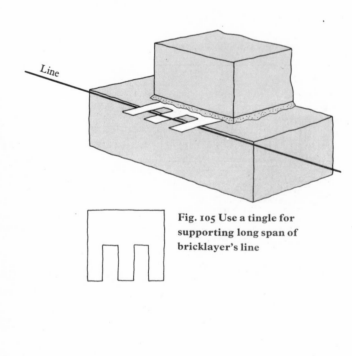

Line

Fig. 105 Use a tingle for supporting long span of bricklayer's line

BRICKLAYING TOOLS

Much of the equipment used for concreting is included in the bricklaying tool kit.

At the end of the day, it is always worthwhile taking the time to clean and store all equipment. True, you might not feel like extending the work period when you are tired, but it is preferable to start the day with a clean slate and avoid spending time then getting a layer of caked mortar off the trowel or hawk.

Here is a list of the main tools involved. Some smaller items not covered here are mentioned later as their need arises. Your local hardware shop should stock all the items listed.

Spade: For digging foundation trenches.

Builder's Square: For setting out a building site; see concrete section (pages 452-453).

Wheelbarrow: For transporting bricks and mortar to the site; see concrete section (page 434).

Shovels, Buckets and a Watering Can with a fine rose: For mixing mortar; see concrete section (page 433).

One metre (3 ft) Combined Spirit Level and Plumb Rule: For levelling foundations, and for ensuring that the bricks are being laid true. A lot of people prefer to use a plumb bob and line for checking verticals; keep one handy as a check against the spirit level.

150 mm (6 in) Spirit Level: This I always consider is a necessity for the beginner. In the early stages, it is advisable for him to level each brick individually after it has been laid. Later on when there is less risk of a wall being constructed out of true, this smaller level will not be used at all.

Bricklayer's Line and a pair of Steel Pins: By anchoring the pins at the ends of the walls, the line can be stretched taut along the course being built as a guide to the bricks being laid level. The line must not sag and should be checked regularly with a spirit level. On really long spans, sagging will be inevitable. Here, midway support should be provided with a slotted, metal plate called a tingle (Fig. 105).

Large-laying Trowel: This is used for spreading the mortar on to the bricks. The size to use is largely a matter of choice.

Though a professional, who is used to spreading sufficient mortar on to three bricks in one action, will prefer something in the region of a 250 mm (10 in) long trowel, a beginner should use a smaller version.

A large trowel, when weighted with a layer of mortar, can be cumbersome to manoeuvre – and the mortar will be less easy to spread accurately on the bricks.

Try a 175 mm (7 in) trowel at first and gather only sufficient mortar for one brick at a time. Incidentally, a trowel is measured from the tip of the point to the base of the handle.

Pointing Trowel: Pointing, in essence, means filling irregularities in the mortar joints between the bricks.

Initially, when a course of bricks has been laid, gaps and bulges will be apparent along the joints. The excess mortar causing the bulges is cleaned off first of all. Then any gaps are filled in with this excess mortar using the pointing trowel. A weathered or flush joint can be made (see illustrations) using this trowel.

Hawk: This is used for holding the mortar on while working. You can make one from a square of board and a short length of broom handle.

Bricklayer's Hammer: This is needed for cutting bricks when only a little has to be trimmed off. One end of the hammer head is shaped like a chisel.

Professionals often use the handle of the trowel to tap a brick into position on the mortar. The trouble with this is that any mortar on the trowel blade tends to become dislodged and can fall on the face of the finished brickwork below (this never seems to happen with professionals, only with beginners). A beginner would be better off using a spare trowel or a hammer handle for this job.

Bolster Chisel and Club Hammer: These two go together. They are needed when a whole brick has to be cut.

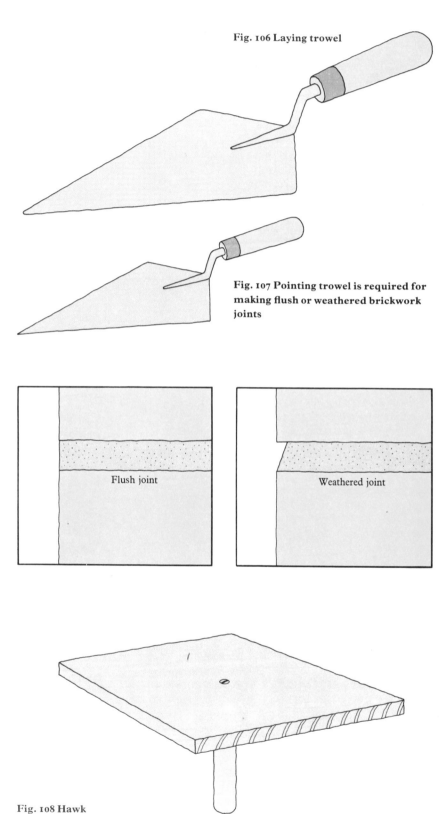

Fig. 106 Laying trowel

Fig. 107 Pointing trowel is required for making flush or weathered brickwork joints

Flush joint

Weathered joint

Fig. 108 Hawk

The correct procedure for cutting a brick is as follows.

Lay the bricks on a firm, level surface and cut grooves on both sides of the 112.5 mm (4½ in) face of the brick by placing the bolster chisel at right angles on the intended cut line and tapping gently with the hammer on its handle. Then a couple of sharp blows with the hammer on the chisel should leave a clean break. Do practice this technique on old bricks first, just to get the hang of things.

Round Jointer: This is used to leave a concave finished appearance in the mortar joints. It is simply drawn along the joint leaving a concave impression. Choosing to finish with this joint – called a rubbed joint, see section on Concrete Blocks, page 478 – as opposed to other kinds of joint (weathered or flush) is a matter of personal taste; though a weathered joint is preferable where a wall is in a particularly exposed situation.

Gauge Rod: Make this yourself with a length of batten (Fig. 112). It is used to check that the joints, and therefore the brick courses, are finishing at the correct heights.

Draw lines at 75 mm (3 in) intervals along the batten. Each 75 mm mark will indicate the top edge of a brick. The rod is placed on a thin piece of metal slipped under the first layer of mortar on top of the foundations – partly protruding to form a level base on which the gauge rod can stand.

BRICK TYPES

There is an enormous selection of bricks available today. The range of colours and textures will certainly satisfy even the most fastidious person who wants to build a feature wall of a particular colour.

Brick merchants or builders' merchants will stock a selection of brick types and probably will be able to order for you any required that are out of the ordinary colour or texture.

Later on I will discuss how to obtain second-hand bricks. Here I want to concentrate of new types. There are

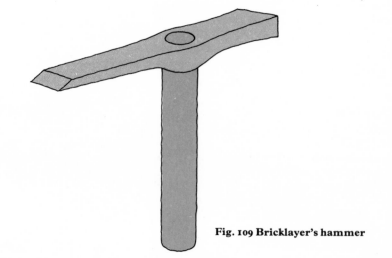

Fig. 109 Bricklayer's hammer

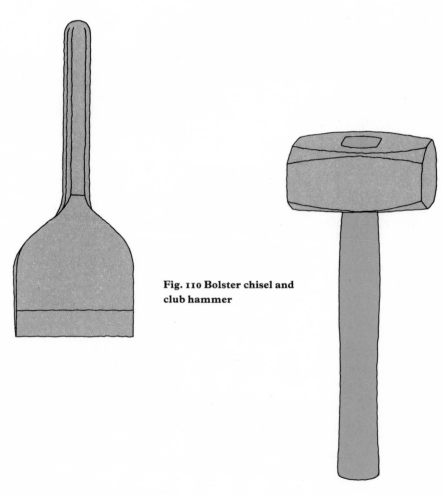

Fig. 110 Bolster chisel and club hammer

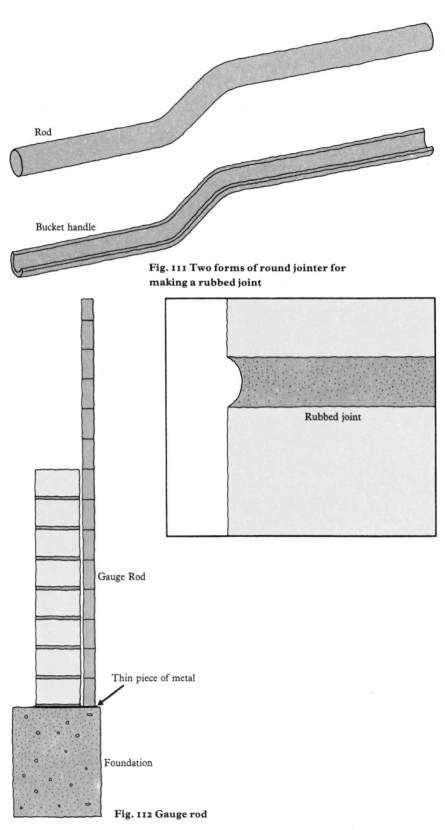

Rod

Bucket handle

Fig. 111 Two forms of round jointer for making a rubbed joint

Rubbed joint

Gauge Rod

Thin piece of metal

Foundation

Fig. 112 Gauge rod

three types of brick: engineering bricks, facing bricks and common bricks.

The home handyman can forget about the first type, more or less, since these are used mainly in civil engineering.

That leaves us with the two types – common and facing bricks, which are made of clay.

Common Bricks: These are made in a variety of materials from soft, porous quality to hard, medium density material. Common bricks are used for all general building work. They are acceptable for all run of the mill jobs – garden walls, garages and so on where a specific decorative appearance is not aimed at.

In the old days when transport was not the inter-city motorway industry that it is today, a brick could be specified by its place of origin or type of clay, for example, Leicester Red, and was likely to be most used locally.

Now, though, since modern transport can transfer bricks far from their place of origin, a closer, more detailed description is needed.

A brick can be identified closely by six different characteristics. Apart from the place of origin, there is the raw material from which it was made; the method of manufacture, e.g., wire cut; its use (facing or common); its colour; its surface texture – sandfaced, rustic.

Flettons: The best and, indeed, the most widely used type of common brick is made from lower Oxford clay which is found in the regions of Peterborough and Bedford. These bricks are called flettons and they form nearly 50 per cent of all the bricks manufactured in Britain.

Facing Bricks: These are specially manufactured to be used when an attractive finished appearance is required. The treatment usually consists of burning mineral granules or coarse sand into the clay.

There are many varieties of facing

491

Frog

Fig. 113 A 'frog' in a brick

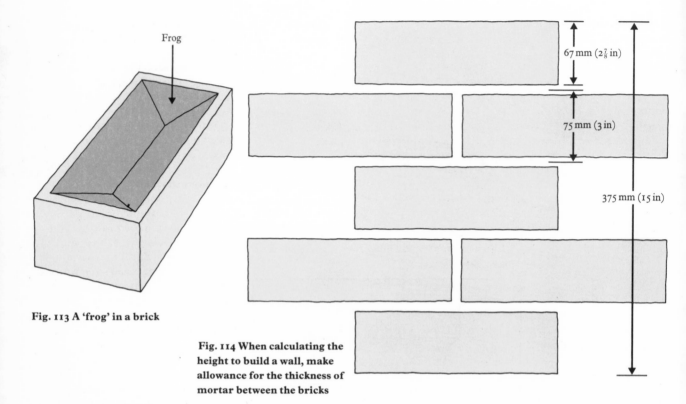

67 mm ($2\frac{7}{8}$ in)

75 mm (3 in)

375 mm (15 in)

Fig. 114 When calculating the height to build a wall, make allowance for the thickness of mortar between the bricks

bricks, but again the most widely used are of fletton clays. Some bricks are faced on all six sides, while others are faced on only three sides. Where a finished item will be viewed from both sides – a wall garden divider is a case in point – the number of sides that are faced must be brought into the reckoning when buying.

Facing bricks are not much more expensive than ordinary flettons. More expensive facing bricks are made in various districts. There are also bricks made from concrete. These are coloured by using pigments.

'London Stock': Bricks manufactured in the South East of England are often referred to as 'stock'. A well-known variety is the yellow coloured 'London stock'.

The yellow colour comes from the Kent and Essex clays used – these contain chalk and are of various grades. Top grade is good facing bricks. The second best grade is called hard stocks; these are a good grade of common brick

and, if carefully selected, make good facings. Mild stocks refer to general purpose common bricks. For foundations and interior walls, there are rough stocks.

Brick Sizes: When buying bricks, at least you do not have to worry about specifying a size, though you might get a little confused about metric sizes. Without prior warning, the beginner could get into a real tangle if he actually measured a brick. Let me explain.

For a long time now, bricks have been sold under a nominal size of 9 in × $4\frac{1}{2}$ in × 3 in. These are nice, even dimensions that are simple to remember.

The confusion starts to creep in when a brick is measured accurately. If you bother to do this, you will find that the actual dimensions are $8\frac{5}{8}$ in × $4\frac{1}{8}$ in × $2\frac{5}{8}$ in. So where has the missing $\frac{3}{8}$ in on all dimensions gone to?

The answer is quite simple. As with concrete blocks, the nominal sizes make allowance for the thickness of the

mortar joints which will be used between the edges of adjoining bricks. Mortar joints of $\frac{3}{8}$ in thickness are assumed to be on the brick when it is sold to you.

When you design a wall, it is far easier to calculate in the nominal dimensions than having to juggle with awkward fractions. That is quite clear. However, the nominal size could cause confusion if a finished part of a project is measured against the original design.

Let me give you an example. Say you are building a carport which has $13\frac{1}{2}$ in wide piers. Each course of bricks in the piers will have only two brick faces shown with a single vertical joint between them.

Simple mathematics shows that one brick face will be $8\frac{5}{8}$ in and one will be $4\frac{1}{8}$ in. Add the thickness of the single mortar joint and the total measurement becomes $13\frac{1}{8}$ in.

In this and all similar cases, it is generally accepted that, for design purposes, the piers can be regarded as being $13\frac{1}{2}$ in wide.

Always design using nominal dimensions. You will be less likely to make mistakes and over or under-estimate on total dimensions of a structure. The most your calculations are likely to be out is $\frac{3}{8}$ in which is hardly going to be critical in any direction.

You will find every aspect of brick-laying simpler if you think only in nominal dimensions. For example, $13\frac{1}{2}$ in wide, as we have just seen, represents one whole brick plus one half of a brick; 18 in wide means two whole bricks; 27 in wide is three whole bricks, and so on.

Regarding heights, it can be seen that if a wall is intended to be 30 in high, then it takes only a fraction of a second to work out that ten courses of bricks will be needed (remember the nominal height of each brick is 3 in).

Earlier I made brief mention of metric sizes. You will find that the vast majority of people still prefer to talk in imperial terms when referring to bricks. This is why both metric and imperial

units are used throughout this book.

For those who prefer to work in metric, a brief explanation of metric brick sizes is given below.

The British Standard laid down for metric size bricks is 225 mm × 112·5 mm × 75 mm (including an allowance for mortar joints).

Manufacturers are producing both metric and imperial sizes, though some are quoting in metric only.

The metric size corresponds very closely with the imperial size. Since it has been rounded off, for the sake of convenience, the metric brick is very slightly smaller.

A final word: batches of bricks do tend to vary, but the variation is slight and usually of little consequence since adjustments can be made in the joints to overcome the problem.

You will notice a V-shaped indentation in one face of most bricks (Fig. 113). This is called a frog; the indentation is filled with mortar during bricklaying, thus a stronger bond is supposed to be gained.

Plain bricks without a frog are called wire cuts. There is no reason why these should not be used for most types of garden construction work.

There is little further to discuss about buying new bricks. It is a simple matter of calculating the number you need very carefully and then shopping around to compare prices.

I have never found a huge difference in the price of new bricks from one source to another, and when I have, delivery charges have tended to equal things up again – especially where the cheaper bricks were being brought a greater distance.

However, if there is more than one supplier locally, it is worthwhile checking each one before ordering.

BUYING SECOND-HAND BRICKS

Second-hand bricks are altogether different. There is nothing wrong in using these for any garden work – many people, in fact, prefer the antique appearance since it tends to merge more

Fig. 115a Pick out your own bricks on a demolition site

successfully with the overall appearance of the flowers, grass and trees.

Certainly, for those people who think that a rustic, rambling appearance is essential in a garden, then second-hand bricks are a must.

There is a snag with second-hand bricks; more about this later. First, where to obtain supplies.

Whenever a demolition team get to work on old walls or houses, there will be a home handyman making inquiries about the prices of the bricks. Demolition sites are not generally advertised in the same way that a jumble sale would be through the local paper or a printed notice popped through the letter box. Very often a hand painted notice on the site entrance is the only guide – this could indicate that floorboards, timber and bricks are for sale.

Don't wait around for a sale notice to be displayed though, one might never actually be put up. Inquiries on site are an accepted part of demolition work. A word with the foreman will establish the selling price per hundred bricks. There is generally a standard price in local second-hand bricks which will not vary greatly from site to site. It is still worth asking around, though.

You will probably be allowed to pick out your own bricks from the mound on the site. Search for whole bricks which have a minimum of mortar clinging to them – as you will see later, these can save a lot of time.

Usually the bricks can be delivered, but it is cheaper to collect them yourself. Though, with petrol costs so high, you might not consider that several trips back and forth with the car is cheaper than having the bricks delivered.

Another advantage of buying bricks locally is that there is a fair chance of picking up bricks of the right shade and weathered appearance to match your existing brickwork.

Cleaning Second-hand Bricks:

Earlier I mentioned a snag. The trouble with second-hand bricks is that they may have to be cleaned up before they

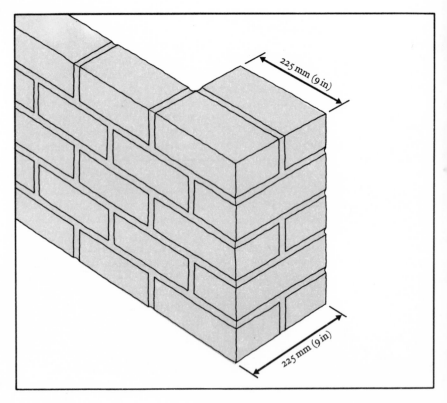

Fig. 115b Stretcher bond

can be re-used. This means that all the old mortar clinging to each brick must be cleaned off. This can be a lengthy, laborious job.

How long it takes to clean off the old, hard mortar depends on the strength of the original mix. Should a really stiff cement mix have been used, then it could take five minutes work with a bolster chisel and a club hammer to clean each brick.

Very likely, as well, when you are getting a little frustrated with chipping away, a few bricks will get broken.

On the other hand, you might be lucky. I have cleaned off old mortar with a wire brush. Clearly a very sandy mortar was used originally, most of which crumbled away over the years and the rest dislodged during the demolition work, leaving just a thin coating in most places.

So, if appearance is not a deciding

factor in whether to use old or new bricks, then the possible time element must be weighed against economy. Assuming an average of two minutes to clean each brick, one hundred could take over three hours work.

Comfort is the main essential before tackling the cleaning of a pile of bricks – a stool and a firm, even 'table' are important. An old packing case makes an excellent table.

A bolster, used in woodworking chisel fashion, is often sufficient to dislodge the old mortar. With stiffer material, a hammer might have to be used with the chisel to produce the desired effect. If this extra force needs to be used, just apply sufficient force to break up the mortar. If you overdo it the brick will break.

So, if you encounter a brick covered with stubborn mortar, do not spend too long on it. Put it on one side; when a similar brick comes up again, rub the two together – this often wears away the mortar quite quickly. If this fails, then keep the bricks for hardcore.

The intention of brick cleaning is not to remove every possible trace of old mortar. Provided that they are reasonably clean, they will do. Odd patches of mortar of not more than about 3 mm ($\frac{1}{8}$ in) thick are permissible.

BONDING

Brickwork gets its strength from the position of each course of bricks in relation to those in the course above and below. The mortar joints between the bricks are the weakest part of the wall so these must be lapped to avoid a continuous joint spanning two courses of bricks.

Arranging the bricks to meet this necessity is called bonding. The stretcher bond is the simplest to understand and to arrange (Fig. 115). Every brick in a wall is laid lengthwise in such a way that the vertical joint between two bricks in one course lies in the centre of a brick in the courses above and below.

Most of the jobs that the beginner is likely to tackle will involve a single 'skin' of bricks laid to stretcher bond. Constructions which fall into this category are low garden walls, up to 0·9 m (3 ft) high, walls of greenhouses, garages, and so on.

Because the bricks are laid lengthwise, the thickness of the wall will be 112·5 mm ($4\frac{1}{2}$ in). Thus walls built in this way are generally referred to as a half-brick wall.

Under current Building Regulations, if the height and length of a wall are both under 2·4 m (8 ft), no piers are required. A shed, therefore, could be 2·4 m × 2·4 m (8 ft × 8 ft) without piers. Piers are merely support pillars which have to be built into walls.

If a pier is needed at the corner of a half-brick wall, it can be allowed for by interlocking the stretcher bond at the corners.

If piers are needed in the run of a wall, then you will have to cut bricks in alternate courses to bond the pier to the wall.

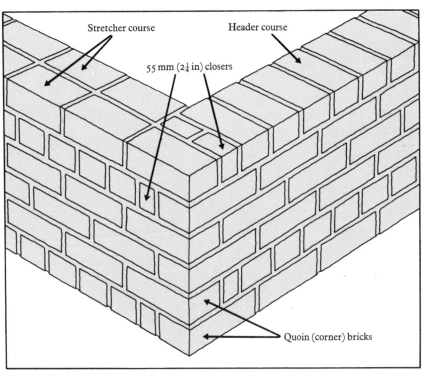

Fig. 116 **English garden wall bond**

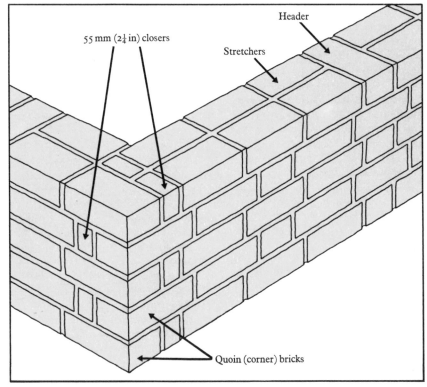

Fig. 117 **Flemish garden wall bond**

For a stronger wall without the need for piers, a 225 mm (9 in) wall is more suitable. It is sometimes thought, however, that the inclusion of piers, if only for effect, is desirable since they can add much to a wall's appearance.

English and Flemish Bonds: The bonding arrangements traditionally used with a 9 in wall are called English and Flemish. The English bond involves the use of alternate courses of headers and stretchers, while the Flemish bond involves a sequence of headers and stretchers in each course. However, since facing bricks are used extensively in these bonding arrangements, traditional, more economical modifications are popularly used.

These modifications are rather misleadingly called garden wall bonds. This implies that these bonding arrangements can be used only to build garden walls. This is not so. They are popular for building construction being strong and economical.

The English garden wall bond (Fig. 112) means that three courses of stretchers are sandwiched between a course of headers, while the Flemish garden wall bond (Fig. 113) uses an alternating sequence in each course – three stretchers to one header.

Earlier, when discussing brick sizes, I mentioned that bricks can vary slightly from batch to batch. When using one of these garden wall bonds, if there are longer bricks in your stack, then use these for the headers. This will make sure that both sides of the wall are flat. The important thing, though, is obviously to make certain that the 'show' side of the wall is absolutely correct.

Garden wall bonds do become a little complicated at corners and this involves some reasonably delicate cutting of bricks. Figs. 116 and 117 show this clearly. Narrow sections of brick adjoin the headers on both sides of the corner. These narrow sections are called closers. Since these will be about 55 mm ($2\frac{1}{4}$ in) wide they must be cut with a bolster chisel and a club hammer. The object is to produce an overlap of $2\frac{1}{4}$ in between the bricks in the courses above and below.

MORTAR

At the start of a bricklaying session, the first thing to be done is to knock up some mortar. The ingredients which are used are cement, sand and hydrated powder lime – all mixed with water to the correct consistency.

Your local builder's merchant will be able to supply and deliver all these ingredients. Ordering materials was covered earlier in the section on concrete. Here it is sufficient to say that the cement used is Portland cement and the sand should be clean building sand.

If you envisage having to do a lot of bricklaying in the coming months, then it will be more economical to buy the materials separately and mix them yourself.

However, should you be contemplating only a small one-off job in the immediate future and have no plans for taking bricklaying any further, then you would probably be better off with a bag or two of dry mortar mix. There is no doubt that dry mortar mixes do save a lot of time and trouble. And, though more expensive, they do ensure that the mix is always of the right proportions and also that it is of the correct strength, colour and workability.

The Marleymix range of dry mixes includes a mortar mix. Bag sizes are 20 and 40 kilos. As a rough guide, a 20 kilo bag is sufficient for laying about 80 bricks.

An acceptable mortar mix that will contend with most situations is 1 : 1 : 6. This means that one part of cement, one part of lime and 6 parts of sand are mixed together with water.

The consistency to aim at is a stiff but workable mix. If excessive water is used, the mortar will certainly not support the weight of a brick – remember that a brick weighs about 2·3 kg (5 lb). Even if it is sufficiently strong to support the brick, there will certainly be a continuous trickle of mortar/water running down the wall during construction.

I think it is probably safe to say that most people would probably set aside a complete day for their bricklaying. So, the first thing to do is to mix up a sufficient quantity of sand and lime to last all day. Add clean water gradually through a watering can rose and mix the ingredients thoroughly.

Lime and sand (in a ratio of 1 : 6) itself makes a weak mortar. In the trade it is referred to as coarse stuff.

The object in mixing up this coarse stuff in a large batch is that, as it is required, a small amount can be mixed quickly with one part of cement. A small amount, in this context, means six parts. This is important if the correct consistency is to be maintained in the mortar mix to be used.

After mixing in the cement, you will have only about two hours to use up the mortar before it becomes useless. There is no point in adding water to bring it back to life, this will make it too weak. The coarse stuff, on the other hand, will last all day, by adding clean water and turning it over if it starts to stiffen.

It is not possible to give exact quantities to mix up since individual working speeds are the criteria.

For economy's sake don't overdo it at your first attempt. Mix only a little coarse stuff to begin with – say six shovelsful of sand and one shovelful of lime, then add the cement as required. If you run out at the end of a morning's work, it will not take long to knock up a batch for the afternoon session.

A word about foreign bodies that can find their way into the mix – and cause annoyance.

By foreign bodies I mean stones or weeds which can infiltrate into the mix through the pile of sand that may have been lying around uncovered in a corner of the garden. Dead leaves and other plant life will almost certainly have been blown into the sand. These must be extracted before mixing.

More annoying are any small stones or pebbles which find their way into the mortar. These have the irritating habit

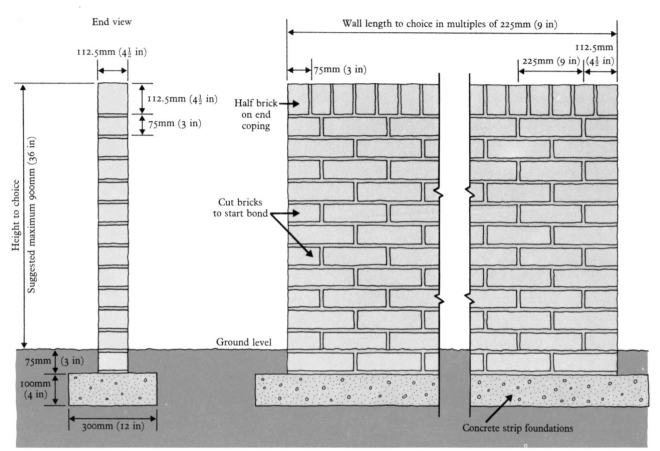

End view

112.5mm (4½ in)

112.5mm (4½ in)

75mm (3 in)

Height to choice
Suggested maximum 900mm (36 in)

Wall length to choice in multiples of 225mm (9 in)

75mm (3 in)

112.5mm

225mm (9 in) | 112.5mm (4½ in)

Half brick
on end
coping

Cut bricks
to start bond

Ground level

75mm (3 in)

100mm (4 in)

300mm (12 in)

Concrete strip foundations

Fig. 118 Estimating foundations

of ending up under one edge of a brick preventing it from lying down flush with its neighbour. These small stones have then to be extracted and thrown away.

Weather conditions have an effect on the mortar. In hot sunlight it can become stiff and unworkable in less than an hour. If this happens, try adding a little water – no more than a cupful to enliven it. If you catch it in time you may be lucky. If more than a cupful is needed, then forget it. Better still, in hot weather, mix up smaller batches.

A strong mortar mix is needed for exposed garden walls, steps, copings and sills. Use one part of cement to 3 or 4 parts of sand. The addition of some

liquid plasticiser will make it easier to work. Proprietary mixes are available from builders' merchants – check the instructions and follow them carefully.

FOUNDATIONS

Earlier, in the section on concrete, the techniques of trenching out foundations were described. When tackling a brick wall, the same basic procedures should be adopted using a builder's square, string lines, pegs and profiles. This applies whether you are setting out a building site or a straight wall.

Where the wall is being built on earth, then a trench with a strip of concrete at the bottom is required. The bottom of the trench must be levelled at the correct depth.

The foundations are very important. If these are not adequate then trouble will be encountered later on through the

bricks cracking and the wall possibly collapsing.

Fig. 118 illustrates minimum dimensions recommended by the Brick Development Association. The dimensions are based on the assumption that the concrete is standing on a firm, solid base that will be sufficient to support the weight of the brickwork.

If you study Fig. 118 things will become clear. For example, take the case where a 100 mm (4 in) depth of concrete is indicated and one course of brickwork 75 mm (3 in) is below the level of the ground. Here the trench must be at least 175 mm (9 in) deep.

Having dug down to this level, it might be found that the subsoil is not a really firm bearing surface. In this case keep digging until such a surface is found. The extra depth can be filled with hardcore, well compacted.

So, should the final depth of the trench be 600 mm (2 ft), it will be filled with 300 mm of hardcore, then a 225 mm layer of concrete and, finally, the course of bricks which make up the extra 75 mm.

If you live in an area where there is shrinkable clay below ground, get expert advice, on the spot, about the depth of foundations. Shrinkable clay can cause problems with brickwork and piers.

Depending on the size of the foundations, you might choose to use dry mix concrete. If you mix your own, then use Mix A.

BUILDING A WALL

So the foundations have been laid and allowed time to harden; string guide lines have been set out, the mortar is mixed and your tools are at the ready.

Since the string guide lines will be attached to profiles well outside the building line, the exact point for the first brick will have to be established and marked on the foundations.

Hang a plumb bob, or place a spirit level/plumb rule at the right-angled intersection of the string guide lines (Fig. 119). This applies only, of course, if you are building a rectangular structure such as a fuel bunker or shed.

Importance of Laying the First Brick Correctly: Where a straight wall is being built, the first brick must be laid parallel with the string guide lines so that the successive bricks will follow a central line through the foundation concrete.

By repeating this plumbing process at intermediate points, and marking the positions on the concrete, the line of the wall can be etched along the concrete by holding the point of the trowel against a straight-edge.

Taking a good trowelful of mortar, spread it thickly along the foundation from the starting point. A layer about 300 mm (1 ft) long and about 19 mm ($\frac{3}{4}$ in) thick is what you should aim at. The excess thickness will be accounted for when the weight of the brick sinks

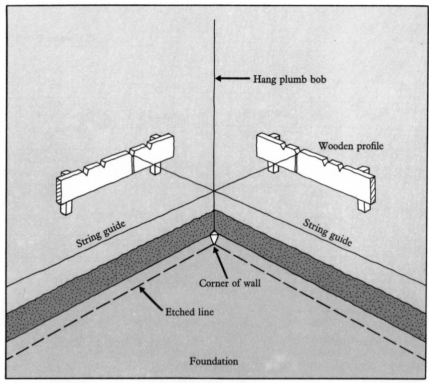

Fig. 119 Ascertaining the position of the first brick

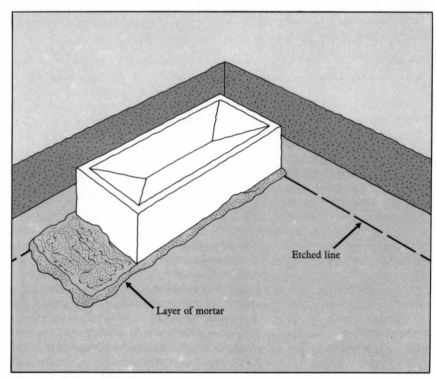

Fig. 120 Laying the first brick

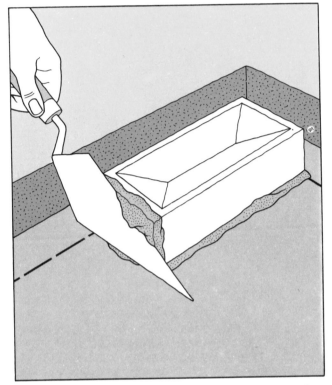

Fig. 121 Turn up the mortar on to the edge of the first brick

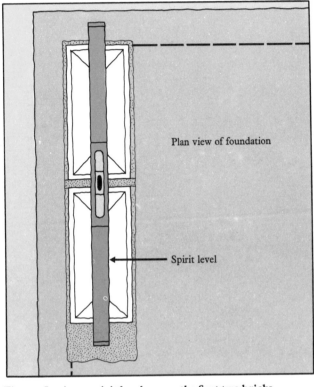

Fig. 122 Laying a spirit level across the first two bricks

into the mortar and compacts it to the required 10 mm ($\frac{3}{8}$ in).

Take your first brick and lay it on top of the mortar. Check with a spirit level that it is level.

The 75 mm (3 in) of mortar protruding along the foundation can be turned up with the trowel along the 75 mm edge of the brick. Now, spread another 300 mm long layer and lay the second brick.

At this point you begin to see the importance of getting that first brick absolutely plumb. That is going to be the guide for the second and all subsequent bricks in the first course. And the first course is the guide to all the bricks in the courses above. The message, I am sure, is clear.

Lay the spirit level across the two bricks and adjust the second one until the spirit level bubble is central. Turn up the excess mortar on to the edge of the second brick as before.

Repeat this process right along the length of the wall. A light tap with the

handle of the trowel or a light hammer handle is sufficient to knock each brick down into the mortar or move it closer to the previous one so that the desired 10 mm ($\frac{3}{8}$ in) mortar joint is maintained.

Do not forget to position the strip of sheet metal under the first layer of mortar on which to stand the gauge rod (see page 491).

Bearing in mind that the mortar will start to dry out quickly in warm weather, it is probably better for the slower beginner to point the joints after each half dozen bricks are laid. In cool, moist conditions, attend to the pointing at a maximum of hourly intervals.

Building up the Corners: The corners of the wall should be built up so that, throughout the building, the pattern will always be similar. That is to say, the courses above the course being completed will be stepped at the corners (Fig. 123).

As each course is completed, stretch the bricklayer's line between the corner

bricks of the next course, as a guide to the positions of the top edges of the bricks being laid.

Great care must be taken to get the corner bricks plumbed truly vertical or the wall will be thrown askew.

That, then, is the technique of building a brick wall. Of course, there will be times when things seem to be going wrong – there is too much or too little mortar being spread, mortar drops on to the brick faces. Many things can happen so here are a few tips to bear in mind.

Hints and Tips when using Mortar:
It sounds simple enough to spread an even layer of mortar but, most likely, you will find that when the brick is plumbed into position, the mortar will be bulging out in some places whilst, elsewhere, there will be cavities.

The simplest thing to do is to skim off the excess mortar immediately and use it to fill in the cavities.

Occasionally, a layer of mortar will be

Fig. 123 Build up the corners

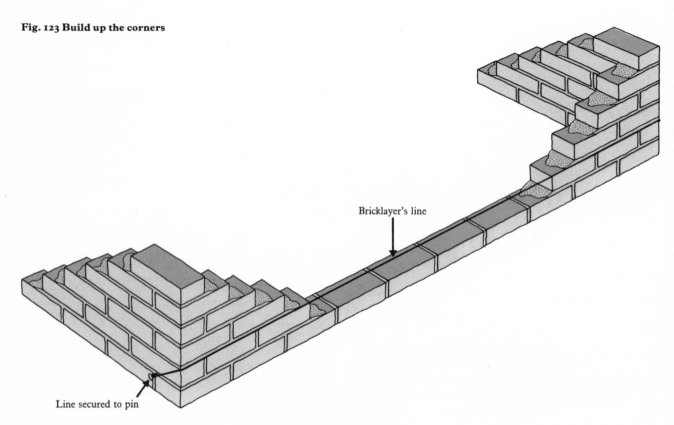

Bricklayer's line

Line secured to pin

far too thick and the brick placed on it will be much higher than the previous one. The immediate reaction is to remove the brick and try to scoop some of the mortar off – before replacing the brick. The trouble is that immediately a brick is laid, some of the moisture from the mortar is absorbed into the bricks in contact with it. So, if you remove the brick and the excess mortar then, when replaced, the brick will not be held so well in position.

It is better to tap down the brick firmly into position and scrape off the excess mortar that bulges out from the sides, rather than remove the brick. However, if the mortar is more dry than wet, and the brick will not sink down to the required level, then you can try removing the brick before slicing off an even skim of the excess mortar using the side of the trowel.

The brick may not be as firm as it should be, or possibly there is no grip at all. In this case the mortar is probably too dry, so scrape off all the mortar

before restarting with fresh material.

The opposite can also happen – the mortar layer can be too thin. Not so difficult to put right, this one, since the brick can be removed and extra mortar laid. This still probably means that the brick will not be as well laid as it should be but provided that the bricks that eventually surround it are sound, then it will be well gripped on three of its sides.

If you find that the mortar on the hawk is a little drier than when mixed, a likely event on a hot day, then make it a routine to sprinkle water on every half dozen bricks before laying them. This prevents the moisture in the mortar sinking into the bricks too quickly which will happen if the bricks are dry and warm from the sun.

Position of Frog: Whether the bricks should be laid with the frog facing upwards or downwards is a question that never occurs to a beginner until he is faced with the decision. The frog is

the depression found in one side of some types of bricks.

It is traditionally accepted that the frog should always face upwards so that the layer of mortar will fill up the indentation giving a stronger grip. Placing the frog face down would not guarantee it being filled.

Recent findings by the Building Research Station, however, say that there is no significant difference in strength or damp resistance whichever method is adopted.

Brick Piles for Ease of Working: It is good practice, before starting work, to lay out a few bricks in stacks along the building line. This avoids you having to trundle back and forth to collect a load when supplies run out.

The Coping Course: It is important to lay a coping course on top of a wall to protect it from the elements.

Pre-cast coping blocks are neat and convenient to use. These can be bought from builders' merchants. Alternatives are to use bricks standing on edge.

On 9 in walls, whole bricks standing on edge make a neat finish. Cut bricks in half to stand on edge for $4\frac{1}{2}$ in walls. Coping bricks must be dense – ordinary

Fig. 124 Looking at the wall from above helps to make sure it is straight and even. At the end of the day, protect new brickwork with polythene sheeting

flettons should not be used.

Inspecting Wall from Above: As well as checking with spirit levels and plumb bob, looking at the wall from above helps to ensure that it is straight and even.

When lower courses are being built, then it is easy to get a bird's eye view of the construction. Once the courses have reached a reasonable level – say 0·9 or 1·2 m (3 ft or 4 ft) – depending on your height, it is not possible to get a straight

down view. So have a pair of step ladders handy for the later stages of construction.

Protecting Brickwork: At the end of the day, the work should be protected from the elements in some way – especially important at a time of the year when frosts are likely. It is equally important to protect bricks from the elements until they are used. They must be kept on a clean, dry base, ideally covered with polythene sheeting.

GARDEN PATHS

A garden path, patio area or a terrace can be formed using bricks. As can be seen from the few examples shown in Fig. 125, it is possible to create many patterns by either standing the bricks on their flat faces or edges.

Bricks can also be used in conjunction with paving stones thus opening up many other possibilities.

It is more economical to choose a pattern where the bricks are laid flat. Here, only 32 bricks are needed to the square yard. Where they are laid on edge, 48 bricks per square yard are needed – half as many again.

Fig. 126 gives details of how to lay brick paving; the polythene membrane should be continuous over the whole area. Weep holes should be set into the mortar joints at 12 in intervals along the perimeter.

INTERNAL BRICKWORK

Though the beginner can confidently tackle an interior project involving brickwork – building a feature fireplace, for instance, it is probably better to have some practice on an exterior project first.

Exactly the same techniques are used for interior work, but far greater care must be taken at every stage.

In an exterior construction, should the visual effect not be all that it should in odd areas, it will not be so important. The construction is not likely to be studied that closely. An interior feature, on the other hand, is going to be closely scrutinised and even minor errors will stick out like a sore thumb. So work even more carefully and patiently on interior jobs.

When choosing the materials – bricks and mortar – remember that the finished effect is something that you are going to have to live with for a long while. It is not like hanging a wrong wallpaper or putting on a coat of paint which proves to be the wrong colour.

So make sure that the final effect is going to be right – and one that will blend with other decorative effects and

colours in case you want to change the scheme later on.

An important consideration is to provide a damp-proof course beneath any interior brick wall construction. So lay a length of damp-proof course material (your builders' merchant will supply this) that spans the whole base.

Alternatively, use a layer of polythene. This has a double advantage: it can be spread out across the floor in the room to protect it during building work; then, when the job is complete, the excess can be trimmed off round the base.

Fig. 125 Some possible patterns for brick garden paths

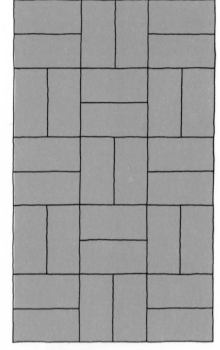

Bricks on flat (basket weave)

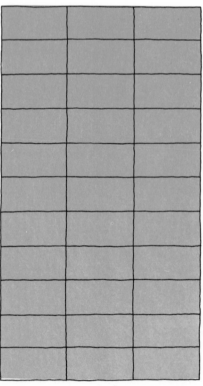

Bricks on flat (stack bond)

Bricks on edge

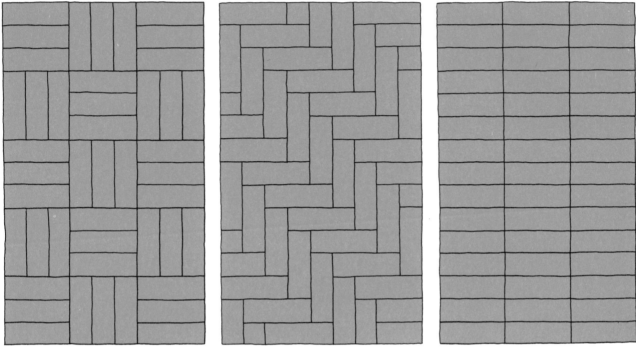

Bricks on edge (wood block)

Bricks on edge (herringbone)

Bricks on edge (stack bond)

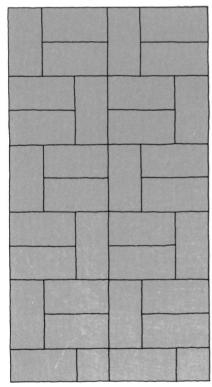

Bricks on flat

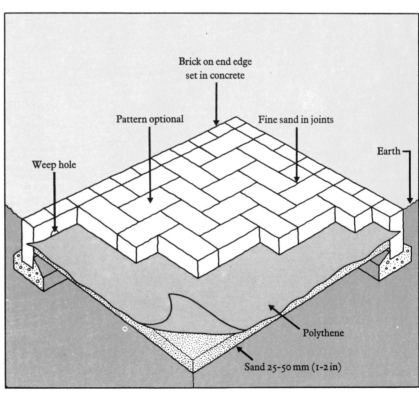

Brick on end edge
set in concrete

Pattern optional

Fine sand in joints

Earth

Weep hole

Polythene

Sand 25-50 mm (1-2 in)

Fig. 126 Laying brick paving

Ideas in Stone

Stonework can be used equally effectively inside or outside the house. Indoors, stone makes a pleasant change from the more usual tiles which are used for fireplace surrounds. The two fireplaces shown in the picture may look complicated to build, but both are made from reconstituted stone and are supplied in kit form. With every stone numbered and keyed into position on the plans supplied, assembling one of these should be within the capabilities of most people.

The third picture shows stone paving for a courtyard. The hexagonal shape makes a change from square or rectangular slabs and its decorative effect is enhanced by the use of bricks for edging and for the sides of the circular raised portion.

In contrast to the rather formal stone paving of the courtyard on the previous page, irregular stone slabs can be used (top right) which give a more rustic feel to this corner of a town garden. The raised surround of the pool is also of stone.

The picture (bottom right) is of a low stone wall, built cavity-fashion so that plants can be grown along the top of it. Here the bed for the plants is quite narrow, but it can be made to any width which you have room for.

The pool (far right, top) is concrete-lined and with a grass surround. It is given character by the informal placing of large, rough-hewn, stone slabs, surrounded by plants, at each end. And finally (far right, bottom) we are back to plant containers. These in brick and concrete have been shown earlier in the book. Here stone has been used instead.

Today the home handyman often uses man-made reconstructed stone as his building material. Various manufacturers produce a variety of units from walling blocks to paving slabs in different types of reconstructed stone.

None of the delicate skills of the stonemason are needed to work these units. The only requirement could be to cut the occasional unit to fit say, a corner or a wall end. Even this can be eliminated with attention to basic planning.

NATURAL STONE
Nevertheless, to gain a true appreciation of the material, it is useful to know something of the origin and uses of natural stone.

Stone has long been man's natural building material. Of all the crafts, that of the stonemason (together with the carpenter) is the oldest. Certainly it is the craft that has changed the least, since the raw material itself is virtually unalterable.

Stone is taken from quarries all around the country and, dependent on the region, different quality and colour of stone is obtained.

The long disused quarry is a familiar sight – today it is often used to dump the mountains of waste that we generate. Quarry waste, on the other hand, is virtually non-existent. There is a use for stone dust and every other size of fragment or piece obtained.

The earliest and more primitive methods of building made use of quite small pieces of stone in what is described as a random rubble wall. Having gone to the trouble of finding the stone in the first place, it made sense to make the most use of every scrap. At the other extreme, huge pieces of stone were cut and hauled long distances to make lasting monuments such as the Pyramids and Stonehenge.

The individual qualities of naturally occurring stone of a particular area has greatly influenced local architecture. Aberdeen, the granite city, and Bath where the local stone graces the Georgian terraces and crescents are

Fig. 127 A random rubble natural stone wall built with a full out mortared joint. The use of occasional large stones adds strength to the wall

examples of this and of how traditional styles of building with stone have come about.

The hardness of granite makes it difficult to shape but easy to polish. The result is fine angular buildings with few ornamentations.

The softer and more easily worked Bath stone lends itself to shaping and so

to columns and scrollings. There are few sharp corners which would be liable to damage.

These are but two examples showing the extremes in the treatments of stone influenced by the nature of the stone itself. There are many variations in between and also differences, within limits, brought about by the stonemason adding his individual treatments in the dressing of stone.

Tooling in Natural Stone: One can actually find marks on the stone that show, if not individuals, at least the different quarries operating in the locality. Often these consist of chisel marks on the surface of an otherwise flat-faced stone. Such chisel marks (called tooling) a widely used means of giving stone a surface texture, but the angle and spacing of these scorings often give a clue to a particular source of the stone.

Natural Stone Treatments:
Although some stones of similar characteristics occur in different parts of the country, their treatments are not always the same, even though the basic style is followed.

In the Cotswolds where a chopped stone is used (that is stone cut with flat sides and a smooth or slightly textured face) houses are built with walls made up of different course heights, these different heights being spaced more or less uniformly throughout so that there is no apparent change in effect from ground to roof level.

East of the Pennines, the practice has been to use the wider course heights nearer to the ground, and then have diminishing heights nearer to the eaves.

Why this difference, using the same basic materials should have happened is unexplained – but if nothing else it

Fig. 128 A section of Masonry Block reconstructed stone wall with the mortar rebated from the face

gives variety and creates both visual contrast and the characteristics of a local or regional environment.

RECONSTRUCTED STONE
There are areas where stone is not considered to be the traditional building material and is replaced by brick, but where stone is predominant our planners, environmentalists and others are seeing to it that at least the look of stone is maintained in new buildings. This, however, had proved difficult for two reasons, the availability and the cost of natural stone. An answer to the problem has evolved in recent years in the form of reconstructed stone.

Across the range of imitation stones now being made there is a wide choice between those that give an impression of stone, at least in texture, and others which are specifically made to mirror, not only the colour and texture of natural stone, but also the way in which it has been traditionally used in building houses or free-standing walls.

In broad terms natural building stones can be classified as: granite and other igneous rocks; limestones (including marbles), and sandstones.

Within these limits there are variations of each type often depending on the age of the stone or its position in a seam so that one quarry can produce stone of quite different characteristics.

The same stone can, as already stated, be worked by the mason in different

ways to give either a smooth face or a highly profiled rocky texture.

While reconstructed stone equivalents are not available for all the natural stone finishes, there are man-made versions that very closely resemble most of their natural counterparts both in suface finish and colouring.

Types and Properties of Reconstructed Stone: A British Standard (BS 1217) defines cast or reconstructed stone as building material manufactured from cement and natural aggregate for use in a similar manner and for the same purpose as natural stone. Usually applied to walling units, the term is also used for other components of a house such as sills, lintels, window surrounds and roofing slates which resemble stone.

There are three main manufacturing methods. First, hydraulically pressed concrete which is then split to produce a rough texture on the face. Second, facing for concrete blocks where the face and the sides of the block are formed first and then a core of concrete added. Third, casting from a range of natural stone masters where the block is of the same colouring and mix throughout.

This third manufacturing method is usually known as reconstructed stone since it is aimed at a faithful reproduction of natural stone.

The first two types are generally

Fig. 129 A cottage built in Masonry Block. The roofing slates are also in reconstructed stone (Traditional Roofing Slates), a reproduction of stone slates

referred to as split blocks and faced blocks, respectively.

Man-made stone has certain physical advantages over natural stone. If cast in moulds it has consistently accurate dimensions and flat beds or faces that make laying easier.

The thickness, usually 100 mm (about 4 in), means that it is used in just the same way as brick for the outer skin of a cavity wall. (Natural stone walls, although built today with a cavity, tend to be very much thicker to allow for

irregular sizes of the stones. Although thickness, in itself, is not a bad thing, the result is either a loss of internal square footage or longer walls.

Other advantages of all types of cast stone are that it has a greater compressive strength than most natural stones and, because of its homogeneous nature, it is far less liable to failure through frost attack.

A question often asked is 'how will it weather?' The answer is simply 'Just like natural stone.' However it is worthwhile explaining that there is frequently some misunderstanding over this. Much will depend on the location and architectural detailing. It could be pollution rather than weathering. In this case using a suitable proprietary

cleaner, following manufacturer's recommendations, may freshen up the surface, but a stiff brush, water and elbow grease is probably the most foolproof method.

Lichens and other vegetable growths will appear on free-standing reconstructed stone walls such as garden walls, but not if a damp-proof course is used. And the same holds good for natural stone.

RECONSTRUCTED STONE EQUIVALENTS OF NATURAL STONE

The following information on the types of reconstructed stone available is based on details kindly supplied by E. H. Bradley Ltd on their Bradstone range.

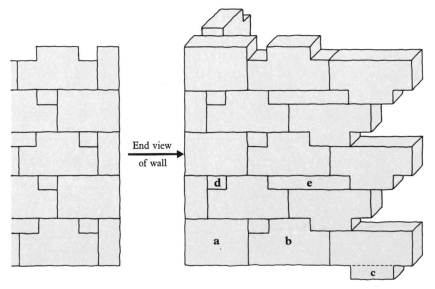

End view
of wall

Chopped Stone, Coursed: In many quarries it was the practice to sort stone into batches each of different thicknesses, roughly square the ends to give a vertical joint and, depending on the local practice, dress the exposed face to give an even textured or near smooth finish.

In building a wall, the stones were laid in level courses but to make use of the different thicknesses of the batches the courses would vary in height throughout the wall (Fig. 131).

The range of course heights found can be in 25 mm (1 in) steps between about 100 mm (4 in) and 225 mm (9 in), the width usually being in the proportion of four times the height.

Coursed Chisel Dressed: This is an indication of how the natural stone is treated and used, 'coursed' indicating the level horizontal jointing running the length of the wall and 'chisel dressed' to show that the face was worked on to give an overall similarity of appearance.

In practice it has been found that it is possible to rationalize the course

Fig. 130 Bonding of Masonry Block
(a) Masonry End or Dressed End
(b) T-shaped Masonry Block, laid 'stem up'
(c) T-shaped Masonry Block, laid 'stem down' – immediately above damp-proof course, stems are bolstered off; these can be used for infill pieces
(d) Infill pieces
(e) Make-up Block

down and by introducing false joints so that each block appears to be made up of more than one stone, the geometric pattern disappears. Small infill pieces have to be cut to complete the bonding arrangement (Fig. 130).

Added to this, many different master casts are used in the production and blocks of identical profiles can be so widely spaced that they are undetectable without a search.

Fig. 131 Natural chopped stone, built coursed

Random Rubble: As the name implies, walls of this construction (Fig. 127) are built of stones of irregular sizes and shapes, the mason virtually taking pieces straight from a haphazard pile of broken stone so that there are no long runs of vertical or horizontal joints.

Closer inspection will show that larger stones are placed at frequent intervals throughout a wall to add to its strength.

In some localities, random rubble is 'brought to courses' and in this case there are level joints running transversely at intervals varying from about 300 to 915 mm (1 to 3 ft) in height.

To meet the essential characteristics of a random rubble wall – its irregularity – a reconstructed stone called *Masonry Block* is produced. Instead of being rectangular it is 'T'-shaped.

By building the T's stem up and stem

Fig. 132 This type of Coursed Chisel
Dressed reconstructed stone is made in
four course heights

Fig. 133 In this house, the right-hand
wing has been built in reconstructed
stone (Bradstone Coursed Chisel
Dressed) to match the natural stone of
the original building on the left

Fig. 134 Squared rubble natural stone wall – this is a common treatment of stone used both in urban and rural buildings

heights of Coursed Chisel Dressed to four, this being sufficient to give the necessary variation throughout the wall. The blocks are all made 450 mm (18 in) long, but, by using many different moulds and incorporating false joints that are pointed up on site to look like actual joints, repetition of profiles is again avoided.

As a finishing touch, the blocks are made with the textured face standing a little proud so that arrises show as irregular but the internal beds are absolutely flat and true.

Squared Rubble: This is a finish applied to all three basic stones, but as you can imagine the appearance is affected according to whether it is granite, sandstone or limestone.

The commonly seen form of squared rubble is laid uncoursed so that there are few horizontal or vertical joints running into one another.

A rule of thumb for laying this stone is to avoid vertical joints greater than the height of the largest stone; also avoid joints that result in a symmetrical cross.

Individual stones have their sides squared off although over an area the different shapes used may range from flattish rectangles to squares, the largest being about 250 mm (10 in) square.

In mason's terminology, the stones are referred to as risers (or jumpers) and stretchers, as in brickwork, indicating those whose greatest measurement is its height or length. Where awkward voids may have otherwise been left, small stones introduced to aid bonding are known as 'snecks'.

The surface texture can best be described as rocky with the larger stones having a more pronounced profile in the centre of the face.

One of the earliest forms of reconstructed stone was made to resemble squared rubble. When it was made in the 1930's there was little, if any, variation in profile and none in the size of the block. The result was (and still is) a repetitive and uninteresting wall.

Rough Hewn Finish: This has long since passed the day of the one mould block. Rough Hewn is made in nine co-

Fig. 135 Rough Hewn Finish is a reconstructed stone version of squared rubble. It is laid random, i.e. no long vertical or horizontal joints

Fig. 136 A bungalow built in Rough Hewn Finish

ordinated sizes of risers and stretchers. There is also a choice of face profiles between high and low relief, the latter having a more prominent profile suited to some parts of the country.

This finish lends itself to making features within a brick or reinforced concrete building. It is also popular for chimney stacks and as a visual contrast in texture for porches, panels below ground floor windows, whole gable ends, garages and retaining walls.

SHADES OF RECONSTRUCTED STONE

Since Bradstone is representative of reconstructed stone and, as already pointed out, one that is found in the three basic natural stones, it is worthwhile mentioning the range of shades in which most Bradstone finishes are produced.

The natural colour is the warm, honey brown of Cotswold stone since the aggregates used are drawn from beds on the borders of Wiltshire and Gloucestershire on the edge of the Cotswolds. To achieve most other shades of natural building stone, a pigment is added to the mix.

There is the creamy grey tone of a weathered limestone – a match for some stones as quarried in Gloucestershire and North Somerset.

The blue grey shade has natural stone counterparts in places as far apart as the Mendips and West Wales.

Varying colourings of sandstones, where the redness is the result of iron oxides, are mostly covered by two shades – ginger brown and light rust brown. The former is generally suited to ironstone areas where the presence of iron is more concentrated such as Northants, parts of Oxfordshire and Warwickshire.

Light rust brown has applications in Somerset, Dorset and Devon as well as in the ironstone areas.

Opposite
Fig. 137 This retaining wall has been made a feature to match the Rough Hewn Finish used in the terrace

Fig. 138 This manor house in Georgian style has been built in Bradstone Brushed Finish which has the appearance of finely-dressed ashlar

For Dartmoor, which has a natural stone colouring not found elsewhere in Britain, a special shade is manufactured.

While the light and shade of the surface texture and weathering combine to give the effect of subtle colour changes within an individual block, until recently there was only a single colour throughout a block. Now, some new shades are being produced with two pigments to give the face a mottled effect found in some building stones that have an inherent colour variation.

Ashlar: This is a square hewn stone or masonry consisting of blocks of stone, finely square dressed to given dimensions and laid in courses not less than 300 mm (1 ft) high with thin joints.

Most of us know Ashlar through the many fine cathedrals, mansions and public buildings built in this finish. Usually it refers to limestones and is particularly associated with Portland stone, although many other quarries produce Ashlar.

Limestones such as Portland are comparatively soft when quarried but harden quickly afterwards. Nowadays it is more common to use Ashlar as a facing only to a steel or reinforced concrete framed building.

Georgian style architecture almost always used Ashlar finished stone and it has come to be considered, rightly, as the best examples of the stonemason's art, at least so far as limestone and sandstone are concerned.

Ashlar Reconstructed Stone Treatments: Three representations of Ashlar treatments are as follows:

Brushed Finish: Flat faced with a light vertical texture simulating the marks left by steel tooth-edged tools used to dress the surface.

Combined Finish: A similar texture but with a higher profile.

Fig. 139 Tooled Finish represents an ashlar finish on which vertical chisel marks add to the texture

Tooled Finish: Has the texture of brushed plus deeper vertical scoring representing chisel markings given to some Ashlars.

DRY STONE WALLING

This is really another form of random rubble walling.

Many country fields are bounded by dry stone walls and farm buildings too are frequently built in this manner, often up to 6 m (20 ft) high.

Dry earth is sometimes used as a form of bonding agent and the thicker walls will be double skinned with a central core of small stones.

There are deceptive skills in building dry stone walls to last. The principle is that the stones should be laid in such a way that rain penetrating the outer face runs out again at a lower level, other- wise the frost action on the wet core would soon cause problems.

If you have ever visited an agricul- tural show, you may have seen a demonstration of building a dry stone wall and noticed that it is not a job that can be hurried.

Some shaping of stones is necessary and it is more a matter of finding or shaping a stone to fit snugly with its neighbours than making it fit by chance. Incidentally, dry stone walls usually make use of stratified rocks, the flat stones showing clearly how they originated in layers.

Being used to seeing dry stone walling in rural settings, it is natural that gardeners should wish to introduce them in their own gardens. To make this more straightforward, there is a reconstructed stone version of dry stone walling known as Cotswall. Although it looks as if it is made up of individual stones, a 530 mm (21 in) long Cotswall block is the equivalent of three layers of stones, all in one piece. The false joint technique and deeply revetted spaces between the 'single' stones enhances the natural look as does the Cotswold colouring.

RIVEN PAVING

This reconstructed stone paving is also used in the garden. Not all man-made paving is produced to look exactly like stone. The reconstructed stone version of York stone slabs, shown in Fig. 144, is produced in moulds made from actual York stone masters to ensure that the authentic surface characteristics are reproduced.

Fig. 140 Natural stone used in dry stone walls commonly seen bounding fields and in farm buildings

Fig. 141 Garden features such as a sun
dial or barbecue can be built easily
from Cotswall reconstructed stone
blocks

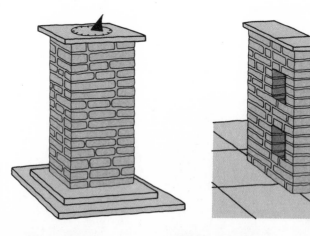

Fig. 142 Cotswall reconstructed stone
block. This enables the look of dry stone
to be built easily in the garden, each
block apparently being made up of a
number of individual stones built in
three courses

The slabs have irregular arrises, just
as the natural stone, and the four edges
are textured to look more natural when
exposed in steps or garden seats.

BUILDING IN STONE

Visitors to old stone buildings are often
heard to remark on the thickness of the
walls. The impression they gain is of
solid walls two or three feet thick.

In the largest structures – churches,
cathedrals and the like – this may be so,
but very often there is a cavity. This
cavity is either left empty or otherwise
filled with a core of small stones, which
would certainly act like a course type of
the modern foam infill, in that movement of air would be restricted, so
reducing heat loss between the inner
and outer skin.

However, it will most probably give
rise to damp penetrating to the inside of
the house, the small stones providing a
bridge for moisture finding its way
through very small cracks, usually in
the mortar.

In the days before damp-proof
courses and clear cavity walls, damp
was probably less of a worry than it is
today. With no wallpaper to peel off or
plaster to fall away, plus a much freer
ventilation through glass-less windows
and enormous chimneys, our fore-
fathers hung the walls with tapestries
and other less permanent linings and
forgot about the damp.

**Fig. 143 Checking level of newly laid
paving slab. Slabs should be laid to
provide a slight slope for water
drainage. Bed the slab on weak and
rather dry sand and cement mortar – 8
parts builder's sand to 1 part cement or
lime**

**Fig. 144 Cutting Riven Paving. Use a
bolster and club hammer to chip along
the intended cut line on one side of the
slab. Then reverse the slab and apply a
sharp blow to the back of the intended
cut line. A clean break should result. It
is most important to provide a flat,
firm backing (as shown) when chipping
along cut line**

Damp-proof Courses: Once the process of capilliary action was discovered and damp-proof courses built in to stop rising damp, it also made sense to stop the damp coming through from outside when it rained by having an internal cavity in which moisture could simply fall to the ground without wetting the inner skin.

In modern house construction damp-proof courses are used in several places, their function being not only to prevent the passage of water from external sources but also to prevent moisture in the fabric of the building from moving from one part to another. Hence there are damp-proof courses under sills, at jambs over openings, in roof parapets and in chimneys, and these precautions apply to brick, stone and reconstructed stone buildings.

Hints and Tips when using Reconstructed Stone: Anyone thinking of

building a large structure with stone should always consult an expert, but simple structures should not be beyond those able to lay bricks soundly and reconstructed stone with its flat beds will present no special problems. However there are a few points which those building, say, a garden wall should bear in mind.

First, always check the colouring of the stone you want against an actual sample. The colouring reproduced in catalogues is only as good as the original photograph and the printing process and, since these both have some limitations, it is always best to see a sample before deciding the shade that you want.

All stone should be handled carefully to avoid damage. Stack it on a hard level surface clear of other materials. Protection from the rain is necessary otherwise unequal weathering can occur giving a blotchy look to a finished wall.

Avoid the temptation to use a strong mortar. A mix of 1 : 2 : 8 (cement : lime : sand) is recommended for reconstructed stone built in normal

situations, or 1 : 1 : 6 where the wall is exposed to severe weather.

If a single skin wall is being built, a waterproofing agent should be added to the mortar in line with the manufacturer's instructions.

Expansion joints are only necessary in designs involving very long lengths of reconstructed stone walling.

The mortar used can make a big difference to the overall job. Unless a special effect is wanted, the mortar should match the stone it is being used with, otherwise the eye tends to see the mortar rather than the stonework.

Quite different effects using the same stone can be had by leaving the joints well rebated or well filled.

Mostly the stone looks better with a rebated joint but with the *Masonry Block*, for example, a full-out mortar is quite acceptable, provided that the mortar and stone match.

Fig. 145 Section through stone wall with centre occupied by small stones and without a damp-proof course

Fig. 146 When using a reconstructed stone facing, the method of incorporating a damp-proof course is the same as used in bricklaying

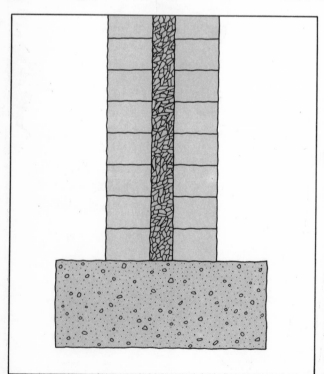

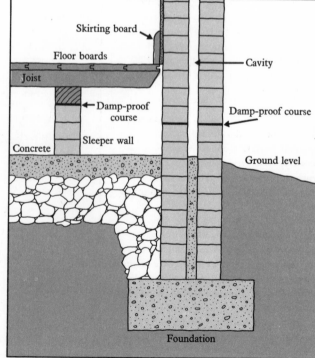

Skirting board
Floor boards
Joist
Concrete
Damp-proof course
Sleeper wall
Cavity
Damp-proof course
Ground level
Foundation

Fig. 147 Laying Cotswall reconstructed stone blocks

(a) Spreading mortar with a trowel ready for laying the next Cotswall block. Footings and sequence of construction follow similar procedures to bricklaying

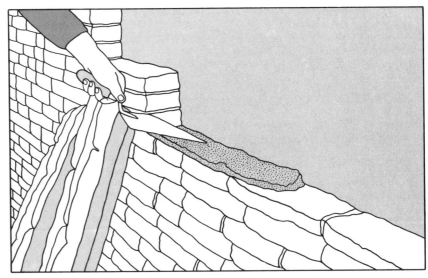

(b) The block placed in position and checked for level with a spirit level. Systematically check for vertical as well as horizontal level with each block

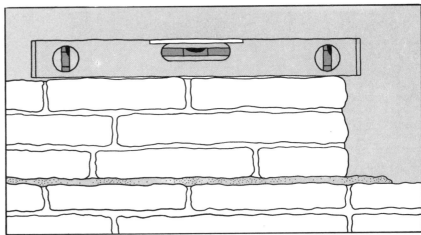

(c) A coping slab is used to finish off the top of the wall

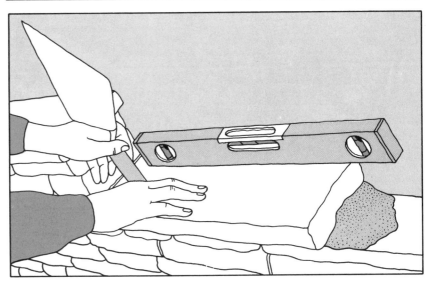

RECONSTRUCTED STONE WITHIN THE HOME

Reconstructed stone also has applications within the home, and any competent handyman should be able to use the material either for a handsome fireplace or a stone wall.

Fireplaces: These are specially designed for the handyman to install –

Fig. 148 Reconstructed stone wall tiles may be used internally or externally. About 13 mm ($\frac{1}{2}$ in) thick they are simply stuck to a sound, flat surface with mortar or pva adhesive

they come in kits with each stone numbered. Often included are a spirit level and trowel.

There is a choice of designs including those with built-in alcoves for flowers or books and you can have stone or slate hearth slabs and stone or hardwood shelving.

Wall Tiles: Reconstructed stone wall tiles can make an effective surround to the fireplace or be used on their own to give an alcove or wall an attractive and lasting finish. The tiles are about 13 mm ($\frac{1}{2}$ in) thick and are simply stuck to any sound, smooth surface using either mortar or a pva adhesive.

The joints are filled with mortar in the usual way and, when complete, the appearance is of a solid stone wall.

Tiles may be used externally to give the look of stone to terraces and patios or as the outer skin of a garage, screen wall or extension, built economically with concrete blocks as the main structure.

RECONSTRUCTED STONE ROOF SLATES

One other use for reconstructed stone in the fabric of a house is in the roof tiles. In such areas as the Cotswolds, Somerset, Oxfordshire, and Northants, roofs have been traditionally built with stone slates.

Supplies of these in their natural state have been getting increasingly difficult to obtain.

To maintain the essential characteristics of many outstandingly beautiful villages and individual houses, roofs in need of repair or replacement on otherwise sound buildings are now being covered with reconstructed stone slates. The *Bradstone Traditional Roofing*, for instance, is made from many different natural stone masters so that the random effect and the uneven texture are reproduced in detail.

THE QUESTION OF COSTS

Finally, we come to the question of costs. Natural building stone, when it can be had, is expensive. Most reconstructed stone walling blocks used in building houses have a laid cost equal to that of good quality facing bricks.

Those who can afford natural stone will no doubt enjoy the satisfaction of knowing they have the real thing, but for the look of stone without the cost, reconstructed stone is the answer and few people will spot the difference.

Opposite
Fig. 149 Reconstructed stone fireplace in a modern design

Index